FACTS AND FIGURES ...

GUIDE TO METRIC COOKING

Use these equivalents to make metric recipes that will fit your cake tins and bowls.

Present Measurement	Approx. Metric Equivalent
1 oz.	25g
2 oz.	50g
3 oz.	75g
4 oz.	100–125g
5 oz.	150g
6 oz.	175g
7 oz.	200g
8 oz.	225g
9 oz.	250g
10 oz.	275g
11 oz.	300g
12 oz.	350g
13 oz.	375g
14 oz.	400g
15 oz.	425g
16 oz.	450g

LIQUID MEASURES

Use a 5-millilitre spoon in place of a teaspoon and a 15-ml spoon in place of a tablespoon. Handy equivalents: a 5-ml pharmaceutical spoon or a set of American measuring spoons.

Present Measurement	Approx. Metric Equivalent
1 fl. oz.	25 ml
2 fl. oz.	50 ml
5 fl. oz.	150 ml
10 fl. oz.	300 ml
15 fl. oz.	400 ml
20 fl. oz.	600 ml
35 fl. oz.	1 litre

OVEN TEMPERATURES

N.B. To convert Centigrade/Celsius temperatures to Fahrenheit, multiply by 9, divide by 5 and then add 32. Conversely, to turn a Fahrenheit temperature into Centigrade/Celsius, subtract 32, multiply by 5 and divide by 9.

Oven	°F	°C	Gas Mark
Very cool	250–275	130–140	$\frac{1}{2}$–1
Cool	300	150	2
Warm	325	170	3
Moderate	350	180	4
Fairly hot	375–400	190–200	5–6
Hot	425	220	7
Very hot	450–475	230–240	8–9

GOOD HOUSEKEEPING

COLOUR
Cookery

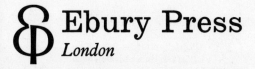
Ebury Press
London

First published in Great Britain October 1967
by Ebury Press, Chestergate House, Vauxhall Bridge Road, London SW1V 1HF
Second impression January 1970
Revised edition 1971
Reprinted 1972
Reprinted 1973
Reprinted 1975
Reprinted 1976
© 1967 The National Magazine Co. Ltd

ISBN 0 7181 3042 1

Photo composition by
Photoprint Plates Ltd., Rayleigh, Essex

Printed in Great Britain by
Fletcher & Son Ltd, Norwich

Colour plates by
Interlitho, Milan

Foreword

Mention Good Housekeeping cookery books in any gathering of women and someone is bound to say, 'Oh, yes—all those lovely colour pictures of food . . . '' and someone else will be sure to add that she's cooked by Good Housekeeping recipes ever since she married.

Here, for addicts of the famous Good Housekeeping recipes and the equally famous food photographs, is a really practical and comprehensive cookery book with something for everyone, whether beginner or experienced cook. Turn to the list of contents and you will see that the sixteen chapters include all the ordinary branches of home cookery, plus some less ordinary items—"The Art of Curry-making", "Buffet Party Catering" and "Bed-sitter Cookery for One", not to mention an invaluable chapter on "Home Preserving".

Throughout the book you will find the cream of Good Housekeeping's recipes, new and traditional, home-grown and foreign, speedily made snacks and some of the great classic dishes.

In addition to the 64 pages of rich colour pictures, there are black-and-white photographs on almost every page, giving how-to-do-it information, showing what the finished dish should look like, offering ideas for serving and presentation and often suggesting at a glance an answer to that eternal question "What shall I give them today?"

As always with a Good Housekeeping book, the recipes have all been tested and re-tested in our Kitchens, and there is a full Index to help you find your way quickly about the book.

And remember, when you buy a Good Housekeeping cookery book, you buy more than just a collection of recipes—you buy nearly fifty years of experience, pioneer research and meticulous testing. You buy too a unique after-service, for the Good Housekeeping Institute staff will gladly answer all your cookery queries personally, if you write to them at the address given below.

CAROL MACARTNEY
Principal, Good Housekeeping Institute

Good Housekeeping Institute
Chestergate House
Vauxhall Bridge Road
London S.W.1

Contents

Colour Illustrations

A GOOD BOWL OF SOUP

Recipes give 4 servings, unless otherwise indicated

Well-flavoured stock is the best possible basis for soups, and with a little forethought you can have a supply of it always at hand. Good stock can be made from bones, meat or poultry and from vegetables; gristle, trimmings and bacon rinds may be included, but fat must not be added. This type of stock is suitable for all types of soup, except consommé, for which a clear bone stock clarified with egg shells is essential. Stock made from raw meat or poultry, not from already cooked pieces, is known as 'first' stock.

To make the stock a stock pot (see first colour picture) is ideal, but by no means essential. Use any saucepan with a well-fitting lid, or a pressure cooker—which saves time and fuel.

Stock will keep for a week in a refrigerator, but when no refrigerator is available, and especially during warm weather, it should be boiled up daily and not kept for more than 2-3 days.

If more convenient, use self-raising flour instead of plain, for thickening soup.

Some Soup-making Do's and Don'ts

Do chop or divide ingredients finely to extract the flavour.

Do sauté the ingredients carefully, to absorb the fat.

Do give long, gentle cooking (with a lid on the pan), to extract the flavours and soften the fibres.

Do stir cream in slowly; single cream is best.

Do skim the stock when it comes to the boil, removing all the scum

Do sieve soup carefully and thoroughly—unless all the vegetables, etc., are put through the sieve, the soup will be flavourless and thin. If you have a blender, it's ideal for this job.

Do add the thickening agent carefully, with the pan off the heat; stir continuously to prevent lumps forming.

Do serve soup hot; heat the individual dishes or tureen.

Don't over-garnish soup.

ACCOMPANIMENTS AND GARNISHES

Certain soups have a recognised accompaniment or garnish, but with others you can ring the changes on a variety of simple and more elaborate finishing touches. Here are notes on some of the most useful additions:

Mushrooms: Slice thinly and sauté in a little butter, bacon fat or dripping before adding to thick soups.

Onion: If a soup lacks flavour, add a little chopped onion and cook for a further few minutes before serving. Onion rings, cut thinly, dipped in egg white and flour and fried until golden-brown and crisp in a little dripping, bacon fat or butter, give a good flavour; they can be added to the soup just before serving.

Leek: Fried, chopped leek is a particularly good addition to potato soup.

Radishes: Slice thinly and add to the soup immediately before serving.

Cucumber: Slice very finely and serve with soup of any flavour, but especially with chicken.

Celery: Pick the tender sprigs from the ends of the stems, wash well and serve one or two in each bowl.

Lemon: Neatly cut wedges are delicious with many of the clear soups and with tomato soups.

Cheese: Freshly grated hard cheese is a pleasant accompaniment to almost any vegetable soup. To add interesting colour, flavour and vitamins, mix freshly chopped parsley or watercress with the grated cheese just before serving. Grated cheese is usually handed separately, but may also be sprinkled on the soup just before it is sent to table.

Cut-out shapes of processed cheese go well with tomato soup.

Bacon: Rind some lean rashers, cut into small strips or dice and fry lightly. Suitable for thick soups.

Sausages and Sausage-meat: Left-over cooked sausages go well with vegetable soups such as spinach. They should be cut into rounds or small strips and heated through in the soup just before serving. Raw sausage-meat may also be used. Roll it into pieces about the size of a marble, dust with flour and grill, fry or bake; alternatively, poach them in the soup for 10-15 minutes.

Melba Toast: Cut stale bread into very thin slices, lay them on baking sheets and dry off in the bottom of a very slow oven. Before serving, brown them lightly in a warm oven (325°F., mark 3) or under a very slow grill.

Fried Croûtons: Cut bread about $\frac{1}{2}$ inch thick and fry until golden-brown in a little dripping, bacon fat or lard. Cut into cubes and serve immediately. (If preferred, the bread can be cubed before frying.)

Toast Croûtons: Make toast just before serving the soup and cut into small dice.

Savoury Fritters: Make a fritter batter with 4 oz. plain flour, 1 egg and about $\frac{1}{4}$ pint milk, season well and add some mixed herbs and, if liked, a little chopped fried bacon or onion; fry in a little hot fat until golden-brown on both sides. Cut into neat strips and add to the soup just before serving.

Rice: Left-over dry boiled rice may be added to soup shortly before it is served, together with some freshly chopped parsley or chives. Rice may also be cooked in the actual soup or broth; in this case, it is added about $\frac{1}{2}$ hour before the end of the cooking time.

Macaroni and Spaghetti: These are good with minestrone and any thin soup. They should be broken into short lengths and are added to the soup about $\frac{1}{2}$ hour before it is to be served. Other types of Italian pasta, such as alfabeto, small conchiglia, cappellini and tagliatelle (broken in small pieces), look more unusual for special occasions; use them in small quantities only.

Scone Topping: Makes a good finish for a family-style casserole or ragoût. Make a scone dough, using 8 oz. self-raising flour, 2 oz. margarine, seasoning and sufficient milk to give a soft, pliable dough. Roll out about $\frac{1}{4}-\frac{1}{2}$ inch thick and cut into rounds. Put these on top of the cooked casserole, brush over with beaten egg yolk and milk and cook in a hot oven (425°F., mark 7) for about 15 minutes.

QUICKLY MADE SOUPS AND BROTHS

Canned and packet soups are an excellent standby and particularly good results can be obtained by adding individual flavourings and garnishes or by combining two different-flavoured soups. The modern bouillon cubes also make it possible to produce stock quickly and easily, since all you have to do is to dissolve them in boiling water; the usual proportion is one cube to $\frac{3}{4}$ pint water, but this may vary with different brands. There are normally two flavours—chicken and beef.

MINESTRONE
(see picture above)

1 lb. finely diced mixed vegetables	A sprig of thyme
2 oz. fat	1 oz. macaroni
2 pints stock	Seasoning to taste
$\frac{1}{2}$ a bay leaf	Grated cheese

Sauté the vegetables in the fat until they are soft—about 15 minutes. Add the stock, herbs and macaroni and boil for 15 minutes to reduce the soup, then simmer for 30 minutes. Check the seasoning and garnish with cheese.

PRAWN SOUP
(see colour picture no. 2)

A 1-lb. pkt. of frozen prawns	1 oz. plain flour
1$\frac{1}{2}$ pints water	2 oz. butter
1 onion, chopped	Salt and pepper
1 lemon	A little grated nutmeg
A pinch of mixed herbs	3 egg yolks
	$\frac{1}{4}$ pint single cream

Put the roughly chopped prawns into the water, add the onion, the lemon rind and herbs and simmer for about 5 minutes, then strain. Make a sauce from this stock with the flour, butter, seasoning and nutmeg. Add the prawns, with the juice of the lemon, and cook for about 2-3 minutes. Mix the egg yolks and cream with 2-3 tbsps. of the soup and add to the pan; re-heat but do not boil. Garnish if desired with parsley sprigs.

CREAM OF SPINACH SOUP
(see colour picture no. 2)

1$\frac{1}{2}$ lb. spinach, cooked	$\frac{1}{2}$ pint milk
1$\frac{1}{2}$ oz. butter	Salt and pepper
1 oz. plain flour	$\frac{1}{4}$ pint cream
1 pint chicken stock	Butter to garnish

Sieve the spinach. Make a sauce with butter, flour, stock and milk; add spinach and season to taste. Stir in the cream and re-heat (but do not boil). Before serving, put a knob of butter on each bowl of soup.

CELERY SOUP
(see picture above)

A head of celery	2 oz. fat
1$\frac{1}{2}$ pints stock or water	2 oz. plain flour
$\frac{1}{2}$ pint milk	$\frac{1}{4}$ pint cream or top of
1 sliced onion	the milk (optional)

Cut up the celery and cook in the stock or water until tender; sieve. Place the milk and onion in a small pan and bring to the boil. Remove the onion and add the flavoured milk to the celery purée. Melt the fat in a pan, add the flour and blend together. Gradually add the purée, with the cream if used, re-heat and season to taste. Garnish if desired with celery leaves.

MIXED VEGETABLE SOUP

1 lb. prepared mixed vegetables	1 level tsp. mixed herbs
1 pint stock	2 oz. fat
1 pint milk	2 oz. plain flour
1 slice of onion	Salt and pepper
	Parsley to garnish

Cook the vegetables in the liquids with the onion and herbs for 20 minutes. Sieve. Melt the fat in a saucepan, make a roux with the flour and gradually add the vegetables, stirring well. Season, re-heat and garnish.

SWEET CORN SOUP
(see colour picture no. 2)

A 4-oz. pkt. frozen whole sweet corn kernels	2 level tsps. cornflour
1 onion	$\frac{1}{2}$ pint milk
1 small red pepper	Salt, pepper and cayenne pepper
1 bay leaf	Chopped chives and
1 pint stock	cayenne to garnish

Put the sweet corn, finely chopped onion and red pepper, bay leaf and stock into a pan, bring to the boil and simmer gently for 15-20 minutes, then sieve. Return the soup to the pan, add the cornflour blended with a little milk and cook for 2-3 minutes. Add the remaining milk and bring to the boil. Season, then garnish with the chopped chives and a little cayenne pepper.

FRESH TOMATO SOUP
(see colour picture no. 2)

2 lb. fresh tomatoes	6 peppercorns
1 level tbsp. cornflour	2 slices of onion
1 pint milk	1 tbsp. tomato purée
1 bay leaf	Salt and pepper
1 clove	

Cut the tomatoes into quarters. Blend the cornflour with a little milk and add the rest of the milk. Pour into a saucepan, add the tomatoes, bay leaf, clove, peppercorns and finely chopped onion. Slowly bring to simmering point (this helps to prevent curdling) and simmer until the tomatoes are soft, then sieve. Add the tomato purée, re-heat and season to taste.

ONION SOUP

8 small onions	2 pints chicken stock
2 oz. butter	1 bay leaf
2 oz. plain flour	6 peppercorns

Slice the onions very thinly into rings. Melt the butter and sauté the onion until quite soft. Add the flour and gently re-cook to absorb the excess fat. Make up the stock, using chicken bouillon cubes, and add to the onion, with the bay leaf and peppercorns, and simmer for 30 minutes; check the seasoning.

CARROT SOUP

1 small potato, sliced	1 oz. fat
6-8 carrots, sliced	2 oz. plain flour
1 onion, sliced	Seasoning
1½ pints chicken stock	Parsley to garnish
½ pint milk	

Simmer the potato, carrot and onion in the stock until soft; sieve, then add the milk. Melt the fat in a saucepan, blend in the flour, gradually add the sieved soup and re-heat, stirring all the time. Season to taste and garnish with parsley.

PIMIENTO SOUP
(see colour picture no. 2)

3-4 red peppers, seeded	A little sugar
2 pints beef stock	1 rasher of streaky bacon
2 onions	for each person
2 tomatoes	A little sage and onion
Salt, pepper, cayenne	stuffing
1 oz. cornflour	Chopped parsley

Simmer the peppers in the stock with the sliced onions and tomatoes until soft. Sieve and season. Mix the cornflour with a little water, add to the soup, re-heat and add a little sugar to taste. Place some stuffing on each bacon rasher, roll up and grill for a few minutes. Serve the soup garnished with the bacon rolls and parsley, or plain, if preferred.

POTATO SOUP

4 medium-sized potatoes, sliced	Celery salt
I small onion, sliced	Grated nutmeg
1 bay leaf	Milk
Salt and pepper	Chopped parsley and grated cheese

Cover the potatoes and onion with water, add the bay leaf and add some salt, bring to the boil and simmer until the onion is soft. Sieve, then season well, adding a pinch of celery salt and a pinch of grated nutmeg. Thin the soup to the required consistency with milk and re-heat at once, garnished with chopped parsley and grated cheese.

PRESSURE-COOKED SOUPS

Using a pressure cooker is an obvious way to produce soups and broths quickly. Remember that the pan should be no more than two-thirds full and the rack should not be used. It is usual to cook at 15 lb. pressure. After cooking, the pressure is reduced under the cold tap—except in the case of dried vegetables, which tend to block the air vent if the pressure is reduced too quickly.
Ordinary soup recipes can be used by reducing the liquid to three-quarters the normal quantity and the cooking time to one-third.

ARTICHOKE SOUP

1 lb. Jerusalem artichokes	2 bacon rinds
1 onion	Salt and pepper
1 oz. fat	3-4 peppercorns
2 pints white stock (e.g., chicken)	1 bay leaf
	A little cream

Scrub and slice the artichokes; peel and slice the onion. Fry both in the fat until golden-brown. Add the stock, bacon rinds, seasonings and flavourings and cook under 15 lb. pressure for 10 minutes, then reduce the pressure under cold water. Strain and add the cream before serving.

LENTIL SOUP

½ oz. dripping or butter	6 oz. lentils
1 onion	1½ pints stock or water
1 carrot	Salt and pepper
2 medium-sized potatoes	A bunch of herbs
	¼ pint milk

Melt the fat in the pan, cut up the vegetables and sauté in the fat with the lentils. Add the liquid, seasonings and herbs. Put on the lid, bring steadily to pressure, lower the heat and cook for 15 minutes. Let the pressure drop slowly to zero, sieve the soup and re-heat. Add the milk to the soup, re-heat again and serve.

OXTAIL SOUP

1 oxtail	A bunch of herbs
2 onions	Salt and pepper
1 carrot	1 oz. plain flour
2 stalks of celery	A little port wine
1 oz. dripping	(optional)
1 quart stock	A squeeze of lemon
1 oz. bacon	juice

Wash and dry the oxtail; prepare and cut up the vegetables. Melt the fat in the pan and sauté the oxtail and vegetables. Cover with stock, bring to the boil, add the bacon, herbs and seasonings, put on the lid and bring to pressure. Lower the heat and pressure-cook for 45 minutes, then reduce the pressure. Strain the stock, cut all the meat off the bones and return the stock and meat to the pan, with extra seasoning if required. Bring to the boil, thicken with the flour blended with the wine or water and boil for 5 minutes, adding the lemon juice.

SCOTCH BROTH (PRESSURE-COOKED)

1-1½ lb. scrag end of mutton	1 quart water
1 small carrot, 1 onion and 1 turnip	Salt and pepper
	1 oz. pearl barley
	Chopped parsley

Cut the meat up small, removing the fat. Dice the vegetables. Place the meat in the pan and add the water, seasonings and barley. Fix the lid and bring steadily to pressure, lower the heat and cook for 20 minutes. Reduce the pressure, open the lid and skim any fat off the surface of the soup. Add the diced vegetables and pressure-cook for 5 minutes, then reduce the pressure. Serve in a tureen, sprinkled with the parsley.

CANNED SOUP VARIATIONS

Note: The number of servings obviously depends on the size of can you use.

Combine 1 can of oxtail and 1 of tomato soup, add lemon juice or sherry to taste and heat thoroughly; serve with grated cheese or croûtons.

Combine 1 can of pea soup and 1 of tomato soup; heat thoroughly. Meanwhile grill 4 bacon rashers till crisp, then chop; alternatively, mince 2 oz. cooked ham. Sprinkle over the soup before serving.

Drain and roughly chop 1 small can of crabmeat, mix with 1 can of asparagus soup and heat thoroughly. Serve sprinkled with chopped parsley.

Mix 1 can of chicken noodle soup with 1 of cream of mushroom and heat. Garnish with watercress.

Combine 1 can of pea soup with 1 can of asparagus soup, heat thoroughly and serve garnished with 1 oz. chopped shrimps.

Combine 1 can of vegetable broth with 1 of tomato soup, then add 1 oz. broken noodles and simmer for 15 minutes. Serve sprinkled with grated Parmesan cheese.

Combine 1 can of celery and 1 of mushroom soup, heat thoroughly; serve garnished with sour cream and sprinkled with chopped chives or about 2 oz. sliced and lightly fried mushrooms.

Fry 1 tbsp. mixed red and green peppers in ¼ oz. butter. Combine with 1 can of cream of chicken soup and simmer for 10 minutes before serving.

Fry 1 tbsp. each finely chopped onion, parsley and almonds in 1 tbsp. oil for 5 minutes. Add 1 can cream of chicken soup and simmer for 10 minutes.

Make up 1 pkt. of French onion soup and simmer for 5 minutes; add 1 can of oxtail soup with 1 bay leaf and 2 level tsps. curry powder; simmer for a further 10 minutes.

Fry 1 tsp. finely chopped onion with 2 oz. chopped mushrooms in ½ oz. butter for 5 minutes. Pour in 1 can of kidney soup and ⅓ can of milk or water and simmer for 10 minutes. Just before serving, add 1 tbsp. instant rice (separately cooked).

CLASSIC SOUP RECIPES

CRÈME DUBARRY

(see picture above)

1 firm white cauliflower	Seasoning and nutmeg
1½ oz. butter	¼ pint cream
1 oz. plain flour	or creamy milk
1½ pints white stock	2 egg yolks

Divide up the cauliflower, discarding the green leaves, and wash well in salted water. Melt the butter in a strong pan, remove from the heat and mix in the flour carefully; return the pan to the heat, then cook for a few minutes. Stir in the stock gradually, add the cauliflower (reserving a dozen well-shaped pieces), bring to the boil and simmer for 30 minutes. Meanwhile, cook the remaining flowerets in salted water until tender but not broken. Sieve the soup, season well and add a pinch of grated nutmeg. Whisk the cream and egg yolks together and add, stirring carefully; re-heat the soup gently (but do not boil) until it thickens. Serve garnished with the cauliflower sprigs.

MOCK TURTLE SOUP

½ a calf's head	A few mushrooms
2-3 quarts stock	A bouquet garni
Salt and pepper	1 bay leaf
2 oz. butter	2 oz. plain flour
2 oz. lean ham or bacon	¼-½ pint sherry
1-2 onions	Lemon juice
2 shallots	Forcemeat balls

Thoroughly wash the head, put it into a pan with the stock, bring to the boil, add the salt and simmer for 3-4 hours, skimming occasionally. Strain off and reserve the liquor, then take the meat from the bones and cut into small pieces. Meanwhile, melt the butter, add the diced ham (or bacon) and prepared vegetables and sauté for a few minutes, then add the herbs, seasoning and enough of the liquor to cover. Lid the pan and simmer gently for about ½ hour. Stir in the flour, blended with a little more liquor, bring to the boil, stirring, and cook for about 5 minutes, then strain into the remaining stock. Add the meat, more seasoning if necessary, sherry and lemon juice; then bring to the boil. Add the forcemeat balls and simmer for a few minutes.

WATERCRESS SOUP

(see picture above)

2 bunches of watercress (about ½ lb.)	Salt and pepper
	1 level tbsp. cornflour
½ oz. butter	¼ pint milk
1 pint stock	2-3 tbsps. cream

Wash the watercress well and remove the coarse stalks. Melt the butter in a saucepan, add the watercress (reserving a few sprigs) and toss over a very gentle heat for 2-3 minutes. Add the stock, salt and pepper, then cover and simmer gently for 20-30 minutes. Sieve, then return the soup to the pan, add the cornflour, blended with the milk, bring to the boil, stirring, and cook for 5-8 minutes. Add more seasoning if necessary and just before serving stir in the cream. Garnish with watercress.

CHESTNUT SOUP

2 onions	Salt, pepper, sugar
1 oz. butter	1 level tbsp. cornflour
A 1-lb. can of unsweetened chestnut purée	A little milk
	2-3 tbsps. cream
2 pints white stock	1 tbsp. chopped parsley

Slice the onions thinly and fry in the butter; add the chestnut purée and cook for about 5 minutes without colouring. Add the stock, seasoning and sugar and bring to the boil. Mix the cornflour with the milk, add to the soup, bring back to the boil and add the cream. Serve hot, garnished with parsley.

CREAM OF PUMPKIN SOUP

2 small onions, chopped	Salt and pepper
1 oz. butter	2 eggs, beaten
Cooked pumpkin (weight about 3 lb. before cooking)	1 pint milk
	A little grated cheese
	Chopped parsley, if
1 pint water	liked

Fry the onions lightly in the butter, put into a pan with the sieved pumpkin, water and seasonings and simmer for about 2 hours. Mix the eggs with the milk, add to the soup and heat very gently for a further few minutes to cook the egg, taking care to prevent curdling. Add the cheese and the parsley (if used) just before serving.

FRENCH ONION SOUP

(see picture above)

½ lb. onions	Seasoning
1½ oz. butter	A bay leaf
½ oz. plain flour	Slices of French bread
1½ pints boiling stock	Grated cheese

Slice the onions or chop finely, then fry in the melted butter until well and evenly browned—take care not to let the pieces become too dark. Add the flour, mixing well. Pour in the boiling stock, season, add the bay leaf and simmer for 30 minutes. Put the slices of bread into a soup tureen, pour on the soup and top with cheese.
Alternatively, put the soup in a fireproof casserole, float the slices of bread on it and cover with grated cheese; the soup is then heated in a hot oven for a few minutes.

GRAVY SOUP

1 lb. shin of beef	2 cloves and a blade
3 pints stock (cold)	of mace
1 oz. dripping	Pepper and salt
1 onion, thinly sliced	½ oz. cornflour or fine
1 carrot and a piece	sago, if required
of turnip (sliced)	Croûtons of toast

Mince the meat and add it to the stock, with any left-over gravy. Melt the dripping in a saucepan and brown the onion. Add the other vegetables and fry lightly, then add stock, meat, herbs and seasoning. Cover and simmer gently for 2-3 hours.
For a thin soup, strain, skim off any fat, then re-heat; re-season if necessary. For a thick soup, sieve, then re-heat. Blend the cornflour or sago with a little cold water, stir in, then bring to the boil, stirring, and cook for about 10 minutes. Serve with croûtons.

CREAM OF MUSHROOM SOUP

½ lb. mushrooms	1 oz. plain flour
½ pint stock	¾ pint milk
1 small onion, sliced	Pepper and salt
1 oz. butter	1 egg yolk

Wash and peel the mushrooms, chop finely and cook for ½ hour in the stock with the onion; sieve when tender. Melt the butter in a saucepan, stir in the flour and add the milk gradually. Bring to the boil, stirring meanwhile, then add the mushroom purée and seasoning and simmer for ¼ hour. Remove from the heat, allow to cool slightly, then stir in the beaten egg yolk. Cook for a few minutes, but do not boil, or the egg is likely to curdle. If desired, add a garnish of cooked mushrooms.

HOLLANDAISE SOUP

(see picture above)

1 tsp. each carrot and	1 pint stock
cucumber 'peas' and	Seasoning
green peas to	¼ pint milk
garnish (see below)	1 egg yolk
1 oz. butter	2-3 tbsps. cream
1 oz. plain flour	

First make the garnish: Cut pea-sized balls from pieces of carrot and cucumber, then cook separately in boiling salted water, drain and rinse. Melt the butter in a thick pan, remove from the heat, add the flour and mix in carefully. Return the pan to the heat and cook the mixture without browning. Slowly add the seasoned stock, stirring constantly, and bring to the boil; add half the milk. Blend the egg yolk, cream and remaining milk. Add the vegetable garnish to the soup, then strain in the thickening and cook gently, without boiling, until the soup thickens.

YOUNG NETTLE SOUP

1½ lb. young nettles	A little cold milk
1 lb. spinach	A few cooked sausages,
1 pint bone stock	cut in small pieces
Seasoning	2 tbsps. yoghourt or
1 oz. plain flour	sour cream

Blanch the nettles and mix them with the washed spinach. Pour the boiling stock over them, add some seasoning and simmer gently for 40 minutes, adding more stock as it becomes necessary. Sieve the soup and return it to the saucepan, then stir in the flour, blended to a smooth cream with the milk. Boil for 2-3 minutes, stirring, and re-season if necessary. Serve with a garnish of sausage and add the yoghourt or sour cream just before serving the soup.

CONSOMMÉ
(see picture above)

4 oz. lean juicy beef
1 qt. 'first' brown
   stock (cold)
2 carrots
2 sticks of celery
1 small onion (scalded)

1 white eggshell
1 blade of mace
6 peppercorns
Salt to taste
Garnish as desired

Trim any fat from the meat, then cut it up finely and soak it in $\frac{1}{4}$ pint cold water for $\frac{1}{4}$ hour. If necessary, skim any fat from the stock. Cut up the vegetables. Place all the ingredients in a pan and bring slowly to the boil, whisking constantly. When boiling point is reached stop whisking and boil fiercely for 1 minute. Let the soup stand for 15 minutes, then strain it through a cloth. Reheat and add any desired garnish.

SPLIT PEA SOUP

6 oz. yellow split peas
2 potatoes, 2 carrots
1$\frac{1}{2}$ pints stock (made
   from pork bones)

$\frac{1}{2}$ level tsp. dried thyme
   (tied in muslin)
8 oz. button onions

Soak the peas for 24 hours, boil until soft and sieve. Prepare and dice the potatoes and carrots. Combine the pea purée and stock and add the potatoes, carrots and thyme. Boil the soup until the vegetables are tender. Boil the prepared onions separately in $\frac{1}{2}$ pint water and when tender add them, with their cooking liquor, to the soup.

LOBSTER BISQUE

1 cooked hen lobster
1 quart stock or water
A small carrot and
   onion
1 bay leaf
A sprig of parsley
Salt and pepper
1 oz. butter

1 oz. plain flour
A squeeze of lemon
   juice
A little cream
$\frac{1}{2}$ glass sherry
Lobster butter
   (see end of recipe)

Remove the lobster meat from the shell and cut it into neat pieces, reserving the coral. Break up the shell and cook with the stock, vegetables, herbs and seasoning for $\frac{3}{4}$-1 hour, then strain. Melt the butter in a saucepan, add the flour and stir in the strained lobster stock by degrees. Bring to the boil, stirring, and cook for about 5 minutes. Add more seasoning if necessary, the lemon juice, cream and sherry. Add the pieces of lobster meat and whisk in the lobster butter.
Lobster Butter: Pound $\frac{1}{2}$ oz. lobster coral with 1 oz. butter and sieve the mixture.

ASPARAGUS SOUP
(see picture above)

1 bundle of asparagus
1 quart of white stock
Salt and pepper
1 oz. butter

1 oz. plain flour
$\frac{1}{4}$ pint milk
A little cream

Prepare the asparagus in the usual way, discarding the woody part, and cut it into short lengths. Cut off a few of the tips and tie in muslin: these are removed from the soup when tender and used as a garnish. Put the asparagus into a pan with the stock, add the seasonings, cover and boil gently until tender. Sieve (reserving the tips for garnish). Melt the butter and stir in the flour to form a roux. Add the asparagus purée and bring to the boil, stirring, then cook gently for 2-3 minutes. Add the milk, re-season if necessary and lastly stir in the cream and asparagus tips to garnish.

CELERIAC SOUP

1 lb. celeriac
1 large potato
1 small onion or leek
1 oz. butter
1$\frac{1}{2}$ pints stock, or
   milk and stock mixed

Pepper and salt
$\frac{1}{2}$ oz. plain flour
2-3 tbsps. milk or cream
Thin slices of toast
Grated cheese, if liked

Peel and slice the vegetables. Melt the butter, add the vegetables and cook for 5 minutes. Add the stock and seasoning, cover and simmer gently until all the vegetables are tender. Blend the flour smoothly with the milk or cream. Sieve the soup, return it to the pan with the blended flour and stir until boiling and creamy in consistency. Re-season and serve with the toast. A little grated cheese stirred into the soup just before serving gives a delicious flavour.

COLD SOUPS FOR SUMMER DAYS

ICED CUCUMBER SOUP

(See picture above)

1 small onion	4 tbsps. cream or
1½ pints stock	top of the milk
1 large cucumber	Seasoning
1 sprig of mint	Green colouring
1 level tsp. arrowroot	

Chop the onion and simmer for 15 minutes in a pan with the stock. Peel the cucumber thinly, cut into small pieces (reserving a little for garnish) and add to the stock, with the mint sprig; simmer until the cucumber is tender. Blend the arrowroot and cream together. Sieve the soup, return it to the pan and season well. Add the cream and arrowroot mixture and slowly re-heat until boiling point is reached; pour into a large bowl to cool. Tint the soup delicately with green colouring and chill it. Serve sprinkled with small cucumber dice or shredded mint.

CRÈME VICHYSSOISE

4 leeks	2 pints chicken stock
2 oz. butter	2 potatoes
1 onion, chopped	⅓ pint cream
Salt and pepper	Chives to garnish

Prepare the leeks, cut up finely and cook gently for 10 minutes in the butter, together with the onion and seasonings: do not allow to brown. Add the stock and the thinly cut potatoes and cook until the vegetables are tender, then sieve. Adjust the seasoning, stir in the cream and chill. Sprinkle with chopped chives before serving.

ICED CURRY SOUP

4 oz. finely chopped	2 pints chicken stock
onion	1 strip of lemon rind
1 oz. butter	1 bay leaf
1 tbsp. curry paste	2 level tsps. arrowroot
1 oz. plain flour	

Fry the onion in ¾ oz. butter until it is soft but not brown; add the curry paste and cook for 5 minutes.

Add rest of butter, stir in the flour and pour on the stock. Bring to the boil, add the lemon rind and bay leaf and simmer for 20 minutes. Strain the soup and return it to a clean pan. Mix the arrowroot with 1 tbsp. water and add to the soup; bring back to the boil, strain and allow to cool. Chill in the refrigerator before serving.

CHILLED BORTSCH

(see picture above)

1 quart good beef stock	2 tbsps. lemon juice
or 2 cans consommé	A good bunch of chives,
¼ pint sour cream or	finely chopped
yoghourt	Cream or sour cream
1 lb. cooked beetroot	Chives to garnish

Beat the stock with the cream or yoghourt until smooth. Add the beetroot, skinned and cut into small, neat dice. Add the lemon juice and chives and chill for several hours. Serve in cups with a spoonful of whipped cream or sour cream on each cup and garnish with chopped chives. (If preferred, this soup may be puréed.)

COLD CREAM OF MUSHROOM SOUP

1½ oz. butter	½ pint cream
1 oz. flour	Mushroom slices or
1½ pints chicken stock	tarragon leaves to
A 7½-oz. can of mushrooms	garnish

Melt the butter, add the flour and cook for 1 minute. Add the stock and blend well, then bring to the boil. Drain and sieve the mushrooms and add to the soup, with the cream. Simmer for about 3 minutes and pour into a bowl; cover and allow to cool, whisking occasionally. When the soup is very cold, whisk again and pour into cups. Sprinkle with the mushroom slices or 2-3 tarragon leaves before serving.

ICED TOMATO SOUP

2 tbsps. water	Salt and pepper
A 15-oz. can of tomato juice	2 level tsps. sugar
¼ pint single cream	Chopped parsley to
1 tbsp. sherry	garnish

Mix all the ingredients together in a basin and chill in the refrigerator. Immediately before serving add the chopped parsley.

CONSOMMÉ

Jellied consommé is a traditional summer delight. Follow the recipe on page 15 and allow to cool.

Here are some variations of cold consommé:

Add 2-3 tbsps. chopped herbs (chives, parsley and tarragon) to 1 quart consommé. Dissolve ¼ oz. of gelatine in a little sherry or Madeira, add to the mixture and chill until jellied. Serve roughly broken up in soup cups and garnish with whipped cream which has been flavoured with curry powder or sprinkled with toasted almonds.

Add ½ pint tomato juice to 1 quart consommé. Stir in 1 envelope of gelatine dissolved in a little lemon juice. Chill until jellied and serve broken up and garnished with sliced lemon and parsley. (See picture above.)

To 1 quart of consommé add some chopped mint leaves. Dissolve ¼ oz. of gelatine in about 4 tbsps. of sherry and add. Chill until jellied, then break up and serve in cups; garnish with whipped cream mixed with chopped mint.

Dissolve ¼ oz. gelatine in 2 tbsps. water and add 1 quart consommé with ½ a cucumber, peeled and finely diced. Chill until jellied. Serve broken up, in soup cups, and garnish each cup with a spoonful of soured cream and a twist of cucumber.

Blanch a red and a green pepper in boiling water for 5 minutes, then dice them, removing the seeds. Dissolve ¼ oz. gelatine in 2 tbsps. white wine and add to 1 quart consommé, with the peppers. Chill until jellied and serve broken up, in soup cups.

FRUIT SOUPS

Though less well-known here than on the Continent, these make a pleasant change on a summer's day.

RED CHERRY SOUP

(see right-hand picture above)

2 lb. cherries	A little red wine, if
2 quarts water	liked
¾ oz. cornflour	Whipped cream
2 oz. sugar	Unsweetened biscuits
Lemon juice	or rusks

Wash and stem the cherries, reserving a few of the best for garnishing, and put the remainder in a saucepan with the water. Simmer gently until tender, then rub through a sieve. Re-heat to boiling point, add the cornflour and sugar, mixed with a little water, and cook for about 10 minutes longer. Lastly, add the lemon juice and the reserved cherries (stoned). A little red wine may also be added to the mixture.

Allow the soup to become quite cold and serve it in glasses or in cups. A small spoonful of whipped cream may be put on the top; serve with biscuits or rusks.

GRAPE SOUP

1 can of grapes	1½ oz. sugar
¾ pint pineapple juice	2 level tbsps. seed pearl
¼ pint water	tapioca
1 piece of stick	1 level tsp. grated lemon
cinnamon	rind

Mix the strained grape juice, half the pineapple juice and the water and add the cinnamon and sugar, then bring to the boil. Add the tapioca and cook for about 30 minutes in a double saucepan, stirring occasionally; remove the cinnamon after 5 minutes. Meanwhile, de-seed the grapes. Take the pan from the heat, stir in the remaining pineapple juice and the lemon rind and put the mixture into the refrigerator. Just before serving, add the seeded grapes to the soup; serve in glasses.

SPICED CHERRY SOUP

1 lb. sweet red	½ level tsp. salt
cherries	1½ pints water
Rind of ½ a lemon	3 level tbsps. quick-cooking
6 whole cloves	tapioca
A 3-inch stick of cinna-	½ pint red wine
mon	Thin lemon slices and
⅓ cup granulated sugar	sour cream (optional)

Wash the cherries and remove the stems. With a vegetable peeler remove the rind from the lemon in strips; stick the cloves into the rind. In a saucepan, combine the cherries, lemon rind with the cloves, cinnamon, sugar, salt and water. Simmer uncovered for 15 minutes.

Gradually stir in the tapioca, bring to the boil, then remove from the heat; stir in the wine and allow to cool. Remove and discard the lemon rind, cloves and cinnamon, then refrigerate the soup.

To serve, ladle the ice-cold soup into individual soup bowls or plates. If desired, top each serving with a lemon slice and a spoonful of sour cream.

TRY A MEAL-IN-ITSELF SOUP

LENTIL SOUP

1 lb. lentils	½ level tsp. pepper
¼ lb. bacon, diced	½ level tsp. dried thyme
2 medium-sized onions	2 bay leaves
2 medium-sized carrots	1 large potato
2 quarts water	1 ham-bone
1 head of celery, sliced	2 tbsps. lemon juice
2½-3 level tsps. salt	

Wash the lentils the night before and leave to soak in cold water to cover. Early the next day drain them, then sauté the diced bacon till golden. Add the sliced onions and diced carrots and sauté till the onions are golden. Next, add the lentils, water, celery, salt, pepper, thyme and bay leaves. Now, using a medium grater, grate the peeled potato into the lentil mixture. Add the ham-bone and simmer, covered, for 3 hours, when the lentils should be quite tender. Remove the bay leaves and the ham-bone, cut all the meat from it and return the meat to the soup. Add the lemon juice and serve at once.

KIDNEY SOUP WITH HERB DUMPLINGS

1 oz. butter	Salt, pepper and thyme
1 onion	to taste
2 sticks of celery	Herb dumplings
1 carrot	(see p. 67)
½ lb. kidney	1 oz. cornflour
1¾ pints stock	⅛ pint milk

Heat the butter, then sauté the cut-up vegetables; add the chopped kidney, the stock and seasonings, bring to the boil and simmer for 2-2½ hours. Meanwhile, make the dumplings. Sieve the soup, add the blended cornflour and milk and simmer for a further ½ hour, until the dumplings are cooked.

ONION SOUP WITH CHEESE

6-8 onions	Salt
2 oz. butter or margarine	3-4 oz. grated cheese
2-3 pints water	Paprika

Peel and mince the onions and brown them lightly in the hot fat in the saucepan; add the water and some salt and allow to simmer until the onions are quite clear. Put the grated cheese in a warmed soup tureen and just before serving, pour the boiling soup over it, stirring constantly. Add some paprika to taste and serve the soup at once, garnished with parsley or croûtons.

LEEK AND POTATO SOUP WITH MEAT BALLS

¾ lb. leeks	Salt
¾ lb. potatoes	Pepper
1 oz. butter	1 tsp. mixed herbs
1¾ pints white stock	1 oz. plain flour
(e.g., chicken)	¼ pint milk

For the Meat Balls

4 oz. minced beef	Pepper
½ an onion, grated	¼ tsp. mixed herbs
2 tsps. tomato ketchup	½ an egg
Salt	1 oz. plain flour

Wash and slice the leeks and dice the potatoes, then sauté both in the butter for 5 minutes. Add the stock, seasonings and herbs; bring to the boil and simmer for 1 hour. Sieve the soup, add the blended flour and milk and re-boil, stirring until thick.

To make the meat balls, mix the meat with the onion, tomato ketchup, salt, pepper and herbs, then bind with the egg. Form into small balls and toss in the flour, add to the thickened soup and simmer for ½ hour.

CHICKEN CREAM SOUP

1 onion	2 oz. mushrooms
½ a green pepper	4 oz. peas
2 oz. butter	Chunks of chicken
2 oz. plain flour	1 bay leaf
1 pint chicken stock	Salt and pepper
½ pint milk	Toast croûtons

Chop the onion and pepper finely and sauté for 5 minutes in the butter. Add the flour and stir until cooked but not brown, then mix in the stock and milk gradually. Add the sliced mushrooms, peas, chicken and seasonings and bring to the boil, stirring all the time. Simmer gently for 1 hour. Serve with croûtons of toast.

MULLIGATAWNY SOUP

1 onion, chopped	2 cloves
1 carrot, grated	1 tbsp. chopped parsley
½ lb. tomatoes, chopped	Sugar, salt and pepper
½ a green pepper,	to taste
chopped	1 oz. cornflour
2 sticks of celery,	¼ pint milk
chopped	Leftovers of cold cooked
1 apple, grated	chicken, cut in neat pieces
1 oz. butter	1 oz. rice, already
1¾ pints chicken stock	cooked
1 level tsp. curry powder	

Sauté the vegetables and apple in the butter for 5 minutes. Add the stock, flavourings and seasonings and simmer for 2-2½ hours, then sieve. Blend the cornflour with the milk and stir it into the soup. Add the chicken and the rice and re-boil to thicken.

THICK TOMATO SOUP

1 oz. butter	Salt, pepper and paprika
1 small onion	to taste
1 carrot	1¾ pints stock
2 sticks of celery	1 oz. cornflour or
1 lb. tomatoes	plain flour
1 clove	¼ pint milk
1 bay leaf	1 oz. pasta or rice
1 level tsp. sugar	Parmesan cheese

Melt the fat and sauté the cut-up onion, carrot and celery for 5 minutes. Add the quartered tomatoes, flavourings, seasonings and stock, bring to the boil and simmer for 1½ hours. Sieve the soup. Blend the cornflour with the milk, add to the soup and re-boil, stirring until thick. Add the pasta or rice and simmer gently for ½ hour. Serve with grated Parmesan cheese.

CABBAGE SOUP WITH MEAT BALLS

(see picture above)

1½ lb. white cabbage	½ level tsp. mixed spice
2 oz. butter	6 peppercorns
3 pints hot beef stock	2 level tsps. salt

For the Meat Balls

¼ lb. minced veal	1 tbsp. chopped onion
¼ lb. minced pork	1 level tsp. salt
2 tbsps. dry bread crumbs	Pepper
	4 tbsps. cream

First make the meat balls. Combine the dry ingredients and gradually mix in the cream. Shape into small balls, using about a teaspoonful for each.

Trim the cabbage and cut into cubes, discarding the core and tough portions. Melt the butter in a thick-based pan, add the cabbage and brown it. Add the stock, flavourings and salt, cover and simmer until the cabbage is tender—up to about 30 minutes. Add the meat balls for the last 5 minutes of the cooking time.

SOUP WITH POACHED EGGS

1½ pints chicken broth	Butter or margarine
½ pint undiluted canned consommé	4 eggs
8 1-inch slices of long Continental bread	Grated Parmesan or Cheddar cheese

Heat the broth and consommé in a saucepan and bring to the boil; meanwhile sauté the bread in hot butter in a large frying pan until browned on both sides. Poach the eggs in the hot (not boiling) soup in the usual way, then place one egg in each soup plate. Pour some broth over the eggs (strain it if desired). Sprinkle the sautéed bread with cheese, place 2 slices beside each egg and hand additional cheese at table.

BEER AND MILK SOUP

1 bottle of beer	1 pint milk
Juice of ½ a lemon	2 egg yolks
A piece of cinnamon stick	Sugar and salt
	Croûtons of fried bread

Heat the beer in a pan with the lemon juice and cinnamon. Heat the milk and pour it over the egg yolks, stirring well. Add to the hot beer and season with sugar and salt. Serve with the croûtons.

LENTIL AND BACON SOUP

(see picture above)

1 lb. lentils	A small bunch of parsley
2 pints water	Salt
Garlic to taste	½ lb. bacon, diced
1 clove	1 lb. potatoes

Wash the lentils and soak overnight. Boil them in the same water, adding the garlic, clove, coarsely chopped parsley and some salt. Add the bacon and allow to simmer until both lentils and bacon are cooked. Then add the potatoes, peeled and cut into very small dice, and cook for a further 20 minutes. If a thicker soup is required, brown some butter with a little flour and add just before serving.

MINESTRA

1¼-1½ lb. cut-up carrots, leeks, celery, cabbage, turnip	3½ pints water
	1 oz. rice
1 onion	1 oz. macaroni
1-2 tomatoes	4 potatoes
1 cup French beans	4 oz. lean bacon
1 clove of garlic	Parsley and basil to taste
1½ oz. butter or fat	Seasoning

Fry all the vegetables in the butter for 20 minutes over a low heat. Add the liquid and cook for 2 hours. Add the rice, macaroni and potatoes and cook for another 25 minutes. Add the diced bacon and herbs and cook for a few minutes more. Season and serve with grated cheese.

CREAMY VEGETABLE SOUP

2 lb. mixed vegetables (e.g. carrots, onions, celery, turnips, tomatoes)	Salt and pepper
	2 oz. pearl barley
	¾ oz. cornflour
	Milk
2 oz. dripping	Carrot, turnip and peas for garnish
2 pints stock	

Cut the vegetables into neat pieces and sauté in the hot dripping until all the fat is absorbed. Add the stock, bring to the boil and season well. Cover and simmer gently for 1 hour, or until the vegetables are tender. Sieve, return to the pan with the barley and continue to cook. Blend the cornflour with a little milk and add a few minutes before the soup is ready. Meanwhile, cut

strips and balls of carrot and turnip, using a Parisian potato-cutter, and cook in boiling salted water; add the peas just before the end of the time. Garnish the soup with these extra vegetables.

BOUILLABAISSE
(see picture above)

2 lb. fish (hake, John Dory, red mullet, sole, crayfish, etc.—weighed after boning)	Peppercorns
	4 cloves
	A sprig of thyme
	A bay leaf
$\frac{1}{2}$ lb. tomatoes	Shredded rind of 1 orange
$\frac{1}{2}$ lb. onions	Olive oil
$\frac{3}{4}$ lb. carrots	1 quart water
2 oz. sliced red peppers	Salt and pepper
1 large bunch of parsley	A pinch of saffron
2 oz. celery	Chopped parsley
1 clove of garlic	Bread slices
2 shallots	Dublin Bay prawns

Prepare the fish and put the chopped heads, tails, bones, shells and trimmings in a large pan with $\frac{1}{4}$ lb. tomatoes and the vegetables and flavourings (except the seasoning, saffron, and chopped parsley). Moisten the mixture with olive oil, stir well, add the water and cook for 1 hour, adding a seasoning of salt, pepper and saffron half-way through.
Strain the liquor into a clean pan, skim and bring to the boil; add the pieces of fish, with the remaining $\frac{1}{4}$ lb. tomatoes (sliced) and 1 tbsp. roughly chopped parsley, and simmer until the fish is cooked. To serve, pour on to thick slices of crusty bread laid in soup plates. The fish is often served separately, garnished with halved Dublin Bay prawns.

FISH CHOWDER
(see right-hand picture above)

1 lb. fresh haddock	2-3 sliced potatoes
$\frac{1}{2}$ pint fish stock	A 15-oz. can of tomatoes
1 sliced onion	Salt and pepper
A few bacon rinds	1 bay leaf
$\frac{1}{2}$ oz. butter	2 cloves

Skin the fish and simmer the skins in $\frac{1}{2}$ pint water to make the stock. Fry the onion and bacon rinds in the

fat for 5 minutes. Add the sliced potatoes and the fish, cut into cubes. Beat the tomatoes to a thick purée, combine with the fish mixture and add the seasoning and flavourings. Simmer for $\frac{1}{2}$-$\frac{3}{4}$ hour. Remove the bay leaf and cloves and garnish with parsley before serving.

EMERGENCY MEASURES
Quick satisfying soups can be made by adding a variety of ingredients to stock made from bouillon cubes. Here are some of the innumerable variations.

ALMOND SOUP
Heat 2 tbsps. olive oil and fry 4 oz. finely chopped almonds, 1 tbsp. chopped onion, $\frac{1}{2}$ tsp. chopped garlic and 1 tsp. chopped parsley, stirring all the time with a spoon. The mixture should be well cooked but not browned. Add 1 oz. breadcrumbs and cook very slowly for a further 3 minutes. Pour on 2 pints stock made from chicken bouillon cubes, season well and simmer for 15 minutes.

SPANISH TOMATO SOUP
Make a roux from 1 oz. butter and 1 oz. flour, add hot stock made from chicken cubes and 1 pint water, blend carefully, then add 1 pint tomato pulp and season well with salt and pepper. Bring to the boil and simmer for 3 minutes. Cook $\frac{1}{2}$ lb. vermicelli in boiling salted water, drain and add to the soup. Serve with grated cheese handed separately.

CHICKEN AND RICE SOUP
Cook 2 oz. instant rice in 1 quart stock made from chicken cubes and water for 10 minutes. Remove from the heat and cool slightly. Pour on to 2 egg yolks, gently whisking all the time. Finally, add the juice of 1 lemon and serve at once.

CHEESE SOUP
Make a roux with 2 oz. butter and 1 oz. plain flour. Add 3 pints stock made from chicken bouillon cubes and water and cook for 10 minutes. Add 2 oz. cooked noodles and 2 oz. grated cheese and heat for a few minutes longer. Serve sprinkled with 1 tbsp. chopped chives or some chopped parsley.

FISH COOKERY

Recipes give 4 servings, unless otherwise indicated

A GUIDE TO FISH BUYING

Whatever fish you buy, the first essential is that it should be absolutely fresh; the fish should smell pleasant, with no trace of ammonia; it should be stiff, not flabby, and scales should be lustrous and easy to rub off. Any spots and markings should be bright, the gills should be red and the eyes bright, clear and not sunken. The largest fish are not always the best—usually medium-sized ones have a better flavour and finer texture.

Here are notes on most of the fish you are likely to see on sale:

Bream: White-fleshed fish of delicate flavour. Sea bream is available all the year; best from June to December; fresh-water bream in season July to February. Bream can be baked, grilled, poached or fried.

Brill: A good-flavoured fish, not unlike turbot and cooked in the same ways. In season practically all the year, but only in small quantities.

Cod: Available all the year; best from October to May. The close, white flesh is somewhat lacking in flavour, but is improved if cooked with herbs, stuffing or vegetables. Can be grilled, baked, fried in batter or used in made-up dishes.
Smoked cod fillet is used like smoked haddock.

Dabs: Small flat fish of the plaice family. Available all the year—best from June to February. Suitable for frying, baking, steaming and poaching.

Eels: Best during autumn and winter. Suitable for baking, frying, stewing or serving jellied.

Flake (sometimes called Dogfish): Available all the year; best from October to June. Suitable for frying, poaching, steaming and for made-up dishes.

Flounders: Resemble plaice, but less good flavour and texture. Available in small quantities most of the year. Suitable for frying, steaming and poaching.

Gurnet and Gurnard: Available all the year but not so good April to June. Suitable for baking, frying and poaching. Excellent cold with salad.

Haddock: Available all the year; best from September to February. Suitable for cooking by all methods.
Smoked haddock, golden cutlets and smoked haddock fillet are usually poached or grilled or used in made-up dishes such as kedgeree.

Hake: Good flavour and texture. Available all the year; best from June to January. Cooked like cod. The dark-coloured Scotch hake is cheaper than Devonshire hake.

Halibut: A large fish with delicate flavour, cheaper than turbot and not quite so good. Available all the year; best from August to April. Suitable for cooking by all methods; excellent cold with salad.

Herring: These inexpensive fish are excellent and nutritious, rich in oils and vitamins. Two main home seasons—May to August and October to December. Suitable for cooking by most methods, including sousing and serving cold. Also prepared in various ways, as under:
Kippers: Herrings that have been split open, soaked in brine, then smoked over wood chips and sawdust to give them their unique smoky flavour. Some of them are now dyed. They are usually poached or grilled.
Bloaters: Herrings that have been soaked in brine, smoked and cured; unlike kippers, they are cured whole and for a shorter period.
Salt Herrings: the fish are gutted and preserved between layers of salt in barrels.
Rollmops: the herrings are filleted, packed in barrels with brine and vinegar, then later rolled up and packed in jars with spices, onions or other flavourings, according to the manufacturer's particular recipe.
Bismark Herrings: are pickled and spiced like rollmops, but left whole.
Buckling: herrings smoked whole, at a higher temperature and for a longer time than kippers, so that they are lightly cooked during the curing. Very delicate in flavour.

John Dory: An ugly fish with delicious flavour. In season October to December. Can be poached or baked whole, or filleted and then cooked as for sole; it may also be served cold, with salad.

Lemon Sole: Available all the year; best from July to February. Cook by any method.

Mackerel: In season October to July; at its best April to June. Cook as for herring. Mackerel must be perfectly fresh.

Plaice: Flat fish distinguished by red spots on dark side. Available all the year; best from May to January. Suitable for all methods of cooking, including serving cold.

Red Mullet: Firm, white flesh with delicious flavour. Best in summer months. Suitable for baking, poaching and grilling; good cold with salad.

Salmon: Small and medium sizes are best. Seasons: English and Scottish, February to August; Irish, January to September. Suitable for poaching, grilling, baking and also for serving cold.

Salmon Trout: In season March to August. Serve poached, grilled, baked or cold with salad.

Skate: A coarse white fish with a large percentage of bone. Suitable for poaching or frying, or to serve cold with salad.

Sole: A flat fish, with firm, deliciously flavoured white flesh. Seasonable all the year. Suitable for any method of cooking.

Sprats: Best from November to March, but supplies affected by weather. Best deep-fried or grilled.

Trout (River): Much prized for its delicate flavour. In season February to early September, but best from April to August. Serve grilled, baked or fried. Delicious served cold.

Turbot: Considered the finest of the flat fish. Seasonable most of the year; best from March to August. Grill, bake or cook by any method. Excellent cold with salad.

Whitebait: Tiny silver fish, the young of the herring and sprat. Most seasonable May to July. Best deep-fried.

Whiting: Available all the year, best in winter months. The traditional fish for invalids. Serve poached, steamed, baked or fried.

WAYS WITH FISH

Grilling: Ideal for thick steaks, cutlets and for herring, trout, etc. See recipes for grilled sole and grilled herrings, etc., and remember these points: season the fish well and brush liberally with fat; score whole fish on each side. Pre-heat the grill, put the fish on to the hot greased grid and turn the heat to moderate; grill gently till tender—5-20 minutes, according to size—turning it once or twice.

Baking: Small cod, hake or haddock (stuffed or plain), and good-sized cutlets are excellent this way. The recipes for Baked Stuffed Mackerel and Cod Véronique show the main methods, in which fish is cooked in fat or liquid. To enjoy baked fish at its best, season it well, cook in a covered dish and bake gently—usually in a moderate oven (350°F., mark 4); allow 10-15 minutes for small pieces, 25 minutes per lb. for stuffed fish.

Poaching: One of the simplest methods, suitable for thin cuts, fillets and smoked fish. Put the fish in a shallow pan, half-cover it with milk or milk and water, add salt and pepper and cook very gently over a low heat, allowing 5-10 minutes. according to thickness. Make a sauce with the liquor.

Boiling: This method is suitable for large whole fish. Put enough water in a fish kettle to cover the fish, bring to the boil and lower the fish in. (Failing a fish kettle, put the fish on a plate and lower it with the aid of a muslin sling.) To improve the flavour, add 1-2 onions, a bay leaf, a blade of mace and some thyme. Simmer slowly, over a low heat, allowing 8-10 minutes per lb.—don't let the water boil again.

Steaming: Steamed fish need not be insipid if you pay attention to seasoning and accompaniments. Small pieces, which take about 10-15 minutes, can be steamed between two plates placed over a pan of boiling water. (See picture below.)
Cook larger pieces or whole fish in a steamer, allowing 30 minutes for cutlets, 15 minutes per lb. for whole fish; adjust the heat so that water in steamer boils steadily. Season the fish and dab with butter before cooking.

Shallow Frying: Excellent for such whole fish as sole, and for fillets, etc.—see Fried Plaice. First coat the fish; the simplest way is to use seasoned flour; other methods are to dip it in seasoned flour, into milk, then into flour again, or to coat with flour, then with beaten egg and finally with breadcrumbs. Use just enough really hot fat to prevent sticking; brown on either side, then fry gently. (See picture below.)

Deep Frying: Used for small fish or pieces, which must be coated with egg and breadcrumbs or batter—see Curled Whiting and Scampi Fritti recipes. The fat is all-important—oil, clarified beef fat or lard is suitable; it must be pure, free from moisture, and heated in a deep pan to 350°-375°F. Put the fish in a frying basket, remove the pan from the heat, lower in the basket, quickly replace over the heat and cook until the fish is golden. Drain well and serve at once.

CHEF'S TIPS

Fish is sufficiently cooked when it will readily separate from the bone (test with the back of a knife), or when the flesh is opaque, white and firm.

When filleting and skinning fish, use a really sharp, pliable knife, and dip your fingers in coarse salt to get a good grip.

To minimise the smell of such fish as herrings cook them in a covered container or wrap in greaseproof paper or aluminium foil.

Wipe fish pans, dishes and cutlery with soft paper immediately after use and rinse in cold water. A little mustard in the washing-up water will kill the smell.

Whenever "olive oil" or "oil" is mentioned, you can use any form of cooking oil.

Frozen fish can be substituted in many of these recipes; canned fish is good in made-up dishes.

FISH RECIPES

GRILLED SALMON CUTLETS
(see picture on page 23)

The cutlets should be about 1 inch thick. Wipe them dry and brush with salad oil or melted butter. Grease the grill pan and cook the fish under a fairly hot grill, allowing about 10 minutes to each side, as necessary, and adding a little more fat as it cooks. Serve garnished with lemon and watercress, accompanied by melted butter, maître d'hôtel butter or Belgian Cucumber (see Vegetables chapter).

BAKED SALMON CUTLETS

4 salmon cutlets, about ½ inch thick	¼ pint dry white wine
4 oz. butter	Cucumber
Lemon	Salt and pepper
	Parsley and watercress

Wipe the cutlets. Melt half the butter and put it into a casserole, then add the salmon, with the juice of half a lemon and the white wine. Cover and bake in a moderate oven (350°F., mark 4) for 25-30 minutes, till the flesh is opaque and will leave the bone readily. Meanwhile peel and dice the cucumber, simmer it in salted water until tender, then drain it and add the rest of the butter, salt, pepper and some chopped parsley. Dish up the fish and garnish with the cucumber, the melted butter and watercress, or with asparagus, when available.

GRILLED SOLE

(see colour picture no. 5)

Wash the sole and remove the black skin. Sprinkle with salt, brush with melted butter and grill under a hot grill for 2-3 minutes on each side. Serve with maître d'hôtel butter.

SOLE MEUNIÈRE

1 small sole, whole or filleted, per person	Butter
Salt and pepper	Lemon juice
Flour	Chopped parsley

Season the sole with salt and pepper, flour it lightly on both sides and fry it in the butter until the fish is cooked and golden-brown on both sides. Serve on a hot dish, sprinkle with lemon juice and parsley, then pour on some lightly-browned melted butter.

SOLE AU VIN BLANC

1 small sole per person	½ oz. flour
2 shallots, finely chopped	A few button mushrooms
½ oz. butter	Salt and pepper
¼ pint white wine	

Put the soles into an ovenproof dish. Fry the shallots in the butter for 3-4 minutes, add the wine and pour over the soles. Cover with greased paper and bake in a fairly hot oven (375°F., mark 5) for 7 minutes. Drain off the liquid and add the flour, blended with a little water. Bring to the boil, add the mushrooms and boil gently for 2-3 minutes. Season well and pour over the sole.

SOLE COLBERT

1 small sole per person	Browned crumbs
1 level dessertsp. seasoned flour	Deep fat for frying
Beaten egg	1 oz. maître d'hôtel butter
	Fried parsley

Ask the fishmonger to clean and skin the soles, leaving the fish whole. With a sharp knife, cut down the centre of the fish on one side, loosening both fillets a little from the bone, so that they can be rolled back, leaving a long depression in the centre of the fish. Dust the fish with seasoned flour, then brush with egg and coat with browned crumbs, shaking off any surplus. Fry the sole in deep fat until golden brown. Serve them garnished with maître d'hôtel butter (placing this in the hollow in the centre of the fish) and with fried parsley.

PAUPIETTES OF SOLE WITH MUSHROOM SAUCE

(see picture below)

8 fillets of sole	2 oz. button mushrooms
A 2-oz. pkt. of frozen shrimps	½ pint milk
1½ oz. butter	Salt and pepper
	1 oz. flour

Roll up the fillets with 2 or 3 shrimps inside each one and stand them upright in an ovenproof dish. Put a very small knob of butter on each and cover with greaseproof paper. Bake in a moderate oven (350°F., mark 4) for 20 minutes. Meanwhile, wash the mushrooms and stew them gently in the milk with salt and pepper for 10-15 minutes. Drain off the liquid. Melt 1 oz. of the butter and add the flour, then gradually add the milk and fish liquor. Bring to the boil, add the mushrooms and pour over the fish.

GLAZED PAUPIETTES OF SOLE

2 filleted sole	¼ pint tomato sauce
Anchovy paste	8 rounds of tomato
Fish stock or water	1 lettuce
½ pint stiff aspic jelly	2 stoned olives

Season the fillets, spread with anchovy paste, roll up neatly and place on a greased tin. Pour on sufficient fish stock or water to come half-way up the fish, cover the tin with greased paper and bake in a moderate oven (350°F., mark 4) for 10-15 minutes. Lift on to a rack and leave to cool. Mix the aspic jelly with the tomato sauce and when the mixture is cold and on the point of setting, glaze the fish with it. Place each fillet on a round of tomato and garnish with crisp lettuce leaves and any remaining aspic jelly, chopped and placed round the dish. Lay half a stoned olive on top of each paupiette.

FRIED PLAICE
(see picture below)

8 fillets of plaice	Fat for frying
Beaten egg	Parsley and lemon
Breadcrumbs for coating	to garnish

First skin the fillets, using a sharp knife; put the fish, skin side down on a board; hold the tail with your left hand and slide the fish off the skin with the knife held in the right hand. Brush the fillets with egg and dip in crumbs. Fry in shallow fat for about 2 minutes on each side. Garnish and serve.

GLAZED FILLETS OF PLAICE

8 plaice fillets	4 tbsps. liquid aspic jelly
2 tbsps. mayonnaise	Radishes and cucumber
1 tbsp. tomato ketchup	to garnish

Skin the fillets, roll them up, steam or poach for 10-15 minutes, then leave to cool on a rack. Mix the mayonnaise, tomato ketchup and aspic jelly together and when on the point of setting, coat the cold fish fillets. Garnish with radish and cucumber skin and serve with radish "roses" and tomatoes.

For a simpler version the cold fillets can be coated with plain mayonnaise and garnished with anchovy fillets.

BAKED RED MULLET

Clean one mullet for each person and put into a well-buttered ovenproof dish. Add salt and pepper, put a little butter on each fish, cover with greased greaseproof paper and cook for about 20 minutes in a moderate oven (350°F., mark 4).

GRILLED TROUT

4 small trout	Lemon and watercress
Olive oil	to garnish
Salt and pepper	

Prepare the trout, then brush them with olive oil and sprinkle with salt and pepper. Put them on a hot grill and cook for 5-10 minutes on each side. Serve at once, garnished with lemon and watercress.

CURLED WHITING
(see picture below)

1 whiting for each person	Deep fat for frying
Beaten egg	Parsley
Browned crumbs	Lemon twists

Clean the fish, but do not cut off the head; remove the eyes. Skin the whiting as follows: slit the skin down the back with a sharp knife, and also cut it round at the tail end of the fish. Dip your fingers in cooking salt, then pull off the skin. Dip the fish in egg and cover with breadcrumbs. Take the tail of each fish and push it through the eye sockets. Fry in deep fat for about 4 minutes, and serve garnished with sprigs of parsley and lemon twists.

TIPSY COD

2 onions, finely chopped	A little chopped parsley
1 oz. butter	Peppercorns
1½ lb. cod fillet	Salt and pepper
1 bay leaf	Brown ale
A little chopped thyme	½ oz. cornflour

Fry the onions in the butter till faintly coloured, then spread in the bottom of an ovenproof dish. Put the pieces of cod fillet on this mixture, add the herbs and seasoning and cover with ale. Cook in a moderate oven (350°F., mark 4) for about 25 minutes. Strain the liquid from the fillets and thicken it with the cornflour, blended with a little water. Bring to the boil, stirring all the time, and pour over the fish.

1. Vegetables are the basis of many a good soup

2. Pimiento, Sweet Corn, Cream of Spinach, Fresh Tomato and Prawn Soups

3. Baked Salmon Cutlets

4. Grilled Herrings

5. Grilled Sole

6. Roast Beef

7. Mixed Grill

8. Baked Ham, Virginian style

COD VÉRONIQUE

4 cod cutlets	Salt and pepper
1 shallot, sliced	1 oz. butter
2 oz. button mushrooms	1 oz. flour
Fish stock	$\frac{1}{4}$ pint milk
A little white wine (optional)	1 cupful white grapes, peeled, halved and stoned

Wash the fish and put into a baking dish. Add the shallot and mushrooms and cover with stock and the wine, if used. Season and bake in a fairly hot oven (375°F., mark 5) for 20 minutes. Drain off $\frac{1}{4}$ pint of the liquid, and arrange the fish on a dish. To make a sauce, melt the butter, add the flour and gradually stir in $\frac{1}{4}$ pint stock and the milk. Season and boil the sauce until it thickens; add most of the grapes. Pour this sauce over the fish and garnish with remaining grapes and mushrooms.

SCALLOPED SMOKED HADDOCK
(see picture below)

1 lb. smoked haddock	1 oz. flour
$\frac{1}{2}$ pint milk	Seasoning
1 level tbsp. chopped onion	Browned crumbs
	Creamed potato
1 blade of mace	Watercress or parsley
1 oz. butter	to garnish

Wash the fish and simmer gently in the milk with the onion and mace. Remove the fish and flake it, then divide between 5 scallop shells. Melt the butter, add the flour, then gradually add the milk, stirring all the time. Bring to the boil, season well and pour the sauce over the fish; sprinkle with crumbs. Pipe the potato all round the edge of the shells, or just across the straight edge. Put under the grill to heat through and brown the potato, garnish and serve.

GRILLED HERRINGS
(see colour picture no. 4)

To clean the fish, cut off the heads with a sharp knife or scissors, removing the inside at the same time. Remove any black skin from inside, and wash clean. Scrape off the scales with the back of a knife and cut off the fins and tails with the scissors. Rinse the fish thoroughly and dry well. Brush the herrings over with melted butter or dripping and put on a hot grid. Cook under a hot grill, browning first one side, then the other, then lower the heat to finish cooking—they should take about 3 or 4 minutes on each side. Serve at once on a hot dish, garnished with lemon slices.

DEVILLED HERRINGS
(see picture below)

2 herrings	2 small tsps. curry paste
2 oz. butter	2 tbsps. lemon juice
$\frac{1}{2}$ level tsp. curry powder	Lemon to garnish

Clean and fillet the herrings. Cream the butter and work in the curry powder, paste and lemon juice. Spread over the fish and grill. Serve at once on a hot dish, garnished with cut lemon.

BAKED STUFFED MACKEREL

4 mackerel	Butter to baste

For the Stuffing

1 oz. shredded suet	1 tsp. chopped parsley
1 oz. ham or bacon, chopped	A pinch of mixed herbs
	Grated rind of $\frac{1}{2}$ a lemon
2 oz. fresh white breadcrumbs	Salt and pepper
	Beaten egg

Cut off the heads and tails of the fish, clean them, remove the roe and take out the backbone. Mix all the stuffing ingredients together, binding them with the beaten egg. Stuff the fish, lay them in a greased baking dish, and cook for 40 minutes in a warm oven (325°F., mark 3), basting well with butter during the cooking.

SOUSED MACKEREL

4 mackerel	4 cloves
1 large onion	1 bay leaf
A blade of mace	Vinegar and water
12 peppercorns	

Clean the mackerel and cut off the heads and tails. Slice the onion and put it into an ovenproof dish with the mackerel and herbs. Cover with equal quantities of vinegar and water. Put a piece of greaseproof paper over the top and cook in a moderate oven (350°F., mark 4) for 1-1$\frac{1}{2}$ hours; leave to cool in the liquor. Serve with salad.

WHITEBAIT

Wipe the fish well with a clean cloth and dust them with flour. Put the whitebait into a frying basket and shake off any excess flour. Heat some lard or oil in a deep frying pan and when the fat is hot enough to brown a cube of bread in 1 minute, plunge the fish into it. Fry it for about 2 minutes, shaking the basket once or twice during the frying. Drain the whitebait on kitchen paper in the oven, and serve piled on a napkin and garnished with cut lemon. Serve brown bread and butter with the fish.

FISH MORNAY

1 lb. cooked white fish	Seasoning
1 oz. butter	1-2 oz. grated cheese
1 oz. flour	2 or 3 tomatoes
½ pint milk	

Remove the skin and bones from the fish and flake it roughly with a fork. Melt the butter and add the flour; cook for a minute, and then gradually add the milk. Bring to the boil, season and add most of the cheese. Mix with the fish and pour into a shallow fireproof dish, together with the cut-up tomatoes. Sprinkle with grated cheese and bake for 30 minutes in a fairly hot oven (400°F., mark 6).

FISH MOUSSE

8 oz. cooked fish	½ oz. gelatine
Pepper	½ pint fish stock
3 tbsps. lemon juice	¼ pint unsweetened
¼ pint salad cream	evaporated milk
½ level tsp. celery salt	

Mix the fish, pepper, lemon juice, salad dressing and celery salt together. Dissolve the gelatine in the stock and allow to cool before adding it to the fish; whisk the evaporated milk. When the fish and gelatine mixture is almost setting, fold the milk into it. Turn out when set and serve with salad.

To make the dish more decorative, line the serving dish with lettuce leaves and garnish with crimped cucumber and tomato twists—see page 126 for directions.

FISH PIE
(see picture below, left)

1½ lb. cod fillet	½ pint white sauce
2 oz. shelled prawns	½ lb. mashed potato
2 hard-boiled eggs	Egg to glaze

Cook the cod, then remove all the bones and skin and flake the fish. Put it in a casserole, together with the prawns and sliced eggs, and cover with the sauce. Cream the potato, adding a little milk if necessary, and cover the pie with it. Brush the potato with the egg, cook in a fairly hot oven (400°F., mark 6) for 35 minutes.

SAVOURY FISH CROQUETTES

½ lb. mashed potatoes	Egg to bind
½ lb. cooked white fish	Egg and breadcrumbs
2 tsps. chopped parsley	Deep fat for frying
1 oz. butter	Lemon and watercress to
Seasoning	garnish

Mix the potatoes, flaked fish and parsley together. Melt the butter in a saucepan, add the fish and potatoes, seasoning and enough egg to bind. Divide the mixture into 8 portions and form into cork-shaped pieces; coat with egg and crumbs and fry in the fat. Garnish and serve.

FISH PASTRY SCALLOPS
(see picture below)

12 oz. shortcrust pastry	8 oz. uncooked white fish
1 oz. butter	1 tsp. chopped parsley
1 oz. flour	A little lemon juice
½ pint milk and stock,	Seasoning
mixed	Egg to glaze

Grease 5 scallop shells and line with pastry, saving some for the 'lids'. Make a sauce with the butter, flour and liquid and add the cut-up fish, flavourings and seasoning. Put some filling in each shell and cover with pastry, sealing the edges firmly. Glaze the scallops and bake in a fairly hot oven (400°F., mark 6) until the tops are brown. Turn out on to a baking sheet, glaze the reverse sides and bake for another 10-15 minutes, till golden. Serve hot or cold, accompanied by a green salad.

SHELLFISH

GRILLED SCALLOPS

8 scallops
Olive oil
Salt and pepper
2 oz. butter

I clove of garlic, finely
   chopped
Chopped parsley
Lemon

Brush the scallops with oil and sprinkle with salt and pepper. Place under a medium grill and grill for 3-4 minutes on each side; put on to a very hot dish. Heat 3 tbsps. olive oil with the butter and garlic and pour over the scallops. Garnish with parsley and lemon wedges.

SCAMPI FRITTI

This is a favourite hors d'oeuvre dish.
Take the flesh from as many Dublin Bay prawns as you need and dip them in coating batter (see below). Fry in smoking hot fat or oil until they are crisp. Pile on a hot dish and garnish with parsley and lemon.
To make the batter, mix 2 oz. flour and a pinch of salt and make a well in the centre. Pour in 3 tbsps. tepid water and 2 tsps. salad oil. Mix to a smooth batter and beat until light. Just before using the batter, add a stiffly beaten egg white.

SCAMPI WITH SAUCE

(see colour picture no. 50)

Frozen scampi, coated with egg and breadcrumbs and fried until golden-brown, can be served hot or cold. Arrange them on a platter, surrounding a dish of tartare or tomato sauce and provide cocktail sticks for easier eating.

OYSTERS

These are at their best when eaten *au naturel* as an hors d'oeuvre. The renowned Colchester and Whitstable oysters are among the best for serving in this way, but oysters from the Helford river beds in Cornwall, though small, have an excellent flavour and are less expensive. Oysters should ideally be eaten as soon as they are opened—and not longer than an hour afterwards. They may be opened by the fishmonger if bought near enough to the serving time, but after a little practice you could learn to open them yourself.
Allow 4-6 per person and serve in the deeper shell, with lemon wedges, cayenne and brown bread and butter.

BAKED LINCOLN LOBSTER

2 medium-sized lobsters
1 small onion, chopped
1 clove of garlic,
   chopped
2½ oz. butter
2 oz. button mushrooms,
   sliced
¼ pint double cream

½ tsp. piquant sauce
1 tsp. made mustard
Chopped parsley
Seasoning
1 oz. grated cheese
1 oz. breadcrumbs
Parsley sprigs and lemon
   butterflies to garnish

Cut the lobsters in half lengthways and remove the flesh, cutting it into large pieces; save the shells. Fry the onion and the garlic in 2 oz. of the butter. Add the mushrooms

and cook gently for a few minutes. Stir in the cream, the piquant sauce, mustard and some chopped parsley; finally add the lobster and season. Return the mixture to the shells and sprinkle with grated cheese and breadcrumbs. Dot with butter and bake in a moderate oven (350°F., mark 4) until golden-brown. Garnish with parsley and lemon.

LOBSTER MAYONNAISE

1 lobster
1-2 lettuces

¼ pint mayonnaise
Cucumber

Remove the flesh from the lobster, retaining the coral for garnishing. (The claws and head may be also used for this purpose.) Flake the flesh, or cut it into small pieces. Wash the lettuce and tear into pieces, keeping the the heart and some of the leaves whole; arrange these on a dish. Mix the lobster flesh with the mayonnaise and pile on to the salad. Decorate with lobster coral in hollowed cucumber chunks, and add any remaining lettuce leaves.

LOBSTER COCKTAIL

½ lb. lobster flesh, or a
   7¾-oz. can of lobster
2 tomatoes

Lettuce
Mayonnaise
Cress to garnish

Dice the lobster flesh and mix with the sliced peeled tomatoes. Line some glasses with lettuce leaves, pile the lobster and tomato in each and coat with mayonnaise. Garnish with cress and serve chilled.
Crabmeat or Dublin Bay prawns, similarly prepared, also provide excellent fish cocktails.

DRESSED CRAB

Pull the top shell from the body of the crab by putting your thumb at the head and pulling the shell gently away. Break off all the claws. Remove the flesh from the shell, keeping the brown meat separate from the white. Discard all the greyish-white "dead man's fingers" and remove the stomach—a small sac near the head. Crack the claws with nut-crackers or a weight and remove all the flesh. If desired, season the flesh with mayonnaise or lemon juice and oil. Wash the shells and replace the meat, putting the brown in the centre and the white on either side. Garnish with paprika, parsley and lemon.

CRAB—STUFFED TOMATOES

1 medium-sized onion,
   chopped
2 oz. celery, chopped
2 rashers of bacon,
   chopped
3 oz. butter
2 oz. fresh white
   breadcrumbs

4 oz. crabmeat
2 eggs
Salt and pepper
6 large tomatoes
Grated cheese
6 small rounds of
   buttered toast

Chop the onion, celery and bacon and fry them in the butter together with the breadcrumbs, until the onion is tender. Flake the crab, lightly beat the eggs and mix all these ingredients together, with the seasoning. Cut the tops off the tomatoes, scoop out the seeds, stuff with the crab mixture and sprinkle with grated cheese. Bake in a moderate oven (350°F., mark 4) for about 20 minutes, then serve the tomatoes on hot buttered toast.

FOREIGN FISH RECIPES

SPANISH TROUT
(see picture above)

4 trout	A few sprigs of parsley,
Olive oil	finely chopped
1 onion, sliced into	Wine or wine vinegar
rings	Lemon juice
1 clove of garlic	Lemon slices

Clean the trout and, if preferred, remove the heads. Dry them with a cloth and fry in the oil for 2-3 minutes. Put into a casserole and keep hot. Fry the onion golden-brown. Put the garlic and parsley into a small pan with equal quantities of wine and water and a squeeze of lemon juice; bring to the boil, add the onions and cook gently for 10 minutes. Dish up the fish, pour the sauce over and garnish with lemon.

PORTUGUESE PLAICE

1 tbsp. chives	8 fillets of plaice
3 tomatoes, skinned	A little white wine
1 oz. butter	Salt and pepper

Chop the chives and fry with the sliced tomatoes in the butter for a few minutes, then pour into an ovenproof dish. Fold each fillet in three and lay on the tomatoes; cover the tomatoes and fish with wine. Add some salt and pepper and bake in a moderate oven (350°F., mark 4) for 25 minutes.

BLUE TROUT (French)

4-6 small river trout	Parsley and lemon
4 tbsps. wine vinegar	to garnish
$\frac{1}{4}$ pint seasoned fish stock	Melted butter

The trout should be very fresh for this—if possible just caught. Clean the fish, but do not scale or wash them or the blue colour will be spoilt. Put the fish in an oven-proof dish and sprinkle each one with vinegar. Add the seasoned fish stock and cook in a fairly hot oven (375°F., mark 5) for 5 minutes, or until the fish is tender. Drain and serve garnished with parsley and lemon. Serve a dish of melted butter separately.

SHRIMPS IN WINE SAUCE (French)

A 12-oz. pkt. of shelled	2 tbsps. warm water
shrimps	Salt and pepper
1 oz. flour	A pinch·cayenne pepper
2 tbsps. olive oil	Sliced lemon and chopped
3 tbsps. white wine	parsley to garnish
2 tsps. tomato paste	

Coat the shrimps with flour and fry them in the oil until golden-brown. Add the wine to the shrimps and cook for about 3 minutes. Add the tomato paste, water, salt, pepper and cayenne, and cook gently for about 2 minutes. Garnish and serve as a hot hors d'œuvre.

SALERNO FISH (Italian)
(see picture above)

4 fillets of hake or cod	1 tbsp. chopped parsley
cutlets	1 level tsp. flour
1 oz. butter	2-3 tbsps. stock
1 clove of garlic, finely	$\frac{1}{4}$ pint white wine
chopped	Salt and pepper
1 tsp. chopped chives	Olive oil
6 mushrooms	Parsley to garnish

Prepare the fish. Melt the butter in a saucepan, add the garlic, chives, sliced mushrooms and parsley, and cook for a few minutes. Stir in the flour, and cook for a further 3 minutes. Add very slowly the stock and wine, season, and bring to the boil. Cover, and simmer gently for 10 minutes. Meanwhile, fry the fillets in oil. Drain, put into a hot dish, and cover with the sauce. Garnish with parsley.

SCAMPI PROVENÇALE

2 small onions, chopped	$\frac{1}{2}$ oz. flour
$\frac{1}{2}$ oz. dripping	$\frac{1}{4}$ pint stock or water
1 rasher of bacon, chopped	Seasoning
$\frac{1}{2}$ lb. tomatoes, skinned	4 oz. shelled scampi

Cut up the onions, and fry them in the dripping until they are just starting to turn a light brown, then add the bacon and chopped tomatoes and continue frying for about 1 minute. Then add the flour and the stock or water, boil over a low heat for 5-10 minutes, then sieve. Season well, and add the scampi. Re-heat and serve as an hors d'œuvre, accompanied by slices of brown bread and butter.

FISH CASSEROLES

FRESH FISH STEW
(see picture above)

1 lb. white fish fillets	1 onion
Flour	2 large tomatoes
Seasoning	4 oz. prawns, shelled
$\frac{1}{2}$ a red pepper	$\frac{3}{4}$ pint fish stock
$\frac{1}{2}$ a green pepper	

Wash the fish, cut up and dip in seasoned flour. Slice the vegetables finely and put with the prawns and fish in a casserole. Pour the stock over, season and cook in a moderate oven (350°F., mark 4) for $\frac{3}{4}$ hour.

FINNISH HERRING PIE
(see right-hand picture above)

4 medium-sized herrings	$1\frac{1}{2}$ lb. potatoes
2 large onions, sliced	2 oz. butter
1 oz. lard	Salt and pepper
4 tomatoes	$\frac{1}{4}$ pint milk

Several hours beforehand, scale and bone the fish, leaving the tails on, and soak in salted water. Fry the onions lightly till golden-brown. Skin and slice the tomatoes. Cut the potatoes lengthwise in thin slices. Put dabs of butter over the inside of a fireproof dish, then put in a layer of potatoes, followed by layers of onion and tomato; season, place the rolled fish on top and surround with tomato and potato. Pour in the milk and cook in a moderate oven (350°F., mark 4) for $1\frac{1}{4}$ hours.

FISH AND BACON CHOWDER

1 lb. white fish	6 bacon rashers
1 large onion	Salt and pepper
1 lb. potatoes	A little milk

Wash and cut up the fish; peel and slice the onion and potatoes. Rind and cut up the bacon rashers and fry lightly. Put a layer of bacon in a casserole, next a layer of fish, then onion and potatoes. Season well and continue until the ingredients are used up. Add milk to cover by about 1 inch and bake in a fairly hot oven (375°F., mark 5) for about 1 hour, or until cooked.

HADDOCK HOTPOT

1 lb. fresh haddock	Salt and pepper
1 onion, chopped	A small can of tomatoes
4 oz. French beans	2-3 large potatoes
4 oz. grated cheese	

Skin the fish and cut into cubes. Cover with the chopped onion, the beans, half the grated cheese and the seasoning. Add the tomatoes, cover with the sliced potatoes and season again. Bake in a moderate oven (350°F., mark 4) for 1 hour. Take from the oven, cover with the remaining cheese and brown under the grill.

AMERICAN TUNA CASSEROLE

2 7-oz. cans of tuna	2 tbsps. sherry or
2 level tbsps. plain flour	piquant table sauce
$\frac{1}{2}$ level tsp. salt	1 cup crumbled potato
A little pepper	crisps
$\frac{1}{2}$ pint milk	

Start heating the oven to fairly hot (375°F., mark 5). Put into a double saucepan 2 tbsps. of the oil from the tuna; gradually stir in the flour, salt, pepper and milk and cook, stirring, until smooth and thickened, then add the sherry or piquant sauce. Cover the bottom of a greased $1\frac{1}{2}$-quart casserole with a quarter of the potato crisps. Add one-third of the tuna, in chunks, then one-third of the sauce. Repeat, making 3 layers; top with the rest of the crisps and bake, covered, for 20 minutes, then take off the lid and bake for a further 10 minutes, or until brown.

FISH AND POTATO CASSEROLE

2 large salt herrings	3 eggs
1 lb. sliced boiled potatoes	1 pint milk
1 tbsp. chopped onion or	$\frac{1}{2}$ level tsp. pepper
spring onion	1 oz. dried breadcrumbs
2 tbsps. melted butter	

Soak the fish for 6 hours, skin and bone them and cut in long strips. Butter a baking dish and put in a layer of potato, then one of herring, with a little onion; repeat, finishing with a potato layer, and pour melted butter over the top. Beat the eggs, add the milk and pepper, pour into the baking dish and sprinkle with breadcrumbs. Bake in a moderate oven (350°F., mark 4) for 30-40 minutes or until browned.

Canned salmon may be used instead of salt herring.

PLAICE AND CHEESE CASSEROLE

(see picture below)

8 fillets of plaice	1 oz. flour
Seasoning	½ pint milk
3 oz. grated cheese	½ lb. tomatoes
1 oz. butter	Tomato to garnish

Fold the fillets of plaice in half, sprinkle with salt and pepper and put in a casserole. Cover with half the grated cheese and bake for 10-15 minutes in a fairly hot oven (375°F., mark 5) until the fish is cooked. Meanwhile, melt the butter, add the flour, cook for a minute or two, then gradually add the milk. Bring to the boil, stirring all the time, and add nearly all the remaining cheese. Cut up the tomatoes and add to the sauce, season well, and allow to cook slowly for about 5 minutes, then pour over the fish. Cover with grated cheese and sliced tomatoes and grill until golden-brown.

SAVOURY FISH STEW

1½ lb. cod or haddock fillet	2 tsps. chopped parsley
1 oz. seasoned flour	¼ pint vinegar
2 oz. lard or dripping	3 tsps. tomato paste
2 onions, sliced	¼ pint water
1 clove of garlic	4 oz. prawns, shelled

Wash the fish, cut in 2-inch squares and coat with seasoned flour. Melt the fat, fry the fish and place in a casserole. Fry the onions until golden and add to the fish, with the crushed garlic and parsley. Pour in the mixed vinegar, tomato paste and water. Cook in a moderate oven (350°F., mark 4) for 40 minutes, adding the prawns 10 minutes before cooking is complete. Serve with spaghetti or rice.

BAKED FISH, SPANISH STYLE

4 cod steaks	4 anchovy fillets
1¼ level tsps. salt	4 tomatoes peeled and cut in thick slices
½ level tsp. pepper	
¼ level tsp. cayenne pepper	3 tbsps. chopped chives
¼ level tsp. grated nutmeg	¼ lb. mushrooms, thinly sliced
1 tbsp. olive oil	
1 large onion, thinly sliced	2-3 tbsps. white wine
	2 oz. melted butter
1½ tbsps. chopped pimiento	4 oz. white breadcrumbs

Wash the fish and dry it. Sprinkle with a mixture of salt, pepper, cayenne and nutmeg. Put the oil into a large ovenproof dish and add the onion and chopped pimiento. Arrange the seasoned fish slices side by side on top of the onion, then place an anchovy fillet on each. Cover the fish with tomato and sprinkle with chives. Scatter the mushroom over all, then pour on the wine. Cover and bake for 30 minutes in a fairly hot oven (400° F., mark 6). Meanwhile, mix the melted butter and breadcrumbs. Sprinkle this mixture on top of the fish and continue baking, uncovered, until well browned—about 5-10 minutes.

SHRIMP CHOWDER

(see picture below)

1 large onion, chopped	2 4-oz. pkts. frozen shrimps or prawns
½ oz. butter	
¼ pint boiling water	1 pint milk
3 medium-sized potatoes, sliced	1-2 oz. grated cheese
	Chopped parsley
Salt and pepper	

Cook the onion in the hot butter for a few minutes till tender, but do not let it brown. Add the water, sliced potatoes, salt and pepper. Cover and simmer gently for about 15 minutes, or until the potatoes are tender. Add the shrimps and the milk and bring to the boil. Stir in the grated cheese and parsley.

HADDOCK WITH LOBSTER SAUCE

1½ lb. haddock fillet	¼ tsp. pepper
Juice of ½ a lemon	A 4½-oz. can of lobster bisque
2 oz. melted butter	
A good pinch of marjoram	3 tbsps. sour cream
	A 4-oz. pkt. of frozen mixed vegetables
½ level tsp. salt	

Wash the fish and cut into 4 portions. Place in a shallow fireproof casserole, sprinkle with the lemon juice and allow to soak for 5 minutes, then discard the juice. Pour the melted butter over the fish and sprinkle with marjoram and seasonings. Grill for about 10 minutes, basting once. Mix the bisque and sour cream together, pour over the fish and cook for 30 minutes in a moderate oven (350°F., mark 4). Serve garnished with the cooked vegetables.

FISH WITH WINE

SOLE WITH ORANGE

4 sole, skinned
Seasoned flour
6 oz. butter
4 small oranges
4 tbsps. sherry
2 tbsps. tarragon vinegar
A little chopped parsley

Coat the fish with seasoned flour. Melt 4 oz. of the butter and fry the fish on both sides. Meanwhile peel the oranges and cut into slices, retaining any juice. Gently heat the orange slices, juice, sherry and vinegar in a small pan. Clean out the frying pan and lightly brown the remaining butter. Put the fish in a serving dish and arrange the orange slices in a line down them. Add the liquid in which the sole were cooked to the browned butter and pour over the fish. Garnish with the parsley and serve at once.

SOLE VÉRONIQUE

2 sole, filleted
2 shallots, chopped
2-3 button mushrooms, sliced
A few sprigs of parsley
$\frac{1}{2}$ a bay leaf
Salt and pepper
$\frac{1}{4}$ pint dry white wine
$\frac{1}{4}$ pint water
4 oz. green grapes
$\frac{3}{4}$ oz. butter
$\frac{3}{4}$ oz. flour
2-3 tbsps. cream

Wash the fillets, fold in 3 and lay in a greased ovenproof dish, with the shallots, mushrooms, herbs, seasonings, wine and water, cover with foil, bake in centre of a moderate oven (350°F., mark 4) for 20 minutes. Meanwhile poach the grapes for about 5 minutes in a little water (or extra wine), then peel them and remove the pips. Strain the liquid from the cooked fish and keep the fish warm while making a roux sauce from the butter, flour and cooking liquid (made up to $\frac{1}{2}$ pint if necessary). When it thickens, remove from heat and stir in the cream and the grapes (retaining a few). Pour over the fish and serve garnished with the remaining grapes.

SOLE WITH MUSHROOMS

2 sole, filleted
2 shallots, chopped
4 oz. button mushrooms
3 tbsps. dry white wine
1 tbsp. water
1 bay leaf
Salt and pepper
$1\frac{1}{2}$ oz. butter
Juice of $\frac{1}{2}$ a lemon
$\frac{3}{4}$ oz. flour
$\frac{1}{4}$ pint milk (approx.)
2-3 tbsps. cream
Mushroom caps to garnish

Wash the fillets of sole, fold each of them in three and place in a greased ovenproof dish with the shallots, the chopped mushroom stalks, wine, water, bay leaf and seasoning, cover and bake for 15-20 minutes in the centre of a moderate oven (350°F., mark 4) until tender. Drain off the cooking liquid; remove the flavouring vegetables and keep the fish warm. Meanwhile simmer the mushroom caps gently in half the butter, with a squeeze of lemon juice and some salt and pepper. Make a roux sauce from the remaining butter, the flour and the cooking liquid, made up to $\frac{1}{2}$ pint with milk. When the

sauce has thickened, remove from the heat, stir in the cream, add a squeeze of lemon juice and adjust the seasoning if necessary. Pour over the fish and serve garnished with mushroom caps.

BAKED STUFFED PLAICE

2 plaice, whole but cleaned
2 oz. fresh breadcrumbs
1 oz. suet
1 tbsp. chopped parsley
$\frac{1}{2}$ level tsp. dried thyme
Grated rind of $\frac{1}{2}$ a lemon
Salt and pepper
Milk or egg to bind
1 oz. butter
$\frac{1}{4}$ pint dry white wine

Get the fishmonger to make a slit down the backbone of the fish and lift the top fillets slightly to form two pockets. Mix together the crumbs, suet, herbs, lemon rind and seasoning and bind with milk or egg. Divide this mixture between the two fish, stuffing it into the pockets. Place the fish in a large, shallow ovenproof dish and dot with the butter. Pour in the wine, cover the dish with foil and bake in a moderate oven (350°F., mark 4) for about 20 minutes, or until tender. Spoon the cooking liquid over the fish and serve garnished with parsley and lemon wedges.

TURBOT WITH CRAB SAUCE

4 pieces of turbot
2-3 slices of onion
A few sprigs of parsley
$\frac{1}{2}$ a bay leaf
Salt and pepper
$\frac{1}{4}$ pint dry white wine
$\frac{3}{4}$ oz. butter
$\frac{3}{4}$ oz. flour
$\frac{1}{4}$ pint milk (approx.)
A $3\frac{3}{4}$ oz. can of crabmeat, drained and flaked
2 level tbsps. grated Parmesan cheese

Wash and trim the pieces of turbot and place them in a greased ovenproof dish with the onion, parsley, bay leaf, seasoning and wine. Bake in the centre of a moderate oven (350°F., mark 4) for about 20 minutes, then strain off the cooking liquid and keep the fish warm. Make a roux sauce from the butter, flour and cooking liquid, made up with milk to $\frac{1}{2}$ pint. When the sauce has thickened, remove from the heat, stir in the crabmeat and adjust the seasoning. Pour over the turbot and sprinkle with the cheese. Place under a hot grill until golden.

TURBOT WITH SHRIMP SAUCE

4 pieces of turbot
$\frac{1}{2}$ a bay leaf
1 clove
Salt and pepper
$\frac{1}{4}$ pint dry red wine
Milk
1 oz. butter
1 oz. flour
2-4 oz. shrimps
2-3 tbsps. cream

Wash the turbot and place in an ovenproof dish or casserole, add the bay leaf, clove and seasoning and pour the wine over. Cover with foil and bake in the centre of a moderate oven (350°F., mark 4) about 20 minutes, or until tender. Remove the bay leaf and clove, strain off the cooking liquid and make up to $\frac{1}{2}$ pint with milk. Make a sauce from the butter, flour and liquid and when it thickens, stir in the shrimps and cream; re-heat for 2-3 minutes. Adjust the seasoning if necessary, then pour over the fish and serve.

HALIBUT AND CUCUMBER IN CHEESE SAUCE

4 steaks of halibut	½ a cucumber, peeled
Salt and pepper	and diced
6 peppercorns	1 oz. flour
A few parsley stalks	Milk
¼ pint dry cider	2 oz. grated cheese
2 oz. butter	

Wash and trim the halibut steaks, place in an oven-proof dish or casserole with the seasoning and flavourings and pour the cider over them. Cover with foil and bake in the centre of a moderate oven (350°F., mark 4) for about 20 minutes, until tender. Using 1 oz. butter, simmer the cucumber with seasoning for about 10 minutes in a covered pan, until tender. When the fish is cooked, remove the peppercorns and parsley and drain off the cooking liquid. Make a sauce from the remaining butter, the flour and the cooking liquid from the fish, made up to ½ pint with milk. When it has thickened, remove from the heat, stir in half the cheese and season to taste. Pour over the fish, sprinkle with the remaining cheese and brown under a hot grill. Serve garnished with the cucumber.

TROUT VIN ROUGE

4 small trout, cleaned	¼ pint dry red wine
2 oz. button mush-	¾ oz. butter
rooms, sliced	¾ oz. flour
1 bay leaf	2-3 tbsps. single cream
1 clove	or top-of-the-milk
Salt and pepper	

Wash the fish and cut off the fins. (Leave the head on, or remove if preferred.) Place in a shallow ovenproof dish and add mushrooms, herbs, seasoning and wine. Cover with foil and bake in the centre of a moderate oven (350°F., mark 4) for about 20 minutes, until tender. Strain off the cooking liquid, retaining the mushrooms, and keep the fish warm. Make a roux sauce from the butter, flour and cooking liquid, made up to ½ pint if necessary with water or stock. When the sauce has thickened, remove it from the heat and stir in the mush-rooms and the cream. Adjust the seasoning if necessary and pour over the fish.

HADDOCK CASSEROLE

1 lb. haddock or cod	Salt and pepper
fillet, skinned	¼ pint cider
½ lb. tomatoes, sliced	2 tbsps. fresh
2 oz. button mush-	breadcrumbs
rooms, sliced	2 tbsps. grated cheese
1 tbsp. chopped parsley	

Wash the haddock (or cod) fillet, cut into cubes and lay these in an ovenproof dish. Cover with the sliced tomatoes and mushrooms, the parsley and seasonings and pour the cider over. Cover with foil and bake in the centre of a moderate oven (350°F., mark 4) for about 20-25 minutes. Sprinkle with the breadcrumbs and cheese and brown in a hot oven or under a hot grill.

SCALLOPS IN CREAM

6-8 scallops	1 shallot, finely chopped
2 tbsps. olive oil	2-3 tbsps. white wine
Lemon juice	¼ pint single cream
Seasoned flour	Salt and cayenne
2 oz. butter	2 oz. grated Parmesan
2 oz. button mush-	cheese
rooms, sliced	

Clean and cut up the scallops. Mix the oil and 1 tsp. lemon juice and marinade the scallops for 1 hour; drain well, then toss in seasoned flour and cook in the butter. Place the scallops in 4 shells, then fry the mushrooms and shallot lightly in the butter. Add the wine and reduce well, then stir in the cream. Heat gently, season and add a few drops of lemon juice. Pour over the scallops, sprinkle with the cheese and brown under a hot grill. Serve as an hors d'oeuvre.

PRAWN RISOTTO

2 chicken bouillon cubes	Salt and pepper
1 oz. butter	2 oz. button mush-
1 onion, chopped	rooms, sliced
1 clove of garlic,	8 oz. prawns, peeled
chopped	Parmesan cheese for
8 oz. long-grained rice	serving
¼ pint dry white wine	

Make up 1 quart chicken stock with the cubes. Melt the butter and fry the onion and garlic for 5 minutes, or until soft but not coloured. Add the rice and continue cooking gently until the grains are golden and transparent. Stir in the wine and allow to bubble briskly until well reduced. Stir in ½ pint stock, some seasoning and the mushrooms and cook in an open pan until all the stock has been absorbed. Continue adding the stock in ½-pint amounts until it has all been used; with the final addition stir in the prawns and cook for a further 5-10 minutes, or until they are heated through and all the liquid is absorbed. Serve at once, sprinkled with Parmesan cheese.

SNAILS À LA BOURGUIGNONNE

1 can of snails	1 small onion
½ pint dry white wine	6 cloves
Salt and pepper	¼ pint brandy (optional)
A bouquet garni	

For the Snail Butter

4 oz. butter	1-2 tsps. chopped parsley
1 shallot, chopped	A pinch of mixed spice
1 garlic clove, crushed	Salt and pepper to taste

Put the snails into a large saucepan with the remaining ingredients, cover and cook gently for 1 hour. Allow to cool in the cooking liquid, then drain and push the snails into the shells.
To make the snail butter, cream the butter with the other ingredients. Fill up the stuffed snail shells with this butter, place the snails in a shallow ovenproof dish and heat through in a hot oven (425°F., mark 7) for about 10 minutes, or until really hot. Serve as an hors d'oeuvre.

LOBSTER THERMIDOR

2 small cooked lobsters	½ pint well-flavoured white
2 oz. butter	sauce
1 small piece of onion,	1 tsp. made mustard
finely chopped	Salt and paprika
2 tsps. chopped parsley	3 oz. grated Parmesan
2 tsps. chopped tarragon	cheese
4 tbsps. white wine	

Remove and dice the lobster meat (keeping the shells whole). Melt 1 oz. butter, add the onion and herbs, simmer for a few minutes, then add the wine and cook until well reduced. Stir in the sauce and lobster meat; heat well and add the mustard, salt and paprika, 2 tbsps. cheese and the remaining butter, in small pieces. Adjust the seasoning and pour into the cleaned shells. Top with the remaining cheese and brown under a hot grill.

PRAWNS NEWBURG

(See picture above)

½ lb. prawns, peeled	¼ pint single cream
1 oz. butter	Salt and cayenne pepper
4 tbsps. sherry or	Boiled rice or toast
Madeira	Chopped chives or
2 egg yolks	parsley

Sauté the prawns very gently in the butter for about 5 minutes. Stir in the sherry or Madeira and cook for a further 2-3 minutes. Mix the egg yolks and cream and pour into the prawn mixture, add seasonings to taste and heat very gently, until a thickened creamy consistency is obtained. Pour at once over boiled rice or toast. Serve sprinkled with chives or parsley and garnished with whole prawns.
Shrimps can of course be used in the same way.

LOBSTER NEWBURG

2 small cooked lobsters	¼ pint single cream
1 oz. butter	Salt and cayenne pepper
4 tbsps. Madeira or sherry	Boiled rice
2 egg yolks	Chopped parsley

Halve the lobsters, carefully remove all the meat and slice it thinly. Melt the butter, arrange the lobster meat in the pan and heat gently for about 5 minutes. Add the Madeira and continue as for Prawns Newburg.

SEAFOOD COCKTAIL

(See picture above)

4 oz. prawns or shrimps,	1 tbsp. single cream
peeled	1 tbsp. white wine or
1-2 tbsps. dry white wine	medium sherry
2 tbsps. tomato ketchup	Salt, pepper and cayenne
2 tbsps. salad cream	1 lettuce

Sprinkle the prawns with wine and leave for ½ hour, turning them from time to time. Make a sauce by combining the ketchup, salad cream, cream and wine, with seasoning. Wash and shred the lettuce and divide between 4 small dishes. Place the drained fish on the lettuce. Spoon the sauce over just before serving. Serve with lemon wedges and brown bread and butter.

SHRIMP CRÉOLE

1 oz. butter	1 level tsp. dried orégano
1 onion, chopped	or mixed herbs
1 small green pepper,	Salt and pepper
chopped	1 level tsp. sugar
1 oz. flour	¼ pint dry white wine
A 14-oz. can of	8 oz. shrimps (or
tomatoes	prawns)

Melt the butter and fry the onion and pepper until soft (5-10 minutes). Stir in the flour, then add the tomatoes, herbs, seasoning and sugar and simmer for 15 minutes. Stir in the wine and shrimps and cook for a further 5-10 minutes, until the flavours are well blended. Serve in a border of boiled rice.

TURBOT BONNEFOY

4 fillets of turbot	½ lb. mushrooms
Salt and pepper	1 glass of claret
2 medium-sized onions	1 pint tomato sauce

Put the fish into a fireproof dish and add the seasoning. Chop the onions and add to the fish, together with the mushrooms and claret. Cover with buttered greaseproof paper, and bake in a moderate oven (350°F., mark 4) for 10-15 minutes. Put the fish on a serving dish. Re-heat the fish liquor with the tomato sauce, boil for 5 minutes and pour over the fish.

SAUCES AND ACCOMPANIMENTS

EGG SAUCE

1 oz. butter	Salt and pepper
1 oz. flour	2 hard-boiled eggs, shelled
½ pint milk	and chopped

Melt the butter and add the flour. Cook over a low heat for a minute, then add the milk. Bring to the boil, add salt, pepper and the chopped egg and re-heat.
Serve with any plainly cooked fish.

FRESH TOMATO SAUCE

½ lb. tomatoes	½ pint milk
1 oz. butter	Salt and pepper
1 oz. flour	

Hold the tomatoes over a flame until the skin splits or place in boiling water for a few moments, then peel them and cut into small pieces. Melth the butter, add the flour, then gradually stir in the milk and bring to the boil. Season, add the tomatoes and allow to simmer gently for about 5 minutes.

WHITE SAUCE

1 oz. butter	½ pint milk
1 oz. flour	Salt and cayenne pepper

Melt the butter and add the flour, then gradually add the milk. Bring to the boil and add the seasonings.
Caper Sauce: Stir in 1-2 tbsps. chopped capers.
Cheese Sauce: Stir in 3 oz. grated cheese.
Mushroom Sauce: Add 2-4 oz. sautéed sliced mushrooms.

PARSLEY SAUCE

Stir 1-2 tbsps. freshly chopped parsley into a white sauce.
Serve with any plainly cooked fish.

SHRIMP OR PRAWN SAUCE

A 2-oz. pkt. of frozen	1 oz. flour
shrimps or prawns	½ pint milk
1 oz. butter	Salt and pepper

Open the packet of shrimps and let them thaw. Melt the butter and add the flour, then cook over a low flame for a minute. Gradually add the milk, stirring well, and bring to the boil. Season well and add the shrimps.
Serve with baked or steamed fish.

WINE SAUCE

1 shallot	¼ pint red wine
2 oz. butter	½ level tsp. caster sugar
1 tsp. anchovy essence	1 tsp. chopped parsley

Chop the shallot very finely and fry it in the butter until it is golden-brown, then add the anchovy essence, red wine and sugar. Boil together until the mixture is reduced by half, then add the parsley.

PIQUANT SAUCE

A blade of mace	1 oz. butter
A few peppercorns	1 oz. flour
½ pint milk, or	1 tsp. vinegar
milk and stock	1 tsp. chopped parsley

Infuse the mace and peppercorns in the milk for 10 minutes over a low heat. Melt the butter and add the flour to make a roux; strain the milk and gradually add to the roux. Bring to the boil and add the vinegar and parsley.
Serve with steamed fish.

QUICK TOMATO SAUCE

1 oz. mushrooms	1 level tsp. sugar
1 small onion	Salt and pepper
¾ oz. butter	1 level dessertsp.
½ pint tomato juice	cornflour

Wash the mushrooms and peel the onion, then chop them finely; fry in the butter for about 2 minutes. Add the tomato juice, sugar and seasonings and cook for 5-10 minutes. Blend the cornflour with a little water, add to the tomato juice and boil for about 1 minute.
Serve this sauce with steamed or fried fish.

MELTED BUTTER SAUCE

With a fine-flavoured fish such as salmon and sole, plain melted butter is delicious.

BLACK BUTTER SAUCE

2 oz. butter	1 tbsp. vinegar
1 tbsp. chopped parsley	

Melt the butter in a pan and allow it to become a golden-brown colour, then add the parsley and fry until it is crisp. Pour into a sauce-boat. Boil the vinegar in the pan and add to the butter in the sauce-boat.

BEURRE ROUGE

Cook a finely chopped shallot with salt, pepper and a pinch of sugar in a glass of red wine until the wine is reduced. Gradually add about 5 oz. butter, beating all the time, and keeping it warm.
Serve with plain baked or steamed fish.

ROE STUFFING

2 oz. soft herring roes	½ oz. flour
6 tbsps. milk	Cayenne pepper
Salt	Lemon juice
Pepper	1 oz. fresh white bread-
½ oz. butter	crumbs

Wash the roes and cook in a little milk with some salt and pepper. When they are cooked, drain off the milk. Melt the butter and add the flour, then stir in the milk; bring to the boil and add the cayenne pepper and a squeeze of lemon juice. Mash the roes and add them, together with the breadcrumbs, to the sauce.

RICE STUFFING

2 oz. rice, cooked	2 oz. raisins
1 small onion, skinned	2 tbsps. chopped parsley
and chopped	1 oz. butter, melted
2 oz. almonds, blanched	Salt and pepper
and chopped	1 egg, beaten (optional)

Combine all the ingredients, season and bind them well together. This can also be used for chicken, meat or vegetables.

MEAT COOKERY

Recipes give 4 servings, unless otherwise indicated

CHOOSING MEAT

Many housewives find the task of selecting meat quite a problem, especially when they first start catering. They often hesitate to purchase an unfamiliar cut because they don't know how to cook it to the best advantage, so they miss many a good and inexpensive buy. We hope that the wide range of recipes in this chapter will help you choose wisely, cook successfully and provide varied and economical meals for your family.

Try to find a good butcher who sells meat only in prime condition for cooking; even the highest quality meat, if offered for sale without the proper hanging, will lack flavour and be tough. Don't be afraid to ask for the butcher's advice, remembering that he is an expert and will gladly help you to select the meat which is best suited to your particular purpose.

Most butchers nowadays sell both fresh home-killed meat and chilled or frozen imported meats. Imported meat is less expensive than meat from our own farms and this difference may make a considerable saving if you are catering for a family on a limited allowance. While the quality and flavour may not always be quite so delicious as in home-killed meat, this can usually be overcome by skilful cooking. Much imported frozen meat is excellent for all types of cooking.

Most frozen meat is thawed out by the butcher and sold ready to cook. If, however, it is still icy when you buy it, allow it to thaw out at ordinary room temperature before cooking it: never put it in a hot place or pour hot water over it to speed the process. When it is thawed, treat as for fresh meat.

Generally speaking, select meat which has not got an undue amount of fat, as this is wasteful. What fat there is should be firm and free from dark marks or discoloration. Lean meat should be finely grained, firm and slightly elastic. The following points are characteristic of the different types of meat:

Beef: The lean of good beef should be bright red in colour and it should be finely marbled with creamy streaks of fat. The solid portions of fat should be smooth, firm and creamy. Avoid joints which show more than the thinnest line of gristle between fat and lean meat.

Mutton: The flesh is darker and more purple in colour than that of beef. Lean meat should be firm and close in texture: the fat should be white and very firm.

Lamb: The flesh is lighter in colour than in mutton and the joints considerably smaller. The fat should be very white and waxy.

Veal: The meat should be pale in colour (not red, which indicates age), smooth and very finely grained, with a small amount of fat, which should be white.

Pork: Avoid very fat pork. The lean should be pale in colour, firm and finely grained and the fat should be firm and white.

Salted or Pickled Meats: Most butchers sell beef, pork and tongues which they have salted ready for cooking. This saves the housewife time and trouble; although the process is not a difficult one and can be carried out at home if necessary (see page 67), it does take several days before the meat is ready to cook, so often it is more convenient to buy ready-to-cook pickled meat. It is always advisable to consult your butcher in good time if you want to buy salted meat, so that he knows your requirements.

Offal: All internal meats, as well as heads, feet and trotters, are included in this category and a variety of both special-occasion and economical dishes can be prepared from them. Internal organs should be cooked soon after they are purchased and kept in the coolest part of the larder or in a refrigerator until needed.

STORING MEAT

Remove the wrapping papers from meat when you reach home and either put it on to a plate, or wrap it in thin plastic material, leaving the ends open for ventilation. Store it in the coolest place available—the coldest part of a refrigerator, below the freezing unit, is ideal. In some of the larger refrigerators a special meat drawer or container is available and meat need not be wrapped or covered, but is placed straight into this. Although the controlled temperature allows uncooked meat to be safely left for several days, the refrigerator must not be regarded as a storage place for a long period; the low temperature only slows down the process of deterioration and does not completely prevent it. Minced raw meat, sausages and offal are particularly perishable and should be used if possible within 24 hours of purchase.

When no refrigerator is available, keep meat in a cool, well-ventilated place, lightly wrapped and protected from flies.

Cooked meats which are put into a refrigerator should be wrapped to prevent drying. Leftover stews or casseroles should be allowed to become quite cold and then left in a covered dish: re-heat thoroughly before using them the next day.

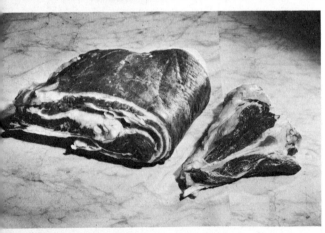

Sirloin, Rolled Ribs, Topside;
Silverside, Brisket of Beef

BEEF

Here is a list of some cuts of beef, with the best ways of cooking them:

Topside	Roast, pot-roast, braise
Sirloin	Roast (on the bone, or boned and rolled)
Ribs	Roast (on the bone, or boned and rolled)
Buttock steak	Braise, stew, pot-roast or use in pies
Rump steak	Grill or fry
Fillet steak	Grill or fry
Chuck steak	Stew
Silverside (pickled)	Boil
Wing rib	Roast
Shin (gravy beef)	Stew, or use for pies, puddings, beef tea
Flank (thick and thin)	Use for pies, stews; boil it if pickled
Aitch bone	Roast; boil it if pickled
Brisket	Braise, stew; boil if pickled

ROAST BEEF
(see colour picture no. 6)

Choose a choice cut—sirloin, ribs or topside. Weigh, then calculate cooking time as follows:

High-temperature Method: In a hot oven (425°F., mark 7). Allow 15 minutes per lb. plus 15 minutes, if required rare; 20 minutes per lb. plus 20 minutes for medium-done. Sirloin and ribs may be cooked in this way.

Moderate-temperature Method: In a fairly hot oven (375°F., mark 5). With sirloin and ribs, unboned, allow 25 minutes per lb. for medium to well-done result; if joint is boned and rolled, 30 minutes per lb.

Slow Roasting: In warm to moderate oven (325°F.-350°F., marks 3-4). For cheaper roasting cuts on the bone (e.g., brisket) allow 40 minutes per lb. to give a medium to well-done result; if boned and rolled, allow 45 minutes per lb.

Cooking and Serving

Place the weighed joint on a rack or straight in the roasting tin. Sprinkle with flour and add some dripping or lard if the meat is lean. When it is cooked, remove it from the tin and keep it hot while making the gravy. Basting is necessary only when the meat is very lean. For "self-basting", use aluminium foil and cook at the high temperature; either brown the joint first and then place it in the foil, or open the foil for the last 20 minutes.

Potatoes, parsnips, carrots, onions and marrow are all good when roasted with the joint; par-boiling (except in the case of marrow) shortens the cooking time and gives an excellent result.

Serve beef with gravy, horseradish cream or sauce and Yorkshire pudding or popovers. The horseradish cream may be put in apricot halves for a special occasion —see the colour picture.

Thin Flank, Shin of Beef;
Fillet and Rump Steak

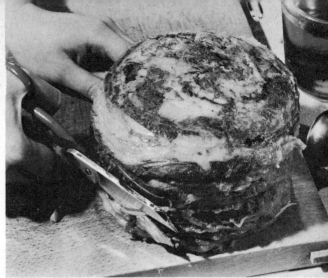

SPICED SILVERSIDE

4 lb. pickled silverside	$\frac{1}{2}$ level tsp. dry mustard
Flavouring vegetables	3 oz. breadcrumbs
8 cloves	1 orange
4 oz. brown sugar	1 lemon
1 level tsp. cinnamon	1 wineglass sherry

Simmer the meat with a few cut-up vegetables for about 2-2$\frac{1}{2}$ hours and allow to cool in the liquor. Put into a greased tin or casserole and stick the cloves in the meat. Mix the sugar with the cinnamon, mustard, crumbs and a little grated orange and lemon rind and spread over the top of the beef. Bake in a moderate oven (350°F., mark 4) for about 40 minutes, basting with the orange and lemon juice and the sherry—pour these over the meat about half-way through the time.

BOILED BEEF

4 lb. salted silverside or brisket	2-3 turnips
6-8 carrots	8 peppercorns
6 onions	A bouquet garni
	Dumplings (optional)

Skewer or neatly tie the meat, cover with cold water, bring slowly to the boil and remove all scum. Add the carrots, cut lengthways, the onions and the thickly sliced turnips, the peppercorns and bouquet garni. Cover and cook very gently, allowing 25 minutes per lb. of meat, plus 25 minutes. Remove the string and serve the meat surrounded by the vegetables (and the dumplings, if included).

GRILLED STEAK WITH ONION RINGS
(see picture above)

Choose fillet or rump steak about 1-1$\frac{1}{2}$ inches thick. If rump steak is used, beat it on a board with a rolling-pin; fillet steak, being very tender, should not require this treatment. Season with salt and pepper (and a little garlic juice, if this flavour is enjoyed). Brush the meat over with oil or melted fat, place under a hot grill and cook for 2-3 minutes on each side first, turning the meat carefully to avoid losing the juices (use tongs if possible). Continue cooking, turning the meat frequently, for about 12-15 minutes, until done; the centre of the steak should be slightly underdone. Serve with fried onion

rings, chipped potatoes and a pat of maître d'hôtel butter. Grilled mushrooms or tomatoes are also favourite accompaniments.

MINUTE STEAKS

Cut some fillet of beef into $\frac{1}{4}$-inch slices, trim neatly and flatten slightly with a wide-bladed heavy knife. Brush over with oil or melted fat and grill quickly for only 1-2 minutes on each side, or fry in a little butter for the same time. Serve with grilled mushrooms and maître d'hôtel butter.

AMERICAN POT-ROAST

4 lb. topside	$\frac{1}{2}$ pint hot water
Salt and pepper	Sliced cooked carrots
1 tbsp. lard or bacon fat	Boiled potatoes
	Chopped parsley

Prepare and season the meat. Heat the fat in a strong pan or casserole, add the meat and turn it several times, in order to brown it on all sides. Add the hot water, cover closely and cook over a gentle heat or in a cool oven (300°F., marks 1-2) for 3$\frac{1}{2}$-4 hours, adding a little more hot water if required. Serve surrounded by the vegetables, sprinkled with chopped parsley.

COLLARED BEEF
(see picture above)

4 lb. salted flank of beef	10 allspice berries
1 bay leaf	1 level tsp. celery seeds
2 cloves	1 onion, sliced
2 blades of mace	Parsley sprigs to garnish
10 peppercorns	

Choose beef that is not too fat for this dish, which must be cooked the day before it is needed. Remove any gristle or bone from the beef, roll into a neat shape and secure with fine string, then tie it in a pudding cloth. Put it in a pan with water to cover and add the spices, herbs and onion; cover and cook gently for about 4 hours. When it is done, lift it out of the pan and press it by placing it on a board, covering it with another board or plate and adding a heavy weight.
Leave till next day. Remove the cloth and string and serve the beef sliced.

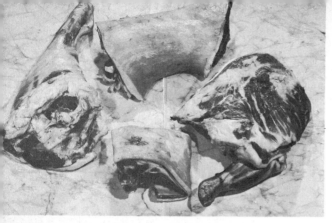

MUTTON AND LAMB

These are the best-known cuts of mutton and lamb:

Leg (whole, or cut into shank and fillet)	Roast: braise or boil a whole leg of mutton
Loin (on the bone or boned, stuffed and rolled)	Roast
Loin chops	Fry or grill
Best end of neck	Roast or braise; as cutlets, fry or grill
Middle neck	Stew, casserole, use in broths and hotpots
Scrag end of neck	Stews, pies, broths
Breast	Stew, braise or roast if boned and rolled
Shoulder (whole or half)	Roast

ROAST LAMB AND MUTTON

Leg, shoulder, loin and best end of neck are the favourite roasting joints. Calculate the roasting time, allowing 27 minutes per lb., plus 27 minutes, according to thickness. Cook in a moderate oven (350°F., mark 4), basting occasionally with the hot dripping. Do not serve lamb or mutton underdone, but avoid overcooking, which tends to dry up the flesh. Serve roast lamb with mint sauce, roast mutton with red-currant jelly or onion sauce, gravy, roast potatoes and vegetables.

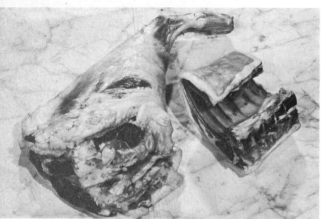

ROLLED STUFFED BREAST OF MUTTON

1 breast of mutton or lamb	A little grated lemon rind
4 oz. breadcrumbs	Beaten egg
1 tbsp. chopped parsley	Dripping
A pinch of mixed dried herbs	Stock
Salt and pepper	Flavouring vegetables (optional)

Ask the butcher to bone the breast, or do it yourself, using a small sharp knife. (Use the bones for stock or soup.) Make the stuffing by mixing the dry ingredients with egg to bind, then spread over the meat. Roll up neatly and secure with string. Melt a little dripping in a heavy flameproof casserole and brown the roll in this; remove any excess dripping, add enough stock to cover the bottom of the pan well, put on the lid and cook the meat slowly for 2 hours; add the vegetables and some extra stock if required.

LAMB KEBABS
(see colour picture no. 12)

¾ lb. lean lamb, cut from the leg	4 mushrooms
	4 tomatoes
2 onions	4 rashers of bacon
2 lamb's kidneys	Olive oil

Cut the lamb into small, neat pieces about 1 inch across. Peel the onions, blanch and cut into quarters. Skin and halve the kidneys, removing the core. Peel and blanch the mushrooms; halve the tomatoes; cut each rasher in

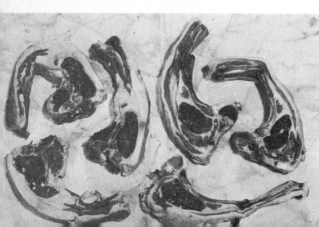

half and roll up. Thread the ingredients on to 4 skewers and brush over with oil. Cook under a hot grill, turning frequently, for about 8 minutes. Serve (still on skewers) on a bed of boiled rice with peas.

BOILED LEG OF MUTTON WITH CAPER SAUCE

1 small leg of mutton or half a larger leg	4 onions, 2 turnips
	1 lb. carrots
Salt and pepper	Caper sauce (see page 66)

Wipe and weigh the meat and put in a pan with fast-boiling water to cover it; boil for a few minutes, skimming frequently, then reduce heat to a gentle simmering. Add salt and pepper and the thickly sliced or quartered vegetables, cover and cook gently, allowing 20 minutes to each lb. of meat, plus 20 minutes. Serve with caper sauce poured over and surrounded by vegetables.

Neck of mutton may be cooked similarly (see picture above). Onion sauce (see page 66) may be served instead of caper sauce.

FRIED CUTLETS

Buy some best end of neck and ask the butcher to saw the rib bones to about 3 inches in length and to remove the chine bone, before cutting it into cutlets. Trim the cutlets and scrape the end of the bone clean. Coat with beaten egg and breadcrumbs and leave for a little while to dry before cooking. Fry in shallow hot fat for about 8 minutes, turning them occasionally, and drain well. Serve with onion or tomato sauce (page 66) and accompanied by potatoes or noodles, fried onions and a green vegetable.

GRILLED CHOP PLATTER

Choose good chops about 1 inch thick. Take out the bone, curl the "tail" of the chop round the "eye" and put a narrow streaky rasher round the edge of each chop, securing it with cocktail sticks. Brush the chops with olive oil and grill on both sides, turning them often, for about 10 minutes. Serve with creamed potatoes, green peas and small whole carrots.
For a simpler dish, omit the bacon and serve the chops with grilled tomatoes (see picture above, right).

LAMB PAPRIKA

1½ lb. middle or best end of neck	1 tbsp. chopped parsley
	1-2 level tsps. paprika
1½ oz. butter	pepper
6 oz. minced onion	Salt
1 lb. tomatoes, skinned and sliced	¼ pint sour cream or yoghourt

Chine the meat and trim away any excess fat, then cut it into chops. Heat the butter and brown the chops on both sides; remove from the pan. Fry the onion in the fat until beginning to brown. Add the tomatoes, parsley, paprika and salt to taste, replace the chops, cover and simmer gently for 1½-2 hours or bake in a covered casserole in a warm oven (325°F., mark 3) for 2 hours.
Stir in the sour cream or beaten yoghourt, re-season and bring back to simmering point. Serve with noodles and buttered courgettes.

MIXED GRILL
(see colour picture no. 7)

The ingredients can be varied to suit individual circum-stances, but a typical mixed grill includes a chop or a piece of steak, a piece of kidney or liver, bacon, a sausage, tomato and mushroom. Prepare the various ingredients according to type and brush them all over with melted fat or oil. Heat the grill thoroughly and begin by cooking the ingredients requiring the longest time. Keep every-thing very hot and serve attractively garnished with watercress, putting a pat of maître d'hôtel butter on each chop or piece of steak. Potato chips or crisps are a popular accompaniment; pineapple rings may be served instead of a vegetable.

The following are the approximate grilling times:

Pork chops	15-20 minutes
Sausages: Thick	15 minutes
Thin	10 minutes
Steak	10-15 minutes
Lamb chops	10-15 minutes
Kidneys	10 minutes
Liver	5-10 minutes
Tomatoes	5 minutes
Mushrooms	5 minutes

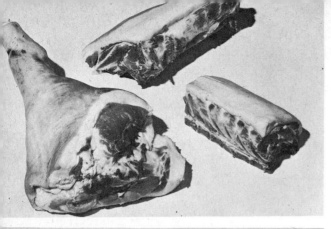

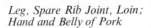

PORK

We give below a list of the most usual cuts of pork:

Leg (whole or divided)	Roast; if pickled, boil it
Shoulder (blade-bone)	Bone and stuff, then roast, pot-roast or braise
Loin	Roast; grill or fry when divided into chops
Belly or streaky	Roast, boil, braise; if pickled, boil or stew
Hand	Roast, boil or stew
Spare rib	Roast; grill or fry when cut into chops
Pork pieces	Stew or use in pies

Pork must always be well cooked and should never be served even slightly underdone. To counteract its richness, it is usually served with a sharp accompaniment.

ROAST PORK

Ask the butcher to score the rind closely and deeply, to make carving easier. Rub the outside with salt and oil before cooking—this gives a good crackling. Put the joint on a rack and roast in one of the following ways:
High-temperature Method: In a hot oven (425°F., mark 7), allowing 25 minutes per lb., plus 25 minutes for joints with bone; this gives very crisp crackling.
Moderate-temperature Method: In a fairly hot oven (375°F., mark 5), allowing 30-35 minutes per lb. for boned and rolled joints; this gives a fairly crisp crackling. Serve with boiled, mashed or roast potatoes and a green vegetable, celery or onions; brown gravy and apple sauce are the accepted accompaniments and cranberry or red-currant jelly may also be served.

SPARE RIBS AND SAUERKRAUT

Season 4 spare rib chops and brush with oil, then brown on both sides under a hot grill. Put 1 lb. sauerkraut into a greased casserole with ¼ pint hot water and sprinkle with 2 oz. brown sugar. Put the meat on top, cover and bake in a moderate oven (350°F., mark 4) for ¾-1 hour.

PORK CHOPS WITH GLAZED APPLES

4 loin pork chops	2 tsps. grated orange
Fat for frying	rind
2 tbsps. minced onion	8 tbsps. orange juice
¼ pint tomato juice	4 oz. granulated sugar
Salt and pepper	4 firm red apples

Choose lean chops (or trim off the surplus fat). Heat a little fat in a thick pan, add the meat and brown on both sides until it is a rich gold. Add the onion, tomato juice and seasoning, cover and simmer gently till the meat is tender—about 30 minutes. Meanwhile, heat the orange rind, juice and sugar until the sugar dissolves. Wipe and quarter the apples, without peeling, remove the core and cook carefully in the orange syrup until soft but unbroken. Put the chops on a dish with the glazed apples and pour any remaining liquid over them.

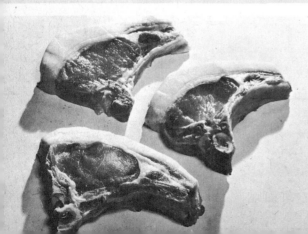

VEAL

These are the usual cuts, with cooking methods:

Shoulder (whole or divided into two)	Roast, stew
Loin	If whole, bone, stuff, roll and roast; if cut into chops, grill or fry
Best end of neck	Roast or cut into cutlets and fry or grill
Scrag-end of neck	Stew
Fillet leg	Roast, cut into slices for frying, or fricassee
	Sometimes boned and stuffed before roasting
Knuckle	Boil, braise, stew
Breast	Stew, braise, boil

ROAST VEAL

Veal for roasting is often boned and stuffed with force-meat, while forcemeat balls may be served with an un-stuffed joint. Veal should be served well cooked and as the flesh lacks fat, it must either be well basted during the roasting, or protected with pieces of fat bacon.

Roast by the moderate-temperature method (in a fairly hot oven, 375°F., mark 5), allowing 20 minutes per lb. for a joint with bone, or 30 minutes per lb. for a boned and rolled joint.

Serve with bacon rolls, gravy, roast potatoes and spring carrots, green peas or other vegetables.

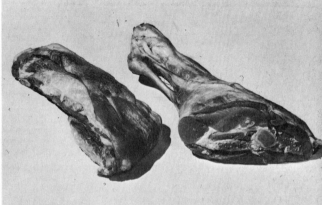

VEAL ROLLS WITH RICE

1-1½ lb. thinly cut fillet of veal	Stock
Herb stuffing	Boiled rice
2 oz. dripping	Sieved spinach
	Gravy

Beat the veal, cut it into even-sized oblongs and spread with forcemeat. Roll up tightly and secure each with thread. Brown in the hot fat and then pour off any excess fat and add stock, almost covering the meat. Cover the pan and cook very gently for about 1 hour. Remove the threads, dish the rolls on a ring of hot rice and fill the centre with spinach; pour round the rolls a gravy made from the veal stock.

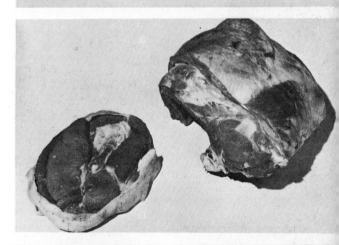

WIENER SCHNITZEL
(see colour picture no. 12)

Veal escalopes (thinly cut slices taken from the fillet)	Beaten egg
	Fine browned breadcrumbs
Seasoned flour	Butter for frying

Beat the escalopes to make them of an even thickness, and if necessary trim them to a good shape. Dip into seasoned flour, then coat with egg and breadcrumbs. Melt plenty of butter in a frying pan and when it is hot, add the meat; turn occasionally to brown both sides evenly. Serve on a hot dish, with any remaining butter strained round.

There are many versions of this popular dish. One is to serve each escalope on a croûte of fried bread spread with anchovy butter.

Sliced Fillet, Loin;
Scrag and Middle Neck

HAM

A whole boiled ham (which may vary in weight from about 10 to 20 lb.) is sometimes required for a large family gathering or for a reception. For smaller parties it may be found more convenient to divide a ham into 2 or 3 sections, which may be cooked separately at different times if required. A whole cured ham, if wrapped in muslin or a cloth and hung in a cool, dry, airy place, will keep for 2-3 months; once it has been cut, it will keep for only 15-20 days.

For most purposes, of course, it is convenient to buy a smaller piece of ham, or cooked ham ready sliced.

BOILED HAM
(see colour picture no. 9)

First weigh the ham to calculate the cooking time.
Small hams and cuts of ham: Allow 20 minutes to each lb., plus 20 minutes, calculating the time from when the covering liquid comes to the boil.
Large hams of 12 lb. and over: Allow 15 minutes to the lb., plus 15 minutes after boiling point has been reached. After weighing the ham soak it for 12 hours in cold water. Choose a pan large enough to hold the ham, put this in and cover it with cold water; bring quickly to the boil and simmer for the required time.
To serve hot: Remove the ham from the liquid, take off the skin and sprinkle with browned crumbs. Serve with broad beans and parsley sauce (when available), or as an accompaniment to roast turkey or chicken.
To serve cold: Allow to cool in the liquid in which it was cooked. Remove the brown skin, sprinkle with fine browned breadcrumbs and put a frill round the bone.

BAKED HAM, VIRGINIAN STYLE
(see colour picture no. 8)

Weigh, soak and boil the ham as above, allowing 20 minutes to each lb. Remove the brown skin, score the surface of the fat with a knife and stud with cloves. Put into a baking tin, brush with warmed golden syrup and sprinkle with equal quantities of flour and brown sugar. Bake in a hot oven (425°F., mark 7) for 30-40 minutes, basting frequently, until surface is golden. Serve with a gravy made from the liquid in the baking tin.

PINEAPPLE-GLAZED HAM

Cook as directed for Virginian Baked Ham above, but after putting it in the baking tin, spread it with a glaze made of 6 oz. canned crushed pineapple mixed with 6 oz. brown sugar; bake in usual way, basting frequently with the glaze. Serve hot or cold, garnished with pineapple, orange slices and walnuts.

HAM AND BEAN CASSEROLE

6 oz. haricot beans, soaked overnight	1 level tbsp. sugar
¾-1 lb. ham or bacon	1 tbsp. treacle
2 stalks of celery, sliced	½ level tsp. dry mustard
1 large onion, sliced	Pepper and salt
	Cold water

Drain the beans. Cut the ham in large pieces, put it in a casserole, surround it with beans, then add the other ingredients, with enough water just to cover. Put on the lid and bake in a cool oven (300°F., marks 1-2) for about 4 hours, adding water from time to time if necessary. About 1 hour before the casserole is ready, remove the lid and raise the ham above the other ingredients. Return the casserole to the oven and cook until the ham is crisp.

BRAISED HAM

½ a ham, either bottom or knuckle end	3 sliced tomatoes
	A few mushrooms (optional)
1 onion	½ pint rich brown sauce
1 carrot	
1 turnip	¼ pint sherry (optional)
1 bouquet garni	
1 quart stock	

Soak the ham for 12-18 hours. Place it in a large pan with the vegetables and herbs, add just sufficient water to cover and simmer for 2½-3 hours, according to size. Remove from the pan and peel off the brown skin. Place the ham in a braising pan or strong deep saucepan and add stock, tomatoes and mushrooms (if used). Cover with a tight-fitting lid, place in a fairly hot oven (375°F., mark 5) or on the top of the cooker and simmer for 1-1½ hours, according to size. Place the ham on a warm dish, strain the stock and reduce to a half-glaze by boiling, then brush over the ham. Add the sauce and sherry (if used) to remaining stock, boil up and serve as gravy.

BOILED HAM AND VEAL FILLETS

4 thin slices of veal fillet	4 tbsps. cooking sherry
4 thin slices of boiled ham	4 tbsps. water
	A few olives
2 oz. lard or butter	Salt and pepper
1 oz. flour	

Beat the veal well, lay a slice of ham on each piece, roll up together and secure. Heat the fat and brown the meat rolls. Sprinkle in the flour, stirring, and add the wine, an equal quantity of water, the sliced olives and salt and pepper. Cover and simmer for about 20 minutes. Remove the strings or skewers and serve with the liquor from the pan (thinned down if necessary).

HAM AND EGG SUPPER DISH

4 hard-boiled eggs	6 tbsps. fresh breadcrumbs, browned
½ lb. cooked ham	
Salt and pepper	½ pint white sauce
4 oz. butter or margarine	Parsley

Roughly chop up the eggs and the ham and season lightly. Melt the fat and mix with the crumbs. Put a layer of this into a pie dish, then a layer of egg mixed with ham, followed by some sauce. Continue, finishing with crumbs. Bake in a moderately hot oven (375°F., mark 5) for about ½ hour and garnish with parsley.

HAM PANCAKES AU GRATIN

Make thin pancakes, cover each with a thinly cut slice of ham which has been spread thinly with made mustard, roll up and put into a well-buttered fireproof dish. Sprinkle with cheese, dot with shavings of butter and grill till the cheese is melted and golden.

BACON

Back and gammon are the choicest cuts for grilling or frying, although streaky bacon, which has fat and lean intermingled, is a more economical cut for this purpose. For boiling in the piece, select forehock, gammon, hock, collar or slipper as an economical cut; middle or corner gammon are the choicest lean joints for cooking in the piece.

Bacon rashers for grilling or frying may be cut to the particular thickness you prefer. A fairly thin rasher is most popular, except for gammon, which is usually preferred thick.

To Fry Bacon: Take off the rind and any bone, using kitchen scissors or a small sharp knife. Put into a frying pan and fry gently, adding no extra fat unless the bacon is very lean. Cook until the fat is transparent and the bacon of the required crispness. Serve with fried eggs, mushrooms, tomatoes, fried bread, etc., as desired. (See picture above.)

To Grill Bacon: Prepare as for frying, brush with melted fat if very lean and cook under a hot grill, turning as required.

To Boil Bacon in the Piece: Soak the bacon in cold water for an hour or two, then put into a pan with cold water to cover, adding herbs or vegetables as required. Simmer gently, allowing 20-25 minutes per lb., plus 20 minutes. Serve hot with parsley sauce, green peas or broad beans and boiled potatoes. If required cold, allow to cool in the liquor, remove the rind and sprinkle with browned breadcrumbs. Serve with salads.

GRILLED GAMMON WITH MUSHROOMS

4 gammon rashers, cut fairly thick	$\frac{1}{4}$ pint milk and water
Oil or melted butter	2 level tsps. flour
$\frac{1}{2}$ lb. small mushrooms	Salt and pepper
1 oz. butter	Chopped parsley
	Cooked green peas

Brush the rashers over with the oil or butter, then grill them, turning them as required and brushing them with more fat when necessary; the cooking time will be about 15-20 minutes.

Meanwhile sauté the mushrooms in the fat for 10 minutes. Blend the liquid and the flour, add to the pan and stir until boiling. Simmer the mixture for 10 minutes and season carefully. Dish up the gammon rashers, then put the mushrooms at one end of the platter, sprinkled with chopped parsley, and place the cooked green peas at the other end.

BACON PANCAKES

4 oz. flour	$\frac{1}{2}$ pint milk
A pinch of salt	4 oz. minced lean bacon
1 egg	Fat for frying

Sieve the flour and salt and mix with the egg and sufficient milk to make a creamy batter. Beat thoroughly until the mixture is covered with bubbles, then stir in the rest of the milk and the minced bacon; put the batter into a jug. Melt a little fat in a frying pan, pour off any excess and then pour in just enough of the savoury batter to cover the bottom of the pan when this is tilted. Cook till golden, toss or turn and cook the other side. Roll up, keep hot while the other pancakes are cooked and serve with spinach, purple sprouting broccoli or other green vegetable. (Serves 2.)

BACON AND LIVER PIE
(see picture above)

$\frac{1}{4}$ lb. streaky bacon	Salt and pepper
$\frac{1}{2}$ lb. calf or pig liver	Stock or water
$\frac{1}{2}$ lb. onions	Some shavings of butter
1$\frac{1}{2}$ lb. potatoes	or margarine
1 level tsp. dried sage	

Cut the bacon and the washed and dried liver into small pieces. Slice the onions and the peeled potatoes. Grease a pie dish and put a layer of potatoes at the bottom, then a layer of onion and a layer of bacon and liver, sprinkled with the herbs and seasonings. Continue until everything is in the dish, finishing with a layer of potatoes. Pour in a little stock or water and put shavings of butter over the top. Cover and cook in a moderate oven (350°F., mark 4) for 1 hour, then remove the cover and bake for 20-30 minutes longer, until the potatoes are browned.

FAMILY-STYLE HOTPOTS

STEAK AND KIDNEY HOTPOT

1 lb. steak and kidney	1 lb. potatoes
Seasoned flour	1 tsp. mushroom ketchup
4 oz. mushrooms	1 tsp. tomato purée
½ lb. carrots	¼ pint water
1 onion	

Cut up the steak and kidney and toss in the seasoned flour. Peel and quarter the mushrooms. Slice the other vegetables thinly. Put the meat and vegetables in layers in a casserole. Mix the ketchup and tomato purée with the water, then pour into the dish, cover with a lid or aluminium foil and cook in a moderate oven (350°F., mark 4) for 2½ hours.

STEAK HOTPOT
(see colour picture no. 10)

1 lb. stewing steak	½ lb. carrots
2 oz. fat	1 orange
1 onion	Salt and pepper
1 stick of celery	

Cut the steak into ¾-inch cubes and fry in the hot fat until brown on every side. Transfer the meat to a casserole. Dice the onion and celery and sauté until golden-brown. Put onion, celery and sliced carrots in the dish, with the grated orange rind and the juice from half the orange. Add salt and pepper and half-cover with water. Cut the remaining half-orange into slices, halve these, arrange round the edge of the hotpot and cook in a moderate oven (350°F., mark 4) for 2 hours.

PORK HOTPOT
(see colour picture no. 10)

4 loin pork chops	2 oz. fat
¼ lb. cooking apples, sliced	3 tomatoes, peeled
	1 lb. potatoes, diced
1 onion, sliced	Salt and pepper

Bone and roll the chops. Fry the apples and onion in the fat until golden-brown. Place the chops in a dish, cover with the apple and vegetables, add seasoning and half-cover the meat and vegetables with water. Cover the dish and cook in a moderate oven (350°F., mark 4) for 1½ hours.

RAGOÛT OF TRIPE

1 lb. tripe	2 cloves
1 oz. dripping	6 peppercorns
1 onion, chopped	1 blade of mace
1 oz. flour	A pinch of mixed herbs
¾ pint stock	1 bay leaf
1 carrot, sliced	2-3 tbsps. vinegar
2 cut-up tomatoes or 1 tbsp. tomato sauce	Gravy browning
	Scone topping if desired
Salt to taste	(see p. 9)

Wash the tripe and cut into neat pieces. Melt the dripping, fry the onion lightly, mix in the flour and add the stock by degrees. Bring to the boil, stirring continuously, then add the carrot, tomatoes, salt, spices and herbs (tied in muslin). Lastly add the tripe and the vinegar, cover and simmer very gently for about 2 hours, until the tripe is really tender, taking care not to let the sauce stick or burn and removing the bag of herbs after about 1 hour. Re-season and if necessary add a little gravy browning to give a rich brown colour. If scone topping is used, place this in position and finish cooking the ragoût in a hot oven (425°F., mark 7) for the last 15 minutes or so of the cooking time, until the topping is nicely browned.

BEEF AND MACARONI HOTPOT

6 oz. macaroni	A 10½-oz. can condensed
2 onions	mushroom soup plus
3-4 sticks of celery	1 can water
1 red pepper	Salt and pepper
2 oz. butter	½ level tsp. dried marjoram
1 lb. minced beef	2 tbsps. chopped parsley

Cook the macaroni in boiling salted water. Prepare and dice the vegetables and sauté in the butter for 5 minutes. Add the meat and cook for a further 5 minutes. Pour in the soup, season with salt and pepper and add the marjoram. Place a layer of macaroni in an ovenproof dish (retaining enough to garnish the dish when cooked) and cover with the meat mixture. Cook for 1 hour in a moderate oven (350°F., mark 4), adding extra stock if necessary. Serve in a border of macaroni, sprinkled with chopped parsley.

LANCASHIRE HOTPOT

1½-2 lb. best end of neck of mutton	1 lb. potatoes
	Salt and pepper
¼ lb. mushrooms	Stock
½ lb. onions	Dripping

Divide the meat into chops, removing any excess fat. Slice the prepared mushrooms, onions and potatoes. Put the meat into the bottom of a casserole and cover with a layer of sliced mushrooms, then add the onions and lastly the potatoes, seasoning each layer. Pour in enough stock to half-fill the casserole and dot the potatoes with shavings of dripping. Cover and cook in a warm oven (325°F., mark 3) for about 2½-3 hours, removing the lid towards the end of the time to brown the potatoes—allow 15-20 minutes.

AMERICAN CABIN CASSEROLE

4 lean lamb chops	4-5 large tomatoes
1 oz. dripping	Salt to taste
1 rasher of bacon	A little curry powder
4-5 large onions	

Fry the chops lightly in the dripping with the chopped bacon. Place the sliced onions and tomatoes in alternate layers in a greased casserole, sprinkling each layer with salt and curry powder. Lay the browned chops on top, cover the dish tightly and bake in a fairly hot oven (375°F., mark 5) for ¾ hour. Remove the lid and cook for a further 30 minutes. Garnish as desired.

CALVES' HEART HOTPOT
(see picture above)

4 calves' hearts	2 level tbsps. dried herbs—
1 onion	marjoram, sage, thyme,
4 sticks of celery	and parsley
4 tomatoes	1 egg
4 tbsps. fresh white	2 oz. seasoned flour
breadcrumbs	2 oz. fat
1 oz. grated suet	1 tbsp. cider

Cut the central membrane of the hearts and trim away any gristle or inedible parts; wash very thoroughly. Prepare and dice the vegetables. Mix together the breadcrumbs, suet and herbs and bind with the beaten egg. Stuff the hearts, sew the edges together and roll them in the seasoned flour. Fry in the hot fat until well browned. Place the hearts in a casserole and add the diced vegetables. Add the remaining flour to the fat and when well browned stir in enough water to make a thick, brown gravy; add the cider. Pour this over the hearts, adding enough water to half-cover the meat and vegetables. Cover the dish and cook in a moderate oven (350°F., mark 4) for 2 hours.

LAMB HOTPOT

1½ lb. scrag of lamb	1 tbsp. pearl barley
2 large carrots	2 level tsps. dried lovage,
2 medium-sized onions	if available
Seasoned flour	½ pint stock and water
1 oz. dripping	2 large potatoes
Salt and freshly ground	Chopped parsley to
pepper	garnish

Trim the meat, removing the excess fat, and chop it into 4 pieces. Slice the carrots and onions thinly. Dip the meat in the seasoned flour. Melt the fat and brown the meat, then remove it and brown the carrots and onions lightly. Season and place in a casserole, arrange the meat on top and sprinkle with pearl barley and lovage. Pour the liquid over and cover with a layer of thinly sliced potatoes. Put on a tightly fitting lid and bake in a warm oven (325°F., mark 3) for 2¼ hours. Raise the heat to hot (425°F., mark 7), remove the lid and brown the potatoes. Serve the hotpot dusted with freshly ground pepper and chopped parsley.

OXTAIL HOTPOT
(see picture above)

1 oxtail, jointed	4 tomatoes, diced
Seasoned flour	2 potatoes, diced
2 oz. fat	Salt and pepper
2 onions, sliced	Dried herbs
½ lb. carrots, diced	Stock or water

Wash the oxtail, dip in flour and fry until golden-brown; place in a casserole. Sauté the onions until golden-brown, then add to the meat, with the other vegetables. Season well, adding some herbs. Half-cover the meat and vegetables with stock, put the lid on the dish and cook in a cool oven (300°F., mark 2) for 4 hours.

VEAL HOTPOT

1 lb. veal fillet	1 onion, chopped
Seasoned flour	¼ lb. peas, shelled
Grated rind of 1 lemon	1 lb. potatoes
½ level tsp. mixed herbs	Salt and pepper
2 carrots, chopped	Stock

Trim, wash and cube the meat, toss in flour, place in a casserole and sprinkle with lemon rind and herbs. Add the vegetables to the hotpot and cover with the potatoes, cut in thin slices. Season and half-cover with stock. Cook in a moderate oven (350°F., mark 4) for 1¼ hours.

BEEFSTEAK HOTPOT

1½ lb. stewing steak	3 carrots
Flour	2-3 potatoes
Seasoning	Ground nutmeg
2 onions	Stock
¼ lb. mushrooms	

Cut the steak into 1-inch cubes and coat with seasoned flour. Put into a casserole with layers of sliced onions, mushrooms, carrots and potatoes, sprinkling each layer with a pinch of nutmeg and some seasoning. Cover with stock and cook in a moderate oven (350°F., mark 4) for 2½ hours.

HAM HOTPOT

(see picture above)

12 oz. finely cut ham	3-4 peppercorns
$\frac{1}{4}$ lb. peas	A pinch of mixed herbs
2 onions	$\frac{1}{4}$ pint water
$\frac{1}{2}$ lb. potatoes	

Cut the ham into 1-inch squares. Shell the peas and slice onions and potatoes thinly. Arrange ham and vegetables in layers in a casserole, with a final layer of potato. Add the peppercorns and herbs, then half-cover with water. Cover and cook in a moderate oven (350°F., mark 4) for 1 hour. Remove the lid for the last 20 minutes to brown the potatoes.

BEEF AND CELERY CASSEROLE

$\frac{1}{2}$ a head of celery	1 lb. minced beef
1 onion	4 tomatoes
2 oz. butter or dripping	$\frac{1}{2}$ pint stock
Salt and pepper	Scone topping (see p. 9)
1 oz. flour	Egg or milk to glaze

Dice the celery, chop the onion and sauté them together in the hot fat; put into a casserole. Season and flour the meat and brown it in the fat, then add to the casserole, with the sliced peeled tomatoes and stock. Cover and cook in a moderate oven (350°F., mark 4) for about $\frac{3}{4}$ hour, then remove the lid, raise the oven temperature to hot (425°F., mark 7) and put on the scone rounds, overlapping them over the top. Glaze and continue to cook for about 15 minutes.

LIVER HOTPOT

$\frac{3}{4}$ lb. liver	1 level tsp. mixed herbs
Seasoned flour	Salt and pepper
1 onion	1 lb. potatoes
2 oz. mushrooms	Stock
3 tomatoes	

Wash and trim the liver, toss in the seasoned flour and place in an ovenproof dish. Dice the onion, peel the mushrooms and tomatoes and slice them thinly. Cover the meat with these vegetables and add the herbs and seasoning; add the thinly sliced potatoes, half-cover the hotpot with stock and bake in a moderate oven (350°F., mark 4) for 1-1$\frac{1}{2}$ hours.

RABBIT HOTPOT

(see picture above)

1 lb. rabbit	1 lb. potatoes
8 oz. carrots	1 pkt. of onion soup mix

Cut up the rabbit into suitable-sized joints and wash well. Blanch by putting into a saucepan, covering with water and bringing to the boil. Remove the rabbit from the pan and place in a dish; over the top arrange the thinly sliced carrots and the potatoes, cut into knobbly pieces. Make up the soup with 1 pint water and pour over the top. Cook in a moderate oven (350°F., mark 4) for 2 hours.

BEEF GOULASH

2 onions	A bouquet garni
1$\frac{1}{2}$ lb. lean stewing beef	Paprika pepper, salt
2 oz. dripping	$\frac{1}{4}$ pint red wine
1$\frac{1}{2}$ oz. flour	Lemon juice
1 pint stock	Creamed potato
2 tomatoes, peeled	Cooked green peas

Slice the onions and cut the meat into cubes. Melt the fat and fry the onion and meat. Transfer them to a casserole, add the flour to the dripping and cook until it browns, then add the stock, cut-up tomatoes, bouquet garni, paprika pepper and salt. Pour over the meat and onions and cook gently in a moderate oven (350°F., mark 4) for about 2 hours, with the lid on; after an hour, stir in the wine and a good squeeze of lemon juice. About 15 minutes before the dish is to be served, remove the lid and pipe rings of creamed potato over the top; allow to brown, then fill with peas.

CASSEROLED LEG OF VEAL

1$\frac{1}{2}$ lb. leg of veal	$\frac{1}{2}$ pint tomato pulp
4 tbsps. oil or lard	$\frac{1}{2}$ pint white wine
2 cloves of garlic	2 sprigs of rosemary
Salt and pepper	A strip of lemon rind

Slice the meat or cut it into small pieces. Heat the oil in a casserole and cook the chopped garlic in it until slightly browned. Add the meat and seasoning and continue cooking until the meat is golden. Stir in the tomato pulp, wine, rosemary and lemon rind, cover tightly and cook gently in a moderate oven (350°F., mark 4) for about 1 hour, or until the meat is tender.

INTERNATIONAL HOTPOTS

FRENCH BEEF AND OLIVE CASSEROLE

(see picture above)

1 lb. rump steak	A bunch of fresh herbs
3 tbsps. olive oil	1 clove of garlic, crushed
1 carrot, sliced	A few peppercorns
1 onion, sliced	Salt and pepper
2-3 sticks of celery,	$\frac{3}{4}$ lb. fat bacon
cut in 1-inch pieces	$\frac{1}{4}$ lb. black and green
$\frac{1}{2}$ pint red wine	olives
$\frac{1}{4}$ pint wine vinegar	3-4 tomatoes

Wipe and trim the meat, then make a marinade. Heat the oil and add the vegetables. Cook until brown, add $\frac{1}{4}$ pint wine, the vinegar, herbs, garlic, peppercorns, salt and pepper, bring to boil and simmer for $\frac{1}{4}$ hour, then leave until quite cold. Cut the meat into thick chunks and cover with the strained marinade.

Fry half the bacon, remove from pan, then fry meat on both sides and put into an earthenware casserole. Add the marinade to the meat with the remaining bacon (diced), wine and olives. Cover with greased greaseproof paper, then with the lid, and cook in a warm oven (325°F., mark 3) for 2½ hours. Shortly before serving, remove any excess fat and add the peeled and sliced tomatoes. Serve with noodles and grated cheese.

GERMAN HARE IN RED WINE

1 small hare	$\frac{1}{2}$ lb. small onions
6 oz. bacon	2 cloves, 2 bay leaves,
2-3 tbsps. dripping	2 peppercorns
2 oz. flour	Salt and pepper
1 pint stock or water	2 glasses of red wine

Cut the hare into small pieces, taking the flesh off the bones when practicable. Cut the bacon into thin strips and mix with the hare. Heat the dripping in a thick stewpan and fry the meat, turning it frequently until brown; take it out and keep hot. Stir in the flour and add the stock. Transfer, with the meat, sliced onions, herbs and seasonings, to a casserole and cook gently in a cool oven (300°F., mark 2) for about 3 hours, then add the wine and continue to cook until the liquor is thick; remove any excess fat. Serve in the casserole, with a piped border of creamed potato.

GREEK MEAT AND POTATO CAKE

(see picture above)

$\frac{3}{4}$-1 lb. meat, minced	1½-2 lb. potatoes, peeled
$\frac{1}{2}$ lb. onions, sliced	and thinly sliced
A little chopped parsley	$\frac{1}{2}$ oz. butter for sauce
2 oz. butter	$\frac{1}{2}$ oz. plain flour
$\frac{1}{4}$-$\frac{1}{2}$ lb. tomatoes, peeled	$\frac{1}{4}$ pint milk
and sliced	1 egg
Salt and pepper	1 oz. grated cheese

Place the meat, onions and parsley in a frying pan with $\frac{1}{4}$ pint water and simmer until all the water is absorbed. Add the butter and cook gently, then add the skinned and sliced tomatoes and season well. Cook slowly for about 20 minutes longer. Grease a cake tin and place a layer of potatoes on the bottom, then a layer of the meat mixture; repeat, finishing with potatoes. Make a white sauce with the butter, flour and milk, remove from the heat and beat in the egg and cheese. Pour over the potatoes and bake in a moderate oven (350°F., mark 4) for about 1 hour.

Serve on a hot dish, accompanied by a green vegetable.

GREEK AUBERGINE MOUSSAKA

2 aubergines	$\frac{1}{4}$ pint stock
3-4 tbsps. olive oil	$\frac{1}{4}$ pint tomato pulp
4-5 medium-sized onions	2 eggs
1 lb. minced beef or lamb	$\frac{1}{4}$ pint cream
4 tomatoes, skinned	Salt and pepper

Slice the aubergines and fry in some of the oil in a frying pan, then arrange them in the bottom of a fireproof dish. Slice the onions and fry till they are lightly browned. Place layers of onion and minced meat on top of the aubergines and lastly add some fried slices of tomato. Pour in $\frac{1}{4}$ pint stock and $\frac{1}{4}$ pint tomato pulp and bake in a moderate oven (350°F., mark 4) for about 30 minutes. Beat together the eggs and cream, add salt and pepper and pour this mixture into the casserole. Put it back into the oven for 15-20 minutes, until the sauce is set, firm and golden-brown.

FINNISH CABBAGE AND LAMB HOTPOT
(see picture above)

2 lb. white cabbage	Seasoning
1 lb. best end of neck of lamb	Tomato purée to taste

Wash the cabbage and chop it finely. Brown the meat on both sides in a saucepan without any extra fat, then add the cabbage, seasoning, tomato purée and a very little water and simmer until the cabbage is quite transparent. Serve like Irish stew.

SWISS BRAISED MUTTON WITH WINE

1½ lb. thickly cut leg of mutton	1 lb. potatoes
Salt and pepper	½ lb. carrots
Cooking fat	1 small celeriac
1 glass of white wine	1-2 medium-sized onions
	1 clove of garlic (optional)

Beat the meat, rub with salt and pepper and fry in the fat in a flameproof casserole until browned on all sides. Add the white wine (or water). Peel and chop the vegetables and place round the meat, cover the casserole with a well-fitting lid and braise in a fairly hot oven (400°F., mark 6) for 1¼-1½ hours.
Pork can be cooked in the same way.

SWEDISH SAILOR'S BEEF

1-1½ lb. chuck steak	Salt and pepper
1½ lb. potatoes	1-2 cups boiling water
2 tbsps. butter	Chopped parsley
2-3 sliced onions	

Wipe the meat, cut into ½-inch slices and beat with a wooden spoon or with a rolling pin. Slice the potatoes thickly. Heat the butter and sauté the onions, then brown the meat. Put alternate layers of potatoes, meat and onion into a casserole, seasoning each layer and finishing with potatoes. Pour a little boiling water into the frying pan, stir well and pour this liquor into the casserole, with just sufficient plain water to cover the contents. Cover and bake in a fairly hot oven (375°F., mark 5) for 1-1½ hours, or until the meat is tender. Sprinkle with parsley and serve from the casserole.

BELGIAN CARBONNADES
(see picture above)

1½ lb. chuck steak	½ pint stock or water
Salt and pepper	1 lb. onions
2 oz. dripping	1 clove of garlic
3 oz. lean bacon	1 oz. sugar
1½ oz. plain flour	A bouquet garni
½ pint beer	2-3 tbsps. vinegar

Cut the meat into neat pieces, season with salt and pepper and brown in the dripping. Add the diced bacon and continue cooking for a few minutes. Remove the meat and bacon from the pan, stir in the flour and brown lightly over very gentle heat. Gradually add the beer and stock, stirring continuously. Fill a casserole with layers of meat, bacon, chopped onion and garlic and a sprinkling of sugar. Pour the sauce over and add the bouquet garni. Cook very gently for 3½-4 hours in a cool oven (300°F., mark 2). Add a little more beer while cooking, if necessary. Just before serving, remove the bouquet garni and stir in the vinegar. Serve with plain boiled potatoes. (About 6 servings.)

AUSTRIAN MUTTON WITH RUNNER BEANS

1½ lb. mutton (without bone)	2 onions
	Pepper and salt
2 lb. potatoes	2 oz. butter
2 lb. runner beans	

Dice the meat; peel the potatoes and cut into thick slices; string the beans and break into 2-inch lengths; peel and slice the onions. Spread some of the butter on the bottom of a heavy, lidded saucepan and fill the pan with layers of onion, meat, beans and potatoes, seasoning each layer and adding dabs of butter. The top layer should be of potatoes. Pour in ½ cup water and cover the pan closely. Simmer very slowly for 1½-2 hours. (Serves 5-6.)

BULGARIAN HOTPOT

1 large aubergine	2 lb. fat beef or veal
3-4 potatoes	2-3 tbsps. butter or oil
5 tomatoes	Salt and pepper
A cup of French beans	1-2 eggs
1 green tomato	1 level tbsp. flour
6 green peppers	Juice of ½ a lemon

(Please turn to page 49)

9. Cold Boiled Ham

10. Steak, Pork and Chicken Hotpots

11. Beef and Kidney Casserole; Veal Surprise Casserole; Savoury Ham
    Spaghetti

12. Lamb Kebabs; Curried Kidneys; Wiener Schnitzel

13. Raised Veal and Ham Pie

14. Madras Curry

15. Ceylon Prawn Curry

Slice the aubergine, sprinkle with salt and allow to stand for 1 hour, then drain off the liquid. Cut up the other vegetables. Cut the meat into small pieces, put in a pan with the butter or oil, salt and pepper and fry gently till brown. Cover with water and simmer for about ½ hour. Now add the vegetables, with more water, stir and simmer for ½-¾ hour, until vegetables and meat are tender. Heap into a baking dish and put into a cool oven (300°F., mark 1). Beat up the eggs, add the flour, lemon juice and a little salt and pour this mixture over the dish. Continue cooking for a few minutes, until the egg is set. (Serves 6-8.)

AUSTRALIAN CORROBOREE HOTPOT
(see picture above)

1-1¼ lb. braising steak	½ pint stock
2 onions	1 level tbsp. plain flour
2 cooking apples	Salt
2 tomatoes	Brown sugar
1 tbsp. dripping	Parsley
2 level tsps. curry powder	3 hard-boiled eggs
2 oz. sultanas	2 pkts. of potato crisps
1 oz. seeded raisins	

Cut up the meat and slice the onions, apples and tomatoes. Heat the dripping in a pan, add the meat, onion and apple and fry until golden-brown. Add the tomatoes and curry powder and cook for a few minutes longer. Place the mixture in a casserole, add the dried fruit and barely cover with stock. Lid the casserole and cook in a moderate oven (350°F., mark 4) for 1½ hours. Blend the flour with a little extra water and stir into the casserole. Season to taste with a little salt and brown sugar, garnish with parsley and sliced egg, surround the casserole with potato crisps and serve at once.

JUGOSLAVIAN BEEF CASSEROLE

1 lb. fat beef	A few haricot beans
¼ of a white cabbage	¼ of a red cabbage
1 small carrot	2 small onions
2 tomatoes	Salt
2 large potatoes	A few peppercorns
1 green pepper	A half-bottle of white
1 small parsnip	wine

Slice the meat and vegetables and lay them in alternate layers in a casserole, lightly salting each layer and adding the peppercorns. Pour the white wine over, cover the casserole closely and simmer for at least 2½ hours. Do not stir or the vegetables will break up. Serve in the casserole.

SCANDINAVIAN PORK CASSEROLE
(see picture above)

4 pork chops	2 eggs
2 fresh herrings	1 pint milk
4 medium-sized potatoes	1 oz. plain flour
4 onions	Salt and pepper to taste
Butter	

Trim the chops, split and bone the herrings and cut off the heads and tails; peel the potatoes and onions and slice fairly thinly. Butter an ovenproof dish, put in a layer of potatoes, a layer of onion, then 2 pork chops, next 2 herring halves and then a further layer of potato and onion. Add the remaining pork chops and herring, then fill in round the sides and cover the top with the rest of the onion and potato. Put a few small knobs of butter over the top and cook, uncovered, in a moderate oven (350°F., mark 4) for 1 hour.
Beat the eggs with the milk, add the flour and seasonings and mix well to give a smooth blend, then pour this mixture over the contents of the casserole. Return the dish to the oven and cook for a further ½ hour, until the savoury custard topping is set.

RUSSIAN CASSEROLED BEEFSTEAK

1½ lb. braising steak	6 small cabbage leaves
1 oz. plain flour	2 carrots
Fat for frying	6 peppercorns
2 thickly sliced raw potatoes	3 tomatoes, skinned

Wipe the steak and beat well, then cut up into 4-inch squares, coat with flour and fry until lightly browned. Put into a deep casserole layers of steak, potato, whole cabbage leaves and sliced carrot, with the peppercorns and sliced tomatoes. Add 1 tbsp. stock or water and a little melted fat if necessary, but the juice from the meat and vegetables may give enough liquid—the casserole should be kept fairly dry. Cover and cook in a moderate oven (350°F., mark 4) for about 2 hours.

SUNDAY-BEST HOTPOTS FOR SPECIAL OCCASIONS

HOTPOT OF BEEF OLIVES WITH ORANGE

¾ lb. rump steak	¼ lb. shelled peas
Fat for frying	Stock
2 carrots	Cornflour or plain flour
2 sticks of celery	to thicken

For the Filling

2 oz. chopped mushrooms	2-3 chopped tomatoes
Grated rind of ½ an	2 tbsps. fresh crumbs
orange	Salt and pepper

Trim the meat and beat until thin, then cut into strips. Prepare the filling by mixing all the ingredients together, adding seasoning to taste. Spread the filling on the strips of meat, roll each up and tie with cotton. Fry lightly in the hot fat and place in an ovenproof dish. Add the diced carrots and celery and the peas, half-cover with stock and bake in a moderate oven (350°F., mark 4) for about 1½ hours. Remove the cottons, thicken the gravy with cornflour or flour and serve with the beef olives.

CASSEROLED BEEF AND TOMATOES

1½ lb. steak	½ pint stock
Seasoning	1½ lb. peeled tomatoes
1 oz. lard or dripping	2 sticks of celery, chopped
1 onion, finely sliced	Mashed potatoes
2 level tbsps. plain flour	Parsley
1 tbsp. Worcestershire sauce	

Trim the steak, cut into even-sized pieces and season with pepper and salt. Heat the fat in a flameproof casserole and fry the onion till soft; add the steak and sprinkle with flour, then brown all together. Add the sauce and stock and bring to the boil, stirring all the time; skim if necessary and add the tomatoes and celery. Cover and cook slowly in a moderate oven (350°F., mark 4) for about 2 hours. Serve with a border of mashed potatoes and sprinkle with chopped parsley or garnish with parsley sprigs.

LAMB AND OYSTER HOTPOT

1½ lb. lamb chops	8 oysters
2 onions	A knob of butter
¼ lb. mushrooms	Salt and pepper
2 lb. potatoes	½ pint rich brown sauce

Trim the chops and remove most of the fat. Slice the onions thinly, quarter the mushrooms and slice the potatoes. Beard the oysters and retain the liquid.
Brush the inside of an ovenware dish over with melted butter. Put a thick layer of the potatoes over the bottom, arrange the chops on this, with a piece or two of mushroom and an oyster on each. Put the remaining oysters and mushrooms in the centre of the dish, scatter the onion over and season well. Add the rest of the potatoes,

taking care to arrange the last layer neatly. Mix about ¼ pint of the gravy with the oyster liquor and pour in at the side of the dish. Brush the potatoes well with the rest of the melted butter and cover with a piece of greased greaseproof paper. Cook in a moderate oven (350°F., mark 4) for 2-2½ hours. About ½ hour before the hotpot is ready, it will be necessary to add the rest of the gravy and to remove the greaseproof paper to allow the potatoes to become attractively browned.

MUTTON WITH APPLES

2 oz. butter	½ pint stock
4 loin chops or a piece of loin of mutton	Seasoning
8 small potatoes, sliced	4 tbsps. white wine or vinegar
4 onions, sliced	4 apples, sliced or quartered
1 level tbsp. plain flour	A little grated cheese

Melt the butter in a frying pan and fry the meat until browned. Arrange some sliced potato and onion at the bottom of a casserole, add the meat and cover with another layer of vegetables. Add the flour to the remaining fat in the frying pan and brown it. Stir in the stock, seasoning and wine, mix and strain over the meat. Place the sliced apple over the top, sprinkle with the grated cheese, put on the lid and cook in a fairly hot oven (375°F., mark 5) for 1-1½ hours, until the meat and vegetables are tender.

PORK AND PRUNE HOTPOT

¼ lb. prunes	1 oz. plain flour
Juice and rind of 1 lemon	Salt and pepper
1 lb. pork	½ oz. dripping

Cover the prunes with cold water, leave to soak for a few hours, then stew them with the rind of the lemon until tender. Strain off the juice and keep it. Remove the stones from the prunes. Wipe the pork, cut it into neat pieces and pass these through the seasoned flour. Melt the dripping in a frying pan and fry the pork until brown. Place the pork and prunes in alternate layers in a casserole. Make some brown gravy with the remaining fat, flour and about ½ pint of the prune juice and pour this over the pork. Add the lemon juice, cover with the casserole lid or a greased paper and stew in a moderate oven (350° F., mark 4) for about 1 hour. Serve in the casserole.

SWEETBREAD HOTPOT

1 lb. sweetbreads	2 oz. plain flour
1 onion, chopped	1 pint stock
8 oz. shelled peas	Salt and pepper
4 oz. mushrooms, sliced	1 level tsp. mixed herbs
1 oz. butter	Toast to garnish

Soak the sweetbreads in salted water until free from blood. Cover with water, bring slowly to the boil, then pour off the liquid. Sauté the onion, peas and mushrooms slowly for 5 minutes in the butter. Add the flour and stir until cooked. Add the liquid slowly, season, add the herbs and bring to the boil. Chop the sweetbreads and add. Cook in a warm oven (325° F., mark 3) for about 2 hours. Serve garnished with triangles of toast.

MEAT CASSEROLES AND STEWS

PINEAPPLE LAMB CASSEROLE
(see picture above)

4 lamb chops	8 mushrooms
Lard or oil	Butter
8 chipolata sausages	Salt and pepper
4 slices of pineapple	¼ pint pineapple juice

Trim the chops and fry in the hot fat till golden-brown. Cut the sausages into small pieces and fry until brown. Place the chops in a casserole, lay a slice of pineapple on each chop and add the sausages. Prepare the mushrooms, leaving them whole, add to the casserole, place a knob of butter on each and sprinkle with seasoning. Pour in the pineapple juice, cover and bake in a moderate oven (350°F., mark 4) for about 1 hour, or until the chops are tender. Dish up as shown.

BRAISED VEAL CUTLETS

4 veal cutlets	1 tbsp. chopped parsley
2½ oz. butter	Seasoning
4 oz. chopped ham	¼ pint red wine
1 tbsp. chopped onion	

Trim the cutlets into a neat shape and fry till golden-brown in 2 oz. butter, remove and put on one side. Fry the ham and onion, add the parsley and season with pepper and salt. Cover the cutlets with this stuffing, place in a casserole and add the wine and a little water to come half-way up the meat. Cook in a moderate oven (350°F., mark 4) with a lid on for about 45 minutes. Take out the cutlets and keep them hot while reducing the liquid slightly; just before serving, add the remaining knob of butter to this liquor and replace the cutlets in it.

SAUSAGE CASSEROLE

¼ lb. bacon	1 green pepper
¼ lb. pork sausages	2-3 tbsps. stock
½ lb. apples	Salt
¼-½ lb. tomatoes	Pepper

Wrap each slice of bacon around 2 sausages, fry (or brown lightly under the grill) and place in a casserole. Peel, core and slice the apples, peel and slice the tomatoes and slice the pepper into strips, discarding the seeds. Arrange the apples, tomatoes and pepper in layers on top of the sausages and bacon. Add the stock and seasoning and cook in a fairly hot oven (400°F., mark 6) for about 40 minutes. (Serves 2.)

BURGUNDY BEEF
(see picture above)

1 oz. lard or dripping	2 tbsps. concentrated
1 large onion, cut into	tomato purée
rings	Seasoning
2 green peppers	A 5-oz. pkt. of frozen corn
1½ lb. chuck steak	kernels
½ pint Burgundy	

Melt the fat and fry the onion until golden-brown; remove and place in a casserole. Cut the flesh of the peppers into thin strips, fry lightly and add these to the onions in the casserole. Cut the meat into 1-inch cubes, removing any gristle, and fry until brown. Stir in the Burgundy and tomato purée and season to taste. When well blended, add to the vegetables in the casserole. Cook in a moderate oven (350°F., mark 4) for 1½-2 hours, then add the corn kernels and continue cooking for a further 10-15 minutes.

VEAL CASSEROLE

1½ lb. stewing veal	¼ pint white wine
2 oz. lard or dripping	½ level tsp. rosemary or sage
2 cloves of garlic	A strip of lemon rind
Salt and pepper	1 level tbsp. plain flour
½ pint tomato pulp	

Slice the meat or cut it into small pieces. Heat the fat in a casserole and cook the chopped garlic in it until lightly browned. Add prepared meat and seasoning and continue cooking until the meat is golden-brown. Stir in the tomato pulp, wine, rosemary and lemon rind, cover tightly and cook gently in a moderate oven (350°F., mark 4) until the meat is tender—about 1-1½ hours. Before serving, thicken the liquid with the flour, blended with a little cold water.

BRAISED PORK CHOPS

2 oz. butter	¼ pint Sauternes
4 loin pork chops,	¼ pint stock
1 inch thick	Salt and pepper
1 onion, thinly sliced	¼ lb. mushrooms, sliced
1 carrot, thinly sliced	½ cup milk and water
A bouquet garni	1 level tbsp. plain flour

Melt the fat and brown the chops on both sides; remove them and sauté the onion and carrot for 5 minutes, remove and place in a casserole, with the chops on top. Add the bouquet garni, wine and seasoned stock and cook in a moderate oven (350°F., mark 4) for 1 hour. Meanwhile put the mushrooms in a pan with the ½ cup milk and water, season, cover and simmer for 5 minutes. Blend the flour with the fat left in the frying pan to make a roux. Drain off the liquid from the casserole and that from the mushrooms and add gradually to the roux, stirring until the sauce has boiled. Add the mushrooms and pour over the chops in the casserole.

VEAL SURPRISE CASSEROLE
(see colour picture no. 11)

2 lb. stewing veal	1 pint boiling water
Salt and pepper	1 bay leaf
1 oz. plain flour	A pinch of thyme
1 oz. butter	A pinch of marjoram
2 tbsps. olive oil	12 stoned black olives
1 clove of garlic	¼ lb. mushrooms
A 2¼-oz. can of concentrated tomato puree	Boiled rice
1 beef bouillon cube	Stuffed olives and onions to garnish

Cut the veal into cubes, dip in seasoned flour and brown it in the butter and olive oil, together with the finely chopped garlic. Add the tomato purée and the bouillon cube dissolved in the boiling water, also the herbs and some seasoning. Bake in a moderate oven (350°F., mark 4) for 1½ hours; half an hour before the end of the cooking time add the stoned olives and sliced mushrooms.
Serve with fluffy white rice, garnished with stuffed olives and with glazed onions, which are made in the following way: cook about a dozen small onions in butter in a saucepan with a lid on, shaking occasionally; meanwhile cook together 2 tbsps. soft brown sugar, 2 tbsps. vinegar and 2 tbsps. port until a thick syrup is obtained. When the onions are cooked, put them into this and boil for a few minutes, until they are all well coated. (Serves 6.)

SAVOURY HAM SPAGHETTI
(see colour picture no. 11)

4 oz. spaghetti	1 oz. plain flour
4 eggs	¾ pint milk
2 tomatoes	4 oz. grated cheese
4 oz. ham	Salt and pepper
1 oz. butter	

Cook the spaghetti in boiling salted water and drain well. Hard-boil the eggs, shell and slice. Skin and slice the tomatoes. Chop the ham. Make a white sauce with the butter, flour and milk, add half the cheese and season. Put alternate layers of spaghetti, tomato, egg and ham in the casserole (reserving some egg and tomato to

garnish). Pour the sauce over and sprinkle the other half of the cheese on top. Cook in a moderate oven (350°F., mark 4) for 30 minutes, until the top is browned. Garnish with slices of hard-boiled egg and tomato.

BEEF AND KIDNEY CASSEROLE
(see colour picture no. 11)

1 lb. stewing steak	¼ lb. mushrooms, sliced
½ lb. kidney	½ lb. potatoes, diced
Plain flour	¾ pint stock
Salt and pepper	A 5-oz. pkt. of frozen
2 oz. lard or dripping	peas to garnish
2 medium-sized onions	(optional)

Trim the steak and kidney, cut into even-sized cubes and coat with seasoned flour. Melt the fat, fry the sliced onions till tender, remove and place in a casserole. Fry the meat until brown and put this also into the casserole. Add the mushrooms and potatoes and pour the stock over. Cook in a moderate oven (350°F., mark 4) for about 2 hours, then add the peas (if used), and cook for a further 15-20 minutes.

CASSEROLED KIDNEYS

1 lb. kidneys	¼ pint stock
3 small onions	Mashed potatoes
1 oz. dripping or lard	Egg or melted butter to
3 rashers of bacon	glaze
Seasoning	Parsley or red pepper to
Plain flour	garnish

Halve and skin the kidneys, removing the cores, then soak them in cold salted water for 5 minutes. Chop the onions finely and fry in the hot dripping or lard until light golden-brown. Place in a casserole and arrange the drained kidneys on top. Cut the bacon into pieces and add to the kidneys; season and dredge lightly with flour. Pour the stock over, cover and cook in a moderate oven (350°F., mark 4) for about 30 minutes, or until tender. Meanwhile line a fireproof dish with mashed potato and glaze the edges with egg or melted butter; brown slightly in the oven. To serve, place the kidneys in the dish and sprinkle with finely chopped parsley or red pepper.
Boiled rice or buttered noodles make an equally good accompaniment to serve as an alternative to the mashed potatoes.

TRIPE AND ONIONS

1 lb. prepared tripe	1 oz. plain flour
4 onions	Salt and pepper
1 pint milk	A pinch of ground mace
1 oz. butter	Chopped parsley

Wash the tripe and cut it into small pieces; peel and slice the onions. Put the tripe and onions with the milk in a casserole, place in a moderate oven (350°F., mark 4) and cook for 2½ hours. When the tripe is done, strain it, keeping the milk. Melt the butter in a pan, stir in the flour and cook until it turns yellow. Add the milk gradually and bring to the boil, stirring all the time. Boil this sauce gently for 5 minutes, adding some seasonings and ground mace to taste, then add the tripe and re-heat. Serve sprinkled with a little chopped parsley.
As this dish has little colour, it is best to accompany it by a vegetable such as grilled tomatoes, Brussels sprouts or French beans.

NORTH COUNTRY CASSEROLE

(see picture above)

4 shoulder of lamb chops	¼ level tsp. ground cloves
1 oz. lard	1 level tsp. salt
1 clove of garlic, chopped finely	⅛ tsp. pepper
4 medium-sized potatoes	A 10½-oz. can condensed mushroom soup
4 small onions	¼ pint stock or water
A 4½-oz. pkt. frozen green beans	Paprika pepper to garnish

Trim some of the fat from the chops. Heat the lard, add the garlic and fry the chops on both sides. Place the chops in a casserole and arrange the halved potatoes and onions round them. Add the beans, cloves, salt, pepper, soup and stock, cover and cook in a moderate oven (350°F., mark 4) for about 1 hour. Sprinkle with paprika pepper before serving.

You can use veal chops in a similar way, and the flavouring can be varied by using other types of condensed soups.

LAYER POTATOES WITH HAM

4 tbsps. sour cream	3 hard-boiled eggs
2 tbsps. double cream	¼ lb. finely diced cooked ham
1 level tsp. salt	
2 oz. butter	3 oz. fresh breadcrumbs
1 lb. cold cooked potatoes, thinly sliced	¼ level tsp. celery salt
	2 oz. melted butter

Mix together in a bowl the sour cream, double cream and salt. Put dabs of butter over the inside of a 1¾-pint fireproof dish, then put in one-third of the potatoes, with a layer of sliced egg on top; pour over them one-third of the cream mixture. Add another third of the potatoes in a layer, sprinkle with two-thirds of the diced ham, then pour the remaining cream mixture over. Top with the remaining sliced potatoes. Toss the breadcrumbs, the rest of the ham and the celery salt in the melted butter and sprinkle this mixture evenly over the potatoes. Bake in a moderate oven (350°F., mark 4) for 30 minutes, or until the topping is bubbly.

PORK CHOPS WITH PRUNE STUFFING

½ lb. prunes	1 oz. fat
4 lean pork chops, 1 inch thick	Seasoning
	4 potatoes
2 tbsps. lemon juice	3-4 tbsps. hot water
1 oz. brown sugar	

Soak the prunes in boiling water for 5 minutes, drain and stone. Bone the chops and make a pocket in each; to do this slit each chop from the bone side almost to the fat. Cut up the prunes with scissors, add the lemon juice, sugar and 1 tbsp. water and cook together for a few minutes. Stuff the chops with this mixture and brown them in the fat, then sprinkle with seasoning. Place in a shallow casserole, cover with thinly sliced potatoes and add the hot water. Bake in a moderate oven (350°F., mark 4) for 1 hour with the lid on, until the chops are tender. If desired, take off the lid for the last ¼ hour to brown the top surface of the casserole.

SUMMER CASSEROLE

(see picture above)

2 lb. shin of beef	1 tbsp. soft brown sugar
1 oz. dripping	1 pint tomato juice
½ oz. flour	Seasoning
½ level tsp. dry mustard	Fresh vegetables as available (see below)
2 chopped chillies	
1 level tsp. celery salt	

Wipe the beef and remove any sinews and skin; cut in cubes, fry in hot fat till golden-brown, drain and place in a casserole. Add the flour, flavourings, etc., to the fat in the pan, bring to the boil, add salt to taste and pour over the meat. Simmer in a warm oven (325°F., mark 3) for 2 hours. Prepare all the vegetables and add to the casserole, then cook for a further ¾-1 hour, until they are tender. (Serves 6.)

Suggested Vegetables
1 small cauliflower, in florets
1 diced carrot
1 sliced onion
¼ lb. tomatoes, quartered
A 5-oz. pkt. frozen sweet corn
A 4½-oz. pkt. frozen French beans.

OXTAIL CASSEROLE
(see picture above)

1 oxtail, cut up	A pinch of mixed herbs
1 oz. dripping or	A bay leaf
lard	2 carrots, sliced
2 onions, sliced	2 tsps. lemon juice
1 oz. plain flour	Seasoning
¾ pint stock	

Fry the oxtail until golden-brown, then place it in a
casserole. Fry the onions and add to the meat. Sprinkle
the flour into the fat and brown it, add the stock gradually and bring to the boil, then pour over the meat.
Add the herbs, carrots and lemon juice, season, cover
and cook in a fairly hot oven (375°F., mark 5) for ½
hour, then reduce to cool (300°F., mark 1) and simmer
very gently for a further 2½-3 hours.
Serve with creamed potatoes and a green vegetable or
green peas.

TRIPE ROMANA

1½ lb. tripe (already	1 oz. flour
prepared)	An 8-oz. can of tomatoes
2 tbsps. vinegar	made into a purée
2 tbsps. oil	Seasoning
4 oz. mushrooms	4 oz. fresh breadcrumbs
1 large or 2 small	1 small pkt. of frozen
onions	peas
2 oz. butter	

Cut the tripe into narrow strips, 2 inches long, and
soak for 30 minutes in the mixed vinegar and oil. Clean
and thinly slice the mushrooms and onions. Melt 1½ oz.
of the butter and fry the onions and mushrooms for 3-4
minutes. Remove vegetables and add the flour to the pan
and brown slightly. Pour in the tomato purée and season
to taste. Grease a casserole or fireproof dish and line
the base with half the tripe. Add the mushrooms and
onions and sprinkle on half the breadcrumbs. Place
another layer of tripe on this, pour the sauce over,
sprinkle the top with the remaining crumbs and dot with
the rest of the butter. Bake in an uncovered dish in a
fairly hot oven (400°F., mark 6) for 25-30 minutes.
Towards the end of the time, cook the peas and use to
garnish the tripe.

LAMB'S HEART CASSEROLE
(see picture above)

4 small lambs' hearts	Salt and pepper
4 oz. fresh crumbs	2 level tbsps. seasoned flour
1 medium-sized onion,	1 oz. dripping
finely chopped	1 pint stock
3 tbsps. melted butter	12 small white onions,
½ level tsp. ground	peeled
ginger	8 quartered carrots

Wash the hearts, slit open, remove any tubes or gristle
and wash again. Fill with a stuffing made from the
breadcrumbs, chopped onion, melted butter, ground
ginger and seasoning. Tie the hearts firmly into their
original shape with string, dredge with seasoned flour
and brown quickly in the hot dripping. Place in a casserole with the stock, cover and bake in a moderate oven
(350°F., mark 4) for 2½ hours, basting and turning them
frequently. Add the whole onions and the carrots for
the last 45 minutes of the cooking time.

RICH CASSEROLED HEART

1 ox heart, weighing	½ pint stock
2½-3 lb.	½ lb. carrots
2-3 oz. butter	½ a small swede
2 onions	Rind of 1 orange
1 oz. flour	6 walnuts, chopped

Cut the heart into ½-inch slices, removing the tubes,
and wash it well. Melt the fat in a frying-pan and sauté
the slices of meat till slightly browned. Remove the
meat, sauté the sliced onions, then put both in a casserole. Add the flour to the remaining fat and brown
slightly. Pour in the stock, bring to the boil and simmer
for 2-3 minutes, then strain over the slices of heart in
the casserole. Cover and cook for 3½-4 hours in a cool
oven (300°F., mark 2). Add the grated carrots and swede
after 2½-3 hours. Remove the rind from the orange,
shred it finely and cook in boiling water for 10-15
minutes, then strain. Add the walnuts and orange rind
to the casserole 15 minutes before the cooking is completed. Alternatively, replace the orange rind and
walnuts by the chopped-up contents of an 8-oz. can of
tomatoes. (Serves 5-6.)

CASSEROLE OF LAMBS' TONGUES

(see picture above)

4 lambs' tongues	1 tbsp. chopped parsley
1 oz. dripping or lard	Salt and pepper
1 onion, sliced	Stock
1 carrot, grated	Bacon rolls (optional)
4 large tomatoes	

Wash the tongues and trim if necessary. Heat the dripping, fry the sliced onion until golden-brown and place it in a casserole. Add the tongues, grated carrot, skinned and sliced tomatoes, parsley and seasoning, and just enough stock to cover. Put into a fairly hot oven (375°F., mark 4) and cook for 1½ hours. If preferred the tongues may be skinned and then re-heated in the liquor before serving. Grilled or baked bacon rolls make a good garnish for this dish.

You could also use canned lambs' tongues to make this dish; re-heat them in the sauce in a covered casserole in a fairly hot oven (375°F., mark 5) for 40 minutes.

BRAISED SWEETBREADS

1 lb. sweetbreads	1 wineglass white wine
1 rasher of bacon	(optional)
1 oz. butter	Salt and pepper
1 carrot, sliced	Stock
1 onion, sliced	Juice of 1 lemon
A bouquet garni	

Wash and soak the sweetbreads in cold water for several hours, changing the water as it becomes discoloured. Blanch by covering with cold water, with a few drops of lemon juice added, bring slowly to boiling point and boil for 5 minutes. Drain, put into cold water, pull off any fat and skin that will come away easily and cut the sweetbreads into even-sized pieces. Fry the cut-up bacon in the butter with the carrot and onion. Put in a casserole with the drained sweetbreads, bouquet garni, wine and seasoning. Almost cover with stock and cook for 2-3 hours in a cool oven (300°F., mark 1). To serve, remove the sweetbreads, vegetables and bacon from the casserole, strain the cooking liquid and boil to reduce it; add the lemon juice and pour this sauce over the sweetbreads.

MEXICAN LIVER WITH RICE

(see picture above)

¾ lb. liver	1 red pepper
1 oz. seasoned flour	1 oz. plain flour
2 oz. dripping	½ pint stock
2 onions	Seasoning
½ lb. skinned tomatoes	4 oz. rice

Wash the liver and remove any skin or tubes. Slice it, toss in seasoned flour, fry lightly in the hot fat, then put in a casserole. Fry the sliced onions, tomatoes and pepper (reserving a few slices of the pepper). When these vegetables are quite soft, add to the liver. Make a sauce with the fat left in the pan, the flour and the stock; season well, pour over the liver and cook in a moderate oven (350°F., mark 4) for ¾ hour.

Meanwhile cook the rice in boiling salted water and poach the remaining slices of pepper for a garnish. Serve the liver on a hot dish, garnishing with the rice and sliced pepper.

For method of cooking rice, see the directions on page 72.

LIVER AND VEGETABLE CASSEROLE

1 lb. liver	½ pint stock
Seasoned flour	1-2 level tsps. dried mixed
2 carrots	herbs
2 small onions	Seasoning
4 potatoes	3 oz. grated cheese

Wash the liver and remove any skin or tubes. Toss it in the seasoned flour. Peel and chop the carrots and onions and slice the potatoes thinly. Place half the carrot and onion in the bottom of the casserole. Sprinkle with half the herbs and some seasoning, then cover with the liver. Add the remaining onion and carrot and finish with the sliced potatoes; pour in the stock. Sprinkle with seasoning and the remaining herbs, cover and bake in a moderate oven (350°F., mark 4) for 1½ hours. Uncover, sprinkle with cheese and bake for a further 15 minutes, or until the cheese topping looks golden and bubbly.

If preferred, the cheese topping may be omitted. Crumbled potato crisps make a good accompaniment.

RICH VEAL STEW

(see picture above)

1½ lb. fillet of veal	1 oz. flour
Cold water	1 pint stock
Salt and pepper	1 tbsp. cream
1 large onion	1 egg yolk
A bouquet garni	A squeeze of lemon juice
Mushrooms to garnish	Chopped parsley
1½ oz. butter or	Bacon rolls if desired
margarine	

Trim the veal and cut it up into neat pieces. Put it into a stewpan with sufficient cold water to cover and add the seasonings, sliced onion and bouquet garni. Cover and cook slowly for about 1 hour, removing any scum from the surface occasionally. Wash and trim the mushrooms and cook them in ½ oz. butter for about 10 minutes, remove them and keep hot. When the veal is tender, strain off and reserve the stock. Make a white sauce, using 1 oz. butter, flour and 1 pint of stock. Mix the cream with the egg yolk and stir into the sauce, with a little lemon juice. Heat, stirring, but do not boil, then add to the veal. Season to taste and serve garnished with the mushrooms and chopped parsley and if liked some small bacon rolls. (Serves 4-5.)
Alternatively, omit the mushroom garnish and use small triangles of fried bread or toast.

IRISH STEW

1 lb. middle neck of	2 large onions
mutton	Salt and pepper
2 lb. potatoes	Chopped parsley

Prepare the meat by wiping thoroughly, removing the marrow and cutting into neat joints. Cut the potatoes and onions in rings and place alternate layers of the vegetables and meat in a pan, finishing with a layer of potatoes. Add salt and pepper and sufficient water to half-cover. Bring to the boil and simmer gently for about 2 hours, or until the meat and potatoes are tender.
Pile the meat, gravy and some of the potatoes in the centre of a hot dish. Place the rest of the potatoes at either end of the dish and sprinkle a little chopped parsley over them.

CASSEROLED BEEF WITH PASTRY RINGS

(see picture above)

1½ lb. chuck steak or	2 onions
shin of beef	½ pint stock
1 oz. flour	½ lb. peeled tomatoes
Salt and pepper	3-4 sticks of celery
1 oz. dripping	8 oz. shortcrust pastry

Cut the meat into even-sized pieces and dip these into seasoned flour. Heat the dripping in a flame-proof casserole and fry the sliced onions and the meat until brown. Add the stock, tomatoes and sliced celery. Cover and cook gently for about 2 hours. Then, if desired, add rings of shortcrust pastry, glazed with egg, and cook for a further ½ hour. Carrots, green peas, beans, etc., may be added.

CASSEROLE OF SHEEP'S HEARTS

4 sheep's hearts	1 oz. dripping
4 oz. breadcrumbs	2 onions
1 oz. chopped suet	2 carrots
1 tbsp. chopped parsley	1 oz. flour
1 level tsp. dried mixed herbs	½-¾ pint stock
Salt and pepper	Creamed potatoes
Beaten egg	

Wash the hearts thoroughly and cut through the central cavity membrane, to make room for the stuffing. Mix together the breadcrumbs, suet, herbs, salt and pepper and bind with beaten egg. Stuff the hearts with this and stitch the top to keep it in place. Melt the dripping, fry the diced vegetables and put these in a casserole. Fry the hearts, then put them on the vegetables. Make a gravy from the remaining fat, with the flour and stock, pour it over the hearts and cook, covered, in a moderate oven (350°F., mark 4) for about 2 hours. Serve with the gravy and with creamed potatoes, small Brussels sprouts or other green vegetable as available.

56

LIVER, HEARTS, KIDNEYS, ETC.

Internal meats, such as liver, kidneys, hearts and brains, and the heads and tails of certain animals, are nearly all very nutritious and valuable foods; some of them are also quite inexpensive.

All offal needs careful washing and preparation before cooking. Kidneys, liver and hearts are often available in a frozen condition and should be allowed to thaw slowly at ordinary room temperature.

Some of the cheapest meats are particularly good for making nutritious soups, broths and stews and recipes are given under the appropriate headings.

As mentioned on page 35, all internal meats (offal) are very perishable and must be used within 24 hours of purchase.

BOILED OX TONGUE

Tongues are frequently purchased already pickled by the butcher and then only need to be cooked. If, however, a fresh tongue is bought, it must be thoroughly scraped and washed, rubbed over with coarse salt (see page 67) and left overnight to drain. The next day it is immersed in a pickling solution and left steeping in this for a week.

Before cooking the pickled tongue, soak it in cold water for several hours (overnight if the tongue has been smoked). Skewer it into a convenient shape if very large and put it into a pan with water to cover. Bring gradually to the boil and drain. Add flavouring ingredients such as sliced carrot, onion, turnip, peppercorns and a bouquet garni, cover with fresh cold water, bring to the boil and simmer for 3-4 hours, until tender. Skin the tongue, taking out any small bones or pieces of gristle.

To serve cold (see picture above): Put the tongue into a convenient sized cake tin (a 7-inch tin is required for a 6-lb. tongue). Fill up with a little of the stock, put a plate on top, weigh down with a heavy object and leave to set. Turn out and garnish.

To serve hot: Sprinkle the skinned tongue with browned crumbs and garnish with sliced lemon and parsley. Serve with parsley or tomato sauce.

GRILLED KIDNEYS
(see picture above)

Cut the washed kidneys in half and cut out the core. Thread them on to a skewer, cut side uppermost, brush over with oil and sprinkle with salt and pepper. Cook under a hot grill, uncut side first and then cut side, so that the juices gather in the cut side. Serve on fried bread, with grilled or fried bacon, or with fried or diced potatoes and maître d'hôtel butter.

Either sheep's or pig's kidneys may be cooked in the same way; the former make delicious savouries when placed on fried croûtes and sprinkled with chopped parsley or served with a small pat of devilled butter (page 66).

STEWED OX KIDNEY

Wash 1 lb. ox kidney thoroughly in cold water. Cut it into pieces, removing the white core with kitchen scissors. Season 1 level tbsp. flour with salt and pepper and roll the pieces of kidney in it. Melt 1½ oz. dripping in a stewpan or casserole and when hot, fry the kidney and a sliced onion until brown. Add 1 pint stock or water, cover and cook very gently for about 1½ hours. If necessary, thicken the gravy with a little flour, blended smoothly with cold water or stock. Serve the kidney in a border of piped or forked creamed potatoes or dry boiled rice.

BRAINS IN BLACK BUTTER SAUCE

4 pairs of lamb brains	1 tbsp. wine vinegar
1 tbsp. vinegar	Black pepper and salt
½ level tsp. salt	Chopped parsley
4 oz. butter	

Wash the brains and soak for an hour in cold water. Remove as much of the skin and membrane as possible and put the brains into a pan with the vinegar, salt and

enough water to cover well. Bring to simmering point and cook gently for 15 minutes. Put into cold water, then dry on a towel. Heat half of the butter in a frying pan, add the brains, brown on all sides and put on to a very hot dish. Add the rest of the butter and heat it until dark brown, without allowing it to burn. Add the wine vinegar and pour over the brains; sprinkle with salt, pepper and parsley.

SWEETBREAD VOL-AU-VENT
(see picture above)

1 pair of sweetbreads	1½ oz. flour
1 oz. butter	2 oz. butter
1 small onion	2 tbsps. cream
Salt and pepper	A vol-au-vent case
4 oz. mushrooms	Parsley to garnish

Clean and skin the sweetbreads and put into a pan with the hot butter and the thinly sliced onion. Brown the sweetbreads lightly, then add salt, pepper and a little water. Cover and simmer gently for about ½ hour. Remove and slice the sweetbread. Peel and slice the mushrooms and cook them in the sweetbread liquor until tender; drain them and mix with the sweetbread. Make a really thick sauce, using the flour, butter and about ½ pint of stock. Add the sweetbread and mushrooms, heat through, add the cream and fill the hot vol-au-vent case. Garnish with parsley.

BRAWN

1 pickled pig's head	Pieces of carrot and
A bouquet garni	turnip
Salt	1 hard-boiled egg
1 large onion	

Cut off the ears and remove the brains and all gristle from the head. Scald the ears, scrape them free of hair and wash well. Place the head in a pan with the bouquet garni, salt, vegetables and pig's ears and cover with water, then bring to the boil. Skim carefully and allow it to cook slowly until the meat is quite tender—about 3 hours is usually sufficient. Strain off the liquid, remove the meat from the bones and cut into small pieces, removing any fat or gristle. Cut the ears into strips. Skim off the fat from the remaining liquid, then boil it until reduced to half. Garnish the bottom of a mould or

cake tin with chopped egg white, pack the meat in tightly and pour some of the liquid over. Put a saucer and weight on it and leave till cold and set. When the brawn is required for use, dip the mould into hot water and turn the brawn on to a dish.

LYONNAISE TRIPE

1½ lb. prepared tripe	Salt and pepper
2 oz. butter	2 large onions, sliced
1½ oz. flour	or chopped
Stock or water	Wine vinegar
1 tsp. tomato paste	Chopped parsley

Cut the tripe into neat pieces and cook until golden in the hot butter. Sprinkle in the flour to absorb the extra fat, and when it has cooked a little while, add just enough stock or water to cover the tripe. Add the tomato paste, salt and pepper, then the onions; cover, and cook gently for 1 hour. Add the wine vinegar and parsley just before serving.

BAKED STUFFED LIVER
(see picture above)

1 lb. liver	4 rashers of back bacon
A little seasoned flour	½ pint stock or gravy
Forcemeat stuffing	

Wash and dry the liver, cut it into 4 pieces, dip into seasoned flour and lay them in a greased baking tin. Put a little stuffing on each piece of liver and lay a piece of bacon on top. Pour the stock round, cover the baking tin with a lid or with greased paper and bake in a moderately hot oven (375°F., mark 5) until the liver is tender—about 40 minutes. Serve the liver on a hot dish and pour the stock or gravy over. Garnish with parsley. Serve accompanied by creamed potatoes and a green vegetable.

LIVER PÂTÉ

Cook some pig's liver with a sliced onion, a little water and seasoning, simmering it until tender. When it is cold, put it twice through a fine mincer. Blend in about one quarter its weight of butter and re-season. Serve on hot toast fingers, for savoury snacks, etc.

MEAT PIES AND PUDDINGS

RAISED VEAL AND HAM PIE
(see colour picture no. 13)

12 oz. plain flour	½ lb. ham or bacon
½ level tsp. salt	1-2 hard-boiled eggs
3 oz. lard	Salt and pepper
¼ pint water	Meat stock
1 lb. fillet of veal	Egg for glazing

Sift the flour and salt and make a well in the centre. Heat the fat and water to boiling point, then pour into the dry ingredients. Mix with a wooden spoon, then knead the dough well until smooth. Keep a quarter of the pastry warm to make the lid and mould the rest into a pie shape, then fasten 3-4 folds of greased greaseproof paper round it to hold its shape; alternatively, line a 5- or 6-inch cake tin or a raised pie mould with the pastry. Cut the veal and ham into small dice and mix with the finely chopped eggs. Fill the pastry case with this mixture, adding seasonings as required and a little meat stock. Put on a pastry lid and decorate the pie as desired, making a hole in the top of it for steam to escape. Glaze with beaten egg and decorate. Bake in a fairly hot oven (400°F., mark 6) for about ½ hour, then reduce the heat to moderate (350°F., mark 4) and cook for about 1½ hours longer; cover the pastry with a double sheet of greaseproof paper when it is sufficiently brown. Fill up the pie with some aspic jelly (made with powdered aspic) and leave until cold. (Serves 6-8.)

STEAK AND MUSHROOM PIE

1½ lb. beefsteak	1 pint stock
4 oz. mushrooms	Salt and pepper
1 onion	½ lb. flaky pastry
Seasoned flour	Egg for glazing
2 oz. dripping	

Cut the steak into neat pieces, discarding any excess fat. Slice the mushrooms and onion. Dip the meat into seasoned flour and fry in the hot dripping until lightly browned; add the mushrooms and onion and when these are fried, add the stock and seasonings. Cover and cook gently for about 1½ hours, or until the meat is tender. Put into a pie dish and if possible leave till cold. Remove any fat from the surface and cover the pie with pastry. Decorate as required, glaze with egg and bake in a hot oven (425°F., mark 7) for about ½ hour.

LARGE CORNISH PASTY

6-8 oz. chuck steak	Salt and pepper
1 large onion	8 oz. shortcrust pastry
8 oz. raw potatoes	Egg to glaze

Remove any excess fat or gristle from the steak and cut the meat into small, neat pieces. Mix with the chopped onion, diced potatoes and seasoning. Roll out the pastry into a round the size of a dinner plate and put the filling in the centre. Damp the edges, draw the pastry together with the join on top, press the edges firmly and knock together with a knife; twist into a wavy line. Brush with beaten egg to glaze. Bake in a

hot oven (425°F., mark 7) for 15 minutes, then reduce to warm (325°F., mark 3) and bake for a further 1¼ hours until the filling is cooked. (Serves 2-3.)

SEA PIE

4 oz. haricot beans or split peas, soaked overnight	1 turnip
	A stalk of celery
½-1 lb. stewing steak or neck of mutton	1 oz. flour
	Salt and pepper
1 onion or leek	About 1 pint stock or water
2-3 carrots	

For the Crust

8 oz. plain flour	Salt and pepper
2 level tsps. baking powder	3 oz. shredded suet

Drain the beans. Cut the meat in neat pieces and mix with the diced fresh vegetables. Mix 1 oz. flour with the salt and pepper. Fill a casserole with layers of the mixed meat and diced vegetables and beans, sprinkle with the seasoned flour, then pour on liquid till the mixture is barely covered.
Make the crust by mixing the dry ingredients and suet and adding enough cold water to make a light dough. Roll out 1 inch smaller than the size of the casserole. Bring the meat and vegetables to the boil, then place the crust on top, cover with a close-fitting lid and simmer for 2½ hours. Serve in the casserole, with the pastry topping cut into triangular slices.

SAVOURY STEAK AND KIDNEY PUDDING

1 lb. steak	4 oz. beef suet
1 sheep's kidney	1 tbsp. chopped parsley
Seasoned flour	1 level tsp. chopped thyme
8 oz. plain flour	A little sour milk or water
¼ level tsp. salt	
2 level tsps. baking powder	½ pint stock

Slice the steak and kidney thinly, dip into seasoned flour and roll up each piece of kidney in a strip of steak. Make a suetcrust pastry with the flour, salt, baking powder, shredded or chopped suet and herbs, mixing it to a fairly moist dough with the milk. Grease a pudding basin, line it with three-quarters of the pastry, put in the meat and stock and cover with remaining pastry. Cover in the usual way and steam for 4 hours.

BACON ROLY-POLY

½-¾ lb. lean bacon	½ level tsp. salt
1 small onion	4 oz. chopped suet
Chopped parsley	Cold water to mix
8 oz. self-raising flour	Tomato sauce or gravy

Mince the bacon and mix it with the finely chopped onion. Fry very lightly and add the parsley. Meanwhile sieve the flour and salt and mix with the suet and enough cold water to give a soft dough. Roll out into an oblong, spread with the bacon mixture to within ½ inch of the sides and damp these with water. Roll up tightly and either tie in a pudding cloth and steam for 2-2½ hours, or put on to a baking tin and bake in a moderately hot oven (375°F., mark 5) for about 1 hour. Serve with tomato sauce or a good brown gravy.

RÉCHAUFFÉ DISHES

MINCED HAM WITH POACHED EGGS
(see picture above)

6 oz. minced or chopped cooked ham
¼ pint white sauce
Mustard
Pepper
A little tomato ketchup
4 rounds of buttered toast
4 poached eggs

Mix the ham with the sauce, mustard, pepper and ketchup. Put on to the hot toast and serve with a poached egg on top. Add extra toast, if desired, as a garnish. Other cold left-over meat, or a mixture of cold meats, may be minced or chopped and served in this way.

NOODLES MILANAISE
(see picture above, right)

½ lb. broken noodles
Salt and pepper
3 eggs
4 tbsps. cream
½ level tsp. grated nutmeg
6 oz. minced ham
Cooked vegetables or green salad

Cook the noodles in plenty of boiling salted water until tender (about 10-15 minutes), then drain them. Season well with salt and pepper and mix with the beaten eggs, cream, nutmeg and ham. Turn into a buttered ring mould and stand this in a baking tin half-filled with water. Bake in a moderate oven (350°F., mark 4) for about 30 minutes, or until set. Turn out, garnish as desired and serve hot with vegetables or cold with a green salad.

BEEF RÉCHAUFFÉ WITH CREAMED POTATO

¾ lb. cooked beef
2 rashers of bacon
2 small onions
Salt and pepper
1 tbsp. chopped parsley
¼ pint stock or gravy
1 tbsp. vinegar
Creamed potatoes

Cut the beef into wafer-thin slices and put a few of them into a greased baking dish. Dice the bacon and fry it with the sliced onions. When these are lightly browned, add salt, pepper and parsley. Put alternate layers of this mixture and of the cold beef into the baking dish. Heat the stock or gravy, add the vinegar and pour into the dish. Cover and bake in a moderate oven (350°F., mark 4) for 30 minutes, then remove the cover, fork some well-seasoned hot creamed potatoes over the top and serve at once.

VEAL SUPRÊME

1 oz. butter
1 oz. flour
½ pint milk
½ lb. cooked lean veal
Salt and pepper
2 hard-boiled eggs
A squeeze of lemon juice
1 wineglass of sherry
Hard-boiled egg to garnish

Melt the butter and stir in the flour. Add the milk gradually and stir until the mixture thickens and becomes smooth. Cut the veal into small cubes and add to the pan, with some salt and pepper. Simmer gently in a covered pan for a few minutes, then add the chopped eggs, lemon juice and sherry. Serve garnished with sliced hard-boiled egg.

BARBECUED LAMB SLICES

¾-1 lb. cold lamb
1½ oz. melted butter
3 tsps. vinegar
4 tbsps. red-currant jelly
¼ pint stock
A little dry mustard
Salt and pepper
Pickled walnuts (optional)

Cut the lamb into neat slices. Make a piquant-flavoured sauce by melting the butter and adding the vinegar, red-currant jelly, stock and seasonings. (It is convenient to do this in a frying pan.) Add the slices of meat and turn them in the sauce until they are well covered and heated through. Place on a heated serving dish, pour the remaining hot sauce over the meat and serve at once.
A few pickled walnuts may be chopped up and added to the sauce if desired.

IDEAS FOR THE COLD TABLE

MEAT PLATTER
(see colour picture no. 50)

A variety of sliced meats can be served on a platter garnished with radish roses, celery curls, tomato lilies, etc. English cold meats can be supplemented by the wide variety of Continental specialities, sausages and salamis now available.

Alternatively, spread the meat slices with a savoury filling and serve rolled up and secured with cocktail sticks. Suggested combinations:— ham with cream cheese and raisins or cranberry jelly; beef with horseradish sauce or potato salad; pork with sage and onion stuffing or apple sauce.

Rounds of salami or Continental sausage can be rolled into cones and filled in a similar way with mixed vegetables in salad cream, asparagus tips, cream cheese, pimiento or cocktail onions.

HAM POTATO SALAD
(see colour picture no. 47)

Make a potato salad, using new waxy potatoes and flavouring it well with onion and chopped parsley, then mix in some strips of lean cooked ham before adding the mayonnaise. Garnish with watercress, hard-boiled egg and small tomatoes.

Alternatively, make a jellied tomato ring mould containing sliced eggs, peas, etc., and put the salad in it.

VEAL, HAM AND TONGUE MOULD
(see colour picture no. 47)

1 pint aspic jelly	$\frac{1}{2}$ lb. cooked tongue
3 hard-boiled eggs	$\frac{1}{2}$ lb. cooked ham
$\frac{1}{2}$ lb. cooked veal	

Line an oblong cake or bread tin with almost-setting aspic jelly and decorate it with slices of hard-boiled egg. Chop up any remaining egg and mix it with the diced meats. Put the mixture into the tin and cover with aspic. When set, turn out and serve cut into 8 slices.

A colourful accompaniment is a salad of cooked asparagus and tiny red tomatoes stuffed with cubes of cucumber and green peas in mayonnaise.

BEEF MAYONNAISE

$\frac{1}{2}$-$\frac{3}{4}$ lb. cold beef	2 egg yolks
2 lettuce hearts	Salt and pepper
$\frac{1}{2}$ lb. tomatoes	About $\frac{1}{2}$ pint olive oil
$\frac{1}{4}$ lb. cucumber	Juice of $\frac{1}{2}$ a lemon
Radishes	1 hard-boiled egg

Cut the meat into small dice. Line a salad bowl or platter with some of the larger lettuce leaves; cut the firm hearts into quarters and place these at intervals round the sides. Put the meat, sliced peeled tomatoes, sliced cucumber and radishes into a bowl and mix with the mayonnaise, made as follows: Put the egg yolks into a bowl with the salt and pepper, mix with a wooden spoon and then gradually stir in the oil drop by drop,

adding a squeeze of lemon juice at intervals. The mayonnaise should be thick and creamy when ready. Pile the meat and mayonnaise mixture on the lettuce and decorate the dish with sliced hard-boiled egg and a few tomato slices, etc.

Ready-made mayonnaise may also be used.

HAM AND ASPARAGUS MOULD
(see colour picture no. 50)

Aspic jelly	$\frac{1}{2}$ level tsp. salt
A can of asparagus tips	3 eggs, slightly beaten
	6 tbsps. vinegar
$\frac{1}{2}$ oz. gelatine	$\frac{1}{2}$ pint single cream
2 tbsps. cold water	$\frac{3}{4}$ lb. cooked ham, cut
3 oz. granulated sugar	into 1-inch slivers
1 level tbsp. dry mustard	Watercress and tomato

Line a 1$\frac{1}{2}$-pint mould with aspic jelly (made according to the directions on the packet) and decorate the sides with some asparagus tips. Dissolve the gelatine in the cold water. Mix the sugar, mustard and salt together and add to the eggs. Heat the vinegar just to boiling point and gradually add the egg to it. Return the mixture to the heat and cook slowly till it thickens but does not boil. Remove from the heat, add the dissolved gelatine and chill, stirring occasionally, until the mixture thickens. Add the cream, the ham and the rest of the asparagus, cut into small pieces. Pour into the prepared mould and chill until firm. Unmould and garnish with watercress and tomato wedges. (Serves 4-6.)

PORK CHEESE
(see colour picture no. 47)

1 lb. cold roast pork	$\frac{1}{2}$ tsp. dried sage
$\frac{1}{4}$ lb. pork fat	A little grated nutmeg
Salt and pepper	1 tsp. finely grated
2 tsps. chopped parsley	lemon rind
A pinch of	$\frac{1}{4}$ oz. gelatine
powdered mace	$\frac{1}{3}$ pint stock

Cut the cold pork and fat into small, even-sized pieces. Season well and add the parsley, mace, sage, nutmeg and lemon rind. Mix all the ingredients thoroughly and put into a greased basin or mould. Dissolve the gelatine in the hot stock and pour into the mould until full. Cover and bake in a moderate oven (350°F., mark 4) for 1 hour. When cold, turn out and serve sliced, with salad. (Serves 4-6.)

MARBLED VEAL

Chop up or mince $\frac{3}{4}$ lb. each cold cooked tongue and veal, keeping them separate. Line a mould or glass pie dish with jellied stock and decorate with a pattern of sliced hard-boiled egg and tomato. When this is set, fill up the mould with irregular layers of the two meats, adding jellied stock to cover. When set, turn out and serve sliced, with salad. (Serves 4-6.)

In the Salads chapter of this book are recipes for a wide range of both well-known and unusual salads, English and cosmopolitan, many of which would be excellent with these cold meat dishes.

SAUSAGES

Both beef and pork sausages are made in several styles, so choose the size and type most suitable for your particular purpose. Sausage-meat is the most convenient purchase for made-up dishes, where separate sausages are not required. 1 lb. of sausages serves 4 people when used as a main dish. The smallest chipolata sausages are used mainly for buffet and cocktail party snacks—they are grilled or fried and served on sticks. Pork sausages require longer cooking than beef.

To Fry: Separate the links, pierce them in several places with a fine skewer, or prick once or twice with a fork. Coat with flour and cook in a little hot fat until evenly browned, turning them over to cook all sides. Serve as desired—on fried bread, with bacon or with mashed potatoes and gravy.

To Grill: Prick as for frying, place under a hot grill and cook for 10-18 minutes according to type, turning frequently. Serve with grilled tomatoes, etc.

To Bake: Prick, place on a greased tin and cook in a moderate oven (350°F., mark 4) for about 30 minutes.

TOAD-IN-THE-HOLE

Skin ½ lb. sausages or not, as preferred. If they are skinned, roll them lightly in a little flour to form each into a roll. Heat ½ oz. dripping in a Yorkshire pudding tin until smoking and pour in ½ pint Yorkshire pudding batter (see page 67). Arrange the sausages in rows and bake in a hot oven (425°F., mark 7) for about ¾ hour.

SAUSAGE-MEAT BALLS WITH SPANISH RICE
(see picture above)

1 lb. sausage-meat	1 onion
Seasoned flour	1 small green pepper
Fat for frying	2 sticks of celery
6 oz. long-grained rice	An 8-oz. can of tomatoes
2 oz. margarine	Salt and pepper

Form the sausage-meat into about 6 balls or cakes and roll them in a little seasoned flour. Fry on all sides until well cooked, turning them carefully to prevent them from breaking.

Boil the rice in plenty of salted water until tender and drain it. Melt the margarine, stir in the finely chopped onion, pepper and celery and cook gently for about 15 minutes. Add the tomatoes and the seasoning and when hot stir in the rice. Heat all together, stirring, then put on to a hot dish. Arrange the sausage-meat balls over the top and garnish with parsley.

SAUSAGE POTATO PIE
(see picture above)

1 lb. sausages	A little milk
1 onion, sliced	Butter or margarine
¾ lb. tomatoes, skinned	Salt and pepper
1 lb. cooked potatoes	Chopped parsley

Fry the sausages and then let them cool slightly. Skin most of them, cut in half lengthways and put into a pie dish. Fry the onion in the same pan, also the quartered tomatoes. Meanwhile cream the potatoes with milk and butter and season well. Put the vegetables over the sausages, cover with the potatoes and fork the top. Slice the remaining sausages and place round the edge of the dish, add some onion rings, dot with small shavings of fat and bake in a hot oven (425°F., mark 7) for 15 minutes to brown the potatoes. Sprinkle with parsley.

SAUSAGE FLAN
(see picture on page 203)

4 oz. shortcrust pastry	¾ lb. sausage-meat
(see p. 140)	1 level tsp. mixed herbs
1 onion, skinned	Salt and pepper
4 streaky bacon rashers	1 egg, whisked
½ oz. lard	Tomato to garnish

Line a 7-inch pie plate with the pastry, trim and crimp the edges. Chop the onion finely; rind the bacon and cut into ½-inch strips. Melt the lard in a frying pan and fry the onion and bacon until golden; drain well. Mix the sausage-meat, onion, bacon, herbs, salt and pepper, add the egg and beat well. Spread over the pastry case and bake in a fairly hot oven (400°F., mark 6) for 15 minutes, or until the pastry is set; turn the oven to moderate (350°F., mark 4) and cook for a further 25 minutes, until the sausage-meat is cooked. Decorate with sliced tomato or as desired.

MEAT COOKED WITH WINE

HAM BAKED IN CIDER

3-4 lb. gammon hock or	4 peppercorns
corner gammon, in a piece	4 oz. brown sugar
2 onions, quartered	1 level tsp. dry mustard
2 carrots, quartered	Whole cloves
1 bay leaf	¼ pint cider

Soak the joint for 3-4 hours, then calculate the cooking time, allowing 20 minutes per lb. and 20 minutes over. Put the joint with the onions, carrots, bay leaf and peppercorns into a large pan, cover with fresh water and bring slowly to the boil. Simmer gently for *half* the calculated cooking time. Remove the joint, wipe it dry and wrap in foil. Bake in a fairly hot oven (375°F., mark 5) for the remaining time.

About 20 minutes before the end of the cooking time, remove the joint from foil and take off the skin, using a sharp knife. Mix the sugar and mustard and spread this over the joint. Stud with cloves, pour the cider round the joint and return it to the oven for the last 20 minutes—baste frequently.

Garnish the joint with apricot halves and glacé cherries, peach slices or pineapple rings. For another variation, try a Raisin Sauce: to make this, blend 1½ level tbsps. cornflour with ½ pint cider in a pan, add 2 oz. brown sugar, a pinch of salt, 2 oz. seedless raisins, 4 cloves and a pinch of cinnamon. Simmer together for 10 minutes, stirring, then stir in ½ oz. butter before serving.

HAM MONTMORENCY

2 oz. lard	A bouquet garni
1 onion, chopped	1 tbsp. sherry or cider
1 carrot, sliced	24 black sweet cherries
2 rashers of bacon,	4 thick gammon rashers
chopped	A little oil
2 oz. flour	1 tbsp. red-currant jelly
1 pint stock (made from	1 tbsp. horseradish
1 bouillon cube)	cream
1 tbsp. tomato paste	

Melt the fat in a pan, add the onion, carrot and bacon and fry gently until lightly browned. Remove these, draining the fat back into the pan, then stir in the flour and fry until well browned, to give the sauce a good colour. Gradually stir in the stock, return the vegetables, add the tomato paste, bouquet garni and sherry or cider. Bring to the boil and simmer, stirring the sauce occasionally, for 30 minutes. Alternatively, pour the sauce into a casserole and put in a cool oven (300°F., mark 1-2) for 4 hours, where it will cook slowly with little attention.

Stone the cherries. Trim the gammon rashers and snip the edges to prevent their curling. Fifteen minutes before serving the meal, brush the rashers with oil and grill for 7 minutes. Meanwhile strain the sauce and return it to the pan. Turn the rashers over, brush with some more oil and grill for a further 7 minutes. Stir the red-currant jelly and horseradish cream into the sauce,

bring to the boil and simmer for 4 minutes. Add the cherries and allow them to heat through. Serve the gammon rashers with the sauce poured over them.

BOEUF BOURGUIGNON

1½ lb. braising beef,	4 oz. mushrooms, sliced
cut into 1-inch cubes	½ oz. flour
2 oz. lard	¼ pint Burgundy
½ lb. onions, sliced	½ pint stock
2 rashers of bacon,	A bouquet garni
chopped	Salt and pepper

Brown the meat quickly in the hot fat, then remove it from the pan and add the onions, bacon and mushrooms. Fry slowly, then stir in the flour. Put the meat in a 4-pint casserole and add the wine, stock, bouquet garni and seasoning. Cook in the centre of a warm oven (325°F., mark 3) for 1½ hours. Add the onions, bacon and mushrooms and cook for 1 hour longer.

STUFFED BEEF ROLLS

¾ lb. lean beef, cut into	Salt and pepper
thin slices	1 wineglass red or
1 onion, sliced	white wine
1 carrot, sliced	¼ pint stock
2 rashers of bacon,	A bouquet garni
chopped	1 tbsp. tomato paste

For the Stuffing

1 rasher of bacon,	2-3 tbsps.
chopped	breadcrumbs
1 clove of garlic,	Grated rind of ½ a lemon
crushed	Salt and pepper
1 tbsp. chopped	Grated nutmeg
parsley	

Make the stuffing. Fry the bacon until brown, add the remaining ingredients and mix well. Divide the stuffing between the slices of beef, roll up and tie with string or thread. Put the onion, carrot and bacon into a pan, lay the meat rolls on top, season, cover and cook gently until the meat is brown and sticky. Pour in the wine and stock and add the bouquet garni and tomato paste. Put into a casserole and cook in the centre of a warm oven (325°F., mark 3) for 2½ hours, until the meat is tender. Untie the rolls, strain the sauce and pour it over the meat.

BEEF AND ONION CASSEROLE

1½ lb. chuck steak	½ pint red wine
Salt and pepper	½ pint stock or water
2 oz. dripping	1 lb. onions, chopped
3 oz. lean bacon,	1 clove of garlic, chopped
chopped	A bouquet garni
1½ oz. plain flour	

Cut the meat up neatly, season and brown in the dripping. Add the bacon and continue cooking for a few minutes. Remove the meat and bacon from the pan, stir in the flour and brown lightly over very gentle heat. Gradually add the wine and stock, stirring continuously. Fill a casserole with layers of meat, bacon, onion and garlic. Pour the sauce over and add the bouquet garni. Cook very gently for 3½-4 hours in a cool oven (300°F., mark 1-2). Add a little more wine while cooking, if necessary. Just before serving, remove the bouquet garni. Serve with plain boiled potatoes.

SAUTÉ FILLET OF BEEF

1½-2 lb. fillet of beef	1 medium-sized onion,
Salt and pepper	sliced
2 oz. butter or fat	½ level tbsp. flour
A pinch of mixed herbs	¾ pint beef stock
1 tbsp. finely	4 tbsps. sherry
chopped parsley	

Wipe and trim the meat, season and tie into shape if necessary. Heat the fat in a heavy frying pan and fry the meat until the whole surface is well browned. Add the herbs, parsley, onion, salt and pepper, cover with a well-fitting lid and cook very slowly for 1½ hours, basting frequently. When the meat is cooked, remove it and keep warm.
Stir the flour into the remaining fat, add the stock gradually, stirring all the time, and bring to the boil. Season and add the sherry. Place the meat on a hot serving dish and serve the sauce separately. (Serves 4-6.)

STEAK AND POTATO CASSEROLE

1 oz. butter	An 8-oz. can of tomatoes
2 oz. bacon, chopped	1 clove of garlic,
2 oz. ham, chopped	crushed
1-1½ lb. chuck or shoulder	½ pint red wine or
steak, in 1-inch cubes	wine and stock
½ lb. onions,	A bouquet garni
sliced	Salt and pepper
2 carrots, sliced	½ lb. potatoes, diced

Melt the butter, add the bacon and ham and fry for a few minutes. Add the meat and brown well on all sides. Add the onions, carrots, tomatoes and garlic, pour in the wine, add the bouquet garni and season. Put into a 4-pint casserole and cook in the centre of a warm oven (325°F., mark 3) for 2 hours. Stir in the potatoes and cook for a further 30 minutes.

GOULASH WITH BEER

1 lb. stewing steak	Grated nutmeg
Seasoned flour	2 oz. flour
2 medium-sized onions	½ pint stock
1 green pepper	2 large tomatoes, cut up
A little dripping	A bunch of mixed herbs
3 tbsps. tomato paste	¼ pint beer
Salt and pepper	2 level tsps. paprika

Cut the steak up small and dip in seasoned flour. Chop the onions and pepper and fry lightly in a little dripping. Add the meat and fry lightly on all sides. Stir in the tomato paste, seasonings and flour and add the stock, tomatoes and herbs. Put into a casserole and cook in a warm oven (325°F., mark 3) for 1 hour. Add the beer and paprika and cook for another ½-1 hour, or until the meat is tender; remove the herbs. Serve with sauerkraut and caraway-flavoured dumplings, or with a green salad.

VEAL À LA ROYALE

2 lb. veal, cut into ·	3 tbsps. brandy
1-inch cubes	2 oz. flour
2 oz. lard	Salt and pepper
5 rashers of bacon,	¼ pint red wine
chopped	¾ pint stock
½ an onion, sliced	A bouquet garni

Brown the cubes of veal in the hot lard with the chopped bacon rashers; drain them carefully and put into a 4-pint casserole. Fry the onion until golden and add to the meat. Add the brandy to the pan, set it alight, then when the flames die down, stir in the flour, salt, pepper, wine and stock. Pour over the meat, add the bouquet garni, cover with the lid and cook for 2 hours in the centre of a moderate oven (350°F., mark 4). (Serves 5-6.)

VEAL FLAMBÉ

4 veal cutlets	4 oz. mushrooms, sliced
Salt and pepper	2 tbsps. stock or water
½ an onion, finely	A dash of sherry and of
chopped	Worcestershire sauce
2 oz. butter	¼ pint double cream
2-3 tbsps. brandy	

Season the cutlets with salt and pepper, then fry with the onion in half the fat until golden. Add the brandy and set it alight. When the flames die down, add the mushrooms, remaining fat, stock, sherry and sauce. Simmer gently for 10 minutes. Lift out the cutlets and put on a warm serving dish. Add the cream to the sauce, stir well, then pour it over the meat.

ESCALOPES FINES HERBES

2 oz. butter	2 oz. mushrooms, sliced
1½ oz. flour	½ level tsp. mixed herbs
Salt and pepper	4 tbsps. thin cream
4 escalopes of veal	An 8-oz. can of tomatoes
½ tbsp. tomato paste	1 level tsp. sugar
1 wineglass sherry	2 oz. grated cheese
1 wineglass red wine	

Heat 1 oz. butter in a frying pan. Mix 1 oz. flour with seasoning and toss the meat in this. Cook the escalopes gently for 2-3 minutes on each side in the hot fat; remove and keep hot. Add the remaining ½ oz. flour to the pan, stir in the tomato paste, sherry and wine and bring slowly to the boil; add the mushrooms, herbs and lastly the cream. Season as required. Cook very gently for 5 minutes.
Heat the remaining butter in a pan, add the canned tomatoes and sugar and heat through. Pour into a dish, put the meat on top, pour the sauce over, sprinkle with the cheese and brown under the grill.
Fresh tomatoes may be used instead of canned; peel and chop them and omit the sugar.

KIDNEYS IN RED WINE

2 oz. butter	¼ pint stock
1 onion, chopped	A bouquet garni
4-6 sheep's kidneys	1 tbsp. tomato paste
1 oz. flour	Salt and pepper
¼ pint red wine	4 oz. mushrooms, sliced

Melt the butter and fry the onion until golden. Skin and core the kidneys and cut them into small pieces, add to the pan and cook for 5 minutes, stirring occasionally. Stir in the flour, pour in the wine and stock and bring slowly to the boil, then add the bouquet garni, tomato paste and some salt and pepper. Simmer for 5 minutes. Add the mushrooms and simmer for a further few minutes. Remove the bouquet garni before serving and check the seasoning.

CARVING

Beef Joints
This meat, particularly when cold, is best carved thinly.

Sirloin or Ribs (unboned) (see picture 1 on right): Remove the chine or end bone and cut the meat from the top of the joint in thin slices from the outer fat down to the rib bone. Turn the sirloin over and cut rather thicker slices from the fillet or undercut, this time cutting again down to the bone in even slices. Serve a slice of undercut with a slice of top meat and a little fat.

Rolled Ribs, Rolled Sirloin: When carving boneless joints of meat, slice across the round, in thin slices.

Fillet: Carve across the grain, but rather thickly, in ¼-inch slices; cut downwards towards the dish.

Mutton and Lamb
These are carved in rather thicker slices than beef.

Best end of Neck: If chined, this is easy to carve, as it has only to be divided by cutting between the bones.

Loin: Cut the joint right through downwards between the bones, to divide it into individual chops.

Shoulder (see picture 2 on right): Place the joint so that the bladebone points away from the carver. Insert the fork securely in the meat and with the aid of the fork, raise the far side of the joint slightly, then make a vertical cut through the centre of the meat up to the bone; this will cause the joint to open out slightly, making it appear as if a slice had already been removed. Cut thick slices from each side of this gap, as far as the bladebone on the one side and the knuckle on the other. Slices of the knuckle also may be carved for those who appreciate it. Next turn the joint so that the bladebone faces the carver and carve the meat on top of the blade-bone downwards in strips, parallel with the central "fin" of the bone. Finally, turn the joint upside down and slice meat horizontally from underside.

Leg: Start cutting at the thick end and work towards the shank, cutting in slices down to the bone, then turn it over and cut rather more sloping slices, working from the shank to the fillet end.

Stuffed Breast of Lamb or Mutton: Cut downwards right through the joint in fairly thick slices.

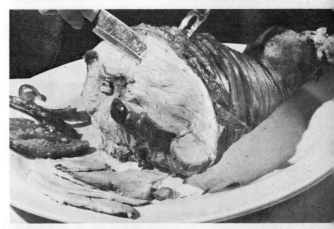

Pork Joints
This meat is cut moderately thick.

Leg (see picture 3 on right): This is cut in the same way as a leg of lamb or mutton, but the cuts should be made between the cuts in the crackling and each person should be given a piece of crisp crackling with the meat.

Loin: Divide between the bones to form chops, or cut into thinner slices for more economical carving.

Spare Rib: Cut between the score marks into moderately thick, even-sized slices.

Veal Joints
Loin (see picture 4 on right): Slice the meat downwards towards the serving dish, in medium-thick slices.

Fillet: If the bone is left in, cut the meat down to the bone on one side, then turn the joint over and do the same on the underside. The joint is often boned and stuffed and when this is done it can be cut right through into slices of medium thickness.

Best End of Neck: Divide by cutting between the bones.

Shoulder: Carve as for shoulder of lamb and mutton.

SAUCES AND OTHER ACCOMPANIMENTS

APPLE SAUCE

1 lb. cooking apples	Sugar, if required
1-2 oz. butter	Lemon juice

Peel, core and slice the apples with a stainless knife and cook them gently to a pulp in a covered pan. Beat with a wooden spoon until smooth and add the fat. Sugar may be added if desired, but a tart apple sauce is just the right accompaniment to pork. If the apples are sweet, add a little lemon juice.

MINT SAUCE

1 level tsp. sugar	2 tbsps. chopped mint
1 tbsp. boiling water	1½ tbsps. vinegar

Dissolve the sugar in the boiling water in a sauce-boat, add the mint and stir in vinegar to taste.

BROWN SAUCE

1 small onion	¾ oz. flour
1 small carrot	½ pint stock
1 piece of turnip	Pepper and salt
¾ oz. dripping	

Prepare and slice the vegetables and fry the onion in the dripping, then stir in the flour and cook it, allowing it to become a golden-brown colour before removing it from the heat. Stir in the stock gradually and add the other vegetables. Simmer for 20-30 minutes, season, strain and re-heat before serving.
For a richer sauce, add about 2 tbsps. sherry.

MUSHROOM SAUCE

To ½ pint well-seasoned white sauce add 2-4 oz. sautéed mushrooms.

ONION SAUCE

Add 1-2 chopped boiled onions to ½ pint white sauce.

CAPER SAUCE

Make some white sauce in the usual way, but use half meat liquor and half milk. Add about 1½ tbsps. coarsely chopped capers to ½ pint sauce.

DEVILLED BUTTER

Beat 2 oz. butter until soft, then mix in a little lemon juice, cayenne pepper and ½ level tsp. curry powder.

MAÎTRE D'HÔTEL BUTTER

1 oz. butter	1 tsp. lemon juice
1 tsp. chopped parsley	Salt and pepper

Mix thoroughly into a creamy paste, using a fork or wooden spoon. Shape into pats and chill before serving.

HORSERADISH CREAM

1-2 tbsps. grated horseradish	Single cream or evaporated milk
1 tbsp. vinegar	Salt, pepper, sugar

Soak the grated horseradish in the vinegar for 10-15 minutes. Stir in enough cream to give a soft consistency and season with salt, pepper and sugar.

GRAVY
(see picture above, left)

Either clear or thickened gravy is always served with roast joints and with many other meat dishes. Stock or vegetable water should be used for gravy, if possible, and it should be made in the baking tin, in order to make use of the juices which may have run into the fat.
Thin Gravy: Pour off all the fat from the tin and add a little boiling stock or water, stirring well in order to mix in any meat juices. Add as much extra liquid as required, season and add gravy browning, if necessary.
Thick Gravy: Pour off all but about 1 tbsp. dripping from the tin and add to this 1-2 level tsps. flour, according to the thickness of gravy required. Stir it over a low heat until smooth and lightly browned, then draw the tin off the heat and add about ½ pint stock or vegetable water. Return the tin to the heat and stir until the gravy boils and thickens. Season to taste and colour if necessary.

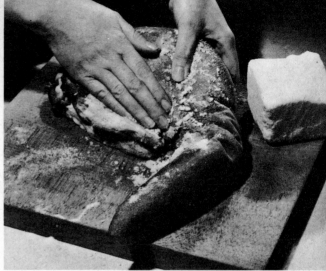

SAGE AND ONION STUFFING

2 large onions
½-1 oz. butter
4 oz. fresh breadcrumbs
2 level tsps. dried sage
Seasoning

Blanch the onions, strain and cover with fresh boiling water, cook until tender. Drain well and chop finely. Add to the other ingredients and mix well.

HERB (PARSLEY) STUFFING
(see right-hand picture opposite)

2 oz. suet
1-2 oz. ham or bacon
4 oz. fresh crumbs
2 tsps. chopped parsley
½ level tsp. mixed herbs
Grated rind of ½ lemon
Salt and pepper
1 egg yolk

Chop the suet and ham finely and mix with the crumbs; add parsley, herbs and lemon rind, season and bind with beaten egg. Use as required; for example to stuff bacon rolls or to make forcemeat balls. (This is sometimes called Veal Forcemeat.)

DUMPLINGS
(see picture above)

4 oz. self-raising flour
¼ level tsp. salt
1½-2 oz. chopped suet
A few fresh or dried herbs (optional)
Cold water to mix

Mix the dry ingredients with water to a soft, elastic dough, roll into balls and add to soups or stews ½ hour before serving.

Herb Dumplings: Include ½ an onion, finely grated, and ½ level tsp. mixed dried herbs.

YORKSHIRE PUDDING

Sift 4 oz. plain flour and ¼ level tsp. salt and make a well in the centre. Add 1 egg and enough milk or milk and water (about ¼ pint) to give a creamy, smooth batter. Beat thoroughly with a wooden spoon until full of air bubbles, then stir in about another ¼ pint liquid. Heat ½ oz. dripping in a Yorkshire pudding tin or in several deep patty tins and pour in the batter, only half-filling small tins. Bake in a hot oven (425°F., mark 7) for about 45 minutes (15-20 minutes for small puddings).

PICKLING MEAT

Ox tongue, pig's head, leg or belly of pork and silverside or brisket of beef are particularly suited to pickling. Trim and wash the meat, then rub it over with salt to remove all traces of blood (see picture above). Use a large earthenware crock, bowl or basin, or a polythene bowl or pail and cover with a board to exclude the dust.

Wet Pickle: This is the easier method. Put 1 gallon water, 1½ lb. bay or common salt, 1 oz. saltpetre and 6 oz. brown sugar in a large pan, bring to the boil and boil for 15-20 minutes, skimming carefully. Strain into a bowl, allow to cool, put in the meat and cover.

Dry Pickle: Pound ½ lb. bay salt, mix with ½ lb. common salt, ½ lb. brown sugar, 1 oz. saltpetre, ½ oz. black pepper and 1 level tsp. allspice. Rub the meat daily with this mixture, working it well in. Leave the meat in the covered crock.

Times for Pickling Meat: Home-pickled meat is best done in the cold weather and the meat may remain in the salt mixture for a variable length of time. A thick cut of beef needs about 10 days, whereas a thinner cut, or a pig's head split in half, may be sufficiently salted in 4-5 days.

Cooking Salted or Pickled Meat: Remove the meat from the pickle and wash it thoroughly in cold water. If desired, it may be soaked for 1 hour in cold water before cooking. Put the meat (neatly tied up if necessary) into a pan of cold water, bring slowly to the boil and skim. The first water may be thrown away and this process repeated if required. Add herbs and vegetables if desired, then allow the water to simmer very gently for the required time. (Retain the liquid for use in making soups, etc.)

For salt beef and pork allow 50 minutes cooking time per lb. Ox tongue requires 3-4 hours, according to size; test for tenderness with a small skewer.

If the meat is to be pressed or collared (see page 37), it is best to remove the skin and any bones before the meat becomes cold; do this as soon as it is cool enough to handle. Tongue and ham skin comes away quite easily, but take care not to break up the meat.

THE ART OF CURRY-MAKING

Recipes give 4 servings, unless otherwise indicated

Whether you use ready-prepared curry powder and/or paste, or mix your own, do remember that thorough cooking, especially during the preliminary frying, is needed to remove the raw flavour of the spices.

Always cook curries slowly, to develop the characteristic richness. Indian curry is rarely thickened with flour —the long cooking should give the required consistency.

Cut the meat, poultry or fish into bite-sized portions, so that the curry can be eaten with a spoon.

When you are frying the onions (and perhaps garlic), cook them slowly, with a lid on, to prevent browning.

Although true Indian curries do not include apple, in this country it is often used as a substitute for mangoes; again, the sultanas which we also include, might be used in an accompanying pellao (pilaff), but not in curry.

The custom of garnishing a dish of curry with rice, which has become traditional in Europe, is not seen in the East, where the rice is served separately.

The rice should be the Patna or long-grain type.

In the East, curries are usually accompanied by a variety of side dishes—see the notes on pages 72-74.

CURRY POWDER AND PASTE

Providing you buy a reliable brand and use it while fresh, you can obtain a very pleasing result with a ready-prepared mixture. (Paste, incidentally, usually contains certain ingredients that keep better in this form than in a dry, powdered state.) However, you can achieve even better results by making your own mixtures from fresh spices, bought in seed or 'whole' form or already ground. Buy only a little at a time and keep spices and curry powder in airtight containers. Here is one reliable recipe:

HOME-MADE CURRY POWDER

(see right-hand picture on page 74)

1 oz. turmeric	2 oz. cumin seed
½ oz. coriander seed	1½ oz. fenugreek
½ oz. red chillies	½ oz. powdered ginger
½ oz. black pepper	¼ oz. poppy seed

Any ingredients which are not already powdered must first be crushed by means of a pestle and mortar. Mix all well together, then sift to remove any imperfectly crushed seeds and pound these again before re-mixing. Store in an airtight jar.

This gives a powder of medium strength; for a hotter flavour, increase the quantity of chillies.

COCONUT AND COCONUT MILK

Grated fresh coconut or desiccated coconut may be added to a curry to give a mellow flavour.

Coconut milk is also a very common ingredient. For best results it should be made from a fresh nut, but desiccated coconut can be used. Grate the coconut and pour over it enough boiling water to cover. Leave for 20-30 minutes, to obtain a well-flavoured infusion, then squeeze the liquid out through a fine strainer. A thinner milk is obtained by using the coconut a second time.

CALCUTTA BEEF CURRY

1 lb. stewing steak	½ pint thick coconut
1 level tsp. coriander	milk
powder	1 onion, sliced
1 level tsp. turmeric powder	1 clove of garlic,
1 level tsp. chilli powder	crushed
A pinch of black	1 oz. butter
pepper	Stock
A pinch of ground	Salt and lemon juice
ginger	

Cut the meat into pieces, removing any fat. Mix the powdered ingredients and make into a paste with a little of the coconut milk. Fry the onion and garlic in the butter until tender and add the paste, then fry for a further 3-4 minutes. Add the meat and a little stock, bring slowly to the boil and simmer for about 1 hour. Add the remaining coconut milk, some salt and lemon juice and serve at once, accompanied by boiled rice and a fruit or vegetable sambol (see page 74).

MARROW CURRY

1 lb. prepared marrow	2 level tsps. turmeric
2 large onions, sliced	powder
1½ oz. butter	2 level tsps. salt
2 level tsps. curry	2 large tomatoes, sliced
powder	2 tsps. lemon juice

Cut the marrow into cubes. Fry the onions in the butter until golden-brown. Stir in the curry powder, turmeric and salt, add the tomatoes and cook for a few minutes. Add the marrow, stir well and cook gently for 15-20 minutes, then shake the pan over the heat without the lid until the marrow is dried. Sprinkle on the lemon juice and cook for 1 minute. Serve with a pellao (p. 72).

CURRIED CRAB

A medium-sized crab	Salt
(or 1 can)	½ tsp. curry paste
1 small onion	2 tsps. chutney
1 small apple	1 oz. sultanas
1 oz. butter or lard	1 tsp. lemon juice
¾ oz. rice flour	2 tbsps. single cream
1 level tsp. curry powder	(optional)
½ pint stock	

Cut the crab meat up neatly. Peel the onion and peel and core the apple; chop both finely. Melt the butter and fry the onion, then the apple, rice flour and curry powder. Add the stock gradually and stir until boiling. Add salt to taste, the curry paste, chutney, sultanas and lemon juice, cover and simmer for 1 hour, stirring frequently. Add the fish, re-heat and stir in the cream. Serve with boiled rice.

KABAB ZEERA (CROQUETTES)

1 lb. lean lamb	2 level tsps. cumin
1 onion	1 tbsp. chopped parsley
A pinch of cayenne	Salt
pepper	Fat for frying

Mince the lamb and onion twice. Season and blend thoroughly, then shape into sausages about 4 inches long and ¾ inch thick. Fry in shallow fat until evenly browned. Serve in a curry sauce—for example, the one given for Curried Eggs on page 69.

CURRIED EGGS
(see picture above)

5 eggs, hard-boiled	1 oz. flour
2 small onions	½ pint stock
A small piece of apple	Salt
2 oz. butter	2 tsps. lemon juice
1 level tsp. curry powder	Rice: stuffed olives

Slice 3 of the eggs. Chop the onions and apple finely. Melt the butter, fry the onion lightly, add the apple, curry powder and flour and cook for a few minutes. Gradually add the stock, salt and lemon juice, boil up and skim, then simmer for about ¼ hour. Heat the sliced eggs in this sauce, then turn the mixture into a hot dish and surround with boiled rice. Decorate with olives and the remaining eggs, cut in wedges. Serve this mild curry with lemon, preserved ginger and coconut.

CHICKEN DOPYAZA

1½ lb. skinned jointed chicken	2 level tsps. powdered turmeric
½ level tsp. powdered ginger	1 level tsp. powdered cumin
½ level tsp. salt	2 level tsps. powdered coriander
1 lb. onions	
½ a garlic clove	¼ pint yoghourt
1 oz. butter	½ pint water
Seeds of 1 cardamom	4 peppercorns

If possible, use an enamelled iron casserole for this curry. Wipe the chicken, prick with a skewer, rub in the ginger and salt and leave for ½ hour. Chop half the onions, fry the onion and crushed garlic in the butter until brown, then remove from the pan, draining well. Cook the cardamom in the fat for 1 minute, then add the other spices, yoghourt and chicken; simmer gently till nearly all the yoghourt has been absorbed. Pound the cooked onions (or put them in a liquidizer) and add with the water to the chicken. Sprinkle the peppercorns and remaining onions (sliced) over the chicken. Cover and cook in a warm oven (325°F., mark 3) for 1 hour. 'Dopyaza' means 'twice onion'—strictly speaking, this curry should contain onions in two different forms, added at two different stages of the cooking.

CEYLON PRAWN CURRY
(see picture above and colour picture no. 15)

1 pint prawns or 1 doz. Dublin Bay prawns	1 level tsp. ground cloves
	1 level tsp. ground cinnamon
1 onion	
1 clove of garlic	1 level tsp. salt
2 oz. butter	1 level tsp. sugar
1 level tbsp. flour	¼ pint coconut milk (p. 68)
2 level tsps. turmeric	½ pint stock
	1 tsp. lemon juice

Shell the prawns and chop the onion and garlic finely. Melt the butter and fry the onion and garlic lightly, then add the flour, turmeric, cloves, cinnamon, salt and sugar. Cook gently for 10 minutes and add the coconut milk and stock. Simmer gently for 10 minutes, add the cooked prawns and lemon juice, re-season as necessary and cook for a further 10 minutes. Garnish with a few prawns heated separately; serve this mild curry with boiled rice and a hot chutney.
Shrimps may be used in a similar way.

CURRIED KIDNEYS
(see colour picture no. 12)

¾ lb. lamb's kidney	1 oz. flour
1 onion, peeled	½ pint stock
2 sticks of celery	1 oz. sultanas
1 oz. dripping	Seasoning
1-2 level tsps. curry powder	6 oz. rice

Wipe the kidney with a damp cloth and chop it finely, removing the skin and central core. Chop the onion and celery finely. Melt the dripping, add the onion, celery and kidney and cook over a low heat for 10 minutes, until the vegetables are soft. Stir in the curry powder and flour and add the stock gradually, stirring all the time. Bring to the boil, still stirring, add the sultanas, season to taste and simmer for about 30 minutes, or until the kidney is tender. Cook the rice in boiling salted water, then drain, rinse and dry it. Serve the curried kidney with a border of the dry boiled rice arranged round it.

PORK AND PINEAPPLE CURRY

(see picture above)

1 lb. pork fillet ·
2 oz. butter
1 clove of garlic
1 medium-sized onion
1 red pepper
1 tbsp. shrimp or
  anchovy essence
1½ oz. fresh (or green)
  ginger, chopped
  finely

1 level tbsp. grated lemon
  rind
1 level tsp. coriander powder
2 oz. chopped blanched
  almonds
½ pint water
An 11-oz. can of pineapple
  chunks
¼ level tsp. saffron

Cut the pork into small pieces and sauté in the hot butter with the crushed garlic, chopped onion and sliced pepper. Combine the fish essence, ginger, lemon rind, coriander powder and almonds. Add this mixture to the pork and continue frying gently for a few minutes, then add the water and cook until the meat is tender—about 1½ hours. Finally, add the pineapple chunks and saffron and cook for a few minutes longer. Serve with boiled rice.

If you cannot obtain the fresh ginger or coriander powder, use root ginger and ¼ oz. coriander seeds; tie in muslin and remove when the curry is cooked.

FISH CURRY

1 lb. filleted fish (e.g.,
  cod or halibut)
2 small onions, sliced
A clove of garlic, skinned
  and crushed

2 oz. butter
1 tomato, quartered
2 level tsps. curry powder
Salt to taste

Prepare the fish in the usual way. Fry the sliced onions and garlic in the fat, then add the tomato and 1 tbsp. water, to make a thick paste. Sprinkle the fish with curry powder and salt, add to the pan and cook until golden-brown. Pour in 1 teacupful warm water and let the curry cook in the pan with the lid on till the fish is tender when tested; take care not to let it break up. Serve with rice or puris.

Lemon juice may be included if desired, and the tomato may be replaced by tomato paste, a little extra stock or water being added.

VEGETABLE CURRY

(see picture above)

1 cauliflower, cut in
  large pieces
6 tomatoes
6-8 small potatoes,
  quartered
¼ lb. peas
¼ lb. French beans,
  sliced

1 level tbsp. turmeric
1½ level tbsps. mild curry
  powder
½ level tsp. salt
2 oz. butter
6 small onions
1 clove of garlic
½ pint stock

Place the raw vegetables on a large plate. Mix the spices and salt and sprinkle over the vegetables. Melt the butter in a heavy pan and sauté the finely shredded onions and garlic. Add the vegetables, then a little stock, cover, bring to the boil and simmer until tender. Serve with plain boiled rice, as this is a hot curry.

LAMB KOFTA (MEAT BALL CURRY)

1 lb. lean lamb
2 large onions, sliced
4 oz. butter
1 full garlic bulb,
  peeled and minced
2 level tsps. chilli powder
2 level tsps. coriander
  powder
½ level tsp. turmeric powder

1 level tsp. cumin seed
  powder
¼ level tsp. ground ginger
1 level tsp. allspice
1 lb. tomatoes, skinned
1½ cups water
2 level tsps. salt
1 sprig of mint

Mince the lamb. Fry the onions in the butter until soft and browned. Mix the garlic and the powdered ingredients (except for ½ tsp. of the allspice) and blend with 1 tbsp. water. Add to the onions, with the tomatoes; mix well and fry until the tomatoes are soft. Remove 1 tbsp. of this mixture, then add the water and salt to the remainder and simmer for 10 minutes.

Mix the remaining ½ tsp. allspice, the 1 tbsp. tomato mixture, the mint and the minced meat and knead well. Form into small balls and drop them into the sauce. Simmer gently for 30 minutes, shaking the pan so that the koftas are well coated with the sauce.

Koftas, which are very popular in the Deccan and Central India, may be made from a great variety of ingredients.

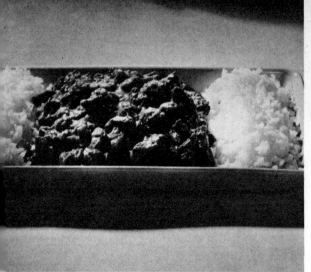

"DRY" CURRIES

BENGAL CURRY
(see picture above)

4 oz. butter	1 tbsp. lemon juice
2 thinly sliced onions	1-1½ lb. tender meat or
1 clove of garlic	parboiled chicken, cut
2 level tbsps. curry powder	in pieces and boned
2 level tsps. mixed spice	1 level tsp. salt
A good pinch of saffron	¾ pint stock

Heat the butter and fry the onions and crushed garlic until well browned, then add the curry powder, spice, saffron and lemon juice and fry again for 5-10 minutes. Add the meat, salt and stock and cook, stirring occasionally, for about ½ hour, by which time the stock should be partly absorbed and the curry thickened. Serve with pellao and a sambol.

DRY VEAL CURRY

1 lb. lean veal	Salt to taste
2 medium-sized onions	A few pickled gherkins
1 clove of garlic	2 tsps. chutney
1 oz. butter	Juice of ½ a lemon
2 level tsps. curry powder	¼ pint stock
1 tsp. curry paste	

Cut the meat up small. Chop the onions and garlic very finely and fry lightly in the butter. Add curry powder and paste and cook thoroughly for about 5 minutes, stirring all the time. Add the meat and salt and cook until well browned. Finally, add gherkins, chutney, lemon juice and stock and cook very slowly for 2-2½ hours, stirring occasionally. Serve with rice and lemon.

BINDALOO CURRY

1 lb. stewing steak	¼ pint vinegar
4 oz. butter	A pinch of salt
6 medium-sized onions	Gherkins and olives,
2 level tbsps. curry powder	sliced

Cut up the steak, removing excess fat. Heat 2 oz. butter in a saucepan and brown the sliced onions for 5 minutes with the lid on. Add curry powder and fry for a further 5 minutes. Brown the steak slightly in the remaining butter, then add it. Gradually add the vinegar and salt and simmer for 2 hours, or cook in a cool oven (300°F., mark 1). Garnish with gherkins and olives.

MADRAS CURRY (HOT)
(see colour picture no. 14)

2 oz. chopped almonds	A small piece of
2 oz. butter or fat	cinnamon stick
2 chopped onions	½ level tsp. ground cloves
1 clove of garlic	2 level tsps. flour
1 level tsp. coriander	1 pint stock or water
powder	1 lb. meat (cut small)
1 level tsp. black pepper	2 level tsps. turmeric
½ level tsp. chilli powder	powder
½ level tsp. cardamom	1 level tsp. sugar; salt
powder	Juice of 1 lemon
½ tsp. cumin powder	

Cover the almonds with ¼ pint boiling water and leave for 15 minutes, then strain the infusion. Melt the fat and lightly fry the onions. Add the garlic, spices and flavourings (except turmeric), with the flour, cook for 5 minutes, then add stock and meat. Simmer till tender—1½-2 hours. Add the almond infusion, turmeric, sugar and salt and simmer for ¼ hour; finally, add lemon juice to taste.

DRY BEEF CURRY
(see picture above)

1 lb. stewing steak	Tamarind water or diluted
1 level tbsp. coriander	vinegar
powder	2 oz. butter
1 level tsp. turmeric powder	1 finely chopped onion
1 bay leaf	1 finely sliced clove of
2 cloves	garlic
¼ level tsp. chilli powder	1 tsp. curry paste
½ level tsp. cumin powder	½ pint stock or water
A pinch of ground	Salt to taste
cinnamon	

Cut up the meat. Mix the spices and tamarind water to form a paste. Melt the butter and fry the onion and garlic, then fry the spices and curry paste thoroughly, stirring constantly. Add the meat and cook slowly for about 1 hour, stirring occasionally. Add the stock, cover, and cook gently for another hour, till liquid is absorbed. Adjust the seasoning, if necessary. Serve with rice or dhal, kabab zeera (page 68) and chutney.

ACCOMPANIMENTS FOR CURRIES

Besides rice, these can include poppadums, chapattis, puris, chutneys, pickles, Bombay duck and innumerable 'sambols'. Some are usually bought ready prepared, like Bombay duck and poppadums; others can be made at home and some recipes are given here.

Sambols (see page 74) are served with the curry in scallop shells, silver bowls or other little dishes, which are grouped either on a large tray or in the centre of the table. Each guest is given a large platter and takes a little of everything.

Some simple accompaniments which need little or no preparation are gherkins, water-melon, guava jelly, green olives, preserved ginger and pickled mangoes.

BOILED RICE

Method I: Allow ½ lb. Patna rice, 3 pints water and 1 level tsp. salt for 4-6 persons. Put the washed rice in fast-boiling salted water and boil for 10 minutes, then drain it in a sieve and pour cold water through to get rid of the loose starch. Put the rice back into fresh boiling water and cook for 2-3 minutes, keeping the pan uncovered throughout the cooking. Drain the rice and serve at once, or keep it warm in a cool oven (300°F., mark 2), covered with aluminium foil or a cloth.

Method II: Soak the rice for ¼-½ hour in cold water and drain (see picture above). Put in a pan with fresh cold water, which should come about 1 inch above the rice; add salt. Put the pan over a high heat, stirring occasionally to prevent sticking. Reduce the heat and cook gently until all the water is absorbed—about 20 minutes—by which time the rice should be tender. Remove from the heat, pour cold water over it, then drain thoroughly. Cover with a cloth and warm through in a cool oven (300°F., mark 2).

To Re-heat Rice: Put it in a pan of boiling salted water, stir and bring to the boil; drain well.

YELLOW RICE

½ lb. Patna rice	4 whole black pepper-
2 level tsps. salt	corns
6 cloves	½ level tsp. saffron
1 stick of cinnamon	2 tsps. milk
3 bay leaves	A little melted butter

Place all the ingredients except the saffron, milk and butter in a pan with 1½ pints rapidly boiling water. Reduce the heat and gently "bubble" the water until the rice is just tender—15-20 minutes. Drain, removing the spices. Mix the saffron with the hot milk and fork through the rice, to colour it evenly. Place the rice in a dish and pour a little melted butter over it. Serve with meat curries.

PELLAO

2 onions	A little ground
2 oz. butter	cardamom
1 lb. rice	A few pieces of stick
Chicken stock	cinnamon
Salt to taste	A few peppercorns
A few cloves	A few sultanas

Mince 1 onion, fry it in the hot butter until pale golden-brown, then add the uncooked rice and fry for about 5-6 minutes. Now add some stock, salt and the spices, adding more stock as the rice swells. When the rice is well cooked, put the pellao in a moderate oven (350°F., mark 4) for ½ hour to dry it off (or it may be dried by placing it in a saucepan over a very gentle heat—but Indian cooks generally find the oven more satisfactory). Slice the other onion, fry with a few sultanas until it is golden-brown and crisp and sprinkle the mixture over the rice. (Serves 8-10.)

SAFFRON PELLAO

½ lb. Patna rice	Seeds from 3
6 oz. butter	cardamoms
2 small sliced onions	2 bay leaves
2 tbsps. stoned raisins	8 peppercorns
or sultanas	Salt
2 tbsps. blanched and	Stock or water
toasted almonds	A few cooked peas
1 inch cinnamon stick	1 tbsp. saffron water

Wash and drain the rice. Heat 2 oz. butter in a sauce-pan and fry the onions till golden-brown. Now add the

rice with the remaining fat and cook, stirring frequently, until the rice has absorbed most of the fat. Add the raisins, almonds, cinnamon, cardamoms, bay leaves, peppercorns and salt. Just cover with hot stock or water, cover the pan and simmer until the rice is tender and all the liquid absorbed. Add the peas and saffron water, stir lightly, put in a heatproof dish and dry off in a moderate oven (350°F., mark 4).

PURIS (FRIED BREAD)
(see right-hand picture opposite)

4 oz. wholemeal flour   Water to mix
Salt and pepper   Fat for frying

Mix the flour and a little salt and pepper with some water to form a stiff dough. If time permits, allow the dough to stand for one hour. Roll out thinly and cut into 4-inch rounds. Fry in the hot fat, one or two at a time, holding them down with a wide draining slice to distribute the air, which gives the characteristic puffy shape. When golden-brown, remove carefully, drain on absorbent paper and serve at once.
The puris may be rolled out and shaped beforehand; cover them with a damp cloth and cook immediately before they are required for serving.

CHAPATTIS
These large, thin unleavened girdle cakes may be bought from some shops specializing in Eastern foods and from Indian restaurants.

POPPADUMS
(see picture above)

Poppadums are savoury wafer-like biscuits, which are usually purchased, as they are laborious to make at home; stored in an airtight tin, they will keep for several months. White ones are fairly mild, red ones very hot. To cook poppadums, choose a frying pan much larger than the size of the raw biscuit, as they expand considerably during cooking. Allow 1-2 per person. Place them one at a time in hot fat and fry for about 20-30 seconds, keeping them flat by holding under with a flat draining spoon. When crisp, drain and serve hot.

Alternatively, the poppadums may be heated through in the oven or under the grill.
Use as an accompaniment to rice or curry, or crumble them over the surface.

DHAL (LENTIL PURÉE)

4 oz. red lentils   1 medium-sized onion
½ pint cold water   Fat for frying
Pepper and salt   1 oz. butter or dripping

Wash the lentils—there is no need to soak them—put them in the water, add pepper and salt and cook steadily, adding more water if they get too dry. Meanwhile, chop the onion finely and fry it. When the lentils are tender, remove from the heat and stir vigorously. Add the dripping and onion and stir well over the heat.

BOMBAY DUCK
(see picture above)

This is actually a fish (bummalo), which is sold salted and dried. It is a very popular accompaniment to many curries and is also often used as an ingredient. The smell when it is being prepared is rather unpleasant, but the taste is appetizing.
Bake in a hot oven or toast under the grill until crisp and brown; if necessary, flatten during the cooking. Alternatively, fry in hot fat and drain well.
Break the Bombay duck into small pieces or crumble up and sprinkle over the curry at table.

YOGHOURT AND CUCUMBER

½ a cucumber, peeled   ½ green pepper or 2
   and sliced thinly   small green chillies
1 level tsp. sugar   ¼ level tsp. pepper
1 tbsp. vinegar   ½ level tsp. salt
2 chopped tomatoes   ½ pint plain yoghourt
½ small chopped onion   Chopped parsley

Place the cucumber in a bowl, sprinkle with sugar and vinegar and marinade for 10 minutes. In another bowl mix lightly the tomatoes, onion and green pepper; add the drained and seasoned cucumber. Mix with the yoghourt and garnish with parsley.

PICKLES, CHUTNEYS AND RELISHES

Very hot, pungent chutneys and pickles are served in the East, but in this country somewhat milder types are probably more popular. Mango chutneys, prepared in different ways to give a very sweet, a hot or a mild effect, are among the best-known kinds. We give a recipe for a good home-made chutney.

Salted mangoes are served as an accompaniment to fish curries; cut-up mangoes, both green and ripe, also mango sauce, are often included in the actual curries.

Other items sold by firms specializing in Eastern foods include lime, green chilli, lemon, aubergine (brinjal), bamboo, sweet turnip and mustard pickles, tamarind chutney and guava jelly. The taste for some of these is, however, only gradually acquired by most Europeans.

HOT INDIAN CHUTNEY

1½ lb. marrow	¼ oz. bruised root
2 lb. tomatoes	ginger
1 lb. onions	4 level tsps. chillies
¼ lb. shallots	4 level tsps. cloves
1 clove of garlic	4 level tsps. white pepper-
1 lb. sugar	corns
1 oz. salt	1 oz. mustard seed
1½ lb. apples	1½ pints vinegar

Prepare and chop the vegetables and the garlic, sprinkle with the sugar and salt and leave overnight. Peel, core and chop the apples and put them with the prepared vegetables into a pan. Add the spices, tied in a muslin bag, and the vinegar, and boil together slowly for at least 4 hours, until the mixture is thick. Pot and cover. Store for several months before use.

SAMBOLS

Coconut: Slice or grate some fresh coconut (see picture above) and serve with chopped green and red peppers. Desiccated coconut may be substituted for fresh, when necessary.

Peppers: Red and green peppers can be parboiled, sliced, egg-and-crumbed and then fried, or they can be sliced and used raw.

Bananas: Use firm bananas; slice and sprinkle with salt, lemon juice and a little chilli powder.

Aubergine (Egg Plant): Boil until soft, then skin, mash the pulp and add a little finely chopped onion, 1-2 chopped chillies, a little coconut milk to moisten and salt to taste.

Cucumber: Fry a chopped onion and a garlic clove in a little oil until soft but not coloured; add chopped cucumber, with a little crumbled Bombay duck and curry powder, a squeeze of lemon juice and a little coconut milk. Simmer until the cucumber is just soft. Serve hot or cold.

Tomato: Skin and slice several tomatoes, mix with some fresh or pickled green chillies, cut lengthwise, a pinch of ground red chillies and a squeeze of lemon juice; add salt to taste. Sprinkle with freshly grated or desiccated coconut and a little chopped onion.

Onions: Slice thinly and add lemon juice, seasonings and some chopped fresh (or pickled) chillies.

Potatoes: Cut several cold cooked potatoes into cubes and blend lightly with a few chopped green chillies, a little finely chopped onion or spring onion and some olive oil; season them to taste and add a little lemon juice. Alternatively, mix some cold mashed potato with desiccated coconut, coconut milk, a little chopped onion and a few coarsely chopped red chillies; add a little olive oil and lemon juice and season to taste.

Dried Peas: Soak the peas overnight, then simmer them until tender, drain and serve sprinkled with lemon juice and paprika pepper.

Eggs: Cut 2 hard-boiled eggs lengthwise into quarters and lightly blend with 1 finely chopped small onion, 2 fresh green (or pickled) green chillies, coarsely chopped, 1 tbsp. lemon juice and salt to taste; sprinkle with fine desiccated coconut or preferably with fresh scraped coconut if this is available.

POULTRY

Recipes give 4 servings, unless otherwise indicated

Poultry includes chickens (fowls), guinea fowls, ducks, geese and turkeys. Quite a lot of it nowadays is frozen, which means there is a good all-the-year-round supply (see notes below on frozen poultry). Most poultry is sold ready for cooking—that is, cleaned, plucked and trussed. Both fresh and frozen chickens and ducks, and occasionally turkeys are available in separate joints as well as whole.

Hanging and storing: Poultry should be hung for 2-3 days after killing before it is cooked. In cold weather it can if necessary be hung for about a week, but unlike game it is not kept until it is "high". Poultry is usually plucked before hanging (see below), though this is not essential, but the inside should be left in.
Hang the bird by the feet in a cool, airy larder and protect it from flies, using muslin if the larder is not fly-proof. If poultry is to be put in a refrigerator, remove the inside and wrap the bird loosely or put it in a covered dish.

Frozen poultry: Deep-frozen poultry should be allowed to thaw out at room temperature; the time required depends on the size of the joint or bird—single joints take from about 1 hour and large turkeys up to 24-48 hours. If you need to speed up the defrosting process, hold the bird under cold (not hot) running water.
The giblets are usually wrapped in polythene and placed inside the body cavity, so remove them before cooking the bird. Frozen birds are usually sold ready for stuffing. We include also a few recipes for game.

STUFFINGS, ETC.

Recipes for Herb Stuffing and Sage and Onion Stuffing appear on p. 67. Here are some others:

SAUSAGE STUFFING

1 large onion, skinned and chopped	2 level tsps. chopped parsley
1 lb. pork sausage-meat	1 level tsp. mixed herbs
1 oz. lard	1 oz. fresh breadcrumbs (optional)
Salt and pepper	

Mix the onion with the sausage-meat. Melt the lard and fry the sausage-meat and onion lightly for 2-3 minutes, add the rest of the ingredients and mix well. Use with chicken; for turkey, double the quantities.

CHESTNUT STUFFING

2 oz. bacon, rinded and chopped	Grated rind of a lemon
4 oz. fresh white bread-crumbs	8 oz. chestnut purée (see note)
1 level tsp. chopped parsley	Salt and pepper
1 oz. butter, melted	1 egg, beaten

Fry the bacon gently in its own fat for about 3-5 minutes, until crisp. Drain and add the rest of the ingredients, binding with the beaten egg.
This stuffing is suitable for a turkey.

Note: Chestnut purée may be made from fresh chestnuts. Boil 1 lb. chestnuts for 2 minutes to soften the skins, remove from the heat and peel them while they are hot. Simmer the peeled chestnuts in milk for about 40 minutes, until soft. Sieve them or put them in an electric blender.

APRICOT STUFFING

3 oz. dried apricots	$\frac{1}{4}$ level tsp. pepper
3 oz. fresh breadcrumbs	1 tbsp. lemon juice
$\frac{1}{4}$ level tsp. mixed spice	1 oz. butter, melted
$\frac{1}{4}$ level tsp. salt	1 small egg, beaten

Soak the apricots overnight in cold water. Drain off the liquid, chop the fruit, stir in the remaining ingredients and bind with the egg.
Use for stuffing a chicken, or make double the quantity for stuffing the neck end of the turkey.

BREAD SAUCE

1 medium-sized onion	$\frac{3}{4}$ oz. butter
2 cloves	3 oz. fresh white bread-crumbs
$\frac{3}{4}$ pint milk	
Salt	$\frac{1}{2}$ a small bay leaf
A few peppercorns	

Peel the onion and stick the cloves into it, place in a saucepan with the milk, salt and peppercorns, bring almost to boiling point and leave in a warm place for about 20 minutes, in order to extract the flavour from the onion. Remove the peppercorns and add the butter and crumbs, with the bay leaf. Mix and cook very slowly for about 15 minutes, then remove the onion.
If liked, remove the onion before adding the breadcrumbs, but a better flavour is obtained by cooking it with the crumbs, as this allows the taste of the onion to penetrate them.
Serve with roast chicken, turkey or pheasant.

CHICKEN

When buying a fresh (non-frozen) bird, feel the tip of the breast-bone with the thumb and finger. In a young bird it is soft and flexible; if it is hard and rigid the bird is probably too old to roast satisfactorily and will have to be steamed or boiled. Look at the feet also—in a young bird they are smooth with small (not coarse) scales and with short spurs.
Many different terms have been used at times to classify chickens, but the main categories seen nowadays are:

Poussins: Very small chickens, 1-2 lb.; 6-8 weeks old; one serves 1-2 people.

Broilers: Small birds, $2\frac{1}{2}$-$3\frac{1}{2}$ lb.; 12 weeks old; one serves 3-4 people. (Frozen chickens are usually broilers.)

Large Roasters: Generally young cockerels or hens, but may be capons. "Young roasters" are 4-5 lb. and one serves 5-6 people; capons weigh up to 8 lb. and one serves 6-10 people.

Boiling Fowls: Older, tougher birds; 4-7 lb. They should be 18 months old, but may in some cases be older. Usually served in casseroles or made-up dishes; allow 4-6 oz. meat per person.

ROAST CHICKEN

When you buy a chicken it will usually be already prepared for cooking, so all you need do is stuff it if you wish. Different stuffings can be used, to give variety.

Make up the chosen stuffing. Loosen the chicken's wings, so that you can pull up the flap of skin over the breast, and fill the cavity with the forcemeat, making the breast a good shape. Remember that the stuffing, being made of bread or rice, will swell somewhat, so don't pack too tightly. Pull the flap down again and secure it with a skewer. (See pictures above.)

Put the chicken in a roasting tin, cover the breast with fat bacon and put some dripping over the rest of the bird. Roast in a fairly hot oven (400°F., mark 6) for 45-60 minutes, according to size; baste occasionally.

Serve the chicken with bread sauce and gravy and if desired, garnish with bacon rolls and chipolata sausages. As very young chickens are delicately flavoured, you may not always want to stuff them, so try just rubbing the inside with a piece of garlic and adding a knob of butter; reduce the cooking time to about $\frac{3}{4}$ hour.

Gravy: remove the chicken to a hot dish, and pour away most of the dripping from the tin, leaving about 1 tbsp.; add 2 level tsps. flour and stir in $\frac{1}{2}$ pint giblet stock, season well and bring to the boil, stirring well all the time. Add a little gravy browning if necessary.

CHICKEN ROASTED IN ALUMINIUM FOIL

Wrap the chicken entirely in aluminium foil, making the join along the top, and roast in a fairly hot oven (400°F., mark 6) for 1 hour. Undo the join and loosen the foil for the last 10 minutes of the cooking time, so that the bird can brown, which makes it look more attractive. Serve with the usual accompaniments.

CHICKEN ROAST ON A SPIT

Some cookers are provided with a spit which can be attached to the roasting tin. This provides a very good way of roasting young chickens, as the birds can be evenly browned all over and the fat simply drips into the tin.

Put the chicken onto the spit and brush it with melted fat, place in position and roast for 50-60 minutes, according to size—see the book given with your cooker for details. Baste the chicken with the fat in the tin. Serve in the usual way, or with salad.

BAKED CHICKEN WITH CHEESE SAUCE

(see colour picture no. 22)

Divide a chicken into joints, put in a roasting tin with some fat and cook in a fairly hot oven (400°F., mark 6) for about 45 minutes, until tender. Place in a heatproof dish, coat with $\frac{1}{2}$ pint well-flavoured cheese sauce and put under the grill for a few minutes, until pale golden-brown.

FRIED CHICKEN

Joint the chicken and cut the breast away from the bone, keeping the pieces as large as possible. Dip each piece in egg and fresh white breadcrumbs and fry in hot fat until golden-brown and tender—10-15 minutes. Serve at once with peas, sweet corn fritters and mushroom sauce. Alternatively, garnish with grapes which have been peeled and tossed in melted butter.

FRENCH FRIED CHICKEN

1 broiler	1 egg
4 oz. flour	$\frac{1}{2}$ oz. melted butter
$\frac{1}{4}$ pint milk	Fat for frying

Cut the chicken into pieces. Make a batter with the flour, milk, egg and melted butter, beating it well. Dip each piece of chicken into the batter and then fry in hot fat until golden-brown. Finish cooking in a moderate oven (350°F., mark 4) until the chicken is tender—about 30 minutes. Serve with a good tomato sauce.

SOUTHERN-STYLE FRIED CHICKEN

Cut a broiler into 4 pieces, dip quickly in and out of cold water and drain. Dip each piece into seasoned flour until thoroughly coated. Fry the chicken in hot fat until each piece is tender and brown on both sides. Arrange on a hot dish, garnish with peas and keep hot while you make the gravy. Put 2 tbsps. of the fat used for frying into a saucepan, add 1 level tbsp. flour, and stir in $\frac{1}{4}$ pint milk or cream and $\frac{1}{4}$ pint giblet stock; if desired, add a few sliced mushrooms, and allow to cook for a minute or two. Season well before serving.

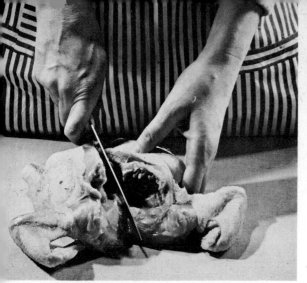

DEEP-FRIED WHOLE CHICKEN

Small, tender birds are excellent fried whole—in fact, it is the quickest way of cooking them and gives a deliciously appetising crisp finish to the skin. Buy a roaster weighing about 2½ lb. and get ready a pan big enough to hold it, with enough fat to cover the bird. Remove the giblets from inside the chicken and dry the bird. Let the fat become smoking hot and carefully lower the bird into it. Cook (uncovered) over a moderate heat for 20 minutes, turning the bird several times during the cooking. Serve the chicken either hot or cold.

The above method of cooking can be used when you wish to make chicken flambé—an excitingly spectacular dish for a special occasion.

Put the cooked chicken on a warmed serving dish. Warm 1 wineglass of brandy and just before serving the chicken, set light to the spirit and pour it over the bird while it is still flaming.

Serve with a green salad and new potatoes.

CHINESE FRIED CHICKEN

1 large chicken	2 spring onions
6 tbsps. soy sauce	Flour
6 tbsps. sherry	Deep fat
1 level tsp. sugar	

Cut the chicken into about 12 pieces and soak them in the soy sauce, sherry, sugar and chopped onions for about an hour. Drain the chicken and dip each piece in flour. Fry in hot fat for about 5 minutes, until golden-brown. Serve with plain boiled rice, adding a little soy sauce and sherry. (Any soy sauce and sherry that is left over can be used in sauces and soups. (Serves 4-6.)

MATABELE FRIED CHICKEN

(see colour picture no. 16)

1 chicken, jointed	1 green pepper, sliced
Olive oil	1 large onion, sliced
Seasonings	12 oz. rice
4 rashers of bacon, sliced	2 rounds of pineapple
1 red pepper, sliced	Chopped chives

Marinade the chicken in seasoned olive oil for about 30 minutes. Boil the giblets to make stock for the rice. Heat 2 tbsps. oil in a frying pan and fry the bacon, peppers and onion, then add the rice and fry till it becomes opaque. Add enough chicken stock to cover the rice, then pour in one and a half times as much again. Season well and simmer gently until all the liquid is absorbed and the rice is tender. Add the diced pineapple 5 minutes before the rice finishes cooking. Meanwhile, fry the chicken in hot oil until tender and golden-brown. Serve it on the rice, sprinkled with chopped chives. This makes a good buffet party dish.

GRILLED CHICKEN

Young, small and tender broilers are very good when grilled. Split the chicken down the back, but without cutting through the skin of the breast, then flatten the bird out, removing the breastbone and breaking the joints where necessary. Skewer the legs and wings closely to the body. Alternatively, divide it into portions. Brush over with melted butter or oil, sprinkle with salt and pepper and put on the greased grid, skin side up. Cook under a moderate heat for 15 minutes, then turn the chicken and grill on the underside for a further 15 minutes or until tender. Serve garnished with watercress and accompanied by a clear giblet gravy.

Another method is to split the chicken then, after brushing it with oil, to sprinkle it with a mixture of very finely chopped onion, parsley and fresh white breadcrumbs and cook as above. Serve garnished with watercress and accompanied by brown or tomato sauce. (See pictures above.)

DEVILLED GRILLED CHICKEN

1 chicken	4 tbsps. French
1½ level tbsp. curry powder	mustard
4 tbsps. honey	Rice and green salad

Cut the chicken into 4 pieces and rub all over with curry powder. Mix the honey, mustard and remaining curry powder and brush some of the mixture over the chicken. Grill the chicken for about 15 minutes, turning it every 5 minutes and basting with the sauce. Serve on rice, accompanied by a green salad.

CHICKEN POACHED IN WHITE WINE
(*see picture above*)

Cut the chicken into joints and put these into a flat saucepan. Add a bay leaf and a piece of parsley. Pour in enough white wine to cover the chicken almost entirely. Simmer very gently for 40 minutes, until the chicken is tender, then lift out the bird, drain it and place in a serving dish. Make a sauce as follows: Melt 2 oz. butter, add 2 oz. flour and gradually stir in 1 pint of the strained wine; add some salt, bring to the boil and add 1 tbsp. cream or top of the milk. Pour this over the bird and serve at once.

CHICKEN POACHED IN TOMATO

1 chicken	2 stalks of celery,
A little flour	sliced
Fat for frying	Seasoning
12 small onions,	$\frac{1}{2}$ pint tomato purée
sliced	Boiled rice
2-3 carrots, sliced	

Joint the chicken, dredge the pieces with flour and sauté in hot fat until well browned all over. Pour away the fat and add the onions, carrots and celery, salt, pepper and tomato purée. Simmer gently for $\frac{3}{4}$-1 hour, until the chicken is tender, and serve with dry boiled rice.

CHICKEN KIEV

This famous Russian dish is rather extravagant and not quite so easy to make as the more familiar ones, but once you have mastered it, you will find it well worth the trouble.

First of all, clarify enough butter to fry the chicken: to do this, put the butter in a saucepan with some water, bring to the boil, pour into a basin and allow to cool; when the butter is solid, drain the water away from underneath and the fat is then ready for use.

Remove the leg joints and the skin from a broiler. Scrape the meat from the part of the wing nearest the body back to the first wing joint. Break the scraped wing bone just below the joint. (This forms a "handle" to hold

later.) Carefully remove the whole of the two breasts from the bird, together with the little bits of wing to which they are attached. Remove the fillet from each (this is the loose piece of meat inside the breast) and flatten with a knife. Make an incision in the underside of the piece of breast about 2 inches long and $\frac{1}{4}$ inch deep. Open up the incision on either side with the point of your knife to make a pocket. Roll a piece of butter up in each fillet and put this into the pocket, squeezing it gently together to make a good shape and to enclose the fillets. Dip the pieces in fresh white breadcrumbs, then in egg and again in breadcrumbs, and fry in deep fat for 10-12 minutes. Serve with sauté or chipped potatoes.

CHICKEN "SOUS LA CLOCHE"
(*see picture above*)

1 small chicken, drawn	A bay leaf
and trussed	$1\frac{1}{2}$ oz. butter
$\frac{1}{4}$ pint white wine	$1\frac{1}{2}$ oz. plain flour
$\frac{1}{4}$ pint chicken stock	$\frac{1}{2}$ pint milk
4 oz. mushrooms, sliced	Cooked asparagus tips
Seasoning	(fresh or canned)

Place the chicken in a casserole and add the wine, stock, mushrooms, a little salt and a bay leaf. Cover and cook in a moderate oven (350°F., mark 4) for about $1\frac{1}{4}$ hours, or until tender. Drain off the liquid—it should make about $\frac{1}{2}$ pint—and retain the mushrooms. Melt the butter, add the flour, stir over a low heat for 1-2 minutes, then gradually stir in the milk and the chicken liquid. Bring to the boil, season well and add the asparagus and mushrooms. Boil for 2-3 minutes and pour over the chicken (after removing the strings).

CHICKEN RISOTTO WITH BANANAS

$1\frac{1}{2}$ lb. cooked chicken	4 oz. mushrooms
A bouquet garni	$1\frac{1}{2}$ oz. dripping
Seasoning	12 oz. rice
$1\frac{1}{2}$ pints chicken stock	4 bananas
2-3 onions	Grated cheese

Cut the chicken flesh into neat pieces and boil the bones with the bouquet garni and seasoning to make the stock. Cut up the onions and half the mushrooms and fry in the dripping, then add the rice and fry this till opaque. Add the boiling stock and some salt and cook gently until the liquor is absorbed and the rice tender: do not stir while it is cooking, but if necessary fork it gently. Lay the chicken on top of the rice for about 10 minutes, to heat through. Fry the remaining mushrooms and the bananas for a garnish. Put the rice and chicken on an ovenproof dish, sprinkle with cheese and brown under the grill. Serve with green salad. (Serves 6.)

CHICKEN JAMBALAYA

½ a cooked chicken	¾ lb. fresh tomatoes,
2 onions, sliced	skinned and quartered
1 green pepper, chopped	¼ pint chicken stock
2 sticks of celery,	¼ pint dry white wine
sliced	6 oz. long-grained rice
2 tbsps. oil	¼ lb. ham, chopped
¼ lb. mushrooms, sliced	Pepper

Cut the chicken flesh into cubes. Sauté the onions, pepper and celery in the oil until they are golden-brown. Add the mushrooms, tomatoes, stock, wine and rice and cook gently on top of the stove until the rice is tender (15-20 minutes). Add the chicken and ham and heat through. Season to taste and turn into a serving dish.

CHICKEN À LA CRÈME

1 roasting chicken	1 oz. flour
2 small onions, sliced	¼ pint dry white wine
1 oz. butter	A bouquet garni
2 tbsps. oil	¼ pint cream
Salt	Black pepper (optional)

Joint the chicken. Sauté the chicken joints and onions in the butter and oil. Season with salt, reduce the heat, cover and cook for 20 minutes. When the joints are nearly done, remove the onions (which are used for flavouring only) and stir in the flour; cook for a minute or two, without browning. Add the wine and bouquet garni and continue to cook for a further 10-15 minutes. Add the cream very carefully to the wine in the pan, but do not allow to boil. Remove the joints and place on a serving dish. Discard the bouquet garni, pour the remaining sauce over the chicken and grind some black pepper over it before serving.

SWEET-SOUR CHICKEN

1 small can of	1 oz. butter
pineapple pieces	¼ pint sour cream
6 oz. mushrooms,	½ pint chicken stock
quartered	2 tsps. lemon juice
⅛ pint dry white wine	1 level tbsp. cornflour
4 chicken joints	1 oz. roasted almonds
1 tbsp. oil	Salt and pepper

Drain the pineapple pieces and place them in a saucepan with the mushroom quarters and white wine; simmer gently for 5-7 minutes. Sauté the chicken joints in the oil and butter until they are a light golden-brown. Transfer to a 3-pint casserole. Remove the mushrooms and pineapple from the heat and carefully blend a little of the liquor with the sour cream. Return this mixture to the pan and heat gently, but do not boil. Pour the pineapple and mushrooms over the chicken joints. Blend the stock, lemon juice and cornflour together and add to the fat remaining in the pan; bring to the boil and boil for 1 minute. Add the roasted almonds and seasoning and pour over the chicken joints. Cook in a cool oven (300°F., mark 2) for 1½ hours.

COQ AU VIN

3 oz. bacon, chopped	¾ bottle of red wine
6 oz. mushrooms, sliced	1 level tbsp. cornflour
15 button onions (or	⅛ pint brandy
4 medium-sized	1 level tsp. sugar
onions, sliced)	A pinch of grated
1 oz. butter	nutmeg
1 tbsp. oil	Salt and pepper
4 chicken joints	A bouquet garni

Sauté the bacon, mushrooms and onions in the butter and oil until they are golden-brown. Remove from the pan and place half of the mixture in a 3-pint casserole. Sauté the chicken joints until golden-brown; remove from the pan and place in the casserole. Add the remaining bacon, mushrooms and onions to the casserole. Gradually stir the blended wine and cornflour into the fat remaining in the pan; bring to the boil and allow to cook for 1-2 minutes. Add the brandy and pour over the joints in the casserole. Finally, add the sugar, nutmeg, salt, pepper and bouquet garni and cook in a moderate oven (350°F., mark 4) for ¾ hour, or until the chicken is tender. Before serving, remove the bouquet garni.

FRENCH-STYLE ROAST CHICKEN

A 2½-3 lb. roasting	2 oz. butter, melted
chicken	2 rashers of bacon
5-6 sprigs of tarragon	¼ pint chicken stock
or parsley	¼ pint dry white wine
3 oz. unsalted butter	Watercress to garnish
Salt and pepper	1 oz. flour

Wipe the inside of the chicken, then put the sprigs of tarragon or parsley inside it, with the unsalted butter and some pepper. Brush the breast of the bird with the melted butter. (Alternatively, cover with the rashers of bacon or if preferred, use both butter and bacon.) Put the bird in a roasting tin, add the stock and wine and cook in a fairly hot oven (400°F., mark 5) for 45-50 minutes, basting every 15 minutes with the stock. Alternatively, roast it on a spit, if available. Remove the bacon during the last ¼ hour, to let the breast brown. Place the chicken on a serving dish and garnish with watercress. Thicken the liquor with 1 oz. flour and season to taste; serve separately.

CHICKEN MARENGO

4 chicken joints (frying)	½ pint chicken stock
3-4 tbsps. oil	1 tsp. tomato paste
¼ lb. mushrooms, sliced	2 tbsps. medium sherry
¼ pint rich brown sauce	A bouquet garni
¼ pint tomato sauce	Salt and pepper

Sauté the chicken joints in the oil until golden-brown. Transfer them to a large casserole. Add the mushrooms to the fat remaining in the pan and sauté until tender; remove from the pan and add to the casserole. Mix together the brown sauce, the tomato sauce, chicken stock, tomato paste and sherry and heat, then pour over the chicken joints. Add the bouquet garni to the casserole, season, cover and cook for ¾ hour in a moderate oven (350°F., mark 4). Remove the bouquet garni.

PORTUGUESE CASSEROLE OF CHICKEN WITH RICE

Put 2 chopped onions and 2 carrots in a casserole; add chopped parsley, seasoning and a chicken, jointed and skinned. Braise for 1 hour or until the chicken is nicely browned, then remove it and sieve the gravy. Add enough water to give about 1 pint stock, with 8 oz. long-grain rice and cook until the rice is done. Put a layer of rice in a fireproof dish, then the chicken, and cover with remaining rice. Top with sausage (preferably paprika type) and brown in a moderate oven (350°F., mark 4). Garnish as desired.

CHICKEN BOURGUIGNON

1 chicken	Salt and pepper
Butter	1 glass of red
3-4 button onions	Burgundy
3 rashers of bacon, diced	2 oz. mushrooms, sliced
A bouquet garni	Mashed potatoes

Joint the chicken, put it in the butter with the onions and bacon and fry until brown. Add the bouquet garni, salt, pepper and wine, cover with a lid and simmer gently until the chicken is tender—about 30 minutes. Meanwhile fry the mushrooms; 10 minutes before the end of the cooking time remove the bouquet garni and add the mushrooms. Serve in a border of mashed potato.

CHICKEN AU GRATIN

A 4-lb. chicken	1½ oz. flour
Seasoned flour	Salt and pepper
Dripping	4 tbsps. fresh white
Heated stock	breadcrumbs
2 oz. butter	4 tbsps. grated cheese

Cut the bird into convenient-sized serving joints and dredge with seasoned flour. Brown in hot fat on all sides. Cover with the stock and simmer until the chicken legs are tender. Lift out the chicken and put into an ovenproof dish. Melt the butter and stir in the flour, cook without colouring and then add about ¾ pint of the chicken stock. Season well to taste and pour over the chicken. Sprinkle with the breadcrumbs and cheese mixed together and bake in a fairly hot oven (400°F., mark 6), or place under the grill until the surface is brown. (Serves 6.)

VIENNESE CHICKEN

1 chicken	Breadcrumbs
Juice of 2 lemons	Fat for frying
Olive oil	1 egg yolk
A bay leaf	¼ pint milk
A little thyme and parsley	¼ lb. small mushrooms
1 egg	Seasoning
	Parsley to garnish

Joint the chicken and marinade for about 2 hours in the juice of 1 lemon and some olive oil, with the bay leaf, thyme and parsley. Drain the chicken, dip in beaten egg, coat with breadcrumbs and fry in hot fat until golden-brown and tender. Meanwhile mix the egg yolk with the milk, mushrooms, salt and pepper and cook until thick. At the last minute pour in the remaining lemon juice and pour the sauce around the fried chicken. Garnish with chopped parsley.

CHICKEN HOTPOT
(see colour picture no. 10)

4 pieces of chicken	½ lb. carrots
Seasoned flour	4 tomatoes
2 oz. fat	2 oz. Patna rice
1 onion	Seasoning
2-3 rashers of bacon	¼ pint chicken stock
½ lb. shelled peas	2-3 oz. frozen prawns

Dip the chicken pieces in seasoned flour and fry until golden-brown in the hot fat; put on to a plate. Sauté the onion until golden. Rind and dice the bacon. In a basin mix together the onion, bacon, peas, sliced carrots, skinned and sliced tomatoes and rice; add the seasoning. Arrange this mixture and the chicken pieces in layers in a casserole, then pour the stock over. Cover and cook for 1 hour in a fairly hot oven (375°F., mark 5); 10 minutes before serving, add the prawns.

CHICKEN LOUISETTE

4 chicken joints	¼ pint medium white wine
1 tbsp. oil	A bouquet garni
2 oz. butter	½ a cucumber, peeled
1 onion, sliced	and sliced
1 clove of garlic, peeled	2 oz. ham, chopped
	Salt and pepper
1 oz. flour	2 egg yolks
¼ pint stock	3 tbsps. cream

Sauté the chicken joints in the oil and 1 oz. of the butter until they are golden-brown, then remove from the pan. Add the onion and garlic to the fat and continue to brown. Sprinkle on the flour and cook for 1 minute. Gradually add the stock and wine, bring to the boil and cook until thickened. Replace the chicken joints, add the bouquet garni and simmer on top of the stove for 20-30 minutes. Cook the cucumber in the remaining butter. Add the ham and seasoning and simmer for a further 4-5 minutes. When the chicken joints are tender, strain off the liquor. Mix the egg yolks and cream and add a little of the chicken liquor to blend. Add this mixture and the remaining chicken liquor to the pan containing the cucumber and ham and heat very gently until the sauce thickens. Place the chicken joints on a serving dish and pour the sauce over.
As a variation, mushrooms may replace cucumber.

SPANISH STEWED CHICKEN

1 chicken	2 green peppers, prepared
Seasoned flour	½ lb. tomatoes, skinned
2 oz. bacon, diced	¼ pint sherry or stock
2 oz. butter or dripping	Salt and pepper
	Chopped parsley
2 Spanish onions, sliced	Crescents of pastry

Joint the chicken and dip the pieces in the seasoned flour. Fry the bacon until cooked, then take it out and add the butter or dripping. Fry the chicken several pieces at a time, until all are browned on the surface, then return the bacon and the chicken to the stewpan or casserole and add the onions, peppers and tomatoes, the sherry or stock and a little seasoning. Cover the pan closely, cook gently for ½ hour and serve the chicken garnished with chopped parsley and crescents of pastry.

CHICKEN CASSEROLE

(see picture above)

1 chicken	$\frac{3}{4}$ pint giblet stock
3 tbsps. olive oil	Seasoning
4 bacon rashers, diced	1 tbsp. tomato paste
1 small onion, chopped	2 oz. mushrooms, sliced
1 level tbsp. flour	Parsley to garnish

Cut the chicken into joints and fry in the olive oil with the bacon and onion until lightly browned. Remove from the saucepan, add the flour and cook for a minute or two, then add the giblet stock and bring to the boil. Season well and add the tomato paste and the mushrooms. Return the chicken, bacon and onion to the sauce and allow to simmer gently for about 1 hour, until the chicken is tender. Serve garnished with chopped parsley.

BARBECUED CHICKEN

Tender young chickens are one of the best things to roast at an open-air barbecue.

Make a good fire—a glowing red fire without smoke—and if possible erect a revolving spit over it. Put the chicken on the spit, brush it over with fat or oil and roast over the hot coals for about 40 minutes, turning it round at intervals to cook and brown evenly. When the bird is cooked, it should be so tender that you can pull it apart. Serve it plain, or with a bowl of barbecue sauce (see below), into which the joints may be dipped.

BARBECUE SAUCE FOR CHICKEN

1 oz. dripping	$\frac{1}{4}$ pint stock
3 large onions	Salt and pepper
1 lb. tomatoes, skinned	A pinch of sugar
2 level tbsps. flour	A pinch of mixed herbs

Melt the dripping, chop up the onions and fry them in the fat until almost tender, then cut up the tomatoes and add them. Continue frying for a few minutes, then add the flour and mix it well in. Gradually add the stock, bring to the boil and add the seasonings, with a pinch of mixed herbs. Allow to simmer gently for about 10 minutes, then sieve and re-heat before serving.

CHICKEN IN ASPIC

1 cooked chicken	Asparagus tips
1 pint aspic	A 5-oz. pkt. of frozen
Hard-boiled egg	peas

Cut up the chicken into small pieces. Make up the aspic and when it is cold, pour a little in an oblong mould; when this sets, decorate with hard-boiled egg and asparagus. (You could represent chicks with the egg and tufts of grass with the asparagus.) Pour a little more aspic over the decoration and allow to set in the refrigerator. Mix the chicken with most of the aspic, just keeping enough back to mix with the peas, and pour it in; put the mould in a cold place to set. Meanwhile cook the peas, and when they are cold, mix with the remaining aspic and pour into the mould. Leave to set and turn out when required. Serve with salad.

CHICKEN GALANTINE

1 chicken	1 stick of celery
12 oz. sausage-meat	1 glass of sherry
A piece of ham	Stock or water to cook
2 hard-boiled eggs	the galantine
Pepper and salt	Aspic, sliced tomato and
A little powdered spice	lettuce to garnish
1 onion, 1 carrot	

First, bone the chicken. To do this, first cut off the end joints of the wing pinions and the feet, severing these at the first joint of the leg. Begin boning at the neck and down the backbone. Using a small, sharp knife, carefully turn the flesh back from the bone. To do the wings and legs, cut through from the inside out to withdraw the bone, then turn them back again.

Spread the chicken out skin side downwards and spread the sausage-meat over it. Cut the ham in chunks or long pieces and arrange these over the sausage. Put the hard-boiled eggs along the centre, sprinkle with salt and pepper and a little spice. Roll up, making into a neat shape and tie securely in muslin.

Put the galantine into a saucepan with the vegetables, salt, sherry and stock and simmer it gently for about 2 hours. Take it out, re-tie the cloth as tightly as possible, then put it on a dish and put a weight on top. When it is cold, remove the cloth, brush with liquid aspic and garnish with chopped aspic, tomato and lettuce. (Serves 8.)

CHAUDFROID OF CHICKEN
(see picture above)

1 chicken	Aspic jelly
Radish, cucumber, truffles, hard-boiled egg, etc.	Salad

For the Chaudfroid Sauce

Tomato purée	½ pint liquid aspic jelly
½ pint good white sauce	

Steam the chicken, skin it and allow to become cold. Next make the chaudfroid sauce. Add sufficient tomato purée to the white sauce to colour it well, then mix with the aspic; pour over the skinned chicken when cold but not set. Allow to set firmly, then decorate with pieces of radish, cucumber skin, etc., dipping these in cold liquid aspic jelly. Finally pour a thin layer of cold aspic over the chicken to hold the decorations in place.

CHICKEN TERRAPIN

1 cold roasted chicken	Salt and pepper
⅛ pint sherry	1½ oz. cooked rice per
¼ pint double cream	person

Cut the chicken flesh into cubes, place in a thick-based pan and add the sherry. Heat gently, turning the pieces the whole time. When they are heated through, pour a little sherry into the cream, blend and season. Return this carefully to the pan and heat gently, but do not boil. Serve the chicken with the rice (or on toast).

COLD CHICKEN SOUFFLÉS
(see right-hand picture above)

½ oz. gelatine	8 tbsps. evaporated milk
½ pint aspic jelly	(A 6-oz. can)
½ pint white sauce	2 egg whites
8 oz. minced chicken	Radish, cucumber,
Salt and pepper	lettuce, etc.

Tie some greaseproof paper firmly round 4 individual soufflé dishes. Dissolve the gelatine in the liquid aspic jelly, mix with the sauce and chicken, season and leave till nearly set. Whip up the evaporated milk and when it is stiff, fold it into the mixture; lastly add the stiffly beaten whites of egg; pour quickly into the soufflé dishes and leave in a cold place to set. When firm, remove the

papers carefully with the help of a hot wetted knife and decorate with radish or cucumber and parsley sprigs. Serve with lettuce.

OTHER POULTRY

ROAST GOOSE

Pluck the bird and remove the stumps from the wings. Cut off the feet and the wing tips at the first joint. Cut off the head, then, forcing back the neck skin, cut off the neck where it joins the back. Draw the bird and clean the inside with a cloth wrung out in hot water. Put a thick fold of cloth over the breast-bone and flatten it with a mallet or rolling pin. Stuff with sage and onion stuffing or a fruit stuffing.

Working with the breast side uppermost and tail end away from you, pass a skewer through one wing, then through the body and out again through the other wing. Pass a second skewer through the end of the wing joint on one side, through the thick part of the leg, through the body and out the other side in the same way. Pass a third skewer through the loose skin near the end of the leg, through the body and out the other side in the same way. Enlarge the vent, pass the tail through it and fix with a small skewer. Wind string round the skewers, keeping the limbs firmly in position, but avoid passing the string over the breast of the goose. Tuck the neck skin in under the string.

Sprinkle the bird with salt, put in a baking tin on a rack or trivet (as goose tends to be fatty) and cover with the fat taken from inside, then with greased paper. A sour apple put in the tin during the cooking adds flavour to the gravy.

Roast in a fairly hot oven (400°F., mark 6) for 15 minutes per lb. plus 15 minutes, basting frequently. To cook by the slow method, roast in a moderate oven (350°F., mark 4) for 25-30 minutes per lb. Remove the paper for the last 30 minutes, to brown the bird.

Serve with giblet gravy (made in the roasting tin after the fat has been poured off) and apple or gooseberry sauce. Apple rings which have been dipped in lemon juice, brushed with oil and lightly grilled, also make an attractive garnish.

ROAST DUCK
(see colour picture no. 17)

Pluck, draw and truss in the usual way, except that the wings are not drawn across the back; tie the legs with fine string.

A young duckling does not require stuffing, but it is usual to stuff an older bird with sage and onion stuffing at the tail end. Sprinkle the breast with salt and pepper. Cook just above the centre of a fairly hot oven (400°F., mark 6); allow 20 minutes per lb. Remove the trussing strings and skewers; serve the bird garnished with water-cress and accompanied by apple sauce, potatoes, peas and thin brown gravy. Orange salad is also a favourite accompaniment for roast duck.

DUCK À LA PORTUGAISE

1 roasting duck	½ a small can of
1 tbsp. oil	pimientos, finely
1 oz. butter	chopped
1 small onion, chopped	1 oz. flour
1 green pepper, finely	¼ pint chicken stock
chopped	¼ pint red wine
½ lb. tomatoes, skinned	A bouquet garni
and quartered (or an	A dash of paprika
8-oz. can)	Salt and pepper

Joint the duck and sauté in the oil and butter until the joints are golden-brown; remove from the heat and place in a 2-pint casserole. Sauté the onion and green pepper in the remaining fat until lightly browned. Add the tomatoes and pimientos and sprinkle in the flour; cook for 1-2 minutes. Gradually add the stock and wine and bring to the boil. Add the bouquet garni, a dash of paprika and seasoning to taste. Pour over the duck joints and cook in the centre of a moderate oven (350°F., mark 4) for 1-1½ hours, or until the duck is tender. Remove the bouquet garni before serving.

ROUEN DUCK

1 large duck	½ pint chicken stock
2 oz. butter	1 wineglass claret
1 oz. shallots, chopped	A bouquet garni
1 oz. flour	Lemon juice

For the Stuffing

Heart and liver of the	1 tsp. chopped parsley
duck, chopped	1 oz. butter
2 tbsps. fresh crumbs	Seasoning
1 small onion, chopped	

Mix the ingredients for the stuffing and stuff the duck with it. Sauté the duck lightly in the butter until golden-brown; remove and place in a 3-pint casserole. Add the shallots to the remaining fat and lightly sauté until golden-brown; add to the casserole. Make a roux with the remaining fat and the flour and gradually add the stock; finally add the claret. Pour over the duck in the casserole, add the bouquet garni and a good squeeze of lemon juice and cook for 1½ hours, in the centre of a moderate oven (350°F., mark 4). Remove the trussing strings and put the duck on a serving dish. Strain the sauce over it.

DUCK WITH GOOSEBERRIES

1 duck	½ oz. butter
½ pint gooseberry	1 tsp. lemon juice
purée	1 wineglass medium
1 oz. sugar	sherry

Place the cleaned and trussed duck in a roasting tin and cook for 1 hour (or till tender) towards top of a hot oven (425°F., mark 7), basting every 20 minutes with the fat that runs out. Mix the gooseberry purée, sugar, butter and lemon juice and heat slowly. Before serving, add the sherry and serve this sauce separately.

DUCK IN RED WINE

1 duck	A bay leaf
½ a clove of garlic	Sprigs of parsley
2 oz. flour	½ level tsp. dried thyme
¾ pint red wine	1 level tsp. salt
2 oz. mushrooms,	1 lb. small onions
sliced	1 lb. small carrots

Remove the skin and fat from the duck and put them with the giblets into a pan. Cover with water and simmer for 1 hour. Skim off the fat and cool the stock.
Cut the duck into joints. Heat 2 tbsps. of the duck fat in a pan, then brown the duck joints on all sides. Remove them from the fat and put in a casserole. Add the crushed garlic to the fat and fry for 1 minute. Stir in the flour. Add the wine, mushrooms, bay leaf, parsley, thyme and salt. Bring to the boil, stirring constantly, until the sauce thickens.
Put the peeled onions, scraped carrots and duck giblets in the casserole, pour the sauce over, cover and cook in a moderate oven (350°F., mark 4) for about 1¼ hours.

BRAISED DUCK WITH PINEAPPLE

An 11-oz. can of pineapple	Dripping
½ pint cheap white	½ pint rich brown
wine	sauce
1 duck	1 tsp. tomato ketchup

Drain the pineapple and soak it in the wine overnight. The next day, brown the duck with some dripping in a hot oven (425°F., mark 7) for about 40 minutes, then drain off all the fat. Drain the wine from the pineapple, mix it with the brown sauce and tomato ketchup and pour over the duck; cover the whole tin with aluminium foil or a lid and return it to a moderate oven (375°F., mark 5) for ¾ hour. Before starting to dish up, put the pineapple pieces in a saucepan to heat while you carve the bird; put the duck on a hot dish, garnish with pine-apple and cover with sauce.

SALMI OF POULTRY
(see colour picture no. 18)

1 duck (or any poultry or	½ pint rich brown sauce
game in season)	¼ pint rough red wine
roasted	1 tbsp. port
1 orange	Red-currant jelly
1 shallot, chopped	2 oz. white grapes,
1½ pints chicken stock	skinned

Cut the bird into joints, remove the skin and break up the carcase into small pieces; put into a saucepan. Peel the orange and divide into sections. Add the orange peel, shallots and stock to the duck; bring to the boil and simmer for ½ hour. Mix together the rich brown sauce, red wine and ¼ pint of the strained stock. Place the duck joints in a pan, add the mixed stock and sauce and simmer until heated through. Arrange the joints on a serving dish. Add the port to the sauce and reduce until the mixture is of coating consistency. Pour over the duck and garnish as seen.

DUCK AND ORANGE CASSEROLE

(see picture above)

1 duck, jointed	2 oz. flour
Seasoned flour	$\frac{3}{4}$ pint stock
$\frac{1}{2}$ oz. lard or dripping	$\frac{1}{4}$ pint orange juice
$\frac{1}{4}$ lb. mushrooms	1 orange

Coat the duck with flour. Melt the fat and fry the duck on all sides until well browned; transfer to a casserole: Fry the sliced mushrooms lightly and add to the casserole. Stir the flour into the fat and brown over a very low heat, then gradually add the stock and orange juice and bring to the boil, stirring. Pour over the duck and cook in a moderate oven (350°F., mark 4) for 1 hour. Peel the orange with a vegetable peeler, cut the rind into very thin strips, then remove the pith with a sharp knife; divide the orange itself into segments. Simmer the strips of rind in water till tender and sprinkle over the cooked casserole; garnish with orange segments.

ROAST TURKEY

It is usual to stuff the neck end of a turkey with herb stuffing or chestnut stuffing; allow 1 lb. made stuffing for a bird of up to 14 lb.; twice this amount for a larger bird. For the body cavity, sausage-meat or sausage stuffing is generally used—allow 1-2 lb., according to size.

Make the turkey as plump and even in shape as possible, then truss it with the wings folded under the body and the legs tied together. Before cooking the bird, spread it with softened dripping or butter; the breast may also be covered with strips of fat bacon. If you are going to cook it by the quick method (see below) it is best to wrap the bird in aluminium foil to prevent the flesh drying and the skin hardening. Foil is not recommended for the slow method of cooking, as it tends to give a steamed rather than a roast bird.

For the slow method cook in a warm oven (325°F., mark 3); for the quick method cook in a very hot oven (450°F., mark 8), calculating the time as follows:

Weight in lbs.	Time in hours: Slow method	Time in hours: Quick method
6-8	$3-3\frac{1}{2}$	$2\frac{1}{4}-2\frac{1}{2}$
8-10	$3\frac{1}{2}-3\frac{3}{4}$	$2\frac{1}{2}-2\frac{3}{4}$
10-12	$3\frac{3}{4}-4$	$2\frac{3}{4}$
12-14	$4-4\frac{1}{4}$	3
14-16	$4\frac{1}{4}-4\frac{1}{2}$	$3-3\frac{1}{2}$
16-18	$4\frac{1}{2}-4\frac{3}{4}$	$3\frac{1}{4}-3\frac{1}{2}$

Unless the bird is cooked in foil, baste it regularly, turning it round once to ensure even browning. Foil, if used, should be unwrapped for the last $\frac{1}{2}$ hour, so that the bird may be well basted and then left to become crisp and golden.

Garnish and Accompaniments: Small sausages, forcemeat balls, rolls of bacon and watercress may be used to garnish the turkey. Serve it with brown gravy and bread sauce. Cranberry or some other sharp sauce can also be served. Sliced tongue or ham is a favourite accompaniment.

TURKEY AND CRANBERRY CASSEROLE

(see picture above)

2 medium-sized onions	2 tbsps. chopped
2 oz. butter or dripping	parsley
$\frac{1}{2}$ lb. sliced mushrooms	A pinch of thyme
$\frac{1}{2}$ lb. diced cooked	Salt and pepper
turkey	4 oz. rice
4 oz. diced cooked	2 level tsps. curry powder
ham	$\frac{1}{2}$ pint chicken stock
4 oz. leftover stuffing	4 oz. cranberry sauce

Chop the onions and sauté them in 1 oz. butter until tender. Add the mushrooms and sauté for 2 minutes. Put into a casserole and add the turkey, ham, crumbled stuffing, herbs and seasonings in layers. Heat the oven to moderate (350°F., mark 4). Brown the rice in the pan with remaining butter and the curry powder; add to the casserole and pour in the stock. Cook in the oven for about $\frac{1}{2}$ hour, or until the rice is tender and the liquid absorbed. Garnish with the cranberry sauce (or jelly) arranged in a border round the dish.

BLANQUETTE OF TURKEY

12 oz. cooked turkey	Salt and pepper
1 oz. butter	2 egg yolks
1 oz. flour	Parsley, bacon rolls
$\frac{1}{2}$ pint milk or turkey	and crescents of fried
stock	bread

Cut the turkey into neat pieces. Melt the butter and the flour and cook for a minute over a low heat, then gradually add the milk or stock and bring to the boil. Season well and beat in the egg yolks. Add the pieces of turkey and heat slowly and gently, until thoroughly hot. Serve garnished with parsley, bacon rolls and golden-brown crescents of fried bread.

GUINEA FOWL CASSEROLE

Slices of salt pork, thinly cut	1 oz. flour
1-2 guinea fowl	¼ pint stock
3-4 oz. dripping or butter	½ lb. prepared mushrooms
	¼ pint tomato purée
	Creamed potatoes

Tie the pieces of pork round the birds with fine string. Melt the fat in an enamelled iron casserole and fry the guinea fowl on all sides. Cover and simmer slowly for about 10-15 minutes. Remove the birds from the pot and stir in the flour, cooking it until it is brown, then add the stock, mushrooms and purée. Replace the guinea fowl and cook it covered for about 30-40 minutes Remove the string and fat from the birds and serve with the liquor and creamed potatoes; boiled bacon and broad beans are good with this dish.

PIGEONS WITH GREEN PEAS

2 pigeons	Salt and pepper
2 oz. dripping	Stock or water
12 small onions, peeled	¼ pint tomato purée
1 oz. flour	2 lb. green peas, parboiled

Brown the pigeons in the hot dripping, turning the birds over one at a time and adding extra dripping if required. Brown the onions in the same way. Remove the birds and onions and stir in the seasoned flour, some stock or water and the tomato purée. Add the pigeons and onions. Cover and simmer gently for about an hour. About 10 minutes before serving, add the peas.

CASSEROLED PIGEONS

2 pigeons	1 onion, sliced
Seasoned flour	1 oz. plain flour
Dripping	1 pint stock or water
2 stalks of celery, sliced	A large pinch of dried thyme
2-3 carrots, sliced	Mashed potatoes

Halve the pigeons and dip in flour. Heat the fat and fry the pigeons until light brown, then remove from the fat and place in a casserole. Sauté the vegetables, remove and add the flour, then gradually add the stock and thyme, with more seasoning if necessary. Bring to the boil, then pour into the casserole, together with the pigeons and vegetables, and cook for 2-3 hours in a warm oven (325°F., mark 3). Pile a border of mashed potato round the edge of the casserole before serving.

TIPSY PIGEONS

2 pigeons	4 slices of garlic sausage
8 black olives	1 level tbsp. flour
4 tbsps. sherry	½ pint chicken stock
1 tbsp. oil	2 tbsps. brandy
1 large onion, sliced	Salt and pepper
¼ lb. bacon, chopped	

Wipe the pigeons. Marinade the olives in the sherry for 2 hours. Sauté the pigeons in the oil until golden-brown, then transfer to a 3-pint casserole. Sauté the onion, bacon and sausage until golden-brown, then add to the casserole, with the olives and sherry. Add the flour to the fat remaining in the pan and blend to make a roux. Gradually add the stock and brandy and bring

to the boil; season and add to the casserole. Cook in the centre of a moderate oven (350°F., mark 4) for 45 minutes.

PIGEONS À LA CATALANE

2 pigeons	¼ pint chicken stock
1 tbsp. oil	¼ pint dry white wine
1 oz. butter	1 strip of orange peel
1 oz. ham, roughly chopped	3 cloves of garlic, peeled
1 oz. flour	A bouquet garni
1 tbsp. tomato paste	Salt and pepper

For the Stuffing

Pigeon livers, chopped	1 garlic clove, chopped
4 oz. fresh breadcrumbs	1 tbsp. chopped parsley
2 oz. ham, chopped	1 egg, beaten

Prepare the pigeons. Make the stuffing by combining the livers, breadcrumbs, ham, garlic and parsley with the beaten egg. Stuff the pigeons and sauté them in the oil and butter until golden-brown, then transfer them to a 3-pint casserole. Sprinkle the chopped ham over the pigeons. Blend the flour with the fat remaining in the pan and make a roux. Gradually add the tomato paste, stock and wine, bring to the boil and cook for 1 minute. Remove from the heat and pour over the pigeons. Add the orange peel, garlic, bouquet garni and seasoning, then cook in the centre of a moderate oven (350°F., mark 4) for 35-45 minutes. Remove the bouquet garni before serving.

CASSEROLED PHEASANT

1 pheasant	¾ pint stock
2 oz. butter	¼ lb. button mushrooms
¼ lb. diced cooked ham	4 tbsps. red-currant jelly
Salt and pepper	

Prepare the bird and fry on all sides in the melted fat until browned. Put in a casserole, add the ham, salt, pepper and stock and cook in a moderate oven (350°F., mark 4) for 2 hours. Add the mushrooms after about 1½ hours and stir in the jelly just before serving.

WILD DUCK WITH RAISIN STUFFING

2 wild ducks	Salt and pepper
6 oz. fresh white breadcrumbs	1 egg
4 sticks of celery, chopped	1 cup of hot milk
1 onion, sliced	Slices of fat bacon
6 oz. seedless raisins	Orange-flavoured gravy or orange salad
Chopped nuts	Watercress

Dress the birds and stuff with the following mixture: Combine together the breadcrumbs, celery, onion and raisins. Some chopped nuts may also be added. Season and bind together with the beaten egg and the milk. Sew up the birds or secure with small skewers. Place pieces of fat bacon over the birds and roast in a fairly hot oven (400°F., mark 6) for 20-30 minutes, taking care not to over-cook. Serve with a good gravy, with some orange juice added, or with a simple salad made by tossing sliced peeled oranges in a French dressing. Garnish with watercress if available.

EGG AND CHEESE COOKERY

Recipes give 4 servings, unless otherwise indicated

EGGS

Store eggs in a cool place; if they are put in the refrigerator, keep them well away from the freezer and take them out some time before using, to give them time to reach room temperature, otherwise they crack when being boiled and are also difficult to whisk. Use the refrigerator racks or boxes provided, as these are designed to protect the eggs. Don't store eggs next to cheese, fish or onions, as they absorb strong flavours.

The more lightly egg dishes are cooked, the better (except in the case of hard-boiled eggs). This applies particularly to fried and baked egg dishes and to omelettes, where too long cooking makes the eggs tough.

Cook custards and similar dishes containing eggs very slowly over a low heat or stand them in a water bath or double saucepan.

CHEESE

Though cheese often requires months—sometimes years —to bring it to full maturity, once ripe it deteriorates comparatively rapidly. So buy only enough to last a few days to a week and store it in a cool place, such as a cold larder; cover it loosely to protect it from the air, but do not make it air-tight. If entirely exposed to the air, cheese will become hard and dry and if tightly covered it is likely to mould.

A refrigerator is not ideal for storing cheese, but if it must be used, the cheese should first be wrapped in waxed paper or foil or tightly covered.

The less cooking cheese has, the better. Over-heating tends to make it tough, so when making a dish such as Welsh Rarebit or cheese sauce, heat the cheese very gently and don't cook the mixture more than necessary once the cheese is added.

QUICK WAYS WITH EGGS

BAKED EGGS

Place the required number of individual ovenproof dishes or cocottes on a baking sheet, with a knob of butter in each dish. Put them in the oven for 1-2 minutes, until the butter has melted. Break an egg into each dish, sprinkle with a little salt and pepper, place in the centre of a moderately hot oven (350°F., mark 4) and leave until the eggs are just set—about 5-8 minutes. Serve at once, plain for breakfast or with vegetables as a snack. If you don't wish to use the oven, prepare the eggs as above, sprinkle them with white breadcrumbs or grated cheese, then cook them under the grill until the yolks are just setting.

FLAMENCO EGGS

(see colour picture no. 20)

2-3 slices of cooked ham	A little good stock
1 tbsp. chopped onion	½ lb. continental-type
Olive oil or butter	sausage, sliced
½ lb. tomatoes, skinned and cut up	6 asparagus tips, cooked
½ lb. cooked peas	Strips of sweet pepper
½ lb. cooked potatoes	4 eggs

Cut the ham up small and fry with the onion in the oil or butter until they begin to colour. Add the tomatoes, peas and potatoes, with stock to moisten, then sauté gently for a few minutes, stirring carefully. Add the sausage and put into an ovenproof dish; garnish with asparagus tips and sweet pepper, break the eggs on top and put into a hot oven (425°F., mark 7) for a few minutes, until the eggs are set.

SAVOURY MERINGUE EGGS

(see colour picture no. 20)

Grill ½ lb. skinless sausages, slice, mix with the contents of a 15-oz. can of baked beans and pour into an ovenproof dish. Separate 4 eggs, whisk the whites stiffly and pile into the dish, making 4 hollows in the top. Place the egg yolks in the hollows, sprinkle with 2 oz. grated cheese and bake in a fairly hot oven (400°F., mark 6) for 10-15 minutes, until the meringue is crisp.

SCRAMBLED EGGS

Break the eggs separately, then beat them together lightly, season to taste and add 1 tbsp. milk for each egg. Melt a little butter in a small pan, allowing about 1 oz. for 4 eggs, then add the egg-and-milk mixture, stirring. Stir and cook slowly until creamy, pile the mixture on to buttered toast and serve at once.

Variations

Try adding (to a 4-egg mixture) 2 oz. lightly cooked chopped mushrooms; 2 skinned tomatoes, chopped and cooked with a diced rasher of fried bacon; 3-4 tbsps. well-drained canned sweet corn; 2 oz. chopped ham, tongue or other meat; leftovers of cooked fish, e.g., fresh haddock, smoked haddock, kipper, removing all bones and skin and flaking it carefully.

EGGS À LA MORNAY
(see picture above)

Slice 4 hard-boiled eggs and lay them in a fireproof dish, reserving a few slices for garnish. Season well ½ pint white sauce, add 1 oz. grated cheese and pour the sauce over the eggs. Sprinkle another 1 oz. of cheese over the top, dot with shavings of butter and brown under a hot grill for a few minutes. Garnish with sliced egg and parsley.

FRIED EGGS WITH TOMATO SAUCE

Pipe some creamed potato round the edge of a hot dish, pour a little tomato sauce in the middle and put 4 hot fried eggs into it; serve at once.

FLUFFY FRIED EGGS

2 eggs, separated	Buttered toast or
Salt	chopped cooked
Dripping	spinach

Whisk the egg whites with a pinch of salt until stiff. Heat a little dripping in a frying pan and drop in the beaten egg white, in two portions. Drop an egg yolk in the centre of each white and fry until set. Serve on hot buttered toast or chopped spinach. (Serves 2.)

ASPARAGUS WITH POACHED EGGS

1 bundle of asparagus	Seasoning
4 rounds of buttered toast	Chopped parsley or paprika pepper
4 eggs	

Cook and drain the asparagus and keep it hot. Make and butter the toast and poach the eggs. Arrange the asparagus on the toast and top with the eggs; season and sprinkle with parsley or paprika pepper.

BAKED EGG RISOTTO

Cook some rice in a little well-flavoured stock, as for a risotto, until all the liquid is absorbed; add some chopped shrimps and chopped parsley. Put 2-3 tbsps. of this mixture in the bottom of each cocotte or ramekin dish and break an egg into each. Dot with pieces of butter, season lightly and bake in a moderate oven (350°F., mark 4) until the eggs are set—about 15 minutes.

CRISP STUFFED ROLLS
(see picture above)

4 crisp dinner rolls	1 oz. butter
1 small onion	3 eggs
2 oz. mushrooms	Seasoning
3 tomatoes	

Remove a lid from each roll and scoop out some of the soft inside. Skin and grate the onion, chop the mushrooms and peel and chop the tomatoes. Melt the butter, add the vegetables and sauté gently for 5-10 minutes, until soft. Beat the eggs with some seasoning, pour into the pan and stir with a wooden spoon over a low heat until the mixture thickens. Pile it into the bread shells, replace the lids, put on a baking sheet and cook in a moderate oven (350°F., mark 4) for about 15 minutes, until the rolls are crisp and the filling thoroughly heated. Garnish as desired. Serve at once.

SIMPLE CURRIED EGGS

Hard-boil some eggs, allowing 1-2 per person. Fry 2 small chopped onions in some butter until they are soft, then stir in 2 level tsps. curry powder and ½ oz. flour. Add ½ pint stock and stir until the sauce boils. Season and add a little chutney. Cut the eggs in half lengthways and add to the sauce, then simmer for a few minutes, to heat them through. Serve within a border of cooked rice or creamed potato.

EGGS IN BAKED POTATOES

4 large raw potatoes	2 tbsps. top of milk
1 oz. butter	4 eggs
Salt and pepper	

Scrub the potatoes then, using a sharp-pointed knife, mark around the tops in a circle. Bake the potatoes in a moderate oven (350°F., mark 4) for 1 hour, or until soft. Remove the insides of the potatoes and mash with butter, seasoning and milk. Return about half the mixture to each potato skin, break an egg in each, return them to the oven and cook until the egg has set. If desired, the rest of the creamed potato may then be piped round the top and the potatoes browned under the grill.

POTATO NESTS

(see picture above)

1 lb. creamed potatoes	Seasoning
4 eggs	1 oz. grated cheese

Pipe a border of creamed potato round 4 scallop shells or dishes (or put the potato into a greased heat-proof dish and make 4 wells in it). Break an egg into each dish (or well) and sprinkle with salt, pepper and grated cheese. Bake in a moderate oven (350°F., mark 4) until the eggs are set—about 10-15 minutes—and serve with green peas.

EGG RAMEKINS

4 oz. cooked ham	½ pint milk
Butter	Salt and pepper
1 oz. flour	4 eggs

Chop the ham very small. Make a white sauce with 1 oz. butter, the flour and the milk; season to taste and mix with the ham. Lightly butter 4 small individual dishes and spread the bottom and sides with the mixture. Break the eggs one by one into a cup, slide one into each dish, dot with butter and bake in a moderate oven (350°F., mark 4) until set—about 12 minutes.

EGGS WITH MUSHROOM STUFFING

2-3 oz. mushrooms, chopped	4 hard-boiled eggs
	Piquant table sauce
2 tsps. chopped parsley	½ cup tomato pulp
Butter or margarine	Grated cheese

Fry the mushrooms with the parsley in the butter or margarine. Halve the eggs and remove the yolks; mash these with the mushroom mixture and the sauce and season to taste. Fill the egg-white cups with this stuffing and place the eggs in a greased fireproof dish. Pour the tomato pulp over them and sprinkle with grated cheese. Place under the pre-heated grill for 5-10 minutes.

SAVOURY EGGS

4 crumpets (pikelets)	4 poached eggs
Butter	Chopped parsley
Anchovy paste	

Toast and butter the crumpets, spread with paste, top with the eggs and sprinkle with parsley.

EGGS À LA FLORENTINE

(see picture above)

1 lb. spinach	4 eggs
Salt and pepper	2-3 tbsps. single cream
½ oz. butter	A sprig of parsley
2 oz. grated Parmesan cheese	to garnish

Wash the spinach well, put it into a pan with a little salt and just the water that clings to the leaves and cook for 10-15 minutes, until tender. Drain well, chop roughly and mix with the butter and seasoning. Put into an oven-proof dish and cover with most of the grated cheese. Break the eggs into a saucer and slide side by side into the cheese; bake in a moderate oven (350°F., mark 4) for 10 minutes. Remove from the oven, spoon the cream over and sprinkle with the remaining cheese. Return the dish to the oven and bake for a further 10-15 minutes, until the eggs are firm. Serve garnished with parsley.
Alternatively, line small individual casseroles with the spinach purée, add cheese and an egg to each and finish as above.
For a simpler dish, serve poached eggs on creamed spinach.

SCALLOPED EGGS

Grease 4 scallop shells and put a sliced hard-boiled egg in each. Cut 4 anchovies in small pieces and mix with 1 tbsp. capers and ½ pint white sauce. Pour this over the eggs, sprinkle with browned crumbs and re-heat for 10 minutes in a moderate oven (350°F., mark 4).

MIMOSA EGGS

Hard-boil 4 eggs, cut them in half, sieve the yolks and slice the whites; put the latter in a hot fireproof dish, pour ½ pint well-seasoned white sauce over them and sprinkle thickly with the sieved yolks. Serve very hot.

EGG AND TOMATO SAVOURIES

Remove the pulp from 4 tomatoes and bake the cases in a moderate oven (350°F., mark 4) until tender but unbroken. Meanwhile scramble 2-3 eggs in the usual way, season and use to fill the tomato cases. Garnish with parsley and serve with noodles, spaghetti or macaroni.

OMELETTES—AS SAVOURY AND SWEET

The first essential for omelette-making is a reliable pan, either a special omelette one or a small-sized frying pan; whichever is used, it must be thick and smooth-surfaced. Before use, prepare it as follows: heat it gently, rub it over with salt and a small pad of kitchen paper and wipe it out with a dry cloth. Heat the pan thoroughly and evenly before putting in the egg mixture and try always to use clarified butter for the cooking.

PLAIN OMELETTE

Beat 3 eggs lightly, add a little pepper and salt and cook as shown in the pictures above:
1. Heat $\frac{1}{2}$ oz. butter, tilting the pan, then carefully pour in the egg mixture.
2. At once begin to stir gently with a fork, continuing until no more liquid egg can be seen.
3. When the mixture is just set, tilt the pan and fold omelette over, inserting any filling that is to be used.
4. Turn the omelette into a hot dish, garnish according to the type of filling and serve at once. (Serves 2.)

VARIATIONS

Mushroom: Fry 2 oz. sliced mushrooms in a little fat till tender and sprinkle over surface of cooked omelette before folding. Add a little sherry to egg mixture before cooking, if desired.
Herb: Add chopped parsley, chives, thyme or other herbs to the eggs before cooking.
Kidney: Cut up 1-2 sheep's kidneys, add 1 tsp. finely chopped onion and fry lightly until cooked. Bind with sauce or gravy and fold into omelette.

SPANISH OMELETTE

1 tomato, skinned	Olive oil
2 cooked potatoes	2 tbsps. cooked peas
2 canned pimientos	4 eggs
1 small onion, chopped	Salt and pepper

Slice and chop the tomato, dice the potatoes and cut up the pimientos. Fry the onion lightly in a little oil; add the vegetables and cook for a few minutes, stirring. Beat the eggs, season well and pour them into the pan. Cook the omelette in a very little oil, shaking the pan occasionally. When one side is lightly and evenly browned, cover with a plate, turn the omelette and cook the other side. Do not fold; serve hot, with tomato sauce. Spanish omelette, served cold, makes an excellent picnic dish.

OMELETTE CARDINAL

4 eggs	6 oz. prawns
Salt and pepper	1 tbsp. single cream
1 oz. butter	$\frac{1}{4}$ pint white sauce
1 orange	

Mix the eggs with a fork and season. Heat the butter, pour in the eggs and cook in the usual way. Peel the orange thinly and carefully, in order to obtain only the outer rind, then cut this into very thin Julienne strips. Finish peeling the orange, remove the pith and slice the flesh. Just before folding the omelette, fill it with half the Julienne strips and half the prawns, mixed with the cream. Fold the omelette and slide on to a hot serving dish, make a lengthwise incision and fill with remaining prawns. Pour the sauce over both ends. Arrange the orange slices around and sprinkle the rest of the Julienne strips on top.

SOUFFLÉ OMELETTE

3 eggs, separated · Seasoning
3 tbsps. milk or water · ½ oz. butter

Beat the egg yolks and add the liquid, with seasoning if required. Continue as in pictures above:
1. Whisk the egg whites stiffly, then fold into yolk mixture; work lightly and avoid overmixing.
2. Melt the butter and tip the pan so that the sides are greased. Spread the egg mixture over the surface.
3. Cook the omelette carefully over a moderate heat until it is an even golden-brown on the underside.
4. Lightly brown the top under a grill, add any required filling and fold the omelette in half. (Serves 2.)

VARIATIONS

Cheese: Sprinkle the surface liberally with grated cheese before browning the top.
Shrimp: Heat 2 oz. picked shrimps in a little white sauce. Add a few drops anchovy essence to the yolks and insert the shrimps before folding omelette.
Ham or Meat: Add 2 oz. minced ham, cooked meat, liver, tongue or chicken to the yolk mixture.

FRANKFURTER CRUMB OMELETTE

1½ oz. fresh bread-crumbs · 1 level tsp. salt
¼ pint boiling water · ¼ level tsp. pepper
4 eggs, separated · 6 heated and sliced
½ tsp. chopped herbs · Frankfurter sausages

Put the crumbs in a basin, add the boiling water and then leave to stand for 10 minutes. Beat the egg yolks

with the herbs and seasonings, then add the soaked breadcrumbs to the mixture. Fold in the stiffly whisked egg whites, pour the mixture into a prepared frying pan, add the Frankfurters and cook as usual. Put under a hot grill until the top is firm, fold and serve on a hot plate.
Note: Chervil, tarragon, summer savory and rosemary are all suitable herbs to include.

ASPARAGUS OMELETTE

A few cooked or canned asparagus spears · Salt and pepper
4 eggs, separated · 4 oz. grated Cheddar cheese
1 tbsp. water

Cut off the green tips of the asparagus, with about 1 inch of the stalk; chop the rest. Make a soufflé omelette in the usual way, adding the chopped asparagus and 3 oz. of the grated cheese to the egg yolks. Cook as usual, but do not fold; slide it on to a warm plate, make a slight incision in the middle of the omelette with the point of a knife, put in the asparagus tips in a bundle and sprinkle with the rest of the cheese.

SWEET SOUFFLÉ OMELETTES

Make as above, but omit the seasoning.
Jam: Spread the cooked omelette with hot jam, fold and sprinkle with sugar.
Rum: Add 1 good tbsp. best quality rum to the egg yolks. Put the cooked omelette on a hot dish and pour 3-4 tbsps. warmed rum round, ignite and serve.
Apricot: Add the grated rind of an orange or tangerine to the egg yolks. Spread thick apricot pulp over the omelette before folding and serve liberally sprinkled with caster sugar.

SUPPERS AND SNACKS WITH CHEESE

CHEESE AND ONION PIE
(see picture above)

6 oz. shortcrust pastry	1 level tbsp. seasoned flour
2 medium-sized par-boiled onions	3-4 oz. grated cheese
	2 tbsps. milk

Divide the pastry in half and roll out one part to cover an ovenproof plate. Slice the onions finely, dip into seasoned flour, place on the pastry and add the cheese and milk. Cover the pie with the rest of the pastry, cut into strips and worked lattice-fashion. Bake in a hot oven (425°F., mark 7) for about 40 minutes, until the pastry is golden-brown.

Alternatively, mix the onions with a little well-flavoured cheese sauce, sprinkle with grated cheese and finish as above.

CHEESY GAMMON SAVOURY

Grill 4 gammon rashers on both sides for about 7 minutes. Turn out a 15-oz. can of jellied cranberry sauce and cut into thick slices; place one slice on each rasher, cover with strips of processed cheese and grill until the cheese melts. Serve at once, with potato straws and mushrooms, or as desired.

CHEESE AND FISH PIE
(see colour picture no. 22)

2 lb. potatoes	1½ oz. flour
2½ oz. butter	6 oz. grated cheese
Milk	Tomatoes, mushrooms,
Salt and pepper	stuffed olives, etc., to
1 lb. white fish	garnish

Cook the potatoes and mash with 1 oz. butter, a little milk and seasoning to taste. Pipe a border of this creamed potato round an ovenproof dish and leave to brown under the grill. Meanwhile place the fish in a pan, cover with water, put on the lid and bring slowly to the boil, turn off the heat and leave the fish for 5 minutes. Drain the fish well (reserving ¼ pint of the liquor), skin and flake it. Make a white sauce with the remaining butter, flour, fish stock and ¼ pint milk. When it thickens, remove from the heat, stir in 4 oz. of the cheese and season. Combine with the fish and pour into the piped potato border. Sprinkle with the remaining cheese and grill till the cheese bubbles. Garnish as desired with tomatoes, mushrooms, stuffed olives, etc.

WELSH RAREBIT
(see picture above)

6 oz. Cheddar cheese	Beer or stout
¼ level tsp. dry mustard	Worcestershire sauce
A little pepper and salt	Hot buttered toast

Shred the cheese, put it into a double saucepan and allow it to melt slowly over hot water. Add the seasonings, then stir in slowly as much beer or stout as the cheese will take up, and flavour to taste with Worcestershire sauce; the mixture should be smooth and creamy. Pour it over the hot toast and brown under the grill, if desired. Serve at once, garnished with parsley and accompanied by tomatoes.

Buck Rarebit: Make as above and serve topped with a poached egg.

Yorkshire Rarebit: Top with a slice of boiled bacon and a poached egg.

CHICKEN CHEESE

4 portions of chicken	¼ pint dry cider
4 oz. butter	¼ pint single cream
2 slices of onion	Salt and pepper
Thyme	2 tsps. mild mustard
¼ pint stock	4 oz. strong Cheddar
1½ oz. flour	cheese, grated

Simmer the chicken in the butter until tender (about 20 minutes). Put the pieces on to a heatproof dish and keep hot. Simmer the onion with a pinch of thyme in the stock. Strain and add the flour, stirring all the time. Stir in the cider, cream, seasonings and half the cheese; allow to simmer for 10 minutes. Pour this sauce over the chicken, sprinkle with the remaining cheese and brown under a very hot grill.

CARNIVAL MACARONI CHEESE
(see colour picture no. 21)

4 oz. macaroni	1 oz. flour
1½ oz. butter	1 level tsp. salt
3 oz. button mushrooms	A dash of pepper
	¾ pint milk
2 tbsps. chopped canned pimiento	6 oz. Cheddar cheese, shredded
2 tbsps. sliced green pepper	Buttered breadcrumbs

Cook the macaroni in boiling salted water for 15 minutes. Meanwhile, melt the butter in a saucepan, then add the mushrooms, pimiento and green pepper (reserving a little of each for garnish) and brown lightly. Stir in the flour, salt and pepper. Add the milk gradually and cook until thickened, stirring constantly. Add the cheese, stirring well to make a smooth sauce.

Rinse the macaroni in warm water and drain well. Fold it into the cheese sauce, pour into a casserole, top with breadcrumbs and garnish. Bake in a moderate oven (350°F., mark 4) for 25 minutes.

CHEESE HAM CROQUETTES
(see picture above)

3 hard-boiled eggs	4 oz. grated cheese
3 oz. cooked ham	1 tsp. chopped parsley
1 oz. butter	Beaten egg and
1 oz. flour	white breadcrumbs
¼ pint milk	Deep fat for frying
Seasoning	

Chop the eggs and ham very finely. Melt the butter in a small pan, stir in the flour, add the milk and bring to the boil. Season, add the cheese, parsley, eggs and ham and turn on to a plate to cool. When the mixture is cold, shape into croquettes, coat with egg and breadcrumbs and fry in deep fat until golden-brown. Garnish with watercress.

STUFFED PEPPERS
(see colour picture no. 22)

4 green peppers	Seasoning
1 onion	4 oz. Cheddar cheese,
4 oz. mushrooms	grated
2 oz. butter	4 rashers of streaky
4 tbsps. fresh bread-	bacon
crumbs	¼ pint stock

Halve the peppers lengthwise, remove the seeds and cook the cases in boiling salted water for 5 minutes, then drain and put into an ovenproof dish. Chop the onion and mushrooms and cook in the butter until tender. Add the breadcrumbs, seasoning and most of the cheese. Put this mixture into the peppers, sprinkle with the rest of the cheese and put half a rasher of bacon on each. Put the stock in the dish, cover and bake in a fairly hot oven (400°F., mark 6) for about 20 minutes; remove the cover and cook for a further 10 minutes.

HAM AND LEEKS AU GRATIN
(see picture above)

8 medium-sized leeks	4 oz. Gruyère cheese,
Seasoning	grated
Butter or margarine	8 slices of cooked ham
2 oz. flour	Toasted breadcrumbs
½ pint milk	Chopped parsley
Nutmeg	

Trim, wash and clean the leeks, put into boiling salted water and boil slowly for 20 minutes. Drain in a colander, keeping back about ½ pint of the liquid, and leave for about 5 minutes. Make a well-seasoned cheese sauce with 2 oz. butter, the flour, milk, leek liquor, a little grated nutmeg and 2 oz. of the cheese.

Wrap each leek in a slice of ham and put in a fireproof dish, pour the sauce over, top with breadcrumbs and the remaining cheese, dot with butter and put under the grill until golden-brown. Garnish with parsley.

TUNA CHEESE CASSEROLE

2 oz. butter	2 7-oz. cans of
1 oz. plain flour	tuna fish
¾ pint milk	6 oz. Cheddar cheese,
Salt	grated
Pepper	1½ lb. potatoes (creamed)
1 tsp. salad cream	

Melt 1 oz. butter in a small saucepan, add the flour and cook, stirring, for 1 minute. Add the milk gradually, stirring constantly, and cook until smooth. Remove from the heat and stir in some seasoning, the salad cream, tuna fish and cheese. Butter a deep ovenproof dish and arrange in it a deep layer of potato; pour in the cheese mixture, top with remaining potato and brush well with melted butter. Bake in a moderate oven (350°F., mark 4) for 1 hour.

EGGS WITH CHEESE

VEGETABLE CHEESE BAKE

4 eggs, separated
½ pint milk
3 slices of white bread
with the crust
removed
1 level tsp. salt
½ level tsp. dry mustard
⅛ level tsp. pepper
6 oz. strong Cheddar
cheese, grated
6 oz. ham, chopped

10 oz. finely chopped
cooked vegetables
1 tbsp. finely chopped
onion
2 tbsps. chopped green
pepper or parsley
An 11-oz. can of con-
densed tomato soup
(undiluted)
2 tbsps. butter or
margarine

Start the preparations on the previous day. Put the
egg yolks in a mixing bowl and beat with a fork. Add
the milk, bread and seasonings. Let the bread soften,
then break it up with a fork; add the cheese, ham,
cooked vegetables, onion and green pepper or parsley,
then refrigerate the mixture.
About 1 hour before the dish is required start heating
the oven to cool (300°F., mark 2). Beat the egg whites
till stiff and fold them into the cheese mixture. Pour into a
greased casserole or dish and bake for 45 minutes or
until firm; serve hot, with a sauce made by heating the
soup with the butter. (Serves 4-6.)

BELGIAN EGG SAVOURY

4 eggs
Butter
A few shelled prawns
A little chopped
chervil and parsley

French mustard
½ pint cream
Salt and pepper
2 oz. grated cheese

Boil the eggs for 6-7 minutes, put them into cold water for
1-2 minutes, then shell them and slice into a saucepan.
Add a little butter, most of the prawns and the other
ingredients (except the cheese) and mix well; pour into
a greased fireproof dish, sprinkle with cheese, dot with a
little butter, put into a hot oven (425°F., mark 7) and
cook till the top browns. Garnish with prawns, or as
desired.

CAULIFLOWER AU GRATIN

1 cauliflower
4 eggs
1½ oz. butter
1½ oz. flour

¾ pint milk
Salt and pepper
4 oz. grated cheese
4 tomatoes

Prepare the cauliflower, leaving it whole, but cutting
a cross in the base of the stem part to help it to cook.
Quickly cook it in boiling salted water for 15-20 minutes.
Hard-boil the eggs. Make a roux with the butter and
flour and then gradually add the milk; stir until the sauce
boils, season to taste and add 3 oz. of the grated cheese.
Halve the tomatoes and grill lightly. Drain the cauliflower and place in a fireproof dish. Shell and drain the
eggs, quarter them and arrange round the cauliflower,
keeping back a few pieces for garnish. Quarter the
tomatoes and arrange these also round the cauliflower,
keeping a few pieces for garnish. Coat the cauliflower,
tomatoes and eggs with the sauce, sprinkle with the
remaining cheese, garnish with egg and tomato and place
under the grill for 5 minutes. Serve hot.

EGG SALAD CASSEROLE

6-8 coarsely chopped
hard-boiled eggs
6 sticks of celery,
diced
2 oz. chopped nuts
1 tsp. minced onion
¼ level tsp. pepper

2 tbsps. chopped
parsley
½ level tsp. salt
¼ pint mayonnaise
4 oz. grated cheese
2 pkts. potato crisps

Start heating the oven to moderate (350°F., mark 4).
Combine all the ingredients except the cheese and potato
crisps and toss lightly. Put into 4 individual casseroles;
sprinkle with the cheese and crushed crisps and bake
(uncovered) for 25 minutes; serve immediately.

EGG AND CHEESE FLAPJACKS

4 eggs
1 tbsp. grated onion
1½ oz. flour
½ level tsp. salt
⅛ level tsp. pepper

1 level tsp. baking powder
3 oz. American pro-
cessed cheese, grated
⅓ cup of fat or
salad oil

Beat the eggs and add the onion; sift in the flour, salt,
pepper and baking powder and blend well. Stir in the
cheese. Heat some of the fat in a frying pan; drop in
large spoonfuls of the egg mixture and brown on both
sides, turning once. Add more fat as needed. Serve at
once, with canned cranberry sauce, marmalade or
sautéed bananas.

EGG FLIP AND POTATO PIE

2 eggs
¼ pint milk
Salt and pepper
½ lb. cooked potatoes

¼ lb. tomatoes,
skinned
4 oz. Cheddar cheese
Parsley to garnish

Beat the eggs thoroughly and add the milk, salt and
pepper. Slice the potatoes and tomatoes and grate the
cheese. Butter a pie dish and put in a layer of potatoes
and tomatoes, adding a sprinkling of cheese, salt and
pepper. Add 2-3 tsps. of the egg mixture and then
another layer of potatoes, tomatoes and cheese. Finish
with a layer of grated cheese and pour in any remaining
egg mixture. Bake slowly in a moderate oven (350°F.,
mark 4) for about 40 minutes, until the egg flip has set
and the cheese topping is golden-brown. Garnish with
parsley. (Serves 2-3.)

POTATO EGGS

¾ lb. boiled potatoes
Salt and cayenne
pepper
3 oz. grated cheese
1 beaten egg
4 hard-boiled eggs

Flour
Breadcrumbs
Deep fat for frying
Rounds of fried
bread
Tomato sauce

Mash the potatoes and season with salt and cayenne
pepper. Add the grated cheese and sufficient beaten egg
to produce a fairly stiff paste, then beat very thoroughly
until smooth. Shell the eggs and flour them lightly.
Turn the potato mixture on to a floured board, divide
into 4, flatten out each piece, put one of the eggs on each
and mould the potato around it, keeping the egg shape.
Coat with beaten egg and breadcrumbs and fry in the fat
until golden-brown. Cut in half crosswise and serve on
rounds of fried bread, accompanied by tomato sauce.

CHEESE PUDDING
(see picture above)

6-8 thin slices of bread and butter	2 tsps. tomato sauce
2 eggs	4 oz. grated cheese
A little made mustard	1 pint milk
Salt and pepper	1 oz. breadcrumbs
1 onion, chopped	Toast to garnish

Cut the buttered bread into neat pieces and put into a pie dish. Beat the eggs with the seasonings, onion and sauce; add 3 oz. of the cheese and the milk. Pour this mixture over the bread and allow to stand for 10-15 minutes. Mix the remainder of the cheese with the breadcrumbs and sprinkle over the top. Bake in a moderate oven (350°F., mark 4) for about ¾ hour, until set and golden. Garnish with toast triangles and serve with baked tomatoes.

HOT STUFFED EGGS

2 hard-boiled eggs	Salt and pepper
½ oz. butter	Egg and breadcrumbs
½ oz. flour	Deep fat for frying
2-3 tbsps. milk	Fried parsley for garnish
¾ oz. grated cheese	Cheese sauce

Split the eggs in half lengthways, remove the yolks and sieve them. Melt the butter, stir in the flour and milk and cook, stirring, until the mixture leaves the sides of the pan. Add the cheese, seasoning and sieved egg yolks, mix well and fill the egg-white cases with this mixture. Coat with egg and breadcrumbs and fry in hot fat until golden-brown. Garnish with fried parsley and serve with cheese sauce. (Serves 2.)

CHEESE AND EGG FLAN

6 oz. cheese pastry	3 hard-boiled eggs
¼ pint aspic jelly	Mayonnaise, anchovies,
3 small, firm tomatoes	etc., to garnish

Line a flan ring with the cheese pastry and bake "blind", then allow to cool. Dissolve the aspic and cool it until it is on the point of setting again. Meanwhile skin the tomatoes and slice thinly and slice the eggs; arrange both of these in the flan case, pour the jelly over and allow to set. Garnish.

SPICY HAM AND EGGS
(see picture above)

6 eggs	1 tbsp. chilli sauce
1 oz. butter	A dash of tabasco sauce
1 oz. flour	½ lb. diced cooked ham
1 level tsp. dry mustard	A few sliced stuffed olives
¾ level tsp. salt	
⅛ level tsp. pepper	4 oz. diced sharp processed cheese
½ pint milk	
1 tsp. grated horseradish	Grated cheese and breadcrumbs for topping
1 tbsp. piquant table sauce	

Hard-boil the eggs, peel and slice them. Start heating the oven to fairly hot (400°F., mark 6). Make a spicy sauce as follows: melt the butter in a saucepan, stir in the flour, mustard, salt and pepper, then the milk. Cook, stirring until the mixture thickens. Stir in the horseradish and the piquant, chilli and tabasco sauces. In a 1¼-pint casserole, arrange layers of egg, ham, sliced olives, cheese and sauce (reserving some egg and olives). Sprinkle with cheese and breadcrumbs and bake (uncovered) for 25-30 minutes. Garnish with the remaining egg and olives. (Serves 6.)

OEUFS SOUBISE AU GRATIN

1 lb. onions	2 oz. fresh crumbs
Pepper and salt	4 eggs
Butter	1 level tbsp. flour
3 oz. well-flavoured cheese, grated	½ pint milk
	A pinch of marjoram

Roughly slice the onions and boil in salted water for 5 minutes; drain and chop finely. Melt 2 oz. butter, add the onion and cook with the lid on the pan until tender but not coloured; season. Meanwhile mix together the cheese and breadcrumbs and place half over the bottom of a buttered heatproof dish. Cover with half the onion. Soft-boil the eggs (i.e., cook in boiling water for 4 minutes), then put immediately into cold water; carefully remove the shells. Place the eggs on the bed of onion, cover with a white sauce made from ½ oz. butter, the flour and ½ pint milk; season with pepper, salt and marjoram. Spoon the remainder of the onion on top of the sauce and finally add the rest of the cheese and the crumbs, then dot with pieces of butter. Place in a hot oven (425°F., mark 7) and cook for 15 minutes.

CHEESE AND EGG FRICASSEE

(see picture above)

4 hard-boiled eggs	1 tsp. finely chopped
½ pint white sauce	parsley
A pinch of salt	2 oz. grated cheese
A little pepper	Browned breadcrumbs

Quarter the eggs, add to the white sauce and season well. Heat through without allowing to boil, then add the parsley and put into individual dishes. Cover the top thickly with the grated cheese and breadcrumbs and brown for a minute or two under a hot grill. Serve immediately, with toast and watercress.

HAM AND CHEESE PANCAKES

2 oz. flour	4 slices of ham
Salt	3 oz. grated cheese
1 large egg	Rings of green pepper
¼ pint milk and water	to garnish
Fat for frying	

Put the flour into a bowl, add the salt and the egg, then gradually stir in the liquid, mixing to a smooth batter. Heat the fat in a frying pan and when it is really hot, pour in sufficient batter to form a thin layer over the base of the pan. Cook the pancake on one side, turn and cook the other side; keep it hot while making 3 more pancakes. Put a slice of ham on each pancake, sprinkle it with cheese and roll up. Arrange the pancakes in a serving dish, sprinkle the rest of the cheese over the top and brown lightly under the grill. Serve garnished with the green pepper rings.

SWEET CORN SPECIAL

3 large eggs	Salt and pepper
A 15-oz. can of	3 large tomatoes
sweet corn	3 oz. grated Cheddar
3 oz. margarine	cheese

Hard-boil the eggs. Heat the corn in a saucepan with 2 oz. margarine and some seasoning for 6 minutes. Halve the tomatoes, dot with the rest of the margarine and grill for 5 minutes. Drain and shell the eggs. Drain the sweet corn and pour into an ovenproof dish. Halve the eggs lengthwise and arrange down the centre of the dish, on top of the corn. Season, cover with cheese and brown for 4 minutes under the grill. Put the tomatoes round the edge of the dish, garnish with parsley and serve at once. (Serves 3.)

CROQUE-MONSIEUR WITH EGGS

(see picture above)

4 slices of toasted bread	4 tomatoes
Butter or margarine	Salt
4 rashers of bacon	4 eggs
4 slices of cheese	

Butter the bread generously and grill briefly on the buttered side. Trim the bacon rashers, lay them on the slices of bread and grill lightly. Place the bread and bacon in an ovenproof dish and lay the cheese over the top. Halve the tomatoes and put alongside the bread in the dish; sprinkle with salt and again grill lightly. Melt some butter in a frying pan and fry the eggs briskly; lift them from the pan and place on the cheese. Put the whole back under the grill for 1 minute and serve piping hot.

DEVILLED HAM CASSEROLE

2 oz. minced ham	6 thin slices of bread
2 tbsps. chilli sauce	A little butter
1 tsp. made mustard	3 eggs, beaten
1 tsp. minced onion	½ level tsp. salt
1 tsp. piquant table	¾ pint milk
sauce	3 oz. grated cheese
1 tsp. horseradish sauce	

Combine the ham, chilli sauce, mustard, onion, piquant sauce and horseradish and spread the bread with this mixture. Place in a single layer in a baking dish and dot with knobs of butter. Mix together the eggs, salt and milk, pour over the bread and sprinkle with cheese. Place in a pan of warm water and bake in a warm oven (325°F., mark 3) for 1-1¼ hours. (Serves 2-3.)

EGGS WITH CHEESE FILLING

8 small plain biscuits	A little whipped
Anchovy paste	cream
4 hard-boiled eggs	Salt and pepper
2 oz. grated Cheddar	Chopped parsley or red
cheese	pepper to garnish

Spread the biscuits with anchovy paste. Cut the eggs in half lengthwise and remove the yolks. Cut off a small piece of white from the bottom of each half-egg and stand the cup on a biscuit. Pound the sieved egg yolks with cheese and cream and season to taste. Pipe this mixture back into the egg whites and put a little finely grated cheese, chopped parsley or red pepper on each.

CHEESE SAVOURIES AND PASTRIES

CHEESE PASTRY

3 oz. butter or margarine	3 oz. grated cheese
	4 oz. plain flour

Blend together the butter and cheese until soft. Add the flour gradually and stir until the mixture begins to stick together. Collect it into a ball, knead until smooth and if possible refrigerate before using.

CHEESE STRAWS
(see colour picture no. 23)

Roll out some cheese pastry fairly thinly and cut into fingers about 3 inches long and $\frac{1}{4}$ inch wide. Stamp out some rings, using 2 greased cutters, put all on a baking sheet and bake in a fairly hot oven (400°F., mark 6) for about 10 minutes. When the biscuits are cold, dip the ends of the straws into paprika pepper or finely chopped parsley and insert into the rings.

CHEESE GONDOLAS
(see colour picture no. 23)

Line some boat-shaped tins with cheese pastry (see above) and bake "blind". When they are cold, fill with grated Cheddar cheese mixed with thick cream. Place on each boat a "sail" made of thinly cut processed cheese or rice paper and decorate with sliced radish.

HOT CREAM CHEESE TARTLETS

Shortcrust pastry	$\frac{1}{4}$ pint thick white sauce
1 oz. cream cheese	
Salt and pepper	1 egg, separated
$\frac{1}{2}$ tsp. Worcestershire sauce	Finely grated Parmesan cheese

Roll out the pastry and use it to line some small tartlet tins. Beat the cream cheese until soft, then add the seasonings, the sauces and the egg yolk. Beat the egg white until stiff and fold it into the mixture. Three-quarters fill the pastry cases with this mixture and bake in a fairly hot oven (375°F., mark 5) for about 15 minutes. Before serving, sprinkle a little grated Parmesan cheese on top of each tartlet.

FISH AND CHEESE FLAN

An 8-inch flan case	A 4-oz. carton of cottage cheese
1 oz. butter	
1 oz. flour	A 7-oz. can of tuna fish or salmon
$\frac{1}{4}$ pint milk	
4 tbsps. single cream	1-2 tomatoes to garnish
2 eggs	

Make the flan case in the usual way and bake it blind. Make a thick white sauce with the butter, flour and milk. Add the cream, 1 whole egg, 1 egg yolk and the cheese, then the fish, drained and flaked. Beat in the stiffly beaten egg white. Turn the mixture into the pastry case and bake it for about $\frac{1}{2}$ hour in a fairly hot oven (400°F., mark 6); 10 minutes before the end of the time, arrange thin tomato slices round the edge. Serve hot.

COCKTAIL STICK TITBITS
(see colour picture no. 23)

Arrange a variety of appetising morsels on cocktail sticks and skewer these into a small cheese, a grapefruit or whole rosy apples. Choose from the following:
Cheddar cheese with celery, a cocktail onion or a chunk of pineapple and a cocktail cherry.
A tiny sausage, a piece of Cheddar cheese and a cocktail onion.
Stoned dates or prunes, or split and seeded grapes, filled with cream cheese.
Savoury Bacon Rolls: Roll a strip of bacon round a piece of pineapple or apricot, a prune or date stuffed with cheese, a stuffed olive, pickled onion or cocktail sausage, then grill until crisp. Serve hot.
Cheese Balls: Form some cream cheese into balls and roll them in chopped parsley, walnuts or minced ham.

QUICHE LORRAINE
(see colour picture no. 23)

6 oz. shortcrust pastry	A pinch of cayenne pepper
6 oz. Gruyère cheese	
6 oz. bacon	A pinch of grated nutmeg
2 eggs	
Salt	$\frac{1}{4}$ pint double cream

Line a 7-inch flan case with the pastry. Slice the cheese thinly; rind the bacon and cut it into 1-inch cubes. Place a layer of cheese on the pastry, then a layer of bacon, and repeat until all these ingredients have been used up. Beat the eggs with the salt, cayenne and nutmeg, add the cream and pour over the cheese and bacon mixture in the flan case. Bake it in a fairly hot oven (400°F., mark 6) for 40 minutes, until golden-brown. Serve immediately.

CURRY CHEESE BALLS
(see colour picture no. 23)

12 oz. cream cheese	2 level tbsps. curry powder
4 oz. coarse-cut coconut	Parsley

Roll the cheese into small balls and chill them. Blend the coconut and curry powder, brown under a moderately hot grill and cool. Roll the balls in the coconut mixture and chill again before serving. Serve spiked on cocktail sticks or as desired. Sprinkle with chopped parsley.

BACON, DATE AND CHEESE
(see colour picture no. 23)

Rind some bacon rashers and cut each into two; stone some dates. Stuff each date with a strip of cheese and wrap a piece of bacon round. Grill for 8-10 minutes.

HOT CHEESE PUFFS
(see colour picture no. 23)

2 egg whites	4 oz. grated cheese
$\frac{1}{4}$ level tsp. baking powder	Small toast canapés
Salt and pepper	Watercress

Whisk the egg whites stiffly and whisk in the baking powder and seasonings. Fold in the cheese and pile the mixture on to the canapés. Cook under a moderately hot grill until golden and puffy and serve hot. Garnish with watercress.

16. Matabele Fried Chicken

17. Roast Duck

18. Salmi of Poultry

19. Eggs and Cheese—indispensable for good cooking

20. Savoury Meringue Eggs and Flamenco Eggs

21. Carnival Macaroni Cheese

22. Baked Chicken with Cheese Sauce; Cheese and Fish Pie; Stuffed
    Peppers

23. Cheese Savouries and Titbits

CAMEMBERT CANAPÉS

Butter some fingers of toast about 3 inches long by ½ inch. Cut slices of Camembert cheese slightly smaller, place on the toast, then toast quickly under a hot grill. Sprinkle with paprika pepper and serve at once.

CHEESE SCRAMBLE

1 oz. butter	1 teacupful grated
1 teacupful milk	cheese
½ teacupful fresh	Salt and pepper
breadcrumbs	1 beaten egg

Put the butter and milk into a pan and bring to the boil, add the crumbs and cheese and season to taste. Stir over a low heat until the cheese has melted, add the egg and when the mixture is very hot, serve it on fingers of hot buttered toast.

SAVOURY WAFERS

Cream cheese	Chopped chives
Celery salt and pepper	Ice-cream wafers

Beat the cheese with a little celery salt, pepper and finely chopped chives. Spread it on half the ice-cream wafers, top with more wafers and serve at once on a dish garnished with watercress.

CHEESE ÉCLAIRS

(see picture above)

2 oz. butter or	4 oz. plain flour, sieved
margarine	3-4 eggs
¼ pint boiling water	Filling (see below)

Put the butter and water into a small pan and when the fat has melted, add the flour and stir vigorously. Cook gently until a smooth ball of paste is formed, then remove from the heat, cool slightly and mix in the eggs, adding them one at a time and beating very thoroughly. The paste should finally be of such a stiffness that it can be piped easily, but will retain its shape. Using a forcing bag fitted with a ½-inch nozzle, pipe 2-inch lengths of the paste on to a baking tin and bake these in a hot oven (425°F., mark 7) for 20-30 minutes, or until the éclairs are well risen and light. When they are cooked, split them open, cool and fill with a rich, creamy cheese

sauce or with softened cream cheese mixed with a little anchovy paste.

CHEESE DARTOIS

(see colour picture no. 50)

4 oz. flaky pastry	Salt, pepper and
1 egg	cayenne pepper
2 oz. finely grated	1 oz. butter or
Parmesan cheese	margarine

Roll the pastry out thinly and divide it into two portions. Beat the egg and add the cheese, seasonings and melted butter; spread the mixture over one half of the pastry, damp the edges and place the other piece of pastry on top, press the edges well together and mark across in strips. Bake in a very hot oven (450°F., mark 8) for about 15 minutes, until the pastry is golden-brown. Divide into fingers and serve either hot or cold.

CROÛTES OF FRIED CHEESE

6 Petit Suisse cheeses	Rounds of bread
(or ¼ lb. Gruyère)	1-2 oz. butter
1 beaten egg	Watercress
2 oz. breadcrumbs	

Divide each small cheese in half (or cut rounds of the Gruyère cheese). Brush over with beaten egg, coat with breadcrumbs and repeat this process twice, to make a really firm covering. Fry the rounds of bread golden-brown in the butter, then fry the cheese. Place the cheese on the croûtes and garnish with watercress.

YORK FINGERS

4 oz. flaky pastry	Finely grated cheese
4 oz. Wensleydale or	Minced ham
processed cheese	Horseradish sauce
Beaten egg	

Roll out the pastry thinly and cut the cheese into very thin slices. Put the cheese on to one half of the pastry, fold the other half over and roll it out again. Cut the pastry into fingers about 3 inches long and ½ inch wide, brush with beaten egg and sprinkle with grated cheese. Bake in a very hot oven (450°F., mark 8) until golden, then spread with ham mixed with horseradish sauce.

COLD BUFFET

SCOTCH EGGS

4 hard-boiled eggs	Beaten egg
A little flour	Breadcrumbs
10 oz. sausage-meat	Deep fat for frying

Peel the eggs and dust with flour. Coat each with 2-3 oz. sausage-meat, keeping it a good shape. Brush with beaten egg, coat with breadcrumbs and fry in deep fat for about 7 minutes. Drain well and allow to cool. Serve cut in halves with salad.

CHEESE CREAMS

¼ pint aspic jelly	3 oz. grated cheese
Sliced radishes or cucumber, cress or other garnish	Salt
	½ tsp. made mustard
	¼ pint white sauce
½ oz. gelatine	½ pint evaporated milk

Place about 1 tsp. jelly in each of 8 dariole moulds and allow to set. Garnish each with radish, cress or other colourful decoration and cover this with a little more aspic. Dissolve the gelatine in any remaining aspic jelly and mix with the cheese, seasonings and sauce. Whip the milk until it is thick and fold in. When the mixture is almost setting, pour into moulds and set. Turn out to serve and garnish with cress.

EGGS IN ASPIC

Hard-boiled eggs	Chopped chives
Seasoning	Aspic jelly
Cream cheese	Cooked carrots and peas

Cut the eggs in half and cream the sieved yolks with the seasoning, cream cheese and chives. Place this mixture in the egg-white cups and put the eggs together again. Set them in small jelly moulds in aspic jelly with pieces of carrot and green peas. Unmould when set and serve with a green salad.

SALMON DUNK

A 4-oz. can of salmon	2 gherkins, chopped
¼ lb. cottage cheese	Seasoning
2 rashers of streaky bacon	1-2 tbsps. mayonnaise
	Parsley
A 3-oz. carton of dairy sour cream	Potato crisps

Drain the excess liquid from the salmon and flake it into a basin; add the cottage cheese. Fry the bacon till crisp, crush and fold into the salmon mixture, then add the sour cream and gherkins. Check the seasoning and finally fold in the mayonnaise. Garnish with a sprig of parsley and serve with potato crisps for dunking.

PICKLED EGGS

6 hard-boiled eggs	1 oz. pickling spice
1 pint white wine or cider vinegar	A small piece of orange peel
6 cloves of garlic, skinned	A piece of mace

Boil all the ingredients (except the eggs) for 10 minutes in a heavy pan with a well-fitting lid. When the mixture is cool, strain it into a wide-mouthed glass jar with a screw-lid or a tight cork. Put in the eggs (shelled but whole) and leave for at least 6 weeks before eating.
More hard-boiled eggs can be added as convenient, but they must always be covered by the liquid.
Serve as a buffet dish or snack, with salad.

LANCASHIRE CHEESE LOG

½ lb. grated Lancashire cheese	1 hard-boiled egg, chopped
1 tsp. chopped chives	½ level tsp. salt and pepper
2 gherkins, chopped	2 tbsps. mayonnaise
¼ tsp. French mustard	2 tsps. top of the milk
2 stuffed olives, chopped	Lettuce to garnish

Mix all the ingredients together, moistening with the mayonnaise and top of the milk. Shape into a roll, wrap in greaseproof paper and chill. Serve sliced, on a bed of lettuce.

RAISIN AND CHEESE PYRAMIDS

4½ oz. seedless raisins	Salt and pepper
4 oz. rice (cooked and drained)	1 small red pepper
	1 egg, lightly beaten
6 oz. grated cheese	

Grease 8 dariole moulds and arrange a layer of seedless raisins in the bottom of each. Mix the rice, cheese and remaining raisins together, with some seasoning. Remove the seeds from the pepper and chop. (If using a fresh pepper, blanch it in boiling water for 5 minutes and drain well.) Stir this and the egg into the rice mixture. Fill the dariole moulds, place on a baking sheet, cover well and bake in a moderate oven (350°F., mark 4) for 30-35 minutes, until set. Allow to get cold and chill if possible. Turn out on to a plate and serve with salad.

SAVOURY CHEESE SLICE

8 oz. self-raising flour	1 small onion, skinned and finely chopped
3 oz. butter or margarine	
5 oz. cheese, grated	4 oz. streaky bacon, chopped
1 egg, beaten	½-1 level tsp. mixed herbs
A little milk (if needed)	Seasoning

Rub 2 oz. of the fat into the flour until it resembles breadcrumbs. Stir in 3 oz. of the cheese, then mix to a fairly soft dough with egg and some milk if necessary. Fry the onion and bacon gently for about 5 minutes in the remaining 1 oz. fat. Divide the dough into 2 pieces and roll out each piece into an 8-inch square. Place one piece on a greased baking sheet, cover with the onion and bacon and sprinkle with the herbs and seasoning. Wet the edges and cover with the second piece of dough, pressing the edges together. Brush with milk and sprinkle with the remaining cheese. Bake towards the top of a fairly hot oven (400°F., mark 6) for about 20 minutes, until crisp and golden. Serve cut in fingers or wedges; you can eat it hot or cold.

Variation: Fry 2-3 skinned and chopped tomatoes with the onion and bacon.

VEGETABLES AND VEGETARIAN RECIPES

Recipes give 4 servings, unless otherwise indicated

Keep vegetables in a cool, airy place—for example, in a vegetable rack placed in a cool larder or in the vegetable compartment of the refrigerator. Green ones should be used as soon as possible after gathering, while their Vitamin C value is at its highest.

Prepare all vegetables as near the time of cooking as possible, to retain both flavour and Vitamin C content.

Serve fried vegetables very hot and don't cover them with a lid or they will become soggy.

Add a knob of butter to boiled and steamed vegetables. A sprinkling of chopped herbs added before serving also improves vegetables—try parsley on carrots, mint on peas, tarragon on courgettes. A little grated nutmeg gives an interesting flavour to cabbage.

A well-flavoured white or cheese sauce makes a change with such vegetables as cauliflower, marrow, leeks and onions, broad beans and carrots.

A platterful of assorted vegetables, arranged in rows or circles, looks attractive and is a good accompaniment to boiled meat. (See colour picture no. 24.)

AN ALPHABET OF VEGETABLES

Artichoke (Jerusalem): Scrub the artichokes; using a stainless knife or peeler, peel quickly and immediately plunge them into cold water, keeping them under water as much as possible to prevent discoloration. A squeeze of lemon juice (or a few drops of vinegar) in the water helps to keep them a good colour. Cook in boiling salted water to which a little lemon juice (or vinegar) has been added, until just soft—about 30 minutes. Drain, garnish with chopped parsley and serve with melted butter or a white, cheese or similar sauce. Allow 6-8 oz. per portion.

Artichokes (Globe): The artichokes should be of a good green colour, with tightly clinging, fleshy leaves—leaves that are spreading, and fuzzy, purplish centres indicate over-maturity. Cut off the stem close to the base of the leaves and take off the outside dry or discoloured leaves. As globe artichokes have close-growing leaves, they need soaking in cold water for about $\frac{1}{2}$ hour, to ensure that they are thoroughly cleaned; drain well. Cook in boiling salted water until the leaves will pull out easily—20-40 minutes, depending on size. Drain upside-down. Serve with melted butter.

Globe artichokes may also be served cold, with a vinaigrette dressing (see Salads chapter).

When eating them, pull off the leaves with the fingers; the soft end of each leaf is dipped in the sauce and sucked. When you reach the centre, remove the choke (or soft flowery part), if it has not already been taken out, and eat the bottom—the chief delicacy—with a knife and fork. Allow 1 artichoke per person.

Asparagus: Cut off the woody end of the stalks and scrape the white part lightly, removing the coarse spines. Tie in bundles with the heads together and place upright in a pan of boiling salted water. Boil for 10 minutes, then lay them flat and cook until just soft—a further 10-15 minutes. Don't over-cook asparagus —the tips should not be mushy. Drain and untie before serving with melted butter.

Asparagus may also be served cold, with a vinaigrette dressing or mayonnaise.

To eat, hold a stick by the stem end and dip the tip in the butter or sauce. It is not usual to eat the stem end.

Allow 8-12 stems per serving.

Aubergine or Egg Plant: Aubergines should be of a uniform purple colour, firm, smooth and free from blemishes. Cut off the stem, wash the vegetables and if necessary peel them. Aubergines are usually fried or stuffed and baked.

Allow about 6 oz. per serving.

Beans (Broad): Shell beans and cook in boiling salted water until soft—20-30 minutes. If liked, serve with parsley sauce. When the beans are very young and tender the whole pods may be washed, cooked and eaten.

Allow $\frac{1}{2}$-$\frac{3}{4}$ lb. (weight as bought) per serving.

Beans (French and Runner): Top, tail and string the beans. Slice runners thinly; French beans may be left whole. Cook in boiling salted water until soft—15-20 minutes. Remove any scum that rises during cooking. Drain and toss with salt and pepper and a knob of butter.

Allow $\frac{1}{4}$-$\frac{1}{2}$ lb. per serving.

Beetroot: Cut off the stalks 1 inch or so above the root, then wash the beetroots, taking care not to damage the skin or they will "bleed" when boiled. Boil in salted water until soft—the time depends on age and freshness, but 2 hours is the average. Peel off the skin and slice or cube. Serve hot, coated with a white sauce, or cold, sliced and in a little vinegar.

The cooking time may be much reduced if the beets are peeled and sliced and then cooked until tender in a very little water in a covered pan, the liquid being used to make a sauce; the time varies, but is about $\frac{1}{2}$ hour.

Allow 4-6 oz. per serving when served as a vegetable.

Broccoli: There are several varieties of this vegetable, the chief being:

White broccoli, with a fairly large flower head, which is cooked and served in the same way as cauliflower. Buy by the head, judging by size.

Purple broccoli and Calabrese (a green sprouting broccoli), with a more delicate flavour. Cook like cauliflower,

allowing 15-20 minutes. Serve plain, or with melted butter sauce.

Allow 6-8 oz. per serving.

Brussels Sprouts: Wash the sprouts, removing discoloured leaves, and cut a cross in the stalks. Cook in boiling salted water until soft—10-20 minutes—drain, return them to the pan and re-heat with a knob of butter and salt and pepper.

Allow 4-6 oz. per serving.

Cabbage—Green, Red, Kale, Greens: Remove coarse outer leaves, cut the cabbage in half and take out the hard centre stalk. Wash thoroughly, shred finely and cook rapidly in about 1 inch of boiling salted water for 15-20 minutes, or until cooked. For red cabbage add 1 tbsp. vinegar to the water. Drain well and toss with a knob of butter, a sprinkling of pepper and a pinch of grated nutmeg (optional).

Allow 4 oz. per serving.

Carrots, New: Trim off the leaves, then scrape lightly with a sharp knife. Small new carrots are usually cooked whole. Simmer in salted water for about 15 minutes, or until cooked. Serve tossed with a little butter, pepper and chopped parsley. *Old:* Peel thinly, cut up, cook and serve as above, but simmer for about 20 minutes.

Allow 4-6 oz. per serving.

Cauliflower: Remove the coarse outer leaves, cut a cross in the stalk end and wash the cauliflower. Cook stem side down in fast-boiling salted water for 20-30 minutes, depending on size. Drain well and serve coated with white or cheese sauce.

Cauliflower can also be divided into florets and cooked as above for about 15 minutes; drain and serve tossed with butter and a sprinkling of pepper, or with sauce.

A medium-sized cauliflower serves 4 people.

Celeriac (The root of turnip-rooted celery): Peel fairly thickly; small roots may be cooked whole, but larger ones are sliced thickly or diced. Cook in boiling salted water or stock until soft—1 hour or longer. Drain well and serve with melted butter or white sauce.

Allow $\frac{1}{4}$-$\frac{1}{2}$ lb. per serving.

Celery: Wash, scrub and cut into even lengths. Cook in boiling salted water until tender—$\frac{1}{2}$-1 hour, depending on its coarseness. Drain well and serve with a white parsley or cheese sauce.

Allow 1 head of celery per serving if small, 2-3 sticks if really large.

Chicory (Succory): To prepare, cut off a thin slice from the base; using a pointed knife, remove the core. Pull away any damaged outer leaves and wash quickly under

100

cold water—don't soak. To cook, put into boiling salted water with a little lemon juice added and cook gently for about 20 minutes. Serve plain or with a cheese or tomato sauce.

Allow 1-2 heads per serving.

Corn on the Cob: Choose cobs which are plump, well formed and of a pale golden-yellow colour and use them while still really fresh. Remove the outside leaves and silky threads, put the cobs into boiling unsalted water (salt toughens them) and cook for 12-20 minutes, depending on size, but don't overcook, which also makes them tough. Drain well and serve with melted butter, salt and freshly-ground pepper.

Allow 1-2 cobs per serving.

Courgettes: These are a variety of small vegetable marrow, normally cooked unpeeled, either left whole or cut in rounds. They may be boiled (allow 15-20 minutes), steamed or fried and are served with melted butter and chopped parsley or tarragon.

Allow $\frac{1}{4}$ lb. per serving.

Leeks: Remove the coarse outer leaves and cut off the roots and tops. Wash the leeks very well, splitting them down the centre to within 1 inch or so of the base, to ensure that all grit is removed; if necessary, cut them right through. Cook in boiling salted water until soft—20-30 minutes. Drain very thoroughly. Serve coated with a white or cheese sauce.

Allow 1-3 leeks ($\frac{1}{2}$-$\frac{3}{4}$ lb.) per serving, according to the amount of waste.

Marrow: Large ones must be peeled; the seeds are removed and the flesh cut in even-sized pieces. Cook in boiling salted water until soft—about 20 minutes—and drain well. Serve coated with a white or cheese sauce. Marrow can also be roasted in the dripping round the meat or stuffed and baked—either whole or in thick rings.

Allow 6 oz. per portion when cooked unstuffed.

Mushrooms: Most of the mushrooms bought today are cultivated and require only washing and draining before being used. Cut off the earthy end of each stalk—the rest of the stalk can be included in the dish or as an ingredient in stuffing. Field mushrooms need skinning and should be well washed.

Allow 1-3 oz. per serving, depending on whether the mushrooms are to be used as a garnish or vegetable.

Onions: These vary considerably in both size and flavour. Shallots are smaller than the average true onion, but have a stronger flavour. Spanish onions are larger but milder than English ones. Skin and trim, cut up if desired and cook in boiling salted water for 30-45 minutes. Drain and use as required. Onions may also be fried, braised and stuffed and baked.

Allow 4-6 oz. per serving.

Parsnips: Wash, peel, quarter and remove the hard centre core. Cut in slices, strips or dice and leave in water until required for cooking. Cook in boiling salted water for 30-40 minutes, until soft. Drain and toss in butter, salt and pepper, with a little grated nutmeg if liked. To roast parsnips, par-boil for 5 minutes in salted water, drain and put in the fat round the joint for 1 hour.

Allow 6-8 oz. per serving.

Peas: The season for fresh peas lasts for about 6 weeks only, but they are sold preserved in various ways— canned, bottled, dried, dehydrated and frozen. De- hydrated and frozen peas are very similar to fresh when properly cooked and presented—follow the directions on the packet.

Allow, for one serving, 8 oz. fresh peas (as bought), 2-3 oz. canned, frozen, etc.

To cook fresh peas, shell, wash, place in boiling salted water with about 1 level tsp. sugar and a sprig of mint and cook until tender—20-30 minutes. Drain, remove the mint and if liked toss the peas with a knob of butter. For Petis Pois (a particularly small, sweet type of pea much used on the Continent), cook with the addition of a little chopped onion and some butter.

Potatoes: Peel as thinly as possible, using either a special peeler or a sharp, short-bladed knife. New potatoes are scraped or brushed. Cook potatoes as soon as you can after peeling or scraping; if it is necessary let them stand for a while, keep them under water, to prevent discolora- tion. Cook in boiling salted water for 15-30 minutes; drain and finish as desired. (See potato recipes pp. 102-3.)

Allow 6-8 oz. per portion.

Spinach: Wash well in several waters to remove all grit, and strip off any coarse stalks. Pack into a saucepan with only the water that clings to the leaves. Heat gently, turning the spinach occasionally, then bring to the boil and cook gently until soft—10-15 minutes. Drain well and re-heat with butter and seasoning.

Allow $\frac{1}{2}$ lb. per serving.

Swedes, Turnips: Peel thickly and put under water to prevent discoloration. Swedes are cut up. Young turnips can be left whole, but older ones are sliced or diced. Cook in boiling salted water, allowing 30-60 minutes for swedes, 20-30 for turnips. Swedes and older turnips are usually mashed with butter and seasoning. Whole turnips may be tossed in butter or a little top of the milk, with seasoning, or served in a white sauce.

Allow 4-6 oz. per serving.

CANNED, FROZEN AND DEHYDRATED VEGETABLES

There is a wide and ever-increasing selection of these products, and most people find it convenient to keep some canned (or bottled) and dehydrated kinds in store for emergency use. They require practically no time for preparation, cook quickly (follow the directions on the container) and may be used in many ways to make either accompaniments or main dishes.

Here are a few quick ways of presenting some of the most popular of these prepared vegetables:

Peas: Cook and serve with chopped skinned tomatoes and spring onions which have been lightly fried in butter. Alternatively, cook some chopped celery in $1\frac{1}{2}$ inches of water until tender, add a packet of peas and cook for a further 5 minutes.

Peas and Carrots: Add to the cooked vegetables a chopped onion which has been fried in butter.

Cut Green Beans: Slice 2 oz. mushrooms, fry in butter and add to the cooked beans.

Sliced Green Beans: Add some crisply fried bacon and chopped cooked onion to the cooked beans.

Broad Beans: Add the cooked beans to a cheese sauce, sprinkle with grated cheese and brown under the grill.

Spinach: Add horseradish sauce to the cooked spinach.

Broccoli: Fry some chives or grated onion in a little butter, add a few drops of lemon juice and pour over the broccoli. Top with toasted shredded almonds.

Sweet Corn: Cook, and add 2 tbsps. double cream.

VEGETABLE RECIPES

POTATOES WITH ONIONS

2 lb. potatoes   1 pint stock
2 large onions   A little butter
Pepper and salt

Wash and peel the potatoes, halve lengthways, then cut across into slices about ½ inch thick. Slice the onions. Grease a fireproof casserole and put in alternate layers of potato and onion, finishing with potato. Sprinkle with pepper and salt, add the stock and put knobs of butter on top. Bring to the boil, cover with greased paper and cook in a moderate oven (350°F., mark 4) for 1-1½ hours.

POTATO MATCHES
(see picture above)

Peel some potatoes, slice and cut in thin fingers. Dry them in a tea towel. Heat some deep fat or oil in a pan till a faint blue haze rises, place a few "matches" in the frying basket, gently lower this into the fat and cook until the potatoes are golden-brown. Lift out the basket, tap it lightly on the edge of the pan to shake off the surplus fat, and turn the potato matches on to crumpled absorbent paper to drain. Repeat until all the potato matches are cooked.

CREAMY JACKET POTATOES

4 potatoes   Salt, pepper and
Butter   nutmeg
2 egg yolks   Parsley
3-4 tbsps. cream

Scrub the potatoes well, prick them and bake slowly till soft. Cut a hole in each and remove the inside, using a small spoon. Sieve the potato, and mix with a generous amount of butter, the egg yolks and the cream. Season, add grated nutmeg to taste and return the mixture to the potato cases. Dot with shavings of butter and bake in a moderate oven (350°F., mark 4) till golden on top. Garnish with parsley.
Alternatively, the potatoes may be stuffed with tomatoes or chopped fried mushrooms.

BAKED CHEESE POTATOES

4 large potatoes   Seasoning
4 tbsps. hot milk   A little butter
4 oz. grated cheese   Paprika and parsley

Wash and scrub the potatoes, prick several times and bake in a moderate oven (350°F., mark 4) until well cooked—1½-2 hours. Cut in half lengthwise and scoop out the centre, leaving the skins intact. Put the potato in a basin and work with a fork till free from lumps. Add milk, most of the cheese, and seasoning to taste. Mix until blended, then fill the potato shells with the mixture. Sprinkle the rest of the cheese on top, brush over lightly with a little melted butter and brown in the oven. Sprinkle with paprika before serving, and garnish with parsley.
Alternatively, cut a cross in each potato after baking and add seasoning and a piece of soft cheese—see picture on page 203.

POTATOES DAUPHINE
(see picture above)

¾ lb. cooked potatoes   1-2 eggs
1½ oz. butter   Seasoning
¼ pint water   Fat for frying
2½ oz. flour   Fried parsley

Sieve the potatoes. Melt the butter, add the water and bring to the boil, then toss in the flour and mix well, until the mixture forms a ball. Beat in the eggs to give a soft mixture and finally beat in the sieved potato and season to taste. Heat some fat until it is smoking hot, drop in spoonfuls of mixture and fry until golden. Serve very hot, with parsley. (Serves 3-4.)

LYONNAISE POTATOES

1½ lb. potatoes   Seasoning
Butter   ½ lb. chopped onions

Boil the potatoes in their skins, peel and leave to become almost cool. Slice them thinly and toss them in a pan with some very hot butter, adding the salt and pepper. When the potatoes are beginning to colour, add the onions. Continue cooking until the potatoes and onions are all golden-brown.

POMMES ANNA

Wash and peel 4 large potatoes, slice them thinly and
dry in a cloth. Butter a round cake tin or a small baking
tin and arrange the potatoes in it in layers, with 1 oz.
butter and seasonings between the layers; fill the mould
two-thirds full. Put 1 oz. butter on top and bake in a
fairly hot oven (375°F., mark 5) for about 1 hour. Test
by inserting a skewer; when the potatoes are soft and
brown, turn them out onto the serving dish and garnish
with sprigs of parsley.

DUCHESSE POTATOES

1 lb. cooked potatoes	1 tbsp. cream or milk
1 oz. butter	Salt and pepper
1 egg	

Sieve the potatoes. Melt the butter in a saucepan, add
the potatoes, and when warm add the beaten egg yolk
and cream; season well and mix thoroughly. Put the
mixture into a forcing bag with a large star nozzle and
pipe on to a greased tin in rosettes or other shapes, as
desired. Glaze with beaten egg, and brown in a hot oven
(425°F., mark 7) for about 10-15 minutes.

ARTICHOKES WITH
VINAIGRETTE SAUCE

Allow one globe artichoke per person. Trim the stalk
and cut the ends of the coarse outside leaves with
scissors and wash the vegetables. Boil in salted water for
about ½ hour (or until the outer leaves will tear off easily),
remove from the water and turn upside-down to drain.
Pull out the centre in one piece and remove the "choke".
Replace the centre, and decorate with parsley. Serve hot
or cold, with vinaigrette sauce.

ASPARAGUS WITH EGG SAUCE

Cut off the woody ends of the asparagus, lightly scrape
away any coarse spines, and tie in bundles. Place upright
in a pan of boiling salted water and boil for 10 minutes,
then lay the bundles flat and cook until tender—a further
10-15 minutes. Drain and untie the bundles. Meanwhile
pipe some creamed potato in the base of an ovenproof
dish and keep warm. Arrange the asparagus on top, pour
½ pint egg sauce over and re-heat in the oven. Sieve hard-
boiled egg yolk over the sauce to garnish.

AUBERGINES À LA PROVENÇALE

2 aubergines	1 onion, chopped
Seasoning	2 oz. fresh white
1 oz. butter	breadcrumbs
4 small tomatoes,	2 oz. grated cheese
skinned	Parsley sprigs and baked
1 shallot, chopped	tomatoes to garnish

Do not peel the aubergines, but wipe them and steam or
boil for about ½ hour; when they are tender, cut them in
half lengthways, scoop out the flesh, chop and season.
Heat the fat in a pan and sauté the tomatoes, shallot and
onion. Lastly, add the aubergine flesh and a few breadcrumbs. Stuff the aubergine cases with this, sprinkle with
breadcrumbs and then with grated cheese. Grill till
golden-brown on top and serve garnished with parsley
and baked tomatoes.

SAUTÉED CAULIFLOWER

Cook a cauliflower in boiling salted water till almost
tender. Break off the sprigs and sauté them in 2 oz.
melted butter till golden-brown (toss rather than stir,
to prevent the sprigs from breaking). Arrange on a dish
in the cauliflower shape. Sieve 2 hard-boiled eggs and
chop 1 tbsp. parsley and sprinkle these over the cauliflower. Sauté 2 tbsps. fresh white breadcrumbs in 2 oz.
butter and when hot pour over the cauliflower.

CELERIAC WITH CHEESE SAUCE

Peel a celeriac and cut into slices about ⅛ inch in thickness. Boil in salted water until tender—about 15 minutes
—then drain well. Make some cheese sauce, put a little
in the bottom of an ovenproof dish and arrange the slices
of celeriac on top. Add the rest of the sauce, sprinkle
with grated cheese and brown in the oven.

BUTTERED COURGETTES
(see picture above)

Leave the courgettes (small young marrows) whole,
and parboil them in salted water for 5 minutes, then
drain. Put them in a casserole with 2 oz. melted butter,
cover and cook in a cool oven (300°F., mark 1) till
tender—about 20 minutes—turning them occasionally
while cooking. Serve sprinkled with salt, pepper and
chopped parsley.

BELTED CELERY

4 heads of celery	½ pint milk
4 rashers of bacon	1 tbsp. chopped parsley
1 oz. butter	Salt and pepper
1 oz. flour	Grated cheese

Trim the celery, tie together to prevent splitting and parboil. Drain well, untie and wrap a piece of rinded bacon round each, then lay them in an ovenproof dish. Melt the butter and add the flour, gradually stir in the milk (or milk and celery stock) and add the parsley; season well and pour over the celery. Bake in a moderate oven (350°F., mark 4) for ½ hour; sprinkle with cheese.

BELGIAN CUCUMBER

4 small cucumbers	¼ pint mayonnaise
2 egg yolks	Chopped dill
½ pint yoghourt	

Peel the cucumbers, cut into 2-inch lengths and cook in fast-boiling salted water until tender (about 10 minutes). Drain, and arrange in a hot dish. Beat the egg yolks, mix with the yoghourt and the mayonnaise and warm gently without boiling. Pour over the cucumber and sprinkle with chopped dill.

STUFFED MARROW

A 3-lb. marrow	Salt and pepper
6 oz. rice	A pinch of dried thyme
2 onions, sliced	4 hard-boiled eggs, chopped
2 oz. butter	Baked tomatoes, baked
½ a red pepper, sliced	potatoes and onion-
¼ lb. mushrooms, sliced	flavoured gravy to serve
1 tsp. chopped parsley	

Wash the marrow, then put it into a greased baking tin with a little water. Cover with greased paper and bake in moderate oven (350°F., mark 4) till tender (¾ hour). Meanwhile boil rice for ¼ hour and drain it. Fry the onions in the butter till golden-brown, then add the red pepper and mushrooms and cook for several minutes. Add the onions, pepper, mushrooms and parsley to the rice, with the seasoning and herbs, and mix lightly together. Lastly, add the hard-boiled eggs. When the marrow is tender, remove a portion of the top for a lid, scoop out the seeds and fill up the centre with the rice mixture. Top with the lid and serve with baked tomatoes, baked potatoes or other vegetables, and onion-flavoured gravy. (Serves 4-6.)

MARROW WITH CHEESE SAUCE

Peel a marrow, cut in half lengthways, scoop out the seeds and cut the flesh into cubes. Put into a greased casserole, season, but do not add any liquid; cover with a round of greased paper, then cover with the lid. Cook in a cool oven (300°F., mark 1) for about 1 hour. When the marrow cubes are tender, toss them lightly in the sauce.

STUFFED ONIONS

(see picture above)

4 large onions	2 oz. chopped walnuts
4 oz. grated carrot	4 tbsps. double cream
3 oz. grated cheese	Seasoning

Cook the onions in salted water for ½-¾ hour, scoop out the centres and chop them. Mix the carrot, 2 oz. of the cheese and the walnuts with the chopped onion and the double cream. Season to taste. Fill the onion shells with this mixture, sprinkle the remaining grated cheese on top, and bake in a moderate oven (350°F., mark 4) for about 30 minutes. Serve with French beans and parsley sauce.

SPICED RED CABBAGE

1 small red cabbage	2 cooking apples, peeled,
A little butter	cored and sliced
¼ pint water	1 oz. sugar
3 cloves	2 tbsps. lemon juice
Salt	

Remove the outer leaves of the cabbage, halve it, remove the core, then wash it and shred very finely. Put a little butter and the water in a saucepan. Add the cabbage, cloves, salt to taste and the apples. Cover the saucepan closely and simmer for ¾ hour. Add a little more butter, the sugar and lemon juice, and simmer for another 5 minutes before serving.

CASSEROLED VEGETABLES

RATATOUILLE

(see picture above)

4 tomatoes	$\frac{1}{4}$ a cucumber
2 aubergines	2 tbsps. oil
1 small green pepper	1 oz. butter
2 onions	Seasoning
1 small marrow or 3	1 clove of garlic
courgettes	Chopped parsley

Skin and slice the tomatoes. Wipe and slice the aubergines. Prepare and slice the pepper, removing the seeds. Skin and slice the onions. Peel the marrow (but not courgettes, if used) and slice. Slice the cucumber. Heat the oil and butter in a flameproof casserole and add the vegetables, seasoning and crushed garlic. Stir well, cover tightly and cook in a moderate oven (350°F., mark 4) for 1-1$\frac{1}{2}$ hours, or until tender. Serve with parsley.

MUSHROOM CASSEROLE

$\frac{3}{4}$ lb. mushrooms	1 sheep's kidney
3 tomatoes	(optional)
1 onion	Salt and pepper
1 oz. butter or	1 tbsp. chopped parsley
dripping	4 tbsps. stock or water

Grease a casserole. Wash and slice the mushrooms, skin and slice the tomatoes and cut the onion in rings, then fry in the fat until golden-brown. Cut up the kidney. Fill the dish with alternate layers of kidney and vegetables, seasoning well. Sprinkle with the parsley and finish with a layer of mushrooms. Add the liquid and stew gently in a moderate oven (350°F., mark 4) until tender—about 30 minutes. Pack the ingredients closely to allow for shrinkage during cooking.

CASSEROLED POTATOES

1$\frac{1}{2}$ lb. potatoes	4 oz. butter
2 onions	Paprika and chopped
Salt and pepper	parsley to garnish

Peel the potatoes and slice thinly. Peel the onions and chop finely. Butter a casserole dish and place a layer of potatoes in the bottom, cover with a little onion, season well and dot with butter. Continue adding layers in this way until the dish is filled, finishing with potatoes. Cover with buttered greaseproof paper and bake in a fairly hot oven (400°F., mark 6) for about 45 minutes, or until the potatoes are tender. Sprinkle with paprika and parsley.

VEGETABLE MACARONI CASSEROLE

(see picture above)

$\frac{1}{2}$ lb. carrots	Seasoning
A small turnip	$\frac{1}{4}$ pint tomato juice
2 stalks of celery	2 oz. macaroni
2 leeks	4 tbsps. chopped parsley
2 tomatoes	Fried onion rings to
1 rasher of bacon	garnish
1 oz. dripping	Grated cheese as
1 clove of garlic	accompaniment

Cut up the vegetables and dice the bacon. Heat the fat and sauté first the bacon then the vegetables for 10 minutes. Transfer to a casserole, add the crushed garlic, seasoning and tomato juice and cook in a moderate oven (350°F., mark 4) for 1 hour. Meanwhile cook the macaroni; add with the parsley to the casserole and top with onion. Serve with cheese.

VICHY CARROTS

2 oz. fat	Seasoning
2-3 tbsps. water	A little single cream
1 lb. young carrots	Chopped parsley

Melt the fat in a casserole, add the water and sliced carrots, cover and cook in a moderate oven (350°F., mark 4) for $\frac{3}{4}$-1 hour, until the carrots are tender and the liquid absorbed. Toss in cream and parsley before serving.

BRAISED CELERY

Trim 4 celery hearts and place in a greased casserole with 2 oz. butter. Add a dash of lemon juice and $\frac{1}{2}$ pint stock, cover with greased paper and the lid and cook in a warm oven (325°F., mark 3) until the celery is tender—about 1 hour. Place it on a hot serving dish. If necessary reduce the liquor by boiling, then pour over the celery.

PRESSURE-COOKED VEGETABLES

Vegetables cooked in a pressure pan retain flavour and colour and keep their valuable vitamin and mineral content. Pressure cooking is particularly suitable for root vegetables. Watch these points to obtain good results:
1. Choose vegetables of about the same size, or cut large ones into small, even-sized pieces.
2. Cook at 15 lb. pressure.
3. Time accurately—an extra minute may cause vegetables to be over-cooked: as they vary in size, age and toughness, the times quoted can only be a general guide.
4. Use the rack or separators, unless the vegetables are included as part of a meat dish.
5. Pour $\frac{1}{4}$-$\frac{1}{2}$ pint water into the pan—sufficient to reach the level of the rack—before putting vegetables in; do not add green vegetables until the water is boiling.
6. Season lightly, sprinkling salt over the food.
7. Bring quickly to pressure, and reduce pressure quickly.
8. Use the vegetable stock left in the cooker for making soups, sauces or gravies.
Vegetables with the same cooking times may be cooked together; stand them on the rack in separate piles, or wrap each kind in greaseproof paper or aluminium foil. (Allow an extra $\frac{1}{4}$ pint water if paper is used, as this is absorbent.) If your pan is fitted with separators, use these to keep the vegetables apart. When the cooking times differ, put the vegetables needing the longest time in the pan first, and reduce the pressure part way through the cooking to insert those taking a shorter time; e.g. potatoes take 10 minutes and leeks 3 minutes, so reduce the pressure after 7 minutes to put in the leeks. Sometimes the cooking times can be made the same by leaving some vegetables whole and cutting those that take longer into smaller pieces.
Prepare and serve vegetables as described on pp. 99-101.

Artichokes (Globe): Place on rack with water and a little salt and pressure-cook for 10 minutes. Reduce pressure immediately.

Artichokes (Jerusalem): Put on rack, with water, season and pressure-cook for 8-10 minutes.

Asparagus: When water is boiling stand vegetable on rack and add a little salt. Pressure-cook for 2-3 minutes.

Beans (Broad): Place on rack with boiling water and a little salt and pressure-cook for 2-3 minutes.

Beans (French): Place on rack with boiling water and a little salt and pressure-cook for 3 minutes.

Beans (Runner): Place on rack with boiling water and add salt, then pressure-cook for 2-3 minutes, according to maturity of beans.

Beetroot: Place on rack with a little salt and 1 pint water and pressure-cook for 10-35 minutes, according to age and size.

Brussels Sprouts: When water is boiling, put them on rack, season and pressure-cook for 3-4 minutes.

Carrots: Pressure-cook for 2-10 minutes, according to size and age. Young whole carrots take 4-5 minutes; old ones, if diced about 2 minutes, if sliced 2-3 minutes,

if halved or quartered 5 minutes, if whole 8-10 minutes.

Cauliflower: When water is boiling, put vegetable on rack and season. Whole cauliflowers take 5-6 minutes, depending on size and maturity; sprigs 3 minutes.

Celery: When water is boiling, put celery on rack and season. Pressure-cook for 2-3 minutes.

Corn on the Cob: Add water and a little salt and pressure-cook for 4 minutes.

Green Vegetables (Cabbage, Greens, etc.): When water is boiling, add salt and pressure-cook for 1-3 minutes.

Leeks: Put on rack with boiling water and a little salt and pressure-cook for 3 minutes.

Mushrooms: Put on rack, add water and pressure-cook for 3-4 minutes.

Onions: Olace on rack with some salt and water and pressure-cook for 3-4 minutes in the case of sliced or quartered onions, 10 minutes for whole ones.

Parsnips: If halved lengthwise, they take 7-8 minutes' pressure-cooking; if sliced, 3-4 minutes.

Peas (Green): When the water boils, place the peas on the rack with a sprig of mint. Pressure-cook for 1-2 minutes.

Potatoes: Place on the rack or in a separator and add water and seasoning. Pressure-cook as follows:
    In jackets: 12 minutes
    Peeled, medium-sized: 8-10 minutes
    Peeled and quartered: 4-5 minutes
    New (add mint): 6-8 minutes.

Mashed Potatoes: Melt a little butter in the pan, add $\frac{1}{4}$ pint milk for every $1\frac{1}{2}$ lb. potatoes, with seasoning to taste, and put in the potatoes, cut in small pieces. Pressure-cook for 3-6 minutes, according to size, then mash them in the pan.

Spinach: Place on rack when water boils, season and pressure-cook for 1-2 minutes.

Swedes and Turnips: Place on rack, add water and a little salt and pressure-cook for 4-5 minutes.

Tomatoes: Stand them on the rack, with water, and pressure-cook for 1-2 minutes.

Vegetable Marrow: Put on the rack, add water and some salt, and pressure-cook for 3-4 minutes.

Braised Vegetables: The most suitable kinds are carrots, turnips, parsnips, celery and onions. For every 1 lb. of vegetables, place 1 oz. dripping in the pressure pan and sauté the vegetables over a low heat until the fat has been absorbed. Add $\frac{1}{2}$ pint brown stock and pressure-cook for the time required by the various vegetables. Before serving, thicken the stock with $\frac{1}{2}$ oz. cornflour to $\frac{1}{2}$ pint liquid, or reduce it by boiling in an open pan.

Dried Vegetables: Before cooking, soak dried and split peas, butter beans and haricot beans (but not lentils) for 1-2 hours, or overnight, in boiling water; discard this water. Put the vegetables straight into the pan, without using the rack, and add 2 pints cold water and 2 level tsps. salt for every 1 lb. Never fill the pan more than half-full, as dried vegetables swell during cooking. Bring slowly to 15 lb. pressure and cook butter and haricot beans and peas for 15-20 minutes, split peas and lentils for 10-15 minutes. Reduce the pressure gradually.

VEGETARIAN DISHES

CHICORY AND RICE
(see picture above)

4 heads of chicory	2 tbsps. rice (uncooked)
2 oz. butter	Chopped parsley or
Stock	grated cheese
Seasoning	

Wash the chicory and cut in half lengthways, or leave whole if small. Melt the fat, add the chicory and cook for a few minutes, then half-cover with stock, season, put on a tightly-fitting lid and simmer for 10 minutes. Add the rice and cook until this is soft and almost all the liquor absorbed. Sprinkle with parsley or cheese.

SAVOURY PANCAKES

2 oz. flour	$\frac{1}{4}$ lb. mushrooms, sliced
A pinch of salt	4 tbsps. cooked peas
$\frac{1}{2}$ an egg	2 tbsps. white sauce
$\frac{1}{4}$ pint milk	Fat for frying
4 hard-boiled eggs	

Make the batter by mixing the flour, salt, egg and milk together. Make the filling by mixing the chopped eggs and mushrooms, peas and sauce. Put some fat in a frying pan, pour in a little batter, and cook on both sides: keep hot on a plate over boiling water. Continue adding fat and batter to the pan till all the batter is used and 6 pancakes have been made. Put a little filling in the centre of each pancake and fold over in three. Serve hot, with baked potatoes and a sauce. (Serves 3.)

NUTTY STUFFED TOMATOES

4 large tomatoes	1 tsp. chopped fresh
1 cup fresh white	mint
breadcrumbs	1 egg
2 oz. ground walnuts	Seasoning
2 tsps. raw onion, grated	Butter
2 tsps. chopped parsley	

Cut off a small round from the top of each tomato and reserve it for a lid. Scoop out the inside of the tomatoes and mix with the breadcrumbs, walnuts, onion and herbs. Bind with the egg, season, fill the tomatoes and dot each with a little butter. Put on the lid of each, put them on a greased baking tray and cover with some greased paper. Bake in a moderate oven (350°F., mark 4) for 15-20 minutes.

MUSHROOM RING
(see picture above)

2 oz. butter	2 eggs
1 small onion, chopped	2 oz. grated cheese
8 oz. mushrooms, sliced	2 tbsps. cream or top of
Salt and pepper	the milk
Grated nutmeg	Finely chopped parsley
2 oz. flour	Spaghetti in tomato sauce
$\frac{1}{4}$ pint milk	as accompaniment

Melt the butter and fry the onion and the mushrooms (reserving 1-2 whole ones for garnishing) for 5 minutes. Add salt, pepper and nutmeg. Gently stir in the flour, add the milk and continue stirring until the mixture comes to the boil. Remove from the heat, add the beaten eggs, cheese and cream, turn mixture into a greased ring mould and bake in a moderate oven (350°F., mark 4) for $\frac{1}{2}$ hour, or until firm. Gently turn out onto a warm dish, garnish with parsley and fried mushrooms and serve with the hot spaghetti. (Incidentally, if you do not require it as a strictly vegetarian dish, you can garnish the ring with fried or grilled bacon rolls.) Mushroom Ring is also delicious served cold, with salad.

VEGETABLE PIE

A variety of cooked	Beaten egg or milk
vegetables	Pepper and salt
1 pint cheese sauce	Grated cheese
2 lb. sieved cooked potato	Mushrooms or tomatoes
2 oz. butter	for garnish

Cook the vegetables till tender, and make the sauce, then put vegetables and sauce in layers in a dish. Mix the potato with the butter, egg and seasoning, and spread on top of the vegetables. Sprinkle with a little grated cheese and brown in the oven. Garnish with mushrooms or tomatoes. (Serves 6.)

CHEESE AND LEEK PIE

6 oz. shortcrust pastry (see p. 140)	Seasoned flour
	4 oz. grated cheese
2-3 leeks, parboiled and cut into rounds	2 tbsps. top of the milk
	Egg to glaze

Line a pie plate with the pastry. Put the leeks on the pastry and sprinkle with a little seasoned flour. Cover with the grated cheese and add the milk. Roll out the rest of the pastry and cut into strips, plait these lattice-fashion over the top, brush with beaten egg, and bake in a hot oven (425°F., mark 7) for about 30 minutes.

CHEESE AND EGG PIE

½ lb. shortcrust pastry (see p. 140)	¼ lb. mushrooms or tomatoes
1 pint cheese sauce	2 oz. grated cheese
4 hard-boiled eggs	

Make a flan case with the shortcrust pastry and bake it 'blind'. Make the cheese sauce and add the quartered hard-boiled eggs. Lightly fry the mushrooms (or skin and chop the tomatoes) and add to the sauce. Put the mixture into the pastry case, sprinkle the grated cheese on top and brown in a hot oven or under the grill.

CELERY HOTPOT
(see picture above)

A head of celery	1 level tsp. seasoned flour
2½ oz. butter	¼ pint vegetable stock
4 tomatoes, skinned and quartered	6 oz. self-raising flour
	A pinch of salt
2 onions, finely chopped	Cold water to mix
	Wedges of cheese

Prepare the celery, melt ½ oz. of butter and fry the tomatoes and onions for about 10 minutes, then add seasoned flour and stock. Place in a casserole or other suitable dish, and continue to cook for a further 15 minutes. To make the biscuit crust for the top, rub the rest of the butter into the flour, add the salt and mix with cold water to a soft dough. Roll out lightly on a floured board to about ½ inch in thickness, cut into rounds and place on top of the vegetables. Bake the hot-pot in a hot oven (425°F., mark 7) until the crust is golden-brown—20-30 minutes. Just before the end of the baking, add the wedges of cheese.

BRAISED BEANS

½ lb. haricot beans	Seasoned stock
½ clove of garlic, crushed	1 lb. vegetarian sausages
	Chopped parsley
3 tomatoes, sliced	Chutney
4 oz. mushrooms, sliced	French mustard

Wash the beans, drain, cover with water and leave to soak overnight. Mix the beans, garlic, tomatoes and mushrooms. Add enough stock to cover, and cook in a cool oven (300°F., mark 1) for 3-4 hours, until the beans are tender. Stir occasionally and if necessary add a little more stock: when the dish is cooked, most of the liquid should be absorbed. Bake or fry the sausages and arrange on top of the savoury beans. Garnish with chopped parsley, and serve accompanied by chutney and French mustard.

VEGETABLE DUMPLING

Make 8 oz. cheese suetcrust pastry (see below) and use two-thirds of it to line a greased basin. Chop up a variety of cooked vegetables (e.g. carrots, turnips, parsnips, onions, mushrooms, cauliflower and French beans) and moisten with ½ pint cheese sauce. Put this mixture inside the pastry case and cover with remaining pastry. Cover with greased paper and steam for 2½-3 hours in a pan, with boiling water coming half-way up the basin. Turn out and serve with tomato sauce and small whole carrots.

CHEESE SUETCRUST PASTRY

8 oz. flour	4 oz. grated cheese
A pinch of salt	2 oz. grated suet sub-
1 level tsp. baking powder	stitute
	Cold water to mix

Make the pastry as usual, combining the dry ingredients and adding water to give a soft, elastic dough. Use as desired, e.g. for Vegetable Dumpling above.

SALADS

Recipes give 4 servings, unless otherwise indicated

There are thousands of variations on the salad theme, and plenty of scope for people who enjoy creating recipes or who have artistic flair.

Salads are truly international and we offer here a collection of recipes from all round the world.

From the health point of view salads have much to offer. Since the ingredients are mostly used uncooked and very fresh, their vitamin C value is retained; when the salad is coupled with a protein food such as eggs, cheese, fish or meat, it makes a very nutritious meal. Salads appeal particularly to those on a slimming diet, as the number of calories in the various ingredients is usually low.

Even the best of salads is improved by a good dressing, so we devote a section to salad dressings, with many variations. Remember not to use too much dressing; no surplus should be seen at the bottom of the bowl— there should be just sufficient clinging to the salad ingredients to flavour them appetisingly. A salad intended to accompany a main dish is usually tossed in a simple French dressing. Heartier salads, with mayonnaise or another rich dressing, may be served at a less formal lunch, dinner or supper, where the chief course is not very substantial, or they may indeed form the main course.

Lettuce and other Greenstuff: In this country we tend to include lettuce in almost every salad, and to think of it as the only ingredient for a green salad. The cabbage type is the one most commonly used, since it is available for many months of the year, and is better for tossed salads. However, the distinctive flavour of the long, slender cos lettuce lends extra interest to some salads, while Canadians and Americans also use a crisp lettuce called Iceberg. (Incidentally, they call our cos lettuce Romaine.) Other green ingredients well worth including are:

Endive and Chicory: (which we bracket because there is some confusion between the English and French use of the words. In Great Britain "endive" (or "curly endive") applies to a plant shaped like a spreading cabbage lettuce, but with feathery leaves, while "chicory" means a long, tightly packed head of slender, yellowish-white leaves. Whatever they are called, either is a good salad ingredient.

Cabbage: White cabbage leaves, finely shredded, add both flavour and texture to the salad bowl.

Spinach: Raw spinach leaves can replace lettuce and their dark green colour is a good contrast to other ingredients.

Watercress: This also makes a good colour contrast and its peppery flavour sets off rich meat and poultry.

Herbs in Salads: Parsley is an addition to any salad. Don't chop it very finely but snip it with scissors straight on to the salad, just before serving. A few leaves of fresh mint, sage, thyme, dill or tarragon (one at a time, not all together) can be chopped and sprinkled over a salad. Some people like verbena or rosemary, but don't be too liberal with these slightly scented flavours unless you know the tastes of the people you are serving.

Garlic: Many of those who say they dislike garlic don't really know how to use it. True, it is pungent and needs using with discretion—you will find one "clove" ample for the average bowl of salad.

First remove the papery outside skin of the garlic clove, then crush the clove with a broad-bladed knife (do this on a plate, unless you have a board that you keep specially for onion-chopping). Scrape the crushed garlic into the salad bowl or add it to the dressing. Alternatively, use a garlic press, if you have one.

HOME-GROWN SALADS

GOLDEN SLAW
(see colour picture no. 26)

1 medium-sized Savoy cabbage	Salt and pepper
1 lb. red apples	$\frac{1}{4}$ pint mayonnaise
$\frac{1}{2}$ lb. Gruyère cheese	1 tbsp. prepared mustard
	A little sugar

Wash the cabbage well. Spread out the outer leaves, then cut round the base of the heart and scoop it out, leaving a 'bowl'. Finely shred the cabbage heart. Core and dice the apples. Cut the cheese into fine slivers, put in a basin with the cabbage and apples, sprinkle with salt and pepper and toss gently. Combine the mayonnaise with the prepared mustard and toss the salad mixture in this dressing until the ingredients are well coated. Serve in the scooped-out cabbage 'bowl', sprinkled with sugar.

FRUIT, NUT AND CHEESE SALAD
(see colour picture no. 26)

8 oz. curd cheese	4 walnut halves
1 tbsp. seedless raisins	Cucumber and water-
Lettuce	cress to garnish
4 canned peach halves	

Beat the cheese until smooth. Put the raisins into boiling water for 1-2 minutes to soften them, drain well and cool, then mix with the cheese. Put the lettuce on a dish in about 4 individual portions and place on each a peach half (or 2-3 apricot halves). Top each with a tablespoonful of the cheese and raisin mixture and decorate with a walnut half. Garnish the dish with cucumber and watercress.

SPRING SALAD
(see colour picture no. 26)

4 eggs	A bunch of watercress
A bunch of radishes	Mustard and cress
A bunch of spring onions (optional)	4 tomatoes
1 lettuce	1 beetroot
	$\frac{1}{2}$ a cucumber

Hard-boil the eggs. Wash the radishes and cut into 'lilies' (see p. 126); wash the spring onions (if used) and cut the stalks into curls; soak both in a bowl of iced water to make them open. Wash and drain the lettuce, watercress and mustard and cress and arrange on a platter. Slice the tomatoes, beetroot, cucumber and eggs. Arrange all the ingredients attractively on the platter and serve with mayonnaise (see p. 124).

RAINBOW SALAD

1 clove of garlic	$\frac{1}{2}$ a cucumber
1 small, close cabbage heart	4-6 oz. grated cheese
1 beetroot	2 oz. green peas
2 carrots	French dressing
2 tomatoes	Hard-boiled eggs to garnish

Rub a flat platter or dish with the cut garlic. Chop the cabbage heart, peel the beetroot, grate the carrots coarsely; wash and slice or prepare the other ingredients

according to type. Place the different ingredients in sections radiating from the centre of the dish. Sprinkle with French dressing (or serve this separately) and garnish with the quartered eggs.

CRAB SALAD

2 oz. black olives	6 tbsps. mayonnaise
8 celery stalks	2 tbsps. tomato ketchup
2 $3\frac{1}{4}$-oz. cans of crabmeat	2 tsps. lemon juice
	Lettuce

Cut the olives into wedges, slice the celery thinly and flake the crabmeat. Blend the mayonnaise, tomato ketchup and lemon juice and toss the other ingredients lightly in this mixture. Serve in lettuce 'cups'.

SARDINE AND BEETROOT SALAD

2 7-oz. cans of sardines	4-6 tbsps. seasoned mayonnaise
2 eating apples	Lettuce
1 medium-sized beetroot	

Mash the sardines in a bowl. Grate 1 apple and the beetroot and mix with the sardines. Add mayonnaise to moisten and garnish with lettuce and sliced apple.

MUSHROOM SALAD

4 oz. well-opened cultivated mushrooms	1 tbsp. finely chopped parsley
1 tbsp. lemon juice	Freshly ground black pepper and salt
3 tbsps. olive oil	

Wash and dry the mushrooms, if necessary; do not peel, but remove the stalks. Slice very thinly into a serving dish, add the lemon juice, oil, parsley and pepper and leave to soak in this dressing for $\frac{1}{2}$ hour. Salt lightly just before serving. This is a good accompaniment for fish.

JELLIED TOMATOES

$\frac{1}{2}$ oz. gelatine	1 tbsp. cooked peas
$\frac{1}{2}$ pint stock	1 tbsp. diced chicory
3 large tomatoes	1 lettuce
1 tbsp. diced cooked carrot	1 tbsp. chopped parsley

Dissolve the gelatine in the stock. Cut the tomatoes in halves and scoop out the centres, adding the pulp to the stock. When the jelly is beginning to set, add the carrot, peas and chicory and leave until almost firm. Put the jelly mixture into the tomato cases, piling it up as high as possible. Place each tomato on a leaf of lettuce garnished with parsley; if possible, chill before serving.

ASPARAGUS AND CORN SALAD

2 corn cobs	$\frac{1}{4}$ pint mayonnaise
1 bundle of asparagus, cooked	2 lettuces
1 tbsp. chopped capers	1 hard-boiled egg
	2 tomatoes

Cook and drain the corn and allow to get cold. Cut the asparagus heads off to the depth of 2 inches; keep a few for garnishing and put the remainder in a basin with the corn and capers. Add the mayonnaise (see p. 124) and blend well. Pile into individual salad dishes and garnish with lettuce, sliced egg and tomato.

POTATO AND EGG SALAD

(see picture above)

2 tbsps. vinegar	3 hard-boiled eggs
1 level tsp. sugar	1 grated onion
Salt	A few anchovy fillets,
Pepper	chopped
2 lb. cooked potatoes	1 tbsp. chopped parsley

Combine the vinegar, sugar and seasonings in the bottom of a dish. Cut the potatoes and eggs into slices and place in layers in the dish, sprinkling each layer with onion and anchovy. Finish with a layer of egg and garnish with chopped parsley and a line of grated onion.

MEAT SALAD MOULD

1 oz. gelatine	4 oz. breakfast sausage
1 pint meat stock or	Radishes for garnish
water	1 tomato, sliced
½ tsp. meat extract	Cucumber
Seasoning	1 hard-boiled egg
4 oz. cooked peas	Lettuce, sliced tomato
1 tbsp. chutney	and mustard and cress
4 oz. diced corned beef	to garnish

Dissolve the gelatine in ¼ pint water and add it to the stock, meat extract and seasoning. Place a little of this jelly at the bottom of a mould or cake tin and put this in a cold place to set. Meanwhile, add the peas, chutney, corned beef and breakfast sausage (reserving some for garnish) to the rest of the stock. Slice the radishes, tomato, cucumber and hard-boiled egg and arrange them attractively in the set jelly in the mould, together with the rest of the breakfast sausage. Pour on the rest of the jelly and allow to set in a cold place. Turn on to a dish and garnish.

CHEESE SALAD BOWL

1 lettuce	¼ lb. small new potatoes
Watercress	Mayonnaise
½ lb. tomatoes	A little made mustard
6-8 oz. Cheddar cheese	Chopped chives or parsley

Line a salad bowl with lettuce and watercress. Peel and slice the tomatoes and cut the cheese into small dice (or crumble it if this is easier). Cut up the potatoes, combine them with the cheese and tomatoes and mix with mayonnaise and a little made mustard to bind. Put into the centre of the salad bowl and sprinkle with chopped chives or parsley.

CELERY SALAD

(see picture above)

1 head of celery	⅛ pint salad oil
½ an onion (grated)	1 tbsp. tarragon vinegar
1 hard-boiled egg	1 tbsp. cream
2 tsps. French mustard	2 tomatoes and
Salt and pepper	1 beetroot to garnish

Wash the celery, cut up finely and mix with the onion. To make the dressing, combine the sieved egg with the mustard and seasonings and then gradually add the oil, vinegar and cream. Immediately before serving, pour the dressing over the celery mixture and garnish with slices of tomato and some diced beetroot.

HAM AND CELERY SALAD

4 sticks of celery	1 red or green pepper
6 oz. lean ham	(or a small pepper of
¼ of a cucumber	each colour)
½ lb. cooked new	1-2 hard-boiled eggs
potatoes	Lettuce or endive
Mayonnaise	

Cut the celery, ham, cucumber and potatoes into small, neat pieces. Combine with enough mayonnaise to bind and add any trimmings from the peppers and the eggs that are not required for garnishing the dish. Put some lettuce or endive leaves on a flat plate, pile the salad ingredients in the centre and put slices of hard-boiled egg and pepper rings round the outside.

CHRISTMAS SALAD

8 oz. cooked turkey,	Salt and pepper
boned	1 tsp. lemon juice
6 sticks of celery	Lettuce
¼ pint mayonnaise	

Dice the turkey and celery and combine with the mayonnaise. Season with the salt, pepper and lemon juice, chill and serve on lettuce leaves.

DUCK AND TANGERINE SALAD

2 lettuce hearts	$\frac{1}{2}$ lb. cooked green peas
$\frac{3}{4}$-1 lb. cooked duck	2 tbsps. French
6 tangerines	dressing
A bunch of watercress	Parsley

Arrange the lettuce heart leaves on a flat dish. Slice the duck and arrange neatly on the lettuce. Peel the tangerines, removing as much of the pith as possible, and divide 2 of them into segments. Push a small bunch of watercress into the top of each whole tangerine and put these on the dish. Toss the peas in the French dressing and arrange round the duck. Garnish with parsley and tangerine segments.

SALMON AND RICE SALAD

(see picture above)

6 oz. Patna rice	6 tbsps. mayonnaise
$\frac{1}{2}$ lb. tomatoes	1 level tsp. celery
An 8-oz. tin of salmon	seeds
4 tbsps. finely chopped	Grated lemon rind
chives	A little salt and pepper
6 tbsps. whipped cream	Lettuce and radishes

Cook the rice in boiling salted water in the usual way and drain. Skin the tomatoes, remove the seeds and chop roughly. Drain and flake the salmon, add with the tomato and chives to the rice and mix lightly. Fold the whipped cream into the mayonnaise and add the celery seeds, with lemon rind, salt and pepper to taste. Fold in the rice mixture and press into a 2-pint ring mould. When the salad is set, turn it out on to a platter lined with lettuce leaves and garnish the ring with sliced radishes.

SALAD IN ASPIC

$\frac{1}{2}$ pint aspic jelly	$\frac{1}{4}$ lb. carrots
$\frac{1}{4}$ lb. new potatoes	(cooked)
(cooked)	$\frac{1}{4}$ small cauliflower
$\frac{1}{4}$ lb. shelled green peas	(cooked)
(cooked)	1 lettuce
3 tbsps. mayonnaise	Mustard and cress

Prepare the aspic jelly as directed on the packet. Set a thin layer in the bottom of some small dariole moulds, then put in a layer of potatoes, cut into small rounds; cover this with aspic and allow to set. Add a layer of peas, cover with aspic and allow to set as before. Mix 3 tbsps. mayonnaise with 3 tbsps. aspic and add the remainder of the vegetables, cut into small dice. Fill up the moulds with this, allow to set, turn out and arrange on a bed of lettuce. Garnish with mustard and cress or as desired.

CHICKEN AND ALMOND SALAD

6 oz. seedless raisins	Salt and pepper
4 oz. almonds	1 tsp. lemon juice
12 oz. cold cooked	1 tbsp. grated onion
chicken	1 tbsp. chopped
$\frac{1}{4}$ pint cream	parsley
2 tbsps. mayonnaise	Lettuce
(preferably home-made)	

Cover the raisins with cold water and bring to the boil, leave to stand for 5 minutes, then drain. Blanch and toast the almonds. Cut the chicken into long shreds. Mix the cream with the mayonnaise and season with the salt, pepper and lemon juice. Put all the ingredients except the lettuce in a bowl and combine well with the mayonnaise mixture. Serve the salad on a dish or platter lined with lettuce leaves.

EGG SALAD

(see picture above)

4 hard-boiled eggs	1 level tsp. sugar
1 head of celery	1 tbsp. lemon juice
4 carrots, grated	1 tbsp. orange juice
Radishes	Pepper
$\frac{1}{2}$ a cucumber	1 tbsp. finely chopped
$\frac{1}{2}$ pint yoghourt	parsley
1 level tsp. paprika	

Slice the eggs, lay them on a bed of shredded celery, cover with the raw grated carrot and surround with sliced (unskinned) radishes and cucumber. Cover with a dressing made by mixing the yoghourt with the paprika, sugar, strained fruit juices, a little pepper and the parsley. Chill and serve.

For Salad Dressings see pp. 124-125.

SALADS À LA FRANÇAISE

In France many salads are served either as an hors d'œuvre or as accompaniment to roasts, grills and fried dishes, so we give several of this type.

The French use herbs extensively in salad making, as they improve and intensify the flavour of the various salad ingredients. There are many varieties of herbs and nowadays most of them can be bought in this country, in either dried or fresh form. Herbs are normally chopped finely and sprinkled over the finished salad, though sometimes they are added to a dressing.

GREEN SALAD
(see picture on page 109)

This is the traditional French accompaniment to steak. See that the lettuce is fresh and crisp and take care to use the right proportions of oil and vinegar in the French dressing. Toss the lettuce lightly in the dressing until all leaves are thinly coated.

CHERRY AND CUCUMBER SALAD
(see colour picture no. 28)

1 lettuce heart	A medium-sized can of
1 scallop shell per	cherries
person	French dressing
½ a small cucumber	

Separate the lettuce heart leaves, wash and drain; place 2-3 leaves on each scallop shell. Skin and dice the cucumber and add to the drained cherries. Mix the cherries and cucumber with the dressing and heap them in the centre of the lettuce leaves.

CHICORY AND ORANGE SALAD
(see picture above)

Remove the root and the outer leaves from 4 heads of chicory, wipe the heads clean and cut into chunks. Peel 2 oranges and divide into segments; mix the two and sprinkle with French dressing.
Orange Salad: Use 4 oranges and omit the chicory.

DRESSED FENNEL
(see colour picture no. 28)

Slice the fennel finely, sprinkle with salt and cover with lemon and oil dressing.

TOMATO AND BLACK OLIVES
(see picture above)

4 tomatoes	Black pepper
½ a clove of garlic	8 olives, stoned and
3 tbsps. mayonnaise	coarsely chopped

Peel the tomatoes and scoop out the seeds and pulp. Put pulp in a bowl, mix well with the crushed garlic and add the mayonnaise. Pour this dressing over the tomatoes, filling each, and sprinkle lightly with pepper. Scatter the olives over the tomatoes.

CARROT HORS D'OEUVRE

1 lb. carrots	1 tsp. lemon juice
1 small onion or shallot	A pinch of salt
2 tbsps. olive oil	A pinch of sugar

Peel the carrots and grate coarsely; grate the onion and add. Mix oil, lemon juice, salt and sugar, pour on to the mixture and toss well before serving.

TOMATO SALAD
(see colour picture no. 28)

4 tomatoes	Finely chopped chives
⅛ pint French dressing	to garnish

Slice the tomatoes. Pour the French dressing over them and sprinkle with chopped chives.

FILLED ARTICHOKES
(see colour picture no. 28)

4 globe artichokes	Seasoning
4 tbsps. mayonnaise	1 hard-boiled egg yolk

Wash the artichokes, pull off the hard outer leaves and cut stems close to leaves. Cut off the tops ¾ inch down and stand the artichokes upside-down in cold water for ½ hour. Drain, cover with boiling salted water (1 level tsp. salt to 1 quart water) and cook until tender—25-40 minutes. Drain and chill. Remove the centre "chokes", fill the hollows with seasoned mayonnaise, and sprinkle with sieved egg yolk.

SALAD NIÇOISE

(see picture above)

1 lb. tomatoes	4 oz. cooked French
1 small cucumber	beans
Salt and freshly	2 oz. black olives
ground black pepper	½ a clove of garlic
1 tsp. chopped basil	French dressing
1 tsp. chopped parsley	8 anchovy fillets
Grated rind of 1 lemon	

Put the tomatoes in a bowl, pour boiling water over, peel and slice. Slice the cucumber, then lay this and the tomato in a small dish and season well with salt and pepper. Sprinkle the herbs over the cucumber and tomato. Grate the lemon rind over the whole, then scatter the beans over. Halve and shred the olives, scatter these over the salad and season. Chop the garlic, add to the dressing and pour over the salad. Halve each anchovy fillet and make a lattice pattern on top of the salad. Serve with bread and butter and lemon.

MINT AND ONION SALAD

1 bunch spring onions	1 level tbsp. caster sugar
1 dozen mint leaves	Vinegar

Slice the onions thinly and chop the mint finely. Arrange in layers in a small glass dish, sprinkling sugar between the layers. Cover with vinegar and let stand for ½ hour before serving. This is good with cold lamb.

LEEK SALAD

Clean 4 young leeks and blanch them in boiling salted water for 8 minutes; lift out and drain carefully, then chill well. Sprinkle them with freshly ground black pepper and toss in French dressing.

TOMATO HERB SALAD

1 tbsp. lemon thyme	1 tbsp. basil
1 tbsp. tarragon	4 tomatoes
1 tbsp. marjoram	2 oz. seedless raisins
1 tbsp. chives	French mustard dressing

Chop the herbs very finely. Peel and quarter the tomatoes. Chop the raisins roughly and add to the tomatoes. Sprinkle with the herbs, pour the French mustard dressing over and chill well.

FILLED BEETROOTS

(see picture above)

4 small beetroots	1 orange
Salt and pepper	1 tbsp. grated horseradish
1 tbsp. lemon juice	1 level tsp. sugar
4 sticks of celery	French dressing

Peel and hollow out the beetroots, season with salt and pepper and sprinkle with lemon juice. Chop the celery coarsely, peel and cut up the orange and use both to fill the beetroot cups. Add the horseradish and sugar to the dressing and sprinkle this over the beetroots. Garnish with celery curls, or as desired.

BROCCOLI SALAD

¾ lb. broccoli heads	2 tsps. chopped capers
3 tbsps. French dressing	3 tbsps. cream dressing
2 tbsps. chopped chervil	Sprigs of watercress

To prepare the broccoli, plunge it into rapidly boiling water, bring back to the boil and boil fast for ¼ hour. Immediately it is tender, drain it in a colander and when cool, pile in a bowl and chill. Sprinkle with some of the French dressing and leave for about 1 hour. Add the chopped chervil and capers to the cream dressing and pile this on the broccoli. Dip the watercress in the French dressing and arrange round the broccoli.

TOMATO ICE

1 lb. tomatoes	1 tsp. tomato purée
½ a clove of garlic	Juice of 1 lemon
1 bay leaf	Grated rind of 1 orange
1 tsp. chopped basil	½ gill cream
½ pint thick mayonnaise	A pinch of sugar
sauce	Salt and pepper

Make a tomato pulp by stewing the tomatoes with the garlic, bay leaf and chopped basil; sieve this mixture. Mix the pulp with the mayonnaise and add the tomato purée, lemon juice and orange rind. Partially whip the cream and add the tomato mixture, with the sugar, salt and pepper to taste. Pour into an ice tray and freeze in the refrigerator, stirring every ½ hour until the mixture is half-frozen, then leave it to freeze completely.
This is often used to accompany grilled sole.

For Salad Dressings see pp. 124-125.

SALADS FROM THE MEDITERRANEAN

FENNEL AND CUCUMBER SALAD
(see picture above)

1 orange	Chopped mint
½ a cucumber	Lemon and oil dressing
1 fennel root	1 clove of garlic
8 radishes	2 hard-boiled eggs

Peel the orange and divide into segments. Cut the unpeeled cucumber into ¼-inch slices, then cut each slice across into 4 pieces. Cut the fennel into short, thin strips; slice the radishes. Mix all these together and add a little chopped mint. Make the lemon and oil dressing (see p. 124), add the chopped garlic and pour over the salad. Quarter the eggs and arrange on the salad.

FENNEL AND GRUYÈRE CHEESE

Shred 1 fennel root and cut 4 oz. Gruyère cheese into slivers. Season well with freshly-ground black pepper and pour lemon and oil dressing over.

AUBERGINES WITH TONGUE

3 small aubergines	2 thick slices of
6 tbsps. olive oil	cooked tongue
1 clove of garlic	2 red peppers
4 tbsps. chopped parsley	Lemon and oil dressing

Do not peel the aubergines, but cut them into small dice and sauté gently in the oil. Chop the clove of garlic and add to the cooked aubergines, with the chopped parsley. Cut the tongue into dice and the peppers into strips, then add to the mixture. Toss in the dressing (see p. 124).

SALAD OF MUSHROOM AND SHELLFISH
(see right-hand picture above)

1 clove of garlic, crushed	An 8-oz. pkt. frozen scampi
½ lb. mushrooms	Lemon and oil dressing

Rub 2 bowls with the crushed garlic. Slice the raw mushrooms thinly, then put them in one bowl and the shellfish in the other. Pour half of the dressing over the mushrooms and the rest over the fish. Just before serving, mix the two and sprinkle with parsley.

MARGUERITE SALAD
(see colour picture no. 28)

4 heads of chicory	A 16-oz. can of grapefruit
1 large apple	segments
2 sticks of celery (optional)	4 tomatoes
	Watercress
4 mushrooms	Mayonnaise

Cut off the root end of the chicory, remove the outer leaves and wash in cold water. Peel, core and slice the apple; cut the celery and mushrooms into Julienne strips; drain the grapefruit segments; scald and peel the tomatoes; wash the watercress. Arrange the chicory leaves round the edge of a dish, next add the grapefruit segments; then the tomatoes, with mushroom (and celery, if used) piled between them. Lastly, add a circle of apple slices with a heap of watercress in the middle. Serve with mayonnaise.

ITALIAN CAULIFLOWER SALAD

1 medium-sized cauliflower	1 tbsp. minced shallot or onion
7 anchovy fillets, cut into small pieces	1 tbsp. bottled capers
	Freshly ground pepper
10 stoned and sliced ripe olives	3 tbsps. olive or salad oil
	1 tbsp. wine vinegar

Wash and trim the cauliflower and break into small flowerets. Cook in 1 inch of boiling salted water for about 10 minutes, or until tender-crisp. Drain, cool, then put in the refrigerator. Place the chilled cauliflower, anchovy fillets, olives, capers and shallot in a bowl, sprinkle generously with pepper and pour the oil and vinegar over all; toss well and refrigerate for ½ hour before serving.

YELLOW PEPPER SALAD

4 tomatoes	2 sticks of celery
4 large raw yellow peppers	4 tbsps. olive oil
	Salt and freshly ground
A bunch of radishes	black pepper

Peel and slice the tomatoes; cut the peppers into rings; slice the radishes and the celery. Mix together, pour the olive oil over and season with salt and pepper.

PANZANELLA (ITALIAN BREAD SALAD)

2 cups of stale bread, cut into small squares
½ cup water
1 garlic clove, cut up
1 sprig of fresh basil
1 medium-sized onion, minced

2 medium-sized red, ripe tomatoes
1 level tsp. salt
⅛ level tsp. freshly ground pepper
2 tbsps. olive oil
1 tbsp. wine vinegar

Briefly soak the bread in the water, draining it while still firm. Meanwhile, rub the salad bowl well with the garlic and fresh basil. (Or sprinkle a pinch of dried basil into the bowl.) Toss the bread in the salad bowl with the onion, cut-up tomatoes, salt and pepper. Add the oil and vinegar and mix lightly but well.

ANTIPASTO

This Italian word means either hors d'œuvre or a salad. Most basic Antipasto recipes contain tuna fish, anchovies, tomatoes and peppers. The flavours should contrast—spicy, sharp and bland—and the colours should be as varied and attractive as possible.

HAM AND SALAMI ANTIPASTO

(see picture above)

4 slices of Parma ham
4 slices of tomato
4 slices of Italian salami
4 sticks of celery, each cut in 4 2-inch strips
A 3½-oz. can of tuna

4 anchovy fillets, divided in halves
A 5-oz. can of red pimientos, cut in strips
4 black olives
4 green olives
4 tsps. capers

Lay the slices of ham on a platter, lengthwise and overlapping each other. Between them arrange the slices of tomato and salami alternately. Pile the celery at either end of the dish. Place the tuna fish across the centre and cover with anchovy fillets. Pile the pimiento at one side of the dish. Stone the olives and slice into strips, then pile the black ones in two opposite corners and the green ones in the remaining corners. Place the capers down both sides of the fish.

GALICIAN SEAFOOD SALAD

(see picture above)

½ a cooked lobster
2 hard-boiled eggs
1 medium-sized onion
1 green pepper
2 tbsps. olive oil
1 tbsp. vinegar

¼ tsp. prepared mustard
Salt and pepper
¼ lb. shelled shrimps
Lettuce
Lemon and gherkin fans
Chopped basil

Remove the lobster meat from the shell and cut into chunks. Slice the eggs, onion and green pepper. Make a dressing with the oil, vinegar and seasonings. Toss the lobster, shrimps and most of the egg in this and arrange on a layer of lettuce. Garnish with the onion rings, green pepper slices, half-slices of lemon, gherkin fans and sliced egg; sprinkle with basil.

FRENCH BEANS WITH TUNA FISH

Cook 1 lb. French beans until just tender. Dice the contents of a 3½-oz. can of tuna fish. Make a French dressing, pour over the warm beans and top with the fish.

COURGETTE AND RICE SALAD

2 courgettes
4 oz. quick-cooking rice
2 tomatoes

8 black olives
French dressing
4 sprigs of mint
2 tsps. chopped basil

Cook the courgettes in boiling salted water until just tender. Boil the rice, drain and allow to dry a little. Slice the tomatoes, stone and chop the olives. Toss all in the dressing and garnish with herbs.

ENSALADA ISABELLA

2 celery hearts
1 lb. cooked potatoes
4 apples
1 clove of garlic

1 egg yolk
Pepper and salt
Oil
Lemon juice

Remove the outer stalks of the celery, leaving the crisp hearts; wash and leave in cold water until required. Slice the potatoes; peel and slice the apples. Pound the chopped garlic thoroughly in a mortar, add the egg yolk and seasoning and stir in the oil, a few drops at a time, until the mixture is thick, then stir in a little lemon juice to taste. Cut up the celery and toss this with the apples and potatoes in the mayonnaise.

SALADS FROM CENTRAL EUROPE

TOMATOES STUFFED WITH APPLE AND CELERY

4 large tomatoes	1 level tsp. sugar
Salt	4 tbsps. sour cream
Pepper	3 tbsps. olive oil
4 sticks of celery	1 tbsp. grated horseradish
2 apples	Chives, watercress and
4 tbsps. lemon juice	radishes to garnish

Cut a $\frac{1}{4}$-inch slice from the stem end of each of the tomatoes; using a spoon, scoop out and reserve the pulp. Sprinkle the tomato cups with 1 level tsp. salt and $\frac{1}{4}$ level tsp. pepper, then place them upside-down on a plate. Finely slice the celery, grate the unpeeled apples coarsely and put in a bowl; add the lemon juice, sugar and $\frac{1}{2}$ level tsp. salt. Combine the sour cream, olive oil, horseradish, $\frac{1}{2}$ level tsp. salt and $\frac{1}{4}$ level tsp. pepper. Drain the tomato pulp and chop it coarsely. Chill all these ingredients. Combine the apple and sour cream mixtures, then add the tomato pulp. Use to fill the tomato cups, arrange these on a large dish and sprinkle with chopped chives. Garnish with watercress and radish roses (see p. 126) or as desired.

LETTUCE AND BACON SALAD

(see colour picture no. 29)

1 lettuce	1 level tbsp. brown sugar
2 oz. diced bacon	3 tbsps. vinegar
6 tbsps. olive oil	

Wash the lettuce and arrange in a salad bowl. Fry the bacon in the oil until crisp; add the sugar and vinegar and pour this hot dressing over the lettuce. Serve at once, while the lettuce is still warm from the dressing.

CELERIAC SALAD

(see colour picture no. 29)

2 lb. celeriac	1 tsp. prepared mustard
Boiling salted water	4 small pickled beet-
3 tbsps. mayonnaise	roots

Wash and peel the celeriac and cut into Julienne strips. Put into boiling salted water and cook for about 5 minutes, until tender; drain and allow to cool. Mix the mayonnaise with the mustard and combine with the celeriac. Garnish with a ring of the sliced pickled beet-roots.

"SWISS CREST" SALAD

(see colour picture no. 29)

2 lb. asparagus	$\frac{1}{2}$ lb. Gruyère cheese
Salted water	$\frac{1}{2}$ lb. tomatoes
6 oz. ham (preferably uncooked Grisons)	3 tbsps. mayonnaise

Wash and prepare the asparagus and cook in salted water; strain and cool. Divide into 4 equal portions and place on a large round plate, forming a cross. Fill the gaps between the arms of the cross alternately with rolled slices of ham and slices of cheese. Surround with sliced tomatoes and fill the centre of the cross with mayonnaise. Serve cold.

GREEN PAPRIKA SALAD

$1\frac{1}{2}$ lb. green peppers	1 level tsp. salt
2 tbsps. vinegar	1 level tsp. sugar

Wash the peppers, remove the cores and seeds and cut the flesh into crosswise rings, then scald these. Mix the vinegar with a little water and add the salt and sugar. Mix with the sliced peppers and leave to stand for 2 hours.

GUNDEL SALAD (HUNGARIAN)

6 oz. mushrooms	$\frac{1}{4}$ lb. cooked asparagus
5 tbsps. salad oil	tips
1 green pepper	1 level tsp. salt
2 large tomatoes, skinned and sliced	A dash of pepper
	2 tbsps. vinegar
$\frac{1}{4}$ of a cucumber, thinly sliced	1 head of lettuce

Trim and quarter the mushrooms, brown them in the oil and cool. Slice the green pepper, fry in the oil for a few seconds and cool. Mix the tomatoes, cucumber, asparagus tips and green pepper and season well with salt, pepper and the vinegar. Shred the lettuce and add it immediately before serving. Finally, add the oil used for browning the mushrooms.

CHEESE SALAD

1 lettuce	1 medium-sized onion,
3 tbsps. French dressing	finely chopped
1 tsp. prepared mustard	$\frac{1}{2}$ lb. Gruyère cheese

Wash and drain the lettuce and arrange in a salad bowl. Make the French dressing and add the mustard and the onion. Cut the cheese into small, thin slices and mix with the dressing. Allow to stand for 1 hour, then serve on the lettuce.

CABBAGE SALAD

A small white cabbage	1 level tsp. caraway seeds
1 onion, chopped	$\frac{1}{2}$ level tsp. dried marjoram
3 tbsps. French dressing	1 tbsp. chopped parsley

Trim the cabbage, removing the outer leaves, then wash and shred it. Place in a bowl and pour some boiling water over it; after 10 minutes drain, then add the chopped onion. Make a French dressing, adding the caraway seeds and marjoram. Pour this mixture all over the cabbage and sprinkle the salad with the chopped parsley.

DANDELION LEAVES SALAD

1 lb. dandelion leaves	Salt and pepper
$\frac{1}{4}$ pint sour cream	$\frac{1}{2}$ level tsp. paprika

Wash the dandelion leaves very well indeed and put them in a bowl, pour boiling water over them and drain well. Put 3 tbsps. of boiling salted water into a saucepan and put in the leaves, cover the pan and cook for 10 minutes, shaking about 3 times during the cooking. Drain the leaves and chop coarsely. Heat the sour cream in a thick-based pan and add the salt and pepper. Stir the chopped dandelion leaves into the mixture, reduce the heat and slowly bring the cream just up to boiling point, but do not allow to boil. When cool, sprinkle with paprika pepper.

FROM RUSSIA AND NORTHERN EUROPE

SALAD OF HERRINGS

(see top picture on left)

4 salted herrings	¼ lb. mushrooms
½ tsp. mustard	4 new potatoes
French dressing	1 cooked beetroot
1 pickled cucumber	

The salted herrings must be prepared as follows: wash the fish very thoroughly to remove the brine. Cut off the head and fins, clean out the insides and bone the fish; soak in cold water for 12-24 hours, then remove the skin. Add the mustard to the French dressing. Slice the cucumber and raw mushrooms; dice potato and beetroot. Place the herrings in a dish and arrange the other ingredients around them. Pour the dressing over and serve very cold.

SALAD WITH SCRAMBLED EGGS

(see middle picture on left)

4 eggs	1 oz. butter
Salt and pepper	3 raw carrots
1 tsp. chopped mint	1 small onion
1 tsp. chopped parsley	3 tomatoes, skinned
1 tsp. chopped	¼ of a cucumber
marjoram	3 tbsps. French dressing

Beat the eggs lightly, season with salt and pepper and add the chopped herbs, then scramble them in the butter in the usual way; when cold, cut into small pieces. Grate the carrots, chop the onion finely and slice the tomatoes and cucumber. Add the carrots and onion to the scrambled egg, place this on a dish and surround it with the sliced tomato and cucumber. Pour the French dressing over the tomato and cucumber.

POTATO AND APPLE SALAD

4 medium-sized potatoes	1 tbsp. capers
2 medium-sized apples	White wine dressing

Cook the potatoes in their skins in boiling salted water, then peel and allow to cool. Peel and core the apples. Slice apples and potatoes very thinly and mix with the capers. Toss well in the white wine dressing and serve cold.

RAW CELERIAC SALAD

2 young celeriac roots	French dressing
2 apples	

Peel and shred the roots carefully. Peel, core and shred the apples. Toss both thoroughly in the French dressing and chill for 3-4 hours before serving.

BEETROOT SALAD

(see bottom picture on left)

1 lb. cooked beetroot	½ level tsp. caraway
1 horseradish root	seeds
1 level tsp. sugar	The juice of 3 lemons
1 level tsp. salt	

Peel and slice the beetroot and grate the horseradish. Mix the horseradish with the sugar, salt, caraway seeds and lemon juice and pour over the beetroot.

SAUERKRAUT SALAD

1 small can of sauerkraut	Sugar to taste
1 carton of plain yoghourt	

Rinse the sauerkraut in cold water, drain and mix with the yoghourt, adding sugar to taste.

RED CABBAGE SALAD

1 lb. red cabbage	French dressing
2 cooking apples	1 hard-boiled egg

Quarter the cabbage and take out the root. Shred the cabbage finely. Shred the apples and put them straight into the dressing. Add the cabbage, toss lightly before serving and garnish with the sliced egg.

MUSSEL SALAD

4 small potatoes	Lettuce leaves
8 mussels	1 hard-boiled egg
1 tsp. each chopped parsley, dill and chives	1 canned truffle, if available
White wine dressing	

Cook the potatoes, drain, cool and dice them. Thoroughly clean the mussels and cook in boiling salted water until their shells open; remove from the shells, discard the beards and dice the mussels. Chop all the herbs and mix them with the dressing. Toss the potatoes and mussels in the dressing and arrange on lettuce leaves. Garnish with chopped egg and truffle strips.

MACARONI-TOMATO SALAD

(see colour picture no. 28)

4 oz. macaroni	Salt
¾ lb. tomatoes	Vinegar to taste
1 tbsp. horseradish sauce	Mustard and cress and tomato slices
A 4-oz. can of cream	to garnish

Boil the macaroni until just tender. Cut the tomatoes into small pieces and mix with the macaroni. Blend the horseradish sauce, cream, salt and vinegar and mix all the ingredients together. Put in a dish and garnish with the cress and slices of tomato.

POTATO AND CELERY SALAD

4 potatoes	Salt
1 head of celery	Pepper
French dressing	Sliced tomatoes

Boil the potatoes, drain and cool. Shred the celery and soak in dressing. Slice the potatoes and mix with the celery, season well and serve with tomatoes.

RUSSIAN SALAD

½ lb. cold cooked meat	½ a cucumber
2 cooked beetroots	2 hard-boiled eggs
4 cooked potatoes	French dressing
4 gherkins	½ tsp. made mustard

Dice the meat and mix with the diced beetroots, potatoes, gherkins and cucumber and the chopped eggs. Mix the French dressing with mustard and combine with salad.

HUZARENSLA

½ lb. stewing steak	Salt and pepper
1 lb. potatoes	1 lettuce
2 medium-sized cooked beetroot, diced	2 tomatoes
1 large cooking apple	½ a cucumber
A bunch of spring onions	2 hard-boiled eggs
8 gherkins	Parsley sprigs, spring
4 tbsps. mayonnaise	onions in curls and
½ tsp. French mustard	gherkin fans to garnish

Stew the meat in water with a pinch of salt until tender and cut into small pieces. Boil the potatoes and mash thoroughly; when cold mix with the meat, beetroot and shredded apple. Add the chopped onions and gherkins. Make the mayonnaise and add mustard and seasoning. Mix all the above ingredients and put on a flat dish. Garnish with the lettuce, sliced tomatoes, cucumber and eggs, the parsley sprigs, spring onion curls and gherkin fans.

SCANDINAVIAN SALADS AND COLD TABLE

In Scandinavia, salads as we know them are not very often eaten, but their place is taken to some extent by the almost universal Smørrebrød, which often consist of salad ingredients. Smørrebrød are often eaten as hors d'oeuvre and in Norway they may form the midday meal, while together with a variety of fish, meat and other dishes, they play an important part in the Scandinavian cold table.

Roughly translated, Smørrebrød means "buttered bread", but it has come to mean bread and butter with a topping of some kind—in other words, an open sandwich. Some Danish and Swedish restaurants serve certain traditional Smørrebrød, always made up in the same way, but since such an enormous range of different ingredients can be used, it is simpler to leave yourself a free hand, using your imagination and your artistic ability to create your own tempting open sandwiches. Smørrebrød are becoming more and more popular in this country as a "party piece" which can be prepared beforehand.

The base is usually Scandinavian ryebread, which, like many varieties of crispbread, can now be bought in this country. Failing either of these, firm white or brown bread is quite satisfactory. The secret is to butter the bread or crispbread very well, so that the ingredients will stay firmly in place. Arrange the topping and garnish carefully, remembering that both in colour and in taste the garnish should suit the topping.

ASSORTED SMØRREBRØD

(see colour picture no. 27)

Lettuce, smoked salmon, sliced cucumber, lemon twists.
Liver sausage, slices of tomato, chopped chives.
Lettuce, sardine, caviare, lemon twist.
Liver pâté, ring of pimiento, cucumber cones, radish rose.
Salami slices, onion rings, chopped chives, black olives, mayonnaise.
Lettuce, smoked salmon, horseradish cream, lemon slice, parsley.
Salami, mayonnaise, half-slices of cucumber, parsley.
Sliced tomato, sliced hard-boiled egg and chives.
Caviare, chopped raw onion, raw egg yolk.

OTHER EASY SMØRREBRØD

Lettuce, ham, scrambled eggs, cress.
Pork luncheon meat, sweet pickle, cucumber.
Tongue, Russian salad and a tomato twist.
Crisply grilled bacon, scrambled eggs.
Chopped pork, potato salad, watercress, sliced tomato.
Chopped hard-boiled eggs and chopped chives.

GARNISHES FOR SMØRREBRØD

These can include anything from a simple sprig of parsley to radish roses, curled celery, cucumber cones, gherkin fans, onion rings, tomato twists and red pepper Julienne (see p. 126 for instructions) or one of the following:

Egg Strips: Allow 4 eggs to $\frac{1}{2}$ pint milk, beat well, strain and season; cook slowly over warm water until set, then leave till cold and cut in strips. As a quick alternative, scramble the eggs in the usual way and press lightly while cooling.

Horseradish Salad: Grate fresh horseradish into whipped cream; flavour with lemon juice and a little fine sugar.

Herbs: Fresh dill is one of the most traditional garnishes, but when it is not in season, it is quite permissible to use parsley sprigs.

FRIKADELLER (MEAT BALLS)

(see colour picture no. 27)

1 lb. meat without bones	4 oz. plain flour
(e.g. $\frac{1}{2}$ lb. pork and	Pepper
$\frac{1}{2}$ lb. veal or beef)	Chopped onion or onion
1-1$\frac{1}{2}$ level tsps. salt	juice
1 egg	Mashed potato (optional)
$\frac{1}{2}$ pint milk	Lard for frying

Wash the meat, remove the sinews and cut the flesh into small pieces; mince 2 or 3 times, adding the salt. Whip the egg and milk and stir into the flour, then add gradually to the meat. Add more salt, if necessary, a pinch of pepper and onion (or juice) to taste. If desired, add potato, in proportion of 1 part potato to 2 parts meat—the mixture should be fairly thick. Heat the fat in a frying pan and spoon in the mixture in small balls. Cook on all sides, until light brown and cooked through.

THE COLD TABLE

This usually includes a very large platter of cold meats such as pork, ham, tongue, liver pâté, beef, salami, chicken, etc. In addition there would be a large cheese-board containing traditional Scandinavian and other cheeses such as goat's milk, Samsoe, Danish Blue, Gorgonzola, Danish Port Salut and so on. Assorted crispbreads are also offered, plus a liberal amount of butter. Herrings, Frikadeller and Fågelbo are almost indispensable. Here are some typical recipes:

SUMMER SALAD

(see picture above)

Lettuce	Parsley to garnish
6 oz. mushrooms	2 tbsps. cream
4 oz. ham	4 tbsps. mayonnaise
5 stuffed olives	$\frac{1}{2}$ level tsp. curry powder
1 hard-boiled egg	$\frac{1}{4}$ level tsp. garlic salt

Wash the lettuce and arrange on a large round dish, then place a small bowl in the centre to hold the mayonnaise. Clean the mushrooms, discard the stalks and cut the caps in halves. Arrange the half-mushrooms in a garland round the base of the small bowl. Cut the ham into strips and arrange these round the mushrooms. Slice the olives and sprinkle amongst the ham. Slice the egg and arrange round the outer edge of the dish. Garnish the salad with sprigs of parsley. Blend the cream and mayonnaise together, add the curry powder and garlic salt and pour this mixture into the little bowl.

SOUSED SALT HERRINGS

(see colour picture no. 27)

1 large salt herring	$\frac{1}{3}$ cup sugar
$\frac{1}{2}$ cup vinegar	2 tbsps. chopped onions
2 tbsps. water	5 peppercorns, crushed
10 whole allspice,	Fresh dill sprigs and
crushed	onion rings to
2 sprigs fresh dill	garnish

Clean the herring, removing the head, rinse under cold running water, then soak it in cold water for 10-1 hours; change the water a few times. Cut the herring along the back, remove the big backbone and as many small ones as possible and pull off the skin. (The bone

(Please turn to page 12)

24. Mixed Vegetable Platter

25. Green Salad and dressing

26. Golden Slaw; Fruit, Nut and Cheese Salad; Spring Salad

27. Scandinavian salads and cold table

28. French and Mediterranean salads

29. Lettuce and Bacon Salad; Swiss Crest Salad; Celeriac Salad

30. Spanish Paella

come out easily after the soaking.) Drain on absorbent paper, then place the fillets together one on another, so that they look like a whole fish. Slice thinly with a sharp knife, and remove to a long narrow dish, using a spatula. Mix the remaining ingredients in a saucepan, bring to the boil and simmer for a few minutes, cool, strain and pour over the herring. Garnish, chill and serve with small boiled potatoes.

PRAWN SALAD

(see picture above)

1 tbsp. mayonnaise	1 tbsp. chopped parsley
1 oz. cream cheese	2 sticks of celery
2 tbsps. whipped cream	$\frac{1}{2}$ lb. frozen prawns
1 finely chopped green pepper	Lettuce
	1 lemon, sliced

Mix the mayonnaise and cream cheese and add the cream, pepper and parsley; place in a small bowl in the centre of a platter. Cut the celery into fine strips and mix with the prawns. Place the lettuce on platter, cover with the prawn-and-celery mixture and garnish with lemon.

CUCUMBER SALAD

2 cucumbers	Juice of $\frac{1}{2}$ a lemon
1 level tbsp. salt	2-3 level tbsps. sugar
$\frac{1}{4}$ pint vinegar	A dash of black
$\frac{1}{4}$ pint water	pepper

Do not peel the cucumbers unless the skin is tough. Wash them well, slice very finely, sprinkle with salt, put in a bowl with a weighted plate on top and leave for some hours or overnight. Discard the juice, rinse the slices and dry in a cloth. Make a dressing of the remaining ingredients, then pour it over the cucumber and leave for about $\frac{1}{2}$ hour. Serve as a side dish with fried meats, roasts and chicken, or use to garnish Smørrebrød.

PICKLED BEETROOTS

Wash 2 lb. small beets but do not peel; cook in plenty of water till tender for $1\frac{1}{2}$-2 hours. Allow to cool, then peel, slice and put into a jar. Bring 1 pint vinegar, pint water and 2-4 oz. sugar to the boil and pour over to cover the beets completely.

These will keep for 2-3 weeks—longer if strips of raw horseradish are boiled with the vinegar. Serve with any kind of roast, liver pâté or salads.

FAGELBO (BIRD'S NEST SALAD)

(see picture above)

8-10 chopped anchovy fillets	2 tbsps. chopped chives
	2 tbsps. capers
2-4 tbsps. diced pickled beetroot	2 tbsps. diced cold cooked potato
2 tbsps. finely chopped onion	4 raw egg yolks

In the middle of a shallow dish put 4 small mounds of anchovy, with a little beetroot between. Now arrange concentric rings of the other salad ingredients around the heaps, pinching the rings in a little at the middle of each side. Make a slight depression in the centre of each of the original mounds and put a raw egg yolk in each 'nest'. Serve chilled. The first person to help himself stirs the ingredients well together to blend them completely.

FAIRY-TALE SALAD

(see left-hand picture opposite)

$1\frac{1}{2}$ lb. boiled potatoes	2 tsps. French mustard
2 tbsps. gherkin	Salt and pepper
2 tbsps. cocktail onions	A little sugar
2 tbsps. olive oil	Chopped parsley and dill
1 tbsp. vinegar	

Slice the cold potatoes, chop the gherkins and mix both with the onions. Blend the oil, vinegar and mustard, then season with salt, pepper and sugar. Toss the salad in this dressing and marinade for 2 hours. Sprinkle with the herbs before serving.

PIQUANT POTATO SALAD

2 small onions	Pepper and salt
$\frac{1}{3}$ pint stock or milk	A little sugar
2 oz. butter	2 lb. cooked potatoes,
$\frac{1}{4}$ pint vinegar	sliced $\frac{1}{4}$ inch thick

Slice the onions and boil until tender in the stock and butter. Add the vinegar, seasonings and sugar, then the potatoes, bring to the boil and cook for a few minutes.

AMERICAN-STYLE SALADS

WATER LILY SALADS
(see picture above)

4 globe artichokes
8 oz. cold lamb, cut into dice

½ pint mayonnaise
2 tbsps. capers

Soak the artichokes in cold salted water for 2 hours, drain and wash. Drop them into boiling salted water and cook until tender—about 25 minutes. Drain and leave to cool. Trim the stems and level the leaves, then take out the hairy 'choke' and the central leaves, so that only the base and a ring of outside leaves are left. Lightly toss the meat in ¼ pint mayonnaise and fill the artichokes. Sprinkle some capers over each. Serve the remaining artichoke leaves separately, tossed with the rest of the mayonnaise.

WALDORF SALAD

2 lb. eating apples
Lemon juice
1 level tsp. sugar
¼ pint mayonnaise

1 head of celery
2 oz. shelled walnuts
1 lettuce

Peel and core the apples; dice all but one, then slice this apple, dip in lemon juice to prevent it discolouring and reserve it for garnish. Toss the diced apples with 2 tbsps. lemon juice, the sugar and 1 tbsp. mayonnaise. Just before serving, slice the celery, crumble the walnuts (keeping a few whole for garnish) and add both to the apple mixture. Add the rest of the mayonnaise and toss together very well. Serve in a bowl lined with lettuce leaves and garnish with the apple slices and the whole walnuts.

LAYERED COLESLAW

1 small head of white cabbage
½ a cucumber
1 large green pepper

2 onions
1 bunch of radishes
Gold dressing (see p. 125)

Finely shred the cabbage. Score the cucumber from end to end with a vegetable knife, remove alternate strips of peel with a pointed knife, then cut the cucumber crosswise in thin slices. Wash and seed the pepper and cut into ¼-inch rings. Cut the peeled onions into rings.

Prepare and wash the radishes and slice very thinly. Arrange about a quarter of the cabbage in a salad bowl; on this arrange the cucumber in a layer, cover with another quarter of the cabbage, then a layer of green pepper rings. Next cover with the remaining cabbage, then a complete layer of onion rings; finally, heap the other half of the cabbage in the centre. Arrange the radish slices round the outer edge of the coleslaw and serve with a small jug of gold dressing.

ENDIVE AND TANGERINE SALAD
(see picture above)

1 head of curly endive or lettuce
4 tangerines
4 tomatoes

8 slices of lemon
2 tsps. olive oil
Salt, pepper and sugar

Wash and drain the endive or lettuce and arrange on a platter. Peel and segment the tangerines and slice the tomatoes. Arrange these and the lemon slices on the endive or lettuce leaves, sprinkle with the olive oil and season with salt, pepper and sugar.

COLD CURRIED CHICKEN SALAD

6 oz. quick-cooking rice
2 pints water with 1 level tsp. salt
1 small ready-cooked chicken
1 small cauliflower
3 tbsps. French dressing
¼ pint mayonnaise

3 level tsps. curry powder
½ level tsp. salt
¼ level tsp. pepper
2 level tbsps. milk
1 small green pepper
2 sticks of celery
2 onions (finely sliced in rings)
1 cos or round lettuce

Cook the rice in the salted boiling water over a low heat until it feels tender; drain very well and dry off in a slow oven. Cut the chicken into chunks. Remove the green outer leaves of the cauliflower and cut the 'flower' into ¼-inch strips, then toss with the rice in the French dressing. Combine the mayonnaise, curry powder, salt and pepper in a large bowl, slowly stir in the milk, add the chicken and toss together. Add the rice mixture, the green pepper (seeded and cut in strips), the celery (cut at an angle) and the onion rings. Line a plate with lettuce leaves and turn the mixture on to this. Serve with separate dishes of curry accompaniments—for instance flaked coconut, salted peanuts, pineapple cubes, tomato wedges and red-currant jelly.

VIRGINIA CHICKEN APPLE SALAD
(see picture above)

½ a small cooked chicken	⅛ pint whipped double cream
½ lb. unpeeled apples	1 level tsp. salt
6 tbsps. lemon juice	1 lettuce
½ a head of celery	2 heads of chicory
6 stuffed olives	Unpeeled, cored apple
2 oz. slivered almonds	rings
3 tbsps. mayonnaise	

Cut the chicken into chunks. Cut up the apples and dip into 3 tbsps. of the lemon juice to prevent their discolouring. Slice the celery and olives. Combine the above ingredients with the almonds. Blend the mayonnaise with the cream, 2 tbsps. lemon juice and the salt; toss this with the chicken mixture, then leave to chill. Heap the salad on a layer of lettuce and chicory. Dip the apple rings in the rest of the lemon juice, tuck some chicory leaves in each ring and use to garnish.

JELLIED BEETROOT AND APPLE SALAD

½ a pkt. of raspberry jelly	1 tbsp. lemon juice
¼ pint boiling water	8 oz. cooked beetroot
⅛ pint vinegar	1 eating apple
	1 oz. shelled walnuts

Dissolve the jelly in the ¼ pint of boiling water. Add the vinegar and lemon juice, made up to ¼ pint with cold water. Slice or dice the beetroot; peel, core and slice the apple. Place the walnuts in the base of a ring mould and add the beetroot and apple in layers. Pour on the jelly, leave in a cool place to set and serve with cold meats.

CARROT AND RAISIN SALAD

3 oz. seedless raisins	4 tbsps. mayonnaise
1 orange	1 tbsp. lemon juice
1 lb. grated raw carrots	1 level tsp. sugar
	¼ level tsp. salt

Put the raisins in a bowl, pour boiling water over them and leave to stand for 5 minutes to plump them; drain well. Peel the orange and divide into sections, then chop. Add the orange and carrots to the raisins. Combine the mayonnaise, lemon juice, sugar and salt and toss the carrot mixture well in this dressing.

PEAR AND STUFFED GRAPE SALAD
(see picture above)

2 canned or fresh ripe pears	Salt and pepper
¼ lb. black grapes	1 tsp. chopped chives
2 tbsps. cream cheese	Milk if required
¼ oz. butter	1 lettuce
	2 tbsps. French dressing

Peel, halve and core the pears. Halve the grapes and remove the pips. Blend the cream cheese, butter, seasonings and chives, adding a very little milk if necessary to soften the mixture. Put this mixture between the grape halves. Arrange each half-pear on a crisp lettuce leaf, fill the hollow centres with the stuffed grapes, chill well and sprinkle with French dressing. Serve with rolled bread and butter.

CAESAR SALAD

1 cos lettuce	A 2-oz. can of
French dressing	anchovy fillets,
1 raw beaten egg	finely chopped
2 oz. grated Parmesan cheese	Garlic croûtons (see below)

Wash the lettuce, drain thoroughly and pull apart, then toss in the dressing. Mix the egg, cheese and anchovy and add to the lettuce, mixing well.
Make some garlic croûtons by cutting 3 slices of French bread into cubes and frying them in oil with 2 cut cloves of garlic; when they are golden-brown, remove the garlic and drain the croûtons on absorbent paper. Immediately before serving the salad, add the croûtons.

LEEK AND TOMATO SALAD

4 young tender leeks	1 tsp. chopped basil
4 tomatoes; skinned	1 tsp. chopped chervil
1 cos lettuce	3 tbsps. French dressing
1 clove of garlic	

Wash the leeks and slice the white part coarsely. Cut the tomatoes into sections. Wash and drain the lettuce. Rub round the inside of a salad bowl with the crushed clove of garlic and arrange the lettuce in it. Place the leeks and tomatoes on the lettuce and sprinkle with the basil and chervil. Pour the French dressing over.

SALAD DRESSINGS

FRENCH DRESSING

¼ level tsp. salt	A pinch of sugar
⅛ level tsp. pepper	1 tbsp. vinegar
¼ level tsp. dry mustard	2 tbsps. olive or salad oil

Put the salt, pepper, mustard and sugar in a bowl, add the vinegar and mix well. Beat in the oil with a fork and when the mixture thickens, use it at once. The oil separates out on standing, so if necessary whisk immediately before use. A good plan is to mix the dressing in a salad-cream bottle, then shake up vigorously just before serving.

A little tarragon vinegar is sometimes added. The proportion of oil to vinegar varies with individual taste, but use vinegar sparingly.

FRENCH DRESSING VARIATIONS

With Chives: Mix 2 tbsps. French dressing with 1 tbsp. chopped chives. Good with vegetable salads.

With Herbs: Mix 2 tbsps. French dressing with 1 tbsp. chopped parsley, ½ level tsp. powdered marjoram and a pinch of powdered thyme. Good with vegetable or meat salads.

With Pickles: Mix 2 tbsps. French dressing with 2 tbsps. pickle relish or 2 tbsps. chopped dill pickle. Good with vegetable, meat or fish salads.

With Olives: Mix 2 tbsps. French dressing with a few sliced stuffed olives or a few chopped ripe olives. Good with vegetables, fruit or fish salads.

Vinaigrette Dressing: Add a little chopped parsley, chopped gherkin or capers and chives to 2 tbsps. dressing.

LEMON AND OIL DRESSING

2-3 tbsps. olive oil	1 tbsp. lemon juice
Pepper and salt	

Add the oil gradually to the condiments and when the salt is dissolved, pour in the lemon juice.

MAYONNAISE
(see pictures on left)

2 egg yolks	2 tsps. white vinegar
½ tsp. made mustard	or strained lemon
Pepper and salt	juice
¼ pint (approx.) olive	1 tsp. tarragon vinegar
oil	1 tsp. chilli vinegar

Put the egg yolks into a basin with the mustard and pepper and salt to taste. Mix thoroughly, then add the oil drop by drop, stirring hard with a wooden spoon or a whisk the whole time, until the sauce is thick and smooth. Add the vinegars gradually and mix thoroughly. If liked, lemon juice may be used instead of the vinegars or it may replace white vinegar only.

Note: To keep the basin firmly in position, twist a damp cloth tightly round the base—this prevents it from slipping. In order that the oil may be added 1 drop at a time, put into the bottle-neck a cork from which a small wedge has been cut. Should the sauce curdle during the process of making, put another egg yolk into a basin and add the curdled sauce very gradually in the same way as the oil is added to the original egg yolks.

Caper: Mix 2 tbsps. mayonnaise with 1 tsp. capers, 1 tsp. chopped pimiento and ½ tsp. tarragon vinegar. Good with fish and vegetable salads.

Cream: Mix 2 tbsps. mayonnaise and ¼ pint whipped double cream. Particularly good with salads containing fruit.

Cucumber: Mix 2 tbsps. mayonnaise with ½ a small cucumber (pared, chopped and drained). Good with fish salads, particularly those made with crab, lobster and salmon.

Herb: Mix 2 tsps. mayonnaise with 2 tsps. chopped chives and 1 tbsp. chopped parsley. Good with meat or fish salads.

SPICY MAYONNAISE SAUCE

(Made in an electric mixer)

2 egg yolks	A pinch of pepper
1 tsp. French mustard	1 tsp. lemon juice
1 level tsp. sugar	½ pint best olive oil
1 level tsp. salt	2 tbsps. white wine
A very small pinch of	vinegar
Cayenne pepper	

Place the egg yolks, mustard, sugar, salt, peppers and lemon juice in the mixer bowl and blend, using speed 3-5. Place the oil in the juice extractor bowl, regulate the dripper and add the oil very gradually at first. When the egg and oil emulsify, the oil may be allowed to run through the dripper more rapidly. When all the oil has been incorporated, add the vinegar gradually until the sauce is of the right consistency, i.e., until it is stiff enough to hold its shape. Use as required; this mayonnaise is particularly good with grilled fish.

FOAMY MAYONNAISE

2 egg yolks	2 small tbsps. lemon
Salt and pepper	juice
Salad oil (about ¼ pint)	1 egg white

Cream the yolks and seasonings and add the oil drop by drop, stirring hard all the time until the mayonnaise is thick and smooth. Stir in the lemon juice. Put in a cool place until required; just before serving, fold in the stiffly whisked egg white.

WHITE SALAD CREAM

¼ pint double cream	2 tsps. lemon juice
2 tsps. tarragon vinegar	2 egg whites, whisked

Beat the cream until fairly stiff, then stir in the vinegar gradually. Season to taste, add the lemon juice and fold in the stiffly beaten egg whites.

SOUR MILK DRESSING

A simple dressing, practical in the summer time, is made from sour milk. Allow the milk to become solid, then beat up with salt, pepper and sugar to taste. It is particularly good with green salads.

FRENCH MUSTARD DRESSING

2 tsps. French mustard	1 level tbsp. sugar
2 tbsps. olive oil	Salt and freshly ground
Juice of ½ a lemon	black pepper

Blend mustard and oil and slowly mix in lemon juice; add sugar and seasoning and use as required.

CREAM DRESSING

Salt and cayenne	¼ pint double cream
pepper	2 tbsps. vinegar

Add the seasoning to the cream and whip until thick, then very gradually add the vinegar (French wine, for preference). Chill and use as required.

BOILED SALAD DRESSING

1 oz. flour	2 eggs, beaten
1 level tbsp. sugar	2 oz. butter
2 level tsps. dry mustard	¼ pint vinegar
1 level tbsp. salt	¼ pint sour cream or
¼ pint milk	salad oil

Mix the dry ingredients, blend with the milk and bring to the boil, stirring continuously; boil for 5 minutes. Cool a little, add the eggs and butter, beat well and cook until thick, but do not boil. Add the vinegar gradually and beat well, then stir in the cream or oil and bottle the dressing. Shake well before using.

HORSERADISH DRESSING

Fresh horseradish	1 tsp. lemon juice
¼ pint thick sour	1 tsp. vinegar
cream	Salt
A pinch of sugar	Cayenne pepper

Clean and grate the horseradish to give 3 tbsps. Whip the cream until thick and add the horseradish, sugar, lemon juice and vinegar; season to taste.

SOUR CREAM SALAD DRESSING

¼ pint thick sour cream	½ level tsp. sugar
2 tbsps. white vinegar	1 level tsp. salt
2 tbsps. chopped onion	A little pepper

Mix all the ingredients thoroughly.

SPANISH SALAD DRESSING

2 level tsps. caster sugar	1 tbsp. cold water
1 level tsp. salt	1 tsp. piquant sauce
1 tsp. made mustard	1 tbsp. tomato ketchup
A pinch of paprika	5 tbsps. salad oil
1 tbsp. lemon juice	

Mix together in a basin the sugar, salt, mustard and paprika. Moisten these with the other ingredients, beat thoroughly and serve on any plain salad.

WHITE WINE DRESSING

⅛ pint olive oil	1 tsp. lemon juice
⅛ pint white wine	Salt and pepper

Blend oil and wine as for a French dressing, stir in lemon juice and season to taste.

GOLD DRESSING

½ pint mayonnaise	2 tbsps. vinegar
½ level tsp. salt	2 tbsps. milk
¼ level tsp. pepper	2 tsps. prepared
⅛ level tsp. paprika	mustard
2 level tsps. sugar	2 egg yolks

Combine the ingredients as listed and blend well.

Note: In all salad recipes where mayonnaise is suggested, this can be replaced by commercial mayonnaise or salad cream when speed is important.

SALAD INGREDIENTS AND GARNISHES

Beetroot: Thinly peel the cooked beetroot (see Vegetables chapter). Cut into thin slices, if the beetroots are small; grate or dice them if large. The prepared beetroot can be sprinkled with salt, pepper and 1-2 level tsps. sugar and covered with vinegar or vinegar and water—this helps it to keep and also gives it a better flavour.

Cabbage: Wash the leaves in salted water, drain and cut into shreds with a sharp knife.

Celery: Separate the sticks and wash them well in cold water, scrubbing to remove any dirt from the grooves. Slice, chop or make into curls (see Salad Garnishes).

Chicory: Trim off the root end and any damaged leaves, wash the chicory in cold water and drain.

Cucumber: Wipe the skin and either leave it on if liked or peel it off thinly. Slice the cucumber finely, sprinkle with salt and leave it for about 1 hour; pour off the liquid and rinse. Alternatively, you can soak the cucumber in a little vinegar, with salt and a pinch of sugar. If you like the cucumber crisp use it when freshly sliced.

Endive: Trim off the root end, remove the coarse outer leaves, separate remaining leaves, wash and drain well.

Lettuce: Remove the outer coarse leaves. Separate the inner leaves and wash them under a running cold tap or in a bowl of cold water. Drain them in a sieve or colander or shake them in a clean tea towel.
To "revive" a withered lettuce, wash it in cold water, shake slightly to remove the excess moisture, place in a polythene bag or a bowl covered with a plate and put in the bottom of the refrigerator or in any cool place. In an hour or so the leaves will have crisped up.

Mustard and Cress: Trim off the roots and lower parts of the stems with scissors and place the leaves in a colander or sieve. Wash them (under a fast-running cold tap if possible), turning the cress over and removing the seeds.

Radishes: Trim off the root end and leaves and wash the radishes in cold water. Slice thinly or cut into "lilies" or "roses" (see Salad Garnishes).

Spring Onions: Trim off the root end, remove the papery outer skin, trim the green leaves down to about 2 inches of green above the white and wash.

Tomatoes: Remove the stem and wash or wipe the tomatoes. To remove the skins from tomatoes, plunge them for a minute into boiling water, then lift them out and put them immediately into cold water; when they are cool, the skins will peel off easily with a knife. Alternatively, spear a tomato on the prongs of a fork and turn it gently over a gas jet until the skin bursts, then peel it off with a knife.

Watercress: Trim the coarse ends from the stalks, wash the watercress and drain well before using.

SALAD GARNISHES

The classic green salad needs no garnish and only the simplest of touches is required to set off many other types—a dusting of chopped herbs on potato salad, a sprinkling of chopped onion or some thinly cut onion rings on a tomato salad, a few leaves of watercress on an orange salad. However, for those occasions when you want something a little more ambitious to set off a mixed salad or to garnish, say, a cold veal and ham pie, here are some attractive salad decorations that can quite easily be produced.

Radish Roses: Choose round radishes and wash them well, removing the root but leaving 1 inch or so of the stalk. Using a small, sharp knife or potato parer, peel the skin down in sections to look like petals, starting at the root end and continuing nearly as far as the stalk. Repeat all round, leaving the middle of the radish as the flower centre. Soak in cold water for a short time to make the petals open out; shake well before using.

Radish Lilies: Wash and trim the radishes, then cut each into sections down from the root end towards the stalk. Leave in cold water until they open like flowers.

Curled Celery: Cut into very thin shreds lengthwise and soak in cold or iced water until curled—about 1 hour. Drain well before using.

Curled Spring Onions: Prepare as for celery, above.

Cucumber Cones: Cut thin slices. Take one slice, cut from centre to rim, then wrap one cut edge over the other to form a cone.

Crimped Cucumber: Working lengthwise on a whole or half cucumber, remove strips of the cucumber skin about ⅛ inch wide at intervals of about ⅛ inch. Now cut the cucumber crosswise into thin slices.

Gherkin Fans: Choose long, thin gherkins. Cut each lengthwise into thin slices, but leave these joined at one end. Fan out the slices.

Lemon Fans: Cut ¼-inch slices; now halve each, making semi-circles. Cut rind again in half, leaving centre membranes attached, then open each piece out to form a "fan" or "butterfly".

Onion Rings: Cut the onion crosswise. Use the rings in graduated sizes or singly to enclose another garnish such as chopped egg or beetroot.

Tomato Twists: Slice a firm tomato crosswise. Slit each piece up to the core, leaving a piece at the top holding the halves together; turn halves in opposite directions to make the twist.
Use beetroot, lemon or cucumber similarly.

Tomato Lilies: Choose firm, even-sized tomatoes. Using a small sharp-pointed knife, make a series of V-shaped cuts round the middle of each, cutting right through to the centre. Carefully pull the halves apart.

Red Pepper Julienne: Cut a red (or green) pepper into very thin strips, cutting across the vegetable and removing any pith or seeds.

Quick Garnish: Sprinkle finely chopped parsley on potato salad; finely chopped onion on beetroot; chopped spring onion on tomato; chopped mint, chives, tarragon or parsley on green salad.

PASTA & RICE

Recipes give 4 servings, unless otherwise indicated

Though so different in origin and character, these two foods can be used in much the same ways.

PASTA

Pasta, which is Italian in origin, is made from special 'hard' wheats. Some continental shops sell freshly-made pasta, which should be used straight away, though the packeted kinds sold throughout the country will keep indefinitely. The main practical difference between fresh and packeted pasta is that the former takes about 5 minutes to cook, the packet pastas up to 20 minutes.

COOKING AND SERVING PASTA

Italians would reckon about 3-4 oz. per person, but in this country 1½-2 oz. is enough for most people. Pasta should be cooked in a large quantity of fast-boiling salted water (see chart for times) until *al dente*, or just resistant to the teeth—it should never be mushy or slimy. Drain it as soon as it is cooked and serve on a heated dish.

These are the average times; if the pasta has been stored for some time, slightly longer may be needed.

Vermicelli, Spaghettini	5 minutes
Spaghetti	12-15 minutes
Macaroni	15-20 minutes
Fancy-shaped, e.g. Farfalette;	
Tagliatelle, Noodles	10 minutes
Lasagne	10-15 minutes
Canneroni, Large shells	20 minutes
Stuffed, e.g. Ravioli	15-20 minutes

RICE

There are three main kinds of rice grain—long, medium and short. Long grains are best for made-up savoury rice dishes and for rice used as a savoury accompaniment. Medium grains are very suitable for rice rings, stuffings and croquettes. The short-grain type is usually used for rice puddings and other sweet dishes.

PREPARING AND COOKING RICE

Rice sold in unbranded packs or loose should be washed in a strainer under the cold tap.

Boiled Rice—the 1-2-1 Method
Place 1 cup of long-grain rice in a saucepan with 2 cups water and 1 level tsp. salt. Bring quickly to the boil, stir well and cover with a tight-fitting lid. Reduce the heat and simmer gently for 14-15 minutes. Remove from the heat and before serving separate out the grains gently, using a fork—the rice will not need draining. For a drier effect, leave covered for 5-10 minutes.

Boiled Rice—Ordinary Method
Allow 1½-2 oz. long-grain per person. Half-fill a large pan with water (about 1 pint to each oz. rice), bring to the boil and add about 1 level tbsp. salt to 6 oz. rice. Add the rice and continue to boil rapidly, uncovered, until the rice is just soft—15-20 minutes. Drain the rice in a sieve and rinse by pouring hot water through it, then return it to the pan with a knob of butter; cover with a tea towel or a lid and leave on a very low heat to dry for 5-10 minutes, shaking pan from time to time.

PASTA RECIPES

SPAGHETTI NAPOLITANA

8 oz. spaghetti	Salt and pepper
1 oz. butter	1 oz. Parmesan cheese,
1/4-1/2 pint tomato sauce	grated

Cook the spaghetti in fast-boiling salted water in the usual way for 12-15 minutes. Drain and return it to the pan, with the butter, and shake it over a gentle heat for a minute or two. Serve on a heated dish, with the tomato sauce poured over it and the cheese sprinkled on top; if you prefer, the sauce and cheese may be served separately.

BUTTERED SPAGHETTI

Have ready a large pan of boiling water. Allow 2 oz. spaghetti per person; hold the end of the bunch of spaghetti in the water and as it softens, coil it round in the pan. Boil rapidly for 12-15 minutes, moving the spaghetti occasionally to prevent sticking, until it is just cooked. Drain well and return it to the pan with 1-2 oz. butter and a good sprinkling of grated Parmesan cheese. Stir and leave for a few minutes for the butter and cheese to melt. Serve with more grated cheese in a separate dish. Any form of tubular or ribbon pasta can be cooked and served in this way.

SPAGHETTI ALLA BOLOGNESE

8 oz. spaghetti	Grated Parmesan cheese

For the traditional Italian meat sauce

2 oz. bacon, chopped	8 oz. minced beef, raw
1/2 oz. butter	4 oz. chicken livers,
1 small onion, skinned and chopped	chopped (optional)
	1 level tbsp. tomato paste
1 carrot, peeled and chopped	1/4 pint dry white wine
1 stick of celery, scrubbed and chopped	1/2 pint beef stock
	Salt, pepper, nutmeg

Make the sauce first. Fry the bacon lightly in the butter for 2-3 minutes, add the onion, carrot and celery and fry for a further 5 minutes until lightly browned. Add the beef and brown lightly. Stir in the chicken livers, if used. After cooking them for about 3 minutes, add the tomato paste and wine, allow to bubble for a few minutes and add the stock, seasoning and nutmeg. Cover and simmer for 30-40 minutes, until the meat is tender and the liquid in the sauce is well reduced. Re-season if necessary.

Meanwhile cook the spaghetti in the usual way in fast-boiling water for about 12-15 minutes. Drain and serve on a heated dish with the sauce poured over. Serve the cheese sprinkled over the sauce or in a separate dish.

MACARONI CHEESE

(see left-hand picture below)

6 oz. macaroni	A pinch of grated nutmeg
1 1/2 oz. butter	or 1/2 tsp. made mustard
1 1/2 oz. flour	6 oz. cheese, grated
1 pint milk	2 tbsps. fresh white
Salt and pepper	breadcrumbs (optional)

Cook the macaroni in fast-boiling salted water for 15 minutes only and drain it well. Meanwhile melt the fat, stir in the flour and cook for 2-3 minutes. Remove the pan from the heat and gradually stir in the milk. Bring to the boil and continue to stir until the sauce thickens; remove from the heat and stir in the seasonings, 4 oz. of the cheese and the macaroni. Pour into an ovenproof dish and sprinkle with the breadcrumbs (if used) and the remaining cheese. Bake in a fairly hot oven (400°F., mark 6) for about 20 minutes, or until golden. Quick macaroni can also be used—cook it as directed.

Variations

Add to the sauce any of the following:
1 small onion, skinned, chopped and boiled
4 oz. bacon or ham, chopped and lightly fried
1/2-1 green pepper, seeded, chopped and blanched
1/2-1 canned pimiento, chopped
2 oz. mushrooms, sliced and lightly fried

MEDITERRANEAN PASTA

(see right-hand picture below)

6-8 oz. pasta	A 5-oz. can of tomato
2 medium onions, skinned and chopped	paste
	1 level tsp. dried marjoram
1 1/2 oz. butter or 2-3 tbsps. oil	or rosemary
	1 level tsp. sugar
1 clove of garlic, crushed	Salt and pepper
A 15-oz. can of Italian tomatoes	4 oz. mushrooms, sliced

Cook the pasta in the usual way. Fry the onions gently in 1 oz. of the butter for 5 minutes, until soft but not coloured. Stir in the garlic, tomatoes, tomato paste, herbs, sugar and seasoning, cover and simmer for 30 minutes, until the sauce is thick. Fry the mushrooms gently for about 3 minutes in the remaining 1/2 oz. butter and add. Adjust the seasoning and serve over the pasta.

MACHERONI ALLA CARBONARA
(Macaroni with Ham and Eggs)

6 oz. macaroni, in short lengths	2-3 eggs, beaten
1 oz. butter	Salt and pepper
4 oz. cooked ham	2 tbsps. grated Parmesan cheese

Cook the macaroni in the usual way in fast-boiling water for 15-20 minutes, until soft, and drain it well. Fry the ham lightly for 2-3 minutes in the butter, until heated through, and stir in the drained macaroni, beaten eggs and seasoning. Stir over a gentle heat until the mixture is well blended and the eggs are just beginning to thicken. Add the cheese, mix well and serve straight away.
Quick macaroni can also be used—cook as directed on the packet.

STUFFED CANNERONI WITH TOMATO SAUCE

8 oz. canneroni	1 can of tomato soup

For the Stuffing

4 oz. fresh white bread-crumbs	2 tbsps. chopped parsley
A little milk	Salt and pepper
8-12 oz. lean bacon, finely chopped	1 egg, beaten
	4-6 oz. cheese, grated

Cook the canneroni in fast-boiling salted water for 15 minutes only and drain it. Soak the breadcrumbs in the milk. Fry the bacon lightly in its own fat for about 5 minutes, until soft, adding a little butter if it tends to stick. Mix together the crumbs, bacon, parsley and seasoning and bind with the egg. Stuff the canneroni with this mixture, lay half of them in a greased ovenproof dish and cover with half the cheese. Add the remaining pasta, pour the soup over and add the remaining cheese. Bake for about 20 minutes towards the top of a fairly hot oven (400°F., mark 6) until golden on top and bubbling.
Note: In the traditional recipe fresh tomato sauce is used, but the soup saves a good deal of time.

LASAGNE AL FORNO
(Baked Lasagne)

2 8-oz. cans of Italian tomatoes	1 level tsp. sugar
A small (3-oz.) can of tomato paste	8 oz. cooked veal or ham, diced
½-1 level tsp. dried marjoram	4 oz. lasagne
Salt	6 oz. Ricotta or cream cheese
Pepper	2 oz. Parmesan cheese
	8 oz. Mozarella cheese

Combine the canned tomatoes, tomato paste, marjoram, seasonings and sugar, simmer gently for about 30 minutes and add the veal or ham. Cook the lasagne in boiling salted water in the usual way for about 10-15 minutes (or as stated on the packet) and drain well.
Cover the base of a fairly deep ovenproof dish with a layer of the tomato and meat sauce. Add half the lasagne, put in another layer of the sauce, then cover with the cheeses, using half of each kind. Repeat these layers with the remaining ingredients, finishing with a layer of cheese. Bake towards the top of a fairly hot oven (375°F., mark 5) for 30 minutes, until golden and bubbling on top. Serve at once. The special sauce can be replaced by a Bolognese sauce (see opposite).

RAVIOLI
In Italy, supplies of ravioli and its variants are made and cooked fresh daily. In this country, freshly made ravioli can be bought in some Italian shops and restaurants. Failing this, you can find ready-cooked ravioli in some delicatessen shops and it can also be bought in cans.
To cook fresh Ravioli: Put the ravioli into boiling salted water, adding about 10-15 pieces at a time, and cook for 15-20 minutes (don't cook more than this at any one time, as the pieces tend to break up if the pan is crowded). Remove them with a slotted spoon and keep warm until all are cooked. Toss them with a little butter and then serve sprinkled with finely grated Parmesan cheese.
As a variation, the cooked ravioli can be layered with tomato sauce in a greased ovenproof dish, sprinkled with grated Parmesan cheese and baked in a fairly hot oven (400°F., mark 6) for about 15 minutes, until golden.

RICE RECIPES

FLAVOURED RICE
1. Rice may be cooked in various liquids to give extra flavour and variety. Replace water by any of these:
Chicken or beef stock (fresh or made from a cube).
Canned tomato juice, undiluted or used half-and-half with water.
Orange juice—used half-and-half with water.
2. Alternatively, rice can be flavoured as follows:
Savoury Rice: Fry chopped onion, pepper, celery or bacon in a little butter in the pan before adding the rice.
Herby Rice: Add a pinch of dried herbs with the cooking liquid (e.g. sage, marjoram, thyme, mixed herbs).
Raisin Rice: Add stoned raisins (or currants or sultanas) and if liked a pinch of curry powder.
Variety Rice: When the rice is cooked stir in: diced pineapple, chopped canned pimiento, slivered browned almonds, grated cheese, or chopped fresh herbs.

FRIED RICE WITH EGG

4 oz. long-grain rice	2 oz. mushrooms, thinly sliced
2 eggs, beaten	
4 tbsps. oil	2 tbsps. frozen peas
½ level tsp. salt	2 oz. cooked ham, diced
½ an onion, finely chopped	2 tsps. soy sauce

Boil the rice. Make a plain omelette from the eggs, cut it into thin strips and set aside. Fry the drained rice for about 5 minutes in 2 tbsps. of very hot oil with the salt, stirring all the time; remove from the pan and set aside. Clean the pan and add the remaining oil. Fry the onion for about 3 minutes, till lightly browned, add the remaining vegetables and the ham and fry lightly for a further 3 minutes, stirring well. Slowly add the rice and when well mixed, stir in the soy sauce and shredded omelette; serve hot, to accompany chicken.

RISOTTO
Risotto is the main rice dish in the north of Italy, where rice takes the place of pasta. Risotto is usually a dish complete in itself (with the exception of Milanese Risotto, which is served as an accompaniment to such well-known Italian dishes as Osso Buco).
The difference between a risotto and a pilau is that the former is moister, being made from a special type of rice with short, fat grains. In this country a long-grain rice may have to be substituted, but the risotto should still be made more moist than a pilau.

CHICKEN RISOTTO

½ a boiling chicken or 2-3 good-sized chicken portions (uncooked)	2 oz. mushrooms, sliced
	2 oz. bacon or ham, chopped
3 oz. butter	¼ pint dry white wine
2 small onions, skinned and finely chopped	Chicken stock
	Salt and pepper
1 stick of celery, scrubbed and finely chopped	Chopped fresh herbs as available (e.g. marjoram thyme or basil)
1 clove of garlic, crushed (optional)	8 oz. long-grain rice
1 green pepper, seeded and finely chopped	Grated Parmesan cheese

Skin the chicken, bone it and cut the flesh in strips. Melt 1 oz. of the butter and fry one of the onions gently for 5 minutes, until soft. Add the chicken, the remaining vegetables and the bacon or ham and fry for a further few minutes, stirring all the time. Add the wine and let it bubble until well reduced; just cover with chicken stock and add the seasoning and herbs. Put on the lid and leave to simmer for about 1 hour, until the chicken is really tender.
Fry the remaining onion in 1 oz. of the remaining butter for about 5 minutes, until soft. Add the rice and stir until transparent. Add about ½ pint of chicken stock and cook over a moderate heat, uncovered, until the stock has been absorbed; continue to cook, adding more stock as required, until the rice is just soft (15-20 minutes). Pour in the chicken mixture, stir well and continue cooking until the two mixtures are well blended and the liquid all absorbed. Stir in the remaining butter and some Parmesan cheese and serve.

SHELLFISH RISOTTO

1 onion, skinned and finely chopped	Salt and pepper
	1 clove of garlic (optional)
3 oz. butter	8 oz. frozen scampi or prawns, thawed
8 oz. long-grain rice	
¼ pint dry white wine	Grated Parmesan cheese
1½ pints boiling chicken stock	

Prepare the risotto as above, using 2 oz. of the butter. Just before the rice becomes tender, gently fry the garlic (if used) and the shellfish in the remaining 1 oz. butter for 5 minutes. Stir into the risotto and serve with the cheese.
A few sliced button mushrooms can be fried with the shellfish or a few frozen peas or strips of canned pimiento can be added to the risotto just before the rice is cooked. Other shellfish, such as crab or lobster meat (fresh or canned) may also be used; a mixture of shellfish, with possibly a few mussels (canned or fresh) will give a more unusual touch.

PAELLA
(see colour picture no. 30)

6-8 mussels, fresh or bottled	4 tomatoes, skinned and chopped
2-4 oz. Dublin Bay prawns (or frozen scampi)	8-12 oz. long-grain rice
1 small cooked lobster	2-3 pints chicken stock (made from a cube)
1 small chicken	
4 tbsps. olive oil	Salt and pepper
1 clove of garlic, crushed	A little powdered saffron
1 onion, chopped	A small pkt. of frozen peas
1 green pepper, seeded and chopped	Garnish

This famous Spanish dish takes its name from the pan in which it is cooked—a shallow oval metal dish with handles at each side. There are few hard-and-fast rules about making a paella, although the following ingredients are traditionally included—chicken, lobster, shellfish of various kinds, onion, green or red peppers and rice. Paella is rather elaborate and somewhat expensive to prepare in this country, but it makes an attractive party dish. The quantities given should serve at least 8 people. Shell or drain the mussels and peel the prawns, if fresh. Remove the lobster meat from the shell and dice it, retaining the claws for decorating. Cut the meat from the chicken into small pieces. Put the oil into a large *paella* or frying pan and fry the garlic, onion and green pepper for 5 minutes, until soft but not browned. Add the tomatoes and chicken pieces and fry until the chicken is lightly browned. Stir in the rice and add half the stock, the seasoning and saffron (blended with a little of the stock). Bring to the boil, then reduce the heat and simmer for about 20-25 minutes, until the chicken is tender and the rice just cooked.
Stir in the mussels, prawns, lobster meat and peas and simmer for a final 5-10 minutes, until heated through. Serve garnished with a few extra strips of green pepper or pimiento and the lobster claws. Mussels in their shells can also be used as a garnish.

BASIC PILAU

8 oz. long-grain rice	3 pints boiling chicken stock
2 oz. butter	Salt and pepper

Fry the rice gently in the melted butter for about 5 minutes, stirring all the time, until it looks transparent. Add the stock pouring it in slowly, as it will tend to bubble rather a lot at first. Add the seasoning, stir well, cover with a tight-fitting lid and leave over a very low heat for about 15 minutes, until the water is absorbed and the rice grains are just soft. (The idea is that the rice should cook in its own steam, so don't stir meanwhile.) Remove the lid, cover the rice with a cloth, replace the lid and leave in a warm place to dry out for at least 15 minutes before serving. (This is a traditional part of making a pilau.)
To serve, stir lightly with a fork to separate the grains, add a knob of butter and serve at once.

LIVER PILAU

½ lb. calf's liver, cut in strips	A pinch of mixed spice
2 oz. butter	2 oz. currants
2 onions, finely chopped	2 tomatoes, skinned and chopped
1 oz. shelled peanuts or almonds	1½-2 pints chicken or meat stock (boiling)
6-8 oz. long-grain rice	
Salt and pepper	A little chopped parsley

Fry the liver lightly in the butter for 2-3 minutes and remove it from the fat with a slotted spoon. Fry the onions for 5 minutes in the same fat until soft but not brown. Add the nuts and rice and fry for a further 5 minutes, stirring all the time. Add the seasoning, spice, currants, tomatoes and stock, stir well, cover with a tight-fitting lid and simmer for about 15 minutes, until all the liquid has been absorbed. Stir in the liver and parsley, cover again and before serving leave for 15 minutes in a warm place (but without further cooking). The liver if preferred may be replaced by cooked chicken or lamb.

HOT PUDDINGS

Recipes give 4 servings, unless otherwise indicated

Although the modern trend is towards serving a light sweet or fresh fruit at the end of a meal, there are still times when a good, substantial hot pudding is just what the family needs. Here is a wide selection for all occasions, including hearty steamed, suet and baked puddings, lighter milk puddings and batters and delicious soufflés, not forgetting the ever-popular fruit pie in many guises.

Note: Use plain flour unless otherwise directed.

STEAMED PUDDINGS

SAXON PUDDING

(see picture above)

4 oz. sponge cake crumbs	2 oz. butter
2 oz. ground almonds	2 eggs
2 tbsps. cream or top of milk	2 oz. shredded or diced pineapple
2 tbsps. milk	Grated rind of 1 lemon
2 oz. sugar	

Grease a plain mould thoroughly. Put the crumbs and ground almonds into a basin, pour on the cream and milk and leave to soak for about 30 minutes. Cream together the sugar and butter and beat in the egg yolks alternately with the soaked mixture and the drained pineapple. Beat in the lemon rind and lastly fold in the stiffly beaten egg whites. Steam carefully for 1½-2 hours, turn out, decorate with pieces of pineapple and serve with pineapple sauce (see below).

PINEAPPLE SAUCE

4 oz. sugar	2 level tbsps. shredded pineapple
¼ pint water	
2 level tbsps. apricot jam, sieved	2 level tsps. cornflour
2-3 tsps. lemon juice	A little red colouring if desired

Dissolve the sugar in the water and add the apricot jam, lemon juice and pineapple. Blend the cornflour with a little cold water and add to the hot syrup, bring to the boil and add colouring.

RICH CHOCOLATE PUDDING

(see picture above)

2 oz. plain chocolate	1½ oz. sugar
¼ pint milk	1 egg
4 oz. fresh white bread-crumbs	Vanilla essence
	¼ level tsp. baking powder
1½ oz. butter	Almonds to decorate

Break the chocolate into small pieces, melt it in the milk, pour on to the crumbs and leave to soak for 15-20 minutes. Cream together the fat and sugar until soft and light, beat in the egg yolk, then beat in the soaked crumbs. Add a few drops of vanilla essence and the stiffly beaten egg white. Lastly, fold in the baking powder, put the mixture into a greased mould and steam gently for 1 hour, until well risen and firm. Turn it out on to a hot dish, decorate with a few blanched almonds and serve with chocolate sauce—see recipe below.

CHOCOLATE SAUCE

1½ oz. unsweetened chocolate	2 oz. sugar
	A few drops of vanilla essence
⅓ pint water	
1 level tsp. cornflour	½ oz. butter
A pinch of salt	

Break up the chocolate, add half of the water and dissolve over a gentle heat. Mix the cornflour and salt to a smooth cream with a little of the remaining cold water, heat the remainder, and when boiling pour on to the blended cornflour, stirring. Return it to the saucepan and bring to the boil, still stirring. Add the dissolved chocolate and sugar and cook for 4-5 minutes, stirring and beating. Lastly, stir in the vanilla essence and butter.

For some other sweet sauce recipes, see p. 158.

CANARY PUDDING

4 oz. flour	4 oz. caster sugar
A pinch of salt	2 eggs
½ level tsp. baking powder	2 tbsps. milk
4 oz. butter	A few drops of vanilla essence

Sift together the flour, salt and baking powder. Cream the butter and sugar until soft and white, then beat in the eggs separately, with a sprinkling of flour. Stir in the remaining flour lightly and add the milk and essence. Put into a greased 2-pint basin, two-thirds filling it, cover with greased greaseproof paper and steam for 1½ hours. Turn out and serve with jam sauce.

Some variations of Canary Pudding are given below.

JAM CANARY PUDDING
(see colour picture no. 32)
Put 2 tbsps. jam (or marmalade or golden syrup) in the basin before adding the pudding mixture.

ORANGE OR LEMON SPONGE
Add the grated rind of 1 lemon or orange and serve with a sauce made with the fruit juice.

CHERRY SPONGE
Add 2 oz. cut up glacé cherries to the Canary Pudding mixture, combining them with the dry ingredients. Serve with a custard sauce flavoured with Maraschino or sherry.

CHOCOLATE SPONGE
Add 1½ oz. cocoa and a pinch of baking powder to the flour and mix to a soft dropping consistency, adding a little more milk if necessary. Serve with chocolate or custard sauce.

SPONGE RING
(see picture above)

4 oz. butter or margarine	Grated rind of 1 lemon
4 oz. sugar	Mixed stewed fruits, e.g., cherries, apricots, currants, gooseberries
2 eggs	
6 oz. flour	
½ level tsp. baking powder	A little cornflour

Grease a ring mould. Cream together the fat and sugar until fluffy and light, beat in the eggs one at a time, then lastly fold in the flour, baking powder and grated lemon rind. Put the mixture into the mould, cover, and steam for 1½ hours. Turn it out, then pile the hot mixed fruit into the centre and round the dish. Serve the pudding with some of the fruit juice, thickened with a little cornflour.

LAFAYETTE PUDDING

4 oz. butter	2 oz. fine fresh white breadcrumbs
4 oz. sugar	
2 eggs	½ level tsp. baking powder
4 oz. flour	2 oz. glacé cherries
3 oz. ground almonds	3 tbsps. milk

Cream together the fat and sugar, then beat in the eggs separately. Mix together the dry ingredients and add the cut up cherries. Fold the dry ingredients into the first mixture, alternately with the milk. Put into a greased basin and steam gently for 2 hours. Serve with almond-flavoured sauce or custard.

MARMALADE PUDDING

4 oz. flour	3-4 oz. shredded suet
¼ level tsp. salt	1 egg, beaten
1 level tsp. baking powder	4 tbsps. marmalade
	Milk to mix
4 oz. fresh white breadcrumbs	Marmalade sauce

Sift the flour, salt and baking powder together. Add the crumbs and suet and mix well, then add the egg, marmalade and sufficient milk to give a soft dropping consistency. Put the mixture into a greased basin, cover with greased paper and steam for at least 2 hours. Turn out and serve with marmalade sauce—see below.

MARMALADE (OR JAM) SAUCE

1 tbsp. marmalade (or jam)	½ level tsp. cornflour
1 level tsp. caster sugar	A little lemon juice
¼ pint water	Colouring (optional)

Put the marmalade (or jam), sugar and water in a saucepan and bring to the boil. Add the cornflour, mixed with a little cold water, and boil up until the sauce is clear and the cornflour cooked—about 5 minutes. Add the lemon juice and colouring (if used). Strain if necessary.

SYRUP SPONGE PUDDING

(see picture above)

8 oz. flour
A pinch of salt
$\frac{1}{4}$ lb. shredded suet
1 level tsp. ground
  ginger

2 tbsps. golden syrup
1 level tsp. bicarbonate
  of soda
Milk to mix

Put the flour, salt, suet and ginger into a basin, make a well in the centre and add the syrup. Dissolve the bicarbonate of soda in 1 tbsp. of the milk. Mix the pudding to a very soft dough with milk and add the bicarbonate of soda. Put the mixture into a greased basin, cover with greased paper and steam for $2\frac{1}{2}$ hours. Turn out and serve with syrup or custard sauce. Decorate if desired with chopped crystallised ginger.

SPOTTED DICK OR PLUM DUFF

4 oz. flour
A pinch of salt
1 level tsp. baking
  powder
4 oz. shredded suet

4 oz. fresh white
  breadcrumbs
4 oz. currants
Water to mix

Sift the flour, salt and baking powder together. Add the breadcrumbs, suet and currants and mix to a soft dough with water. Turn out on to a floured board and shape into a roll, put this into a piece of greaseproof paper, then roll it in foil. Boil for 2 hours or steam for $2\frac{1}{2}$-3 hours. Unwrap and serve with butter and brown sugar, or with custard sauce.

STEAMED OR BOILED FRUIT PUDDING

(see right-hand picture above)

2 lb. fruit
8 oz. suet crust pastry
  (see p. 140)

2-4 oz. sugar
A little water, as
  required

Thoroughly grease a 3-pint basin and prepare the fruit. (Apples, rhubarb, apricots, gooseberries, plums and so on are all suitable.) Cut off a quarter of the pastry, roll the rest out into a round and line the basin with it. Fill the basin well with fruit until it is piled high, putting a good sprinkling of sugar between the layers, and add a very little water—the amount varies according to the fruit, juicy ones needing least water. Roll out the rest of the pastry into a round for the top, damp the edges and fix firmly. Cover with greaseproof paper, then with foil, and tie down lightly. Steam for $2\frac{1}{2}$-3 hours or boil for 2 hours. Turn out and serve with custard or a sauce.

CHRISTMAS PUDDING

(see colour picture no. 31)

6 oz. plain flour
1 level tsp. mixed spice
$\frac{1}{2}$ level tsp. grated nutmeg
3 oz. fresh white bread-
  crumbs
4 oz. shredded suet
4 oz. raisins, stoned
  and chopped

8 oz. currants, cleaned
8 oz. sultanas, cleaned
4 oz. peeled, cored and
  chopped apple
3 oz. Demerara sugar
Grated rind of 1 lemon
2 eggs, beaten
$\frac{1}{3}$ pint strong ale

Grease a 2-pint basin. Sift together the flour and spices. Add the breadcrumbs, suet, dried fruit, apple, sugar and lemon rind. Mix well and gradually stir in the eggs and ale. Stir again thoroughly. Turn the mixture into the basin, cover with greased greaseproof paper and then with aluminium foil or a pudding cloth. Either place the pudding in a pan with water half-way up the sides of the basin and, after bringing it to the boil, reduce the heat and simmer for 6 hours, or alternatively cook it in a steamer for 8 hours. Leave the greaseproof paper in position, but when the pudding is cold, cover with a fresh piece of foil or cloth before storing.
Re-boil for 3-4 hours before serving with Fluffy Sauce or Brandy Butter—p. 158. (Serves 5-6.)

FLUFFY SAUCE FOR CHRISTMAS PUDDING

2 oz. butter
4 oz. icing sugar,
  sifted

2 eggs, separated
2 tbsps. brandy
$\frac{1}{4}$ pint double cream

Cream the butter and sugar. Beat in the beaten egg yolks. Gradually beat in the brandy and add the cream. Place in a double saucepan and cook over a gentle heat until of the consistency of thick custard. Pour slowly on to the beaten egg whites, whisking all the time. Keep warm in the double pan, but don't continue to cook. Stir before serving.

BAKED PUDDINGS

MIXED FRUIT COBBLER

(see picture above)

8 oz. self-raising flour	Sweetened cooked fruit (apples, cherries, black-currants, bananas, goose-berries or apricots)
2 level tbsps. sugar	
2 oz. butter	
1 egg	Beaten egg and sugar to glaze
Milk to mix	

Mix the dry ingredients and rub in the fat, then mix to a soft scone dough with egg and milk. Knead lightly on a floured board and cut into rounds or rings $\frac{1}{2}$ inch thick. Heat the fruit in a pan and when it boils pour it into a pie dish. Place the scones on top (in an overlapping circle round the edge of the dish), brush lightly with egg and sprinkle with sugar. Bake in a hot oven (425°F., mark 7) for 5-10 minutes, until the scones are well risen and brown.

BAKED JAM ROLL

Roll 8 oz. shortcrust pastry into an oblong, damp the edges with a little water and spread to within 1 inch of the sides with jam. Roll up and put into a greased ovenproof dish. Pour à little milk into the dish and bake in a moderate oven (350°F., mark 4) for 30-40 minutes, until brown and crisp. Serve with more jam, if required.

PINEAPPLE UPSIDE-DOWN PUDDING

(see colour picture no. 32)

1 small can of pineapple rings	6 oz. self-raising flour
1 oz. glacé cherries	4 oz. butter
3-4 tbsps. melted golden syrup	4 oz. caster sugar
	2 eggs
	2-3 tbsps. milk

Grease the base of a 7-inch square cake tin well and line with greased greaseproof paper, arrange the pineapple and cherries decoratively in it and cover them with the syrup. Using the same method as for Canary Pudding, make a cake mixture from the remaining ingredients and spread it carefully and evenly over the fruit. Bake in the middle of a moderate oven (350°F., mark 4) for about 45 minutes. Turn out on to a plate and serve hot or cold,

accompanied by whipped cream or by the pineapple juice thickened with arrowroot. (Allow 2 level tsps. arrowroot to $\frac{1}{4}$ pint juice.)

ADAM AND EVE PUDDING

(see picture above)

1 lb. cooking apples	2 oz. sugar
3 oz. Demerara sugar	1 egg
Grated rind of 1 lemon	2 oz. flour
2 oz. butter	$\frac{1}{4}$ level tsp. baking powder

Peel, core and slice the apples; add the Demerara sugar and lemon rind and put them into an ovenproof dish or pie dish with 1 tbsp. water. Cream the butter and sugar thoroughly, add the egg and beat well, then stir in the flour and baking powder and spread on top of the apples. Bake in a fairly hot oven (400°F., mark 6) for about $\frac{1}{2}$ hour, or until the apples are tender and the cake mixture well risen and firm.

APPLE-ANNA

Peel and slice an apple, put in a casserole and sprinkle with 2 level tbsps. brown sugar. Slice a banana and arrange on top, then slice another 2 apples and put over the banana. Sprinkle with 3 level tbsps. sugar and dot with a little butter. Cover the casserole and bake for 20 minutes in a fairly hot oven (375°F., mark 5), then take off the lid and bake for about 15 minutes longer, or until the fruit is tender. Serve with cream.

DANISH APPLE CAKE

$2\frac{1}{4}$ lb. cooking apples	Jam or marmalade
4 oz. sugar	Ground cinnamon
4 oz. butter or margarine	$\frac{1}{4}$ pint double cream (whipped) to decorate the cake
4 oz. coarse breadcrumbs (preferably half white, half brown)	

Wash, peel and slice the apples, then stew them with or without a little water, according to type. Add half the sugar. Melt the fat and mix in the breadcrumbs, then add the remaining sugar, stirring this into the fat until light brown in colour. Grease a cake tin and in it place alternate layers of crumbs, apples, jam or marmalade and a light sprinkling of cinnamon, finishing with crumbs. Press down firmly, then cook for $\frac{1}{2}$ hour in a moderate oven (350°F., mark 4). Turn it out and decorate the top with whipped cream and jam or marmalade.

PEACH UPSIDE-DOWN PUDDING

(see picture above)

2 tbsps. golden syrup	2 eggs
$\frac{1}{2}$-$\frac{3}{4}$ lb. peaches, sliced, or an 11-oz. can of sliced peaches, drained	$\frac{1}{2}$ level tsp. baking powder
	6 oz. flour
4 oz. butter	Milk to mix
4 oz. caster sugar	

Grease well a 6-inch cake tin and put a round of greased paper at the bottom. Coat the base with golden syrup and arrange the peaches decoratively over this. Cream the fat and sugar and beat in the eggs. Sift together the baking powder and flour and fold into the mixture, with a little milk to give a soft dropping consistency. Put the mixture into the tin and bake in a fairly hot oven (400°F., mark 6) until well risen and brown—about 35-40 minutes. Turn the pudding out upside-down and serve with syrup sauce—see recipe below.

Upside-down Pudding can be varied by using other fruits —fresh, bottled or canned—or the sponge mixture can be flavoured with ginger, chocolate, lemon, orange, coffee, etc. Serve with a suitably-flavoured sauce.

SYRUP SAUCE

4 tbsps. water	Juice of $\frac{1}{2}$ a lemon
2 tbsps. golden syrup	

Mix all together and boil rapidly for a few minutes.

ORANGE PUDDING

4 oz. butter	5 oz. flour
4 oz. sugar	$\frac{1}{4}$ level tsp. baking powder
3 eggs	Orange curd
Grated rind and juice of 1 orange	4 oz. caster sugar for meringue topping

Cream the fat and sugar until light and creamy. Beat in 2 of the egg yolks and one whole egg, the orange rind and the juice, then fold in the flour and baking powder. Put into a greased dish and bake in a moderate oven (350°F., mark 4) until well risen and firm—30-40 minutes —and then spread the top with a little orange curd. Whisk the remaining egg white until stiff, fold in the caster sugar and whisk well. Pile on top of the pudding and bake in a cool oven (300°F., mark 1) until golden-brown—15-20 minutes.

RAILWAY PUDDING

(see picture above)

8 oz. flour	1 egg
1 level tsp. baking powder	Milk to mix
4 oz. butter and lard mixed	Finely grated rind of 1 lemon
3 oz. sugar	Jam and caster sugar

Sift the flour and baking powder together and rub in the fat. Add the sugar and mix to a dropping consistency with the beaten egg and the milk; flavour with the lemon rind. Put into a greased shallow cake tin and bake in a fairly hot oven (375°F., mark 5) until golden-brown—about $\frac{1}{2}$ hour. Split in half and spread with warmed jam; put together again, cut into squares and sprinkle liberally with caster sugar.

WEST RIDING PUDDING

4 oz. shortcrust pastry	3 oz. flour
Jam	$\frac{1}{4}$ level tsp. baking powder
3 oz. butter	1 oz. ground almonds
3 oz. sugar	Grated lemon rind
1 large egg	Milk to mix

Line a shallow pie dish or an ovenproof plate with pastry, decorate the edges and spread a layer of jam over the bottom. Cream the fat and sugar until light and creamy and beat in the egg. Fold in the remaining ingredients, adding enough milk to give a soft dropping consistency. Spread this mixture over the jam and bake in a moderate oven (350°F., mark 4) for 35-45 minutes, until well risen.

BAKEWELL TART

4 oz. shortcrust pastry	1 egg
2 tbsps. red jam	2 oz. cake crumbs
$1\frac{1}{2}$ oz. butter	2 oz. ground almonds
2 oz. sugar	1 tsp. almond essence

Line a pie plate or a sandwich tin with the pastry and spread the jam over the bottom. Cream the butter and sugar until soft and white, then add the beaten egg a little at a time. Stir in the ground almonds and cake crumbs and add the almond essence. Spread the mixture on the top of the jam and add strips of pastry cut from the trimmings. Bake in a moderate oven (350°F., mark 4) until the mixture is firm and the pastry lightly browned —30-40 minutes. Serve hot or cold, with or without custard.

MILK AND CUSTARD PUDDINGS

SEMOLINA PUDDING

1 pint milk	½ oz. sugar
1½ oz. semolina	1 egg, separated

Heat the milk and when almost boiling sprinkle in the semolina, stirring. Stir until boiling, then simmer for 10-15 minutes, until the grain is soft, stirring frequently. Remove from the heat, add the sugar and cool slightly. Beat the egg yolk into the semolina and mix well. Whisk the white stiffly and fold in. Pour into a greased pie dish and bake in a moderate oven (350°F., mark 4) for about 30 minutes, until the pudding is lightly browned.

ORANGE SEMOLINA MERINGUE
(see picture above)

1 pint milk	An 11-oz. can of mandarin
1½ oz. semolina	oranges
A pinch of salt	2 egg whites
4 oz. sugar	Walnuts to decorate

Boil the milk and sprinkle in the semolina, stirring all the time. Add the salt and 2 oz. sugar and cook for about 5 minutes. Drain the oranges, place most of them in an ovenproof dish and pour the semolina pudding over. Whisk the egg whites till stiff and fold in the remaining sugar. Put this meringue carefully over the pudding and bake in a moderate oven (350°F., mark 4) for about 15 minutes, until crisp and golden. Decorate with orange sections and walnuts.

TAPIOCA SPONGE PUDDING

1 oz. seed pearl tapioca	1 oz. caster sugar
A pinch of salt	1 egg, separated
¾ pint milk	Flavouring

Wash the tapioca and soak it in a little water for ½ hour, then drain it, put with the salt and milk into a saucepan and bring to the boil. Simmer, stirring occasionally, until cooked. Cool a little and add the sugar, egg yolk and flavouring. Whip the egg white stiffly and fold it into the mixture. Put into a greased pie dish and bake in a fairly hot oven (375°F., mark 5) for about 20 minutes.

RICE PUDDING

1½ oz. short-grain rice	A little butter
1 pint milk	Grated nutmeg
½-1 oz. sugar	

Wash the rice and put it into a greased pie dish with the milk and sugar. Put a few shavings of butter over the top, with a little grated nutmeg. Bake in a cool oven (300°F., mark 1) for 2-3 hours, stirring once or twice during the first hour, then leave undisturbed for remaining time.

GROUND RICE PUDDING

1½ oz. ground rice	½ oz. sugar
1 pint milk	½ oz. butter

Mix the rice to a creamy consistency with a little of the milk, heat the rest until nearly boiling, then stir it into the rice. Return the mixture to the pan and boil for several minutes, stirring, until thick and creamy. Sweeten, pour into a greased dish, dot with shavings of butter and bake in a moderate oven (350°F., mark 4) until lightly browned on top—20-30 minutes.

QUEEN OF PUDDINGS

¾ pint milk	Grated rind of 1 lemon
1½ oz. butter	2 eggs, separated
3 oz. breadcrumbs	2 oz. caster sugar
1½ oz. sugar	Jam

Bring the milk to the boil with the butter and pour over the crumbs, sugar and rind; stir and leave to cool. Add egg yolks and mix well, then pour into a pie dish and bake in a moderate oven (350°F., mark 4) till set. Meanwhile whisk the egg whites stiffly and fold in the sugar. Spread the pudding with melted jam and pile or pipe the meringue on top. Bake in a slow oven (300°F., mark 1) till the meringue is crisp—about ½ hour.
If preferred, this pudding may be made and served in individual dishes.

BAKED CUSTARDS

½ pint milk	½ oz. sugar
1 egg	Nutmeg

Heat the milk without boiling it. Beat the egg with the sugar and pour the milk on to it, stirring well. Strain the mixture into individual dishes, sprinkle with a little grated nutmeg and bake in a cool oven (300°F., mark 2) for about 20 minutes, until set.

CARAMEL CUSTARD

4½ oz. sugar   1 pint milk
¼ pint water   4 eggs

Put 4 oz., sugar and the water into a small pan, dissolve, then heat without stirring until the mixture becomes a rich brown colour, but don't make the caramel too dark, or it will taste bitter. Pour it quickly into a hot soufflé tin, then, holding the tin with a cloth, coat the inside well all over. Leave to set. Heat the milk; beat the eggs and remaining ½ oz. sugar and pour the hot milk on to the eggs. Strain the mixture into the tin and cover with greased paper. Steam very gently until the custard is set—about 1-1¼ hours. Turn it out carefully into a warm dish and serve either hot or cold.

CARAMEL CRISP PUDDING

(see right-hand picture opposite)

4 oz. sugar   2 eggs
4 tbsps. water   ¾ pint milk
3 oz. diced white bread

Dissolve the sugar in the water and boil rapidly until it caramelises. Leave to cool slightly, then carefully add another 4 tbsps. water and re-boil. Grease a fireproof dish and put the diced bread into it, then pour the caramel over and leave to soak. Meanwhile, beat the eggs, heat the milk to boiling point and pour on to the eggs. Strain this mixture over the soaked bread and leave to stand for 15 minutes, then bake in a cool oven (300°F., mark 1) for 20-30 minutes, until the custard has set and the bread (which rises to the top) is crisp and brown.

BREAD AND BUTTER PUDDING

(see picture above)

5-6 slices of white bread   1 tbsp. marmalade
  and butter   (optional)
2 oz. dried fruit   2 eggs
1 oz. sugar   1 pint milk

Grease a fireproof dish. Cut the bread and butter into triangles; clean the fruit and mix it with the sugar. Arrange the bread and butter, fruit and sugar in layers in the dish, and spread the top layer with marmalade (if used).
Beat the eggs and pour on the cold milk, then pour this mixture over the bread and butter and soak for 1 hour. Bake in a cool oven (300°F., mark 1) for ¾-1 hour, until the custard is set and the top lightly browned.

CHOCOLATE MARSHMALLOW PUDDING

(see picture above)

¾ pint milk   1 oz. sugar
1 egg   1 tsp. vanilla
2 oz. sponge cake crumbs   essence
3 oz. ground almonds   ¼ lb. marshmallows
1 oz. cocoa

Heat the milk and pour it on to the well-beaten egg. Put the dry ingredients into a bowl and pour on the egg and milk, add the sugar and vanilla essence, then pour into a greased dish and bake in a moderate oven (350°F., mark 4) until set—about 1 hour. Remove from the oven, arrange the marshmallows on top and brown them under a hot grill. Serve with marshmallow sauce—see recipe.

MARSHMALLOW SAUCE

4 oz. granulated sugar   1 egg white
3 tbsps. water   Vanilla essence
8 marshmallows   A little colouring

Dissolve the sugar in the water, then boil together for about 15 minutes. Add the marshmallows, cut into small pieces with scissors. Beat the egg white very stiffly, then gradually fold in the marshmallow mixture. Add essence and colouring.

RICH CABINET PUDDING

A few halved glacé   ¾ pint milk
  cherries   Vanilla essence
3 eggs   4 small sponge cakes
1½ oz. caster sugar

Grease a plain tin mould and line the bottom with a round of greased paper. Decorate with halved cherries. Beat the eggs and sugar, add the milk and vanilla essence and beat well. Cut the sponge cakes into small dice and put them in the tin, strain the eggs and milk over and soak for 20 minutes. Cover with greased paper and steam gently for about 1 hour, until set. Turn out and serve with Mousseline sauce—see recipe below.

MOUSSELINE SAUCE

Whisk 2 oz. caster sugar and 2 egg yolks over hot water, then add ¼ pint cream or top of the milk, and continue whisking until thick and frothy. Add 2-3 tbsps. Madeira or sherry and whisk until sauce thickens again. Serve immediately.

BATTER MIXTURES

PANCAKES

4 oz. flour	½ pint milk or milk
A pinch of salt	and water
1 egg	Lard for frying

Mix the flour and salt, make a well in the centre and break in the egg. Add half the liquid and beat the mixture until it is smooth. Add the remaining liquid gradually and beat until well mixed.

Heat a little lard in a frying pan until really hot, running it round to coat the sides of the pan; pour off any surplus. Pour or spoon in just enough batter to cover the base of the pan thinly and cook quickly until golden-brown underneath. Turn with a palette knife or by tossing and cook the second side until golden. Turn out on to sugared paper, sprinkle with sugar and a squeeze of lemon and serve at once, with sugar and lemon wedges. If you are cooking a large number of pancakes, keep them warm by putting them as they are made between 2 plates in a warm oven. Finally, roll up all the pancakes and serve at once.

PANCAKES WITH A DIFFERENCE

Ginger and Banana Pancakes: Add 1 level tsp. powdered ginger with the flour and cook the pancakes in the usual way. To make the filling, mash 1 banana per person with double cream and add some small pieces of preserved ginger. Spread the filling on the cooked pancakes, roll up and serve with whipped cream.

Layered Pancakes: Instead of rolling the pancakes, use a filling (for instance whipped cream and jam) to layer the pancakes one on top of the other. Cut in wedges.

A mixture of drained canned fruit (such as peaches, apricots, strawberries and raspberries) and whipped cream, makes another delicious filling.

Surprise Pancakes: Make the pancakes in the usual way, spoon some ice cream into the centre of each pancake and fold in half, like an omelette. Serve with jam sauce or a sauce made from sieved raspberries.

FRENCH PANCAKES

2 oz. butter	2 oz. flour
2 oz. caster sugar	½ pint milk
2 eggs	Jam

Cream the fat and sugar, add the eggs one at a time, with some of the flour, then fold in the rest of the flour and lastly stir in the very slightly warmed milk. (At this stage the mixture will probably curdle, but this does not matter.) Half-fill 4-6 greased patty tins or saucers with the mixture and bake in a fairly hot oven (400°F., mark 6) for 10-15 minutes. Turn the pancakes out on to a sugared paper, place a spoonful of hot jam in each and fold over like an omelette, or sandwich together with jam *(see left-hand picture above)*.

FRITTERS

(see picture above)

4 oz. flour	Deep fat for frying
A pinch of salt	4 bananas, 16 apple
A tbsp. olive oil	slices, or 10
¼ pint tepid water	pineapple rings
2 egg whites	Caster sugar

Sift together the flour and salt, make a well in the centre and add the oil and half the water. Draw in the flour from the sides and mix and beat well. Add sufficient water to bring to a coating consistency. Just before using the batter, whisk the egg whites until stiff and fold them into the mixture. Heat the fat until a faint smoke appears on the surface. Dip the pieces of fruit into the batter, drain well and lower carefully into the hot fat. Allow to brown on one side, then turn the fritters and cook on the other side until they are golden-brown. Remove, draining well, then put on to crumpled kitchen paper to finish draining. Serve the fritters sprinkled with caster sugar.

AMERICAN WAFFLES

6 oz. flour	½ pint milk
A pinch of salt	2 oz. melted butter
1½ level tsp. baking powder	A few drops of vanilla
1 level tbsp. caster sugar	essence
2 eggs	

Sift the flour, salt and baking powder into a basin, and stir in the sugar. Make a well in the centre of the dry ingredients and add the egg yolks. Mix these in, adding the milk and melted fat alternately, then stir in the vanilla essence. Whip up the whites of egg very stiffly and fold in lightly. Pour the batter into the heated waffle iron and cook according to the maker's directions. Serve the waffles immediately, with butter and maple syrup, if available, or with golden syrup.

HOT SOUFFLÉS

STEAMED VANILLA SOUFFLÉ

1 oz. butter	2 level tsps. caster
1 oz. flour	sugar
¼ pint milk	3 egg yolks
½ tsp. vanilla essence	4 egg whites

Prepare a soufflé tin by greasing it well with olive oil or melted butter. Cut a round of greaseproof paper to fit the bottom of the tin, place in position and grease it well. Tie a band of strong greased paper round the sides—this should extend 3 inches above the top of the tin. Well grease a square of paper to put on top of the soufflé during the steaming. Melt the butter and add the flour, gradually add the milk and stir this panada mixture until it thickens, then boil, beating well, until it leaves the sides of the pan. Remove the pan from the heat and beat in the essence and sugar. Beat in the egg yolks one at a time and lastly fold in the stiffly beaten egg whites. When the mixture is thoroughly blended, pour it into the prepared tin and steam very gently for about 45 minutes —the soufflé should be well risen and firm to the touch when cooked. Turn out carefully on to a hot dish and serve with a good custard or jam sauce.

This is the foundation soufflé recipe, which can be varied by the addition of other flavourings. The mixture can be either steamed or baked—see recipe below.

BAKED ORANGE SOUFFLÉ

(see picture above)

1 oz. butter	2 level tsps. caster sugar
1 oz. flour	3 egg yolks
¼ pint milk	4 egg whites
Grated rinds of 2 oranges	Icing sugar

Prepare a soufflé dish by greasing it well with a little butter, then dredging with caster sugar. Tie a band of stiff paper round the dish, so that it extends 3 inches above the top and grease the paper well. Make a panada as above with the butter, flour and milk. Add the grated orange rind and the sugar, then beat in the egg yolks one at a time. Lastly fold in the stiffly beaten egg whites, mix well and put into the prepared dish. Bake in a fairly hot oven (400°F., mark 6) for 35-40 minutes, until well risen and golden-brown. Sprinkle with icing sugar and serve immediately with orange sauce.

CHERRY SOUFFLÉ

(see picture above)

Add 2 oz. glacé cherries (each cut in four). Steam (or bake), and serve with a sweet white sauce flavoured with sherry or Maraschino.

LEMON SOUFFLÉ

2 oz. butter	2 eggs
2 oz. caster sugar	½ oz. flour
Juice of ½ a lemon	Grated lemon rind

Cream together the butter and sugar, then beat in the lemon juice and egg yolks. Stand the basin over boiling water and whisk until the mixture is thick and creamy. Fold in the flour and grated lemon rind and add the stiffly beaten egg whites. Grease and flour a soufflé tin and half-fill it with the mixture, stand the tin in another tin half-filled with water and bake in a moderate oven (350°F., mark 4) for ½ hour. Turn out and serve with Mousseline sauce (p. 137).

CHOCOLATE SOUFFLÉ

Use the same recipe and method as for Vanilla Soufflé, but dissolve 1½ oz. chocolate in the milk before using it for making the panada mixture.

LIQUEUR SOUFFLÉ

2 sponge cakes	1 oz. plain flour
5 tbsps. Kirsch	¼ pint milk
2½ oz. mixed glacé fruits	2 oz. sugar
2 oz. butter	3 eggs

Cut the sponge cakes into fingers and soak in 1 tbsp. Kirsch. Rinse the glacé fruits in very hot water to remove the excess sugar, cut into small pieces and allow to soak in 1 tbsp. Kirsch. Prepare a soufflé dish and set the oven to hot (425°F., mark 7).

Melt the butter, add the flour and beat well. Remove from the heat and gradually beat in the milk; when the mixture is free from lumps, return it to the heat and cook for 5 minutes. Cool slightly and beat in the sugar, egg yolks and 3 tbsps. Kirsch, then fold in the stiffly beaten egg whites. Pour half this mixture into the prepared soufflé dish, place over it a layer of sponge cakes and glacé fruit, cover with the remaining soufflé mixture and place in a hot oven (425°F., mark 7) for 15 minutes; lower the heat to moderate (350°F., mark 4) and continue to bake for 30 minutes. Serve at once.

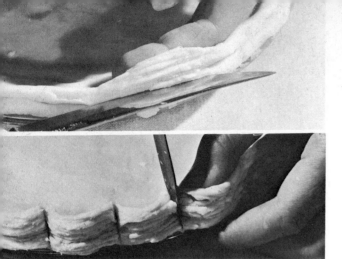

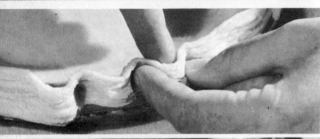

PASTRY RECIPES

FLAKY PASTRY

8 oz. flour
A pinch of salt
6 oz. margarine and
lard, mixed

A squeeze of lemon
juice
Cold water to mix

Sift the flour and salt into a basin. Soften the fat and divide it into 4 portions. Rub one quarter well into the flour and mix to a stiff paste with lemon juice and water. Knead the paste on a lightly floured board, then roll it into an oblong and flake another quarter of the fat over two-thirds of the pastry: to prevent the fat working through at the edges when the pastry is rolled out, keep it about $\frac{1}{2}$ inch in from the edges. Fold the pastry into three, first bringing the bottom third up, then the top third down to cover it. Seal the edges lightly with the rolling pin and turn the pastry towards the left. Repeat the processes of flaking, folding and turning with the two remaining portions of the fat. Fold and roll once more, then leave the pastry in a cool place for $\frac{1}{2}$ hour before using it as required.

RICH SHORTCRUST OR FLAN PASTRY

8 oz. flour
A pinch of salt
5 oz. butter (or mar-
garine and butter)

1 level tsp. caster sugar
1 egg yolk
Cold water

Sift the flour and salt into a basin. Rub in the fat with the tips of the fingers until the mixture resembles fine breadcrumbs: do this very lightly or the mixture will become greasy and heavy. Add the sugar. Beat the egg yolk and add 1-2 tbsps. cold water, then add just sufficient of this liquid to mix to a firm dough. Turn on to a floured board, knead or pat lightly into a round, roll out and use as required.

PIE EDGINGS
(see pictures above)

The appearance of a tart or pie can be greatly improved by means of a decorative edge. After putting on the top crust of the pie a better finish is obtained if the edges are "knocked up" with a sharp knife—see picture 1. This applies particularly to the richer pastries, such as flaky or rough puff. For a decorative finish suitable for a plate pie, a scalloped edge can be made, as shown in picture 2; the width of the scallops can be varied as required, but is usually fairly small for sweet pies. Picture 3 shows a fluted edge, made by pressing the forefinger on one side of the pastry, against the finger and thumb held on the other side. A further decoration for a plate pie is shown in picture 4; this is made by cutting strips of pastry and twisting them on to the damped edge of the top crust. Several other pastry decorations can be devised which will use the leftover pastry trimmings.

SHORTCRUST PASTRY

8 oz. flour
A pinch of salt

4 oz. fat
Cold water to mix

Sift the flour and salt into a bowl, put in the fat, cover with flour and break into pieces. Using the finger-tips, rub the fat into the flour till the mixture is as fine as breadcrumbs; raise the hands high in the basin to incorporate as much cold air as possible. Add the water slowly, using just enough to make the mixture bind when stirred. Use a round-ended knife to mix. Finally, knead gently into a smooth ball, leaving the bowl clean. The pastry is now ready to roll out and use.

SUET CRUST PASTRY

8 oz. flour (or 6 oz.
flour and 2 oz. fine
breadcrumbs)
1 level tsp. baking powder

$\frac{1}{2}$ level tsp. salt
3-4 oz. suet, shredded
or chopped
Cold water to mix

Sift the flour, baking powder and salt, mix in the suet and add the breadcrumbs, if used. Make a well in the centre and pour in enough cold water to give a soft but not sticky dough. Place this on a lightly floured board and gently knead it. Use as required.

FRUIT AND BERRY PIES

FRUIT PIE
(see top picture on right)

8 oz. shortcrust pastry   Cold water
2 lb. fruit (approx.)   Milk or egg white
Sugar to sweeten   to glaze

Make the pastry as directed opposite, and prepare the fruit according to kind. Half-fill a pie dish with fruit, sprinkle well with sugar, and well fill the dish with the rest of the fruit. Add sufficient water to cover the bottom of the dish. Roll the pastry out $\frac{1}{8}$-$\frac{1}{4}$ in. in thickness, making it the shape of the pie dish but about 1 in. larger all round. Cut off a strip of pastry about 1 in. wide to cover the rim of the dish. Damp the dish rim, press on the strip and damp the pastry edge. Lift the rest of the pastry on a rolling pin, lay it over the fruit and press lightly on to the rim, then trim off the rough edges. "Knock up" the edges and mark with a fork. Glaze with milk or egg white and make a hole at each end to allow the steam to escape. Bake in a hot oven (425°F., mark 7) for 15-20 minutes, until the pastry has set and lightly browned, then reduce the heat and cook until the fruit is quite tender. Serve hot dusted with caster sugar.

SPICED APPLE AND CHEESE PIE
(see colour picture no. 33)

6 oz. shortcrust pastry   1 level tsp. powdered
1 lb. cooking apples   cinnamon
4 oz. sugar   Milk to glaze
2 level tbsps. flour   2 slices of cheese

Divide the pastry into 2 even-sized pieces, roll out and use one piece to line a shallow pie dish. Peel, core and slice the apples; add the sugar, flour and cinnamon and mix well. Put this mixture into the dish, wet the edges of the pastry and cover with the second piece; flake and scallop the edges and brush the top with milk. Bake in a hot oven (425°F., mark 7) for 10 minutes, then lower to moderate (350°F., mark 4) and bake for a further 20-30 minutes to cook the fruit. Just before serving, decorate the top of the pie with triangles of cheese and return it to the oven until they just begin to melt. Serve hot, with cream or custard.

SUMMER BERRY PIE

2 lb. mixed berry fruits   Egg white
8 oz. shortcrust pastry   Caster sugar
4 oz. sugar

Strawberries, raspberries, loganberries, gooseberries, red and black currants, etc., can all be used in this pie. Pick the fruit over and wash it, half-fill a pie dish with the mixed berries and sprinkle well with sugar, then pile the rest of the fruit high in the dish. Roll out the pastry and cover the dish as for fruit pie. Glaze with beaten egg white and caster sugar, and bake in a fairly hot oven (375°F., mark 5) for about 30 minutes, until the pastry is brown and the fruit tender. Serve hot or cold, with whipped cream.

APPLE CINNAMON PIE
(see picture above)

8 oz. flaky pastry   2-3 oz. sugar
1 lb. cooking apples   Egg for glazing
Ground cinnamon

Roll the pastry out $\frac{1}{4}$ inch thick. Cut a round of pastry the size of a fireproof plate and put it to one side. Roll out the rest of the pastry into a round and line the plate with it. Slice the apples and place on the pastry and sprinkle well with cinnamon and with plenty of sugar. Damp the edges of the pastry and place the first round over the fruit. Press the edges well together, "knock up" the sides and decorate with flutes or scallops. Brush the pastry with a little egg and bake in a hot oven (425°F., mark 7) for 15-20 minutes, until the pastry is well risen and crisp, then put it into a cooler part of the oven, cover the pastry with a piece of greaseproof paper and continue cooking until the fruit is quite tender. Sprinkle with caster sugar before serving.

RED CURRANT LATTICE PIE

(see top picture on left)

8 oz. shortcrust pastry	1 lb. red currants
Egg for glazing	2-3 oz. sugar

Line an ovenproof plate with pastry, trim the edges and keep the trimmings to make the lattice. Flute the edges of the pastry and brush with a little egg. Prepare and wash the red currants and fill the dish, sprinkling sugar between the layers of the fruit. Roll out the rest of the pastry and cut into strips. Damp the inner side of the pastry rim and place the strips in a lattice on top of the fruit. Brush the lattice with egg and bake the pie in a fairly hot oven (400°F., mark 6) for about ½ hour, till brown and crisp. Sprinkle well with sugar and serve with whipped cream.

BLACKBERRY TRELLIS PIE

(see lower picture on left)

6 oz. flaky pastry	1-2 oz. sugar
Milk or egg for glazing	2 tbsps. condensed milk
1 lb. blackberries	Grated rind of 1 lemon

Line a plate with the pastry, flute the edges with a sharp knife, prick the bottom of the pie and put some baking beans in the centre. Brush the edges with a little milk or egg and bake in a hot oven (425°F., mark 7) until well cooked—about 15 minutes. Roll out the pastry trimmings and make into a trellis, glaze and bake separately for 5-10 minutes, then allow to cool. Mix the blackberries, sugar, condensed milk and lemon rind, put into the pie case and place the trellis on top. Serve immediately.

APPLE SAUCE PIE

12 oz. shortcrust pastry	3-4 tbsps. thin royal
½ pint thick apple purée	icing
Ground cinnamon	Flaked or halved
1-2 tbsps. sultanas or	almonds
stoned raisins	

Line a dish or tin with half the pastry. Put the apple purée in the dish with a sprinkling of cinnamon and the dried fruit. Cover with the rest of the pastry, brush the top with royal icing and sprinkle the icing with almonds. Bake in a fairly hot oven (400°F., mark 6) for about 30 minutes, until the pastry is brown and firm. Serve hot or cold.

GOOSEBERRY PLATE PIE

8 oz. flaky pastry (see	1 level tsp. cornflour or
recipe on p. 140)	arrowroot
1 lb. gooseberries	Egg white to
¼ pint water	glaze
2-4 oz. sugar, as	Caster sugar
required	

Line a pie plate with half the pastry. Prepare gooseberries, rinse, then place in a saucepan with about ¼ pint water. Cover and cook very gently until tender, taking care to keep the berries whole. Drain in a colander. Measure ¼ pint of the juice, put this back in the saucepan with the sugar and add the cornflour or arrowroot blended with a spoonful of cold water. Cook, stirring, until the mixture boils and thickens. Add the gooseberries and set aside to cool, then pour into the lined pie plate. Cover with the pastry, glaze with beaten white of egg and dust with caster sugar. Bake in a hot oven (425°F., mark 7) for about 10 minutes, then reduce the heat to moderate (350°F., mark 4) and cook for about 30 minutes, until the pie is well risen and nicely browned. Serve hot, with cream.

SWISS PLUM TART

6 oz. shortcrust pastry	A little sugar
½ lb. plums	¼ oz. butter

Line a pie plate with shortcrust pastry and decorate the edges. Cut the plums in half, remove the stones and then cut them in quarters. Arrange these quarters in over lapping circles on the pastry. Sprinkle with sugar and some fine shavings of butter and bake in a hot oven (425°F., mark 7) until the pastry is lightly browned—1 minutes—then cook at moderate (350°F., mark 4) unti the fruit is tender—about 30 minutes in all.

Sliced apples or black cherries (stoned) may also b used for making this type of tart.

COLD PUDDINGS

Recipes give 4 servings, unless otherwise indicated

Cold sweets and desserts can range from hearty fruit tarts and flans to feathery confections of cream and meringue, but they all share the advantage of being easy to prepare in advance. Although for the really elaborate ice-cream creations a refrigerator is essential, there are dozens of delicious and simply made sweets which will become sufficiently chilled in a cool larder.

FLANS AND PASTRY SWEETS

TO MAKE A FLAN CASE

Make flan pastry as directed on page 140. Grease a piece of greaseproof paper, place it on a baking sheet and set the flan ring on this. Roll the pastry out into a round $\frac{1}{8}$-$\frac{1}{4}$ inch thick and about 1 inch larger than the ring, and press into position, making it quite flat at the base; trim the edges and prick the bottom lightly. If the flan is to be filled after cooking it is necessary to bake it "blind". For this place a piece of paper inside the pastry and half-fill with baking rice or beans; bake in a hot oven (425°F., mark 7) until the pastry is set (about 15 minutes), then take out the beans and paper and carefully remove the ring. Put the pastry case back into the oven to finish cooking; when it is golden-brown, remove it from the oven and cool on a rack.

When a flan ring is not available, a flan case can be made in a shallow sandwich tin; in this case, place strips of paper under the pastry to facilitate removing it from the tin when baked. Oblong flans also look attractive—see picture below.

Flan cases are usually made with flan (rich shortcrust) pastry, but plain shortcrust may be used if desired.

FRUIT FLANS
(see colour picture no. 33)

Most fruits, when attractively arranged in a flan case, make good summer or party sweets. Hard or soft fruits, fresh or canned can be used equally well, and a mixture may also be used. Such soft fruits as loganberries, rasp-berries and strawberries are generally used raw, but other fruits are better if cooked beforehand in a syrup made with fruit juice or water, sweetened with sugar. Stone fruits should be halved if large, the stones being removed. When cooking the fruit take care to stew it very gently so that it will remain a good shape. Having arranged the fruit neatly in the flan case, cover it with one of the following: fruit jelly (which should be quite cold and just on the point of setting); sugar syrup (boiled until it is thick enough to coat a spoon); a fruit purée. When the coating has set, the flan can be decorated with cream.

HARLEQUIN FRUIT TART
(see left-hand picture below)

8 oz. shortcrust pastry	$\frac{1}{2}$ pint lemon jelly
A variety of cooked fruits	Whipped cream (optional)

Roll the pastry out to fit a Swiss roll tin, carefully fit it into the tin, flute the edges and bake "blind" in a fairly hot oven (400°F., mark 6) until brown and cooked through; cool on a rack. Prepare the fruit (e.g., cherries, raspberries, blackberries, apricots, sliced peaches, sliced pears and damsons), and arrange in separate rows across the pastry case. Make up the jelly and leave it in a cool place until nearly set, then quickly pour it over the fruit and leave to set. Serve piped with cream, if desired.

As an alternative, the pie shell can be divided into sections before baking, by means of twisted strips cut from the pastry trimmings; damp the ends to fix them.

CREAM CHEESE AND APRICOT FLAN
(see picture below)

6 oz. shortcrust pastry	2 tbsps. red-currant
8 oz. cream cheese	jelly
4 oz. sugar	2 tbsps. water
An 8-oz. can of apricots, halved	1 tbsp. lemon juice
	Angelica to decorate

Roll out the pastry and line a flan case (7-8 inches); bake the case blind in a hot oven (425°F., mark 7) until crisp and golden-brown. Cream the cheese and sugar together, then spread evenly over the bottom of the flan case. Arrange the halved apricots on top, cut side down. Make a glaze as follows: put the red-currant jelly, water and lemon juice into a small, thick saucepan and stir over a gentle heat until dissolved; boil briskly until slightly tacky, then spoon carefully over the fruit. Decorate the flan with cut angelica.

GOOSEBERRY MARSHMALLOW TART
(see picture above)

1 lb. gooseberries	1 level tsp. ground cloves
¼ pint water	A little grated nutmeg
6 oz. sugar	½ lb. shortcrust pastry
1 oz. cornflour	1 oz. butter
A pinch of salt	½ lb. marshmallows
1 level tsp. ground cinnamon	

Top and tail the fruit and cook with the water and 4 oz. sugar. Mix the rest of the sugar, the cornflour, salt and spices. When the fruit is tender, add this mixture and cook, stirring, till thick. Line a deep pie plate with pastry and decorate the edges. Fill with fruit mixture and dot with butter. Cover with strips of the remaining pastry, arranged in a lattice pattern, and bake in a fairly hot oven (375°F., mark 5) for about 25-30 minutes. Place a marshmallow in each lattice "hole" and return the pie to the oven to finish browning; alternatively, serve with whipped cream or custard.

ORANGE CREAM TART

½ oz. gelatine	Grated rind of 1 lemon
½ oz. cornflour	¼ pt. dbl. cream, whipped
½ pint milk	An 11-oz. can of
2 eggs, separated	mandarin oranges
5 oz. caster sugar	9-in. pastry case

Dissolve the gelatine in a little water. Blend the cornflour with a little of the milk and heat the remainder. Pour the boiling milk on to the cornflour, return the mixture to the pan and cook for 2-5 minutes. Remove from the heat and add the egg yolks, 1 oz. sugar, the gelatine and lemon rind. Cool, then fold in the cream. Arrange most of the mandarin oranges in the pastry case, spoon on the cream mixture and leave to cool. Beat the egg whites until stiff, whisk in half the remaining sugar and fold in the rest. Pile this mixture on to the cream filling, carefully covering right to the edge. Bake at 425-450°F (mark 7-8) for about 2-3 minutes until lightly brown. Decorate with the remaining orange.

CHOCOLATE PEAR FLAN

Place scoops of plain ice cream in a flan case made from chocolate and ginger crust (see this page). Top with drained pear halves and flaked almonds.

Chocolate and Ginger Crust: Melt 4 oz. chocolate and 2-3 oz. butter in a bowl over hot water. Combine with ½ lb. crushed gingernuts, line a pie dish with the mixture and chill until set.

APRICOT AMBER
(see picture above)

2 lb. apricots (or ¾ lb. purée)	A flan or pastry case
2-3 oz. sugar	2 oz. caster sugar
2 eggs, separated	Angelica and glacé cherries
2 oz. melted butter	to decorate

Sieve the apricots, mix with the sugar, egg yolks and melted butter, then pour the mixture into the prepared flan or pastry case. Bake in a fairly hot oven (400°F., mark 6) for 20-25 minutes, till firm. Whisk the egg whites until stiff and then whisk in half the caster sugar; fold in the rest of the sugar and pile this meringue in a ring on the filling. Sprinkle well with sugar and put into a cool oven (300°F., mark 1) until it is light brown and crisp—about 25 minutes. Decorate as seen.

LEMON MERINGUE PIE
(see colour picture no. 34)

4 oz. shortcrust pastry	4 oz. sugar
3 level tbsps. cornflour	2 eggs, separated
¼ pint water	3 oz. caster sugar
Juice and grated rind	Glacé cherries and
of 2 lemons	angelica

Roll out the pastry and line a 7-inch flan case or deep pie plate. Trim the edges and bake blind towards the top of a hot oven (425°F., mark 7) for 15 minutes. Remove the paper and baking beans and return the case to the oven for a further 5 minutes; reduce the oven temperature to moderate (350°F., mark 4). Mix the cornflour with the water in a saucepan, add the lemon juice and grated rind and bring slowly to the boil, stirring until the mixture thickens, then add the sugar. Remove from the heat, cool the mixture slightly and add the egg yolks. Pour into the pastry case. Whisk the egg whites stiffly, whisk in half the caster sugar and fold in the rest. Pile the meringue on top of the lemon filling and bake in the centre of the oven for about 10 minutes, or until the meringue is crisp and lightly browned. Decorate before serving with the glacé cherries and angelica.

31. Christmas Pudding and Fluffy Sauce

32. Pineapple Upside-down Pudding; Jam Canary Pudding; Raspberry Tapioca Creams

33. Sliced Apple and Cheese Pie; Chocolate Coffee Pie; Fruit Flan

34. Lemon Meringue Pie

35. New-style Cheese Cake

36. Mille-feuilles

37. Brandied Melon and Ginger; Cherries in Red Wine; Pears in Port
Wine; Orange Ambrosia

38. Pineapple Salad; Fruit Salad Pavlova; Fruit-filled Avocado Pears

CRISP PEACH TART
(see picture above)

4 oz. shortcrust pastry
A 15-oz. can of peaches
Grated rind of 1 lemon
2 oz. butter
2 oz. brown sugar

2 oz. flour
1 level tsp. mixed spice
2 oz. chopped nuts or
    coconut

Line a pie dish with the pastry. Drain the peaches, place most of them in the tart and cover with the lemon rind and a little peach juice. Rub together the butter, sugar, flour and spice until the mixture resembles fine bread-crumbs. Mix in the nuts and spread this crumbly topping over the fruit. Bake in a hot oven (425°F., mark 7) for about 20 minutes, until crisp and golden. Decorate with the remaining peaches and serve with custard or cream. Vary by using other fruit, e.g., apricots, pears, stewed apples, gooseberries, rhubarb.

MILLES-FEUILLES
(see colour picture no. 36)

8 oz. puff pastry
Raspberry jam
$\frac{1}{4}$ pint double cream

An 11-oz. can of pineapple
Green glacé icing
Chopped nuts

Roll the pastry out $\frac{1}{8}$-$\frac{1}{4}$ inch thick and cut into 7-inch rounds—it should make 5-6. Put on a baking tray and prick them, then bake in a very hot oven (450°F., mark 8) for 8-10 minutes, until brown and crisp. Cool on a rack. Spread one layer of pastry with jam, place another round on this and cover with whipped cream and chopped pineapple (reserving a few pieces). Repeat to the last layer, which is iced and decorated with pineapple and chopped nuts.

CHOCOLATE COFFEE PIE
(see colour picture no. 33)

6 oz. shortcrust pastry
1 pint milk
1 oz. cornflour
2 level tbsps. cocoa
1 level tsp. coffee extract

1 oz. butter
4 level tbsps. sugar
Whipped cream and
    grated chocolate
    to decorate

Line a pie plate with pastry, brush over with milk, prick the bottom and bake in a hot oven (425°F., mark 7) until cooked through. Meanwhile bring $\frac{3}{4}$ pint milk to the boil; blend the cornflour, cocoa and coffee extract with 2 tbsps. cold milk to a smooth paste and pour on the hot milk. Return to the pan and bring to the boil, stirring; boil for a minute or two, then add the butter and sugar and beat for 2 minutes. Pour this mixture into the pie shell and allow to become quite cold before decorating with cream and chocolate.

LEMON CORNFLAKE FLAN
(see picture above)

Make up a lemon jelly, using only $\frac{3}{4}$ pint liquid. When it is on the point of setting, add a small can of evaporated milk or cream and beat very well until the mixture is pale and fluffy. Pour into a flan case of cornflake refrigerator crust (see below) and allow to set. Serve decorated with pieces of crystallised lemon.

Cornflake Refrigerator Crust: Heat 2 oz. butter, 2 oz. sugar and 1 tbsp. golden syrup until melted. Roughly crush 3 oz. cornflakes, mix with 1 level tsp. powdered cinnamon and combine with the melted mixture. Line a flan case or pie dish with the crust, pressing it firmly together, and chill in the refrigerator until set.

NUTTY MERINGUE PIE

4 oz. shortcrust pastry
2 egg whites

4 oz. soft brown sugar
2 oz. chopped walnuts

Roll the pastry out to fit a 9-inch pie plate or shallow heat-proof dish and bake "blind" in a hot oven (400°F., mark 6) for 25 minutes. To make the filling, whisk the egg whites until stiff, then fold in the sugar and nuts, put into the pastry case and bake in a cool oven (300°F., mark 1) for about $1\frac{1}{2}$ hours.

CUSTARD PIE

4 oz. shortcrust pastry
$\frac{1}{2}$ pint milk
2 eggs, beaten

2 tbsps. sugar
Nutmeg

Line a pie dish with the pastry. Warm the milk to blood heat and pour it on to the eggs and sugar. Strain the mixture into the pie dish, sprinkle well with grated nutmeg and bake in a hot oven (425°F., mark 7) for 10 minutes, till the pastry is set, then reduce to moderate (350°F., mark 4) and continue cooking for 40 minutes in all, until the custard is set.

FRUIT DESSERTS

RASPBERRY AND PINEAPPLE RINGS

(see picture above)

Cream 2 squares of demi-sel cheese or a mild cream cheese spread with the grated rind of 1 lemon, 2 level tsps. sugar and enough lemon juice to give a soft consistency. Sandwich some pineapple rings together in pairs with this mixture; decorate and serve with raspberry sauce. Chill both the pineapple rings and the sauce before serving.

To make the sauce, blend 2 level tsps. arrowroot with $\frac{1}{4}$ pint of juice taken from a can of raspberries, boil until the sauce thickens and then fold in the drained raspberries. Alternatively, use fresh raspberries crushed with sugar.

SAVARIN À LA POMPADOUR

(see colour picture no. 49)

A little rice flour	1 pint rum syrup
4 oz. flour	1 oz. browned almonds
$\frac{1}{4}$ oz. fresh yeast	Macédoine of fruit (peaches,
$\frac{1}{2}$ level tsp. sugar	red-skinned apples,
$\frac{1}{8}$ pint milk	mandarin oranges,
2 eggs	bananas, cherries, black
$2\frac{1}{2}$ oz. butter (melted,	and green grapes)
then cooled)	Whipped cream (optional)

Grease a mould and dust it with rice flour. Heat and sift the flour. Cream the yeast and sugar, add the tepid milk and strain this mixture into the flour. Leave in a warm place for about $\frac{1}{2}$ hour; when bubbles form, work in the flour, beat in the eggs and the butter (melted, then cooled) and beat until the mixture is of a dropping consistency. Three-quarters fill the prepared mould. Leave to prove, again in a warm place, until mixture has risen to top of tin, then bake in a fairly hot oven (400°F., mark 6) for about $\frac{1}{2}$ hour. Turn out, saturate with rum syrup and decorate with spikes of browned almonds. Fill the centre with the fruit macédoine and for a more decorative effect pipe with whipped cream. Strain the rum syrup, add the rest of the fruits to it and pour it round the savarin.

Rum Syrup: Boil $\frac{3}{4}$ pint water and 6 oz. sugar for about 7 minutes until it forms a syrup. Add 3 tbsps. rum and the juice of $\frac{1}{2}$ a lemon.

SUMMER PUDDING

1 lb. soft fruits (raspberries,	Sugar
currants, blackberries,	Thin slices of bread
etc.)	Custard or whipped cream

Stew the fruit with sugar and water, keeping it as whole as possible. Arrange the fruit and bread in alternate layers in a basin, retaining some of the juice; pour this over the mixture, then place a piece of bread on the top, cover with a plate and press down with a heavy weight. Leave for $1\frac{1}{2}$-2 hours or overnight. If possible chill before serving with the custard or cream.

GALA PINEAPPLE

Select a fairly large pineapple with a good crown of green leaves. Following the markings in the pineapple skin, stick in slanting rows of cocktail sticks; on these fix rows of fresh fruits, e.g., grapes, cherries, strawberries, slices of banana, chunks of red-skinned apple, pieces of pineapple and also chunks of cheese. (Dip the apple and banana slices in lemon juice to prevent their discolouring.) This makes a good item at a buffet or cocktail party.

MELON AND FRUIT SALAD DE-LUXE

Choose a medium-sized ripe honeydew or cantaloup melon. Cut a slice off the top and scoop out the seeds and then the flesh, leaving a rim of flesh round the top edge. Cut the melon pulp into cubes, retaining the juice, and mix with a selection of fresh or canned fruits, the juice of a lemon and a little Kirsch and leave to stand. Just before serving, fill the melon with the fruit salad, top with scoops of ice cream and sprinkle with some chopped nuts. Place on a dish, decorate with extra fruits and serve at once.

CHERRIES IN RED WINE
(see colour picture no. 37)

1 lb. red cherries	2 tbsps. red-currant jelly
Red wine	Arrowroot

Stew the cherries in just enough red wine to cover, with the red-currant jelly. Strain off the juice and thicken with arrowroot ($\frac{1}{2}$ oz. to 1 pint juice). Put the fruit in individual glasses and pour the juice over. Chill.

BRANDIED MELON AND GINGER
(see colour picture no. 37)

1 canteloupe melon	Caster sugar (about
1-2 level tsps. powdered	4 oz.)
ginger	$\frac{1}{8}$ pint brandy

Halve the melon, scoop out the flesh and dice it; place in a bowl with the ginger and sufficient sugar to sweeten (the amount depends on your own tastes). Chill until the sugar has dissolved and the juice flows, then stir in the brandy. Serve in the half melon shell or in individual dishes, accompanied by cream.

ORANGE AMBROSIA
(see colour picture no. 37)

4 sweet oranges	1-2 tbsps. Curaçao
Caster sugar to taste	or Grand Marnier
2 oz. desiccated coconut	

Peel the oranges, removing as much of the pith as possible; slice across very thinly. Place the oranges in individual glasses, layered with the sugar, coconut and liqueur, and chill before serving.

PEARS IN PORT WINE
(see colour picture no. 37)

4 large ripe pears	Rind of 1 lemon
$\frac{1}{4}$ pint port	2 tbsps. red-currant
$\frac{1}{4}$ pint water	jelly (or to taste)
3 oz. sugar	Cream

Peel the pears, cut in quarters lengthwise and remove the cores. Make a syrup from the port, water, sugar and lemon rind. Add the pears and simmer gently until tender. Remove the fruit, add the red-currant jelly, then boil the syrup rapidly until it is well reduced. Place 4 pear slices in each glass and pour the syrup over. Allow to cool and serve with cream.

PEACHES IN WHITE WINE

Allow one or more yellow peaches per person. Peel and slice each into a wine glass, pour on some white wine and leave for a few minutes. The peach is eaten first, then the wine is drunk. (The most suitable wine is a sweet white Italian one, such as Orvieto.)

RASPBERRY AND BANANA CREAM
(see left-hand picture above)

2 eggs, separated	3 bananas
3 oz. caster sugar	$\frac{1}{4}$ pint double cream
$\frac{1}{4}$ pint raspberry purée	Whipped cream and rasp-
$\frac{1}{2}$ oz. gelatine	berries to decorate
2 tbsps. raspberry juice	

Whisk the egg yolks, sugar and fruit purée over boiling water until the mixture is thick and creamy. Dissolve the gelatine in the raspberry juice and add it to the mixture; sieve and add 2 of the bananas. Whip the cream and whisk the egg whites until stiff. When the fruit mixture is cool add the whipped cream and lastly the egg whites. Pour into a dish and when set add some piped cream, sliced banana and a few raspberries.

BLACKBERRY FOOL
(see picture above)

1 lb. blackberries	Sugar to taste
(or a 15-oz. can)	$\frac{1}{2}$ pint custard and/or cream

Stew the blackberries in a little water with sugar as required (unless canned fruit is used); sieve the fruit. Mix the purée with the custard or cream (or a half-and-half mixture) and sweeten to taste. Pour into glasses, decorate with chopped nuts or as desired. Serve with shortbread or Savoy biscuits.
This sweet is equally good made with other fruits, especially gooseberries, rhubarb and berry fruits.

BROILED GRAPEFRUIT

Cut 2 grapefruit in half and loosen the segments in the usual way. Brush each half well with melted butter, sprinkle with 1 level tbsp. brown sugar, 2 tsps. rum or sherry and a little powdered cinnamon, then grill gently for 10 minutes, until tender and bubbling. Serve alone or with whipped cream.

APRICOT DESSERT
(see picture above)

A 1 lb. 14 oz. can of apricots	2 eggs, separated
1½ oz. cornflour	1 tsp. almond essence
2 oz. ground almonds	2 tsps. lemon juice
2 oz. caster sugar	¼ pint double cream
	Blanched angelica

Sieve the apricots with their juice (keeping 8 for decoration) and make up to 2 pints with water. Mix the cornflour, almonds, sugar and egg yolks to a smooth paste with a little of the cold fruit mixture. Bring the rest of the fruit to the boil, add to the cornflour, return the mixture to the pan and cook for 3 minutes. Remove from the heat and add the essence and lemon juice. Whisk the egg whites stiffly and fold in. Spoon the mixture into individual glasses. When cold, cover with half-whisked cream and put an apricot half and angelica "leaves" on each. Whisk the remaining cream and pipe some into each apricot. (Serves 8.)

FRUIT SPONGE FLAN

3 eggs	Fresh or canned fruits
3 oz. sugar	Whipped cream to
3 oz. flour	decorate
½ pint jelly	

Grease a sponge flan tin and sprinkle it with a little flour. Whisk the eggs and add the sugar, then continue whisking until the mixture is light and thick. Fold in the flour, put the mixture into the tin and bake in a fairly hot oven (375°F., mark 5) for about 20 minutes, then cool on a rack. Fill with the fruit and coat with jelly which is just on the point of setting (or with arrowroot glaze), then pipe with cream.

FRUIT SALAD PAVLOVA
(see colour picture no. 38)

8 oz. caster sugar	½ lb. fresh or canned fruit
1 oz. cornflour	(oranges, grapes,
3 egg whites	cherries, banana, etc.)

Draw a circle 6 inches in diameter on a piece of waxed or greaseproof paper, then place this on a greased tray. Sieve the sugar and cornflour together very thoroughly.

Beat the egg whites until foamy, add half the sugar-and-cornflour mixture and beat until stiff. Now add the rest of the sugar-and-cornflour and fold in until it is well blended. Place in a forcing bag fitted with a vegetable star pipe and pipe round the pencil line on the paper and over the entire centre. Pipe round the edge to build up a "basket" shape. Bake in a very slow oven (250°F., mark ¼) for 2-3 hours, until quite dry and crisp. While the meringue case is cooking, peel and slice oranges and apples, halve and seed grapes, stone cherries, slice banana and cut pineapple into chunks.

Take the meringue case off the paper while it is still warm and lift it on to a cooling rack. When it is cool, arrange the fruit attractively in the meringue basket.

HEDGEROW DELIGHT

½ lb. blackberries	1 sponge sandwich
½ lb. damsons	Whipped cream
Sugar to sweeten	Chopped almonds

Stew the two fruits separately with sugar to sweeten, adding no water with the blackberries and very little with the damsons. Remove the stones from the latter then cook the damsons with the blackberries for a few minutes. Lay the first sponge layer in a dish, pour over it half of the fruit and put the other cake layer on top, then add the rest of the fruit. Leave for 4-6 hours in a cool place, then transfer to a glass dish. Put some cream on top and sprinkle with chopped almonds.

STUFFED PEARS
(see picture above)

2 oz. seedless raisins	2 level tbsps. sugar
2 tbsps. rum	A 1 lb. 14 oz. can of pear
2 tbsps. water	halves
1 oz. chopped crystallised ginger	Maraschino cherries to decorate
¼ pint double cream, whipped	Savoy biscuits

Simmer the raisins gently in the rum and water for about 10 minutes, until the fruit is soft and has absorbed the spirit. Allow to cool, drain the fruit and mix with the ginger, cream and sugar. Pile this mixture on the well-drained pear halves, decorate each with a cherry and chill well. Serve with Savoy or shortbread fingers.

FROSTED FRUIT PYRAMID

(see colour picture no. 39)

This makes an excellent centrepiece for a formal dinner table or buffet. For it you need a selection of fruits, for example, green and black grapes, clementines, dessert dates, green and red-skinned apples. Leave the apples whole; leave some clementines whole but divide 2-3 of them into segments; separate grapes into small bunches. Dip the fruits into lightly beaten egg white, then into caster sugar, making sure that the whole surface of each is thoroughly coated; leave overnight for the frosting to become firm. The next day, build the fruit up into a pyramid, using a silver cakeboard as base and securing the layers of fruit with cocktail sticks. Decorate the base of the pyramid with sections of clementine and sprays of frosted fern.

MERINGUE PYRAMID

(see colour picture no. 48)

4 egg whites	½ lb. green and black
8 oz. caster sugar	grapes
½ pint double cream	2 oz. shelled walnuts
Sugar to sweeten cream	Chocolate curls or flakes

Whisk the egg whites very stiffly. Add the sugar a little at a time, beating well after each addition. Put the mixture into a forcing bag fitted with a plain nozzle and pipe on to lightly oiled greaseproof paper in small round meringues. Bake in a very cool oven (250°F., mark ¼) for 3-4 hours, until crisp and dry but not coloured.
Whip and sweeten the cream. Remove the seeds from the grapes and chop the nuts roughly. Place a layer of meringues on a plate and cover with some of the cream and grapes. Continue piling up layers of meringue, fruit and cream in this way (retaining a little cream for decoration); form into a pyramid and finish with meringues. Pipe stars of cream between the meringues and decorate with grapes and walnuts, then sprinkle with chocolate flakes.

DAMSON WHIP

1 lb. damsons	1 egg white
3 oz. sugar	Double cream and nuts to
½ oz. gelatine	decorate
¼ pint evaporated milk	

Stew the damsons with the sugar and ¼ pint water until tender, then sieve them. Dissolve the gelatine in ¼ pint hot water and stir it into the fruit purée; add the milk and leave to cool. When the mixture is almost set, add the egg white and whisk until light and frothy. Pile into glasses and decorate with whipped cream and some chopped nuts.

RASPBERRY TAPIOCA CREAMS

(see colour picture no. 32)

1 pint milk	A 15-oz. can of raspberries,
1½ oz. tapioca	well drained
oz. sugar	Whipped cream and
2 eggs, separated	angelica to decorate
Vanilla essence	

Boil the milk and sprinkle in the tapioca, cook for several minutes, until the mixture thickens, then add the sugar and beaten egg yolks; allow to cool and then fold in the stiffly beaten egg whites and the flavouring. Pour into a bowl and chill if possible. Spoon alternate layers of raspberries and tapioca cream into 4 sundae glasses and decorate.
To vary, rice or semolina can be used instead of tapioca and any fresh or canned fruit can replace the raspberries.

CHERRY TRIFLE

6 oz. sugar	½ pint custard
1 lb. stoned cherries	2 oz. almonds
Sponge cakes or cake	¼ pint double cream
crumbs	Chopped pistachio
Cherry jam or red-currant	nuts
jelly	

Make a syrup with the sugar and sufficient water to cover the fruit; wash the cherries and stew them in the syrup. Split the sponge cakes and spread them with cherry jam or red-currant jelly; if cake crumbs are used, a thin layer of jam may be spread on top of them. Pour the stewed cherries over and leave for about ½ hour for the sponge cakes to soak, then cover with the custard. Blanch the almonds and shred each into about three; sprinkle these on top of the custard, reserving a few for decoration. Whip the cream stiffly with a little caster sugar and pile in rocky heaps on top of the nuts. Decorate with pistachios (or almonds).

ORANGE AND RASPBERRY BAVAROIS

(see colour picture on back of jacket)

1 pkt. of raspberry jelly	½ pint milk
1 pkt. of orange jelly	¼ pint single cream
¼ lb. fresh raspberries	¼ pint double cream
2 level tbsps. custard powder	Whipped cream and orange
1 level tbsp. sugar	slices to decorate

Place the jelly cubes in a measure, make up to ¾ pint with boiling water and stir to dissolve. Make up ¼ pint of the liquid jelly to ½ pint with cold water, then pour into the base of a 2½-pint fancy mould. Drop in the ¼ lb. prepared fruit and leave to set.
Make up a custard, using the custard powder, sugar and milk, and leave to cool. Stiffly whisk the single and double creams. Whisk the cooled custard into the remaining jelly when this is on the point of setting. Fold the cream through the mixture and pour into the mould; chill. Turn out, and decorate with orange slices and whipped cream.

ORANGE BASKETS

4 large oranges	A few canned apricots
¼ lb. grapes	A few canned or glacé
2 bananas	cherries
1 dessert pear	Angelica

Wipe the oranges and cut the top off each. Remove the pulp carefully without piercing the skin and squeeze it in muslin to obtain the juice. Stone the grapes, slice the bananas and cut up the other fruit. Pour the orange juice over the mixed fruit. Notch the edges of the orange baskets with scissors and fill with the fruit mixture. Soak the angelica in a little water and cut it in strips to form basket handles.

ICE CREAM SWEETS, JELLIES, ETC.

VANILLA ICE CREAM

$\frac{1}{2}$ pint milk	3 egg yolks
3 oz. sugar	$\frac{1}{4}$ pint double cream
$\frac{1}{2}$ level tsp. salt	Vanilla essence

Boil the milk. Mix sugar, salt and egg yolks in a basin, pour milk over and cook in a double saucepan till the mixture thickens, stirring all the time. Let it cool; when cold pour into a freezing tray of the refrigerator and freeze for 20-30 minutes. Turn out and whip till creamy. Add cream and essence, return mixture to tray and freeze until firm, stirring occasionally. (Serves 8.)

PINEAPPLE ICE CREAM

Drain contents of a 15-oz. can of crushed pineapple. Whip $\frac{1}{2}$ pint double cream, then add the juice of $\frac{1}{2}$ a lemon, 1 oz. sugar and the pineapple pulp. Put into the ice tray and freeze; stir at intervals of 15-20 minutes until half-frozen, then leave until hard.

STRAWBERRY LIQUEUR ICE CREAM

$\frac{1}{4}$ pint double cream	1 tbsp. rum or
8 oz. strawberries, puréed	Maraschino
to give $\frac{1}{4}$ pint	2 oz. sugar (if fresh
$\frac{1}{2}$ tsp. vanilla essence	strawberries are used)

Whip the cream, then mix with all the other ingredients. Pour into a freezing tray of the refrigerator and freeze for $\frac{3}{4}$-1 hour. Turn out and whisk until smooth, then return the mixture to the tray and freeze until firm.
Variations: Use raspberries instead of strawberries; in this case the purée may need sieving to remove the pips. Use a can of pineapple; drain off the juice from the can and crush the pineapple pieces well before adding to the cream.

PEACH AND STRAWBERRY ROMANOFF

4 peaches	1 glass of Curaçao
1 lb. strawberries	Vanilla ice cream
Caster sugar	1 tbsp. cream

Skin and slice the peaches, place with three-quarters of

the strawberries in a dish and sprinkle with caster sugar. Crush the remaining strawberries to a pulp, add the Curaçao, ice cream and cream, then mix well together. Pour over the fruit and chill before serving.

ICE CREAM TULIP
(see left-hand picture above)

Make a sponge sandwich cake and before it is quite cold, put one half on a dish, then spread with a thick layer of red cherry jam, which should begin to soak into the cake. Cover with some ice cream, piling it up in the centre. Cut the top half of the cake into wedges and arrange upright round the ice cream. Fill the centre with cherries and pipe with whipped cream.

SUNDAES

Sundaes can be quickly and simply made, using the following basic ideas with your own individual variations:
(1) Ice cream in various flavours with layers of fresh fruit that has been lightly crushed, mixed with sugar and a little liqueur (optional), then left to stand; top with cream.
(2) Alternate layers of two ice creams, say, coffee and orange or vanilla and chocolate, topped with a chocolate, butterscotch or jam sauce and chopped nuts or flaked chocolate.
(3) Alternate layers of chopped or whipped jelly, fruit and ice cream.

STRAWBERRY MOUSSE
(see right-hand picture above)

$\frac{1}{2}$ pint strawberry purée	$\frac{1}{2}$ pint double cream, lightly
2 oz. caster sugar	whipped
Juice of 1 lemon	2 egg whites, stiffly whisked
$\frac{1}{2}$ oz. gelatine	Strawberries and cream
$\frac{1}{2}$ gill water	to decorate

To make the purée, sieve some fresh or canned strawberries; add the sugar and lemon juice. Dissolve the gelatine in the water over gentle heat and add. When the mixture is about to set, fold in the cream and lastly the egg whites. Put into a wetted mould and leave to set. Turn out and decorate with whole strawberries and a little whipped cream.
Alternatively, omit the gelatine and $\frac{1}{2}$ gill water and put the mixture into the freezer of the refrigerator to make a frozen mousse.

APPLE MOUSSE

(see picture above)

4 large apples, peeled and cut up	3 eggs
Juice and grated rind of 1 lemon	½ pint thick cream
	2-3 oz. sugar (according to tartness of apples)
½ oz. gelatine	1 red eating apple

Cook the apples with the lemon rind and a little water, then sieve into a basin. Melt the gelatine with ½ gill lemon juice (add some water if necessary), leave to cool and when it starts to thicken add to the apple.

Whisk the eggs in a bowl over boiling water until thick and creamy; cool, stirring from time to time, add to the apple mixture, sweeten to taste, then fold in the cream. Pour into an 8-inch cake tin and leave to set, then turn out.

Cut wafer-thin slices of the eating apple, leaving the peel on to give extra colour, and use as decoration. (To prevent the slices going brown, dip them in a sugar syrup made by boiling 2 level tbsps. sugar and ½ pint water together with 2 tbsps. lemon juice.)

CHARLOTTE RUSSE

(see right-hand picture above and colour picture no. 51)

½ pkt. of yellow or red jelly	¼ pint double cream, whipped
Glacé cherries and angelica or fresh fruit	Kirsch or Cointreau
	½ oz. gelatine
1 pkt. of sponge fingers	3 tbsps. water
½ pint custard (cold)	Whipped cream to decorate (optional)

Make up the jelly and set ¼ inch of it in the bottom of a straight-sided mould. When it is set, decorate with pieces of cherry and angelica or fresh fruit; carefully cover with a little more jelly and allow to set.

If necessary, trim the sides of the sponge fingers, then brush the edges with liquid jelly. Line the sides of the mould with the fingers, pressing them closely together. Combine the custard, cream and liqueur. Dissolve the gelatine in the water and add to the cream mixture. When this is on the point of setting, pour it into the centre of the mould and allow to set. Trim off any surplus from the top of the sponge fingers.

Dip the bottom of the mould in hot water and then turn the charlotte out on to a serving dish. Any leftover jelly may be set in a thin layer, chopped and put round the charlotte. If you wish, tie a ribbon round the charlotte before serving.

As a variation, make a fruit-flavoured cream for the centre—add ¼ pint fruit purée to the mixture before adding the dissolved gelatine.

SHERRY PRUNE MOULD

1 lb. prunes	1 tbsp. sherry
½ pint water	2 oz. split almonds
Rind of 1 lemon	Whipped double cream
2 oz. sugar	Browned almonds to decorate
½ oz. gelatine	

Soak the prunes for several hours, then cook them with the water, lemon rind and sugar until they are tender. Strain off ½ pint of the juice, dissolve the gelatine in it and add the sherry. Pour a little of the jelly into the bottom of a mould and when firm decorate with a few of the split almonds, then put another layer of jelly over these. Meanwhile sieve the prunes, add remaining nuts (chopped into rough pieces) and mix in the rest of the jelly. Pour into the decorated mould and leave to set. When the mixture is firm, turn it on to a glass plate and decorate with cream and a few browned almonds.

NEW-STYLE CHEESE CAKE

(see colour picture no. 35)

12 oz. curd or cottage cheese	2 eggs, beaten
	½ pint soured cream
6 oz. digestive biscuits	Vanilla essence
3 oz. caster sugar	Lemon peel to decorate
3 oz. butter, melted	

Sieve the cheese. Crush the biscuits and mix them with 1 oz. of the sugar and the butter. Butter a shallow oven-proof dish about 9 inches in diameter and press the crumb mixture against the sides and base. Bake in the centre of a moderate oven (350°F., mark 4) for 10 minutes.

Meanwhile beat the cheese until it is softened. Mix in the eggs, the rest of the sugar and the cream. Flavour with a little vanilla. Pour into the biscuit case, return it to the oven and cook for 30-35 minutes, until set. Decorate with a long twist of thinly pared lemon peel.

LEMON SOUFFLÉ
(see colour picture no. 50)

3 lemons	¼ pint double cream
4 eggs, separated	Crystallised lemon slices,
6 oz. sugar	finely chopped nuts
½ oz. gelatine	and whipped cream to
2 tbsps. water	decorate

Prepare a 6-inch soufflé case: cut a band of firm paper 3 inches deeper than the sides of the case and fix it round the outside, making sure that it is a good shape.

Combine the finely grated rind and the juice of the fruit with the egg yolks and sugar and whisk over hot water until thick and fluffy. Remove from the water and add the gelatine (dissolved in the water over very gentle heat). Leave in a cool place till the mixture begins to thicken, then fold in the whipped cream and stiffly whisked egg whites; pour into a prepared soufflé dish and leave to set. Remove the paper and decorate.

Alternatively, set in paper cups—see picture on p. 203.

CHOCOLATE SOUFFLÉ

3 eggs	2 oz. melted chocolate
3 oz. caster sugar	½ pint double cream
¼ pint milk	Whipped cream to
½ oz. gelatine	decorate
3 tbsps. water	

Prepare a case as described for Lemon Soufflé above. Put the egg yolk, sugar and ¼ pint milk in a basin over boiling water and whisk till thick and light.

Meanwhile dissolve the gelatine in the water and add to the mixture with the melted chocolate, and allow to cool. Whisk the cream and also the egg whites. Fold the cream into the egg yolk mixture, and lastly fold in the whisked egg whites. Pour into the prepared soufflé case and leave to set firmly. Carefully remove the paper and decorate the soufflé with piped cream or as desired. Evaporated milk can be substituted for cream, if preferred.

COFFEE SOUFFLÉ

Make as for Chocolate Soufflé, but use ¼ pint strong black coffee to flavour. Decorate with halved walnuts and angelica.

APRICOT SOUFFLÉ

A 15-oz. can of apricots	1-2 tbsps. orange liqueur
3 eggs, separated	or rum
3 oz. caster sugar	¼ pint double cream
1 tbsp. lemon juice	2 oz. walnuts, chopped
½ oz. gelatine	Cream to decorate

Prepare a 7-inch soufflé case by cutting a band of firm paper about 3 inches deeper than its sides and fixing round the outside—make sure it is a good shape. Drain and reserve the syrup from the apricots. Sieve the fruit to make ¼ pint purée. Put the egg yolks, sugar, lemon juice and 2 tbsps. fruit syrup in a basin over hot water and whisk till thick and creamy.

Dissolve the gelatine in 2 tbsps. fruit syrup over gentle heat and add the liqueur. Fold into the whisked mixture, then fold in the fruit purée. Whisk the cream and egg whites separately. Fold the cream, then the egg whites into the fruit mixture. Pour into the prepared soufflé case and leave to set. Carefully remove the paper. Decorate the sides with nuts and the top with cream.

APPLES À LA ROSEBERY

1 lb. apples	¼ pint double cream
A ½-inch piece of	A little sherry
cinnamon stick	Pink colouring
Juice and rind of 1 orange	½ oz. gelatine
and 1 lemon	Cream for piping
Caster sugar	½ pint chopped fruit jelly

Stew the apples with 1 gill water, the cinnamon, grated orange and lemon rind and a little sugar. Sieve the pulp, measure and make up to ½ pint with a little water. Half-whip the cream, add the apple pulp, fruit juices, sherry and sugar to taste and some colouring. Add the gelatine, dissolved in a little water, and when the mixture begins to thicken, put it into a mould. Turn out when set and decorate with piped cream and chopped jelly.

HONEYCOMB MOULD

2 large eggs	Vanilla essence
1 pint milk	½ oz. gelatine
1½ oz. sugar	2 tbsps. water

Separate the eggs. Make a custard with the egg yolks, milk and sugar and flavour it with vanilla. Dissolve the gelatine in the water and add it to the custard. Whisk the egg whites very stiffly and fold lightly into the cool custard mixture. Pour into a glass dish or mould and turn out when set. Serve with chocolate sauce or with stewed fruit (or jam) and whipped cream.

This is the traditional Honeycomb Mould, but if you wish you can replace the vanilla by grated orange or lemon rind or coffee essence. Chopped glacé fruit and nuts may be added.

LEMON CHIFFON CREAM

3 eggs, separated	Grated rind of ½ a lemon
3 oz. sugar	½ lb. fresh strawberries
Juice of 1 lemon	(optional)
2 tbsps. dry white wine	

Beat the egg yolks and sugar together until creamy, then gradually add the lemon juice, wine and lemon rind. Put into the top of a double boiler and heat gently, stirring all the time, until it thickens—do not overheat or it will curdle. Allow to cool. Whisk the egg whites stiffly and fold into the lemon cream mixture. Pile into individual glasses and chill before serving, with the strawberries, if used.

CHOCO-RUM

6 oz. plain chocolate	¼ pint double cream,
4 eggs, separated	whipped
2 tbsps. rum	1 oz. nuts, chopped

Melt the chocolate in a bowl over a pan of hot water and cool slightly. Beat the egg yolks into the chocolate, then add the rum. Whisk the egg whites until stiff and carefully fold into the chocolate mixture. Put into individual glasses and chill. Decorate with whipped cream and nuts.

ZABAGLIONE

6 egg yolks	6 tbsps. Marsala or
2 level tbsps. sugar	Madeira wine

Whisk the egg yolks and sugar together until light and creamy. Add the wine and blend well. Heat the mixture over boiling water, whisking all the time and taking care not to let it curdle. As soon as it thickens, pour into individual glasses and serve hot; it may also be served over fruit.

SYLLABUB

(see picture on right)

This old English sweet was traditionally made with milk straight from the cow poured from a height into wine, cider or ale: this gave a frothy mixture, which was sweetened to taste and flavoured with spices and spirit. Here are two modern recipes—the first separates out and when eating it you dip a spoon through the frothy honeycomb layer into the wine-lemon whey; the second, which is more solid, may be made beforehand and kept for up to 2 days in a cool place (but not the refrigerator). Serve boudoir biscuits or macaroons separately.

Recipe I

2 egg whites	¼ pint sweet white wine
4 oz. caster sugar	½ pint double cream,
Juice of ½ lemon	lightly whipped

Whisk the egg whites until they form stiff peaks. Fold in the sugar, lemon juice and wine. Finally fold in the cream. Spoon into glasses and leave to separate. Decorate with a twist of lemon peel.

Recipe II

Thinly pared rind of 1	2 tbsps. brandy
lemon and 4 tbsps. juice	2-3 oz. caster sugar.
6 tbsps. white wine or	½ pint double cream
sherry	Grated nutmeg

Place the lemon rind, juice, wine and brandy in a bowl; leave for several hours or overnight. Strain into a large bowl, add the sugar and stir until dissolved. Add the cream slowly, stirring all the time. Whisk until the mixture forms soft peaks, spoon into ¼-pint glasses and sprinkle with nutmeg. For the version shown in the picture, prepare the glasses by painting the rims with egg white and dipping into coloured sugar; decorate the syllabub with crystallised lemon slices.

CRÈME WAFLAN

Sandwich about 10-12 pairs of wafer biscuits together with royal icing and press them between 2 boards for a few hours. Coat the sides of a thin sandwich cake with warmed sieved apricot jam and stand the biscuit sandwiches upright round it; hold them in place with a fine string, then pipe over the joins with royal icing. Make up a raspberry jelly, using ½ pint of the juice from a 1 lb. 14-oz. can of raspberries. When it is on the point of setting, beat thoroughly until pale and fluffy. Fold in ½ pint whipped cream and the drained raspberries (reserving a few for the decoration). Pour the mixture into the Waflan case and leave to set. Decorate the sides and top of the biscuits with royal icing and arrange the remaining raspberries on the cream filling. Replace the string by a satin ribbon and serve as soon as possible.
An alternative filling for summertime is fresh raspberries or strawberries, crushed and mixed with stiffly whipped cream.

LEMON SNOW

½-¾ oz. gelatine	3 egg whites
½ pint boiling water	Preserved lemon and glacé
6 oz. sugar	cherries to decorate
¼ pint lemon juice	

Dissolve the gelatine in the boiling water and add the sugar and lemon juice; leave to cool but do not allow it to set. Add the egg whites and whisk until light and fluffy. Put the snow into individual glasses and decorate.

FRUIT SALADS ROUND THE WORLD

BASIC FRUIT SALAD
(see colour picture no. 50)

Make a syrup by boiling together 4 oz. sugar and ½ pint water and when cool add the juice of 1 lemon. Prepare according to type 2 oranges, 2 bananas, 2 red-skinned apples, 4 oz. black or green grapes, 1 small can of cherries and 1 can of peaches or pineapples. Add all to the syrup. Supplement with other fruits in season, e.g., strawberries, raspberries, apricots, melon, plums or pears; 2-3 tbsps. fruit liqueur or spirit can be added to the syrup. Chill before serving.

Serve in a glass dish or, for a change, in hollowed oranges or melons (serrate the edges with a knife) or in a brandy balloon or punch bowl. The rim may be frosted by painting it with egg white and coating with sugar crystals.

BULGARIAN BRANDIED FRUIT SALAD
(see picture above)

2 apples	½ a small melon
2 pears	3 oz. sugar
1 orange	¾ pint white wine
An 8-oz. can of cherries	¼ pint brandy

Peel and thinly slice the apples, pears and orange. Stone the cherries. Scoop out balls from the melon with a Parisian cutter and mix the fruit thoroughly. Combine the wine and brandy, pour over the fruit and mix well, taking care not to break up the fruit pieces. Chill in the refrigerator and serve very cold indeed.

DELICIOUS SALAD (SOUTH AFRICA)

2 oranges	4 guavas
1 pineapple	4 oz. sugar
2 bananas	

Peel and thinly slice the apples, pears and orange. pineapple, remove the core and cut the remaining flesh into slices. Peel and slice the bananas. Do not peel the guavas, as their skins are attractive in colour—just slice them. Arrange the fruits in layers, generously sprinkle each layer with sugar and finish with a layer of orange slices. Leave the salad for several hours, so that the sugar can dissolve and form a syrup with the fruit juice.

APPLE SALAD (GERMANY)

6 large eating apples	Juice and grated rind of
3 oz. chopped hazelnuts	1 lemon
3 oz. chopped walnuts	3 oz. icing sugar, sifted
3 oz. seedless raisins	½ pint double cream

Peel and slice the apples, mix with the nuts and raisins and sprinkle with lemon juice. Mix with sugar and lemon rind, toss in the cream and serve chilled.

DRUNKEN PRUNES
(see picture above)

¾ lb. prunes	½ oz. gelatine
1 pint water	⅛ pint port
3-4 oz. sugar	A few canned pears or
Grated rind and juice of	apricots
1 lemon	

Simmer the prunes in the water with the sugar, lemon rind and juice until tender. Sieve the fruit and juice to make a purée. Dissolve the gelatine in a little hot water, add to the fruit, then add the port. Pour the mixture into a refrigerator tray and leave to set. Chop it into large cubes and serve with the pears or apricots. (Serves 6.)

FRUIT SALAD IN GLASSES (FRENCH)

½ lb. strawberries (hulled)	1 liqueur glass of
2 bananas (sliced)	Maraschino
¼ lb. cherries (stoned)	1 liqueur glass of brandy
Juice of 1 lemon	⅛ pint sugar syrup
¼ pint sweet clear jelly (liquid)	

Put the 3 fruits in layers into individual goblet glasses. Strain the lemon juice and mix with other liquids. Pour a little of this syrup over the fruit in each glass; chill well before serving.

PINEAPPLE AND PEACH SALAD (GERMANY)

¼ pint water	1 glass Rhine wine
4 oz. granulated sugar	2 oz. black grapes
4 fresh peaches, halved	Icing sugar
4 slices fresh pineapple	

Make a syrup with the water and granulated sugar, cool and pour over the peaches; leave for 1 hour. Cut the pineapple slices into halves and arrange these in a circle on a flat dish, then fill the centre with the peach slices. Add the wine to the sugar syrup and pour over the fruit. Halve and seed the grapes, roll them in icing sugar and use to garnish the salad. Chill before serving.

SYRIAN CHILLED FRUIT SALAD

(see picture above)

4 oz. dried apricots	2 oz. almonds
4 oz. prunes	2 oz. pine kernels
4 oz. dried figs	2 oz. pistachio nuts
Other dried fruit as	2 tbsps. rose-water
available	Sugar syrup or fruit syrup
2 oz. seedless raisins	to taste

Wash the dried fruit, cover with cold water and leave to soak in a cool place for 24 hours. Blanch the nuts and add to the fruit, with the rose-water and enough syrup to sweeten. Keep in a cold place (preferably in a refrigerator) until needed; if possible, serve with ice cubes floating in the juice.

SCANDINAVIAN FRUIT SALAD

¼ lb. redcurrants	¼ lb. raspberries
¼ lb. blackcurrants	5 oz. caster sugar
¼ lb. loganberries	½ pint red wine

Prepare the fruits and put them in a bowl. Sprinkle with the sugar, pour the wine over and leave to stand in a cool place for 1 hour before serving.

PAW-PAW SALAD (NEW ZEALAND)

4 paw-paws	4 slices of pineapple
2 sweet oranges	(fresh or canned)
4 passion fruit	¼ pint pineapple juice

Peel the paw-paws, discarding the seedy pulp, and dice the flesh. Peel and dice the oranges and scoop out the pulp from the passion fruit. Arrange the fruits in a bowl and decorate with pineapple. Pour pineapple juice over and leave for an hour or so.

SALADE MARIETTE (MEDITERRANEAN)

1 lettuce	2 Jaffa oranges
2 red-skinned apples	Cream

Line a salad bowl with lettuce. Core but do not pare the apples, quarter them, then slice each quarter. Fill one side of the bowl with these slices. Peel the oranges (keeping the peel), and place at the other side of the bowl. Scrape away the pith from the rind, cut the coloured part into thin Julienne strips and place as a dividing line between the apples and oranges. Serve with cream.

ORANGE SALAD (SWITZERLAND)

4 Jaffa oranges	1 tsp. Curaçao
2 tsps. Kirsch	

Peel and quarter the oranges, place them in a salad bowl, sprinkle with the mixed liqueurs and chill.

FRUIT SALAD PLUS

(see picture above)

Combine a can of peaches with 2 sliced red-skinned apples (unpeeled) and ½ lb. seeded black grapes. Mix 2 pkts. cream cheese with 1 oz. sugar, the grated rind of 1 orange, 1 oz. chopped walnuts and enough orange juice to give the consistency of thick cream. Serve the fruit salad topped with the cheese mixture and sprinkled with more walnuts.

FRUIT-FILLED AVOCADO PEARS (USA)

(see colour picture no. 38)

4 oranges	8 strawberries
2 avocado pears	Caster sugar
Lemon juice	

Peel and segment the oranges. Halve the avocados and sprinkle with a little lemon juice to prevent discolouring. Wash and halve the strawberries. Pile the orange segments in the pear halves, decorate with the strawberries and dredge with sugar.

FILLED MELON (WEST AFRICA)

1 melon
½ pint sugar syrup
1 orange, peeled and segmented
1 grapefruit, peeled and segmented
2-3 tbsps. whisky
Ice cream

Cut the top off the melon, then remove and dice the flesh. Mix the syrup with the melon, diced orange and grapefruit segments and add the whisky. Put all this in the melon shell and top with ice cream.

PINEAPPLE SALAD (WEST AFRICA)
(see colour picture no. 38)

1 large pineapple
1 large paw-paw
½ a water melon
2 oranges
1 grapefruit
Honey
½ lb. black grapes

Slice the pineapple lengthwise into two halves, scoop out the flesh from the centre and cut into strips. Dice the paw-paw and melon and mix with the pineapple strips. Peel and segment the oranges and grapefruit, then mix with the other fruits and sweeten with honey. Halve and seed the grapes. Pile the diced fruit mixture into the pineapple and decorate with grapes. (Failing melon and paw-paws, use 4 oranges and 2 grapefruits.)

FRUIT SALADS FOR SLIMMERS

MELON FRUIT SALAD

Choose a ripe cantaloup melon; cut a slice off the top and scoop out the seeds, with some of the pulp, then turn the melon upside-down to drain whilst preparing the filling. Cut the melon pulp up into small pieces and mix with some fresh fruit. (Raspberries, strawberries or redcurrants are probably the best fruits to choose.) Pile the fruit and melon mixture into the melon, pour on some lemon juice sweetened with Saxins, and replace the lid.

CITRUS SALAD

1 grapefruit
2 oranges
1 mandarin or clementine
Saxin

Remove the skin from the fruit, and remove the sections from the central pith with a sharp knife. The mandarin need not be cut, but should be sectioned and the outer pith removed with warm water. Sweeten with Saxin.

FRESH FRUIT SALAD

2 dessert pears
1 dessert apple
1 orange or tangerine
3 dessert plums
1 peach
4 oz. white and black grapes mixed
1 banana
A few cherries
1 bottle of gooseberries or other fruit (optional)
Saxin
Juice of 1 lemon

Prepare the pears and remove the centres with the aid of a teaspoon; peel and core the apple, and cut up into sections. Peel the orange or tangerine and divide into segments. Cut the plums and the peach in half and remove the stones, then slice into convenient-sized pieces. Place all these fruits in a chilled bowl, together with the grapes, sliced banana, cherries, and gooseberries. Sweeten ¼ pint water with Saxin to taste, add the lemon juice, and pour over the fruit.

RASPBERRY DELIGHT
(see left-hand picture below)

Arrange ¾ lb. fresh raspberries in 4 sundae glasses. Pour 1 tbsp. strained fresh orange juice into each, decorate with sprigs of mint and chill before serving.

SUMMER COCKTAIL
(see right-hand picture below)

1 small honeydew melon
Juice of 1 large grapefruit
Saxin
Mint and glacé cherries to decorate

Use a parisienne cutter to scoop out balls from the melon flesh. Fill sundae glasses two-thirds full with melon. Sweeten the grapefruit juice if necessary with Saxin, pour over the fruit and chill. Garnish each cocktail with mint (if available) and half a cherry.

QUICK SWEETS

POIRES HÉLÈNE

Put some lemon or vanilla ice cream into sundae glasses, place one canned pear in each, top with chocolate sauce and decorate with almonds or crystallised violets.

PÊCHES AURORE

½ pint single cream
Vanilla ice cream
1 glass of Kirsch

Red colouring
4 large peaches, skinned
1 tbsp. whipped cream

Make a sauce by mixing thoroughly the single cream, a little ice cream, Kirsch and a few drops of red colouring. Halve the peaches. Serve each peach with a little ice cream and pour the sauce over. Decorate with cream.

SPEEDY ICE CREAM SWEETS

1. Place some ice cream in individual dishes, add 2 meringue halves to each and top with fruit, chocolate or butterscotch sauce and cream.
2. Fill éclairs or choux pastry balls with ice cream and serve sprinkled with chopped nuts.

MERINGUE BALLS

(see left-hand picture above)

Cut 4 rounds of Swiss roll, place on a baking sheet, top with fresh or canned fruit and sprinkle with sherry. Whip 2 egg whites until stiff and beat in 2 level tbsps. caster sugar. Pile this meringue over the cake and fruit, taking it right down to meet the baking tray, and bake in a hot oven (425°F., mark 7) for a few minutes, until the meringue is just coloured. Serve at once.

FRUIT CREAM FLAN

(see right-hand picture above)

Instant whip puddings and flavoured custard and blanc-mange powders make a creamy filling for a flan. They can be alternated with layers of fruit, or the fruit can be folded into the mixture.

Suggested fillings and toppings: Raspberry cream, whole raspberries decorated with crushed ratafias.

Chocolate cream, mandarins or oranges, decorated with cream.
Butterscotch cream, sliced bananas, decorated with crushed praline or toasted coconut.
Lemon cream, crushed pineapple, decorated with walnuts or crystallised ginger.

QUICK APPLE FLAN

Spread a prepared flan case with raspberry jam and cover this with a layer of sweetened stewed apples. Make up some thick custard, using 2 level tbsps. custard powder, 2 level tbsps. sugar and ½ pint milk, and pour it carefully over the fruit. Sprinkle with flaked chocolate and serve chilled, with cream if desired.
Vary by leaving out the jam, by using other types of fruit (fresh, canned or stewed), by flavouring the custard, or by sprinkling with chopped nuts or coconut.

CREAM CHEESE AND PINEAPPLE FLAN

1 prepared flan case
2 pkts. cream or lactic cheese
3-4 tbsps. chopped pineapple

2 oz. chopped walnuts
Sugar to taste
Grated rind of 1 lemon

Mix together the cream cheese, pineapple, 1 oz. of the walnuts, 1-2 oz. sugar and lemon rind. Stir until well mixed, adding a little pineapple juice if necessary to give the consistency of whipped cream. Pile into the flan case and decorate with remaining nuts.

FRUIT CREAMS

Put alternate layers of instant pudding mixture or flavoured custard and soft fruit in sundae glasses and decorate with cream, nuts, chocolate, praline, angelica, crystallised fruit or fresh fruits. Use similar combinations to those given for Fruit Cream Flan.

RICE CONDÉ

Add 1 level tbsp. sugar, the grated rind of 1 lemon and a pinch of salt to a 15-oz. can of rice pudding. Pour into individual dishes, top with half a peach, flat side downwards, and pour some jam sauce over.

157

BAKED FRUIT ALASKA

1 sponge round	2 egg whites
1 block of ice cream	4 oz. caster sugar
Canned or stewed fruit	

Place the cake on a fireproof dish and put the ice cream on top. Pile on some fruit, taking care it does not slip off. Whisk the egg whites until stiff and fold in almost all the sugar. Coat the Alaska well with this meringue. Sprinkle with remaining sugar and bake in a hot oven (425°F., mark 7) for 4-5 minutes, until lightly coloured.

SWISS APPLE CHARLOTTE

2 lb. cooking apples	2 tbsps. golden syrup
2 oz. sugar	½ oz. cornflakes
1½ oz. butter	Cream or evaporated milk

Peel, quarter and core the apples; cook in a little water until soft, then sieve. Add just a little sugar. Spoon into a bowl or individual glasses. Melt fat and syrup in a saucepan and add cornflakes, carefully turning them until evenly covered with syrup. Pour the cream or milk over over the apple, then pile the cornflakes on top.

CHOCOLATE BANANAS

1 sponge cake	1 oz. chocolate
1 tbsp. sherry	Chopped browned
2 bananas	almonds

Put the cake in the bottom of an individual glass dish and soak it with the sherry. Split the bananas and put on the sponge cake, pour on the melted chocolate, and decorate with a few chopped nuts. (Serves 1.)

BANANES FLAMBÉES

6 fairly firm bananas	3 tbsps. Demerara sugar
3 oz. butter	3 tbsps. Kirsch

Peel the bananas, halve lengthwise and fry for 2 minutes in the hot butter. Sprinkle with the sugar, add the Kirsch then light this and allow to burn for 1 minute. Serve the bananas at once.

QUICK CHARLOTTE RUSSE

½ pint double cream	2 oz. chopped glacé
1 egg white	cherries
2 oz. icing sugar	Flavouring (e.g., vanilla,
1 oz. chopped nuts	almond)

Whip the cream until thick. Beat the egg white stiffly and fold in the sugar, cream, nuts, cherries and flavouring. Spoon the mixture into dishes and decorate with chopped nuts or cherries. Serve with Boudoir biscuits or sponge fingers.

NEGRITAS

4 oz. plain chocolate	A little chocolate or
3 eggs, separated	whipped cream to
3 tbsps. sherry	decorate

Grate the chocolate and put it in a bowl over a pan of hot water. Beat in the egg yolks and stir for several minutes, then remove from the heat and stir in the sherry (or 1 tbsp. brandy). Whisk the egg whites until stiff and fold into the mixture. Pour immediately into glasses and leave to become cold. Serve decorated with melted or grated chocolate or cream.

SALADE D'ORANGES AU LIQUEUR

Skin 4 oranges and cut into thin slices, removing any pips. Lay in a shallow dish, sprinkle with 2 oz. caster sugar and pour over them ½ gill of rum, brandy or Kirsch.

SWEET SAUCES

WHITE SAUCE

1 oz. butter	Sugar to sweeten
1 oz. flour	1 tbsp. cream (optional)
¾ pint milk	

Melt the butter, stir in the flour and blend thoroughly then add the cold milk gradually and bring to the boil. Add the sugar, and boil for 5 minutes, stirring meanwhile. Lastly, stir in the cream.

EGG CUSTARD SAUCE

½ pint milk	1 egg or 2 yolks
A strip of lemon rind	1 oz. sugar

Heat the milk and lemon rind together, but do not boil, then pour on to the well-beaten egg, stirring. Return the mixture to the pan and cook over hot water until the sauce coats the back of the spoon thinly. Add the sugar, strain and cool, stirring occasionally, or serve hot if liked.

LEMON OR ORANGE SAUCE

1 large lemon or orange	½ oz. flour or cornflour
1-2 level tbsps. sugar	½ pint water
1 oz. butter	1-2 egg yolks

Wipe the lemon or orange, grate the rind and rub it into the sugar. Melt the butter in a saucepan and stir in the flour or cornflour, then add the water gradually and stir until boiling. Simmer slowly for 2-3 minutes, and add the sugar and strained lemon or orange juice. Then remove the saucepan from the heat, and quickly stir in the egg yolks. Pour at once into a sauce-boat.

BRANDY BUTTER

Cream together 2 oz. butter and 4 oz. icing sugar until light and creamy, then beat in 2-3 tbsps. brandy. Pile into a small dish, and put in a cool place to harden; sprinkle with a little more icing sugar just before serving.

TO WHIP FRESH CREAM

Use double cream: it should be as cool as possible, and the whipping should be done in a cool place. Put the cream in a bowl and sweeten with a little fine sugar if desired. If there is a large quantity, whip it with a hand or electric whisk; for a small amount use a fork. Continue beating until the cream is thick enough to stand up in points, but on no account over-beat, or it will separate out and turn into butter.

TO WHIP EVAPORATED MILK

Prepare evaporated milk as follows: boil the tin of milk for 20 minutes in a pan of water, then leave it to become quite cold. The milk will then whisk up quite stiffly, but a still better result is obtained if it can first be chilled for at least 30 minutes in a refrigerator. This whisked milk should be used immediately. If required for later use add ½ oz. gelatine, dissolved in 2-3 tbsps. water, and whisk this in well, adding sugar and flavouring to taste.

YEAST COOKERY
AND SCONE-MAKING

HOME BAKING

The wonderful smell of hot, fresh bread and the sight of the crisp golden loaves are an inspiration to any house-wife to try her hand at breadmaking. Nowadays, the process is so much more simple than in our grandmother's time. In many dough preparations the preliminary "sponging" is not now considered necessary, while the refrigerator can play an important part (see below).

THE FLOUR AND THE YEAST

Plain flour is always used, but a wide range is available, especially:

White flour. For bread making, and any other yeast mixtures, use flour which contains plenty of gluten—called "strong" flour. In the south of England this is not always available; where a branded make is not obtainable, it is worth asking a local baker if he will sell you some plain bread flour.

Wholemeal: 100 per cent. wheat.

Wheatmeal: 85-90 per cent. wheat (i.e., some of the bran omitted).

Stone-ground: more expensive, but very good flavour.

Rye flour: gives the characteristic Continental rye bread. Remember that while white flour keeps well, wheatmeals should be used up quickly.

The yeast used may be either baker's or dried yeast, which is sold in tins.

Fresh yeast should be moist and crumbly to the touch, resemble putty in appearance and have a clean, pleasant smell. It should be purchased only in small quantities, since it does not keep well, except in a refrigerator, where it may be stored for up to 3 weeks in an air-tight plastic container or securely sealed polythene bag. When it is required, remove it from the refrigerator and leave it for 2 hours at room temperature.

Dried yeast will keep for several months if the tin is kept tightly closed. The instructions are always given on the tin, but as a guide use half as much dried yeast as fresh yeast—that is, $\frac{1}{2}$ oz. dried yeast equals 1 oz. of the fresh form. Please note that the recipes in this book give the quantities for fresh yeast.

YEAST COOKERY

Yeast is a living plant and must be given the right conditions—warmth, moisture and food—for it to grow. In so doing, it gives off a gas which will "raise" the dough; then, when it is no longer needed, the yeast is killed off by baking.

Temperature: An even, warm temperature is required for the preparation of yeast mixtures except when the action of the yeast is being deliberately retarded (see this page). Thus bowl, flour and mixing liquid must all be warmed before use and all draughts avoided; use warmed greased tins.

Creaming or dissolving the yeast: Work it with a little sugar, using a teaspoon. The milk or water must then be added to this immediately. Another method is to stir the yeast in with the warmed liquid until it is dissolved

and then add the sugar. Continue as given below.

Setting the sponge: Make a well in the centre of the flour pour in the liquid yeast mixture and leave in a warm place for 15-20 minutes to start the yeast working.

Mixing: Add the remaining liquid. (Wholemeal mixtures need more water than plain white flour.)

Kneading: This process distributes the yeast throughout the dough. It is usually easier to work on a lightly floured board.

Rising: The dough should be left in a warm place in a greased bowl covered with a damp cloth or greased poly-thene, until it doubles its size—usually in about one hour. If for convenience you want a quicker rise ($\frac{1}{2}$ hour), put the dough in a really warm place; for a slower rise ($1\frac{1}{2}$ hours) put it in a cold larder. Remember, the slower the rise, the better the bread.

Shaping: Turn the dough on to a floured board and knead for 2-3 minutes to ensure the bread has no large holes; when it is smooth, shape as required.

Proving: After the shaping, leave for a second rising in a warm place for 10-20 minutes (or until loaves reach top of tins).

Baking: Generally in a very hot oven (450°F., mark 8) for 10-20 minutes; then in a fairly hot oven (400°F., mark 6 or 375°F., mark 5) to finish baking.

Testing: Tap the loaves underneath with the knuckles; if they are ready they sound hollow.

Glazing: Brush with either milk or beaten egg before baking. Sometimes buns, etc., are brushed with a sugar glaze when they come out of the oven; to make this, dissolve 2 oz. sugar in 3 tbsps. water, bring to the boil, and boil until syrupy—3-4 minutes.

THE MODERN WAY—USE THE REFRIGERATOR

Store yeast dough in the refrigerator and you will be able to make your bread whenever it is most convenient. Both the effect of the cold in the refrigerator and a high pro-portion of fats, liquid and sugar contained in a mixture, serve to retard the action of the yeast. You can leave such a dough in the refrigerator for several days and it will have risen only very slightly.

This method may be applied to any of the yeast recipes in this book. Remember that:

(a) Doughs mixed with milk will keep 4 days.

(b) Doughs mixed with water will keep 7 days—except plain bread dough, which will keep 3 days.

Follow these simple rules:

1. Store the dough immediately after kneading or beating. Place in a large greased bowl and cover closely with foil. If it is to be stored for several days, cover the foil over with a damp tea towel.

2. Remove dough from refrigerator when you want to make your bread, and if it is too stiff to handle, allow it to return to room temperature first. After shaping, leave it in a warm place to double in size (1-1$\frac{1}{2}$ hours) before baking.

3. Alternatively, the dough can be shaped before refrigerating. On taking out, leave to double its size (1-1$\frac{1}{2}$ hours) before baking.

1. White Bread: dissolve the yeast in ⅓ of water, add sugar and pour into well in the flour and salt. Set to sponge.

2. Add remaining water and mix with the hand till it forms soft but non-sticky dough. Turn on to a board.

3. Knead thoroughly; put into a greased bowl, cover with damp cloth and leave it in a warm place.

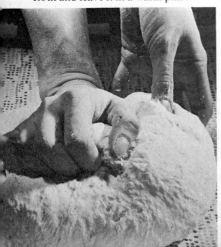

4. Leave to rise till doubled in size —about 1 hour. Turn out and knead lightly 2-3 minutes till smooth.

5. Divide into two and make each into loaf shape. Put in tin and set to prove in a warm place 15-20 minutes.

6. When the dough fills the tins, glaze (if desired) and then bake as directed in recipe this page.

WHITE BREAD

(See pictures on this page and bottom picture opposite.)

3 lb. flour
6 level tsps. salt
1 oz. yeast
1 level tsp. sugar
1½ pints tepid water

Make the bread as shown in the pictures on this page; see also the general notes overleaf. Bake for 20 minutes in a very hot oven (450°F., mark 8), then a further 40 minutes in a fairly hot oven (375°F., mark 5). This makes 3 loaves in 1-lb. tins or 2 in 2-lb. tins.

FARMHOUSE LOAF

To make a farmhouse loaf, shape 1½ lb. white bread dough and put into a shallow loaf tin, taking care that the ends of the loaf do not touch the tin. Make a lengthwise cut in the loaf and put to prove for 20-30 minutes in a warm place. Bake in a very hot oven (450°F., mark 8) for 40-50 minutes, reducing the heat to fairly hot (375°F., mark 5) after 20 minutes. If a floury appearance is liked, brush it with milk and water, and sprinkle with flour before baking.

MILK LOAF

1¼ lb. flour
2 level tsps. salt
1 oz. lard
½ oz. yeast
1 level tsp. sugar
½ pint tepid milk

Sift the warmed flour and salt and rub in the fat. Cream the yeast with the sugar and add the milk. Make a well in the flour, add the liquid and sprinkle with a little flour. Cover and put in a warm place for ½ hour to set the sponge. Mix to a soft dough, knead well on a floured board and leave in a warm place to rise to double its size. Knead lightly, then divide into two and shape each into a ball. Press lightly into greased and floured 1-lb. tins and prove in a warm place for 20-30 minutes, until the dough has risen to the top of the tins. Bake in a very hot oven (475°F., mark 9) for 15 minutes, then reduce the heat to fairly hot (375°F., mark 5) and bake for ¾-1 hour in all. Glaze with sugar syrup.

COTTAGE LOAF

Divide 1 lb. white bread dough into two portions, one larger than the other. Shape into rounds, place the smaller on top and push a floured finger down centre of both to fix firmly together. Prove and bake as usual for about ¾ hour.

FRENCH BREAD

1 lb. plain flour   1 level tsp. sugar
1 level tsp. salt   ½ oz. butter
½ oz. yeast   Beaten egg to
½ pint warm   glaze
    water

Warm the sifted flour and salt in a mixing bowl. Dissolve the yeast in the warm water, add the sugar and butter and stir well until melted. Pour the liquid ingredients into the flour and beat well with the hand until the dough leaves the bowl and hands clean. Knead for 3 minutes on a floured board and return it to the bowl. Cover and set to rise in a fairly warm place until double its size—the longer this process takes, the better the resulting bread (1½-2 hours). Turn the dough out on to a floured board and knead. Roll the dough out to an oblong 15 by 10 inches, then cut in half lengthwise. Roll up each loaf tightly from the long edge, sealing the ends thoroughly. Point the ends, and place on greased baking sheets. Prove in a warm place for 20 minutes, brush with beaten egg and bake in a very hot oven (450°F., mark 8) for 10 minutes, then reduce heat to fairly hot (375°F., mark 5) for a further 10-15 minutes. Allow to cool, then brush with water to wet them thoroughly, and replace in the oven for 10 minutes longer. This produces a crisp crust similar to that on continental breads.

WHOLEMEAL BREAD

(see first two pictures on right)
3 lb. wholemeal flour or 1 lb.
    white and 2 lb. wholemeal
1 oz. salt   1½ pints tepid
2 oz. lard   water
1 oz. yeast   1 oz. sugar

Add the salt to the flour, rub in the lard and put the bowl in a warm place. Dissolve the yeast in half the tepid liquid and add the sugar. Make a well in the flour and add the yeast mixture and enough water to give a rather soft dough. Knead well, then put to rise till it doubles its size. Re-knead, shape and put into tins (previously

greased and dusted with whole-meal), half-filling them, or else shape into round cobs. Prove for 20 minutes, and bake in a very hot oven (475°F., mark 9) for 15 minutes, then reduce to fairly hot (400°F., mark 6) and bake until the loaves are brown and sound hollow when tapped. Wholemeal generally requires more moisture than white flour and takes some-what longer to cook.

To make a twisted loaf, divide the dough into three and knead each portion until smooth, then place in the prepared tin diagonally, pushing into place with the knuckles. During the proving, the three pieces will rise together.

This quantity makes 2 large loaves, or one loaf, the moulded loaf and the boat, as seen in our pictures.

WHOLEMEAL BOAT

To shape the "boat", take off a small piece of dough and put on one side. Shape the remainder into a fairly fat but tapering oval. Roll out the small piece with the hands until it is long enough to put along the middle of the loaf, and tuck both ends underneath. Place on a greased and floured baking sheet and bake in a very hot oven (450°F., mark 8) for 20-30 minutes.

QUICK WHOLEMEAL BREAD

2 lb. wholemeal flour
1 lb. white flour
2 level tbsps. salt
2 level tbsps. sugar
2 oz. yeast
1¾ pints water
Cracked wheat (optional)

Mix the flour, salt and sugar. Dissolve the yeast in a little of the tepid water. Make a well in the centre of the flour and pour in the yeast mixture and remaining tepid water. Mix to a soft dough, then knead well for about 5 minutes, until smooth. Shape and half-fill 3-4 greased 1-lb. loaf tins, and set to rise in a warm place until doubled in size (about 30 minutes). Bake in a very hot oven (450°F., mark 8) for 20-30 minutes. The tins may first be dusted with cracked wheat, and some of this may be sprinkled on top of the loaves before proving, if liked.

This dough may be used as basis for various sweet tea breads—for example, the Apricot and Currant Bread on p. 168.

MORE LOAVES

a warm place for 15-20 minutes. The loaves may then be glazed with beaten egg and sprinkled with caraway seeds or left as they are, before baking in a very hot oven (450°F., mark 8) for 40 minutes.

QUICK WHITE LOAF

1 lb. flour	½ pint water
1 level tsp. salt	1 level tsp. sugar
½ oz. yeast	Egg and milk to glaze

Sift the flour and salt into a bowl. Dissolve the yeast in the tepid water and add the sugar. Make a well in the centre of the flour and pour in the yeast mixture. Mix to a dough and knead for 10 minutes on a floured board, to distribute the yeast and to make the dough very smooth. Place it in a greased and floured bread tin, and allow to rise in a warm place until double its size. Glaze with beaten egg and milk and bake for 45 minutes in a very hot oven (450°F., mark 8), reducing the heat to moderate (350°F., mark 4) after 15 minutes.

CURRANT BREAD

1¼ lb. flour	1 oz. chopped candied peel
2 level tsps. salt	½ oz. yeast
1 oz. lard	1 level tsp. caster sugar
8 oz. currants	¾ pint tepid milk (approx.)

Sift the warmed flour and salt and rub in the fat. Add the currants and peel and mix well. Cream the yeast with the sugar and add the milk. Make a well in the flour, add the liquid, sprinkle a little flour over the top, cover and put in a warm place for about ½ hour to set the sponge. Mix to a soft dough, knead well on a floured board and leave in a warm place to rise for 1 hour, or till doubled in size. Divide into two pieces, and knead each into a ball. Press lightly into greased and floured 1-lb. tins, or shape into smooth cobs, and place on a baking sheet. Prove in a warm place for 20-30 minutes, until the dough has filled the tins. Bake the loaves in a very hot oven (475°F., mark 9) for 10 minutes, then reduce to fairly hot (375°F., mark 5) and bake until cooked—¾ hour in all—then brush over if desired with sugar glaze.

RYE BREAD

1½ lb. rye flour	1 level tsp. sugar
1 lb. white flour	¾ oz. yeast
3 level tsps. salt	1⅛ pint milk and water
1 oz. butter or lard	Beaten egg for glazing
2 level tsps. caraway seed	

Warm and sift the flours and the salt. Rub in the fat and add the caraway seeds. Cream the sugar and the yeast and add most of the tepid liquid. Make a well in the flour, pour in the yeast mixture, and mix to a firm dough, adding the remaining liquid as required. Knead until smooth on a floured board, then place in the bowl and cover. Leave to rise in a warm place for about 1½ hours. Turn out and knead again, divide into two and shape into either an oval boat-shaped loaf or a round (the top of the boat-shaped loaf may be scored, if desired). Put on to greased and floured baking sheets, and set to prove in

CHOLLA AND CROWN LOAVES

1 lb. flour	1 level tsp. salt
1 level tsp. sugar	2 oz. butter or margarine
½ oz. yeast	1 egg
⅓ pint milk and 3 tbsps.	Poppy seeds

These are made from an enriched white bread dough, which may also be used for rolls, etc.
Into the mixing bowl put one-third of the flour, with the sugar, yeast and milk, and mix well together to a batter. Leave in a warm place until frothy. Mix remaining flour with the salt and rub in the fat. Add the beaten egg to the batter (reserving a little to glaze), then stir in the flour mixture and mix well with the hand to a firm dough. Turn on to a floured board and knead until smooth and elastic. Put to rise in a bowl in a warm place until doubled in size (50-60 minutes), then turn on to a floured board and knead lightly.
To make a Cholla, divide the dough into two and roll each piece into a strip 12-14 inches long. Arrange the strips in a cross on the board. Then take the two opposite ends of each strip and cross them over in the centre. Cross each strip alternately 2 or 3 times. Finally, gather the short ends together, seal with water and lay the plait on its side.
Place on a floured tin, and put to prove in a warm place for 30-40 minutes. Brush with beaten egg, sprinkle with poppy seeds and bake in a fairly hot oven (375°F., mark 5) for 45-50 minutes.
To make a Crown Loaf, take half the risen dough and divide it into six. Roll each piece to a smooth ball, place five in a ring in a greased sandwich cake tin, then put the sixth in the centre. Prove, glaze and finish, etc., as above, and bake in a fairly hot oven (375°F., mark 5) for 30-35 minutes.
The crown looks particularly attractive for a dinner or lunch party, and it breaks easily into separate "rolls".

VIENNA LOAF

1 lb. flour	½ oz. yeast
1 level tsp. salt	1 level tsp. sugar
1½ oz. butter	1 egg
½ pint milk	

Warm the sifted flour and salt in a bowl. Melt the butter in the milk and, when tepid, pour on to the yeast, add the sugar and beaten egg, then pour all into a well in the flour. Mix to a soft dough and beat well, until the mixture leaves the hand clean. Leave to rise in a warm place until it has doubled its size. Knead on a board and shape into 3 loaves. Cut slits along the length of each loaf. Place on a greased baking sheet, and prove for 15 minutes in a warm place. Glaze with milk or beaten egg, and bake in a very hot oven (450°F., mark 8) for 20-30 minutes, reducing the heat to fairly hot (375°F., mark 5), after 8 minutes.

ROLLS AND BREADSTICKS

MILK ROLLS

1 lb. flour
½ level tsp. salt
2 oz. lard

½ oz. yeast
About ½ pint milk
Milk or egg to glaze

Warm the flour, add the salt and rub in the lard. Cream the yeast and add most of the tepid milk. Make a well in the flour and pour in the liquid. Mix to a soft elastic dough, adding the remaining milk as required. Knead well and put to rise in a warm place for about an hour, or until double its size. Turn out on to a floured board and knead. Divide the mixture into small pieces and shape as desired. Apart from round balls and long finger rolls, favourite shapes are:

Plaits: (divide each piece into three and pull these out into long strips; stick the ends together and plait loosely).

Twists: (divide each piece into two and pull into long strips; twist the pieces together, sealing the ends with a little water).

Crescents: (bend long finger rolls round to form a half-moon shape).

Place the rolls on a greased baking sheet and put in a warm place to prove for 10-20 minutes. Glaze with milk or beaten egg, and bake in a very hot oven (450°F., mark 8) for 15-20 minutes, according to size, until well risen, golden-brown and hollow-sounding when tapped underneath. (Makes about 16.)

BRIDGE ROLLS

½ lb. flour
A pinch of salt
½ oz. yeast
1 level tsp. caster sugar

4 tbsps. tepid milk
1 egg
2 oz. butter
Egg to glaze

Sift the flour and salt into a basin and make a well in the centre. Cream the yeast with the caster sugar, add half the liquid and pour into the flour. Beat the egg with the remainder of the milk and stir it into the flour with the melted butter, mixing to a soft, smooth dough. Stand the dough in a warm place until it has doubled its size. Turn on to a board and cut into narrow strips the size of bridge rolls, about 3 inches long. Roll in the hands, place them on greased baking tins and prove for 10 minutes. Brush with beaten egg, and bake in a very hot oven (450°F., mark 8) for about ¼ hour. (Makes 12-16.)

BISCOTTES
(picture above left)

1½ oz. yeast
1½ pints milk
2 lb. flour
6 oz. butter or margarine

4 oz. caster sugar
2 eggs
Egg to glaze

Cream the yeast and add a little tepid milk to it. Make a well in the centre of the sifted flour, and add the yeast with half the remaining milk. Sprinkle the top lightly with flour, and leave in a warm place to sponge for 20 minutes. Cream the butter with the sugar and beat in the eggs. Add this creamed mixture to the flour, together with the remaining milk, and knead to a smooth dough. Cover and allow to rise in a warm place until treble its size. Knead and shape into long fat rolls. Place on a baking sheet, brush with egg and prove for 10 minutes. Bake in a fairly hot oven (400°F., mark 6) for 20-25 minutes. The next day, cut in slices ⅓ inch thick, and bake in a cool oven (325°F., mark 2) until brown and crisp—about 30 minutes; turn after 20 minutes.

DINNER ROLLS
(picture above right)

1 lb. white bread dough
Egg to glaze

Poppy seeds, cardamom, coriander

Knead the dough till smooth, divide it into pieces, and shape.

There are endless variations, as shown in picture, e.g.:

Small Cottage Loaves, made as described on p. 161.

Knots: Make by pulling dough into a strip and knotting.

Trefoils: Make by dividing each piece into three balls and arranging on a baking sheet so that they are just touching.

Snails: Coil a strip of dough from the outside to the centre.

Glaze with beaten egg and sprinkle with poppy seeds, cardamom or coriander. Bake in a very hot oven (450°F., mark 8) for 10-15 minutes.

These rolls are crusty and have quite a different texture from the richer, soft milk roll. (Makes about 16.)

BRIOCHES
(picture above)

1 lb. flour	4 whole eggs and 4 yolks
1 level tsp. salt	4-6 oz. melted butter
$\frac{1}{2}$ oz. yeast	1 oz. caster sugar
2-3 tbsps. warm water	Beaten egg to glaze

Sift the flour and salt together and make two wells in the flour. Dissolve the yeast in a little of the warm water and pour into one well. Put the beaten eggs and yolks, melted butter and sugar into the other well. Beat thoroughly with the hand, adding more water if required to make a soft, sticky mixture. Cover and allow to rise in a warm place for 1 hour. Brush about 24 deep patty pans with melted butter. Shape the dough into an even number of large and small balls. Put a large ball at the bottom of each patty pan, make a hole in the centre and put in a small ball. Prove for 20 minutes, brush with beaten egg, and bake in a very hot oven (450°F., mark 8) for 5-10 minutes.
Brioches are delicious served with coffee.

BREADSTICKS
(picture on right)

1$\frac{1}{2}$ lb. flour	2 level tsps. sugar
2 level tsps. salt	$\frac{3}{4}$ pint milk
$\frac{3}{4}$ oz. yeast	2 oz. butter

Warm the flour and sift with the salt. Cream the yeast with the sugar and add half of the tepid milk. Make a well in the centre of the flour and pour in the yeast mixture. Sprinkle with flour and put in a warm place to sponge for 15 minutes. Add the remaining milk and melted butter, and mix to a dough. Knead well and put to rise for 15-20 minutes. Turn out on to a floured board and knead. Divide the dough into small pieces, then roll and pull these into sticks 6-8 inches long and as thick as a finger. Place on a greased baking sheet, and prove in a warm place for 15-20 minutes. Bake in a fairly hot oven (400°F., mark 6) for about 30-35 minutes, reducing the heat to moderate (350°F., mark 4) after 10 minutes.
For salted breadsticks, brush over with milk and water before baking, and sprinkle with crushed rock salt.
These breadsticks will keep for about two weeks in an airtight tin, and can be crisped up again in a slow oven before serving.

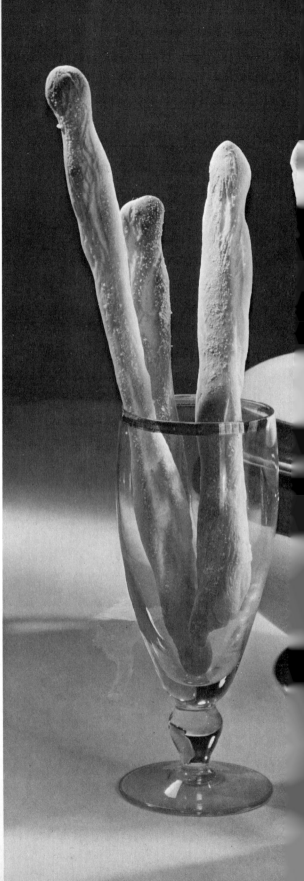

TEA-TIME SPECIALS

SALLY LUNN TEACAKES
(see picture left above and colour picture no. 40)

12 oz. flour	1 egg, beaten
¼ level tsp. salt	1 oz. lard or margarine
½ oz. yeast	Egg or milk and sugar to
1 level tsp. sugar	glaze
⅓ pint milk and water	Glacé icing

Sift the flour and salt into a basin. Cream the yeast with the sugar, stir in the tepid liquid and pour into the centre of the flour. Add the beaten egg and melted fat, and mix to a light, soft dough, then knead well. Divide into 2 or 3 pieces, shape into rounds and put into small greased and floured tins, half filling them. Set in a warm place till the dough rises to the top of the tins, then bake them in a very hot oven (450°F., mark 8) for 15-20 minutes. Glaze a few minutes before finally removing from the oven, using a sugar glaze. When cold, cover with glacé icing. (If preferred slice across before icing.)

YORKSHIRE TEACAKES

Follow the recipe for Sally Lunn Teacakes, adding 2 oz. currants or sultanas and omitting the egg, if preferred. Allow the dough to rise in the bowl, then knead again, shape into flat, round cakes and prove in warm place a few minutes. Bake in a very hot oven (450°F., mark 8) for about 15 minutes. Glaze and leave on a rack to cool.

DEVONSHIRE SPLITS

1 lb. flour	½ oz. yeast
1 level tsp. salt	About ½ pint warm milk
2 oz. margarine	Egg or milk to glaze
1 level tsp. sugar	

Warm the sifted flour and salt and rub in the fat. Cream the sugar and yeast and add some milk; put this in the middle of the dry ingredients, cover and allow the mixture to stand in a warm place to start the yeast working. Mix with enough liquid to give a soft dough. Knead it well and return it to the floured mixing bowl; cover and put in a warm place to rise. Turn it out and knead well, then roll out to about ¾ inch thick. Cut out with a scone cutter, making about 24 splits, and put on a greased and lightly floured tin. Leave to prove for about 10 minutes, or until the scones double their bulk. Glaze with milk, and bake in a very hot oven (450°F., mark 8) for 10-15 minutes.

CRUMPETS (PIKELETS)
(see picture right above)

½ oz. yeast	A pinch of bicarbonate of
1 pint milk and water	soda
1 lb. flour	1 level tsp. salt

Cream the yeast with a little of the tepid liquid, add the rest and pour into the flour. Beat very thoroughly with the hand for 5 minutes, then cover and leave it to stand in a warm place for 1 hour. Dissolve the bicarbonate of soda and salt in a little warm water and add to the sponged mixture. Beat up and put to rise again for ¾ hour. Have ready a greased girdle, moderately hot; grease some crumpet rings and let them heat on the girdle. Pour in enough batter to cover the bottom of each ring thoroughly; cook gently until the top is set, remove the rings, turn the crumpets over and allow to dry for a few minutes on the underside. To serve, toast on both sides, butter and serve hot.

MUFFINS

1 oz. yeast	3 level tsps. salt
1 pint water	1½ lb. flour

Mix the yeast with the warm water, add the salt to the sifted flour, and add the liquid and yeast by degrees. Beat well with the hand for 15 minutes; thorough beating at this stage is most essential. Stand the batter in a warm place for 5 hours and cover with a cloth. Beat up again and leave for a further ½ hour. Meanwhile, take a deep baking tin, dust very liberally with flour and put in a warm place. When the muffin mixture is ready, turn on to a floured board and cut into even-sized pieces. Although the mixture is very soft, only sufficient flour should be used to make handling easy. Roll the portions of dough into flat cakes, rather smaller than the muffin rings, and put them in the floured tin. Allow to prove for 20 minutes. Have ready a moderately hot floured girdle or hot-plate, grease some muffin rings, and heat them. Drop the muffins in the rings and cook for 5 minutes; turn, and cook for another 5 minutes. Remove the rings and press the sides of the muffins to see if they are quite cooked. Butter generously.

RICH YEASTY PASTRIES

CINNAMON PINWHEEL RING

(see picture above)

1 lb. flour	1½-2 oz. melted butter
1 level tsp. salt	Ground cinnamon
2 oz. butter or margarine	Ground almonds
½ oz. yeast	Caster sugar
½ oz. sugar	A little beaten egg to
½ pint tepid milk (approx.)	glaze

Warm the flour, add the salt and rub in the fat. Cream the yeast and sugar and add most of the warmed milk. Pour into the flour and mix to a soft, elastic dough, adding more milk if required. Knead well and put to rise in a warm place for 1 hour, until double its size.

Turn the dough on to a floured board and knead well, until smooth. Roll out to an oblong ⅛ inch thick, spread with melted butter and sprinkle with cinnamon, ground almonds and sugar. Roll the dough up to form a long roll and join the ends to make a ring. Place on a greased and floured baking sheet and with scissors snip almost through into slices about ½ inch thick; then open these out and arrange as shown in the picture. Put in a warm place to prove for 10-15 minutes. Brush with beaten egg and bake in a fairly hot oven (375°F., mark 5) for 25-30 minutes.

DANISH PASTRIES

(see colour picture no. 40)

1 oz. yeast	Confectioner's custard or
¼ pint milk	almond paste for
A pinch of salt	filling
11 oz. plain flour	Egg to glaze
2 eggs, beaten	Glacé icing
1 oz. sugar	Roasted, flaked, or
6 oz. butter or margarine	chopped almonds

Cream the yeast with a little tepid milk. Add the salt to the flour, make a well in the centre and drop in the eggs, with the yeast and sugar. Gradually mix in the flour,

beat the dough well, cover and leave in a warm place for ¼ hour. Roll out the dough fairly thinly on a floured board, and place the fat in the centre. Fold the dough over the butter and give two "turns" as for puff pastry. Allow to stand for 10-15 minutes, then give two further turns, followed by another rest in a cool place. Roll out the pastry ¼ inch thick and finish as desired—for instance:

Almond Crescents: Cut the pastry into triangles with bases of 6½ inches. Place a "sausage" of almond paste near the base roll it up, bend round to form a crescent, and place on a greased baking sheet. Prove in a warm place for about 20 minutes, brush with egg, and bake in a hot oven (425°F., mark 7) for 15-20 minutes, until golden-brown. Whilst still hot, brush with icing and sprinkle with nuts.

Custard Pastries: Cut the pastry into ½-inch strips, twist each strip by turning the two ends in opposite directions, then, holding both the ends, coil it on to a baking sheet, starting at the centre. Push the centre down to form a hollow and prove. Before baking place a little confectioner's custard (see below) in the middle of each pastry.

Cranberry Turnovers: Cut the pastry into 4-inch squares. Place a spoonful of stewed cranberries (or gooseberries) in centre and fold over into a triangle, sealing edges.

Almond Catherine Wheels: Cut the pastry into 4-inch squares. Snip each corner almost to the centre and place a small ball of almond paste there. Draw alternate corners to centre, overlapping them, and seal with egg white.

Almond Paste: Use ½ oz. butter, 3 oz. caster sugar, 3 oz. ground almonds, 1 beaten egg, almond essence (optional). Cream the butter and sugar, stir in the almonds and add enough egg to make a soft spreading consistency; add a few drops of almond essence if liked.

Confectioner's Custard: Use 1 oz. flour, 1 oz. sugar, 1 beaten egg, ¼ pint milk and a little vanilla essence; blend the flour, sugar and egg to a smooth cream; bring the milk to the boil and pour on to the blended mixture, stirring all the time. Return the mixture to the pan and bring to the boil, stirring all the time until the custard thickens. Cook for 1-2 minutes, flavour with vanilla essence, cover and cool before using.

AUSTRIAN TOFFEE BUNS

1 lb. flour	2 eggs
4 oz. sugar	10 oz. butter
1 oz. yeast	Stoned raisins
$\frac{1}{3}$ pint milk plus 3 tbsps.	Brown sugar
$\frac{1}{2}$ level tsp. salt	Ground cinnamon

The dough is made the day before. Into a large mixing bowl put $\frac{1}{2}$ lb. flour and 1 level tsp. sugar; rub in the yeast, add the milk and mix well together to a batter. Leave in a warm place until frothy (15 minutes). Mix the remaining $\frac{1}{2}$ lb. flour with the salt and add this to the yeast mixture, together with the beaten eggs, remaining sugar and 8 oz. softened butter. Beat the dough thoroughly for 5-10 minutes, then cover with aluminium foil, place in the refrigerator and leave overnight.

The next day, turn the dough out on to a floured board and leave for 5-10 minutes to soften up, as it will be firm. Then knead lightly, dealing with half at a time. Roll out into an oblong $\frac{1}{8}$ inch thick, as for Chelsea Buns (overleaf). Brush with melted butter and sprinkle with raisins, brown sugar and cinnamon. Roll up tightly and cut into 1-inch slices. Prepare some patty tins by brushing with fat and putting a small knob of butter and 1 level tsp. brown sugar in each.

Place a slice in each tin and set to prove in a warm place for 15-20 minutes, until well risen. Bake in a moderate oven (350°F., mark 4) for 10-15 minutes, until golden-brown. Turn out immediately and leave upside-down. The butter and sugar will have formed a delicious toffee topping.

LARDY CAKE

1$\frac{3}{4}$ lb. risen white bread dough	6 oz. caster sugar
	3$\frac{1}{2}$ oz. currants
5 oz. lard	Sugar and water glaze

Make the white bread dough as described on p. 160, then roll it into an oblong and spread on it half the lard, half the sugar and half the currants, covering only two-thirds of the dough. Fold the dough into three, bringing the uncovered portion up first, then fold over again; seal the ends by pressing them with a rolling-pin. Turn the dough half-way round, and again roll into an oblong. Spread the remaining lard, sugar and currants on to two-thirds of it, then fold and turn as before. Roll out to fit a tin about 7 inches square—the dough should be 1-1$\frac{1}{2}$ inches thick. Mark with a criss-cross pattern, using a sharp knife, and leave in a warm place to rise for about 20 minutes. Bake in a fairly hot oven (400°F., mark 6) for $\frac{3}{4}$-1 hour. When cooked, brush over with hot sugar and water glaze: to make this, dissolve 1 level tbsp. sugar in 1 tbsp. water and bring to the boil.

HONEY AND ALMOND KUCHEN

A third of the Toffee Bun dough (this page)	2 oz. blanched almonds
	2 oz. currants
Melted butter	Brown sugar

For the Honey Topping

oz. softened butter	$\frac{1}{2}$ oz. flour
oz. caster sugar	1 oz. chopped almonds
tbsps. thick honey	

Divide the dough into three, then divide 2 pieces in halves again. Shape the 4 small pieces into rounds and

roll out or flatten with the hand to fit a 6- or 7-inch cake tin. Place one round in the well-greased tin, brush with melted butter and sprinkle with the chopped almonds, currants and brown sugar. Place another round on top, treat in the same way, and repeat yet a third time; place the last round on top, leaving it plain. Roll the large piece into a strip about 16 inches long and coil it loosely into the tin.

Put in a warm place to prove for 20-30 minutes, until well risen. Meanwhile, blend all the ingredients for the topping, spoon this on to the Kuchen and bake in a fairly hot oven (400°F., mark 6) for 30-40 minutes, until well risen and golden-brown. If it browns too quickly, turn the oven down to moderate (350°F., mark 4) after 20 minutes.

This cake is delicious eaten either hot or cold.

PINWHEEL SLICES

Prepare a roll as for Cinnamon Pinwheel Ring (opposite), but do not join it into a ring. Cut into slices 1$\frac{1}{2}$ inches thick, make 2 or 3 cuts almost through each slice, and arrange, opened out, on a baking sheet. Leave to prove in a warm place for 15 minutes, then bake in a fairly hot oven (375°F., mark 5) for 10-15 minutes. While it is still hot, brush with glacé icing.

FRUIT BRAID

$\frac{1}{2}$ lb. flour	2 oz. caster sugar
A pinch of salt	1 egg
$\frac{1}{2}$ oz. yeast	Egg to glaze
$\frac{1}{4}$ pint milk	Glacé icing
2 oz. butter	

For the Filling

1 cooking apple, grated	2 oz. Demerara sugar
3 oz. stoned raisins, halved	Grated rind of $\frac{1}{2}$ a lemon
1 oz. finely chopped mixed candied peel	A pinch of ground cinnamon

Sift the flour and salt into a bowl and set to warm. Dissolve the yeast in the lukewarm milk and add the melted butter, sugar and beaten egg. Make a well in the flour, pour in the liquid and beat thoroughly until the mixture leaves the hands clean. Cover, and set to prove in a warm place for about $\frac{3}{4}$ hour. Knead on a floured board and roll out into a strip 14 by 6 inches, then transfer to a baking sheet. Place the well mixed filling down centre third of the strip. Slash the sides diagonally at $\frac{3}{4}$-inch intervals and fold the ends in alternately over the filling. Prove in a warm place for 20-25 minutes. Brush with beaten egg and bake in a fairly hot oven (400°F., mark 6) for 30-35 minutes. While still warm, brush with a little glacé icing.

MINCEMEAT RING

Make some dough as for Chelsea Buns (page 168) and leave it in a warm place for about 1 hour, until doubled in size. Knead lightly and roll out into an oblong. Spread thinly with 1 oz. softened butter, then add a generous layer of mincemeat. Roll up tightly, join the ends and put into a ring tin. Using scissors, cut three-quarters of the way through the ring at $\frac{1}{2}$-inch intervals. Leave in a warm place until doubled in size, then brush with sugar glaze (see p. 159) and bake in a very hot oven (450°F., mark 8) for about 40 minutes. While it is still warm, decorate with a little thin glacé icing (p. 199).

YORKSHIRE SPICE BREAD
(see left-hand picture opposite)

1 lb. flour	1 dsp. golden syrup
¼ level tsp. salt	2 oz. sultanas
4 oz. butter	4 oz. currants
4 oz. lard	1 oz. chopped candied peel
½ oz. yeast	4 oz. caster sugar
1 level tsp. sugar	1 level tsp. grated nutmeg
1 egg	1 level tsp. ground cinnamon
Approx. ¼ pint milk and water	Sugar glaze

Sift the flour and salt together and set to warm. Rub in the butter and lard and make a well in the centre of the flour. Cream the yeast with the sugar and pour over the beaten egg. Warm the liquid and the syrup gently, then add to the flour, together with the yeast mixture. Mix to a soft dough with the hand, and knead well until the mixture leaves the hand clean. Leave to rise until the dough has doubled its size (approx. 1 hour). Turn the dough on to a floured board and knead until smooth, adding 1-2 oz. more flour if necessary. Work in the prepared fruit, sugar and spices. Divide the dough into two, shape it and place in 2 greased and floured 1-lb. bread tins. Put in a warm place to prove for about 20 minutes, until the dough reaches the top of the tins, then bake in a very hot oven (450°F., mark 8) for 1¼ hours, reducing heat to moderate (350°F., mark 4) after 10 minutes. Brush with sugar glaze while still hot.

YEAST FRUIT LOAF

1 lb. flour	1 egg
4 oz. butter	½ pint tepid milk and water
4 oz. sugar	6 oz. sultanas and currants
1 level tsp. salt	½ level tsp. grated nutmeg
¾ oz. yeast	

Warm the flour, rub in the butter and add the sugar and salt. Cream the yeast. Beat the egg, pour on the warmed milk and add, together with the creamed yeast, to the flour. Mix and beat thoroughly, then cover and allow to rise for about 1¼ hours. Beat in the fruit and nutmeg very thoroughly, and put into 2 greased loaf tins (6 by 4 by 3 inches). Prove for about 30 minutes. Bake in a hot oven (425°F., mark 7) for 15 minutes, and then reduce heat to moderate (350°F., mark 4) for 30 minutes, or until well risen and brown.

APRICOT AND CURRANT BREAD

Into ¾ lb. risen Quick Wholemeal Dough (p. 161) work 4 oz. chopped dried apricots, 2 oz. currants and 1 oz. sugar. Knead well together, then place in a greased 1-lb. bread tin. Prove in a warm place until it reaches the top of the tin, then bake in a very hot oven (450°F., mark 8) for 40-50 minutes. Brush with melted butter after baking.

RICH DOUGH CAKE

8 oz. flour	½ oz. chopped peel
A pinch of salt	2 oz. currants
A pinch of grated nutmeg	2 oz. chopped glacé cherries
1½ oz. butter	
½ oz. yeast	1 oz. sugar
¼ pint milk and water	Egg to glaze
1 egg	Sugar glaze

Sift the flour, salt and nutmeg, and rub in the butter. Mix the yeast with a little tepid milk and water. Make a well in the centre of the flour and pour in the yeast mixture, the remaining liquid and the beaten egg. Knead thoroughly on a floured board for 5 minutes, then knead in the peel, currants, cherries and sugar. When smooth, put into a greased and floured 6-inch cake tin; press lightly into the tin, and allow to rise in a warm place until the dough reaches the top of the tin. Glaze with beaten egg, and bake in a hot oven (425°F., mark 7) for about ½ hour, turning the heat down to fairly hot (375°F., mark 5) after 20 minutes. Brush with sugar glaze whilst still hot.

This cake may also be baked in a loaf tin and served cut into slices and buttered.

CHELSEA BUNS

8 oz. flour	¾ gill milk and water
A pinch of salt	1 oz. butter
3-4 oz. currants and sultanas, mixed	1 egg
	A little melted fat
2 oz. sugar	Sugar glaze
½ oz. yeast	

Sift the flour and salt and put to warm. Clean the fruit and mix it with 1 level tbsp. sugar. Cream the yeast with 1 level tsp. sugar, mix with the warm liquid, add to one-third of the flour and set to sponge. Rub the butter into the rest of the flour and add remaining sugar. Gradually beat in the egg and then the sponged mixture. Beat thoroughly with the hand and put in a warm place to rise. When it has doubled its size, knead lightly. Roll the risen dough to an oblong, brush with fat, add the fruit and sugar, and roll up. Cut slices 1 inch thick and place close together in a greased straight-sided tin. Prove for about 25 minutes. Bake in a very hot oven (475°F., mark 9) for 15-20 minutes, until well risen and golden. When the buns are cooked, but still warm, brush them over with a sugar glaze.

HOT CROSS BUNS
(see right-hand picture opposite)

1 lb. flour	¼ pint milk or milk and water
¼ level tsp. salt	
4 oz. currants	3 oz. caster sugar
1 oz. chopped candied peel	3 oz. butter
1 level tsp. ground cinnamon	2 eggs
	Shortcrust pastry (optional)
1 level tsp. grated nutmeg	Milk and sugar to glaze
1 oz. yeast	

Sift the flour and salt into a bowl. Add the fruit and spices. Dissolve the yeast in the tepid milk and add the sugar, melted fat and beaten eggs. Pour into a well in the flour and salt and mix well together. Beat with the hand until smooth, then cover and set to rise until doubled in size. Flour the hands and shape small portions of dough into about 16 round buns. Place on a well-greased and floured baking tin (allowing room to spread). Mark a cross on top by cutting deeply or by placing thin strips of shortcrust pastry across the buns (as in the picture) and put in a warm place to prove for about 20-30 minutes. Glaze with milk before putting the buns into a very hot oven (450°F., mark 8) for about 15 minutes. Remove from the tray, brush immediately with sugar glaze and leave until this is set. Eat while still warm, or re-heat before serving.

39. Frosted Fruit Pyramid

40. Sally Lunn Teacakes: Danish Pastries

41. Oven Scones; Drop Scones; Oatcakes; Scotch Bun; Shortbread;
Gingerbread

42. Grasmere Cake

43. Victoria Sandwich Cake; Swiss Roll; Iced Sandwich

44. Lemon Gâteau

45. Cream Horns; Meringues; Madeleines; Petits Fours

46. Cream Cheese Sandwich Loaf

CREAM BUNS

Prepare the dough as for Devonshire Splits (p. 165). Shape into small round balls and place fairly close together on a greased and floured baking tin, so that during the proving the buns spread and touch each other. Prove for 10-15 minutes, then bake in a very hot oven (450°F., mark 8) for about 15 minutes.

When cool, split and fill with jam, then pipe with a line of whipped cream.

PINE KERNEL BUNS

4 oz. butter	1 oz. sultanas
½ lb. flour	1 oz. chopped candied peel
½ oz. yeast	2 oz. pine kernels or
2 oz. sugar	almonds
4-6 tbsps. warm milk	Grated rind of 1 lemon
2 eggs	Glacé icing

Rub the fat into the flour. Cream the yeast and 1 level tsp. sugar and add the milk, then put in a warm place for ½ hour. Add the eggs and mix the dough thoroughly, then knead very well. Leave to rise until it has doubled its bulk; turn on to a board and knead in the remaining sugar, fruit, chopped nuts and lemon rind, leaving a few nuts for decoration. Grease 8-12 patty tins, form the dough into walnut-sized balls, and put three into each tin. Leave to prove, and bake in a very hot oven (450°F., mark 8) for about 10 minutes. Cool on a rack; when cold, run a little icing over each, and sprinkle with a few toasted pine kernels.

NUTTY TWISTS

Make up the mixture given for Chelsea Buns (opposite) and divide the risen dough into about 12 even-sized pieces. Cut each in half, form the halves into 2 rolls and twist them together. Put to rise on a greased tin, and brush over with a sugar glaze. Bake in a very hot oven (450°F., mark 8) for 15-20 minutes, and just before baking is complete, brush over with more sugar glaze and sprinkle with chopped almonds or pine kernels.

BATH BUNS

8 oz. flour	2 oz. caster sugar
A pinch of salt	2 oz. sultanas
3 oz. margarine	1 oz. chopped candied peel
⅛ pint milk (approx.)	Egg and milk to glaze
½ oz. yeast	1 oz. loaf sugar
1 beaten egg	for topping

Sift the flour and salt and rub in the fat. Warm the milk and use a little to cream the yeast. Pour the yeast and liquid into the flour, add the egg, beat very thoroughly, cover with a cloth and put to rise in a warm place until it doubles its size—about 1½ hours. Add the sugar and fruit, knead well, and form into 8-12 small balls; put on to greased tins, and prove until they double their size. Glaze, sprinkle with crushed loaf sugar, and bake in a very hot oven (450°F., mark 8) for 15-20 minutes.

LEMON YEAST BUNS

Follow the recipe for Bath Buns (above), replacing the fruit by 2 tbsps. grated lemon and omitting the crushed sugar topping. Bake in a very hot oven (450°F., mark 8) for 15-20 minutes, then cool on a wire tray. Prepare a glacé icing from icing sugar, lemon juice and yellow colouring, and ice the buns when cold, decorating with lemon jelly slices (optional).

SUGAR CURRANT BUNS

Use Currant Bread dough (p. 162), divide it into even-sized pieces and form into buns. Place on a greased baking tin and put in a warm place to rise. Brush over with sugar glaze and bake in a very hot oven (450°F., mark 8) for 15-20 minutes; when nearly cooked, glaze again, and sprinkle with brown sugar.

SWISS BUNS

Make dough as for Sally Lunn Teacakes (p. 165), but shape into finger-length rolls; glaze, and bake in a very hot oven (450°F., mark 8) for about 20 minutes. When the buns are cold, coat them with a little white glacé icing.

CHERRY TREFOIL BUNS

Make some dough as for Chelsea Buns (opposite), but replace the dried fruit by 2 oz. chopped glacé cherries. Cover the dough and put to rise for at least 1 hour. Turn on to a floured board, knead, and divide into small balls. Put 3 balls into each greased patty tin and put to rise. Brush lightly with beaten egg and milk, put a glacé cherry in centre of each, and bake in a very hot oven (450°F., mark 8) for about 20 minutes.

SCONES AND QUICK BREADS

PLAIN OVEN SCONES
(see colour picture no. 41)

8 oz. self-raising flour	Milk to mix (about
¼ level tsp. salt	¼ pint)
1-2 oz. fat	

Sift the flour and salt into a basin and rub in the fat. Make a well in the centre and stir in enough milk to make a light, spongy dough—just firm enough to handle. Turn on to a floured board, knead very lightly if necessary to remove any cracks, then roll out lightly to 1 inch thick, or pat out with the hand. Cut in rounds with a sharp cutter dipped in flour, or shape into triangles with a sharp knife. Place on a floured baking sheet, glaze if liked with beaten egg or milk, and bake near the top of a very hot oven (450°F., mark 8) for 7-10 minutes, until well risen and nicely browned. Cool the scones on a wire cake rack.

Sour milk may be used in making these scones.

FRUIT SCONES
(see first picture)

Follow the above recipe but add 2 oz. currants, sultanas or raisins to the dry ingredients; chopped dates may be used if preferred.

OATCAKES
(see colour picture no. 41)

6 oz. medium oatmeal	½ level tsp. salt
2 oz. plain flour	1½ oz. butter
¼ level tsp. bicarbonate of soda	Boiling water to mix

Mix the oatmeal, flour, bicarbonate of soda and salt in a basin. Add the softened butter, with sufficient water to give a soft binding consistency. Knead lightly and roll out very thinly on a board sprinkled with a little oatmeal or flour. Cut into about a dozen rounds or triangles, place on a greased baking tray and bake towards the top of a fairly hot oven (400°F., mark 6) for about 15 minutes, or until the edges curl up and the oatcakes are crisp. Cool and serve with butter.

GIRDLE SCONES
(see second picture)

Make the mixture as for Plain Oven Scones, adding 2-3 oz. currants if desired. Roll out ¼ inch thick, cut out, and place on a moderately hot greased girdle or heavy-based frying-pan. When the scones are brown, turn them and cook on the other side for about 5 minutes altogether.

DROP SCONES
(see third picture and colour picture no. 41)

8 oz. plain flour	1-4 oz. granulated
1 level tsp. bicarbonate of soda	sugar
	2 eggs
2 level tsps. cream of tartar	½ pint milk

Sift the dry ingredients and add the sugar. Whisk the eggs and stir into the dry ingredients, with enough milk to make a batter the consistency of thick cream. Do this as quickly and lightly as possible, using a large metal spoon—do not beat. If a thin pancake is wanted, add rather more milk. Have ready a girdle, hot and lightly greased all over. Put the mixture in spoonfuls on the girdle; for round pancakes, drop from the point of the spoon, for oval, from the side. Keep the girdle at a steady heat, and when bubbles rise to the surface of the pancakes and burst, turn the cakes over, using a knife, and cook until golden-brown on the other side—4-6 minutes in all. Put the pancakes on a cloth, cover with another and cool on a rack; this keeps in the steam and the pancakes do not become dry. Serve with butter or with whipped cream and jam.

BAKING POWDER BREAD

1 lb. plain flour	Milk or water to mix
4 tsps. baking powder	(about ½ pint)
1 level tsp. salt	

Sift the flour, baking powder and salt into a basin, make a well in the centre and stir in enough liquid to make a soft, spongy dough. Turn on to a floured board, knead very lightly, and form into 2 flat loaves. Cut three marks on each with a knife. Put on a floured baking sheet and bake in a hot oven (425°F., mark 7) for about 45 minutes, or until well risen, nicely browned on top and firm underneath.

See also Malt Loaf, p. 172.

CAKES, BUNS AND BISCUITS

In just over thirty pages we have tried to gather together some of the most popular recipes from the many Good Housekeeping books on this favourite subject.
At the end of the chapter you will find recipes for icings and frostings, with many variations, and some helpful notes on icing and simple decoration for formal cakes.
Note: Cake tins should be greased and lined with grease-proof paper before use.

FAMILY CAKES

GINGERBREAD
(see colour picture no. 41)

1 lb. plain flour	½ lb. brown sugar
1 level tsp. salt	6 oz. butter
1 level tbsp. ground ginger	6 oz. treacle
1 level tbsp. baking powder	6 oz. golden syrup
1 level tsp. bicarbonate of soda	½ pint milk
	1 egg

Sift together the flour, salt, ginger, baking powder and bicarbonate of soda. Warm the sugar, butter, treacle and syrup, but do not allow to get hot. Warm the milk and beat the egg. Combine all the ingredients, mixing very thoroughly, pour into a prepared 8-inch square tin and bake in a moderate oven (350°F., mark 4) for about 1¾-2 hours, or until firm to the touch.

FRUIT GINGERBREAD
(see picture below)

12 oz. plain flour	2 level tsps. mixed spice
4 oz. margarine	1 level tsps. bicarbonate
3 oz. sugar	of soda
2 oz. chopped candied peel	12 oz. golden syrup
3 oz. sultanas	2 eggs
2 oz. chopped nuts	A little preserved ginger
½ oz. ground ginger	to decorate

Sift the flour and rub in the fat. Add the sugar, peel, sultanas, nuts, spices and bicarbonate of soda. Stir in the warmed syrup and the beaten eggs and mix thoroughly. Put into a prepared 8-inch square tin and bake in a cool oven (300°F., mark 2) for 1¾-2 hours. Decorate with pieces of preserved ginger as seen in the photograph.
If preferred, omit the peel and sultanas and substitute 4 oz. cut-up preserved ginger.

MADEIRA CAKE

8 oz. plain flour	5 oz. caster sugar
A pinch of salt	3 eggs
2 level tsps. baking powder	Lemon essence
	Milk to mix
A little finely grated lemon rind	A slice of citron peel for the top of the cake
5 oz. butter or margarine	

Prepare a 7-inch cake tin. Sift the flour, salt and baking powder together and add the grated lemon rind. Put the butter and sugar into a basin and work together until they are of a creamy consistency. Beat in the eggs, adding a little at a time. Fold in the dry ingredients, a little lemon essence and some milk if required. Put into the prepared tin, place in a moderate oven (350°F., mark 4) and bake for 1-1¼ hours. Put the slice of citron peel on top of the cake as soon as it is set—if it is added before the cake is put in the oven, it is inclined to sink.

SPICE CAKE
(see picture below)

½ lb. margarine	½ level tsp. ground cinnamon
½ lb. moist brown sugar	
3 eggs	½ level tsp. ground cardamoms
3 oz. chopped almonds	
A little grated orange peel	½ pint single cream
	¾ lb. plain flour
½ level tsp. ground cloves	2 level tsps. baking powder

Grease and flour an 8-inch square tin. Cream the fat and sugar until light and fluffy. Beat in the eggs a little at a time and mix in the nuts, flavourings and cream. Sift together the flour and baking powder and stir into the mixture. Put into the prepared tin and bake for 1 hour in a moderate oven (350°F., mark 4).

GRASMERE CAKE

(see colour picture no. 42)

1 lb. plain flour	1 level tsp. mixed spice
7 oz. margarine	2½ level tsps. bicarbonate
½ lb. sugar	of soda
½ lb. currants	¾ pint sour milk
¼ lb. sultanas	

Rub the fat into the flour and add the other dry ingredients. Mix with enough sour milk to form a dropping consistency and leave to stand overnight. Put in a loaf tin (5½ by 9½ inches) and bake in a warm oven (325°F., mark 3) for 2-2½ hours.

ROSEYLANGEN CAKE

1 lb. plain flour	1 level tsp. mixed spice
½ lb. butter	Grated rind of 1 lemon
½ lb. currants	1 small bottle of brown
½ lb. raisins, stoned	ale
¼ lb. chopped mixed	1 level tsp. bicarbonate
candied peel	of soda
¾ lb. brown sugar	4 eggs

Sift the flour and rub in the fat, then add the fruit, sugar, spice and lemon rind. Warm the ale, pour over the bicarbonate of soda and quickly add to the other ingredients. Beat the eggs and mix in. Beat well for 5 minutes, then put into a loaf tin (5½ by 9½ inches approx.) and bake in a warm oven (325°F., mark 3) for about 3 hours.
This cake is best kept for a week before cutting.

DATE AND NUT FAMILY CAKE

12 oz. plain flour	1 level tsp. ground
6 oz. butter or mar-	cinnamon
garine	½ pint apple purée
6 oz. sugar	¾ level tsp. bicarbonate
12 oz. chopped dates and	of soda
nuts	2-3 tbsps. milk

For the Cake Topping

1 heaped tbsp. chopped	2 level tsps. sugar
nuts and dates, mixed	½ level tsp. ground
together	cinnamon

Put the flour into a bowl and rub in the fat until the mixture resembles fine breadcrumbs. Add the sugar, dates and nuts and cinnamon. Make a well in the centre and add the apple purée. Lastly dissolve the bicarbonate of soda in the milk and add to the mixture; mix well and put into a prepared loaf tin measuring about 8 by 5 inches. Mix the ingredients for the topping, sprinkle over the surface and bake the cake in a moderate oven (350°F., mark 4) for 1½ hours.

FRUIT LOAF

1 lb. self-raising flour	A pinch of salt
6 oz. sugar	8 tbsps. milk
12 oz. mixed fruit	2 tbsps. treacle
(currants, sultanas and	1 tbsp. golden syrup
stoned raisins)	2 eggs

Put all the dry ingredients into a basin and gently heat the milk, treacle and syrup. Beat the eggs until frothy, then add the eggs and the syrup mixture alternately to the dry ingredients, a little at a time, until they are well mixed. Stir well, put into an oblong loaf tin (approx. 5½ by 9½ inches) and bake in a warm oven (325°F., mark 3) for 1½ hours.

DATE LOAF

½ lb. plain flour	1 level tsp. baking powder
¼ lb. margarine	1 level tsp. bicarbonate of
½ lb. chopped dates	soda
¼ lb. sugar	¼ pint milk, approx.
2 oz. chopped nuts	1 egg, lightly beaten

Rub the fat into the flour and add the dates, sugar and nuts. Dissolve the baking powder and bicarbonate of soda in the milk and mix with the egg, into the dry ingredients, adding more milk if necessary to give a stiff dropping consistency. Put into a loaf tin (4½ by 8½ inches) and bake in a moderate oven (350°F., mark 4) for 1 hour.

CHERRY CAKE

12 oz. glacé cherries	8 oz. sugar
10 oz. plain flour	4 eggs
2 oz. self-raising flour	Vanilla essence
8 oz. butter	Milk to mix, if required

Wash the cherries, cut in half, dry on a tea towel and dust with a little of the measured flour. Grease and line an 8-inch tin. Cream the butter and sugar, then lightly whisk the eggs and beat into the mixture. Lightly fold in the cherries and flour, with a few drops of vanilla essence. Add a little milk if the mixture is stiff. Put into the prepared tin and bake in a warm oven (325°F., mark 3) for about 1 hour 50 minutes.

SEED CAKE

6 oz. plain flour	4 oz. butter
½ level tsp. baking powder	4 oz. sugar
A pinch of salt	2 eggs
2 level tsps. caraway seeds	A little milk

Sift the flour, baking powder and salt together and add the caraway seeds. Put the butter and sugar into a basin, cream until pale in colour, then beat in each egg separately. Stir in the sifted flour, adding a little milk to make the mixture of a dropping consistency. Put into a prepared 7-inch tin and bake in a fairly hot oven (400°F., mark 6) for about 1 hour.

MALT LOAF

3 tbsps. malt extract	3 oz. chopped dates
3 tbsps. golden syrup	1 egg
⅓ pint milk	1 level tsp. bicarbonate of
8 oz. self-raising flour	soda

Put the malt, syrup and milk in a saucepan and beat until well blended. Sift the flour and add the chopped dates. Beat the egg and add to the flour, together with the malt mixture, stirring all the time. Dissolve the bicarbonate of soda in a little water and add it to the mixture, then pour into a greased bread tin and bake in a fairly hot oven (375°F., mark 5) for about 1 hour, or until firm.

LAYER AND SPONGE CAKES

VICTORIA SANDWICH CAKE
(see colour picture no. 43)

4 oz. butter or margarine	$\frac{1}{2}$ level tsp. baking powder
4 oz. sugar	A little milk, if necessary
2 eggs	Jam
4 oz. plain flour	Caster sugar to dredge

Cream the fat and sugar together until light and creamy, then beat in the eggs, adding a little at a time so that the mixture does not curdle. Sift the flour and baking powder together and fold very lightly into the mixture, together with a little milk if necessary to give a soft dropping consistency. Put into 2 greased 7-inch sandwich tins and bake in a fairly hot oven (375°F., mark 5) for 25-30 minutes. Cool on a cake rack and when cold sandwich together with jam. Dust lightly with caster sugar or decorate as desired.

The Iced Sandwich shown in the same colour picture is finished as follows: coat the sides with warmed sieved jam or with coffee butter icing (p. 199) and roll them in chopped nuts. Cover the top with coffee glacé icing (p. 199) and pipe a border of coffee butter icing round the edge. The flowers consist of split blanched almonds and chocolate dragées.

CHERRY SPONGE CAKE
(see picture above)

4 eggs	$3\frac{1}{2}$ oz. plain flour
4 oz. caster sugar	1 oz. melted butter

For the Filling

1 lb. black cherries	$\frac{1}{2}$ pint whipped cream
3 tbsps. Kirsch	A little grated bitter
3 oz. caster sugar	chocolate

Combine the eggs, sugar and flour as for a whisked sponge (see Swiss Roll recipe, overleaf). Lastly, fold in the melted butter (which must not be too hot). Pour the mixture into a greased 8-inch cake tin and bake in a moderate oven (350°F., mark 4) for about 1 hour. Cool on a rack.

Wash the cherries, remove the stems and stones and put the fruit into a bowl. Mix the Kirsch and sugar, pour over the cherries and let them stand for at least 2 hours. Heat the mixture to boiling point, then cool.

Put one of the sponge cakes on a plate. Make a border round the edge with whipped cream and spread the cooled thickened cherry mixture over the centre. Place the second sponge cake on top and press down lightly—just enough to make the layers stick together. Cover the top and part of the sides with the remaining cream and sprinkle a ring of grated chocolate on the top.

COFFEE NUT GÂTEAU
(see picture above)

6 oz. butter	A pinch of salt
6 oz. caster sugar	Coffee butter cream (p. 199)
3 eggs	Chopped and whole
6 oz. plain flour	walnuts
$\frac{3}{4}$ level tsp. baking powder	Coffee glacé icing (p. 199)

Cream the butter and sugar until light and fluffy, then beat in the eggs one at a time. Sift the flour, baking powder and salt and fold in a little at a time. Divide the mixture equally between 2 greased 7-inch sandwich tins and bake in a fairly hot oven (375°F., mark 5) for 30 minutes, until golden-brown and firm to the touch; cool. Make the butter cream with 3 oz. butter and 6 oz. icing sugar and add sufficient coffee essence to give a good flavour. Sandwich the layers together with this icing and use the remainder to coat the sides of the cake. Roll the sides in chopped walnuts and coat the top with glacé icing flavoured with coffee; decorate with whole nuts.

ORANGE SANDWICH CAKE

3 egg whites and 2 yolks	1 level tsp. baking powder
4 oz. butter	Grated rind of 1 orange
4 oz. caster sugar	A little milk
6 oz. plain flour	Orange butter cream (see (p. 199)

Beat the egg whites stiffly. Cream the fat and sugar until very light. Beat in the egg yolks. Sift the flour and baking powder and mix in the orange rind. Add to the creamed ingredients alternately with the milk; the mixture should be of a dropping consistency. Lastly, fold in the stiffly beaten egg whites. Put into 2 prepared 6- or 7-inch sandwich tins and bake in a moderate oven (350°F., mark 4) for about 25 minutes. When cool, sandwich together with orange butter cream.

CARAMEL NUT GÂTEAU

(see colour picture no. 50)

3 eggs	2½ oz. ground almonds
2½ oz. caster sugar	3 oz. browned flaked
2 level tsps. instant coffee	almonds
1½ oz. self-raising flour	

For the Filling

6 oz. icing sugar	2 level tsps. instant coffee
3 oz. margarine	3 tsps. water

For the Caramel and Topping

6 oz. granulated sugar	Whole almonds
4 tbsps. water	

Beat the eggs and sugar, with the coffee, as for a whisked sponge (see Swiss Roll, below). Fold in the sifted flour and ground almonds, put into two prepared 7-inch sandwich tins and bake in a fairly hot oven (375°F., mark 5) for 20 minutes. Turn out and allow to cool. Make the filling: blend the icing sugar and margarine and flavour with the coffee dissolved in the water. Sandwich the cakes together with half this mixture and spread most of the remainder round the sides of the cake (reserving a little for decoration); press the flaked almonds into the butter cream.

Make a caramel by dissolving the sugar in the water in a pan (without stirring), then boiling until golden. Pour on to the top of the cake and mark into portions with a knife before the caramel sets completely. Pipe with butter cream and decorate with almonds.

LEMON GÂTEAU

(see colour picture no. 44)

6 oz. self-raising flour	Juice and finely grated
2 oz. cornflour	rind of 1 lemon
A pinch of salt	2 eggs, lightly beaten
8 oz. butter	6 tbsps. apricot jam
8 oz. sugar	Decoration as desired

For the Frosting

2 egg whites	Finely grated rind of 1
12 oz. caster sugar	lemon
A pinch of salt	A pinch of cream of
2 tbsps. water	tartar
2 tbsps. lemon juice	Yellow colouring

Grease and flour three 8-inch sandwich tins. Sift the flour, cornflour and salt on to a plate. Cream the fat, sugar and lemon rind until light and fluffy and gradually add the eggs, beating well. Fold in the flour and lightly stir in the lemon juice. Divide the mixture evenly between the tins and bake in a moderate oven (350°F., mark 4) for 30 minutes, till golden-brown and springy to the touch. When the cakes are quite cold, spread jam evenly over 2 and sandwich all 3 layers together.

To make the frosting, whisk all the ingredients (except the colouring) lightly together; place the bowl over hot water and whisk until the mixture thickens sufficiently to hold peaks. Add a few drops of colouring, to tint it pale lemon-yellow. Using a palette knife, spread frosting over top and sides of cake. Rough up the surface and decorate with angelica and mimosa balls, or as desired.

SWISS ROLL

(see colour picture no. 43)

3 eggs	1 tbsp. hot water
4 oz. caster sugar	Caster sugar to dredge
4 oz. plain flour	Warmed jam

Prepare a Swiss roll tin, 9 by 12 inches. Put the eggs and sugar into a large basin and stand this over a saucepan of hot water, then whisk very briskly until the mixture is light, thick and firm enough to retain the impression of the whisk for a few seconds. Remove the basin from the heat. Sift about one-third of the flour over the surface of the mixture and fold in very slightly, using a large metal spoon. Add the remaining flour in the same way and lightly stir in the hot water.

Pour the mixture into the prepared tin, allowing it to run over the whole surface. Bake in a very hot oven (450°F., mark 8) for 7-9 minutes, until golden-brown, well-risen and firm.

Meanwhile, have ready a sheet of greaseproof paper liberally sprinkled with caster sugar: if desired, place it over a tea towel lightly wrung out of hot water, to help make the sponge pliable. Turn the cake quickly out on to the paper, trim off the crusty edges with a sharp knife and spread the surface with warmed jam. Roll up with the aid of the paper, making the first turn firmly, so that the whole cake will roll evenly and have a good shape when finished; roll more lightly after this first turn. Dredge the cake with sugar and cool on a cake rack.

DEVIL'S FOOD CAKE

(see colour picture no. 52)

8 oz. plain flour	10 oz. caster or soft
¼ level tsp. salt	brown sugar
½ level tsp. bicarbonate of	3 eggs, beaten
soda	1 tsp. vanilla essence
2 level tsps. baking powder	Chocolate butter cream
3 oz. grated chocolate	(p. 199)
8 fluid oz. milk (scant	Quick frosting (see below)
½ pint)	Chocolate flakes or
5 oz. margarine (or	vermicelli
vegetable shortening)	

Line three 7-inch or two 9-inch sandwich cake tins and grease them. Sift the flour with the salt and bicarbonate of soda on to kitchen paper. Warm the chocolate in the milk until it has dissolved. Cream the margarine in a basin and beat in the sugar gradually until the mixture is soft and creamy. Add the eggs a little at a time and beat thoroughly. Stir in the sieved dry ingredients alternately with the chocolate milk. Add the vanilla essence and bake in the prepared tins in a moderate oven (350°F., mark 4) for 30-35 minutes.

When the cakes are cooked, cool on a wire tray, sandwich together with chocolate butter cream (or whipped cream) and coat with quick frosting. Decorate with flaked chocolate or chocolate vermicelli.

Quick Frosting: Put into a bowl 2 egg whites, 12 oz. caster sugar, a pinch of salt, a large pinch of cream of tartar and 4 tbsps. water and whisk lightly. Place the bowl over hot water and whisk until the mixture thickens sufficiently to hold "peaks". Use at once.

CARIBBEAN CAKE

For the Cake

4 eggs, separated	4 oz. self-raising flour
6 oz. caster sugar	

For the Filling

3 oz. butter	1 oz. plain chocolate,
6 oz. icing sugar, sifted	grated
1 oz. preserved ginger,	3-4 tsps. rum (or
chopped	sufficient to taste)

For the Topping

8 oz. plain chocolate	Walnut halves and
8 oz. unsalted butter	preserved ginger to
Rum (optional)	decorate

Grease and line an 8-inch cake tin. Whisk the egg whites until stiff, then fold in the caster sugar and the egg yolks very lightly. Sift the flour into the bowl and fold in carefully. Pour the mixture into the prepared tin and bake in the centre of a moderate oven (350°F., mark 4 for about 40 minutes, or until golden and shrinking from the sides of the tin. Turn out and allow to cool.

To make the filling, cream the butter and icing sugar and stir in the ginger and chocolate, with rum to taste. Cut the cake in three layers and sandwich together with the filling.

To make the topping, melt the chocolate and butter in a basin over a pan of water and add rum to taste (if used). Remove from the heat and cool until the mixture thickens, then spread it over the sides and top of the cake. Decorate with a few walnut halves and pieces of preserved ginger.

BRIDGE CAKE

(see picture above)

6 oz. butter	2 tbsps. lemon juice
6 oz. sugar	½ lb. grapes
3 eggs	½ gill sherry
6 oz. plain flour	½ pint double cream
¾ level tsp. baking powder	Icing sugar

Cream the fat and sugar and beat in the eggs. Fold in the sifted flour and baking powder, then the lemon juice. Divide the mixture between 2 greased 7-inch sandwich tins and bake in a fairly hot oven (375°F., mark 5) until firm and golden-brown—20-30 minutes. When the cakes are cool, cut a 4-inch round out of the centre of one of them and cut this into 6 wedge-shaped pieces. Halve and seed the grapes and leave them to soak in the sherry for 1 hour. Whisk the cream and stir in the drained grapes (reserving a few for decoration).

Sandwich the whole cake and the ring together with the cream and grape mixture. Use the remainder of the mixture to fill the hole in the centre. Place the cake wedges in place, radiating from the centre, sprinkle with icing sugar and decorate with the remaining grapes.

CHESTNUT GÂTEAU

(see picture above)

3 eggs	4 oz. chopped browned
3 oz. caster sugar	almonds
3 oz. plain flour	¼ pint double cream
1 tbsp. warm water	A little chestnut purée
Apricot jam	

Whisk the eggs and sugar until thick and creamy. Fold in the sifted flour with a metal spoon, then fold in the warm water. Pour the mixture into a greased and lined Swiss roll tin (8 by 12 inches) and bake in a very hot oven (450°F., mark 8) for 7-9 minutes, until golden-brown and firm to the touch. Turn out on to a cooling rack. When cool, cut across into 3 and sandwich together again with thin layers of apricot jam, sprinkled with almonds. Coat the sides with jam and press on chopped nuts. Decorate the top with whipped cream and chestnut purée piped in alternate lines.

GENOESE SPONGE

3 oz. butter	3 large eggs
2½ oz. plain flour	4 oz. caster sugar
½ oz. cornflour	Filling and/or icing

First clarify the butter. Heat it gently until melted, then continue heating slowly without browning until all bubbling has ceased—this indicates that the water has been driven off. Now remove it from the heat and let it stand for a few minutes for the salt and any sediment to settle, then gently pour off the fat. If much sediment is present, strain the butter through muslin.

Grease and line a shallow 8-inch square tin. Sift the flour and cornflour. Put the eggs and sugar in a large basin, stand this over a saucepan of hot water and whisk briskly until the mixture is light, thick and stiff enough to retain the impression of the whisk for a few seconds. Remove the basin from the heat. Sift about half of the flour over the surface of the mixture and fold in very lightly. Add the remaining flour in the same way, alternately with the cooled clarified butter—Genoese sponge must be mixed very lightly or the fat will sink to the bottom and cause a heavy cake. Pour the mixture into the prepared tin and bake in a fairly hot oven (375°F., mark 5) until golden-brown and firm to the touch, the time depending on the depth of the cake—about ¾ hour. Use as required for layer cakes, iced cakes, etc.

PARTY SPECIALS

ORANGE LIQUEUR GÂTEAU

6 oz. margarine	½ pint double cream,
6 oz. caster sugar	whipped
3 eggs, beaten	Chopped walnuts
6 oz. self-raising flour,	1-2 tbsps. fresh orange
sifted	juice
2-3 tbsps. Grand Marnier	5 oz. icing sugar, sifted
Grated rind of 1 orange	Thin slices of orange

Grease and line a pair of 7-inch sandwich tins. Cream the margarine and the caster sugar until pale, soft and fluffy. Gradually beat in the eggs, beating well after each addition. Fold in the flour and then divide the mixture evenly between the tins, levelling the top with a knife. Bake just above the centre of a fairly hot oven (375°F., mark 5) for about 35 minutes, until golden and beginning to shrink from the sides of the tin. When cool, sprinkle some liqueur over each half.

Add the orange rind to the cream and use about half of the mixture to sandwich the two cakes together. Spread a little round the sides and then roll the cake in the chopped walnuts. Add sufficient orange juice to the icing sugar to make an icing thick enough to coat the back of a spoon. Spread this over the top of the cake. When set, pipe with whirls of cream and decorate with thin slices of orange.

If preferred, spread the sides of the cake with apricot jam instead of cream; the amount of cream can then be cut down slightly.

MERINGUE TORTE

Prepare 3 rounds of greased greaseproof paper 8-9 inches in diameter, and place on baking trays. Whisk 5 egg whites till stiff, add 5 oz. caster sugar and whisk the mixture till it is again stiff. Gently fold in another 5 oz. sugar and place the mixture in a forcing bag fitted with a plain nozzle. Cover one round of paper with lines of piped meringue, pipe a lattice of meringue over another paper and a double ring round the edge of the last paper round. Dredge each lightly with caster sugar and dry for several hours in a cool oven (300°F., mark 1); when firm, remove from the paper. Drain a can of peaches and slice thinly. Lightly whip ½ pint cream and add a little vanilla essence and sugar. Spread cream over the first meringue, place the ring on top and fill with fruit and cream. Spread cream on the ring and cover with the lattice. Decorate with peaches and glacé cherries.

MALAKOFF CAKE

A 3-egg sponge cake,	2 egg yolks
baked in a Swiss roll tin	6 tbsps. brandy
5 oz. blanched almonds,	3 tbsps. milk
chopped	¼-½ pint double cream and
4 oz. sugar	chopped nuts to decorate
6 oz. butter	Sugar for cream

Divide the cake into 3 even-sized oblongs. Line a small loaf tin with waxed or greaseproof paper and place one piece of the cake in the bottom. Place the almonds and half the sugar in a thick-based frying pan and heat gently, stirring continuously, until the sugar caramelises and the almonds are pale golden in colour; allow to cool. Cream the butter with the remaining sugar, then stir in the egg yolks and gradually add half the brandy. Finally, stir in the coated chopped nuts.

Mix the remaining brandy with the milk, sprinkle 2 tbsps. of it over the first layer of cake and cover with half the nut filling. Continue in this way with another layer of cake, 2 more tbsps. of the brandy, the remaining filling, the final layer of cake and the last 2 tbsps. brandy. Cover and leave in a cool place overnight. Turn out and cover with the whipped and sweetened cream, then decorate with chopped nuts.

Notes: The sponge cake could be replaced by sponge fingers. Rum could be used instead of brandy.

ANGERS GÂTEAU

For the Cake

4 eggs	¼ oz. cornflour
4½ oz. caster sugar	2 oz. unsalted butter,
4 oz. plain flour	melted

For the Syrup

4 oz. caster sugar	Juice and grated rind of
1 tbsp. water	1 large orange
4 tsps. lemon juice	4 tbsps. Cointreau

For the Filling and Decoration

4 oz. unsalted butter	2 tbsps. Cointreau
6 oz. icing sugar, sifted	4 oz. flaked almonds,
2 tbsps. double cream	toasted

Grease and line two 8-inch sandwich tins in the usual way. Whisk the 4 eggs and the 4½ oz. caster sugar in a large bowl over a pan of hot water until the mixture is thick enough to leave a trail. Remove the basin from the heat and continue to beat until the mixture cools. Sift and fold in most of the flour and cornflour. Lightly fold in the melted butter (which should not be too hot), then the remaining flour. Turn the mixture into the prepared tins and bake in the centre of a fairly hot oven (375°F., mark 5) until well risen and golden-brown—25-30 minutes. Cool on a wire tray.

Make the syrup by dissolving the sugar in the water and fruit juices, bring to boiling point and boil for 5 minutes. Remove from the heat and add the grated orange rind and the Cointreau.

Make the filling by creaming the butter and gradually beating in the icing sugar; lightly mix in the cream and Cointreau.

Brush one cake liberally with some of the syrup and cover with two-thirds of the cream filling. Place the second cake on top, brush the sides with syrup and coat with flaked nuts. Decorate with the remainder of the cream filling, piped in whirls.

RICH CHOCOLATE NUT CAKE

(see picture on facing page)

6 oz. butter	2 oz. plain flour
6 oz. sugar	4 eggs, separated
3 oz. melted chocolate	Butter cream (p. 199)
5 oz. ground almonds	Nut cream, chocolate
2 tbsps. fresh white	vermicelli and
breadcrumbs	whipped cream
1 tbsp. rum	to decorate

Cream the fat and sugar and add the chocolate, almonds, the crumbs soaked in the rum, the flour and egg yolks. Beat the whites to a stiff froth and add them to the mixture, beating well. Put into 2 8-inch sandwich tins and bake in a warm oven (325°F., mark 3) for about ¾-1 hour. Cool on a rack, then sandwich with butter cream and top with nut cream and decorate as seen.

To make nut cream, cream 2 oz. butter and 2 oz. sugar, then add 4 oz. ground almonds and 1 tbsp. cream. Beat thoroughly and use as required.

BERRY-WHIP SQUARES

4 oz. fat	Milk if required
4 oz. caster sugar	Topping (see below)
2 eggs	Fruit or chopped nuts
6 oz. self-raising flour	to decorate

Cream the fat and sugar, then beat in the eggs one at a time. Stir in the flour; if the mixture is too stiff, a little milk may be added. Put into a greased and lined Swiss roll tin and bake in a moderate oven (350°F., mark 4) for 20-25 minutes. Turn out and cool, then cut into 2-inch squares. Just before serving, top with Berry-whip (see below) and add a few pieces of canned fruit or chopped nuts to decorate.

BERRY-WHIP TOPPING

1 egg white	¾ lb. strawberries or
A pinch of salt	raspberries
6 oz. caster sugar	

Put all the ingredients into a basin and whisk or beat with an electric beater till the mixture will stand up in stiff peaks when lifted. (If frozen fruit is used, thaw it, then drain before adding.)

MERINGUE NESTS

Make a meringue mixture as given on p. 191, but use eggs and 6 oz. caster sugar. Pipe it into rings on oiled paper, building the rings up to form "nests". Bake as directed. When cool, fill with cream and fresh strawberries (or any other fresh fruit). Alternatively, fill with coffee butter cream mixed with chopped walnuts and decorate each nest with a halved walnut.

HARVEST RIBBON CAKE

6 oz. fat	Grated rind of ½ a lemon
6 oz. caster sugar	2 level tbsps. cocoa
4 eggs	Sea foam frosting (see
8 oz. plain flour	below)
1½ level tsps. baking	Seedless raisins, toasted
powder	almonds and orange
3 tbsps. milk	peel to decorate
Yellow colouring	

Cream the fat and sugar, beat in the eggs one at a time and add the sifted flour and baking powder, with sufficient milk to give a soft dropping consistency. Divide into 3 portions, then add the yellow colouring and lemon rind to one and the cocoa to another, leaving one plain. Put into 3 prepared 7-inch sandwich tins and bake in a fairly hot oven (375°F., mark 5) for 25-30 minutes. Cool on a rack. Sandwich the cakes together with frosting and coat the whole cake with it. Decorate with 2 sprays of raisins and 2 sprays of toasted almonds, making "stems" of finely cut orange peel. If preferred, plain butter cream may be used to sandwich the layers together.

SEA FOAM FROSTING

6 tbsps. golden syrup	A pinch of salt
3 egg whites	1½ tsps. vanilla essence

Heat the syrup in a pan till it is boiling. Beat the egg whites till stiff, add the salt and slowly pour the syrup over the whites. Beat until the frosting is fluffy and stands up in peaks; add the vanilla essence and use at once.

SIMPLE FRUIT GÂTEAU

(see picture on p. 203)

Make up a Victoria Sandwich mixture as on p. 173, but use 6 oz. each of fat, sugar and flour and 3 eggs. Spread it evenly in a greased and lined 8-inch tin. Bake in the centre of a fairly hot oven (375°F., mark 5) for about 45 minutes. When cake is cool, spread sides with 4 oz. butter cream (see p. 199) and roll the sides in finely chopped nuts. Put the cake on a plate and place well-drained canned fruit over the top. Thicken ¼ pint of the fruit juice with 1 level tsp. cornflour and when the mixture clears, pour it over the fruit and allow to set.

GÂTEAU LE PROGRÈS

5 egg whites	Vanilla essence
7 oz. caster sugar	Chopped almonds
5½ oz. ground almonds	Icing sugar

For the Crème au Beurre

2 egg yolks	8 oz. unsalted butter
4 oz. caster sugar	4 oz. plain chocolate
¼ pint milk	

Grease 2 Swiss roll tins generously and flour the insides. Whisk the egg whites until stiff but not dry and fold in the sugar, ground almonds and 2-3 drops of essence. Spread the mixture over the tins and bake in a fairly hot oven (375°F., mark 5) for 30-40 minutes. Trim the edges with a sharp knife while the cakes are still hot, cut each in half lengthwise and carefully remove to a wire rack to cool.

Crème au Beurre: Cream the egg yolks with half the sugar until white. Dissolve the remaining sugar in the milk, bring to the boil and pour on to the yolks. Return the mixture to the pan and stir over a very gentle heat until it will coat the back of the spoon, then allow to cool. Cream the butter until soft and add the cooled custard by degrees. Melt the chocolate, but do not allow it to become really hot; add it to the crème mixture.

Sandwich the meringue oblongs together with the crème au beurre, spread the tops and sides with more of it and press chopped almonds round the sides. Pipe on a decoration with the remaining crème—in France, the word *Progrès* is usually written across the top. Sprinkle icing sugar round the edges. Chill the cake before serving. As an alternative to the crème au beurre, you could use chocolate butter cream (see p. 199).

CHOCOLATE PEPPERMINT RING

A vanilla pod	1 level tsp. baking powder
4 tbsps. milk	8 oz. butter
8 oz. plain chocolate	6 oz. caster sugar
4 oz. plain flour	4 eggs, separated
2 oz. ground rice	

For the Butter Cream and Topping

5 oz. butter	A little green colouring
8 oz. icing sugar, sifted	Chocolate vermicelli
3 tsps. crème de menthe	

Grease a tube cake tin, 9 inches in diameter by 2½ inches deep; place a ring of greaseproof paper in the base and a narrow strip of paper round the top rims, projecting about ½ inch, to raise the height.

Infuse the vanilla pod in the milk for ½ hour, then remove it. Melt the chocolate in the milk, taking care not to overheat. Sift together the flour, ground rice and baking powder. Cream the butter and sugar until light and fluffy. Beat in the egg yolks one at a time and then the cooled but still soft chocolate mixture. Whisk the egg whites and lightly fold into the cake mixture. Turn into the prepared tin and bake in the centre of a moderate oven (350°F., mark 4) for about 1¼ hours, until well risen. Make the butter cream in the usual way. Coat the cooled cake with butter cream and sprinkle with chocolate vermicelli.

Note: Failing a tube tin, use an 8-inch round cake tin and bake for 1¼ hours.

SCOTCH BUN

(see colour picture no. 41)

For the Pastry

10 oz. plain flour	Cold water to mix (about
A pinch of salt	4 tbsps.)
2½ oz. margarine	Egg to glaze
2½ oz. lard	

For the Filling

8 oz. plain flour	1 lb. stoned raisins
1 level tsp. cinnamon	4 oz. brown sugar
1 level tsp. ginger	1 lb. currants
1 level tsp. bicarbonate of soda	4 oz. chopped candied peel
1 level tsp. cream of tartar	4 oz. chopped almonds
	¼ pint whisky (approx.)

This should be made several weeks at least before it is to be eaten (by tradition at Hogmanay parties).

Grease an 8-inch cake tin. Make the pastry in the usual way and leave it in a cool place. Mix together all the ingredients for the filling, using enough whisky to moisten and bind the mixture. Line the cake tin with two-thirds of the pastry—see that it comes well up the sides, so that it may be folded over. Fill with the fruit mixture, packing it well in. Fold over the edge of the pastry and stick the edges firmly. Brush the top with beaten egg, then prick all over with a fork; using a plain 2-inch cutter, mark overlapping circles over the top. Bake in a moderate oven (350°F., mark 4) for 2½-3 hours.

RICH CHRISTMAS CAKE

1 lb. 2 oz. currants	½ level tsp. ground cinnamon
8 oz. sultanas	
8 oz. raisins, stoned	10 oz. butter
4 oz. mixed peel, chopped	10 oz. soft brown sugar
6 oz. glacé cherries, halved	Grated rind of ½ a lemon
10 oz. plain flour	6 eggs, beaten
A pinch of salt	3 tbsps. brandy
½ level tsp. mixed spice	

Line a 9-inch cake tin, using 2 thicknesses of greaseproof paper. Tie a double band of brown paper round the outside.

Clean the fruit if necessary. Mix the prepared currants, sultanas, raisins, peel and cherries with the flour, salt and spices. Cream the butter, sugar and lemon rind until pale and fluffy. Add the eggs a little at a time, beating well after each addition. Fold in half the flour and fruit, using a tablespoon, then fold in the rest and add the brandy. Put into the tin, spread the mixture evenly, making sure there are no air pockets, and make a dip in the centre. Stand the tin on a layer of newspaper or brown paper in the lower part of a cool oven (300°F., mark 1-2) and bake for about 4½ hours. To avoid over-browning the top, cover it with several thicknesses of greaseproof paper after 2½ hours.

When the cake is cooked, leave it to cool in the tin and then turn it out on to a wire rack. To store, wrap it in several layers of greaseproof paper and put it in an airtight tin. If a large enough tin is not available, cover the wrapped cake entirely with aluminium foil. If you like, you can prick the cake top all over with a fine skewer and slowly pour 2-3 tbsps. brandy over it before storing. For icing and decoration see pp. 200-201.

CAKES FROM OTHER COUNTRIES

SACHERTORTE (Austrian)
(see picture above)

8 oz. plain chocolate	3 oz. ground almonds
4 oz. unsalted butter	1½ oz. self-raising
6½ oz. sugar	flour
5 eggs, separated	Jam, almonds, etc.

For the Icing

5 oz. chocolate	5 oz. butter

Melt the chocolate and when soft, cream with the butter, sugar and egg yolks; beat all together thoroughly. Fold in the almonds and sifted flour, then the stiffly beaten egg whites. Put into a greased and lined cake tin and bake in a fairly hot oven (400°F., mark 6) for at least 45 minutes. When the cake is quite cold, cut it in half and fill with a layer of jam.

To make the icing, melt the chocolate and butter, mix well together and allow to become fairly firm, then spread over the top and round the sides of the cake. Decorate as desired—with blanched almonds, piped whipped cream, etc.

SOUR CREAM DEVIL'S FOOD CAKE (USA)
(see right-hand picture above)

8 oz. self-raising flour	¼ pint sour cream
1 level tsp. salt	3 oz. melted chocolate
8 oz. butter	6 tbsps. hot water
8 oz. sugar	1 tsp. vanilla essence
1 egg	Grated chocolate to
1 level tsp. bicarbonate of	decorate
soda	

For the Frosting

4 oz. butter	2 tbsps. cream
10 oz. sifted icing sugar	1-2 tbsps. rum

Sift together the flour and salt. Cream the butter thoroughly, add the sugar gradually and beat until light. Add the well beaten egg and beat well. Dissolve the soda in the sour cream. Add the flour to the creamed mixture alternately with the sour cream, a little at a time; beat well after each addition. Combine the chocolate and hot water and add to the above mixture, then beat until smooth and add the vanilla essence. Put into 2 buttered and floured 9-inch cake tins and bake in a moderate oven (350°F., mark 4) for about 30 minutes.

To make the frosting, cream the butter till very soft, then gradually add the sifted icing sugar. Work in the cream and as much rum as desired. Beat the mixture well until light and fluffy. Using some of the frosting, sandwich the two cakes together, then spread the remainder evenly over the top and sides. Press grated chocolate onto the sides, using a palette knife.

This produces a cake much lighter in colour than the usual Devil's Food Cake.

KARIDOFSITA (Greece)

5-6 eggs, separated	2 level tbsps. cornflour
12 oz. caster sugar	A little milk
12 oz. chopped walnuts	½ level tsp. plain flour
1 oz. dessert chocolate	½ level tsp. baking powder

Beat the egg yolks and sugar together. Add the walnuts, melted chocolate, the cornflour (blended with a little milk), the plain flour, baking powder and lastly the stiffly beaten egg whites. Pour into a greased, lined 9-inch cake tin and bake in a fairly hot oven (375°F., mark 5) for about 1¼ hours. If desired, this cake may be iced with chocolate icing (p. 199), when cooked and cooled.

GÂTEAU DE SAVOIE AU CITRON (France)

2½ oz. potato flour, or	Juice and grated rind
1¼ oz. each of arrow-	of ½ a lemon
root and plain flour	Icing sugar or lemon-
3 eggs	flavoured glacé icing
5 oz. caster sugar	to decorate

Prepare an 8-inch sandwich tin. Sift the flour (or flours). Separate the eggs and cream the yolks with the sugar until light, then add the flour, lemon juice and rind. Whisk the egg whites until stiff and fold them very carefully into the mixture. Turn at once into the prepared tin and bake in a fairly hot oven (375°F., mark 5) for about 40 minutes. When cool, dust with icing sugar or cover with glacé icing, which may be flavoured with lemon if desired (see p. 199).

FLORENTINES

(see picture above)

Rice paper	1 oz. chopped crystallised
3¾ oz. butter	cherries
4 oz. caster sugar	1 tbsp. whipped cream
4 oz. mixed broken	¾ oz. plain flour
walnuts and almonds	4 oz. plain block
1 oz. sultanas	chocolate
1 oz. chopped peel	

Place the rice paper on baking trays. Melt the butter, add the sugar and dissolve, then boil together for 1 minute. Add all the other ingredients (except the chocolate) and mix. Drop the mixture in small, well-shaped heaps on to the lined trays and bake in a moderate oven (350°F., mark 4) for about 10 minutes, until golden-brown. Remove and cool, remove the rice paper, then spread the backs with melted chocolate and mark with a fork.

RETES-STRUDEL (Hungarian)

1½ tsps. salad oil	8 oz. butter, melted
1 small egg	and cooled
6 fluid oz. water (¼ pint	Filling (see recipes
plus 2 tbsps.)	on this page)
10½ oz. flour (unsifted)	Icing sugar

Combine the oil, egg and water; beat until smooth, using a fork. Measure the flour into a large bowl, make a well in the centre, pour in the oil mixture and stir well to form a soft dough. Turn the dough out onto a lightly floured surface and knead until elastic. Lightly brush the ball of dough with melted butter, cover with a large bowl and let stand in a warm place for 30 minutes.

Meanwhile, cover a small table with a clean cloth. Rub just enough flour into the cloth to cover it very well, so that it will prevent the dough from sticking; brush off any excess. Place the dough in the centre of the cloth; using a floured rolling pin, roll the dough out into a square about 16 by 16 inches. Using the fingers, spread the entire surface with more melted butter.

Stretch the dough out so that it hangs well over the table all round and is thin enough to see through. Using scissors, snip off the thick edges all round and let the dough dry for 15 minutes, or until crisp. Start heating the oven to fairly hot (375°F., mark 5) and measure out the ingredients for the desired filling.

When the dough is crisp, sprinkle it lightly with melted butter; then proceed as in the filling recipe (see below). Turn in the overhanging sides of the dough over the filling all the way round, to make a very neat square. Roll up the dough, then, using a sharp knife, cut the roll in half crosswise so as to make 2 Strudels. Using a broad spatula, lift them carefully onto a greased baking sheet or Swiss roll tin, side by side. Brush with melted butter and bake for about 55-60 minutes, brushing often with melted butter. Bake until crisp and golden-brown. Serve warm, thickly sprinkled with sifted icing sugar. If desired, the Strudel may be accompanied by ½ pint commercial sour cream mixed with 1 level tsp. grated nutmeg; chill well.

APPLE STRUDEL FILLING

4 oz. dried white	¼ level tsp. ground cinnamon
breadcrumbs	2 lb. sliced and stewed
3 oz. finely chopped	apples, well drained
walnuts	1 level tbsp. grated lemon
6½ oz. granulated sugar	rind
¼ level tsp. grated nutmeg	2½ oz. raisins, stoned

Combine the crumbs, walnuts, sugar, nutmeg and cinnamon and use to sprinkle over the half of the Strudel dough nearest you. Toss the apples with the lemon rind and raisins and spoon over the crumb mixture.

Proceed as already described.

CREAM CHEESE STRUDEL FILLING

4 3-oz. packages of	1 level tbsp. grated lemon
cream cheese	rind
3 egg yolks	2½ oz. dried white
3 oz. sugar	breadcrumbs
2½ oz. raisins, stoned	

Combine the cheese, egg yolks and sugar and beat until smooth and blended. Stir in the lemon rind and the raisins. Now sprinkle the breadcrumbs evenly over the half of the Strudel nearest you and spread the cheese filling over the crumbs. Proceed with the rolling of the Strudel as already directed.

MONT BLANC AUX MARRONS (France)

(see right-hand picture opposite)

3 eggs	Apricot purée
4 oz. sugar	Browned almonds
3 oz. plain flour	Chestnut purée (see
3 oz. butter	below)

Beat the eggs and sugar together over hot water until thick and frothy. Melt the butter and allow it to cool, then add the sifted flour and melted butter alternately to the whisked mixture and mix well. Pour into a Swiss roll tin and bake in a fairly hot oven (400°F., mark 6) for 20-25 minutes; cool on a rack. Cut the cake into 2-inch rounds, using a scone cutter, and coat the sides and top of the pieces with apricot purée. Roll the sides of the cakes in chopped browned almonds and pipe the chestnut purée into whirls on top of each cake.

Chestnut Purée. Cook, peel and sieve $\frac{1}{2}$ lb. chestnuts. Dissolve 3 oz. granulated sugar in 4 tbsps. water and bring to the boil. Simmer gently until a hard ball forms when a drop of the syrup is put into cold water. Mix with the chestnuts and flavour to taste with a little vanilla essence. Alternatively, use canned chestnut purée (sweetened as above with sugar syrup) or canned chestnut spread.

PAHKINAKAKKA (Finnish Nut Cake)

A little butter	$\frac{1}{4}$ level tsp. salt
1 level tbsp. breadcrumbs	$\frac{1}{2}$ lb. finely chopped
4 eggs, separated	walnuts
1$\frac{1}{2}$ tsps. vanilla essence	1$\frac{1}{2}$ level tbsps. self-raising
$\frac{1}{2}$ level tsp. grated lemon	flour
rind	Icing or whipped cream
3 oz. sugar	to decorate

Butter and crumb a loaf tin (9$\frac{1}{2}$ by 4 'inches). Beat the egg yolks with the vanilla essence and gradually mix in the grated lemon rind, sugar and salt, beating thoroughly. Sprinkle the chopped nuts with the flour, then mix into the egg yolks. Beat the egg whites stiffly and fold into the mixture. Pour into the tin and bake for 1 hour in a fairly hot oven (375°F., mark 5). When cool, this cake may either be topped with glacé icing (see p. 199) or decorated with some whipped cream.

POLISH HONEY CAKE

(see left-hand picture above)

4 oz. sugar	1 level tsp. ground cinnamon
3 egg yolks and 5 egg	$\frac{1}{4}$ level tsp. powdered cloves
whites	$\frac{1}{2}$ level tsp. grated nutmeg
3 oz. chopped walnuts	$\frac{1}{2}$ pint clear honey, heated,
8 oz. self-raising flour	skimmed and cooled

Cream together the sugar and 3 egg yolks, till light and cream-coloured. Add the nuts, sifted flour, spices and honey. Stiffly beat the 5 egg whites and fold into the first mixture. Turn into a greased and floured 8-inch cake tin and bake in a moderate oven (350°F., mark 4) for about 1 hour. Leave plain or decorate as seen with icing sugar, sifted through a paper doyley.

KARDEMUMMAKAKA (Swedish Cardamom Cake)

(see picture above)

4 oz. butter	$\frac{1}{2}$ pint single cream
10 oz. caster sugar	12 oz. self-raising
2 level tsps. ground	flour
cardamoms	Caster sugar to dredge

Melt the butter, pour over the sugar, add the cardamoms and pour in the cream. Sift the flour and fold into the mixture. Pour into a buttered and floured 9-inch ring mould tin and bake in a moderate oven (350°F., mark 4) for 40-45 minutes. Turn out on to a wire rack, and dredge the top of the cake thickly with caster sugar while it is still hot.

TOPFENKUCHEN (Austrian)

5 oz. cream cheese	5 eggs, separated
5 oz. butter	Juice and grated rind
5 oz. ground walnuts,	of 1 lemon
hazelnuts or almonds	1 oz. self-raising flour
5 oz. sugar	

Cream together the cheese, butter, nuts, sugar, egg yolks, lemon juice and grated rind. Fold in the flour and then the stiffly beaten egg whites. Pour the mixture into a greased and lined 8-inch cake tin. Bake for $\frac{1}{4}$ hour in a very hot oven (450°F., mark 8), then for a further 1$\frac{1}{2}$ hours in a moderate oven (350°F., mark 4), until the mixture is dry inside when tested with a skewer.

POLISH CHEESE CAKE
(see picture above)

For the Pastry

4 oz. plain flour	1 egg yolk
2 oz. butter	A little water to
1 oz. sugar	mix

For the Filling

8 oz. cream cheese	8 oz. caster sugar
6 egg yolks	1 tsp. vanilla essence
2 oz. melted butter	Glacé icing (p. 199)

Make pastry as for shortcrust and line an 8-inch square baking tin. Now make the filling. Tie the cream cheese in muslin and squeeze out the moisture. When it is dry, crumble it into a mixing bowl. Add the egg yolks, melted butter, sugar and essence and beat thoroughly until quite smooth. Place in the pastry case and bake in a moderate oven (350°F., mark 4) for about 1 hour, until the cheese mixture is firmly set.
When the cake is cold, cut it into squares and coat each with a little glacé icing.

BLØTKAKE (Soft Sponge Cake from Norway)

4 eggs	4½ oz. plain flour
½ lb. sugar	1 tbsp. cold water to
4½ oz. potato flour	mix
or cornflour	

For the Marzipan Icing and Decoration

1 level tsp. plain flour	6 oz. ground almonds
1 tbsp. milk	1 lb. icing sugar, sifted
Almond essence	1 large egg

For the Filling

3 tbsps. sherry	4 oz. chopped walnuts
¼ pint double cream	or almonds

Whisk the eggs and sugar together over hot water or in an electric mixer until they are very thick and creamy; fold in the sifted potato and plain flours very carefully and finally add the cold water. Put into a round 8-inch cake tin and bake in a cool oven (300°F., mark 2) for 40-50 minutes. Turn out and cool.
Meanwhile, make the marzipan icing. Whisk together the flour and milk in a small saucepan, bring to the boil, remove from the heat and cool, then stir in 5 drops of almond essence. Stir the ground almonds evenly into the sifted icing sugar. Mix well with the milk mixture and add sufficient egg to give a pliable dough. If desired the marzipan may be coloured.
Divide the cake into 3 layers. Sprinkle with sherry and fill with the whipped cream and nuts, then cover the top with the marzipan icing. To do this, roll the marzipan out on a board, with the help of a little icing sugar, to about ⅛ inch in thickness. Place it over the cake, allowing it to hang down over the sides and covering them completely. Decorate with flowers made from marzipan or with almonds or walnuts, according to the type of nut used in the filling.

DOBOZ TORTE (Austria)
(see picture above)

4 eggs	6 oz. icing sugar
6 oz. caster sugar	8 oz. softened butter
5 oz. plain flour	4 oz. melted chocolate
4-6 oz. caster sugar for	Crushed biscuits or
caramel	chopped nuts to
3 egg whites	decorate

Butter and flour 6-7 baking sheets. Whisk the eggs, add the sugar gradually and whisk over hot water until very thick and fluffy. Fold in the sifted flour. Spread the mixture out on the baking sheets into large rounds—about 8½ inches across—and bake in a fairly hot oven (375°F., mark 5) for 7-10 minutes, until golden-brown. Loosen from the tins and trim each cake to a neat shape with a sharp knife—a saucepan lid may be used as a guide. Lift onto wire cake racks to cool.
Take the round with the best surface and lay it on an oiled rack or tray. Now prepare the caramel: put the sugar in a small, heavy saucepan, place over gentle heat and allow the sugar to dissolve without stirring; boil steadily to a rich brown, then pour it over the biscuit round, spreading it with an oiled knife. Mark into sections and trim around the edge.
Make a chocolate butter cream as follows: whip the egg whites and icing sugar over hot water until very thick. Cream the butter thoroughly and beat the meringue into it by degrees; add the melted chocolate. Sandwich the remaining biscuit rounds together in one stack with the butter cream and put the caramel-covered one on top. Spread the sides of the torte with butter cream and press either crushed biscuit crumbs or chopped nuts round the sides. Pipe the remaining butter cream round the top edge to make a decorative border.

NOVELTY CAKES

MERRY-GO-ROUND CAKE
(see picture above)

Bake a Victoria sandwich cake mixture in a pair of 8-inch sandwich tins and when cool sandwich together with vanilla-flavoured butter cream (see p. 199). Coat with white or pastel-coloured glacé icing (p. 199).

Choose a striped or bright-coloured drinking straw for the centre pole, and cut some narrow coloured ribbons into equal lengths; fix one end of each into one of the open ends of the drinking straws, holding them in place with a coloured hat pin. Fix the other ends of the ribbons to the outer edge of the cake with attractive candle-holders (we used tiny wooden dolls) and then carefully twist the centre straw to make the ribbons taut. Decorate the side of the cake with more ribbons.

BALLOON CAKE

Coat an 8-inch cake with coloured glacé icing (p. 199). Before it has quite set, fix some flat round coloured sweets in bunches round the cake to represent bunches of balloons. Using a fine writing nozzle and a little chocolate butter cream (p. 199), pipe in the balloon strings. If the child's name is short, this can also be written in sweets on top of the cake. Place candles round the top edge.

HEDGEHOG CAKES

Bake 18 small cakes in small patty tins, using the Victoria sandwich mixture (p. 173). When cool, coat with chocolate butter cream, then rough it up slightly with the flat edge of a knife. Brown some slivered almonds under the grill and stick them into the cakes to represent the hedgehog's prickles. Use cloves for the eyes and almond halves for the feet.

ALPHABET BRICKS

Make an oblong Victoria sandwich and when it is cool, cut it into 1½-inch cubes. Coat thoroughly with sieved apricot jam, then cover the bricks with a lemon butter cream of fairly soft consistency. Re-shape the bricks and smooth the edges with a knife, then draw a fork over the butter cream to mark all the sides. Make up a little chocolate butter cream and pipe large letters on each side of the bricks.

GUY FAWKES CAKE
(see picture above)

Bake a Victoria sandwich or Madeira cake mixture in an 8-inch tin. When it is cool, coat it with 1 lb. chocolate glacé icing (see p. 199). Use 4 oz. almond paste and cocktail sticks to make the rockets and decorate them as seen with some coloured glacé icing. Still using white icing, pipe some firework shapes round the cake and add hundreds and thousands and coloured balls to represent the sparks. Pile a few chocolate fingers on the top of the cake for a bonfire, and place the rockets around it, as seen in the photograph.

SAILING BOATS

Make an oblong Victoria sandwich. When it is cool use a boat-shaped cutter to cut out foundation shapes for the boats. Make up some vanilla butter cream (p. 199) and coat the boats with it, leaving a little on one side for decoration. Smooth the edges with a warm knife and reshape the sides. Add some chocolate colouring to the remaining butter cream and pipe port-holes on the sides of the boats. Cut sails from rice paper and fix into the butter cream.

PICTURE CAKE

Coat the top of a slab cake with glacé icing (either coloured or plain—see p. 199). Using a plain writing pipe and stiff glacé icing of a contrasting colour, mark it into large squares. In each square outline some simple children's toy, e.g., balloons, a beach ball, a bicycle, a train, a building brick, etc.

JUMBO CAKE

Fill a sandwich cake with a well-flavoured lemon filling and coat it with yellow glacé icing (p. 199). Trace a picture of an elephant on to a piece of cardboard and cut out the shape, leaving a stencil. Place this on the cake and fill the cut-out area with a chocolate butter cream (p. 199); smooth with a knife and leave to set before lifting off the stencil. Using lemon icing, pipe the eyes, ears and other finishing touches. A saddle and decorative trappings may also be added in icing.

MUSHROOM CAKE

(see picture above)

3 eggs	6 oz. butter
5 oz. caster sugar	1-2 level tbsps. cocoa
3 oz. plain flour	A little almond paste
1 egg white	Desiccated coconut
8 oz. icing sugar	Green colouring

Make a sponge (see Swiss roll, p. 174) from the whole eggs, 3 oz. caster sugar and flour and bake in 2 greased and lined 8-inch sandwich tins in a moderate oven (350°F., mark 4) for about 30 minutes. Make up a meringue mixture with the egg white and 2 oz. caster sugar (see p. 191) and form into meringues of varying sizes. Make a butter cream with the icing sugar, butter and cocoa (see p. 199).

When the cakes are cold, sandwich them together with some butter cream; spread most of the remainder over the sides and top, then furrow with a fork or icing card. Make stalks of almond paste and stick them to the base of the meringues with a little butter cream. Using a small writing nozzle, pipe underneath with butter cream to represent gills. Tint the coconut with a little green colouring dissolved in water. Place the cake on a board, surround with the coconut and decorate with the meringue mushrooms, placing some on the board and some on the cake itself.

CANDLE CAKE

6 oz. butter and margarine	6 oz. self-raising flour
6 oz. caster sugar	¼ lb. sieved apricot jam
3 beaten eggs	
For the Icing	
1 egg white	2 tbsps. water
6 oz. caster sugar	A pinch of cream of tartar
A pinch of salt	

Cream the fat and sugar together until light and fluffy. Beat in the eggs gradually and fold in the sifted flour. Put into a well-greased and floured cocoa tin and bake in a moderate oven (350°F., mark 4) for 50 minutes; start cooking with the tin upright, then turn it onto its side when the mixture is set, to ensure even cooking. Cool on a rack. When completely cold, brush the cake on all sides

with the apricot jam and stand it up on end in the centre of a 6-inch round cake-board.

Put all the icing ingredients together in a bowl and whisk lightly. Place the bowl over hot water and continue whisking until the mixture thickens sufficiently to hold 'peaks'.

Cover the cake completely with this icing, so that it gives the appearance of wax dripping down the sides of a candle.

Make a 'flame' out of cardboard, paint it orange and red and fix it firmly in the top of the cake.

'NUMBER' BIRTHDAY CAKE

(see picture above)

6 oz. butter	4 oz. icing sugar for almond paste
6 oz. caster sugar	
3 eggs	Beaten egg
6 oz. self-raising flour	Gravy browning
2 lb. icing sugar for glacé icing (p. 199)	4 oz. icing sugar and 3 oz. butter for butter cream
Yellow colouring	
4 oz. ground almonds	Cocoa

Obtain a cake tin representing the correct numeral and grease it very well; seal the bottom with foil. Make up a Victoria sandwich mixture from the 6 oz. butter, 6 oz. caster sugar, eggs and flour (see p. 173), place in the tin and bake in a moderate oven (350°F., mark 4) for 1 hour. Cool on a rack. Place on a board and coat with 2 layers of pale yellow glacé icing.

Bind the ground almonds and 4 oz. icing sugar with beaten egg and knead in gravy browning until the paste is pale brown. Roll out on a board dusted with icing sugar, then cut out 4 mice of different sizes and a grandfather clock. (This will be easier to do if you first draw paper patterns.)

Make up a plain butter cream with the remaining sugar and butter (see p. 199) and use a little to stick 3 mice in graded sizes round the sides of the cake and a mouse and the clock on top (see picture). Colour a little butter cream with cocoa and pipe a face and pendulum on the clock. With the remaining butter cream, tinted yellow, pipe a border round the base of the cake.

This design may need to be slightly adapted to suit the particular numeral.

TRADITIONAL CAKES

NORFOLK CAKE
(see picture above)

8 oz. plain flour	4 oz. sultanas
1 level tsp. baking powder	2 oz. currants
½ level tsp. mixed spice	Grated rind of 1 lemon
4 oz. butter	and 1 orange
3 oz. sugar	1 tbsp. melted chocolate
2 eggs	2 tbsps. milk

Sift the flour, baking powder and spice and allow to stand in a warm place while you beat the butter and sugar to a light, fluffy cream. Beat the eggs and stir them into the butter mixture, alternately with the flour. Mix in the cleaned sultanas and currants, the orange and lemon rind and the chocolate, then the milk. Put into a greased and lined round 8-inch tin and bake in a cool oven (325°F., mark 3) for about 2 hours.

YORKSHIRE PARKIN

½ lb. plain flour	6 oz. soft brown sugar
½ level tsp. salt	4 oz. butter or lard
¼ oz. bicarbonate of soda	3 oz. golden syrup or
1 oz. mixed spice	black treacle
4 oz. coarse oatmeal	¼ pint milk

Sift the flour, salt, soda and spice, then mix thoroughly with the oatmeal and sugar. Melt the fat with the syrup or treacle and add to the dry ingredients, with the milk. Spread into an 8-inch square tin and bake in a moderate oven (350°F., mark 4) for about 50 minutes.

PITCAITHLY BANNOCK

8 oz. butter	¼ level tsp. salt
2 oz. caster sugar	1 oz. finely chopped
8 oz. plain flour	blanched almonds
2 oz. ground rice	1 oz. chopped peel

Work the butter and sugar together on a smooth surface until thoroughly blended, then draw in the sifted flour, ground rice and salt. Finally, mix in the almonds and peel. Form into a round cake about 1 inch thick, lay it on a greased paper on a baking tin, prick the top and pinch up the edge, then pin a band of greased paper round the edge of the bannock. Bake in a moderate oven (350°F., mark 4) for 30-40 minutes.

POUND CAKE (FRUITLESS)
(see picture above)

8 oz. butter	12 oz. self-raising flour
8 oz. sugar	Juice and grated rind of
4 eggs	1 lemon

Beat together the butter and sugar until light and fluffy. Beat the eggs and add to the mixture, alternately with the flour. Mix in the lemon juice and rind. Turn the mixture into a lined and greased loaf tin (5 by 7½ by 3½ inches) and bake in a cool oven (325°F., mark 3) for about 2 hours.

SIMNEL CAKE

12 oz. currants	1 level tsp. ground
4 oz. sultanas	cinnamon
3 oz. mixed candied peel	6 oz. butter
8 oz. plain flour	6 oz. caster sugar
A pinch of salt	3 eggs
1 level tsp. grated	Milk to mix
nutmeg	A little apricot jam

For the Almond Paste

12 oz. caster sugar	Lemon juice to mix
1 egg	Egg yolk to glaze
8 oz. ground almonds	

Grease and line an 8- or 9-inch cake tin. Prepare the fruit and peel. Make up the almond paste in the usual way, take about one-third of it and roll it out into a round to fit the cake tin.
Sift the dry ingredients and add the fruit and peel. Cream the fat and sugar thoroughly and beat in each egg separately. Stir in the flour, adding enough milk to form a dropping consistency. Put half the mixture into the tin, smooth the top and cover with the round of almond paste. Pour on the rest of the mixture and bake in a warm oven (325°F., mark 3) for 2-3 hours.
When the cake is cool, coat it with a little warmed jam and cover the top with a second round of almond paste, pressing it well down. Shape the remaining almond paste into small balls (eleven is the traditional number) and arrange them round the edge of the cake. Brush the almond paste over with beaten egg yolk and return the cake to the hot oven for a few minutes to brown. Decorations such as an Easter chick or a group of tiny marzipan eggs may be added.

AYRSHIRE SHORTCAKE

(see picture above)

4 oz. plain flour	4 oz. caster sugar
4 oz. ground rice	1 egg yolk
A large pinch of salt	About tbsp. cream
4 oz. butter	

Sift the flour, ground rice and salt. Rub in the butter lightly, then add the sugar and mix well. Beat up the egg yolk and cream and add to the mixture; mix to a firm dough, then roll out thinly, cut into wedges, rounds or fingers and prick with a fork. Place on greased paper on a baking tin and bake in a cool oven (325°F., mark 3) for about 25 minutes.

APPLE CAKE

12 oz. self-raising flour	$\frac{3}{4}$ pint apple purée
$\frac{1}{2}$ level tsp. salt	4 oz. butter
1 level tsp. ground cinnamon	6 oz. moist brown
$\frac{1}{2}$ level tsp. grated nutmeg	sugar
$\frac{1}{2}$ level tsp. ground cloves	1 egg, separated
1 level tsp. bicarbonate of soda	4 oz. stoned raisins

Sift together the flour, salt and spices. Add the bicarbonate of soda to the apple purée, stirring until dissolved. Cream the butter and sugar until light and fluffy, add the egg yolk and beat well. Now add the flour and apple purée alternately to the butter mixture, then add the raisins and lastly fold in the stiffly whipped egg white. Put the mixture into a greased and lined 8-inch round cake tin and bake in a moderate oven (350°F., mark 4) for about 1-1½ hours.

DUNDEE CAKE

10 oz. plain flour	1 orange
4 oz. currants	5 eggs
4 oz. raisins	8 oz. butter or margarine
4 oz. sultanas	8 oz. sugar
4 oz. chopped orange and lemon peel	3 oz. ground almonds
2 oz. whole almonds	A pinch of salt

Sift the flour. Prepare the fruit, blanch and split the almonds, grate the orange rind and beat the eggs. Cream the butter and sugar and add the eggs and flour alternately, beating well. Add the fruit, ground almonds, orange rind and salt. Turn the mixture into a greased and lined 8-inch cake tin, cover the surface with the split almonds and bake in a cool oven (325°F., mark 3) for about 2½ hours. Cool on a wire rack.

LINCOLNSHIRE FARMHOUSE DRIPPING CAKE

1 lb. plain flour	1 tbsp. black treacle
$\frac{1}{2}$ level tsp. salt	$\frac{1}{2}$ pint milk (approx.)
6 oz. dripping	2 eggs, beaten
2 oz. candied peel	1 level tsp. bicarbonate of
$\frac{1}{2}$ lb. raisins	soda
6 oz. granulated sugar	

Sift the flour with the salt and rub in the dripping thoroughly. Chop the candied peel, stone the raisins and add both to the flour, with the sugar. Warm the treacle in $\frac{1}{2}$ gill milk, mix with the eggs and stir into the mixture, with just enough cold milk to make a dough which will just drop from the wooden spoon when shaken. Then add the bicarbonate of soda, dissolved in 1 tbsp. milk; put at once into a prepared 8-inch square cake tin. Bake in a moderate oven (350°F., mark 4) for about 1½-2 hours, reducing the temperature to cool (325°F., mark 3) after the first hour.

This cake is very good if cut into squares or sliced thinly and buttered.

MAIDS OF HONOUR

(see picture above)

1 pint milk	1 oz. chopped blanched
A pinch of salt	almonds
1 level tsp. rennet	2 level tsps. sugar
3 oz. butter	8 oz. puff pastry
2 eggs	A few currants (optional)
1 tbsp. brandy	

Warm the milk to blood heat, add the salt and rennet and leave to set; when firm, put into a piece of fine muslin and allow to drain overnight.

The next day, rub the curds and butter through a sieve. Whisk the eggs and brandy together and add to the curds, with the almonds and sugar. Line some deep patty tins with the pastry, half-fill with the curd mixture and if desired sprinkle currants over the top. Bake in a hot oven (425°F., mark 7) for 15-20 minutes.

REFRIGERATOR CAKES

PEACH MALLOW CAKE

½ lb. marshmallows
A 1 lb. 4 oz. can of peaches
¼ pint peach juice
¼ pint Madeira or sherry
Boudoir biscuits (about 2 pkts.)
2 cartons of double cream (½ pint)

Line the base of a loaf tin (9 by 5 inches) with waxed paper. Cut the marshmallows in quarters. Strain the juice from the peaches, mix with the Madeira or sherry and place with the marshmallows in a pan. Heat gently, stirring until the marshmallows dissolve, then refrigerate until the mixture cools and thickens slightly. Whip three-quarters of the cream and stir into the mixture. Arrange a layer of biscuits on the bottom of the tin, cover with half the peaches, roughly chopped, and half the marshmallow mixture. Repeat these layers, finishing with one of biscuits. Refrigerate overnight, unmould, decorate as desired and serve with the remaining cream.

PINEAPPLE CAKE

2 oz. butter
6 oz. icing sugar
2 egg yolks
½ pint double cream
A 15-oz. can of pineapple pieces
2 oz. chopped walnuts
12 digestive discuits
½ oz. melted butter
Halved walnuts for decoration

Cream 2 oz. butter and the sugar till light and fluffy; beat in the egg yolks. Whip the cream till thick, leaving about 2 tbsps. on one side for decoration. Drain and chop the pineapple and fold with the chopped nuts into the cream. Crush the digestive biscuits. Line the sides and base of a 7-by-3-inch refrigerator box or cake tin with non-stick paper and brush with melted butter. Sprinkle one-third of the crumbs on the base, add the creamed fat and sugar mixture, cover with half the remaining crumbs. Place the cream, pineapple and nut mixture on this and finally top with the rest of the crumbs.

Chill the cake overnight. Leave at room temperature for 1 hour then turn it out on to a serving dish and decorate with the 2 tbsps. whipped cream and a few halved walnuts.

GINGER LAYER CAKE

1 pint cornflour sauce, flavoured with butterscotch, pineapple or vanilla
½ lb. ginger biscuits
½ oz. gelatine
2 tbsps. water
1 "family" block of vanilla ice cream

Line a 7-inch square cake tin with waxed paper. Make the cornflour sauce. Cover the bottom of the tin with a layer of the biscuits. Dissolve the gelatine in the water by heating it in a small basin over a pan of hot water, add to the sauce, then heat gently, adding the ice cream in small pieces and stirring all the time until it dissolves. Cool until the mixture begins to thicken, then pour a layer of it over the biscuits. Repeat these layers, finishing with one of biscuits. Refrigerate overnight, unmould and serve cut in slices.

The sauce can also be flavoured with 1-2 tbsps. rum, or 1-2 oz. chopped chocolate, walnuts or crystallised ginger can be added just before the sauce is used.

STRAWBERRY CAKE

½ lb. sweet biscuits
4 oz. butter
4 oz. sugar
2 eggs, separated
Grated rind of 1 lemon
½-¾ lb. strawberries
½ pint double cream

Line a 7-inch square cake tin with waxed paper. Crush the biscuits and arrange half of them in the tin. Cream the butter and sugar until very soft and fluffy, beat in the egg yolks and lemon rind and gradually fold in the stiffly whipped egg whites. Spread this mixture over the crumbs. Hull, wash and slice the strawberries (reserving a few whole ones for decoration) and place on top of the lemon mixture. Whip the cream lightly, pour over the strawberries and cover with the remaining crumbs. Refrigerate overnight. Unmould and decorate, or serve cut in squares, surrounded with the remaining strawberries.

LEMON COCONUT SPONGE

1 lemon meringue pie filling
Grated rind of 2 lemons
½ pint double cream
4 oz. desiccated coconut
Two 7-inch sponge cakes
Chocolate vermicelli or other decoration

Make up the lemon meringue pie filling and allow to cool, then fold in the lemon rind, the cream and 2 oz. of the coconut. Sandwich the cakes together with part of the lemon mixture and completely coat with the remainder. Refrigerate overnight and serve sprinkled with the remaining coconut and a little chocolate vermicelli.

As a variation, the cake can be made with an orange pie filling or decorated with glacé cherries and angelica.

CHOCOLATE VELVET REFRIGERATOR CAKE

24-26 soft sponge fingers
6 oz. caster sugar
2 level tbsps. cornflour
¾ pint milk
½ pint double cream (unwhipped)
2 oz. cooking chocolate
2 egg yolks
1 oz. butter
1 level tsp. gelatine
Toasted almonds for decoration

Line a cake or loaf tin measuring 7 by 5 by 2½ inches with a strip of greaseproof paper. Arrange some sponge fingers to cover the base and sides. Blend the sugar and cornflour in a saucepan, then gradually add the milk and ¼ pint of the cream. Break the chocolate up roughly, add to the milk and bring slowly to the boil, stirring all the time. Boil for 3 minutes, by which time the chocolate will have melted. Cool a little.

Beat the egg yolks, pour on half the chocolate mixture and return this to the rest of the chocolate in the pan; boil for 1 minute. Beat in the butter. Dissolve the gelatine in 2 tsps. hot water and stir into the chocolate mixture; cool, stirring occasionally. When the mixture is beginning to thicken, pour half over the sponge fingers. Cover with a second layer of sponge fingers and pour on the remaining mixture. Leave overnight in the refrigerator. Turn out. Whip the rest of the cream lightly, cover the top of the cake and strew with the almonds.

SMALL CAKES

CHOCOLATE CAKES

3 oz. butter	1 level tsp. baking powder
3 oz. sugar	Milk to mix
1 egg	White glacé icing (p. 199)
5 oz. plain flour	Chocolate shavings
1 oz. cocoa	

Cream the fat and sugar and beat in the egg thoroughly. Sift the dry ingredients and add them, with milk to give a soft dropping consistency. Put into paper baking cases and bake in a fairly hot oven (400°F., mark 6) for 20-25 minutes. When the cakes are cold, put a little icing on each and sprinkle with shavings of chocolate.

ROCK BUNS

12 oz. self-raising flour	6 oz. sugar
A pinch of salt	3 oz. currants
¼ level tsp. grated nutmeg	1½ oz. chopped peel
¼ level tsp. mixed spice	1 egg
6 oz. butter or margarine	Milk to mix

Sift the flour, salt and spices. Rub in the fat and add the sugar, fruit and peel. Mix with beaten egg and enough milk to bind. Using a teaspoon and a fork, place in rocky heaps on a greased baking sheet and bake in a fairly hot oven (400°F., mark 6) for 15-20 minutes.

RASPBERRY BUNS

8 oz. self-raising flour	4 oz. sugar
A pinch of salt	Milk to mix
3 oz. butter	Raspberry jam

Sift the flour and salt and rub in the fat. Add the sugar and mix to a stiff dough with milk. Knead lightly, divide in pieces, make a hole in each and add jam. Bake on a greased tin in a fairly hot oven (400°F., mark 6) for 15-20 minutes.

PLAIN COCONUT BUNS

12 oz. self-raising flour	4 oz. desiccated coconut
A pinch of salt	1 egg
6 oz. butter	Milk to mix
6 oz. sugar	

Mix and bake as for Rock Buns; if preferred, make the mixture softer and bake it in patty tins or in paper baking cases.

LEMON OR ORANGE BUNS

8 oz. self-raising flour	Grated rind of 2 lemons
A pinch of salt	1 egg
4 oz. butter	Milk to mix
4 oz. sugar	

Sift the flour and salt. Rub in the fat and add the sugar and lemon rind. Mix with lightly beaten egg and enough milk to give a soft dropping consistency. Put into greased patty tins or small paper cases, and bake for 15-20 minutes in a fairly hot oven (400°F., mark 6), until well-risen and firm to the touch.

To make orange buns, substitute the grated rind of 2 oranges for the lemon rind.

QUEEN CAKES

4 oz. butter	½ level tsp. baking powder
4 oz. sugar	A little milk if necessary
2 eggs	2 oz. sultanas
4 oz. plain flour	

Thoroughly cream the fat and sugar and add the eggs a little at a time, beating well. Fold the sifted flour and baking powder into the mixture, together with a little milk if necessary to give a soft dropping consistency. Add the fruit and place the mixture in spoonfuls in greased patty tins. Bake in a fairly hot oven (375°F., mark 5) for 15-20 minutes, until firm to the touch and golden-brown in colour.

FROSTED CUP CAKES

4 oz. butter	Vanilla essence or a little
3 oz. caster sugar	grated orange or lemon
1 egg	rind
6 oz. self-raising flour	White frosting
Milk to mix	Glacé cherries or nuts

Cream fat and sugar and beat in egg thoroughly. Add the sifted flour and enough cold milk to give a soft dropping consistency; flavour with a few drops of essence or the rind. Put into paper cases standing in patty tins, three-quarters filling the cases, and bake in a fairly hot oven (375°F., mark 5) for about 15 minutes. When cool, remove from the paper cases, dip the top of each cake into white frosting (see below) and decorate with a glacé cherry or a piece of nut.

For the frosting, put ½ lb. granulated sugar and ¼ pint water into a saucepan and heat gently until the sugar has dissolved, then boil to 240°F. Whisk 2 egg whites stiffly in a bowl and pour in the hot syrup in a thin stream, whisking vigorously until the mixture is sufficiently thick.

SWISS TARTS

4 oz. butter	Vanilla essence
1 oz. caster or icing	4 oz. plain flour
sugar	Jam

Cream the fat and sugar together until light and fluffy. Add a few drops of vanilla essence and beat in half the flour, mixing well. Beat in the remaining flour and continue beating until the mixture is well blended. Using a large star pipe, force the mixture into paper cases; start at the centre and pipe with a spiral motion round the sides, leaving a shallow depression in the centre. Place on a baking sheet and bake in a fairly hot oven (375°F., mark 5) for about 30 minutes. Fill the centres with jam.

SPONGE FINGERS

2 eggs	2 oz. plain flour
2 oz. caster sugar	Caster sugar to dredge

Whisk the eggs and sugar together until thick and creamy, then fold in the flour. Grease and flour some sponge finger tins. Put the mixture into a forcing bag with a plain ½-inch nozzle and pipe it into the tins, sprinkle the top of each finger with a little sugar and bake in a fairly hot oven (400°F., mark 6) for 7-10 minutes.

When cold, the top of each finger may be iced with glacé icing and sprinkled with hundreds and thousands. Alternatively, sandwich them together in pairs with butter icing, and dip the ends into melted chocolate.

COCONUT CAKES

(see picture above)

3 oz. self-raising flour	1 oz. desiccated coconut
2 oz. butter or mar- garine	Milk to mix
	Glacé icing (p. 199)
2 oz. caster sugar	Coconut and glacé
1 beaten egg	cherries to decorate

Sift the flour on to a plate. Cream the fat and sugar until light and fluffy, then beat in the egg a little at a time. Fold in the flour and coconut, adding enough milk to form a dropping consistency. Spoon the mixture into greased bun tins. Bake in a fairly hot oven (375°F., mark 5) for 15 minutes. When the cakes are quite cold, coat the tops with glacé icing and sprinkle generously with coconut. Decorate with halved glacé cherries.

COCONUT TARTS

4 oz. plain flour	1 level tsp. caster sugar
A pinch of salt	1 egg yolk
2 oz. butter	Raspberry jam

For the Filling

2 oz. margarine	2 oz. desiccated coconut
2 oz. caster sugar	1 oz. self-raising flour
beaten egg	

Prepare 16-18 patty tins. Sift the flour and salt into a basin, rub in the fat lightly and stir in the sugar. Mix in the egg yolk and sufficient cold water to mix to a firm dough. Turn on to a floured board and knead lightly. Roll out this pastry and cut out rounds large enough to fit the patty tins. Line the tins and put a little jam into each.

For the filling, cream the fat and sugar together until light and fluffy. Beat in half the egg a little at a time. Fold in the coconut and flour, then add the remaining egg to give a soft dropping consistency. Place in spoonfuls in the lined patty tins and bake in a fairly hot oven (375°F., mark 5) for 20 minutes.

To make a Coconut Flan, use the same amounts of pastry and filling, place in a 7-inch flan ring and bake for about ½ hour.

MACAROONS

(see picture above)

2 egg whites	8 oz. caster sugar
4 oz. ground almonds	1 tsp. orange-flower water
1 oz. ground rice (good measure)	Rice paper

To Decorate

Split almonds and glacé cherries	A little egg white

Beat the egg whites lightly with a fork. Stir in the almonds, ground rice, sugar and flavouring and mix thoroughly. Cover a greased baking sheet with rice paper and place the mixture on it in small heaps (or pipe with a nylon forcing bag and large plain pipe), leaving room for spreading. Place an almond or piece of cherry on each biscuit, brush with egg white and bake in a warm oven (325°F., mark 3) for about 20-25 minutes, until pale golden-brown. It is important to cook macaroons slowly, so that they colour evenly and acquire a good texture.

ALMOND FINGERS

4 oz. plain flour	1 level tsp. caster sugar
A pinch of salt	1 egg yolk and cold water
2 oz. butter	to mix

For the Filling

1 egg white	4 oz. blanched and
4 oz. icing sugar	chopped almonds

Sift the flour and salt into a basin and rub in the fat lightly. Mix in the sugar and add the egg yolk and sufficient cold water to mix to a firm dough. Turn on to a floured board and knead lightly. Use this pastry to line a tin measuring approx. 10 by 5 inches. Make the filling by whisking the egg white until stiff, then folding in the sifted icing sugar. Spread this mixture over the pastry base and sprinkle the chopped nuts evenly on top. Bake in a moderate oven (350°F., mark 4) for about 30 minutes. When cold, cut into fingers.

GINGER AND DATE CAKES

6 oz. self-raising flour	2-3 oz. chopped dates
A pinch of salt	1 oz. crystallised ginger
3 oz. margarine	1 beaten egg
3 oz. sugar	Milk to mix

Sift the flour and salt into a bowl and rub in the fat lightly. Stir in the sugar, dates and ginger, then mix in the egg and sufficient milk to form a stiff dropping consistency. Place in spoonfuls in greased patty tins and bake in a fairly hot oven (375°F., mark 5) for 15 minutes.

DOUGHNUTS
(see picture above)

½ lb. flour	3-4 tbsps. warm milk
A pinch of salt	1 egg, beaten
2 oz. butter	Jam
½ oz. yeast	Deep fat for frying
Caster sugar	Cinnamon (optional)

Warm the sifted flour and salt in a basin and rub in the butter. Cream the yeast with 1 tsp. sugar and add to it the milk and egg. Pour into the centre of the flour and mix to a soft dough. Beat well with a wooden spoon or the hand and leave to rise until the dough becomes twice the original size, then knead lightly. Divide into small pieces, shape each into a ball, flatten a little and place about ¼ tsp. jam in the centre of each. Gather the edges together over the jam, forming balls. Place on a greased and floured tin and leave in a warm place for a few minutes to prove. Heat the fat until smoking faintly but not too hot, then fry the doughnuts until golden-brown and cooked through (about 5 minutes). Drain, turn out on to a paper and dredge with caster sugar—which can be mixed, if desired, with a little ground cinnamon. Serve very fresh.

BUTTERFLY CAKES

6 oz. self-raising flour	4 oz. caster sugar
4 oz. margarine	2 beaten eggs

For the Filling

4 oz. butter	Almond essence
6 oz. icing sugar	

Sift the flour. Cream the fat and sugar until light and fluffy, then beat in the eggs a little at a time. Fold in flour to give a stiff dropping consistency. Place in spoonfuls in patty cases and bake in a fairly hot oven (375°F., mark 5) for 15-20 minutes.
For the filling, cream the butter until soft, beat in the sifted sugar gradually and add a few drops of essence. When the cakes are quite cold, cut a slice from the top of each and pipe or fork in a generous amount of filling. Cut each cake slice in half and replace at an angle in the cream, to represent the butterfly's wings.

MINCEMEAT SLICES
(see picture above)

8 oz. self-raising flour	1 egg
4 oz. butter or margarine	Milk to mix
	Mincemeat
4 oz. caster sugar	Brown sugar

Sift the flour into a bowl and rub in the fat lightly. Stir in the caster sugar. Mix in the egg and add sufficient milk to make a soft dough. Turn the mixture out on to a floured board, divide into 2 pieces and roll out each piece to an oblong 6 by 8 inches. Lift one piece on to a greased baking sheet, spread with mincemeat, place the other piece on top and press down firmly. Brush the top with milk and sprinkle thickly with brown sugar. Bake in a fairly hot oven (375°F., mark 5) for 15 minutes. When cool, cut into about a dozen 2-inch squares.

QUICK CAKES

If guests arrive at a time when you have no cakes to offer them, use a plain cake mix and add a variation of your own for a quickly made result. A cake mix intended to give one large cake will equally well make 24 small cakes if the mixture is mixed to a slightly stiffer consistency, spooned into patty cases and baked in a fairly hot oven (375°F., mark 5) for 15-20 minutes.

Fruit Buns: Add 2 oz. mixed dried fruit.
Chocolate Buns: Add 2 oz. chopped up plain chocolate to the dry ingredients.
Coffee Buns: Add 1 tbsp. instant coffee powder.
Cherry Buns: Add 4 oz. glacé cherries cut in half, washed and rolled in flour.
Orange Buns: Add the finely grated rind of 1 orange to dry ingredients; use the juice to replace some of the water

SMALL CAKES FOR PARTIES

MADELEINES

(see colour picture no. 45)

4 oz. butter	Red jam
4 oz. sugar	Desiccated coconut
2 eggs	Glacé cherries and angelica
4 oz. self-raising flour	

Beat the fat and sugar to a white cream and gradually add the beaten eggs, beating well. Fold in the flour. Grease 12 dariole moulds and three-parts fill with mixture. Bake in a moderate oven (350°F., mark 4) for about 20 minutes, or until firm and browned. Trim off the bottoms, so that the cakes stand firmly and are of even height. When the cakes are nearly cold, brush with melted jam, holding them on a skewer, then roll them in coconut. On top of each madeleine place a cherry dipped in a little jam, then add 2 small leaves cut from angelica.

PASTRIES

Although strictly speaking not "cakes", dainty fancy pastries are often served with party-type small cakes. Some recipes are given here and others appear on the next two pages.

CREAM HORNS

(see colour picture no. 45)

Roll out thinly some flaky or puff pastry into an oblong about 12 inches long and cut into ½-inch strips. Moisten one edge of each strip and roll round a cream horn tin, starting at the pointed end of the tin and overlapping the pastry very slightly. Bake in a very hot oven (450°F., mark 8) until crisp—10-15 minutes. Slip off the tins and when cold, fill with a spoonful of jam or fruit, top with whipped cream and dredge with icing sugar.

MACAROON PASTRIES

oz. rich shortcrust	1 oz. plain flour
am	5 oz. caster sugar
oz. ground almonds	2 egg whites

Line boat-shaped tins with the rich shortcrust pastry and add a little jam. Mix the almonds, flour and sugar; whisk the eggs very lightly and fold in the dry ingredients. Place a little mixture in each case and put strips of pastry across some. Bake in a fairly hot oven (375°F., mark 5) for 20 minutes, till the pastry and the macaroon mixture are golden.

ALMOND CROSS PASTRIES

Roll some rich shortcrust pastry out to ⅛ inch in thickness and cut into rounds with a 2-inch fluted cutter. Put a spoonful of the almond mixture given above in the centre and arrange 2 narrow strips of pastry on the top to form a cross. Brush with egg and bake in a fairly hot oven 375°F., mark 5) for about 15 minutes.

ALMOND SANDWICH PASTRIES

Roll out rich shortcrust pastry very thinly and cut into small rounds. Sandwich the biscuits in pairs with the above almond mixture and bake in a fairly hot oven (375°F., mark 5) for 15 minutes. When cold, coat the tops with white glacé icing (p. 199) and pipe stars in coffee butter cream (p. 199) round the sides. Decorate edges with browned chopped almonds.

MERINGUES

(see colour picture no. 45)

2 egg whites	2 oz. caster sugar
2 oz. granulated sugar	¼ pint whipped cream

Rub a trace of olive oil over the surface of a really clean baking sheet, or cover it with very lightly oiled grease-proof paper. Whisk the egg whites very stiffly, add granulated sugar and whisk again until the mixture retains its former stiffness. Lastly, fold in caster sugar very lightly, using a metal spoon. Pipe through a forcing bag (or put in spoonfuls) on to the baking sheet and dry off in a very cool oven (250°F., mark ¼) for several hours, until the meringues are firm and crisp but still white. When cool, sandwich together with cream.

Pink meringues can be made by adding 1-2 drops of red colouring to the mixture with the sugar.

Coffee essence can be added when the sugar is folded in; allow 1 tsp. to each egg white.

Chocolate meringues can be made by adding cocoa with the caster sugar—allow 1 level tsp. per egg white.

The cream filling can be varied by adding finely chopped nuts (see the colour picture), coffee essence, melted chocolate or liqueur.

PETITS FOURS

Bake a shallow square or oblong of Victoria or Genoese sponge (see Layer and Sponge Cakes, pp. 173 and 175). This can then be used as the base for many small fancy cakes—for example:

1. Cut it into fancy shapes, glaze completely with sieved apricot jam and allow to dry. Stand the cakes on a wire cooling tray and pour over them glacé icing (p. 199) which has been coloured or flavoured with a fruit essence, coffee, lemon or orange juice or melted chocolate. When the icing is set, decorate with cut glacé cherry and angelica, chopped nuts, mimosa balls, crystallised flowers, etc. or piped butter cream.

2. Cut cake into small squares and coat with sieved apricot jam. Roll the sides in chopped walnuts and pipe stars of coffee butter cream (p. 199) round the top edges. Heat 2 oz. sugar in a saucepan until melted and golden-brown, allow to cool slightly, then pour a little in the centre of each cake.

3. Coat some small rounds of cake with butter cream (p. 199) and roll the sides in chopped walnuts, or coat with raspberry jam and roll the sides in desiccated coco-nut. Colour some almond paste pale green or pink, roll it out and cut into small petal shapes, allowing 5 for each cake. Arrange the petals on top of each cake and mark the centre of the flower with a mimosa ball. *(See colour picture no. 45.)*

4. Cut a long strip of cake, brush with apricot jam and place 3 small rolls of coloured almond paste along the top. Brush these with jam, then coat completely with glacé icing and decorate if desired with chopped nuts, angelica or glacé cherries. When set, cut up and serve in paper cases.

ALMOND JAP CAKES

(see picture above)

2 egg whites	Vanilla butter cream
A small pinch of cream	(p. 199)
of tartar	Chocolate glacé icing
8 oz. caster sugar	(p. 199)
4 oz. ground almonds	

Whisk the egg whites and cream of tartar until very stiff, then whisk in 4 oz. sugar. Mix together the remaining 4 oz. sugar and the ground almonds and blend into the meringue mixture, using a spoon. Spread the mixture evenly on to well greased and floured baking trays, making it about $\frac{1}{4}$ inch thick and smoothing it down with a palette knife, then bake it in a warm oven (325°F., mark 3) for about 30 minutes. Cut into round cakes with a 2-inch plain cutter while the mixture is still soft. When they are cool, sandwich them together with butter cream, spread butter cream round the sides and top and roll the sides in the crushed cake trimmings. Make a dip in the centre of each cake with the finger and put a little glacé icing in this hollow.

CHAMONIX

2-egg meringue mixture	Vanilla essence
An 8-oz. can of chestnut	$\frac{1}{4}$ pint whipped cream
purée	Grated chocolate
Caster sugar	

Make a mixture as for meringues, p. 191; pipe in small rounds on to a baking sheet and dry out in a very cool oven (250°F., mark $\frac{1}{4}$). Using a plain small pipe, pipe on to each meringue a swirl of chestnut purée (sweetened to taste and flavoured with vanilla essence). Fill the centres with a small blob of whipped cream and dust with grated chocolate.

PETITES FEUILLETÉES

Puff or flaky pastry	Chopped nuts
Egg white	Whipped cream
Sieved apricot jam	

Roll the pastry thinly and cut into 3-inch squares. Fold the corners to the centre and join them with a tiny cut-out shape of pastry. Brush with white of egg and bake in a very hot oven (450°F., mark 8) for 10-15 minutes. When cool brush with jam, sprinkle with nuts and pipe with cream.

CHOCOLATE CASES

(see picture above and colour picture no. 50)

6 oz. plain block chocolate	Sherry to taste
4 oz. sponge cake	$\frac{1}{4}$ pint double cream
1 tbsp. raspberry jam	Maraschino cherries

Line 8 small paper cases with melted chocolate and leave to set overnight. Peel off the paper carefully. Mix together the crumbled cake, jam and sherry and fill the cases with this mixture. Top each with whipped cream and a cherry.

PETITS GÂTEAUX MILLEFEUILLES

6 oz. puff or rough puff	Apricot or raspberry jam
pastry	$\frac{1}{4}$ pint double cream
Beaten egg	Chopped nuts

Prepare the pastry and roll it out $\frac{1}{8}$ inch thick. Prick and cut into small rounds, using a 2-inch plain cutter. Brush the top with beaten egg and bake in a very hot oven (450°F., mark 8) for about 8 minutes, until crisp and golden-brown. Cool, then sandwich 3 layers of pastry together with sieved jam and whipped cream. Brush the top with jam, add a cream rosette and sprinkle with nuts.

ALMOND FLOWER PASTRIES

Roll some puff or flaky pastry out to about $\frac{1}{4}$ inch in thickness and cut out, using a small plain, round cutter. Put the rounds on to a baking tin, brush the tops over with a little beaten egg and bake in a very hot oven (450°F., mark 8) for 10-15 minutes. When the pastries are quite cold, put a little blackcurrant jelly on top of each and arrange some whole or halved blanched almonds round the top to resemble flower petals.

COCONUT PYRAMIDS

Whisk 2 egg whites stiffly and fold in 5 oz. sugar and 5 oz. desiccated coconut. Pile in small pyramids on a greased tin covered with rice paper, press into shape and bake in a very cool oven (275°F., mark $\frac{1}{2}$) till pale fawn for about $\frac{3}{4}$-1 hour. If desired, tint pink or green before baking.

47. Party Salads; Ham Potato Salad; Pork Cheese; Veal, Ham and
Tongue Mould

48. Meringue Pyramid for a party

49. Party Savarin à la Pompadour

50. Buffet Party: Scampi; Ham and Asparagus Mould; Meat Platter;
Savoury Horns; Cheese Dartois; Sandwiches; Lemon Soufflé; Fruit
Salad; Caramel Nut Gâteau; Chocolate Cases

51. Party Charlotte Russe

52. Party Cakes: Brandy Snaps; Nut Rocks; Devil's Food Cake; Eclairs;
Chocolate Truffles

53. Liqueur Coffee for a party

PALMIERS

(see picture above)

Roll some puff pastry out evenly, until it is $\frac{1}{4}$ inch thick and about 20 inches long, then sprinkle it thoroughly with caster sugar. Fold the ends over to the centre until they meet and press with the rolling pin. Sprinkle thoroughly with sugar and fold the sides to the centre again. Press and sprinkle with sugar. Place the two folded portions together and press; then, with a sharp knife, cut into $\frac{1}{4}$-inch slices. Place cut edge down on a baking sheet, allowing room to spread, sprinkle with caster sugar and bake in a very hot oven (450°F., mark 8) until golden-brown. Cool on a rack and just before serving spread sweetened whipped cream on half of the slices, sandwich with the remaining ones and dredge with icing sugar. (If liked, use jam with the cream.)

CHOCOLATE TRUFFLES

(see colour picture no. 52)

4 oz. stale cake or cake trimmings	Rum
4 oz. caster sugar	Chocolate glacé icing (p. 199) or covering
4 oz. ground almonds	chocolate
Apricot jam	Chocolate vermicelli

Crumble the cake finely and add the caster sugar, ground almonds and enough hot sieved apricot jam to bind. Add rum (or flavouring essence) to taste. Shape the mixture into 12-18 small balls and leave to become firm. Dip each ball into the glacé icing or covering chocolate and roll in chocolate vermicelli. When dry, put into small paper cases.

LANGUES DE CHAT

2 oz. butter	Caster sugar to dredge
2 oz. sugar	Chocolate glacé icing to
1 egg	decorate (p. 199)
2 oz. self-raising flour	

Cream the fat and sugar and beat in the egg. Work in flour to make a mixture of a consistency suitable for piping. Put in a forcing bag fitted with a plain $\frac{1}{4}$-inch piping nozzle and force on to a greased tin in fingers about 2$\frac{1}{2}$-3 inches long, spaced widely apart. Dredge with caster sugar and bake in a hot oven (425°F., mark 7)

for about 5 minutes. When the fingers are cold, sandwich them together in pairs with chocolate icing, and dip the ends of each in some more of the icing.

ECLAIRS

(see picture above and colour picture no. 52)

1$\frac{1}{2}$ oz. butter	2$\frac{1}{2}$ oz. plain flour
$\frac{1}{4}$ pint water	2 eggs

Place the butter and water in a pan and bring to the boil. Remove the pan from the heat, stir in the flour, then beat until the paste forms a ball in the middle of the pan. Leave to cool very slightly whilst beating the eggs. Add these gradually to the mixture, beating lightly after each addition; use sufficient egg to give a mixture of piping consistency which will just hold its shape.

The paste is now ready for shaping. Put it into a forcing bag with a plain round pipe of $\frac{1}{2}$-inch diameter and force in finger lengths (3$\frac{1}{2}$-4 inches long) on to a greased baking sheet, keeping the lengths very even. Bake in a fairly hot oven (400°F., mark 6) for about 35 minutes, until well risen, crisp and of a golden-brown colour. Remove from the tin, slit down the sides with a sharp-pointed knife to allow the steam to escape and leave on a cake rack to cool. When the éclairs are cold, fill with whipped cream or flavoured custard and ice the tops with a little chocolate or coffee glacé icing (p. 199).

Cream Puffs

Pipe the paste in small balls on to a baking sheet and bake as for éclairs until risen and golden. Split and cool on a rack. When cold, fill with whipped cream, glaze the tops with sieved apricot jam and sprinkle with chopped walnuts.

NUT FRUIT CLUSTERS

2 oz. grated chocolate	1 oz. chopped seeded
$\frac{1}{2}$ oz. butter	raisins
1 oz. chopped nuts	Cornflakes

Melt the grated chocolate and then add the fat, nuts and dried fruit and sufficient cornflakes to make into a mixture which will bind together. Put in small rough clusters on to waxed paper and leave in a cool place to harden. Serve in little paper cases.

As a variation, replace the raisins by cut-up glacé cherries or chopped crystallised ginger.

BISCUITS AND COOKIES

VANILLA BISCUITS

6 oz. plain flour
A pinch of salt
3 oz. butter
3 oz. caster sugar

1 egg
A few drops of vanilla
essence
Milk to mix

Sift the flour and salt. Cream the fat and sugar and when light and fluffy, beat in the egg. Add the essence, stir in the flour and mix to a stiff paste with milk. Roll the dough out $\frac{1}{8}$ inch thick on a lightly floured board, prick and then, using fancy cutters, shape into biscuits and put on a greased baking tin. Bake in a moderate oven (350°F., mark 4) for 10-15 minutes, till golden. (These quantities make about 24 biscuits.)

CHERRY RINGS

Add 1½ oz. chopped glacé cherries to above mixture, and keep ½ oz. for decoration. Roll out dough as above, then, using a round fluted cutter, cut it into rounds. Remove the centres with a small cutter, halve the cut-out pieces and decorate the rings with these; bake as above. (About 30 biscuits.)

SULTANA PINWHEELS

Cut some Vanilla Biscuit dough into 2-inch diamonds. Fold over one point of each diamond, then put three diamonds together, damping the joins to make them hold, and press a few sultanas into the centre. Bake as for Vanilla Biscuits. (Makes 12 to 14 biscuits.)

CHOCOLATE CREAM SANDWICHES

Follow the Vanilla Biscuit recipe, but substitute 1 oz. cocoa for 1 oz. of the flour. Roll the dough out, prick, cut into fingers about 1½ by 3 inches and put on a greased baking tray. Bake as above for 10-12 minutes. When cool, sandwich together with vanilla butter cream (p. 199). (About 12 biscuits.)

CHOCOLATE WALNUTS

Make some chocolate dough as directed in the above recipe and break off pieces the size of a walnut. Roll into balls, put on a greased baking tray, press half a walnut on each and bake as above for 15-20 minutes. (Makes about 30 biscuits.)

GINGER BISCUITS
(see left-hand picture below)

4 oz. butter or lard
4 tbsps. golden syrup
4 oz. sugar
10 oz. plain flour
2-3 level tsps. ground
ginger

1 level tsp. bicarbonate
of soda
White glacé icing
Preserved ginger and
blanched almonds

Warm the fat, syrup and sugar slightly and beat to a cream. Add the flour, ginger and bicarbonate of soda and mix to a stiff dough. Roll out thinly and cut into rounds, place on a greased tray and bake in a fairly hot oven (375°F., mark 5) for 15-20 minutes. Allow the biscuits to cool slightly before lifting them off the tin. When they are cold, decorate some of the biscuits with glacé icing and triangles of preserved ginger and others with split almonds. (About 30 biscuits.)

SHORTBREAD
(see right-hand picture below)

6 oz. plain flour
2 oz. caster sugar

4 oz. butter

Sift the flour and sugar, work in the fat and continue kneading until the mixture binds together. Divide into two, shape into rounds and smooth the top lightly with a rolling pin. Crimp the edges with the finger and thumb, mark each round into 8 sections with a knife and prick the surface, then place on a greased baking tin and if desired, decorate with halved glacé cherries. Bake in a cool oven (300°F., mark 2) for 40-60 minutes.
If you have a shortbread mould, flour it well, press the dough in, invert on to the baking tin and bake. (See colour picture no. 41.)

SHORTBREAD FINGERS
(see picture below and colour picture no. 41)

Roll the shortbread dough out on a board into an oblong about 3 inches wide and ½ inch thick. Score across with a knife or prick with a fork, then cut into about 30 fingers. Put on a greased tin and bake in a cool oven (300°F., mark 1) for 20-30 minutes, until lightly browned.

SPICY BISCUITS

CLOVER LEAF COOKIES
(see left-hand picture below)

2 oz. butter	A few caraway seeds
2 oz. caster sugar	$\frac{1}{2}$ level tsp. ground ginger
$\frac{1}{2}$ an egg	$\frac{1}{2}$ level tsp. grated lemon
4 oz. plain flour	rind

Cream the butter and sugar together and beat in the egg. Gradually add the sifted flour and knead well. Divide into three portions and work a different flavouring into each. Divide the three mixtures into small even-sized pieces and roll these into balls. Group one ball of each flavour together, placing them on a greased baking tray, and press flat with a palette knife to form the clover leaf shape. Bake in a fairly hot oven (400°F., mark 6) for 10-15 minutes. Cool on a wire tray. (About 15 biscuits.)

PEANUT BUTTER COOKIES
(see left-hand picture below)

2 oz. fat	4 oz. plain flour
2 oz. peanut butter	A pinch of salt
2 oz. caster sugar	1 level tsp. baking
2 oz. brown sugar	powder
$\frac{1}{2}$ an egg	Silver balls or walnuts to
1 level tsp. ground	decorate
ginger	

Cream the fat and sugars together and beat in the egg. Add the sifted dry ingredients and mix well. Shape the dough into balls about $\frac{3}{4}$ inch in diameter, place on a greased baking tray and press flat with a fork. Decorate some with silver balls or walnuts and leave the rest plain. Bake in a fairly hot oven (400°F., mark 6) for 12-15 minutes. (About 12 biscuits.)

CINNAMON TWISTS
(see right-hand picture below)

4 oz. butter	1 level tsp. ground
4 oz. caster sugar	cinnamon
2 egg whites	4 oz. plain flour

Beat the butter and sugar together until light, then beat in the egg whites a little at a time, to form a smooth, light batter. Add the cinnamon and finally fold in the sifted flour. Using a $\frac{1}{4}$-inch tube, pipe the mixture into strips about 7 inches long on to a greased baking tray, keeping them well apart, as they spread a good deal. Bake in a fairly hot oven (400°F., mark 6) for 7-10 minutes. (The edges of these biscuits are very thin and rapidly turn golden-brown while the centre part still remains white.) As soon as the biscuits are removed from the oven, twist them into curly shapes and place on a rack. (About 40 biscuits.)

CINNAMON BARS
(see right-hand picture below)

4 oz. fat	2 level tsps. ground
3 oz. sugar	cinnamon
$\frac{1}{2}$ an egg	Chopped nuts to
5 oz. plain flour	decorate
A pinch of salt	

Cream the fat and sugar together until white and fluffy. Beat in the egg, reserving a little of the white for glazing the biscuits. Sift the dry ingredients and gradually add to the creamed mixture. Press the dough into an oblong tin about 8 by 6 inches, brush the surface with egg white and sprinkle with chopped nuts. Bake in a warm oven (325°F., mark 3) for 1 hour. Cut into slices and allow to cool in the tin, then place them on a wire tray and allow to become quite cold before storing. (Makes about 12 biscuits.)

GINGERNUTS

6 oz. plain flour	2 oz. butter or mar-
A pinch of salt	garine
1 level tbsp. ground ginger	4 oz. brown sugar
1 level tsp. mixed spice	Syrup to mix (approx.
1 level tsp. ground	1 tbsp.)
cinnamon	

Sift the flour, salt and spices together. Cream the fat and sugar and stir in the dry ingredients alternately with the syrup (which may be warmed very slightly in order to make the mixing easier); the mixture should make a fairly stiff paste. Roll into balls the size of a walnut, place on a greased baking tin and flatten slightly. Bake in a fairly hot oven (375°F., mark 5) until browned and crisp—about 20 minutes. (Makes 20-24 biscuits.)

RICH PARTY BISCUITS

BRANDY SNAPS
(see colour picture no. 52)

2 oz. butter or margarine	¼ level tsp. ground ginger
2 oz. sugar	1 tsp. brandy or rum essence
2 tbsps. golden syrup	¼ level tsp. grated lemon
2 oz. plain flour	rind

Melt the fat, sugar and syrup in a pan. Remove from the heat, add the other ingredients and stir until well mixed. Drop the mixture in teaspoonfuls on a greased baking tray, 2 inches apart, and bake in a moderate oven (350°F., mark 4) for 7-10 minutes, until just golden-brown. While they are baking, grease 2-3 wooden spoon handles, and get a wire cooling rack ready. Stand the tray on top of the stove, so that biscuits cool without becoming too hard. Using a palette knife, remove the biscuits from the tray and roll them round the spoon handles. When they are quite cold, slip off carefully. If the last biscuits are too hard to get off the tray, place them over gentle heat for a minute. The secret of making good brandy snaps is to keep them warm enough to handle. When the rolled biscuits are cold, pipe or fill them with whipped cream (see p. 158). (These quantities will make about 18 biscuits.)

CHOCOLATE LOGS

4 oz. plain flour	½ tsp. vanilla essence
A pinch of salt	Milk to mix
3 oz. butter	2 oz. chocolate butter
1 oz. sugar	cream (p. 199)
2 oz. chocolate powder	Icing sugar

Sift the flour and salt and rub in fat with the finger-tips. Add the sugar, chocolate powder and essence, bind to-together with a little milk and put the dough on a lightly floured board. Shape into a long roll 1 inch in diameter, then cut into 2-inch lengths. Bake on a greased baking tray in a fairly hot oven (375°F., mark 5) for 20-30 minutes. When cold, cover with the butter cream, mark with a fork to look like logs and finally dust with icing sugar. (Makes about 12 biscuits.)

LEMON FINGERS

4 oz. butter	8 oz. flour
4 oz. caster sugar	Lemon butter cream (p. 199)
1 egg	Caster or icing sugar
Grated rind of ½ a lemon	to dredge

Cream the butter and sugar together and beat in the egg and lemon rind, then gradually add the flour. Pipe the mixture in finger lengths on to greased baking trays, using a large star nozzle. Bake in a fairly hot oven (375°F., mark 5) for 15-20 minutes, or until golden-brown, and cool on a wire tray. Sandwich together in pairs with butter cream and dredge with either caster or icing sugar or dip the ends in melted chocolate. (About 12 biscuits.)

NUT ROCKS
(see colour picture no. 52)

4½ oz. icing sugar	3 oz. shredded blanched
2 egg whites	almonds or finely
Almond or vanilla flavouring	chopped walnut halves

Put the sifted icing sugar with the egg whites into a mixing bowl. Stand this over a saucepan half-filled with boiling water and whisk the mixture until it clings stiffly to the whisk. Add the flavouring and nuts and put in teaspoonfuls on a greased and floured tin. Bake in a cool oven (300°F., mark 2) for 20-30 minutes until crisp outside, soft inside and hardly coloured.

MARSHMALLOW CREAMS

6 oz. flour	Milk to mix
A pinch of salt	1 tbsp. golden syrup
3 oz. butter	Colouring and flavouring
3 oz. caster sugar	Jam
1 egg, separated	Nuts or glacé cherries

Sift the flour and salt and cream the fat and sugar until light and fluffy. Beat in the egg yolk, add the dry ingredients and stir in enough milk to give a soft dough. Turn out on to a floured board, roll and cut into 1½-inch rounds with a scone cutter. Place on a greased baking tray, prick, and bake in a moderate oven (350°F., mark 4) for 10-15 minutes. Allow to cool and meanwhile make mock marshmallow as follows: Whisk up the egg white and syrup over hot water until thick, fluffy and quite stiff; colour and flavour if desired (e.g., with ¼-½ tsp. coffee essence). Sandwich the biscuits together with jam and coat the tops with marshmallow, roughing it up if desired. Decorate, using halved walnuts on the biscuits topped with coffee-flavoured marshmallow. (Makes about 12 biscuits.)

MERINGUE TOPS

2 oz. butter	3 oz. plain flour
4 oz. caster sugar	1 oz. chocolate powder
A few drops of vanilla essence	A pinch of salt
1 egg, separated	Butter cream or apricot jam

Cream the fat and 2 oz. sugar with essence until quite soft. Whisk the egg yolk and lightly beat it into the creamed mixture. Sift the flour, chocolate powder and salt, add and stir in till mixture binds together; knead on a lightly floured board and roll out to ⅛ inch thick. Cut with a small fancy cutter, put on a greased baking tray and bake in a fairly hot oven (400°F., mark 6) for 5-7 minutes. Whisk the egg white and 1 oz. sugar until very stiff, then fold in the remaining sugar. Put the meringue mixture into a forcing bag fitted with a star pipe and pipe in rosettes on to an oiled baking tray. Bake in a cool oven (300°F., mark 1) for 40-60 minutes, or until firm but not coloured. When both biscuits and meringues are cold, join a meringue to each biscuit with a little butter cream or apricot jam. (Makes about 24 biscuits.)

PINEAPPLE FINGERS

4 oz. butter	2 oz. custard powder
4 oz. sugar	7-8 squares of glacé
1 egg yolk	pineapple
6 oz. plain flour	White glacé icing (p. 199)

Cream the fat and sugar very thoroughly, beat in the egg yolk, then stir in the flour and custard powder. Chop 4-5 squares of pineapple and add, mixing well together. Turn on to a lightly floured board, roll out ¼ inch thick, cut into fingers and place on a greased baking tray. Bake in a fairly hot oven (400°F., mark 6) for 10-12 minutes, cool, then coat with icing. Slice the remaining pineapple and decorate the biscuits with it. (Makes about 24 biscuits.)

CHOCOLATE COCONUT GEMS
(see picture above)

1 egg white	4 oz. desiccated coconut
1 tsp. lemon juice	Rice paper
4 oz. caster sugar	2 oz. plain chocolate

Whisk the egg white in a clean basin until very stiff. Add the lemon juice and sugar and again whisk until stiff. Stir in the coconut. Cover some baking sheets with rice paper. Take a little of the mixture at a time and pinch together to form small balls; lay these on the prepared tins and bake in a very cool oven (275°F., mark ½) until firm—about 1½ hours.
Put the broken-up chocolate into a basin which is standing in a pan of hot water and heat gently until the chocolate melts, then dip the base of each biscuit in it. Place on a wire tray to set. (Makes about 12.)

CHOCOLATE COOKIES

4 oz. self-raising flour	A pinch of salt
1 oz. sweetened chocolate powder	4 oz. butter
	2 oz. caster sugar

For the Filling

1 oz. sweetened chocolate powder	3 tbsps. black coffee
	2 oz. butter

Sift the flour, chocolate powder and salt on to a plate. Cream the butter and sugar and stir in the flour mixture. Form into balls the size of a walnut and place well apart on a greased baking sheet; flatten with a wet fork. Bake in a moderate oven (350°F., mark 4) for 15 minutes. Allow to cool before lifting on to a cooling rack.
Mix the chocolate powder and coffee for the filling in a small saucepan and heat gently until they form a thick cream. Cool slightly and beat in the butter. Sandwich the biscuits together with this cream and dust with icing sugar. (Makes about 9.)

COCONUT KISSES

½ cup condensed milk	A pinch of salt
A few drops of vanilla essence	4-6 oz. shredded coconut

Mix the milk, essence and salt and work in the coconut till the mixture binds together. Put in teaspoonfuls on a greased tin and bake for 10 minutes in a moderate oven 350°F., mark 4). (About 18 biscuits.)

MELTING MOMENTS

4 oz. butter or margarine	Vanilla essence
3 oz. sugar	5 oz. self-raising flour
½ an egg	Crushed cornflakes

Cream the fat and sugar and beat in the egg and a few drops of essence. Work in the flour and mix to a stiff dough. Wet the hands, divide the mixture into small portions and roll into balls. Roll these in cornflakes, put on a greased baking sheet and bake in a fairly hot oven (375°F., mark 5) for 15-20 minutes. (Makes about 24 biscuits.)

TIGER BISCUITS
(see picture above)

3 oz. butter	Butter cream (p. 199)
4 oz. plain flour	Sieved apricot jam
1-2 oz. sugar	Finely chopped walnuts
A very little water	

Rub the butter into the flour and sugar and mix to a stiff paste with a very little water, if needed. Roll out, cut into rounds, lay these on a greased baking sheet and bake in a warm oven (325°F., mark 3) for about 20 minutes, then cool. Sandwich together with butter cream (this may, if desired, be flavoured with coffee); brush the top and sides with sieved jam and roll the biscuits in chopped walnuts to coat the sides. (Makes 8-10.)

CHOCOLATE WHIRLS

4 oz. butter or margarine	½ oz. cocoa
4 oz. caster sugar	Milk to mix
1 egg yolk	Melted chocolate or chocolate glacé icing (p. 199)
3½ oz. self-raising flour	Lemon glacé icing (p. 199) or desiccated coconut to decorate
4 oz. custard powder	

Cream the butter and sugar and beat in the egg yolk. Mix in the dry ingredients, with enough milk to give a fairly stiff dough, then knead lightly on a floured board and roll out. Cut out about 24 rounds, remove the centres with a small cutter and place the rings on a greased tin. Prick, then bake in a fairly hot oven (400°F., mark 6) for about 15 minutes. When the biscuits are cold, coat with melted chocolate or chocolate icing (p. 199), swirling it with a fork, and decorate as desired.

REFRIGERATOR COOKIES

If you can use a refrigerator when making cookies, richer mixtures can be used than one can handle when making biscuits or cookies in the ordinary way; also the dough can be rolled out very thinly, so making deliciously thin, crisp cookies. Another advantage is that the mixture can be made up two or three days before you need it, and can be kept in its uncooked state in the refrigerator until you want to cook it. Once the cookies are baked, they can of course be stored in an airtight tin in the normal way.

MINCEMEAT COOKIES

(see picture above)

1 heaped tbsp. mincemeat	2 level tsps. baking powder
2 tbsps. water	7 oz. margarine
12 oz. plain flour	7 oz. soft brown sugar
Salt	1 egg

Cook the mincemeat in the water until the latter has boiled away and the mincemeat is nearly dry. Sift the flour, salt and baking powder together. Cream the margarine and sugar and beat in the egg, then add the dry ingredients and the cooled mincemeat. Form into sausage-shaped rolls, wrap in waxed paper and put in the refrigerator for 8 hours or overnight. When firm, roll out to ⅛-inch in thickness, cut into shapes and bake in a fairly hot oven (400°F., mark 6) for 8 minutes.

CHOCOLATE PINWHEELS

(see picture above)

6 oz. plain flour	3½ oz. sugar
1 level tsp. baking powder	1 egg yolk
	1 tsp. vanilla essence
Salt	1 oz. chocolate
3½ oz. butter	

Sift the dry ingredients. Cream the butter and sugar together and beat in the egg yolk and essence, then stir in the flour. Melt the chocolate and add to one half of the dough, keeping the other half plain. Put both into the refrigerator to chill and harden for about 3 hours; if it is too hard when you remove it, knead it

a little with your hand. Roll each half into an oblong sheet ⅛ inch thick and as nearly as possible the same size. Put one on top of the other and roll up like a Swiss roll. Wrap in waxed paper and put in the refrigerator to harden for about 12 hours, then, using a sharp knife, cut into ⅛-inch slices and bake in a fairly hot oven (400°F., mark 6) for 5-10 minutes; cool on a rack.

MARBLED COOKIES

(see picture above)

After making pinwheels, knead the left-over pieces lightly together, roll into a sausage shape, wrap in waxed paper and put in the refrigerator to harden. Slice ⅛ inch thick and bake for 5-8 minutes in a fairly hot oven (400°F., mark 6). Sprinkle with caster sugar.

ORANGE COOKIES

10 oz. self-raising flour	6 oz. sugar
Salt	1 egg
5 oz. margarine	1 tsp. grated orange rind

Sift the flour and salt together. Cream the margarine and sugar and beat in the egg and the orange rind, then fold in the flour. Either roll the dough into a sausage shape and wrap in waxed paper or put into a small loaf tin that has been lined with waxed paper and chill in the refrigerator for several hours, till firm; turn out and cut into wafer-thin slices with a sharp knife. Bake in a fairly hot oven (400°F., mark 6) for 8-10 minutes.

This recipe can be varied by the addition of grated lemon rind and chopped glacé cherries or desiccated coconut, or other flavourings.

WALNUT COOKIES

4½ oz. plain flour	3½ oz. brown sugar
½ level tsp. baking powder	½ an egg
A pinch of salt	1 tsp. vanilla essence
1 oz. butter	2-3 oz. chopped walnuts
1 oz. lard	

Sift the flour, baking powder and salt together. Cream the fats and sugar until fluffy and add the egg and essence, mixing well, then stir in the dry ingredients and nuts. Shape into a roll, wrap and chill. The next day, slice thinly and bake in a fairly hot oven (400°F., mark 6) for 10-12 minutes.

ICINGS AND FROSTINGS

BUTTER CREAM OR ICING

3 oz. butter	1-2 tbsps. milk or warm
6 oz. icing sugar, sifted	water
Vanilla essence	

Cream the butter until soft and gradually beat in the sugar, adding a few drops of essence and the milk or water. This amount will coat the sides of a 7-inch cake, or give a topping and a filling. If you wish both to coat the sides and give a topping and filling, increase the amounts of butter and sugar to 4 oz. and 8 oz. respectively.

Orange or Lemon Butter Cream: Omit the vanilla essence and add a little finely grated orange or lemon rind and a little of the juice, beating well to avoid curdling.

Walnut Butter Cream: Add 2 tbsps. finely chopped walnuts; mix well.

Almond Butter Cream: Add 2 tbsps. very finely chopped toasted almonds; mix well.

Coffee Butter Cream: Omit the vanilla essence and flavour with 2 level tsps. instant coffee powder or 1 tbsp. coffee essence.

Chocolate Butter Cream: Flavour either by adding 1-1½ oz. melted chocolate or by adding 1 level tbsp. cocoa dissolved in a little hot water (cool before adding).

Mocha Butter Cream: Dissolve 1 level tsp. cocoa and 2 level tsps. instant coffee powder in a little warm water; cool before adding to the mixture.

GLACÉ ICING

Put 4 oz. sifted icing sugar and (if liked) a few drops of any flavouring essence in a basin and gradually add 1-2 tbsps. warm water. The icing should be thick enough to coat the back of a spoon. If necessary, add more water or sugar to adjust the consistency. Add a few drops of colouring if required and use at once.

For icing of a finer texture, put the sugar, water and flavouring into a small pan and heat, stirring, until the mixture is warm—don't make it too hot. The icing should coat the back of a wooden spoon and look glossy.

This amount is sufficient to cover the top of a 7-inch cake.

Orange Icing: Substitute 1-2 tbsps. strained orange juice for the water in the above recipe.

Lemon Icing: Substitute 1 tbsp. strained lemon juice for the water.

Chocolate Icing: Dissolve 2 level tsps. cocoa in a little hot water and replace same amount of plain water.

Coffee Icing: Flavour with either 1 tsp. coffee essence or 2 level tsps. instant coffee powder, dissolved in a little water.

Mocha Icing: Flavour with 1 level tsp. cocoa and 2 level tsps. instant coffee powder, dissolved in a little water.

Liqueur Icing: Replace 2-3 tsps. of the water by liqueur.

AMERICAN FROSTING

8 oz. sugar	1 egg white
4 tbsps. water	

Note: To make this properly, it is necessary to use a sugar-boiling thermometer. If you do not possess one, you can make Seven-Minute Frosting (see below). Gently heat the sugar in the water, stirring until dissolved.

Then, without stirring, heat to 240°F., Beat the egg white stiffly. Remove the sugar syrup from the heat and when the bubbles subside, pour it on to the egg white; beat the mixture continuously. When it thickens and is almost cold, pour it quickly over the cake.

Makes sufficient frosting for a 7-inch cake.

Orange Frosting: Add a few drops of orange essence and a little orange colouring to the mixture while it is being beaten and before it thickens.

Lemon Frosting: Add a little lemon juice while beating.

Caramel Frosting: Substitute Demerara sugar for the white sugar; follow the same method as above.

Coffee Frosting: Add 1 tsp. coffee essence while beating.

CHOCOLATE FROSTING

5 oz. icing sugar, sifted	1 oz. plain chocolate,
1 egg	melted
½ tsp. vanilla essence	1 oz. butter

Beat all the ingredients together over hot water.

FLUFFY FROSTING

7 oz. granulated sugar	A few drops of vanilla
4 tbsps. water	essence
A pinch of cream of tartar	Colouring, if required
2 egg whites, beaten	

Put the sugar, water and cream of tartar into a pan and heat slowly until the sugar dissolves, then cook without stirring until the temperature reaches 240°F. Pour this syrup on to the egg whites, beating all the time. Add the essence and colouring (if used) and beat until the icing is cool and thick enough to spread.

SEVEN-MINUTE FROSTING

1 egg white	2 tbsps. water
6 oz. caster sugar	A pinch of cream of tartar
A pinch of salt	

Put all the ingredients into a bowl and whisk lightly. Place the bowl over hot water and continue whisking until the mixture thickens sufficiently to hold "peaks". The same variations can be made as for true American Frosting, except for the Chocolate and Fluffy versions.

SATIN FROSTING

3 oz. soft butter	3 tbsps. cream
12 oz. icing sugar, sifted	Vanilla essence

Cream the butter and gradually beat in the sugar and cream; when smooth, flavour with vanilla essence.

Maple Satin Frosting: Replace the cream by maple syrup.

Lemon Satin Frosting: Omit the vanilla essence and add the grated rind of ½ a lemon.

FUDGE TOPPING

8 oz. icing sugar	3 oz. sugar
2 level tbsps. cocoa	3 oz. whipped-up
powder	vegetable fat
3 tbsps. milk	

Sift the icing sugar and cocoa into a bowl. Heat the rest of the ingredients gently in a small pan until the sugar and fat are dissolved. Bring to the boil, pour into the icing sugar, stir until mixed, then beat until fluffy. Spread over the cake, using a knife, rough up the surface and leave to set.

ALMOND PASTE

1 lb. icing sugar
1 lb. ground almonds
2 eggs, lightly beaten
1 tsp. vanilla essence
Lemon juice

Sift the sugar into a bowl, then add the almonds, eggs, essence and enough lemon juice to mix to a stiff dough. Form into a ball and knead lightly. (For a slightly less smooth texture, substitute $\frac{1}{2}$ lb. caster sugar for $\frac{1}{2}$ lb. of the icing sugar, sifting the two together.) This makes 2 lb. almond paste—sufficient for a 9-inch cake.

To Apply Almond Paste
(see left-hand pictures below)

Trim the top of the cake if necessary. Measure round the cake with a piece of string. Brush the sides of the cake generously with sieved apricot jam. Take a quarter of the paste, form into a roll and roll out half as long as string and as wide as the cake is deep. Press the strip firmly on to the sides of the cake, smoothing the join with a round-bladed knife and keeping the edges square. Brush the top of the cake with jam. Dredge the working surface generously with icing sugar, then roll out the remaining almond paste into a round to fit the top of the cake. Turn the cake upsidedown, centring it exactly on the paste, and press it down firmly. Smooth the join, loosen the paste from the board and turn the cake the right way up. Check that the top edge is quite level. Leave for 2-3 days before coating with royal icing.

Almond Paste Decorations

Simple but attractive decorations for an iced cake can be made from almond paste and they are particularly suitable for Christmas or birthday cakes. Draw the chosen shape on stiff paper and cut it out. (Stars, candles, holly leaves, Christmas trees, houses or engines make good designs, as they have bold outlines.) Colour some almond paste by working edible colouring in evenly; roll out very thinly on a board sprinkled with icing sugar, lay the pattern on it and cut round with a sharp-pointed knife. For holly berries, roll tiny balls of red-tinted paste. Leave the shapes on a plate till quite dry, then stick them on to the royal icing (which must be firm).

ROYAL ICING

Allow 4 egg whites to every 2 lb. icing sugar; 1 tbsp. glycerine may be added to give a softer texture. Sift the sugar twice. Separate the eggs, place the whites in a bowl and stir slightly—just sufficiently to break up the albumen, but without including too many air bubbles. Add half the icing sugar and stir until well mixed, using a wooden spoon; beat for about 5-10 minutes, or until the icing is smooth, glossy and white. Cover the bowl with a damp cloth or damped greaseproof paper and leave to stand for at least $\frac{1}{2}$ hour, to allow any air bubbles to rise to the surface.

Gradually add the remaining icing sugar until the required consistency is obtained. When the icing is intended for flat work, stand a wooden spoon upright in it—if the consistency is correct it will fall slowly to one side. For rough icing, the mixture should be stiff enough for peaks to be easily formed on the surface when you "pull" it up with the spoon. Add any desired colouring. If possible, leave the icing overnight in an airtight container in a cool place before use. To obtain a really smooth result, just before using the icing, remove 1 tbsp. of it and mix to a coating consistency with water; return it to the rest and mix until smooth.

Sufficient for a 9-inch cake.

To Rough-ice a Cake

Place 1 tsp. of the icing on the cake-board and put on the cake firmly, centring it accurately. Spoon the icing on top of the cake. Working with a palette knife in a to-and-fro motion until the air bubbles are broken, cover the top and sides of the cake evenly. Now draw an icing ruler or palette knife across the top of the cake evenly and steadily, until the surface is smooth. Using a round-bladed knife, draw the icing up into peaks round the sides and in a border round the top of the cake—or as liked. Before the icing is set, you can put on some simple decorations.

If you want a very simply decorated cake, put almond paste on the top only of the cake and then royal icing on the top and down the sides for about 1 inch, so that the almond paste is hidden. Rough-ice the sides and make a border round the cake as above. Decorate as desired and tie a ribbon round the cake below the icing. (For this sort of decoration use half the suggested amounts of almond paste and royal icing.)

Flat-icing a Cake
(see right-hand pictures opposite)

Place the cake on the cake-board. Spoon most of the icing on top of it and cover the top of the cake as described above. Some of the icing will work down the sides of the cake—return this to the bowl. Now draw an icing ruler or the palette knife across the top of the cake evenly and steadily. Draw it across again at right angles to the first stroke until the surface is smooth. If possible, leave the cake for 24 hours. (Put the icing from the bowl into a polythene bag and store in a refrigerator.)

Put the cake and board on an upturned plate or a turn-table and work the remaining icing on to the sides of the cake. Draw a ruler, knife or baker's card round the sides until they are smooth. Smooth out the join between top and sides, then leave to set for at least 24 hours. Finally, remove any unevenness with a sharp knife.

If liked, apply a second layer of icing to give a really smooth finish. Save 4 tbsps. of the royal icing and mix it with a little water to give a coating consistency; pour on to the centre of the cake, then, using a knife, spread it over the top and down the sides. Knock the board gently up and down on the table to bring any air bubbles to the surface, so that they can be burst with a pin before the icing sets. Leave to harden for 2-3 days.

Decorating a Formal Cake

When you are decorating a royal-iced cake, let the flat coat of icing harden for several days before attempting the next stage. Plan out the scheme on a piece of grease-proof paper of the same size as the cake, lay this on the icing and with a pin prick out the design lightly, to act as a guide.

The icing used for piping must be free of all lumps, which might block the nozzles; it must also be of such a consistency that it can be forced easily through the pipe but will retain its shape.

Special icing pumps can be bought, but are more difficult to manage than paper forcing bags (made as follows) or small polythene forcing bags.

To Make and Use a Paper Forcing Bag

1. Fold a 10-inch square of greaseproof or silicone paper into a triangle.
2. Holding the right angle of the triangle towards you, roll over one of the other corners to meet it. Roll the second corner over in the opposite direction to meet the first at the back of the bag. Adjust the two corners over one another until a point is formed at the tip.
3. Fold over the corners several times, to secure them in position.
4. Cut a small piece from the tip of the bag and drop in the required metal nozzle or pipe.
5. To use the bag, place a little icing in it and fold the top over once or twice. When piping, hold the bag in one hand as though it were a pencil, with the thumb in the centre to give an even pressure. If you are inexperienced, first practise piping on an upturned plate. Remember that icing can easily be removed while it is still soft, so mistakes can be corrected.

The Pipes
(see picture below)

For a simple design—which is often the most effective—these types of pipes or nozzles are usually needed:
1. Writing pipes in 3 sizes, to make lines, scallops, dots and words.
2. Star pipes for rosettes, zigzags and ropes.
3. Shell pipe.
For advanced work, use a petal pipe for flowers and bows and a leaf pipe for leaves.

WHAT WENT WRONG? CAKE-MAKING FAULTS ANALYSED

RUBBED-IN AND CREAMED MIXTURES

Close Texture may be due to:
1. Insufficient creaming of the fat and sugar—air should be well incorporated at this stage.
2. Insufficient beating when the egg is added—air is incorporated at this stage also.
3. Curdling of the creamed mixture when eggs are added—a curdled mixture will not hold as much air.
4. Over-stirring or beating the flour into a creamed mixture.
5. Insufficient baking powder.
6. Too much liquid.
7 (a) Too slow an oven—the air expands before the cake is set enough to hold its risen shape.
7 (b) Too hot an oven—the crust sets before the air has time to expand and make the mixture rise.
Uneven and Holey Texture may be caused by:
1. Over-stirring when adding the flour.
2. Uneven or insufficient mixing in of the flour.
3. The mixture being put into the cake tin small amounts at a time—this allows pockets of air to be trapped in the mixture.
Dry and Crumbly Texture may be due to:
1. Too much baking powder.
2. Too long a cooking time in too cool an oven.
Streakiness in the Crust may be due to:
1. Flour being unevenly or insufficiently mixed into the creamed mixture.
2. Faulty mixing—if any of the mixture is left on the sides of the bowl without being combined with the flour and is then scraped into the cake tin, these scrapings will cause streakiness.
Unevenly Risen Cakes may be due to:
1. The mixture not being evenly spread in the tin.
2. The oven shelf being tilted.
3. The tin not being centrally placed on oven shelf.
'Peaking' and Cracking may be caused by:
1. Too hot an oven.
2. The cake being placed too near top of oven.
3. Too stiff a mixture.
4. Too small a cake tin.
Fruit Sinking in a Cake may be due to:
1. Damp fruit. Though fruit needs cleaning, if it is washed, it must be dried by being spread out on trays and left in a warm place for 48 hours before use.
2. Sticky glacé cherries: if covered with thick syrup, they should first be washed, then lightly floured.
3. Too soft a mixture: a rich fruit cake mixture should be fairly stiff, to hold up the weight of the fruit.
4. Opening or banging the oven door while the cake is rising.
5. Using self-raising flour where the recipe requires plain, or using too much baking powder—the cake over-rises, but cannot carry the fruit with it.

Dry Fruit Cakes may be due to:
1. Cooking at too high a temperature.
2. Too stiff a mixture.
3. Not lining the tin thoroughly—for a large cake the tin should be lined with double greaseproof paper.
Burnt Fruit on the outside of a Fruit Cake may be caused by:
1. Too high a temperature.
2. Lack of protection: as soon as the cake begins to colour, a piece of brown paper or a double thickness of greaseproof paper can be placed over the top for the remainder of the cooking time, to prevent further browning.
A Cake that Sinks in the Middle may be due to:
1. Too soft a mixture.
2. Too much raising agent.
3. In the case of a gingerbread, too much syrup in the mixture.
4. Opening or banging the oven door while the cake is rising.
5(a) Too cool an oven, which means that the centre of the cake does not rise.
5(b) Too hot an oven, which makes the cake appear to be done before it is cooked through, so that it is taken from the oven too soon.
6. Too short a baking time.

WHISKED SPONGE MIXTURES

Close, Heavy Texture may be caused by:
1. The eggs and sugar being insufficiently beaten, so that not enough air is enclosed.
2. The egg and sugar mixture being overheated, causing the egg to cook slightly and become rather tough and rubbery.
3. The flour being stirred in too heavily or for too long—very light folding movements are required and a metal spoon should be used.
4. The flour being added in a rush—it should be sieved in gently, so that it will not crush out too much of the air.
5. Too much flour being used in proportion to the eggs and sugar.
Lumps on the Bottom of the Cake may be caused by:
Careless or uneven mixing in of the flour—any unmixed lumps sink to the bottom of the cake.
Cracking of a Swiss Roll may be due to:
1. An unlined tin—lining is necessary to prevent the edges overcooking.
2. Too big a tin—this makes the mixture too thin, giving a brittle instead of a spongy texture.
3. Too hot an oven or too long a cooking time—this makes the cake brittle and difficult to roll.
4. The edges not being cut off: since the edges are the crispest part, they should always be removed or the roll will split.
5. The cake not being rolled quickly enough: it must be rolled while it is still very soft and spongy—i.e. straight from the oven.
Heavy Layer at base of a Genoese Sponge may be due to:
1. The melted fat being too hot—it should be only lukewarm.
2. Uneven or insufficient folding in of fat and flour.
3. Adding all the fat at once—it should be added alternately with the flour.

BUFFET PARTY CATERING

As a general rule, ½ lb. pastry gives about 18-24 savouries, according to size.

ASSORTED SAVOURIES

SAVOURY BOUCHÉES

Roll out ½ lb. flaky pastry ¼-½ inch thick. Using a 2-inch cutter, cut into rounds and put on a baking tin. Cut half-way through the centre of each with a ½-inch round cutter, glaze the tops with egg and bake in a hot oven (425°F., mark 7) for 10 minutes, then reduce the heat to moderate (350°F., mark 4) for a further 5-10 minutes. Remove the soft centres and cool the cases on a rack. Fill the patties when cold.
The basis for most fillings is ½ pint white sauce combined with an ingredient such as the following:
6 oz. picked shrimps, prawns or other shellfish.
4 oz. chopped or minced chicken with 2 oz. minced or chopped ham or 2 oz. chopped fried mushrooms.
4-6 oz. flaked canned or fresh salmon.
4 oz. diced ham and 2 oz. tongue or cooked veal.
6 oz. chopped ham and 2 oz. cooked mushrooms.

CRAB TARTLETS

¼ lb. flaky pastry	2 oz. blanched and
¼ pint white sauce	chopped almonds
A 1½-oz. can of crab	Seasoning
1½ oz. grated cheese	

Roll the pastry out thinly and line some tartlet tins with it. Mix all the other ingredients, reserving half the cheese and the nuts. Fill the cases with this and sprinkle the remaining cheese and nuts on top. Bake in a hot oven 425°F., mark 7) for 15 minutes.

RISOTTO TARTLETS

4 oz. shortcrust pastry	1½ oz. ham
4 oz. cream cheese	1½ oz. smoked salmon
Seasoning	1 oz. Gruyère or Cheddar
1 egg, beaten	cheese

Roll out the pastry and line some tartlet tins with it. Beat the cream cheese, season and stir in the egg by degrees. Cut the ham and salmon into shreds and mix in carefully. Fill the tartlet moulds with this mixture, cut the Gruyère in thin slices and lay these over the top of the tartlets. Bake in a hot oven (425°F., mark 7) until golden-brown and crisp—about 10 minutes.

SAVOURY HORNS

(see picture on p. 205 and colour picture no. 50)

Roll out 4 oz. flaky pastry thinly, cut into ½-inch strips, then wind these round metal "horns", starting from the bottom, overlapping each turn and leaving ½ inch or so of the metal exposed at the top. Glaze with beaten egg and bake in a hot oven (425°F., mark 7) for 10-15 minutes. Remove the metal horns and leave the cases to cool. Fill with a savoury sauce mixture (as given for Bouchées) or a mixture of cream cheese and chopped pimiento or walnuts.

CHEESE AND BACON TARTLETS

(see picture on p. 205)

Roll out 3-4 oz. flaky pastry and line some tartlet tins. Chop 2 oz. cooked bacon (or ham) and put a little in each tin. Beat up 1 egg, some seasoning and ¼ pint milk and divide between the tartlets. Sprinkle 4 oz. grated cheese over the custard filling. Bake in a fairly hot oven (400°F., mark 6) for about 15 minutes.

SAUSAGE ROLLS

6 oz. flaky pastry	Beaten egg to glaze
8 oz. sausage-meat	

Roll out the pastry thinly into an oblong 6 inches wide and cut it into 2 strips. Lay a roll of sausage-meat down the centre of each, brush the edges with egg and fold one side over the filling. Seal the two long edges together by flaking with a knife. Glaze the top of each roll with egg, cut into slices 1-1½ inches long and bake in a fairly hot oven (400°F., mark 6) for about 20 minutes.

CHEESE AIGRETTES

2 oz. plain flour
½ oz. butter
¼ pint water
1 large egg

1½ oz. grated cheese
Seasoning
Deep fat

Make some choux pastry with the flour, butter, water and egg and add the cheese and seasoning. Heat a pan of deep fat until it will brown a cube of bread in a few seconds. Drop the cheese mixture into it in teaspoonfuls and fry for about 5 minutes, until the aigrettes are a pale golden-brown; drain well.

CHEESE BISCUITS

(see picture opposite)

2 oz. cheese pastry
Cream cheese
A little milk

Finely chopped parsley,
    paprika pepper,
anchovies, sliced olives

Roll the pastry out thinly and cut in small rounds. Bake in a fairly hot oven (400°F., mark 6) for 10-15 minutes, then cool. Mix the cheese to a piping consistency with milk and pipe a large star or whirl on each round. Set 2 half-biscuits in the cheese to form wings, or decorate with parsley, paprika, etc.

CHEESE PASTRY, CHEESE STRAWS

See p. 96.

SAVOURY WHIRLS

(see picture opposite)

Roll out 4 oz. cheese or shortcrust pastry thinly into an oblong and spread with yeast or meat extract, leaving the edges free. Brush the edges with water, roll up like a Swiss roll, then slice thinly, put on a greased baking sheet and bake in a fairly hot oven (400°F., mark 6) for 10-15 minutes.

ANCHOVY TWISTS

(see picture opposite)

Scraps of flaky or
    shortcrust pastry
Anchovy fillets

Lemon juice
Beaten egg

Roll the pastry ⅛ inch thick and cut it into strips. Lay a strip of anchovy on top of each and sprinkle with lemon juice. Twist the two together, brush with beaten egg and bake in a hot oven (425°F., mark 7) for about 10 minutes.

SARDINE TRICORNES

(see picture opposite)

6 oz. cheese or shortcrust
    pastry (see recipes on
    pp. 96 and 140)
4 oz. sardines

¼ pint thick cheese-
    flavoured sauce
Egg or milk
Stuffed olives to garnish

Roll the pastry out thinly and cut into rounds 3½-4 inches in diameter. Mix the sardines with the sauce and place a spoonful of this filling in the centre of each round. Brush the outside edge with a little water, draw up over the filling and pinch to form a three-cornered shape. Brush with a little egg or milk and bake in a fairly hot oven (375°F., mark 5) for 15-20 minutes. Decorate with slices of olive or with parsley.

CHEESE DARTOIS

See p. 97.

THREE SMALL SAVOURIES

Thin wedges of melon wrapped round with a thinly cut slice of smoked or roast ham.
Asparagus tips or pineapple spears wrapped in slices of ham.
Asparagus tips wrapped in slices of smoked salmon.

SAVOURY BREAD

Slice a long French loaf diagonally into slices about 1 inch thick, but do not cut through the bottom crust. Spread the cut surfaces with one of these savoury fillings:
Cream cheese mixed with chopped chives
Cream cheese and chopped chutney
Cream cheese and caraway seeds
Cream cheese and tomato purée
Grated Cheddar cheese and chopped mango chutney
Wrap the loaf in aluminium foil and bake in a fairly hot oven (400°F., mark 6) for 10 minutes. Unwrap and serve immediately, with watercress.

DIPS

Cream cheese can be combined with crushed avocado pears, pineapple, flaked salmon or tuna, minced ham, chopped shellfish, celery, onion, hard-boiled egg, crisp bacon, nuts or chutney, or it may be mixed with cream, salad cream, white wine, beer or fruit juice and flavoured with herbs, curry powder or seasoned salt. Serve in a bowl, on a platter surrounded with assorted "dunks"—pumpernickel strips, French bread, fingers of toast, crispbreads, pretzels, potato crisps, celery sticks, radishes, pineapple chunks, avocado chunks, prawns, grilled bacon rolls, chunks of chicken or ham, carrot sticks, cocktail onions, apple segments. Mount these on cocktail sticks if necessary.

Party Edam: Cut the top from an Edam cheese and scoop out the centre. To decorate the outside, cut out shapes in the red skin with a cutter. The scooped-out cheese can then be finely chopped and mixed with extra cheese and any of the savoury ingredients suggested for dips (see above).

CHEESY EGG DUNK

A 6-oz. packet of soft
    cream cheese (preferably
    chive-flavoured)
2 tbsps. mayonnaise
1 tsp. prepared mustard
¼ level tsp. salt

½ tsp. Worcestershire
    sauce
⅛ level tsp. pepper
2 chopped hard-boiled
    eggs
3 tbsps. milk

Mix all the ingredients to a thick cream.

TUNA CHEESE DUNK

A 3-oz. can of flaked tuna
3 3-oz. packages of cream
    cheese
¼ cup dry white wine
1 tbsp. mayonnaise
2 tbsps. chopped parsley

¼ cup well-drained sweet
    pickle
1 tbsp. grated onion
A dash of Tabasco
¼ level tsp. salt
¼ level tsp. garlic salt

Drain the tuna and blend with the cream cheese, then with the remaining ingredients.

BLUE CHEESE DUNK

Mix 2½ oz. blue cheese with ½ lb. cottage cheese, a little grated onion and 1 carton of plain yoghourt.

COCKTAIL STICK TITBITS

See p. 96 for directions for making.

SANDWICH BAR

HINTS ON SANDWICH-MAKING

1. Use a cut loaf (thinly sliced) and soften butter.
2. Prepare the fillings beforehand—they should be moist and well-seasoned. For layer sandwiches (see colour picture no. 50) use well-contrasted fillings.
3. Pair the slices which lie next to each other in the loaf, so that the edges will match.
4. Use a sharp unserrated knife for cutting, as this is less likely to tear the bread. If fancy cutters are used, choose ones with sharp edges.

SANDWICH FILLINGS

Salmon, finely chopped onion and cucumber.
Liver pâté, crisp bacon bits and pickle.
Cream cheese, pimiento and celery or dates.
Scrambled egg and chopped ham or chopped chives.
Chopped turkey or chicken and cranberry jelly.
Chopped shrimps, celery, pineapple and salad cream.

CREAM CHEESE SANDWICH LOAF

(see colour picture no. 46)

A 7½-oz. can of salmon	2 tsps. chopped chives
3 tbsps. salad cream	1 tsp. grated onion
1 tbsp. lemon juice	Seasonings
2 eggs	1 large tin loaf
2 oz. grated cheese	¾ lb. cream cheese
1-2 tsps. made mustard	A little milk
2 oz. butter	Sliced radishes and
2 tbsps. chopped parsley	parsley to garnish

Flake the salmon and mix with the salad cream and lemon juice. Scramble the eggs, add the cheese and mustard and leave to cool. Cream the butter with the herbs and onion. Season all the fillings well. Cut the crusts from the top and short sides of the loaf, slice it into 6 lengthwise and trim off the remaining crusts. Spread one slice with half the salmon mixture, cover with a second slice, then spread with half the egg mixture; add another slice, spread with savoury butter, put on a slice covered with the remaining egg mixture, a slice with the remaining salmon and finally a plain slice. Wrap the loaf in waxed paper, place between two boards and press well. Before serving, cover with cream cheese, softened with milk. Garnish as seen.

SCANDINAVIAN-TYPE OPEN SANDWICHES

(see picture above)

Use small split bridge rolls, thin rounds from a French loaf, toast, crispbread, rye bread or savoury biscuits; spread with butter (possibly flavoured with minced onion, curry powder, mayonnaise or chopped herbs, such as parsley or chives); top with any decorative mixture of ingredients—for instance:
Shrimps, anchovies, crabmeat, tuna fish, salami, cold roast meats, liver pâté, smoked Continental sausage, cheese, cream cheese, eggs (scrambled or hard-boiled and sliced), salad ingredients, olives, gherkins, picked walnuts.

Open sandwich toppings
Herring fillets, potato salad, chopped beetroot.
Cold cooked white fish coated with salad cream, topped with tomato or pimiento.
Scrambled egg topped with smoked salmon, on a base of a lettuce leaf on toast.
Shrimps surrounding hard-boiled egg halves, covered with salad cream and decorated with dill or lettuce.
Shrimps with cheese and cucumber cubes in curry-flavoured salad cream.
Liver pâté, an anchovy fillet, horseradish cream and parsley.
Salami, scrambled egg, slices of leek.
Egg and tomato slices with piped mayonnaise and chopped chives to garnish.

PINWHEEL SANDWICHES

(see colour picture no. 50)

Cut off the end and top crusts from a new white loaf. Stand the loaf on end and cut off very thin slices down its whole length. Put these pieces flat on the table and pass the rolling pin lightly over them—this will make it easier to roll them up. Spread with a soft filling (either dark or brightly coloured, to provide a good contrast to the bread) and cut off the crusts. Roll up, starting at one narrow end, wrap each roll tightly in waxed or greaseproof paper, then put in the refrigerator for ½ hour. When the rolls are firm, cut them in ¼-inch slices, as though cutting Swiss roll.

DRINKS FOR THE PARTY

Elaborate drinks are out of place at a buffet party. Usually the host or hostess has to do the serving and this should not develop into a full-time job. Complicated cocktails, for example, which need mixing on the spot, are a nuisance and anyway rather old-fashioned. A wine or fruit cup, however, is a splendid standby. It can be prepared beforehand and only needs a punch bowl and ladle for quick, easy serving. A large, new goldfish bowl makes a good substitute for a punch bowl—see p. 209. A wide selection of drinks is also unnecessary. Asking the guests what they will have is easy if you offer a choice of only two or three drinks.

At a wine and cheese party, offer both red and white wine. At a beer party, offer bitter, lager and cider. If you rise to a champagne party—*not* so extravagant as it sounds—you only need to offer champagne. At the conventional "come in for drinks", you can get by quite well with sherry and gin plus vermouth and tonic.

Do always offer a non-alcoholic drink as an alternative. You will most likely serve coffee at some stage, but you will also need fruit juice (canned or bottled), fruit squashes, mineral drinks of some kind or a cup (see pp. 208-209) for non-drinkers.

Thirst-quenchers: Alcohol adds to the gaiety of the occasion, but drinks are intended to quench the thirst and this alcohol does not do, so even wine-drinkers may like tonic or lemonade afterwards. Some people like to add water to their wine (a favourite hot-weather trick on the Continent).

"Sale or Return": Your local wine merchant or off-licence will almost certainly let you buy drinks on a "sale or return" basis. This means you can buy enough bottles to cope with your maximum expectations and any unopened bottles can be returned. Glasses can usually be hired.

Apéritifs

These should be served chilled and many of them are improved by ice and a twist of lemon peel.

Sherry	dry, medium or sweet
Port	coming back into fashion as apéritif
Madeira	also becoming popular again
Vermouth	dry, sweet and *bianco* (white)
Dubonnet	excellent iced, with lemon peel
Campari	deliciously bitter-sweet when served with soda or tonic water and ice

Spirits

Whisky	traditionally served neat or with water, but many people like soda or ginger ale
Gin	serve with lime or other fruit squash; bitter lemon or tonic with a lemon peel twist; vermouth, Dubonnet or Angostura bitters (2 or 3 drops) and iced water
Rum	serve with lime, orange or cola drinks
Vodka	use like gin, or serve with tomato juice to make a "Bloody Mary"

Wine

Broadly speaking, wine can be red, white or rosé and still or sparkling. It can cost anything you like to pay, but plenty of the cheaper kinds make excellent party drinking. There is no need to be snobbish about sticking to French wines—splendid wines are imported from other countries and in any case it is a complete waste of a true old vintage to serve it at a stand-up buffet party. Many wines can be bought in ½-gallon, 1-gallon and 2-gallon jars and this generally works out cheaper.

What temperature? White wine is served chilled. Keep it in a cool place or put it in the refrigerator for an hour before serving. (Improvise an ice bucket if refrigerator space is limited.) Red wine is served at room temperature, rosé very slightly chilled.

Champagne is one of the easiest things to serve at a party and you need offer nothing else except a non-alcoholic drink. It can be drunk before, during and after eating and adds an air to any party without necessarily being ruinously expensive. There are plenty of good non-vintage champagnes and the champagne-style Spanish sparkling wines are very reasonable.

French Wines: The main divisions are into Bordeaux and Burgundy—which can be both red or white—and rosé, though there are countless other classifications. Red Bordeaux (also known as Claret), such as St. Emilion or Médoc, is a light, dryish wine. White Bordeaux, such as Graves or Sauternes, is generally semi-sweet—Sauternes is indeed the sweetest of wines. Red Burgundy, such as Beaune and Beaujolais, is fuller and richer than Bordeaux. White Burgundy, such as Chablis and Meursault, is dryish and fairly full. Rosé, such as Anjou rosé or Tavel, is a light wine varying in colour from pale to dark; it can be sweet or dry.

Other Wines: Italian and German wines seem in general to be slightly dearer than the cheapest French. Italian wines include Chianti (red or white) in wicker-basket bottles—probably the most popular, but not necessarily the best or cheapest Italian wine. German wines include the deliciously light and fresh Hocks and Moselles. Every wine merchant now has also a big selection of wines from Spain, Portugal, Algeria, Yugoslavia, Hungary, Cyprus, the Commonwealth countries (even perhaps one from Russia!) and many of these are cheap and very drinkable.

Yield per bottle

Wine	8 glasses
Sherry, Port	10-12 glasses
Champagne	6-8 glasses
Spirits	24 measures (varies a lot; some bars get 28 or even 30 tots from a bottle)
Squash	14-18 long drinks

Beer, Cider

Generally, light ale or lager is served at a party. You can order a small barrel (or pin) of bitter from your local pub and if a knowledgeable host or friend can chock it up, put the bung in and prevent it from dripping, this saves endless bottle-opening. Beer is otherwise available in bottles, cans and 7-pint cans.

Lager-and-lime, which is now superseding the old lemonade shandy, is refreshing after energetic games.

Besides the standard sparkling and still ciders, there are also vintage and champagne types and champagne perry, which are not much cheaper than a cheap wine but are very popular.

WINE CUPS

This assortment should offer something for every taste; the cost varies of course according to the wine used.

MIDSUMMER NIGHT'S DREAM CUP

Ice cubes
1 bottle of Sylvaner
1 bottle of Beaujolais
1 split of lemonade

2 measures of Curaçao
Sliced fresh fruit and
    melon cubes
Sugar to taste

Place the ice cubes in a bowl and pour the wines, lemonade and liqueur over them. Add the fruit and sugar to taste. Serve well chilled. Sweet and very pleasant—about 16 glasses.

LUNAR JULEP

3 bottles of white
    Burgundy
¼ bottle of Pernod
3 tbsps. Crème de Menthe

Crushed ice
Sugar to taste
Finely sliced cucumber
Soda water

Mix the wine, Pernod and Crème de Menthe in a bowl and add the crushed ice and sugar, then chill well. Add the cucumber and soda water just before serving. Very refreshing—about 20 glasses.

PRIDE OF OPORTO

2 lemons
1 bottle of tawny port

4 tbsps. Curaçao
1 siphon of soda water

Squeeze the juice of 1 lemon into a bowl and add the port and Curaçao. Slice the second lemon, float it on top and leave for 20 minutes. Fill glasses two-thirds full and top up with chilled soda water. Sharp and refreshing. About 24 glasses.

CLARET AND SAUTERNES FRAPPÉ

1 bottle of Claret
1 bottle of Sauternes
Strawberries and sliced
    fruit
2 glasses of Curaçao

2 glasses of brandy
Juice of 3 lemons
1 large split of soda water
Sugar to taste
Ice cubes

Place the wines in a bowl, add the fruit and leave for ½ hour. Add the liqueurs and lemon juice. Just before serving, add the soda water, sugar and ice cubes. Serve well chilled. Slightly sharp, very refreshing. About 22 glasses.

BARRIER REEF

2 bottles dry white wine
3 measures of brandy
3 tbsps. Curaçao
1 split of lemonade

¼ lb. grapes, peeled and
    seeded
Crushed ice
Sugar to taste

Mix the wine, brandy, Curaçao, lemonade and grapes. Add the crushed ice and sugar and serve well chilled. Cool and refreshing. Makes about 20 glasses.

EVERYMAN'S BUBBLY

1 bottle of Graves or
    Sauternes

2 pints soda water

Chill both ingredients and combine just before serving, to make a slightly sparkling and very refreshing drink. About 16 glasses.

VERMOUTH CASSIS

Ice cubes
1 bottle of Vermouth
½ a bottle of Crème de
    Cassis

6 splits of soda water
Sliced lemon
Sugar to taste

Place the ice cubes in a bowl and pour the Vermouth over. Add the other ingredients and serve well chilled. Refreshing and not too sweet. About 16 glasses.

HONEYSUCKLE CUP

Ice cubes
1 bottle of medium-dry
    white wine
4 tsps. liquid honey
1 measure of Bénédictine

2 measures of brandy
1 split of lemonade
4 lemons, sliced
1 peach, sliced

Place the ice cubes in a bowl, pour the other ingredients over and leave to stand for 1 hour. Serve very cold. Sweet and slightly bland. About 14 glasses.

"SOFT" DRINKS

Allow individual servings of ¼–⅓ pint per glass. The drinks work out at about 6d.-9d. a glass.

SPICY FRUIT PUNCH

1¼ pints canned or fresh
    orange juice
½ pint canned pineapple
    juice
Juice and rind of 1 lemon
½ level tsp. ground nutmeg

½ level tsp. ground allspice
6 cloves
6 oz. sugar
1 pint water
2 pints ginger ale

Mix together the fruit juices, lemon rind and spices in a large jug. Put the sugar in the water and heat gently to dissolve; cool slightly and add to the other ingredients. Chill and strain; add the ginger ale before serving. About 15-20 servings.

SUNSHINE SHAKE

A 19-oz. can of orange
    juice, chilled
2 pints milk, chilled

1 orange
Fresh mint leaves

Combine the orange juice and milk, preferably in a blender, or failing this, by whisking vigorously with a rotary whisk. Serve in glasses, topped with a slice of orange and a mint leaf. About 9-12 servings.

QUICK QUENCHER

2 pints ginger beer, chilled
¾ pint bottled lime juice

Ice cubes
Fresh mint leaves to garnish

Make this drink just before you wish to serve it. Combine the ginger beer and lime juice, then add the ice cubes and mint. About 9-12 servings.

PINEAPPLE CRUSH

¼ pint stock syrup (see below)

A 19-oz. can of pineapple juice

Juice of 1 orange and 1 lemon

2 ripe bananas, mashed

2 pints ginger ale

To make stock syrup, which is useful for sweetening all kinds of cold drinks, dissolve 1 lb. sugar in ½ pint water over a low heat, then bring to the boil; cool and store in a refrigerator to use as required.

Combine the stock syrup with the first 2 ingredients and chill. Just before serving, add the bananas and chilled ginger ale. About 10-14 servings.

CITRUS PUNCH

Juice of 2 grapefruit

Juice of 2 lemons

Juice of 5 oranges

¼ pint canned pineapple juice

¼ pint stock syrup (see previous recipe)

4 splits of tonic water

1 lemon, thinly sliced

Mix the strained fruit juices in a bowl and chill. Just before serving, add the stock syrup and tonic water and decorate with the lemon slices. About 10 servings.

PINELIME SPARKLE

A 19-oz. can of pineapple juice

3 tbsps. fresh lemon juice

¼ pint bottled lime juice

2 oz. icing sugar

2 splits of bitter lemon

Slices of pineapple to garnish

Put the pineapple, lemon and lime juices together in a jug, sweeten with the sugar and stir well, then chill. Just before serving add the bitter lemon and the pineapple slices. About 9-12 servings.

COFFEE

Although there are many methods of making coffee, the "jug" method is still one of the easiest and best. Use a jug of known capacity, warm it and have some boiling water ready. For each pint of water put into the jug 2 heaped tbsps. finely ground coffee, then pour on the fast-boiling water, stirring vigorously. Stand the coffee in a warm place for about 5 minutes, stirring once or twice, then leave it undisturbed for a further 5 minutes— it will then be ready. If there appear to be many grounds on the top, stir the surface only very lightly with a small spoon or sprinkle with a few drops of cold water—this should clear it, but if any grounds still remain floating, strain the coffee through a fine strainer or muslin.

If the coffee has to be decanted into another pot, be sure that this also is very hot. When coffee has to be reheated, take care not to let it boil.

For white coffee, combine strained black coffee with an equal amount of hot milk, heated separately. If cream is served, the coffee should be strong and black. Hand the cream separately or pour a dessertspoonful of it over the back of a spoon into each cup, so that it spreads over the surface of the coffee.

ICED COFFEE

Make a syrup with 4 oz. sugar and ½ pint water; boil for about 10 minutes, then let it get cold. Chill strong, clear, black coffee and pour into glasses; put a small lump of ice in each glass, sweeten with sugar syrup and top with whipped cream.

COFFEE WITH LIQUEURS

Most liqueurs can be taken with coffee, but some, of course, combine especially well with it.

Coffee to be served in this way should be double-strength—that is, use 3 oz. coffee per pint of water instead of 1½ oz.

If a liqueur coffee is served with cream on top, allow it to stand for 5 minutes before drinking, so that the aroma of the liqueur can penetrate and pervade the cream. Do not stir the cream and coffee together, but drink the coffee through the layer of cream.

We give also recipes for two favourite fruit-flavoured brandies which can be made at home to serve with coffee.

IRISH OR GAELIC COFFEE

You will need 1 part Irish whiskey to 3 parts double-strength coffee. Warm some small goblets, put 1 measure (approx. 1½ fluid oz.) of whiskey in each glass and add 1 level tsp. sugar. Pour in black coffee to within 1 inch of the brim and stir to dissolve the sugar completely. Fill the glasses to the brim with chilled double cream, poured over the back of a spoon. Allow to stand for 5 minutes, then drink the coffee through the cream.

CALYPSO COFFEE

Allow the following ingredients per glass and proceed as for Irish coffee.

1 measure of Tia Maria	Thick double cream
4 measures of double-strength black coffee	1 level tsp. sugar

MEXICAN COFFEE

Allow the following quantities for each glass and make as for Irish coffee.

1 measure of Kahlua	Thick double cream
4 measures of double-strength black coffee	1 level tsp. sugar

WITCH'S COFFEE

Warm some goblet glasses and make sufficient double-strength black coffee. Put 1 measure of Strega in each glass, add 1 level tsp. sugar and pour in 3 measures of coffee; stir to dissolve the sugar. Pour in thick double cream over the back of a spoon and finally sprinkle a little finely grated lemon rind in each glass.

CURAÇAO COFFEE

For each glass allow the following ingredients. Make as for Irish coffee and stir with a cinnamon stick.

1 measure of Curaçao	Sugar to taste
3 measures of double-strength black coffee	A cinnamon stick (optional)

CAFÉ À LA BRÛLOT

1 orange	3 lumps of sugar
2 2-inch sticks of cinnamon	¼ pint Cognac
4 whole cloves	1 pint double-strength black coffee

Peel off the coloured part of the orange skin in one long, thin ribbon. Place the orange peel, cinnamon sticks, cloves and sugar lumps in a saucepan. Pour in the Cognac, warm it for a moment, then set light to it. While the brandy is still flaming, add the black coffee; as the flame subsides, ladle the coffee into 6 coffee cups.

LIQUEUR COFFEE ROUND THE WORLD

Make any of the following as for Irish coffee. The quantities are for 1 glass.

Cointreau Coffee

1 part of liqueur	1 level tsp. sugar
2 parts of double-strength black coffee	Thick double cream

Caribbean Coffee

1 part of rum	1 level tsp. sugar
5 parts of double-strength black coffee	Thick double cream

German Coffee

1 part of Kirsch	1 level tsp. sugar
4 parts of double-strength black coffee	Thick double cream

Normandy Coffee

1 part of Calvados	1 level tsp. sugar
3 parts of double-strength black coffee	Thick double cream

Dutch Coffee

1 part of Hollands Gin	1 level tsp. sugar
4 parts of double-strength black coffee	Thick double cream

Russian Coffee

1 part of Vodka	1 level tsp. sugar
5 parts of double-strength black coffee	Thick double cream

CHERRY BRANDY

2 lb. dark cherries	1 pint brandy
6 oz. caster sugar	

Wash the cherries and cut off the stalks within ¼ inch of the fruit. Prick the cherries in several places with a skewer or darning needle, then pack them with alternate layers of sugar into a wide-necked bottle. Pour on the brandy, making sure that the cherries are quite covered. Cork the bottle securely and store in a cool, dark place for at least 2 and preferably 3 months; shake the bottle at intervals. At the end of this time strain off the liqueur and re-bottle it.

APRICOT BRANDY

12 large apricots	1 pint brandy
½ lb. caster sugar	

Halve the apricots and chop into small pieces. Crack the stones, crush the kernels and add to the apricots. Put the fruit and kernels into a bottle and pour on the brandy; shake the bottle well and cork securely. Store in a cool, dark place and shake the bottle at frequent intervals. After 1 month, strain off the brandy and re-bottle it.

HOME PRESERVING

The principle underlying all preserving is to prevent the decay caused by the growth of minute organisms, yeasts, moulds, and bacteria, which thrive on fruit and vegetables, helped by the chemical action of enzymes. These organisms can all be destroyed by being heated to specified temperatures—different fruits requiring different heats for sterilisation. Once the fruits (or vegetables) have been sterilised they must be kept securely sealed.

The sugar used in preserving helps in the retention of the natural fruit flavour; in jams, it also helps the keeping qualities, as it prevents the growth of yeasts, which are unable to live in a solution containing 60 per cent. or more of sugar.

It is impossible to over-stress the importance of using only fresh, sound fruit, under-ripe rather than over-ripe—in fact, the success of all preserving depends to a large extent on the quality of the fruit (or vegetables).

STEPS IN JAM-MAKING

Wash the fruit thoroughly.

Cooking: The first stage is to cook the fruit, in order to soften it and release the pectin and the acid. This is best done slowly—the fruit and water should only simmer. Extra acid, if needed, is added during this stage. The quantity of water and the cooking time vary for different types of fruit, but the skins must be made really soft, as tough skins in jam are most unpalatable and hard to digest; fruits such as black-currants, damsons and plums need at least $\frac{1}{2}$-$\frac{3}{4}$ hour. This preliminary cooking may be done very satisfactorily in a pressure cooker (see p. 220).

The Addition of Sugar: Many people imagine there is some advantage in using cane rather than beet sugar, or lump rather than granulated. In fact, there is no difference in the keeping qualities of jam made from any of these sugars. Preserving sugar does have one advantage, however—it dissolves more easily.

The sugar must be completely dissolved *before* the mixture comes to the boil again; this is why some recipes state that the sugar should be warmed to help it dissolve more quickly, but this is not essential. Stir the jam while the sugar is dissolving.

Boiling the Jam: As soon as all the sugar is dissolved, bring the jam rapidly to the boil and boil hard and quickly. (At this stage the traditional large, shallow preserving pan proves its usefulness, as it enables the jam to boil quickly without boiling over.) Providing the fruit has been properly cooked beforehand, it should now be boiled for about 5-20 minutes, though some jams need as little as 3 minutes.

Testing the Setting Point: There are several reliable ways of deciding whether jam is ready to set or "jell", but it is at this stage that many people experience difficulty.

Remember when testing jam, particularly in the later stages, that you should always lower the heat, so that it does not go on cooking for too long. If a set is not obtained, continue to boil for a short time.

Of the many different methods of testing, the most common are the "plate" and the "flake" test. For the former, 1 tbsp. of jam is put on a cold saucer and allowed to cool; if the surface is set and crinkles when it is gently pushed with a finger (see picture overleaf), setting point has been reached. For the "flake" test, put a wooden spoon in the jam so that it is lightly coated; when cool, the jam should fall from the tilted spoon in flakes rather than in liquid drops (see picture p. 217).

A very reliable method is to use a sugar thermometer. (This is not expensive and when jam is frequently made, it is a good investment.) When the jam reaches a temperature of 220°F., and providing the pectin and acid content are correct, setting point has generally been reached. With some jams, 221°F., or 222°F., may give better results, but this is a matter of experience. During testing, keep the thermometer in a jug of boiling water when not in use. Stir the preserve thoroughly before using the thermometer. One note of warning: make sure the thermometer is accurate, checking it from time to time by taking a reading in boiling water—212°F.

Potting and Storing: The yield of jam and number of jars needed is easy to ascertain: as the sugar content of the finished jam should not be less than 60 per cent., a recipe that needs 3 lb. sugar should yield 5 lb. jam. The jars must be clean and sterilised and should be warmed in an oven just before use. Be sure to buy packets of covers of the correct size for your jars; wax covers in particular must fit exactly, for air spaces increase the risk of mould.

JAM RECIPES

As the skins of currants are usually very tough, it is important to cook the fruit thoroughly until tender before adding the sugar.

BLACKBERRY AND APPLE JAM

8 lb. blackberries   3 lb. sour apples
1 pint water   Sugar

Place the blackberries in a pan with $\frac{1}{4}$ pint of the water. Simmer slowly until tender and sieve to remove the seeds. Peel, core and slice the apples, add the remaining $\frac{3}{4}$ pint water and cook until tender. Mash by beating with a wooden spoon. Add the sieved blackberries, weigh the pulp and add an equal weight of sugar. Stir, bring to the boil and simmer until the jam sets when tested. Pot and cover immediately in the usual way. (Yield 10 lb.) If the preserving pan is weighed beforehand, the weight of the pulp can easily be calculated.

PLUM JAM

(see pictures above and opposite)

6 lb. plums   6 lb. sugar
1$\frac{1}{2}$ pints water

Wash the fruit and cut in halves, removing the stones. Put the water, kernels and plums into a pan and bring slowly to boiling point. Simmer gently until the fruit is cooked. Add the sugar, stir until dissolved and bring to the boil. Boil briskly for about 10-15 minutes and test for jelling. Pot and cover as usual. (Yield 10 lb.)

BLACK-CURRANT JAM

4 lb. black-currants   6 lb. sugar
3 pints water

Remove the stalks, wash the fruit and put it into the preserving pan with the water. Simmer gently until it is tender and the contents of the pan are considerably reduce. As the mixture becomes thick, stir frequently to prevent burning. Add the sugar, bring to the boil, boil hard for 10 minutes and test on a cold plate for jelling. As soon as it sets, pot and cover immediately. (Yield 10 lb.)

MARROW AND GINGER JAM

4 lb. prepared marrow   Thinly peeled rind and
4 lb. sugar   juice of 3 lemons
1 oz. bruised root ginger

Peel the marrow, remove the seeds and cut into pieces about $\frac{1}{2}$ inch square. Weigh, place in a basin, sprinkle with about 1 lb. of the sugar and allow to stand overnight. Tie up the bruised ginger and the thinly peeled lemon rind in a piece of muslin and place, with the marrow and lemon juice, in a preserving pan. Simmer for $\frac{1}{2}$ hour, add the rest of the sugar and cook gently until the jam sets when tested on a cold plate. Pour into hot, sterilised pots and cover immediately. (Yield 6 lb.)

GOOSEBERRY JAM

6 lb. under-ripe goose-   2 pints water
berries   6 lb. sugar

Top and tail and wash the gooseberries, then put them into a pan with the water. Heat slowly at first, mashing the fruit as it softens, and continue to cook until the contents of the pan are reduced by about one-third. Add the sugar, stir until it is dissolved and bring back to the boil. Boil briskly for about 15 minutes and test for jelling. Pot and cover the jam in the usual way. (Yield 10 lb.)

RHUBARB GINGER

(see colour picture no. 55)

2$\frac{1}{2}$ lb. rhubarb, trimmed   1 oz. root ginger
2$\frac{1}{2}$ lb. sugar   4 oz. stem ginger

Wash the rhubarb and cut it into small pieces; pu it into a basin with the sugar sprinkled on in layers an leave overnight. Put the contents of the basin into pan, with the bruised root ginger tied in muslin. Brin to the boil and boil hard for 15 minutes. Add the ste ginger, cut into small pieces, and reboil for 5 minute or until the rhubarb is clear. Test for jelling; pot an cover immediately. (Yield 4-5 lb.)

DAMSON JAM

5 lb. damsons 6 lb. sugar
1½ pints water

Wash the damsons, put them in a pan with the water, bring to the boil and simmer until the fruit is cooked. Add the sugar, stir until dissolved and bring to the boil. Boil quickly, removing the stones as they rise. After about 10 minutes' boiling, test for jelling; pot and cover. (Yield 9-10 lb., according to the amount of stones removed.)

RASPBERRY JAM

4 lb. raspberries 4 lb. sugar

Place the fruit in a pan, heat gently at first (if necessary adding a very little water), then simmer until the fruit is tender. Add the sugar, stir until dissolved and bring to the boil. Test for a jell and continue to boil until the preserve jells satisfactorily on testing. Pot and cover. (Yield 6-6½ lb.)

STRAWBERRY JAM—I

3½ lb. strawberries, Juice of 1 lemon
hulled 3 lb. sugar

Put the fruit and lemon juice in a preserving pan and simmer gently until the fruit is really soft and the volume of liquid is well reduced. Add the sugar, stir until it has dissolved, then boil rapidly until setting point is reached. (Yield 5 lb.)

STRAWBERRY JAM—II

(Using commercial pectin)

2¼ lb. strawberries, 3 lb. sugar
hulled ½ bottle of commercial
Juice of 1 lemon (about pectin
3 tbsps.)

Wash the fruit and put it in the pan with the lemon juice and sugar; leave for 1 hour, stirring occasionally. Place over a low heat and when the sugar has dissolved, bring to the boil and boil rapidly for 4 minutes. Remove from the heat, stir in the pectin and leave for 20 minutes before potting, to prevent the fruit from rising. (Yield 5 lb.)

BLACK CHERRY JAM

2½ lb. black cherries, 3 lb. sugar
stoned 1 bottle of commercial
¼ pint water pectin
6 tbsps. lemon juice

Put the prepared fruit in a pan with the water and lemon juice and cook gently with the lid on for 15 minutes, then remove the lid. Add the sugar and stir over a low heat until this is dissolved. Bring to a full rolling boil and boil rapidly for 3 minutes. Remove from the heat, add the bottled pectin and stir well. Cool for 15 minutes, stirring occasionally, to prevent the fruit rising. Pot and cover in the usual way. (Yield 5 lb.)

QUINCE JAM

2 lb. quinces Juice of 1 lemon
2½ pints water 3 lb. sugar

Peel, core and slice the quinces. Cook slowly with the water and lemon juice in a preserving pan until the fruit is tender and mashed. Add the sugar, stir until dissolved and bring to the boil. Boil quickly for 10-15 minutes and test for jelling. Pot and cover as usual. (Yield 5 lb.)

PEAR JAM

3 lb. pears 3 tbsps. lemon juice
Thinly pared rind of 1½ 1 lb. 5 oz. sugar
lemons

Peel and core the pears and cut the flesh into chunks. Boil the cores, peel and lemon rind in ¼ pint water for 10 minutes, then strain. Put the juice in a pan with the pear chunks and lemon juice and simmer gently until the fruit is tender. Add the sugar and stir over a low heat until dissolved. Bring to the boil and boil rapidly until setting point is reached. Pot and cover as usual. (Yield 2-2½ lb.)

JELLIES

The main requirement for jelly-making is basically the same as for jams—that is, pectin, acid and sugar must all be present in correct proportions. Only fruit which is rich in pectin should be used (e.g., crab-apples, currants, gooseberries and quinces), though fruit with low pectin and acid content can be combined with one of the above—giving a variety of delectable flavours.

Apart from washing, the only preparation necessary is to remove any unsound pieces and to slice such fruits as apples and plums. Put into sufficient water to cover —using a little more water for hard-skinned fruits such as red and black currants—and cook slowly and thoroughly, to extract all the pectin and acid. Meanwhile, prepare a jelly bag or a linen cloth by scalding in boiling water and tying it to an upturned stool or chair. When the fruit is ready, strain it through the bag or cloth, allowing the pulp to drain until no more drops fall through—it may be left overnight if more convenient. Avoid pressing or squeezing, which would make the jelly cloudy. Fruits rich in pectin can be boiled twice to increase the extract, in which case the pulp is returned to the pan with about half the original quantity of water and simmered for a further ½ hour.

Measure the juice and put in a pan with the sugar; the amount added is usually 1 lb. per 1 pint of juice, but the lower the pectin content, the less the sugar needed. The jelly should set after about 10 minutes' boiling. As soon as setting point has been reached, remove the pan from the heat and quickly remove any scum from the surface, straining the jelly through scalded butter muslin if necessary. Pot and cover as for jams, but use small pots if available.

It is not practicable to quote the yield in jelly recipes because the degree of ripeness of the fruit and the time allowed for the dripping process both affect the quantity of juice obtained.

BLACKBERRY AND APPLE JELLY

2 lb. blackberries   1 pint water
2 lb. crab or cooking apples   Sugar

Wash the blackberries and wash and cut up the apples, without peeling or coring. Put the fruit in a pan with the water and cook for about 1 hour, until tender, mashing occasionally with a wooden spoon. Strain through a jelly bag or cloth and allow to drip. Measure the extract and put in a pan with 1 lb. sugar to each pint. Stir until dissolved, bring to the boil and boil rapidly for about 10 minutes, until it jells when tested. Pot and cover.

CRAB-APPLE JELLY

6 lb. crab-apples   Cloves or root ginger
3 pints water   Sugar

Wash the crab-apples and cut into quarters, without peeling or coring. Put into a pan and add the water. Bring to the boil and simmer for about 1½ hours, or until the fruit is mashed, adding a little more water if necessary. A few cloves or some root ginger may be added while the apples are cooking, if you think they are lacking in flavour. Strain through a jelly cloth. Measure the extract or juice and put into a pan. Bring to the boil, then add 1 lb. sugar to each pint of extract. Stir while the sugar is dissolving, allow it to boil briskly for about 10 minutes and test for jelling; pot and cover as usual.

CRANBERRY AND APPLE JELLY

3 lb. apples   Water to cover
2 lb. cranberries   Sugar

Wash the apples and cut into thick slices without peeling or coring. Wash the cranberries and put all the fruit into a pan; add sufficient water to cover and simmer gently until the fruit is thoroughly tender and mashed. Then strain through a jelly cloth, allowing it to drip overnight. Measure the extract, put into a pan and bring to the boil. When boiling, add 1 lb. sugar to each pint of extract, stir until dissolved, allow it to boil briskly for about 10 minutes, then test for jelling; pour into sterilised jars and cover at once.

This preserve is particularly good with roast turkey, baked ham and other meat, poultry and game dishes.

MEDLAR JELLY

3 lb. ripe medlars   Water (approx. 1½ pints)
1 lemon   Sugar

Cut up the fruit and the lemon, put into the pan, just cover with water and simmer until they become really soft and mushy. Strain through a scalded jelly bag and measure the extract. Return the extract to the pan with ¾ lb. sugar to each pint of juice. Finish in the usual way, pot and cover.

RASPBERRY JELLY

8 lb. raspberries   Sugar

Put the raspberries in a pan without any water and heat them, very gently at first, until they are quite soft and pulped. Strain the pulp through a scalded jelly bag. Measure the extract and return it to the pan, adding 1 lb. sugar to each pint of extract. Finish in the usual way, pot and cover.

ELDERBERRY AND APPLE JELLY

3 lb. elderberries   Water
3 lb. sweet apples   Sugar

Wash the fruits and slice the apples. Cook separately, using sufficient water to cover in each case. Simmer until tender, then strain through a jelly bag or cloth. Allow ¾ lb. sugar to each pint of the mixed juice and finish in the usual way.

MINT JELLY

(see pictures on these pages)

3 lb. tart green apples   Sugar
3 pints water   4 tbsps. chopped mint
1 bunch of mint   A few drops of green
3 pints vinegar   colouring

Wash and quarter the apples and place them in a pan with the water and the well-washed bunch of mint. Simmer until the apples are soft and pulped, then add the vinegar and cook for a further 5 minutes. Put into a scalded jelly bag and leave to drip overnight. The next day, measure the extract and return it to the pan with 1 lb. sugar to each pint of extract. Bring to the boil and boil until setting point is reached. Stir in the chopped mint and a little green colouring and finish in the usual way. Pot and cover.

Windfall apples may be used, providing any bruised parts are cut away.

BLACK- OR RED-CURRANT JELLY

4 lb. black- or 6 lb.   Sugar as
   red-currants   required
2 pints water

Wash the fruit, but do not remove the stalks. Put into a preserving pan with the water, place over a very low heat and simmer gently until the fruit is thoroughly cooked and all the berries pulped. Strain through a jelly bag and allow to drip for several hours. Measure the extract, put it into a pan and bring to the boil. Add 1 lb. sugar per pint of extract, stir until dissolved and bring to the boil, then boil briskly for about 7-10 minutes and test for jelling. When the preserve jells, pot and cover.

RED-CURRANT MINT JELLY

Follow the recipe above, but adding mint in the same way as directed in the recipe for Mint Jelly. This makes a delicious accompaniment to roast lamb.

QUINCE JELLY

4 lb. quinces   ½ oz. citric acid
6 pints water   if fruit is fully ripe
Sugar

Wash the quinces, cut up finely (or mince) and simmer in a covered pan with 4 pints water until tender—about 1 hour—then strain. Add the acid with the remaining 2 pints water to the pulp and simmer for another ½ hour, then strain again. Mix both extracts and allow ¾-1 lb. sugar to each pint. Bring the juice to the boil, stir in the sugar, then bring back to the boil and boil rapidly until setting point is reached. Finish in the usual way, pot and cover.

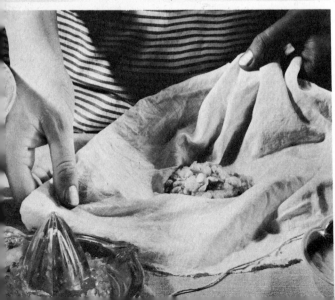

MARMALADE MAKING

Although the methods of marmalade-making are in the main the same as for other preserves, citrus fruits, with their tougher peels, do need much more preliminary cooking, so a greater proportion of water is needed to allow for evaporation at this stage. Many of the problems in marmalade-making could be avoided if it were remembered that during the first cooking the contents of the pan should reduce to rather less than half, if the traditional shallow pan is used. However, if a deep saucepan with a lid is used rather than a preserving pan, less evaporation takes place and less water is needed. Cook marmalade fruits for at least 1 hour in a covered pan after bringing to boiling point, using one-third to half the quantity of water given in the recipe. Then add the sugar and finish in the normal manner, allowing if necessary more time for setting point to be reached. This longer boiling after the addition of sugar gives marmalades a darker colour and mellower flavour, which is particularly advantageous when Seville oranges are not used.

Many recipes advise soaking the cut-up fruit and water overnight to soften the peel, and you may find it convenient to divide the operation into two.

There are many ways of preparing the peel, but the choice is largely a matter of personal taste and convenience. The most usual method is to shred the oranges completely before cooking, but some people prefer to cook the fruit whole and then shred it, removing the pips just before the sugar is added. Another method is to quarter the oranges, tie the pips in a muslin bag and cook the quarters with the water and pips—when softened, the peel is easily sliced.

See pp. 220-221 for pressure-cooked marmalades.

SEVILLE ORANGE MARMALADE

3 lb. Seville oranges   6 pints water
Juice of 2 lemons   6 lb. sugar

Scrub the fruit, cut in half and squeeze out the juice and pips. Slice the peel and put in a preserving pan with the lemon juice, water and pips (tied in a muslin bag). Cook gently until the peel is soft and the water is reduced by a half. Remove the bag of pips after squeezing it, add the sugar, stir until this is dissolved then bring to the boil and boil rapidly till setting point is reached. Remove any scum and let the marmalade cool slightly before pouring into warmed jars. Cover with waxed discs while still hot and seal when cold. (Yield 10 lb.)

DARK THICK MARMALADE

2 lb. Seville oranges   4 pints water
1 lemon   4 lb. sugar

Wash the fruit, cut in half and squeeze out the juice. Put the pips in a muslin bag. Cut the peel into thick shreds and put into a pan with the pulp, pips, juice and water. Mark the level of the contents on the outside of the pan, then boil for 2 hours, or until the depth is reduced by rather more than one-third. Remove the bag of pips. Add the sugar and bring to the boil, stirring constantly, until the sugar is dissolved. Boil for 1 hours, or until the colour has darkened and the preserve sets firmly when tested. Pot and cover immediately. (Yield 6 lb.)

54. Lemon Curd

55. Rhubarb Ginger

56. Bottling Tomatoes

57. Marmalade Making

58. Bacon and Egg Tart for one

59. Quick Pizza for one

60. Grilled Gammon for one

THREE-FRUIT MARMALADE

(see pictures on p. 216 and this page)

2 grapefruit	6 pints water
4 lemons	6 lb. sugar
2 sweet oranges	

The three sorts of fruit should weigh about 3 lb. all together. Scrub the fruit, cut in half and squeeze out the juice and pips. Slice the peel, either by hand or in a marmalade cutter, and put in a preserving pan with the juice, the pips (tied in a muslin bag) and the water. Cook gently for about 2 hours, until the peel is quite soft and the liquid is well reduced. Remove the pips, squeeze out the juice and add the sugar. Stir until it has dissolved, then bring to the boil and boil rapidly for 15-20 minutes, to setting point. Pour into warmed jars and cover at once with waxed discs. Seal when cold. (Yield 10 lb.)

SHRED MARMALADE

(see colour picture no. 57)

2 lb. Seville oranges	4½ pints water
Juice of 2 lemons	3 lb. sugar

Scrub the oranges and remove the peel; cut off the thick pith and shred 4 oz. of the peel finely. Cut up rest of fruit coarsely and simmer in 2½ pints water plus the lemon juice in a closed pan for 2 hours. Simmer the shreds in a closed pan with 1 pint water until tender. Drain off the liquid from the shreds and add to the pulp. Strain this through a scalded jelly or muslin bag and allow to drip for ¼ hour. Return pulp to pan, add remaining 1 pint water, simmer for a further 20 minutes and strain. When dripping stops, put the liquid in a preserving pan with the sugar. Stir over a medium heat, until the sugar has dissolved, then bring to the boil, add shreds and boil rapidly for 15-20 minutes, until setting point is reached. Skim quickly and allow to cool for 10 minutes before potting and covering. (Yield 5 lb.)

LIME MARMALADE

1½ lb. limes	3 lb. sugar
3 pints water	

Scrub fruit and peel rinds off thinly, using a potato peeler; shred the peel finely. Squeeze out the lime juice, then shred rest of pulp and tie it in muslin. Put rind, juice, water and bag of pulp into a pan and cook until well reduced. Remove the muslin bag, add the sugar and stir until it has dissolved. Boil rapidly until a set is obtained, pot and cover. (Yield 5 lb.)

GINGER MARMALADE

5 Seville oranges	6½ lb. sugar
5¼ pints water	½ lb. preserved ginger
3 lb. apples	½ oz. ground ginger

Wash oranges thoroughly, cut off rinds and shred these thinly. Squeeze out the juice and put in a pan with the shreds. Tie pips, pith and stringy parts in muslin and put into pan. Add 5 pints water and boil for 1½-2 hours, until contents of the pan are reduced considerably. Cool, squeeze juice from muslin bag and discard contents. Peel and core the apples, stew gently with the remaining ¼ pint water, mash well and combine with the oranges. Add sugar and gingers, boil for 10-20 minutes and test on a cold plate. When the preserve is boiled sufficiently to set, pot and cover as usual. (Yield about 10 lb.)

FRUIT CURDS, CHEESES AND MINCEMEATS

LEMON CURD
(see pictures above and colour picture no. 54)

4 lemons	1 lb. sugar
4 eggs	4 oz. butter

Wash and dry the lemons and grate the rind from each thinly, then halve the fruit and squeeze out all the juice. Strain the juice into a double saucepan and add the grated rind, beaten eggs, sugar and butter. Stir over a gentle heat with a wooden spoon until the sugar and butter are melted and the curd thickens. Don't boil or the mixture will curdle. Pour into sterilised jars and cover at once.

MARROW CURD

1 lb. prepared marrow	$\frac{3}{4}$ lb. sugar
3 lemons	4 oz. butter

Cut the marrow into small pieces and cook until tender, then strain away the juice. Add the finely grated rind and juice of the lemons and the sugar and butter. Stir whilst bringing slowly to the boil, then simmer to a thick cream. Pot, and at once seal to make airtight.

DAMSON CHEESE

6 lb. damsons	Sugar
$\frac{1}{2}$ pint water	

Put the damsons and water in a covered pan and cook slowly until tender. Sieve and weigh the pulp, which should be about 5 lb., then cook it in an open pan, stirring, until it is reduced to a thick mixture. Add sugar in the proportion of $\frac{3}{4}$ lb.-1 lb. per 1 lb. pulp and continue cooking, stirring all the time to prevent burning, until a spoon drawn across the bottom of the pan leaves a clean line. Press the pulp into a warmed mould or straight-sided jar which has been smeared with a little glycerine. Cover with a waxed disc whilst still hot and seal and store as for jams. For serving, the cheese is usually turned out whole on to a small plate or dish.
Medlars, black-currants, gooseberries and quinces also make excellent cheeses; follow the above recipe.

CRANBERRY CHEESE

3 pints cranberries	$1\frac{1}{2}$ lb. sugar
$1\frac{1}{2}$ pints water	

Wash and pick the cranberries, put in a saucepan with the water and simmer until they are thoroughly tender; if necessary a little more water may be added. When they are cooked, rub through a sieve with a wooden spoon. Wash out the saucepan, return the purée to the pan, add the sugar and bring to the boil, stirring all the time. Boil for 5 minutes, pot and cover.
Cranberry cheese is excellent as an accompaniment to roast game or turkey.

APPLE BUTTER

6 lb. crab-apples or windfall apples	1 level tsp. powdered cinnamon
2 pints water	$\frac{1}{2}$-1 level tsp. ground cloves (optional)
2 pints dry cider	
Sugar	

Wash the fruit, removing any damaged parts, and cut it up roughly. Simmer in the water and cider until pulpy. Rub it through a sieve and weigh it. Allow $\frac{3}{4}$ lb. sugar to every lb. pulp. Return the pulp to the pan and simmer until thick. Add the sugar and the spices and boil until it becomes thick again, stirring frequently. Pot and cover as usual.

MINCEMEAT I

$\frac{1}{2}$ lb. currants	Grated rind and juice of
$\frac{1}{2}$ lb. sultanas	1 lemon
$\frac{1}{2}$ lb. stoned raisins	$\frac{1}{2}$ lb. moist dark brown
$\frac{1}{2}$ lb. cooking apples	sugar
$\frac{1}{4}$ lb. mixed candied peel	2 oz. chopped almonds
$\frac{1}{2}$ lb. beef suet	$\frac{1}{8}$ pint brandy
$\frac{1}{2}$ level tsp. mixed spice	

Wash and prepare the fruit and chop it, together with the suet. Add the rest of the ingredients and mix thoroughly. Leave in a covered container for a week, stirring every day. Turn into jars and seal to make airtight. Keep for a few weeks; stir well before using.

MINCEMEAT II

$\frac{3}{4}$ lb. seedless raisins	Grated rind and juice of
$\frac{1}{2}$ lb. candied peel	1 orange and 1 lemon
$\frac{1}{2}$ lb. sultanas	$\frac{1}{2}$ oz. mixed spice
$\frac{1}{2}$ lb. currants	1 level tsp. grated
1 lb. cooking apples	nutmeg
$\frac{1}{2}$ lb. suet, finely chopped	$\frac{1}{4}$ pint brandy or rum (optional)
$\frac{3}{4}$ lb. brown sugar	

Mince twice or finely chop the cleaned and prepared raisins, the peel, half the sultanas and currants and the apples. Then add the remainder of the fruit and the other ingredients, mix well and leave in a covered jar or bowl. Stir every day for a week, then turn into jars, leaving 1 inch of space at the top. Cover as for jam and keep for a few weeks; stir well before using.

PRESERVING PROBLEMS

When Jam develops Mould

This is most often caused by failure to cover the jam with a waxed disc while it is still very hot—this should be done immediately the jam is potted, or it may become infected with mould spores from the air. Alternatively, pots may have been damp or cold when used or insufficiently full or they may have been stored in a damp or warm place. Other possible causes are insufficient evaporation of water while the fruit is being "broken down" by the preliminary cooking and/or too short boiling after sugar has been added. Mould is not harmful to the jam, but it may affect the flavour slightly. If it is removed, the jam can be boiled up again, re-potted in clean sterilised pots and re-covered; use for cooking purposes.

When Tiny Bubbles Appear

Bubbles indicate fermentation, which is usually the result of too small a proportion of sugar in relation to fruit; accurate weighing of fruit and sugar is very important. This trouble can also occur, however, when jam is not reduced sufficiently, because this too affects the proportion of sugar in the preserve. Fermentation is harmless enough, but it is apt to spoil both flavour and colour. Fermented jam can be boiled up again (see previous paragraph); continue the boiling for a short time if the preserve was not reduced enough in the first instance. Then it can be re-potted and sealed in clean, warm jars and used for cooking purposes.

When Peel or Fruit Rises in Jam

Strawberry jam and shred marmalade are particularly susceptible to this trouble. It helps if they are allowed to cool for 15-20 minutes and are then given a stir before potting, despite the fact that it is normally advisable to pot all preserves as hot as possible.

When Jam Crystallises

This is usually caused by lack of sufficient acid. You should either use a fruit rich in acid or make sure that acid is added to the fruit during the preliminary softening process. Under-boiling or over-boiling of the jam after the sugar has been added can also cause crystallising, as it will upset the proportion of sugar in the finished jam. Crystallisation may also be due to failure to dissolve the sugar completely before bringing the mixture to the boil.

When Jam won't Set

One cause is the use of over-ripe fruit in which the pectin has deteriorated. Other reasons include under-boiling of the fruit, so that the pectin is not fully extracted; there may also be insufficient evaporation of the water before the sugar is added (this can be remedied by further boiling); or over-cooking after adding the sugar (no remedy).

To ensure a set with fruits deficient in pectin, such as strawberries, it is helpful to add an acid such as lemon juice or citric acid; alternatively, mix with a pectin-rich fruit such as red-currants, or a pectin extract —commercially made or prepared at home from apples.

Shrinkage of Jam on Storage

This is caused by inadequate covering or failure to store the jam in a cool, dark place.

MARMALADES AND JAMS WITH A PRESSURE COOKER

If you have a pressure cooker (preferably one with a 3-pressure gauge), it is a good idea to use it for preserving, as it saves quite a bit of time and the fruit retains its flavour and colour.

Rules
1. Always remove the trivet from the pressure pan.
2. Never fill the pan more than half-full.
3. If possible, cook the fruit at 10 lb. pressure.
4. Remember that fruit must receive only its preliminary cooking and softening under pressure—never cook a preserve under pressure after adding the sugar (and lemon juice, if used), but boil it up in the open pan.
5. You can adapt any ordinary jam or marmalade recipe for use with a pressure cooker by using half the amount of water stated in the recipe and doing the preliminary cooking of the fruit under pressure.

Processing Times at 10 lb. Pressure

Marrow	1-2 mins.
Gooseberries	3 ,,
Black-currants	3-4 ,,
Apples	5 ,,
Damsons, plums and other stone fruit	5 ,,
Quinces	5 ,,
Pears (cooking)	7 ,,
Blackberries and apples combined	7 ,,

Notes: Soft fruits such as raspberries and strawberries need very little preliminary softening and are therefore not usually cooked in a pressure cooker. When two fruits (e.g. blackberries and apples) are combined, the cooking times may vary somewhat.

SEVILLE ORANGE MARMALADE

2 lb. Seville oranges	2 pints water
Juice of 2 lemons	4 lb. sugar

Wash the fruit and cut off the rind thinly. Peel off the pith, then cut up the fruit roughly (on a plate, to collect the juice). Place the pith and pips in a muslin bag and chop the rind into fine strips. Place the fruit, rind, lemon juice, muslin bag of pips and 1 pint of the water in the pressure pan, bring to 10 lb. pressure and cook for 10 minutes. Leave the pan to cool and reduce the pressure at room temperature. Remove the muslin bag, squeezing it well, then add the remaining water and the sugar. Return the open pan to a gentle heat and stir until the sugar dissolves, then bring to the boil and boil rapidly until setting point is reached. Pot and cover as usual. (Yield 6½ lb.)

THREE-FRUIT MARMALADE

2 oranges	1½ pints water
1 grapefruit	4 lb. sugar
2 lemons	

The combined weight of fruit should be about 2 lb. Wash it and cut into quarters. Tie the pips in a muslin bag. Put the fruit, muslin bag and ¾ pint water in the pan and pressure-cook at 10 lb. for 10 minutes. Reduce pressure at room temperature and lift out the muslin bag. Chop the fruit finely, then return it to the pan with the remaining water and sugar. When the sugar has dissolved, boil rapidly until a set is obtained. Pot and cover as usual. (Yield approx. 6 lb.)

GRAPEFRUIT AND LEMON MARMALADE

2 grapefruit (about 2 lb.)   1½ pints water
4 lemons (about 1 lb.)   3 lb. sugar

Wash the fruit and cut off the rind thinly. Peel off the pith, then cut up all the fruit roughly. Place the pith and pips in a muslin bag and chop the rind into fine strips. Place the fruit and rind, the muslin bag and ¾ pint of the water in the pressure pan. Bring to 10 lb. pressure and cook for 10 minutes. Allow the pressure to reduce at room temperature, then add remaining water and sugar. Return the open pan to a gentle heat and stir until the sugar has dissolved, bring to the boil and boil rapidly until a set is obtained—about 15 minutes. Pot and cover as usual. (Yield 4½-5 lb.)

SHRED MARMALADE

1 lb. Seville oranges   1¼ pints water
Juice and pips of 2 lemons   1½ lb. sugar

Peel the rind thinly from 2 of the oranges, cut into fine shreds and tie in a muslin bag. Roughly chop the rest of the fruit, pith and peel. Place the fruit, lemon juice and pips, bag of shreds and half the water in the cooker and cook at 10 lb. pressure for 20 minutes. Reduce the pressure at room temperature, then remove the bag of shreds and wash them in cold water. Strain the rest of the contents of the pan through a jelly bag, leaving it overnight. Return the extract and the rest of the water to the pan and bring to the boil, then add the sugar. Boil until setting point is reached and stir in the shreds. Allow to cool for about 15 minutes before potting, so that the shreds do not rise in the jars. (Yield 2-2½ lb.)

BLACK-CURRANT JAM

2 lb. black-currants   2 lb. sugar
½ pint water

String the fruit, then place it in the pan with the water and pressure-cook for 3 minutes at 10 lb. Reduce the pressure at room temperature. Add the sugar, then return the open cooker to a gentle heat and stir until the sugar is dissolved. Boil rapidly until a set is obtained. Pot and cover as usual. (Yield about 3½ lb.)

APRICOT CONSERVE

(see pictures on these pages and on p. 222)

1 lb. dried apricots   Juice of 1 lemon
1½ pints water   3 oz. blanched almonds
3 lb. sugar   (optional)

Soak the apricots in the water overnight or cover with 1 pint boiling water and leave for ½ hour. Put the fruit and water into the pan and pressure-cook at 10 lb. for 10 minutes. Allow the pressure to drop at room temperature, then open the cooker and stir in the sugar, lemon juice and almonds (if used). Bring to the boil and cook without a lid until the jam sets when tested. Pot and cover at once. (Yield 5-5½ lb.)
This recipe does not give a firmly set jam, but the flavour is very good.

APRICOT CONSERVE

DAMSON, GREENGAGE OR PLUM JAM

3 lb. fruit   3 lb. sugar
¼ pint water

Wash the fruit and place it in the pan with the water. Pressure-cook at 10 lb. for 5 minutes, then finish as usual. (Yield 5½ lb. approx.)

MELON AND PINEAPPLE JAM

2 lb. prepared melon   Juice of 3 lemons
½ lb. prepared pineapple   3 lb. sugar

Peel the melon, remove the seeds and cut the flesh into cubes before weighing it. Peel the pineapple and remove the "eyes" and any brown flesh, cut in cubes and weigh. Cook the fruit with the lemon juice at 10 lb. pressure for 10 minutes. Reduce pressure at room temperature, then add sugar and finish in usual way. (Yield 4-4½ lb.)

APPLE GINGER

3 lb. cooking apples   ½ pint water
2 level tsps. ground   3 lb. sugar
   ginger   4 oz. crystallised
Peel and juice of 1 lemon   ginger, chopped

Peel and quarter the apples. Place them in the pan with the ground ginger, lemon juice and water. Tie the apple peel and cores and the lemon peel and pips in a muslin bag and add this. Pressure-cook at 10 lb. for 5 minutes. Reduce the pressure at room temperature. Remove the muslin bag, add the sugar and crystallised ginger and stir over a gentle heat until the sugar has dissolved. Boil until setting point is reached; pot and cover. (Yield 4 lb. approx.)

LEMON CURD

2 eggs, beaten   Juice and grated rind
2 oz. butter, cut up   of 2 lemons
8 oz. caster sugar

Mix all the ingredients together in a basin, then cover this with a double sheet of greaseproof paper. Place on a trivet in the pressure cooker, pour ½ pint water and 1 tbsp. vinegar into the cooker, put on the lid and cook for 12 minutes at 15 lb. pressure. Reduce the pressure at room temperature. Beat the curd really well before pouring it into warmed jars. (Yield 1 lb. or just over.)

JELLY MAKING WITH A PRESSURE COOKER

The fruit used for jelly making can also be softened in a pressure cooker—this method is particularly useful for those fruits which have hard skins, pips, etc.

1. Prepare the fruit according to any ordinary jelly recipe.
2. Place in the cooker (without the trivet) and add only half the amount of water stated in the recipe.
3. Cook at 10 lb. pressure (see the sample times given below), then reduce the pressure at room temperature.
4. Mash the fruit well and pour into the prepared jelly bag. Finish as for ordinary jelly recipes.

Processing Times at 10 lb. Pressure

Gooseberries	3 mins.
Black-currants	4 ,,
Damsons	5 ,,
Apples	7 ,,

UNUSUAL PRESERVES

BRANDIED PINEAPPLE

(see picture on right)

1 large can (1 lb. 13 oz.) of pineapple pieces	A 2-inch stick of cinnamon
3 cloves	$\frac{1}{4}$ pint brandy or Kirsch

Drain the juice from the pineapple and put it into a saucepan; add the cloves and cinnamon and simmer gently together until of a syrupy consistency. Add the pineapple pieces and simmer then for a further 10 minutes. Remove from the heat and add the brandy or Kirsch. Cool, then pack the fruit into a wide-necked bottle. Pour on syrup and seal. Store in cool place.

SPICED PEARS

6 lb. hard pears	2 pints white vinegar
14 oz. sugar	2 sticks of cinnamon
$\frac{3}{4}$ oz. salt	$\frac{1}{4}$ oz. whole cloves
2 pints water	

Use small or medium-sized pears for this preserve. Dissolve 2 oz. of the sugar and the salt in the water and bring to the boil. Peel the pears and if large cut into quarters; add to the boiling water, remove the pan from the heat, cover and leave till cool. Boil together the vinegar, remaining sugar and spices. Remove the pears from the water and drain, then place them in the syrup and bring to the boil. Take from the heat, allow to cool and bring back to the boil. Repeat this process 3 times. Finally, allow to cool and place the pears in small jars. Pour the syrup over them, keeping the surplus, but do not seal. Top up each day for the next 4 days, or until no more syrup is absorbed. Cover as for jam.

SPICED PRUNES

1 lb. prunes	$\frac{1}{2}$ lb. sugar
Cold tea	$1\frac{1}{2}$ level tsp. mixed spice
$\frac{3}{4}$ pint cider vinegar	

Wash the prunes and soak them overnight in the cold tea. Boil together the vinegar, sugar and spice. Cook the prunes in a little of the tea for 10-15 minutes, or until soft; drain. Add $\frac{1}{2}$ pint of the juice to the vinegar. Put the prunes into small jars and cover with syrup. Cover as for jam.

PLUM-RUM JAM

1 lb. plums, finely chopped	2 lemons
$2\frac{1}{2}$ lb. sugar	2 tbsps. dark rum

Put the plums, sugar and lemon juice in a pan, bring to the boil and boil rapidly for 8-10 minutes, stirring all the time, until a light set is obtained. Remove from the heat and add the rum. Allow to cool, stirring at intervals, for 15 minutes. Pour into jars and seal.

RASPBERRY LIQUEUR CONSERVE

Put 1 lb. raspberries and 1 lb. sugar in separate containers in a moderate oven (350°F., mark 4); heat for 15 minutes. Combine them in a large mixing bowl and stir for a few minutes. Leave to stand for 20 minutes. Repeat the stirring and standing 3 times, then add tbsp. Kirsch or Cognac, pot in 1-lb. jars and cover.

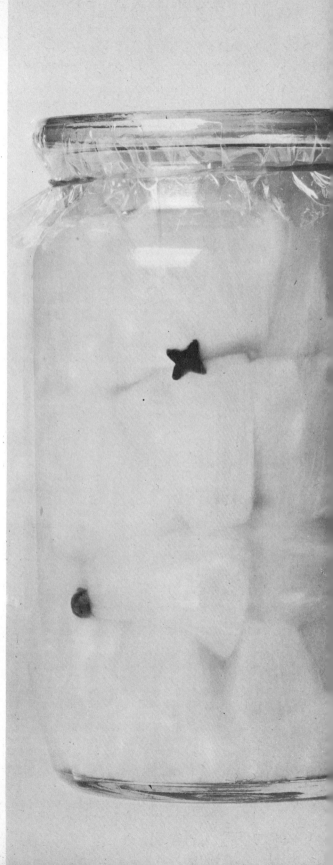

BOTTLING FRUIT

When the season of fresh fruits is at its peak, bottling offers an excellent way of preserving some of these short-lived delights. With a store of home-preserved fruits, you can enjoy summer pies, tarts and puddings all the year round.

THE FRUIT

Fruit chosen for bottling must be fresh, sound, free of disease, clean and properly ripe, neither too soft nor too hard. It is wise to select fruits of similar shape, size and ripeness for a given bottle.

Pick over the fruit and remove any that are damaged, as well as any leaves, stems and so on. Then wash and drain it well and pack into jars.

A few fruits require a little extra preparation, as follows:

Apples, Pears: Peel, core and quarter and drop into a brine solution (2 level tbsps. salt to 1 gallon water) to prevent discoloration. Just before processing, rinse well in fresh water, then drain before packing into the jars.

Peaches: Drop the fruit into boiling water for $\frac{1}{2}$ minute, then transfer to cold water. Skin them, then cut in half and remove the stones. Slice if you wish, and drop into a brine solution, as for apples. Rinse and drain before packing into the jars.

BOTTLING JARS

These are wide-necked glass jars, each covered with a metal sealing disc, with a screw-band to hold it firmly; they can be obtained in 1-lb. and 2-lb. sizes. Both the jars and the screw-bands can be re-used, but a new sealing disc must be used every time. All jars should be checked before use, to make sure that they can be made quite airtight and that they and the fittings are free from flaws. They must be scrupulously clean, so wash them and rinse in clean hot water; they need not be dried, as the fruit slips more easily into position if the inside of the jar is wet.

PACKING THE FRUIT

Place the prepared fruit in the jars layer by layer, using a packing spoon or a wooden spoon handle (see the left-hand picture opposite). When a jar is full, the fruit should be firmly and securely wedged in place, without bruising or squashing; the more closely the fruit is packed, the less chance there is of its rising after processing, when it will have shrunk to some extent.

When the jars have been filled all air bubbles should be dispelled by jarring the bottle on the palm of the hand; alternatively, pack in the fruit and add liquid alternately until the bottle is full. Fill the bottles to the brim before putting on the fittings. With wet-pack methods it is essential to loosen screw-bands by a quarter-turn before processing, to allow steam and air to escape, or the bottles may burst.

SYRUP FOR PRESERVING

Fruit may be preserved in either syrup or water, but syrup certainly imparts a better flavour and colour to the fruit. The usual proportion of sugar used for syrup is 8 oz. to 1 pint water, but the amount may be varied according to the sweetness of the particular fruit. Use granulated sugar, dissolve it in half the required amount of water, bring to the boil and boil for 1 minute, then add the remainder of the water. (This method cuts the time required for the syrup to cool.) If the syrup is to be used while still boiling (see below), keep a lid on the pan to prevent evaporation, which would alter its strength. Bottling syrup can be made with golden syrup instead of sugar, using the same proportions, i.e., 8 oz. syrup to 1 pint water. In this case, put the golden syrup and water into a pan, bring to the boil and simmer for 5 minutes before using.

When the fruit is to be sterilised by the slow water bath method, where the bottles are filled before heating, the syrup is used cold. For the quick water bath method, hot (not boiling) water is poured into the packed jars, which are then processed.

For the wet pack oven method, fill the packed jars with boiling syrup, then process. For the dry pack oven method, boiling liquid is also used, but is not added until after the fruit is processed.

PROCESSING AND TESTING

Sterilise the fruit by one of the methods which are described below, then seal as follows: lift the bottles one at a time on to a wooden surface and screw the band on firmly. When the bottles are cool, test for correct sealing by removing the screw-band and trying to lift the bottle by the sealing disc. If the disc holds firm, this shows that a vacuum has been formed as the jar cooled and it is hermetically sealed. If the disc comes off, there is probably a flaw in the rim of the bottle or on the cap. However, if several bottles are unsealed, the processing may have been faulty. The fruit from such jars should be used up at once or transferred to perfect jars and re-processed without delay.

STERILISING

There are two main methods—in the oven or in a water bath.

Oven Method: This is preferred by many people because quite a number of bottles can be done at one time, and—except for the jars—no special equipment is needed. It is not quite so exact a method as the water bath one, as it is not so easy to maintain a constant temperature and it is easier to over-cook the fruit.

When sterilising fruit by this method, use only one shelf, placed in the middle of the oven, and don't overcrowd the bottles on it, or the heat will not penetrate the fruit evenly.

Water Bath Method: This is considered to be the more exact method, but as it requires some special equipment it is possibly not so commonly used as the above way. For it you need:

1. A large vessel 2-3 inches deeper than the height of the bottling jars; a very large saucepan, a zinc bath or a bucket will serve.
2. A thermometer—a sugar-boiling one will do.
3. Bottling tongs (not essential).

See the detailed notes which follow.

OVEN METHOD OF STERILISING

Wet Pack: Heat the oven to cool (300°F., mark 1-2). Fill the packed jars with boiling syrup to within 1 inch of the top and put on the discs, but do not put the screw-bands in position. Place the jars 2 inches apart on a solid baking sheet, lined with newspaper to catch any liquid which may boil over. Put in the centre of the oven and cook for the time stated in the table. Remove the jars one by one, screw the bands tightly in place and leave to cool.

2. *Dry Pack:* Pack the bottles with the fruit but do not add any liquid. Cover with the discs and place 2 inches apart on a baking sheet lined as above with newspaper. Cook for the time stated in the table, then remove the jars one at a time (not all together). Use the contents of one jar to top up the others if the fruit has shrunk in the cooking. Fill up at once with boiling syrup and place the discs and screw-bands in place. Leave to cool.

The following are the temperatures and processing times recommended by the Long Ashton Research Station:

	Oven—Wet-pack: Pre-heat oven to 300°F. (gas mark 1); process as below:	*Oven—Dry-pack:* Pre-heat oven to 250°F. (gas mark ¼) and process as below:
Soft fruit, in normal packs:		
Blackberries Currants Loganberries Mulberries Raspberries Gooseberries and Rhubarb for pies Apples, sliced	1-4 lb. for 30-40 mins.; 5-10 lb. for 45-60 mins.	1-4 lb. for 45-55 mins.; 5-10 lb. for 60-75 mins. Not recommended for apples

	Oven—Wet-pack:	*Oven—Dry-pack:*
Soft fruit as above in tight packs; also Gooseberries and Rhubarb for dessert		
Stone fruit; dark, whole: Cherries, Damsons, whole Plums	1-4 lb. for 40-50 mins.; 5-10 lb. for 55-70 mins.	1-4 lb. for 55-70 mins.; 5-10 lb. for 75-90 mins.
Stone fruit; light, whole: Cherries, Gages, Plums		Not recommended for light-coloured fruit
Apricots Nectarines Peaches Pineapple Plums, halved	1-4 lb. for 50-60 mins.; 5-10 lb. for 65-70 mins.	Not recommended for these fruits
Figs Pears Whole Tomatoes	1-4 lb. for 60-70 mins.; 5-10 lb. for 75-90 mins.	1-4 lb. for 80-100 mins.; 5-10 lb. for 105-125 mins.
Tomatoes, solid pack (halved or quartered)	1-4 lb. for 70-80 mins.; 5-10 lb. for 85-100 mins.	Not recommended for solid packs

Note: The dry pack oven method is not recommended for fruits which discolour in the air, such as pears, apples and peaches. It will be seen from the above chart that with both oven methods the time required varies not only with the type of fruit, but also with the tightness of the pack and the total load in the oven at one time; the load is calculated according to the total capacity (in lb.) of the jars.

WATER BATH METHOD OF STERILISING

(see pictures on p. 225 and above)

Slow Water Bath: Pack the bottles with fruit and continue as follows:

1. Fill up the bottles with cold syrup.

2. Put the discs and screw-bands in place, then turn the screw-bands back a quarter-turn.

3. Place the bottles in the large vessel (see page 224) and cover them with cold water—immersing them completely, if possible, but at least up to the necks.

4. Heat gently on top of the cooker, checking the temperature of the water regularly; raise the temperature to 130°F. in 1 hour, then to the processing temperature given in the chart in a further ½ hour.

5. Maintain temperature for time given in chart.

6. Remove the bottles with the tongs (or bale out enough water to remove them with an oven cloth).

7. Place the bottles on a wooden surface one at a time and tighten the screw-bands straight away.

Quick Water Bath: If you have no thermometer, this is a good alternative method to the above. Fill the packed bottles with hot (not boiling) syrup, cover and place in the vessel of warm water. Bring the water to simmering point in 25-30 minutes and keep simmering for the time stated in the table.

Fruit	Slow Method	Quick Method
Loganberries Mulberries Raspberries Gooseberries and Rhubarb for pies Apple Slices	165°F., for 10 mins.	2 mins.
Soft fruit as above, tight packs; also Gooseberries and Rhubarb for dessert Stone fruit: Cherries, Damsons, whole Plums, Gages	180°F., for 15 mins.	10 mins.
Apricots Nectarines Peaches Pineapple Plums, halved	180°F., for 15 mins.	20 mins.
Figs Pears Tomatoes (whole)	190°F., for 30 mins.	40 mins.
Tomatoes, solid pack (halved, quartered)	190°F., for 40 mins.	50 mins.

Fruit	Slow Method Raise from cold in 90 mins. and maintain as below:	Quick Method Raise from warm (100°F.) to sim- mering (190°F.) in 25-30 mins. and maintain for:
Soft fruit, normal packs: Blackberries Currants	165°F., for 10 mins.	2 mins.

PULPED FRUIT

Many people like to bottle soft and stone fruits in this way. Prepare as for stewing, then cover with the minimum of water and stew until just cooked. While still boiling pour into hot bottling jars and place the discs and screw-bands in position. Immerse the bottles in a deep pan lined with newspaper and add hot water to come up to their necks. Raise the temperature to boiling point and maintain for 5 minutes. Remove the bottles and allow to cool.

Note.—The fruit may be sieved after stewing and before bottling if you prefer.

BOTTLING FRUIT IN A PRESSURE COOKER

This has the double advantage of shortening the time and ensuring exact control of the temperature. Any pressure cooker will take 1-lb. bottling jars, but if you want to use larger ones, you will need a pan with a domed lid to give the extra depth. (See pictures above and on next page).

1. Prepare the fruit as for ordinary bottling, but see also the additional notes in the chart below.

2. Pack into clean, warm bottles, filling completely.

3. Cover with boiling syrup or water to within $\frac{1}{4}$ inch of the top of the bottles.

4. Adjust the metal discs and screw-bands, screwing these tight, then turning them back a quarter-turn. Next, as an extra precaution, heat the jars by standing them in a bowl of boiling water.

5. Put inverted trivet into pressure cooker and add $1\frac{1}{2}$ pints water, plus 1 tbsp. vinegar to prevent pan from becoming stained. Bring water to boil.

6. Pack bottles into cooker, making sure they do not touch each other by packing newspaper between.

7. Fix the lid in place, put the pan on the heat and heat until steam comes steadily from the vent.

8. Put on the 5-lb. pressure control and continue heating gently to take about 3 minutes to reach pressure. Reduce heat and maintain pressure for time given in chart. (Any change in pressure will cause liquid to be lost from the jars and under-processing may result.)

9. Remove the pan carefully from the heat and reduce the pressure at room temperature for about 10 minutes before taking off the lid.

10. Lift out the jars one by one, tighten the screw-bands and leave to cool.

Fruit	Special Preparation	Processing time in mins. at 5 lb.
Apples	Peel, core and quarter. Keep in brine during preparation to prevent browning. Drain, rinse and pack at once	1
Apricots	If halved, remove stones	1
Blackberries, Raspberries, Loganberries	Pick over to remove damaged fruit, etc.	1
Cherries	Stalk, but leave whole	1
Red, black Currants	String	1
Damsons	Stalk	1
Gooseberries	Top and tail	1
Peaches	Scald in hot water for a few seconds, then transfer to cold water. Peel, halve and stone; slice if liked. Keep in brine during preparation. Drain, rinse and pack at once.	1
Pears	Prepare as for apples. Very hard cooking pears can be pressure-cooked before bottling for about 5 mins.	5
Plums	Prick skins if left whole; alternatively, cut in half and stone	1
Rhubarb	Wipe and cut in 3-inch lengths	1
Strawberries	Not recommended	
Tomatoes	Skin as for peaches; preserve either whole or halved, in brine (see p. 230)	5
Soft Fruit, solid pack	Place fruit in large bowl, cover with boiling syrup (6 oz. sugar to 1 pint water), leave overnight. Drain, pack jars as usual and cover with same syrup. Process as usual	3
Pulped Fruit, e.g., apples, tomatoes	Prepare as for stewing; pressure-cook with $\frac{1}{4}$ pint water at 15 lb. pressure for 2-3 mins., then sieve. While still hot, fill jars to within 1 inch of top, then process	1

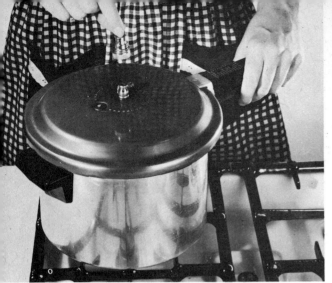

BOTTLING VEGETABLES

Don't attempt this unless you have a pressure cooker and are prepared to take great care to follow the directions exactly—food poisoning can result from faulty processing.

Choose very fresh vegetables and wash them really well, scrubbing them if necessary. Trim, prepare, and grade into even sizes and blanch them, i.e., plunge them into boiling water for the time given in the chart below, then plunge them into cold water. Drain well and fill into jars to within $\frac{1}{2}$ inch of the top—don't pack too tightly. Fill with boiling brine (made by boiling 1 oz. kitchen salt with every quart of water; you can also add a few drops of green food colouring when processing green vegetables). Adjust discs and screw-bands, turning the bands back a quarter-turn as for fruit. Place in a pressure cooker prepared as for fruit bottling, cover and heat: when steam flows from the vent, turn down the heat and allow steam to flow for 7-8 minutes. Put on the 10-lb. pressure gauge and process for the time given in the last column of the chart below. At the end of the processing time, allow to cool very slowly at room temperature before opening the cooker. Remove the bottles, tighten the screw-bands and leave until cold, then test for a seal before storing.

BOTTLING PROBLEMS

When the Seal Fails
Check neck of jar for chips, cracks or other faults. Inspect sealing disc to make sure that there are no faults or irregularities in the metal or the rubber rim. (You must use new sealing disc every time.) The instructions for each method of sterilising must be followed exactly—it is particularly important to tighten screw-bands immediately after processing.

When the Fruit Rises in the Jar
This does not affect the keeping quality of the fruit, but it does spoil the appearance. It can be due to the use of over-ripe fruit or too heavy a syrup, to over-processing, too high a temperature during the processing or loose packing in the jars.

When Mould Appears or Fermentation Takes Place
These are caused by poor-quality fruit, insufficient sterilising or failure of the bottle to seal.

When Fruit is Darkened
If only the top fruit is attacked, it can be due to fruit not being fully covered by liquid or to under-processing. If fruit is darkened throughout, this is probably due to using fruit in poor condition, over-processing or failure to store in a cool, dark place.

VEGETABLE-BOTTLING CHART

Vegetable	Preparation	Blanching	Processing Time at 10 lb. Pressure
Runner Beans	Wash, string, slice	5 mins.	40 mins.
Peas	Wash, shell, grade	2-3 mins.	50 mins.
Carrots	Wash, peel, slice or dice; if young, leave whole	10 mins.	45 mins.
Celery	Wash and cut in even lengths	6 mins.	40 mins.
Beetroot	Use only small ones. Cut off leaves and rub off skins after blanching	5-20 mins., according to size	35 mins.

CANNING

Canning is a very satisfactory method of preserving fruit, but since the apparatus is expensive, its purchase is only justified if there is a real abundance of free or cheap fruit. In some districts a canning machine is made available to the public through some local organisation and canning can then be carried out cheaply and to great advantage.

There are two types of can—those made of tinned steel-plate, which must not be used for red-coloured fruits, and lacquer-lined cans, which can be used for all fruits. If a can is dented do not use it unless you can restore it to shape; one with damaged lacquer should be rejected. Rinse the cans in clean water before use, but do not dry them, as the cloth might scratch the lacquer.

Select fruit as for bottling, seeing that in each can it is uniform in size, shape and ripeness, and pack closely. Cover with boiling hot syrup made from $\frac{1}{2}$-1 lb. sugar per pint of water, pouring it to within $\frac{3}{8}$ inch from the top. Place the lid on at once, and seal as quickly as possible, to prevent the entry of air, which could cause discoloration of the fruit and corrosion of the tin plate; follow the makers' instructions carefully. (See pictures).

Have ready a vessel fitted with a padded bottom and half-full of boiling water. Immerse the batch of cans completely in the boiling water, which must then be brought back to the boil. The processing time required depends on the time the water takes to re-boil, which in turn depends on the number of cans put into the vessel: the longer it takes to re-boil, the shorter the processing time, but 20 minutes should be the limit. (See chart.)

When the processing is completed, place the cans in a sink part-filled with cold water and preferably leave the cold tap running, to prevent over-cooking of the fruit. Remove the cans when at blood heat (test by rolling between the palms for half a minute). As they cool, the ends, which look convex, will resume their normal shape—sometimes with a light pop. Dry and label, stating type of fruit and date.

Store canned fruit in a cool, dry place, as it deteriorates quickly in a warm temperature; do not keep longer than 2 years and take care to use the cans in date order.

Fruit	Time to re-boil water (mins.)	Extra boiling time (mins.)
Apples (in syrup), apricots, black-berries, damsons, gooseberries, loganberries, ripe plums, rasp-berries, red-currants, rhubarb, strawberries	0-5	18-15
	6-10	15-13
	11-15	12-10
	16-20	10-8
Apples (solid pack), black-cur-rants, cherries, pears (ripe des-sert), plums (under-ripe)	0-5	22-20
	6-10	20-18
	11-15	17-15
	16-20	15-13
Tomatoes in brine (solid pack tomatoes should have 10 min-utes extra boiling)	0-5	35-32
	6-10	32-30
	11-15	30-27
	16-20	27-25

CANNING VEGETABLES

Vegetables must be processed under pressure; cans lined with a sulphur-resisting lacquer are required.

Scald or blanch the prepared vegetables according to the chart for bottling vegetables (p. 228), but reduce the time by 5 minutes when using a size A-2$\frac{1}{2}$ can. Pack the vegetables into cans and fill them with brine (2$\frac{1}{2}$ oz. salt to 1 gallon water) to within $\frac{1}{2}$ inch of top. Immediately place a lid on each can and put them into water at simmering temperature; it should come to within 1 inch of top of cans. Leave for 5 minutes, so that the contents of the cans are heated and the air is expelled, then remove the cans one at a time and seal as soon as they are removed from the hot water. Now sterilise the cans under pressure, following the chart for bottled vegetables, but if using size A-2$\frac{1}{2}$ cans, reduce the time by 5 minutes. Cool, dry, label and store as for canned fruit.

229

FRUIT SYRUPS AND JUICES

Fruit too ripe for bottling or jam-making is excellent for making syrups; the best are blackberries, black-currants, loganberries, raspberries and strawberries.

Any fairly small bottles can be used. Seal them as follows:
(a) With a cork, which must be cut off level with the top of the bottle and covered by a screw-cap.
(b) A screw stopper.
(c) A cork alone; it must be tied on with wire or string to prevent its being blown off during sterilisation.
Before use the bottles must be sterilised and corks, stoppers, etc., must be submerged under boiling water for 15 minutes.

In extracting the juice from the fruit no water is needed except for black-currants ($\frac{1}{2}$ pint per lb.) and blackberries ($\frac{1}{2}$ pint per 6 lb.). There are two methods of carrying out this process:

1. Place the fruit in a bowl over a pan of boiling water, break it up with a wooden spoon and leave until juice flows freely from the fruit (about 1 hour for 6 lb.), keeping the pan replenished with boiling water. (This method ensures that the fruit is not over-cooked, which tends to destroy its colour and fresh flavour).

2. Heat the fruit in a pan with the water (if used), and bring quickly to the boil, stirring constantly. Boil for 1 minute, crushing any whole fruit with a wooden spoon. Tip the fruit into a jelly bag and allow to drain overnight; the next day, press and squeeze the pulp thoroughly to remove all the remaining juice. Usually $\frac{3}{4}$ lb. sugar is required for each pint of juice. Stir it into the liquid over a gentle heat until dissolved.

Pour syrup into bottles to within $1\frac{1}{2}$ inch of top, then seal (picture 1). Place in a deep pan padded with thick cloth or newspaper. Fill to the base of the corks or stoppers with cold water, then raise to simmering point and maintain this temperature for 20 minutes. (If you have a thermometer, maintain at 170°F. for 30 minutes.)

Remove the bottles. If using corks only, seal by brushing over with melted candle wax when the bottles are slightly cooled (picture 2). Store in cool, dry place.

RASPBERRY OR RED-CURRANT SYRUP

Wash the fruit and drain it thoroughly. Put it into a large basin and stand this over a saucepan of boiling water, then heat slowly until the juice begins to flow, mashing the fruit with a wooden spoon occasionally. Remove from the heat and strain through a jelly-bag. Transfer the pulp to a clean linen cloth, fold over the ends and twist them in opposite directions, to squeeze out as much juice as possible. Measure the extracted juice and add $\frac{3}{4}$ lb. sugar to every pint. Stir thoroughly over a gentle heat until dissolved and pour into sterilised jars. Sterilise as directed above and wrap the bottles in brown paper to keep the syrup a good colour during storage.

Use this syrup as a sauce to serve with steamed sponge puddings and similar sweets in the winter, or with ice cream in the summer.

ROSE-HIP SYRUP

Rose-hips give a syrup which is particularly rich in Vitamin C, and a different method of making is used to ensure that the highest possible amount of the vitamin is retained. The syrup is valuable both for growing children and for those who are suffering from a deficiency of vitamin C in their diet.

Choose hips which are fresh, fully ripe and deep red. Crush, grate or mince them and put at once into boiling water, allowing 3 pints per 2 lb. hips. Bring back to boiling point, then remove from the heat and allow to stand for 10-15 minutes. Strain through a scalded cloth or jelly-bag and when it ceases to drip, return the pulp to the pan with another $1\frac{1}{2}$ pints boiling water. Re-boil and let stand as before for 10 minutes, then strain. Mix the two extracts, pour into a clean pan and reduce by boiling until the juice measures $1\frac{1}{2}$ pints. Add 1 lb. sugar. Stir until dissolved and boil for 5 minutes. Pour while hot into clean, hot bottles and seal at once. Sterilise as for all fruit syrups.

Rose-hip syrup may be taken neat, or diluted to make a drink; alternatively, it may be used in the same ways as Raspberry or Red-currant Syrup, above.

PRESERVING TOMATOES

Tomatoes can be preserved in a variety of ways; the most usual method is to bottle them, but they may also be stored in the form of purée or juice, they may be canned (see p. 229) or made into sauce or chutney.

BOTTLED TOMATOES

(see colour picture no. 56)

Any method used for bottling fruit is suitable for tomatoes; these are the main variations in the preparation:

1. *With no liquid added:* Dip each tomato in boiling water for about 20 seconds, then remove the skin. Use small tomatoes whole, but halve or quarter larger ones, so that they may be packed really tightly with no air spaces, making it unnecessary to add any water. The flavour is improved if about 1 level tsp. salt and 1 level tsp. sugar are sprinkled among the fruit in each bottle.

2. *In their own juice:* Peel the tomatoes as above and pack tightly into bottles. Stew some extra tomatoes in a covered pan, with $\frac{1}{4}$ oz. salt to each 2 lb. fruit, strain the juice and use to fill up the jars.

3. *Whole unskinned tomatoes (recommended for oven sterilising):* Remove the stalks and wash or wipe the tomatoes. Pack into bottles and fill up with a brine made with $\frac{1}{2}$ oz. salt per quart water.

For the temperatures and times for bottling tomatoes, see the general bottling tables on pp. 225-226.

BOTTLED TOMATO PURÉE

This method enables poorly shaped tomatoes to be used, though they must be sound and ripe. Wash, heat them in a covered pan with a little water and salt and cook until soft. Rub the pulp through a sieve and return it to the pan, then bring to the boil; when it is boiling, pour it at once into hot jars and put the metal sealing discs and screw-bands in place. It is very important that this process should be carried out quickly, as the pulp deteriorates if left exposed to the air. Immerse the bottles in a pan of hot water (padded with thick cloth or newspaper), bring to the boil and boil for 10 minutes. Finish and test as usual.

TOMATO JUICE

Simmer ripe tomatoes until soft and rub them through a hair or nylon sieve. To each quart of pulp add $\frac{1}{2}$ pint water, 1 level tsp. salt, 1 oz. sugar and a pinch of pepper. Process the juice as for Tomato Purée.

RED TOMATO CHUTNEY

4 lb. red tomatoes	$\frac{1}{2}$ lb. sugar (granulated or
1 oz. mustard seed	Demerara)
2 level tsps. allspice	1 oz. salt
$\frac{1}{2}$ level tsp. cayenne	$\frac{3}{4}$ pint white malt
pepper	vinegar

Peel the tomatoes by putting them all in boiling water for 1-2 minutes, then plunging them into cold—the skins will then come off easily. Tie the mustard seed and allspice in muslin and add with the cayenne to the tomatoes. Boil until reduced to a pulp ($\frac{3}{4}$ hour) and add the sugar, salt and vinegar. Continue boiling until the right consistency is obtained ($\frac{3}{4}$-1 hour) and bottle in hot sterilised jars. (Take care to reduce the mixture sufficiently, or the chutney will be too liquid.)

GREEN TOMATO CHUTNEY

3 lb. green tomatoes	$\frac{1}{2}$ oz. mustard seed
$\frac{1}{4}$ lb. cooking apples	$\frac{1}{2}$ level tsp. pepper
$\frac{1}{4}$ lb. onions	$\frac{1}{2}$ level tsp. ground
1 oz. salt	allspice
$\frac{1}{4}$ lb. prunes	$\frac{3}{4}$ pint vinegar
6 oz. sugar	

Wipe the tomatoes and remove the stalks. Peel and core the apples and peel the onions. Put all through a mincer, then add the salt and leave overnight. Soak the prunes overnight. The next day, strain off the liquid from the tomatoes, etc., and turn the pulp into a pan. Stone and chop the prunes and add to the tomatoes, with the sugar, the spices (tied in muslin), and the vinegar. Simmer gently, stirring occasionally, until reduced to a pulp—about 2 hours. Pot and cover.

RED TOMATO SAUCE

4 lb. ripe tomatoes	$\frac{1}{2}$ level tsp. paprika
2 medium-sized onions	pepper
1 oz. salt	4 oz. sugar
A pinch of cayenne	$\frac{1}{3}$ pint spiced
pepper	vinegar (p. 232)

Wash and cut up the tomatoes, place them in a pan with the peeled and chopped onions and simmer gently until the tomatoes are pulped. Rub through a sieve, return the mixture to the pan and add the remaining ingredients. Simmer, stirring occasionally, until of a creamy consistency, pour into warm bottles, seal with sterilised corks and brush the top with melted candlewax when cool.

GREEN TOMATO SAUCE

3 lb. green tomatoes	$\frac{1}{2}$ level tsp. cayenne
$\frac{1}{2}$ lb. apples	pepper
$\frac{1}{4}$ lb. sliced onions	3 cloves
$\frac{1}{2}$ lb. sugar	1-2 blades of mace
$\frac{1}{2}$ oz. salt	$\frac{1}{2}$ level tsp. celery seed
$\frac{1}{2}$ lb. golden syrup	$\frac{3}{4}$ pint vinegar
$\frac{3}{4}$ oz. peppercorns	

Wipe and slice the tomatoes, peel, core and slice the apples, then add the onion, sugar, salt, syrup, spices, etc., and pour the vinegar over them. Boil gently until the sauce is thick, rub it through a fine sieve (adding more vinegar if necessary), then re-heat, stirring, and boil till of a creamy consistency. Pour into warmed sterile bottles and cover immediately.

PICKLES AND CHUTNEYS

EQUIPMENT

The pans used for pickles, etc., should be made of a thick-gauge metal which is not affected by the acid in the vinegar. The best types are aluminium, stainless steel, or those lined with porcelain or enamel (make sure that the lining is not chipped or damaged in any way). Unlined brass or copper pans must not be used, as the acid reacts with the metal, forming traces of a poisonous salt—copper acetate.

The coverings for pickle and chutney jars should be really airtight, to prevent evaporation of the vinegar. Suitable types are: (1) Special vinegar-proof synthetic "skin". (2) Parchment paper brushed over with melted paraffin wax. (3) Greaseproof paper covered with a piece of fine cotton dipped in wax. (4) Properly lacquered metal caps which are lined with discs of a special vinegar-proof paper called ceresin, or with waxed cardboard or with a layer of cork, so that the preserve does not come into contact with the metal and cause corrosion and rusting. Old metal caps should not be re-used unless the lacquer is in perfect condition, and they should always be relined with new ceresin discs.

SPICED VINEGAR FOR PICKLING

The vinegar must be of high quality, with an acetic acid content of not less than 6 per cent; it may be malt, white, wine or cider. To each quart add $\frac{1}{4}$ oz. each of some or all of the following spices: cloves, peppercorns, allspice, chillies, blade mace, mustard seed and root ginger. (Alternatively, buy them already mixed as "pickling spice.")

Bring just to the boil in a covered pan, then remove from the heat, allow to infuse till the vinegar is flavoured —about 2 hours is usually sufficient—and strain.

If you like a very spicy flavour, include the actual spices in the pickle, either in between the layers of vegetables, or placed in the top of each jar—tied if desired in a muslin bag, so that they may easily be removed.

When filling pickle jars, allow at least $\frac{1}{2}$ inch vinegar above the level of the fruit or vegetable, as a little evaporation is inevitable, but do not let the vinegar come in contact with metal caps.

Allow your pickles and chutneys to mature for 2-3 months (except for cabbage, which is better eaten while still crisp); to preserve their colour, it is best to store them in a dark place.

PICKLES

These can be sweet or sour, and are made from uncooked fruit and vegetables (either left whole or cut up, used singly or mixed), which are preserved in clear spiced vinegar. Piccalilli is an exception, and consists of a combination of vegetables preserved in a special thickened mixture.

The first stage in pickle-making, after the preparation of the fruit or vegetables, is the brining process, which should be "dry" or "wet" according to the water content of the particular ingredient. The purpose is to extract liquid and carbohydrates from the tissues, making the pickled food crisp and preventing the growth of bacteria. If the water is not extracted, it dilutes the vinegar, reducing its preserving powers, and also makes it harder for it to penetrate the tissues. After brining, rinse and drain the fruit or vegetables very thoroughly.

Dry Brining is used for watery vegetables such as cucumber, marrow, tomatoes, etc. Place the prepared vegetables in a mixing bowl, sprinkle salt between the layers, allowing about 1 level tbsp. salt to 1 lb. vegetables; cover and leave overnight.

Wet Brining is used for cauliflower, onions, etc. Allow 2 oz. salt to 1 pint water (sufficient for about 1 lb. vegetables), place the prepared vegetables in a mixing bowl, cover with the brine and leave overnight. Root vegetables, such as artichokes, and sometimes beetroot, are cooked in half-strength brine until tender.

Spiced Vinegar is used for covering most simple pickles. Brewed malt vinegar is most commonly used, but for onions, cauliflower and other light-coloured vegetables, white vinegar may be used.

CHUTNEYS

Chutneys are a blend of fruit and vegetables with vinegar, sugar and spices, cooked to a thick consistency; a long simmering time gives a pleasantly smooth, mellow flavour. A vast variety of flavours and colours can be obtained by combining different fruits and vegetables, but the final effect should not be too pungent. To ensure the characteristic soft, even texture, the ingredients must be either minced or evenly and finely chopped, and no whole spices should be included.

PICKLED ONIONS
(see pictures opposite)

Choose small onions or shallots. To make the peeling easier, either do it under cold water, or use a knife and fork (picture 1). Soak in brine made with 2 oz. salt to 1 pint water (picture 2) for 24 hours, then drain and wash well. Pack into jars, using a wooden spoon handle, and pour the cold spiced vinegar over. Seal and store.

PICKLED RED CABBAGE

1 firm red cabbage	1 quart spiced vinegar
Salt	

Quarter the cabbage, removing the outer leaves and centre stalk. Shred each quarter and place in a large basin, sprinkling each layer with salt. Leave overnight, then rinse and drain thoroughly. Pack loosely into bottles or jars, cover with vinegar and tie down. Do not store for more than 2-3 months, or the cabbage will lose its crispness and colour.

PICKLED WALNUTS

Green walnuts	Spiced vinegar
Brine	used cold

Wipe the walnuts, prick well and put into a basin, rejecting any that feel hard when pricked. Cover with brine. Allow to soak for 7 days, throw away the brine, cover with fresh brine and re-soak for 14 days. Wash, dry well, spread the walnuts out and expose them to the air until they blacken. Put into pickle jars, pour hot spiced vinegar over and tie down when cold. Store in a cool place for 5-6 weeks before use.

An interesting variation is obtained by pickling walnuts and onions together. Each should be prepared according to the directions given. Place equal quantities of each in jars, arranged in alternate layers, and pour cold spiced vinegar over them.

PICKLED NASTURTIUM SEEDS

Nasturtium seeds	1 bay leaf
$\frac{1}{2}$ pint white vinegar	3 peppercorns
$\frac{1}{2}$ level tsp. salt	

Pick the seeds on a dry day, wash and examine for insects. Dry well and then put in a cool oven or the sun to dry. To prepare the vinegar, put the salt, bay leaf, peppercorns and vinegar into a saucepan, bring to the boil, remove from the heat and infuse for $\frac{1}{2}$ hour at least, then cool. Pack the nasturtium seeds into jars, cover with the cold spiced vinegar and cork securely in the usual way. Use as a substitute for capers.

APPLE AND ONION PICKLE

¾ lb. tart-flavoured	9 cloves
cooking apples	1½ oz. chillies
¾ lb. onions	1½ level tsps. salt
2 oz. sultanas	¾ pint vinegar
9 peppercorns	

Chop the apples and onions finely and pack them together with the sultanas in hot, dry jars. Tie the spices in muslin, add the salt to the vinegar and steep the spices in it for $\frac{1}{2}$ hour. Bring to the boil and simmer for 10 minutes. Pour on the boiling vinegar and tie down. This is ready for use the next day.

MIXED PICKLES

The following vegetables make a good mixed pickle: Cauliflower, cucumber, green tomatoes, onions and marrow.

Prepare the vegetables, with the exception of the marrow, and soak in brine for 24 hours. Peel the marrow, remove the seeds and cut into small squares, sprinkle with salt and let stand for 12 hours. Drain the vegetables, rinse, pack and cover with cold spiced vinegar, tie down and store for at least 1 month before eating.

MINT PICKLE

$\frac{1}{2}$ lb. tomatoes	1 level tsp. peppercorns
1 lb. sound cooking	1 blade of mace
apples	6 small onions
$\frac{1}{2}$ pint vinegar	1 oz. sultanas
8 oz. sugar	1 teacupful mint
2 level tsps. dry mustard	leaves (pressed
2 level tsps. salt	down)
1 stick of cinnamon	

Cut the tomatoes into four and peel and slice the apples. Boil the vinegar, sugar, condiments and spices together very gently for $\frac{1}{2}$ hour, then strain. Add the remaining ingredients (except the mint) and simmer for 10 minutes. When the mixture is cold, pack the fruit and onions in jars, sprinkling the chopped mint leaves liberally between the layers. Cover with the spiced vinegar, cover the jars and leave for a month before use.

PICCALILLI

1 large cauliflower	1 oz. bruised root
2 cucumbers	ginger
2 lb. shallots	1 oz. black peppercorns
2 lb. apples	2 quarts vinegar
Brine	2 oz. cornflour
1 oz. chilli peppers	1 oz. turmeric
2 oz. garlic	1 oz. dry mustard

Prepare all the vegetables and the apples as required and cut into neat pieces. Cover with cold brine, leave overnight, drain and pack into hot jars. Boil the chilli peppers, garlic, ginger and peppercorns in the vinegar for 5 minutes, then pour in the cornflour, turmeric and dry mustard, previously blended with a little cold vinegar. Stir and boil for 10 minutes to cook the cornflour. Pour on to the vegetables and fruit and cover in the usual way.

SPICED SWEET PICKLE

3 lb. mixed cucumber,	3 level tbsps. cloves
melon rinds, and	1 stick of cinnamon
cooking apples	2 pints vinegar
3 level tbsps. allspice	1½ lb. Demerara sugar

Cut the fruit and vegetables into neat pieces. Stew the melon rind in a little water for 15 minutes, then add the cucumber and apple, cook for a further 10 minutes, and drain thoroughly. Tie all the spices in a muslin bag and boil with the vinegar and the sugar for 10 minutes. Add the fruit and vegetables, bring to the boil and simmer for 5 minutes. Drain the mixture well and pack it into hot jars. Boil the vinegar for a further 10 minutes, remove the bag of spices and pour the vinegar into the jars. Cover in the usual way.

APPLE AND TOMATO CHUTNEY

2 lb. apples	$\frac{3}{4}$ lb. sugar
2 lb. tomatoes	$\frac{1}{2}$ oz. mustard seed
$\frac{3}{4}$ lb. onions	$\frac{1}{2}$ oz. curry powder
1 clove of garlic	1 level tsp. cayenne pepper
$\frac{1}{2}$ lb. dried fruit (seeded)	Salt to taste
	$1\frac{1}{2}$ pints vinegar

Peel and core the apples and stew in a very little water until they are tender and pulpy. Cut up the tomatoes and chop the onions and the garlic (also the dried fruit if necessary). Add these and the sugar to the prepared fruit. Tie the mustard seed in a piece of muslin and add it, with the remaining ingredients, including the vinegar, and cook gently for about 2 hours. When the chutney reaches the required consistency, pot and cover.

APPLE AND GREEN PEPPER CHUTNEY

3 green peppers	12 oz. sugar
1 medium-sized onion	$1\frac{1}{2}$ level tbsps. ground ginger
3 lb. tart apples	$\frac{1}{4}$ lb. red-currant jelly
$\frac{1}{2}$ lb. raisins, seeded	Juice and rind of
1 level tbsp. salt	3 lemons
$\frac{1}{2}$ pint vinegar	

Seed the peppers, peel the onion, peel and core the apples and mince all finely together with the raisins. Place the mixture in a large saucepan with the remaining ingredients and simmer for about 1 hour, or until the chutney is thick; turn it into warmed pots and cover.

APRICOT CHUTNEY

2 lb. dried apricots	1 level tsp. allspice
$\frac{1}{2}$ lb. onions	A pinch of cayenne pepper
3 lb. brown sugar	2 pints wine vinegar
1 level tsp. curry powder	
1 level tsp. cinnamon	

Wash the apricots well, cover them with boiling water and leave for 24 hours. Chop the onions, and stew them with a little of the sugar until tender. Strain the apricots and cut into pieces, put into a pan with the sugar, spices, onions and vinegar and simmer until the chutney is thick—about 2 hours. Pot and cover.

DAMSON CHUTNEY

$3\frac{1}{2}$ lb. damsons	$1\frac{1}{2}$ lb. brown sugar
2 onions	$2\frac{1}{2}$ pints malt vinegar
A clove of garlic	$\frac{1}{2}$ oz. salt
$\frac{1}{2}$ lb. raisins	1 oz. ground ginger
$\frac{1}{4}$ lb. dates	$\frac{1}{4}$ level tsp. ground allspice

Wash the fruit. Chop the onions, crush and chop the garlic, chop the raisins and dates. Mix all the ingredients in a pan and simmer for $1\frac{1}{2}$-2 hours very slowly, until the desired consistency is attained. Remove the damson stones. Pour into jars while hot and cover immediately.

DATE AND APPLE CHUTNEY

1 lb. apples	$\frac{1}{2}$ level tsp. cayenne pepper
1 lb. dates	$\frac{1}{2}$ oz. salt
$\frac{1}{2}$ lb. onions	6 cloves
2 oz. sultanas	1 level tsp. ground allspice
$\frac{1}{2}$ lb. treacle	1 pint vinegar

Peel and core the apple, stone the dates if necessary, peel the onions and put all these ingredients through a mincer, together with the sultanas. Put the remaining ingredients in a pan and bring slowly to the boil. Add the minced fruit, etc., and simmer gently until the chutney is of a thick consistency. Pot and cover at once.

GOOSEBERRY CHUTNEY

3 lb. gooseberries	$\frac{1}{2}$ level tsp. cayenne pepper
$\frac{1}{2}$ lb. stoned raisins	2 level tbsps., salt
4 onions, sliced thinly	$1\frac{3}{4}$ lb. brown sugar
$\frac{1}{4}$ oz. crushed mustard seed	$1\frac{1}{2}$ pints vinegar

Put all the ingredients in a pan and cover with the vinegar. Bring to the boil slowly and continue to cook for 2 hours, until the gooseberries are thoroughly pulped. If the vinegar boils away, add a little more. Put the chutney into warm jars and seal immediately.

PEAR CHUTNEY

3 lb. pears	$\frac{1}{4}$ level tsp. cayenne
1 lb. onions	$\frac{1}{4}$ level tsp. ground ginger
1 lb. green tomatoes	$\frac{1}{2}$ oz. salt
$\frac{1}{2}$ lb. raisins, seeded	5 peppercorns
$\frac{1}{2}$ lb. celery	2 pints vinegar
$1\frac{1}{2}$ lb. Demerara sugar	

Peel, core and slice the pears, peel and chop the onions, wipe and cut up the tomatoes and cut up the raisins. Put all these ingredients into a pan and cook gently until tender. Add the finely chopped celery, the sugar, the spices and the vinegar and simmer for 4 hours, until the chutney is sufficiently thick. Pot and cover.

PLUM AND APPLE CHUTNEY

3 lb. plums	1 level tsp. salt
2 lb. apples	$1\frac{1}{2}$ pints vinegar
1 lb. green tomatoes	$1\frac{1}{2}$ lb. granulated sugar
$\frac{1}{2}$ lb. onions	3 level tsps. finely chopped mint
$\frac{1}{2}$ oz. root ginger	
1 oz. allspice	

Prepare the fruit and vegetables, stoning the plums, peeling and coring the apples, stalking the tomatoes, and skinning the onions, then chop them up and mix well together. Bruise the ginger and tie in muslin with the allspice. Put everything except the sugar and mint into a saucepan and simmer until the mixture begins to thicken. Add the sugar and mint and cook until quite thick. Remove the bag of spices, pot and cover.

RHUBARB CHUTNEY

2 lb. rhubarb	$\frac{1}{2}$ oz. cayenne pepper
$\frac{1}{2}$ oz. garlic	1 lb. sultanas
1 oz. root ginger	2 lb. Demerara sugar
Peel of 2 lemons	1 pint vinegar
1 oz. salt	

Shred the rhubarb finely and chop the garlic. Crush the root ginger and tie in a piece of muslin with the lemon peel. Put all the ingredients into a pan and simmer gently, stirring frequently, until the mixture thickens. Remove the bag of flavourings and pot the chutney while hot. Keep it for 3 months before using.

BED-SITTER COOKERY FOR ONE

QUICK MEALS WITH EGGS AND CHEESE

OMELETTES

Follow the recipe given on page 89, but use 2 eggs only. To make a more satisfying meal, add a filling (which is usually cooked or heated and placed on the omelette before this is folded). Here are some extra suggestions:
Bacon and Mushroom: Lightly fry 1-2 diced bacon rashers, add 2 oz. sliced mushrooms and cook until tender.
Spinach: Cook a 5-oz. packet of frozen spinach in butter and season with salt, pepper and nutmeg. Spread on the omelette and sprinkle with 1-2 oz. chopped ham or grated cheese.
Apple and Bacon: Fry 2-3 diced bacon rashers lightly with 1 diced apple until tender; add a dash of lemon juice and sprinkling of sugar.
Cheese: (1) Grate 2 oz. firm cheese and mix with a little chopped parsley. Sprinkle most of this over the omelette before folding and the remainder on top as it is served.
(2): Melt 2 oz. grated cheese, 1-2 tbsps. milk and ½ oz. butter over a low heat; add ½ tsp. mustard or vinegar before using.
Smoked Haddock: Flake some cooked smoked haddock and heat gently in cheese sauce.
Tuna Fish: Flake a 3-oz. can of tuna and mix with a little condensed mushroom soup.
Tomato: Chop 2-3 tomatoes and fry in butter for 4-5 minutes, till soft and pulped. Add salt, pepper, ½ level tsp. sugar and a pinch of rosemary, sage or mixed herbs.
Prawn: Sauté 2 oz. thawed frozen prawns (or shrimps) in melted butter with a squeeze of lemon. A little chopped green pepper or onion can be added.

SPANISH OMELETTE

Use the recipe on p. 89 but include 2 eggs only; the other ingredients can be slightly reduced—for example, use ½ an onion.
This more filling type of omelette (sometimes called Omelette Paysanne) may be varied at will. Almost any vegetables can be added to or substituted for the onion and pepper and it makes a grand way of using up leftovers. Try these mixtures:
. Add a chopped tomato and a pinch of mixed herbs to the onion, pepper and potato mixture.
. Fry a few strips of canned pimiento or fresh red pepper with the onion and potato and add a few leftover peas.
. Replace the potato by a slice of bread, diced.

SCRAMBLED EGGS

Follow the recipe on p. 86, using 2 eggs.

SAVOURY TOASTED CHEESE

2 oz. cheese, grated	Salt and pepper
A few drops of	A little milk
Worcestershire sauce	Toast, buttered
½ tsp. made mustard	

Mix the cheese and seasonings, bind to a paste with milk, spread on toast and grill until golden.

CHEESEBURGERS

2 oz. minced beef	Salt and pepper
2 oz. cheese, grated	Milk
A little chopped onion	Flour

Mix together the meat, cheese, onion, seasonings and enough milk to bind the mixture together. Divide into small balls and work in enough flour to give a smooth mixture, then form into flat, round cakes and cook under a hot grill for 2 minutes on each side, or until crisp and golden-brown.
For a slightly richer, more filling variation, divide the mixture into smaller balls and wrap round each a rasher of bacon, securing it with a cocktail stick. Cook under a hot grill, turning frequently to brown the bacon evenly.

CHEESE DREAMS

Make some small cheese sandwiches in the usual way and cut off the crusts. Melt some butter in a frying pan and fry the sandwiches until golden and crisp on both sides. Serve at once.

CHEESE AND ONION CRISP

Skin 1-2 onions, slice into thin rings and parboil in salted water for 5-10 minutes. Drain well and lay on slices of buttered toast. Sprinkle with salt and pepper, cover with thin strips of cheese and cook under a hot grill until golden and bubbly.

QUICK PIZZA
(see colour picture no. 59)

4 oz. self-raising flour	½ level tsp. dried sage,
A pinch of salt	mixed herbs or oregano
Cooking oil	3 oz. cheese, diced
3-4 tbsps. water	A few anchovy fillets
An 8-oz. can of tomatoes	A few stuffed olives

Mix the flour and salt with 1 tbsp. oil and the water to a soft dough. Roll out into a 6-inch round and fry the pizza gently in a little oil in a shallow pan for about 5 minutes, or until it is browned on the underside. Turn it over and cover with the well-drained tomatoes, herbs and cheese; garnish with the anchovy fillets and sliced olives. Fry on the second side for a further 5 minutes, then place under a hot grill until the topping is golden-brown. Serve with a simple green salad.
Although the dough is made by a quick method, the topping given above is a traditional one; however, you can vary it by using other mixtures—for instance:
1. Spread with canned tomatoes, sprinkle with chopped ham or crisply fried bacon, add diced cheese.
2. Use sliced mushrooms dotted with butter to replace the anchovies.
3. Spread with canned tomatoes, then sprinkle with chopped sautéed green pepper and diced cheese.
4. Spread with sardines or pilchards in tomato sauce, then sprinkle with diced cheese.

—WITH MEAT AND BACON

STEAK

It is worth while trying to find a butcher who will serve you with good quality steak, well prepared. There are several types of frying steak:

Rump has a very good flavour, but is not always very tender.

Fillet, the undercut of the sirloin, is very tender, but has less flavour than rump and is more expensive; it is often cut into rounds, known as tournedos.

Porterhouse is a thick steak, on the bone, cut from the sirloin and usually incorporating the fillet.

T-bone steak is cut from the sirloin and contains a T-shaped bone.

Entrecôte is a steak without bone, usually cut from the sirloin, though it can be the ribs.

Allow about 6 oz. for an average portion, or 8 oz. for a fairly generous amount.

Cooking

Put the meat on a firm, flat surface and beat well with a rolling pin to break down some of the fibres and make the meat more tender.

Grilling: Brush the steak with oil or put a few small knobs of butter on the top, then season it. Put it under a very hot grill, turn it after 1 minute, brush the second side with oil or add more butter, season and cook for a further minute. Lower the heat and continue cooking, turning the steak once or twice with tongs or 2 spoons, so as not to pierce the flesh and let the juices run out.

Frying: Beat as above, season, put into a pan with a little hot butter and cook for a minute on the first side, turn, season and cook for a further minute. Lower the heat and continue cooking as above.

Cooking Times: For a steak ½ inch thick allow 2-3 minutes each side for rare, 4-5 minutes for medium rare and 6 minutes each side for well done.

Serve with fried potatoes and onions or chipped potatoes, watercress and grilled or fried tomatoes.

For a change, serve with a green salad or have spaghetti instead of potatoes.

BACON AND KIDNEYS

Rind 1-2 rashers of lean bacon and snip the fat so that it does not curl during the cooking. Skin and halve 2 lamb's kidneys and remove the cores. Toss both in seasoned flour. Melt ½ oz. lard and fry the kidneys lightly on all sides. Add the bacon and cook until both kidneys and bacon are done (about 10 minutes). Serve with chopped spinach.

BACON, LIVER AND MUSHROOMS
(see picture below)

A rasher of lean bacon	½ oz. lard
2-4 oz. calf's or lamb's liver	½ small onion, chopped
	1 oz. mushrooms, chopped

Rind the bacon and chop it up. Wash and trim the liver and cut into thin strips. Melt the lard and fry the onion and bacon for 2-3 minutes. Add the liver and mushrooms and continue frying over a gentle heat, stirring from time to time, until the meat is cooked (about 10 minutes). Drain well and serve with rice or crusty bread.

BACON AND EGG TART
(see colour picture no. 58)

4 oz. frozen puff pastry, thawed	2 eggs, beaten
	1 tbsp. milk
2 rashers of back bacon, chopped	Salt and pepper
	1 tbsp. cheese, grated

Roll out the pastry and line a fairly small pie plate. (Use foil if you have no metal plate.) Put in the bacon. Mix the eggs, milk and seasoning and pour over the bacon. Sprinkle with cheese and bake in a fairly hot oven (400°F., mark 6) for 20 minutes, until the filling is well-risen and acquires a golden "crust". This tart will give 2 servings and can be eaten both hot and cold. If you want to make a one-portion tart, allow half the above quantities, with 1 tsp. milk. Use a small foil dish and bake for the same time.

GRILLED GAMMON

Allow 1-2 rashers or 1 steak for a serving. Trim off the rind with scissors and make cuts into the fat at intervals, to prevent the rashers from curling. Place under a medium grill, brushing with a little oil or melted butter, if very lean, and cook on each side for 5-8 minutes, according to thickness. Serve in one of these ways:

With Vegetables (see colour picture No. 60). Grill some mushrooms and/or halved tomatoes alongside the gammon and make a complete course by serving with crisps and spinach; garnish with a slice of pineapple if available.

With Sweet and Sour Sauce: Mix 1 tbsp. red-currant jelly and 1 tbsp. mango chutney, add the grated rind and the juice of ½ a lemon and simmer for 5 minutes, until syrupy. Use hot or cold.

ORANGE-GRILLED GAMMON

Grill the steak on one side, turn and cook for about 2 minutes on the second side, then spread with a mixture of 1 tbsp. white vinegar or lemon juice and 1 tbsp. orange marmalade. Cook until the gammon is tender. Serve with sprigged cauliflower.

DEVILLED GAMMON STEAKS

Mix 1 oz. butter with ½ level tsp. curry powder, 2 tsps. chutney, a pinch of cayenne, a squeeze of lemon juice or a few drops of Worcestershire sauce. Grill the rashers on one side, turn and cook for about 2 minutes on the second side. Spread with the mixture and continue cooking until the meat is tender.
Serve with a green salad.

FRIED VEAL ESCALOPE

Get the butcher to beat the escalope until thin. Coat with beaten egg and either fresh white breadcrumbs (if you have the time) or packet coating crumbs. Melt 1 oz. butter and fry the veal gently on both sides until tender and golden—about 6-8 minutes. Drain well on absorbent paper and serve with lemon and a green salad.

ESCALOPE WITH HAM AND CHEESE

Top the cooked escalope with a thin slice of cooked lean ham and 1 tbsp. grated Parmesan cheese. Spoon a little of the cooking butter over the cheese, cover the pan with a lid or large plate and cook gently for 2-3 minutes, until the cheese has melted. Serve at once with a salad or a green vegetable such as French beans.

PORK FILLET WITH APPLE RINGS

A piece of pork fillet (4-6 oz.)	1 tbsp. oil
oz. butter	1 apple, cored
	1 level tbsp. brown sugar

Beat the fillet with a rolling pin or a wooden spoon until quite thin. Heat the butter and oil together, then fry the meat gently on both sides until tender—about 5 minutes. Cut the apple into thick rings and fry lightly on both sides; sprinkle with sugar and fry for another 1-2 minutes, until the sugar just begins to melt. Drain the meat well and serve with the apple.

PORK LUNCHEON MEAT SAVOURY

½ oz. lard	½ a 7-oz. can of luncheon meat
½ small onion, chopped	A 5-oz. can of baked or curried beans
½ an apple, peeled, cored and chopped	

Melt the fat and fry the onion and apple for 5 minutes. Dice the meat, add to the pan and continue cooking for a further 5 minutes. Stir in the beans and heat until bubbly. Serve alone or with toast.

CASSEROLED BEEF AND TOMATOES

½ a small onion, chopped	2-4 tomatoes, peeled and sliced
1 stick of celery, sliced	1 tsp. Worcestershire sauce
½ oz. butter	
2 level tsps. plain flour	Salt and little pepper
2 tbsps. water	
A 5-oz. can stewed steak	

Sauté the onion and celery in the hot fat until tender. Stir in the flour, brown it, then stir in the water. Add the meat, tomatoes, sauce and seasoning. Bring to the boil and simmer until the tomatoes are tender. Serve with buttered carrots.

CORNED BEEF CASSEROLE

1 oz. butter	A 5-oz. can of baked beans
2-3 cooked potatoes, diced	Salt and pepper
½ small onion, chopped	2 oz. corned beef, diced

Melt the butter in a pan, add the potatoes and fry until lightly browned; remove a quarter of them and set on one side for the topping. Add the onion to the remaining potatoes and brown lightly. Stir in the beans, season well, add the meat, mix well and heat thoroughly. Put into a small fireproof dish and sprinkle the remaining potato over the top, then brown under a hot grill.

HAMBURGERS

Frozen hamburgers or beefburgers of any well-known brand provide a quick meal.

Grill on one side as directed on the packet and turn. To give extra flavour top with one of the following, then continue cooking as usual:

A slice of cheese

1 tsp. butter mixed with 1 tsp. made mustard or a pinch of dried thyme and a good pinch of salt

2 tbsps. grated onion, a thinly sliced tomato or 3 sliced stuffed olives.

Alternatively, make a sauce while the hamburgers are cooking—

Sweet Barbecue Sauce: Melt 1 oz. butter in a pan, add ½ a small onion, grated, and sauté for a few minutes. Stir in 1 tsp. tomato purée and cook for a further 2 minutes. Stir in 2 tsps. vinegar, 2 level tsps. Demerara sugar, 2 tbsps. water, ½ tsp. made mustard and 2 tsps. Worcestershire sauce, simmer for 2 minutes; serve very hot.

Sharp Barbecue Sauce: Warm together in a small pan 1 tbsp. Worcestershire sauce, 1 tbsp. tomato sauce, ½ level tsp. caster sugar, 1 tsp. vinegar, ¼ oz. butter, a pinch of salt, a shake of pepper, 1 tbsp. water, and ½ a small onion, grated.

KIPPERS

To reduce smell, cook by putting into a tall jug, pouring in boiling water to cover, "lidding" with a saucer and leaving for 5-7 minutes. Drain the kippers and serve with a knob of butter.

SMOKED HADDOCK or GOLDEN FILLETS

Wash a 6-8 oz. piece, put into a pan and add milk (or milk and water) to cover. Bring to the boil, remove from the heat, cover with a lid and leave for 5 minutes. Drain the fish well and serve topped with a knob of butter or a poached egg.

FISH AU GRATIN

Cook fresh cod or haddock as for smoked haddock. Use the cooking liquor to make up a packet cheese sauce; pour over the fish, grate a little cheese over and grill until golden. Serve with green peas.

HERRINGS

Grilled: Have the fish cleaned by the fishmonger, but left whole. Scrape off the scales and trim off the fins and tail with scissors. Score the skin diagonally 2-3 times on each side and season. Cook under a medium grill for 5-7 minutes on each side.

A fresh mackerel is equally good cooked this way.

Alternatively, open and bone the fish and put it flesh side upwards on the grill rack; dot with butter and cook until this melts. Sprinkle a few breadcrumbs over and replace under the grill till these are brown and cooked. Serve with lemon.

Herring Fried in Oatmeal—a traditional Scottish way of serving this nourishing and economical fish. Have the fish cleaned and boned. Sprinkle it with salt and pepper, then dip in coarse oatmeal, pressing it well into both sides. Fry on both sides in hot fat until a light golden-brown colour and drain well. With it try a white sauce to which a little made mustard has been added.

Roes on Toast: 2 roes for a snack, 3-4 for a meal. Sprinkle with salt and pepper and dredge with a little flour, then top with a knob of butter. Place under a medium grill and cook first on one side, then on the other. Another way is to shallow-fry the roes and serve on hot buttered toast.

FRIED PLAICE

Buy 2-4 fillets, according to size. Egg-and-crumb, then fry in shallow fat for 3-5 minutes each side, till the fish is cooked and the coating crisp. Serve with broccoli and bought matchstick potatoes.

FROZEN FISH FINGERS

Cook as directed on the packet and serve with frozen mixed vegetables.

TUNA CRISP CASSEROLE

(see picture on left)

Make up half a packet of cheese sauce mix and add 3½-oz. can of tuna fish, flaked; season well, bring to the boil, then put into an individual casserole. Sprinkle with 1-2 oz. grated cheese and some crushed potato crisps, grill until the topping is golden.

QUICK ACCOMPANIMENTS

Vegetables
Don't skimp on vegetables, thinking them too much trouble to cook for one. Small cauliflowers, spring greens, celery, beans, peas, root vegetables—all can be bought in small quantities and used for two meals. Cook rapidly in very little water or drop them into the potato pan or add to the stew.

Tomatoes and Mushrooms are a godsend for single-person catering—they are so easily and quickly grilled, fried or sautéed and go with so many foods.

Frozen and Dehydrated Vegetables: No preparation, no waste, quick cooking—everyone knows their advantages. Leftovers can be kept in a cold place till next day and used up in omelettes, casseroles and other dishes. Follow the manufacturer's directions for cooking.

Potatoes: If you like to cook a batch of "real" potatoes only two or three times a week, it usually pays to prepare double quantities and use up the leftovers in one of these ways:
Sautéed: Fry the sliced cooked potatoes in shallow fat until golden on both sides.
Fried: Mashed potato (either plain or combined with a little finely chopped onion) can be lightly fried in shallow fat till thoroughly heated and crisply golden on the underside. It can also be mixed with diced corned beef and gently fried to make a simple hash.
Potato Salad: Dice cold potatoes, mix with a little chopped onion or dried herbs and bind with salad cream.

Short Cuts: For real speed you can use potato powder or ready-cooked matchstick potatoes and crisps, which need little or no cooking. Frozen chipped potatoes or puffles are more practical than home-cooked chips for the bachelor household.

Salads
See pp. 109-126

Rice, Pasta, Beans
Par-boiled or pre-cooked rice—obtainable at various supermarkets and speciality food shops—takes at most 5-10 minutes to prepare; follow the directions on the pack. When you are less rushed, cook long-grain rice— it need take no longer than cooking potatoes (see p. 127). A quick and tasty meal is made by adding "extras" to canned ravioli, spaghetti or baked beans.
Add ½ level tsp. curry powder to ravioli or spaghetti and heat through; or chop ½ an onion, fry it lightly and stir in.
Chop leftover meat and stir into the contents of the can before heating. Equally tasty additions are chopped cooked sausage, frankfurter, ham, crisp fried bacon, salami or garlic sausage.
Shellfish gives a rather exotic touch to spaghetti or ravioli—add 1-2 oz. prawns or shrimps before heating. A dash of Worcestershire or Tabasco sauce gives a spicy flavour.
Chopped green peppers or mushrooms make a colourful addition to baked beans or pasta.

Bread
Crusty French bread, toast, soft or crisp rolls, breadsticks, crispbread and biscuits ring the changes.

FIFTEEN-MINUTE PUDDINGS

When you want a change from fresh fruit or biscuits and cheese, try some of the following suggestions:

GRILLED GRAPEFRUIT

Loosen the segments of a half-grapefruit, sprinkle the cut surface with brown sugar, dot with butter and grill gently until the fruit is heated through and bubbling.

YOGHOURT PLUS

Both flavoured and plain yoghourt come in small sizes. For a change, sprinkle with Demerara sugar or chopped nuts, pour it over fruit or mix with chopped dates, dried fruit or crystallised ginger.

PACKET PUDDINGS

These mixes, available in several flavours, make quick and easy puddings for two meals. Eat them plain, with fruit or sprinkled with nuts or chocolate.

CANNED CREAMED RICE

Buy this in cans holding a single serving and eat it either hot or cold. To vary it:
1. Top with a drained canned peach or pear half; spoon over it a sauce made by thinning down raspberry jam or red-currant jelly with some juice from the fruit.
2. Layer cold creamed rice with jam or leftover canned or stewed fruit. For a luxury touch, fold in fresh or canned cream or use this as a topping.
3. Heat the rice, flavour with mixed spice or nutmeg and turn it into a small ovenproof dish. Sprinkle with Demerara sugar and grill until golden and bubbly.

ICE CREAM WITH A SAUCE

Here are some "quickie" sweet sauces:
Chocolate: Put 2 oz. plain chocolate (broken in pieces) and a small knob of butter in a small basin standing in a pan of hot water, melt, then stir in 2 tsps. milk. Serve hot or cold.

Mocha: Add ½ level tsp. coffee powder to above sauce.

Chocolate Cornflake: Add ½ cup cornflakes to the finished chocolate sauce and stir until well coated.

Toffee: Melt together 1 level tbsp. sugar, 1 tbsp. golden syrup and 1 oz. butter. Boil for 1 minute, then stir in 1 tbsp. milk. Allow to cool slightly before serving. You can also add some lemon juice or chopped nuts.

Jam: Any jam can be used to make a sauce for ice cream, especially raspberry, black-currant, cherry, apricot and pineapple. Allow about 2 tbsps. jam to an individual portion. Mix with a little lemon juice or water if necessary to give a pouring consistency. Heat through or serve straight away, as you prefer.

Fudge: Chop 2-3 oz. vanilla fudge and melt with 1 tbsp. milk in a small basin standing in a pan of hot water; stir well. Cool slightly before using.

WHEN IT'S ONE-PLUS-ONE

Shopping is often easier when you're planning a meal for yourself and a guest—so many foods come in two-portion packs. If cooking facilities—or time—are very limited it's wise to choose a first course that entails little preparation and perhaps either a main course or a sweet that can be cooked beforehand.

Most of the items mentioned here can be bought in a well-stocked grocer's shop, supermarket or delicatessen.

STARTERS

Melon: This always makes a refreshing hors d'oeuvre. Supermarkets often sell cut portions of honeydew or cantaloup melon and at times you can buy a very small Charentais melon, which is just enough for two people and has a particularly good flavour. Halve the melon or cut the portion in wedges, remove the seeds and serve with caster sugar and powdered ginger. For a special occasion you can add a garnish of a cherry and a pair of mint leaves impaled on a cocktail stick.

Thin wedges of melon can also be served wrapped in a slice of lean ham—traditionally, it should be Italian smoked Parma ham, but any well-flavoured type will do.

Pâté: This is simply sliced, laid on a bed of lettuce and served with toast and lemon. (1-1½ oz. per person.)

Potted Shrimps: Buy in individual pots; turn them out on to lettuce and serve with lemon wedges and brown bread.

Rollmops: Buy these in a screwtop jar. Drain a couple and serve on lettuce, with 1-2 onion rings to garnish. (The rest will keep quite well if the jar is tightly lidded.)

Herring and Mackerel Fillets: These may be bought in a wide variety of sauces—mustard, cream, lobster, lemon, paprika. Serve with lettuce and tomato wedges or with other salad ingredients.

Individual Salads: Sliced tomato looks pretty if given a simple oil and vinegar dressing, served on a bed of watercress or lettuce and sprinkled with a little chopped onion, celery or chives.

Hard-boiled eggs can be sliced and coated with salad cream (diluted, if you are feeling generous, with an equal amount of single cream); serve them on lettuce, with a little chopped parsley or chives and perhaps a dusting of paprika pepper.

Avocado Pear: Rather expensive, but very good for the occasional splurge. One good-sized ripe one will serve two people; make a cut round the middle from top to stem end, twist the two halves in opposite directions to loosen them, pull apart, then remove the stone. Brush the cut flesh with lemon juice to prevent browning, spoon a simple French dressing (see p. 124) over it and sprinkle with a pinch of fresh herbs (parsley, chives, tarragon) if available. Serve with brown bread.

Seafood Cocktail: Allow 2 oz. picked shrimps or prawns or a 1½-oz. can of crab-meat. Pile the shellfish on a bed of lettuce in individual glasses and spoon over it the following sauce: 2 tbsps. tomato ketchup, 2 tbsps. salad cream, 1 tbsp. cream or top of the milk, salt, pepper and a little lemon juice or Worcestershire sauce, all blended together. Serve with lemon wedges.

SOLE À L'ORANGE

Grated rind and juice of 1 orange	Salt and pepper
1½ oz. butter, melted	¾ lb. sole or plaice fillets
2 tomatoes, halved	A sprig of parsley

Add the orange rind and juice to the melted butter. Brush the halved tomatoes with a little of this butter and season them. Place the fish, skin side down, in the grill pan, pour half the orange butter over it and grill for 3-4 minutes. Pour on the remaining orange butter and grill for a further 2-3 minutes. Grill the tomatoes. Garnish the fish with the parsley and grilled tomatoes and serve accompanied by chips and peas.

TROUT AND ALMONDS
(see picture below)

2 trout	1-1½ oz. whole blanched almonds
Seasoned flour	
3 oz. butter	Lemon juice

Coat the trout with seasoned flour and fry for 5 minutes on each side in half the butter. When they are tender, remove from the pan and arrange on individual dishes or plates. To the fat remaining in the pan add the rest of the butter and fry the almonds till golden-brown; remove from the pan and add a squeeze of lemon juice. Pour the butter over the trout and add the almonds. Serve with broccoli (or other vegetables).

PRAWNS ESPAGNOLE

1 onion, finely chopped	A 4-oz. pkt. of frozen prawns
1 oz. butter	
½ a green pepper, chopped	Salt and pepper
An 8-oz. can of tomatoes	2 oz. rice, cooked

Fry the onion in the butter without colouring it. Add the green pepper and cook for 3-4 minutes. Add the tomatoes, prawns, and seasoning and simmer for 15 minutes. Add the rice and continue to simmer for 5 minutes. Turn into a serving dish.

HAM IN SHERRY SAUCE

2-3 oz. noodles	2 tbsps. sherry or Madeira
1½ oz. butter	6 oz. ham, chopped
1 oz. flour	Salt
½ pint chicken stock, made	Pepper
from a cube	

Cook the noodles in boiling salted water for 15-20 minutes, until tender. Melt 1 oz. butter in a saucepan, add the flour to make a roux and cook for 1 minute. Gradually add the stock and sherry and bring to the boil. Add the ham and some seasoning and simmer for 5 minutes, until the ham is heated through. Drain the noodles, return them to the pan and toss in the remaining butter. Arrange the noodles in a ring on a dish and pour the ham and sauce into the centre.

HAM AND CRANBERRIES

2 ham steaks	A 7-oz. can of jellied
A little oil	cranberry sauce
Seasoning	2 oz. grated cheese

Brush the steaks with a little oil and season well on both sides. Grill one side for 7 minutes, then cook for a further 3 minutes on the other side. Place a slice of cranberry jelly on each steak and sprinkle with half the grated cheese. Continue to grill until the cheese is bubbly and the cranberry jelly warmed through.

HAM STEAKS WITH FRUIT

2 ham steaks	Seasoning
Oil	Fruit (see below)

Brush the ham steaks with the oil, season and grill for 7 minutes on one side, then turn. Grill for a further 5 minutes. Arrange on a serving dish, with the chosen fruit, prepared as follows:

Pineapple Rings: Put under the grill for 2-3 minutes before serving, to heat through. Arrange alternately with the ham steaks or on top of them. Pour the juice from the pan over them.

Apple Rings: Cut a peeled and cored apple into ¼-inch slices. Dust them all over with caster sugar and grill for 2-3 minutes on both sides, until soft. Serve as for pineapple.

Peach Halves: Dust canned peach halves with brown sugar and grill until the sugar melts and the peaches are heated through. Serve on the ham steaks.

Orange Slices: Peel an orange, removing the pith and inner skin. Slice the orange across, place the pieces in the grill pan and heat through. Serve the orange slices on top of the ham steaks, or alternating with them. Pour the juice over the steaks.

CHICKEN FRICASSEE

a ready-cooked chicken	½ pint savoury white sauce
onion, finely chopped	made from a packet mix
carrot, sliced	1 tbsp. lemon juice
tbsp. oil	2 tbsps. cream or top-
Salt and pepper	of-the-milk

Dice the chicken meat. Fry the onion and carrot together in the oil without colouring them. Put the diced chicken and sauce into a saucepan; add the drained vegetables and heat through. Blend a little of the sauce in a basin with the lemon juice, return to the pan, heat through, then remove from the heat. Add the cream and seasoning and serve at once. (Do not make beforehand and re-heat, or the cream will separate out.)

PIQUANT FISH TURNOVERS
(see picture above)

½ lb. cooked fish	Seasoning
1 tbsp. chutney	An 8-oz. pkt. of frozen
1 shallot, grated	puff pastry
1 oz. grated cheese	Beaten egg
1 tbsp. chopped parsley	

Skin, bone and roughly flake the fish. Stir in the flavourings and seasonings. Roll out the pastry thinly and cut into 4 squares. Place the filling on the pastry, damp the edges with egg and fold over into triangles; flake and scallop the edges and brush the pastry with egg. Cook on a baking sheet at the top of a hot oven (425°F., mark 7) for about ¼ hour, till golden-brown.

PORK WITH WINE SAUCE

4 prunes	1 orange
2 boneless pork chops	¼ pint water
Salt and pepper	6 tbsps. sherry or Madeira
1 tbsp. oil	

Pour some boiling water over the prunes and simmer them for 15 minutes. Season the chops and fry slowly in the oil, allowing 7 minutes on each side. Peel the orange with a vegetable peeler and cut the rind into thin strips; put these with the water into a saucepan and boil for 5 minutes. Add 2 tbsps. of the orange juice and remove from the heat. Remove the chops from the frying pan and pour in the orange liquid; add the sherry or Madeira and heat through. Serve the chops and prunes with the sauce poured over them.

QUICK FLANS

If you do not want to bake, the following cases or crusts can be made without using the oven. These amounts will line a foil or ovenglass dish large enough for 2-3 servings.

CRUMB FLAN CRUST

½ pkt. (4 oz.) digestive or   2-3 oz. butter or margarine
other plain biscuits   1 level tbsp. sugar

Crush the biscuits into small crumbs and mix with sugar. Melt the butter and add, pressing well with a fork till mixture binds together. Turn into a greased plate or dish, pressing the mixture firmly in place. Leave to set in a cool place before filling.

CHOCOLATE CRUMB FLAN CRUST

½ pkt. digestive or ginger   4 oz. chocolate, in pieces
biscuits   1 oz. butter

Crumble the biscuits. Melt chocolate and butter over a pan of water and use to bind crumbs. Finish as above.

CORNFLAKE FLAN CRUST

1 oz. butter   1 tbsp. golden syrup
1 level tbsp. sugar   3 cups cornflakes

Melt the butter, sugar and syrup together, bring to the boil and boil for 1 minute. Crush the cornflakes, add to the pan and stir until they are well coated. Finish as above.

FILLINGS FOR QUICK FLANS

1. Stewed fruit, e.g. apples, stoned plums or apricots, beaten to a pulp and combined with whipped cream (fresh or canned).

2. A fruit-flavoured blancmange combined with chopped fruit (fresh or canned) and /or whipped cream. (Half a 1-pint pkt. of cornflour or blancmange powder should be ample.)

3. Spoonfuls of ice cream with fruit, grated chocolate or whipped cream.

4. Whipped jelly with fruit, grated chocolate or nuts.

5. Drained canned fruit covered with a glaze made from ¼ pint of the juice thickened with 2-3 level tsps. cornflour.

CHOCOLATE MOUSSE

3 oz. plain chocolate   2 eggs, separated

Break the chocolate into small pieces and melt in a basin over a pan of hot water. Remove from the heat and stir in the egg yolks. Whisk the egg whites stiffly and fold into the mixture. Pour into individual dishes and serve alone or with sponge fingers, whipped cream or a decoration of fruit, e.g., sliced banana or pineapple wedges.

Mocha Mousse: Add 1 level tsp. instant coffee with the egg yolks.
Rum Mousse: Add 1-1½ tbsps. rum with the egg yolks.
Orange Mousse: Add the grated rind of an orange and 1 tbsp. juice, with the egg yolks.
Nutty Mousse: Add 1-2 oz. chopped almonds or walnuts with the egg yolks.

PINEAPPLE SNOW

A 12-oz. can of pineapple   1 level tbsp. sugar
chunks   (optional)
1½ level tbsps. pineapple   Juice of ½ a lemon
blancmange powder   1 egg, separated

Drain the juice from the fruit and if necessary make up to ½ pint with water. Chop the fruit. Blend the blancmange powder and sugar with a little of the juice and bring the rest to the boil; pour on to the blended mixture, return this to the pan and cook until it thickens. Remove from the heat, cool and stir in the pineapple, lemon juice and egg yolk. Whisk the egg white stiffly and fold into the mixture, then pour into individual glasses.
The blancmange powder and the fruit can be varied at will. Try orange or lemon blancmange with mandarin oranges, raspberry flavour with raspberries and so on.

LEMON FLUFF

2 eggs, separated   Grated rind and juice
4 oz. sugar   of ½ a lemon

Put the egg yolks, half the sugar and the lemon rind and juice in a basin and whisk over a pan of hot water until pale and creamy. Whisk the egg whites until stiff, then fold into the lemon mixtures with the remaining sugar. Pile in individual dishes and serve within ½-¾ hour, as the mixture tends to separate out after this.

WITH A JELLY

Half a jelly tablet is sufficient for 2 servings. Here are some possible variations:

1. Make up the jelly in the usual way, leave until it is beginning to thicken round the edges of the bowl, then add a 4-oz. can of cream and whisk thoroughly until the mixture is pale and fluffy. Pile into individual glasses.

2. When making up the jelly, use the juice from a can of fruit (if necessary made up with water to the required amount). Put a layer of the fruit in the glasses and spoon a little of the liquid jelly over. Leave the remaining jelly in a cool place. When it begins to set whisk as above (adding cream if liked) and pour over the fruit in jelly; allow to set before serving.

3. Make up the jelly with fruit juice as above. Whisk when it is on the point of setting and fold in the fruit (cut up if necessary). Pour into individual glasses and leave to set.

4. Make up some jelly in the usual way (using fruit juice if liked). Pour into a large shallow dish or tin and leave to set. Cut into cubes with a wetted knife, pile up in individual dishes and serve with cream or ice cream.

5. Replace a little of the water by wine, liqueur or spirit

INDEX

244